Business Math
Using Excel
2E

Sharon Burton
Brookhaven College
Dallas, Texas

Nelda Shelton
Tarrant County College
Fort Worth, Texas

SOUTH-WESTERN
CENGAGE Learning™

Business Math Using Excel,
Second Edition

Sharon Burton and Nelda Shelton

Vice President of Editorial, Business:
    Jack W. Calhoun

Vice President/Editor-in-Chief: Karen Schmohe

Acquisitions Editor: Jane Phelan

Senior Developmental Editor: Enid Nagel

Senior Content Project Manager: Holly Henjum

Associate Marketing Manager: Shanna Shelton

Media Editor: Lysa Kosins

Senior Frontlist Buyer: Kevin Kluck

Editorial Assistant: Anne Kelly

Production Service: Integra Software Services

Senior Art Director: Tippy McIntosh

Internal and Cover Design: Ke Design, Mason, OH

Cover Images: © Kelly Cline, Peter Close, Nathan
    Maxfield, Ivan Stevanovic: iStock

For product information and technology assistance, contact us at
Cengage Learning Customer & Sales Support, 1-800-354-9706

For permission to use material from this text or product,
submit all requests online at **www.cengage.com/permissions**
Further permissions questions can be emailed to
permissionrequest@cengage.com

Screenshots used with permission of Microsoft. Microsoft® Office Excel® is a registered trademark of Microsoft Corporation in the United States and/or other countries.

Library of Congress Control Number: 2011923634

ISBN 13: 978-0-538-73119-5

ISBN 10: 0-538-73119-2

South-Western Cengage Learning
5191 Natorp Boulevard
Mason, OH 45040
USA

Cengage Learning products are represented in Canada by Nelson Education, Ltd.

For your course and learning solutions, visit **www.cengage.com/school**

Visit our company website at **www.cengage.com**

Printed in the United States of America

1 2 3 4 5 6 7 15 14 13 12 11

Brief Contents

Building Skills for Life & Work
Focus on the Basics

Business Math Using Excel 2e applies a straightforward, easy-to-understand approach to reviewing basic math competencies, then applies those same concepts using the commands and formulas of Excel 2010. This new edition has a brand new look that will engage students right from the start and keep them focused on the essential objectives.

Chapters are divided into bite-size sections.

Math @ Work features an interview with a career professional that connects math concepts to the real world.

CHAPTER

9 Markup and Markdown

9.1 CONCEPTS USED IN PRICING MERCHANDISE
9.2 MARKUP ON COST
9.3 MARKUP ON SELLING PRICE
9.4 MARKDOWN

Retailers buy their merchandise from wholesalers for a certain price. Then they sell the merchandise at a retail, or selling, price that is high enough to cover the cost of the merchandise and the cost of business operating expenses (overhead) and still provide the desired profit for the business to be successful. For example, Southern Charm can't sell a denim shirt for the actual cost, $11.24. If it did, it would lose money, as other expenses (such as salaries, rent, utilities, and insurance) must be covered. This chapter emphasizes the mathematics required to mark up and mark down merchandise.

330

Math@Work

ACCOUNTING ASSOCIATE

Kevin Neihaus is an accounting associate in the Marketing and Communications department at a children's hospital. It is his responsibility to forecast, manage, and track the budget for that department. He also works alongside associates, directors, and vice presidents from many other departments. During a typical week, Kevin could be projecting the expenses of his department, creating new departmental policies and procedures, working with vendors, or trying to improve processes that his department uses in daily operation. He said, "It is my goal to make sure my department runs well, and we have money to do what needs to be done."

Kevin knows that hearing the term "accounting" makes people think of sitting at a desk doing the same thing over and over. He said, "My job is actually filled with changing variables. I often have to consider many different possibilities and conditions to formulate an idea of how the money will be or has been spent. Every day brings something new."

How Math is Used in Accounting
When planning a budget, Kevin uses equations to create and project the department's future expenses. This allows him to predict how much money his department will need in the coming year. Kevin also uses math to calculate exactly how much a newsletter his department is creating will cost. He said, "It is important to know how much each copy of the newsletter will cost. Adding up the costs of producing the newsletter and dividing them by the number we are producing tells me what a single print will cost. I then multiply that figure with the number of newsletters we plan on producing to estimate how much I should budget. This planning allows my department to produce great publications that patients and families want to read while staying within our budget."

What Do You Think?
What skills do you need to improve in order to work in accounting?

Math Skills Used
Addition
Subtraction
Multiplication
Statistics
Percents

Other Skills Needed
Communication
Interpersonal skills
Multi-tasking
Organizational skills

331

Apply Math @ Work activities provide real world connections and practical applications.

APPLY Math@Work ACCOUNTING ASSOCIATE

Math is used in various ways by store owners and their accountants, managers, retail buyers and other retail employees. Consider that people working in retail need to know basic skills, such as addition, subtraction, multiplication and division. However, more complex tasks in retail require more advanced math skills, such as using equations and formulas to calculate gross profit margins, cash flow, and profitability.

You are a new accounting associate and have been asked to apply markdown in the following situation. Your store received 150 vests. Toward the end of the season, 137 vests had been sold at $32.00. It has been decided to mark down the remaining vests to $24.99. Suppose that within two weeks, the remaining vests sold at $24.99, the reduced price. Calculate the percent of expected total sales the markdown cost the store.

1. Calculate the expected total sales.

2. Determine the markdown for 13 vests.

3. Calculate the percent of expected total sales the markdown cost the store.

Focus on Learning

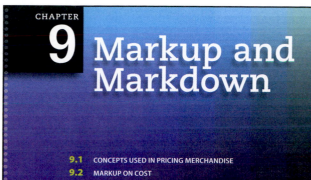

CHAPTER
9 Markup and Markdown

9.1 CONCEPTS USED IN PRICING MERCHANDISE
9.2 MARKUP ON COST
9.3 MARKUP ON SELLING PRICE
9.4 MARKDOWN

Strong, well-defined organization brings key concepts and ideas to students' attention.

Chapters are divided into bite-sized sections.

Exercises apply key concepts immediately, giving students feedback and building confidence along the way.

Objectives are clearly stated to guide learning.

OBJECTIVES

1. Identify terms used with pricing merchandise.
2. Distinguish among basic pricing variables.
3. Calculate the selling price, markup amount, or cost when any two of the three are known.

9.1 Concepts Used in Pricing Merchandise

OBJECTIVE 1 Identify terms used with pricing merchandise.

Selling price (also *retail price*) is what the customer pays. The **cost** is what the retailer pays to the manufacturer. The difference between the cost and the selling price is **markup** (also *gross profit*). Markup is expressed both in dollars (also **markup amount**) and in percentage (also **markup rate**). For instance, an item may be marked up by $23.67 or by 30%. The markup rate can be calculated either on the selling price or on the cost.

Terms are highlighted and defined.

OBJECTIVE 2 Distinguish among basic pricing variables.

The fundamental purpose of a business is to make a profit. A retail business sells goods and services for an acceptable price that is sufficient to cover all expenses and to provide the company with a reasonable profit. Pricing goods is based on an equation that the selling price of an item is equal to the cost

OBJECTIVE 3 Calculate the selling price, markup amount, or cost when any two of the three are known.

Calculating Selling Price
The selling price is found by adding cost and markup.

EXAMPLE

Elliott's Hardware buys a tool set at a cost of $17.40 and adds $8.00 per set as markup to determine selling price. What is the selling price?

STEPS

Add cost and markup to obtain selling price.

Cost + Markup = Selling Price
$17.40 + $8.00 = $25.40   selling price

Worked out, clear **examples** build student confidence by illustrating step-by-step procedures.

Focus on Learning

 NEW **Four Step Problem Solving Plan** helps students solve word problems.

EXAMPLE

Phillip Fontano earns $2,345 a month. He spends one-fifth of his monthly salary for rent. How much does he pay each month for rent?

STEPS

When a math problem uses the word *of*, as in "He spends one-fifth of his monthy salary," the word *of* means to multiply.

Clues   Look for facts. What is the problem asking or what are you trying to find?

Action Plan   Identify the steps to take in the appropriate sequence.

Solve   Perform the steps in the action plan.

Conclusion   Did you answer the question the problem is asking?

Problem Solving Plan

Clues	Action Plan	Solve
Phillip earns $2,345 a month. Phillip spends $\frac{1}{5}$ of his salary.	To determine the rent, multiply $\frac{1}{5} \times 2{,}345$.	$\frac{1}{5} \times \$2{,}345 =$ $\frac{1}{\cancel{5}_{1}} \times \frac{\overset{469}{\cancel{2{,}345}}}{1}$ $\frac{1}{1} \times \frac{469}{1} = \$469$

Conclusion
Phillip's rent for each month is $469.

Use Excel to Do the Math

After learning math concepts in the traditional manner, the concepts are applied using Excel. Excel data files, located on the product website, correlate to each spreadsheet activity in the chapter. Easy-to-read screen captures with callouts make it easy to grasp the concept.

Using the AutoSum Command

home/editing/Σ

Excel's AutoSum button [Σ] is on the Home tab in the Editing group (see Figure 1-6). It is used to add an entire column or row of numbers. Notice the formula in the formula bar does not have any spaces.

FIGURE 1-6

Excel's AutoSum Button

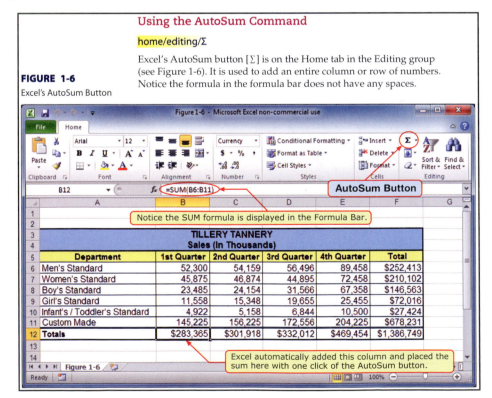

Follow the Path

When a new command is introduced, **follow the path** (Tab/Group/Command) to easily locate the command on the appropriate Excel ribbon. For example, follow the path to AutoSum by clicking the Home tab, Editing group, Σ command.

Excel Data Files

Over 250 preformatted Excel spreadsheets, complete with step-by-step instructions, can be downloaded from the Excel Data Files folder at the product website.

www.cengage.com/businessmath/burton/excel2

Abundant Exercises for Each Concept

All exercises are labeled with the **objective** for quick review.

8.5 Exercises

Name _____ Date _____

Directions   Solve the following problems.

A.   Complete the following.   OBJECTIVE 1

1.   A sales tax is calculated on all sales. True or False?

2.   When calculating a cash discount, you multiply the total amount of the invoice by the discount rate. True or False?

B.   Find the sales tax and the total amount due on these invoices.   OBJECTIVE 1
Round answers to the nearest cent.

Taxable Sale	Sales Tax Percent		Sales Tax Amount		Invoice Total
$3,211.90	7%	3. _____		4. _____	
$1,500.25	8%	5. _____		6. _____	
$380.98	5.5%	7. _____		8. _____	
$234.54	7.5%	9. _____		10. _____	
$867.75	6%	11. _____		12. _____	
$1,111.10	8.75%	13. _____		14. _____	
$1,800.33	5%	15. _____		16. _____	

C.   Determine the sales tax and total amount due on these invoices. Assume   OBJECTIVE 2
shipping charges are not taxable. Round answers to the nearest cent.

Taxable Sale	Sales Tax Percent		Sales Tax Amount	Shipping Charges		Invoice Total
$1,443.22	5%	17. _____		$18.50	18. _____	
$550.15	7%	19. _____		$7.75	20. _____	
$775.30	8%	21. _____		$15.00	22. _____	
$323.12	7.5%	23. _____		$4.50	24. _____	
$9,000.00	7%	25. _____		$25.90	26. _____	
$7,999.00	6.5%	27. _____		$21.98	28. _____	

D.   Solve the following word problems. Round answers to the nearest cent.   OBJECTIVES 1, 2, 3

29.   You are asked to verify an invoice that totals $718.12 before your company pays it. The net price of the merchandise is $635.29; the sales tax rate is 6.5%; and the shipping charge is $39.

a.   Is the invoice amount correct? _____

b.   If not, what error was made, and what should the total amount be? _____

c.   What was the amount of the sales tax? _____

30.   In Exercise 29, the terms of payment are 2/10, n/30.

a.   What is the amount of the cash discount if paid within the discount period? _____

b.   What is the total payment amount? _____

31.   You are preparing an invoice for a customer whose purchase lists for $337.50. The customer is entitled to a trade discount of 10/5; the payment terms are 3/15, n/45; and the sales tax rate is 6%. What should be the total amount of the invoice? _____

32.   Marisa Tallifero bought a cordless phone priced at $49.99. It was subject to 8.75% sales tax. What was the sales tax? _____

What was the total amount Marisa paid for the phone? _____

33.   Jerry Hutchins purchased an assortment of holiday paper. His purchases amounted to $19.97, which was subject to 7.2% sales tax. How much was the sales tax? _____

34.   Penny Holcomb purchased pen and pencil gift sets to give to her employees for the holidays. The total bill was $103.92, which included the sales tax of 6.5%. How much was the actual selling price? _____

What was the amount of the sales tax? _____

35.   For his party, Bobby bought 4 cans of gourmet popcorn and paid $19.96. The tax was 6.2%. How much was the actual selling price? _____

What was the amount of the sales tax? _____

36.   The amount of a sale is $479.50 and the sales tax rate is 7.25%. How much is the sales tax? _____

What is the total selling price? _____

37.   A printer is priced at $524. If a sales tax of $8\frac{1}{2}$% is charged on the printer, what is the total selling price? _____

E.   Use Excel to complete the invoice.   OBJECTIVE 4

38.   Retrieve *ch08ex07.xlsx*. Follow the directions. Save the file as *ch08ex07a.xlsx*.

39.   Retrieve *ch08ex08.xlsx*. Follow the directions. Save the file as *ch08ex08a.xlsx*.

Hone Practical Math Skills for Life & Work

Chapter Review and Assessment

KEY TERMS

adjusted gross income	Federal Unemployment Tax Act (FUTA)	property tax
adjustments to income	Health Savings Account (HSA)	real property
alternative minimum tax	individual retirement account (IRA)	standard deduction
assessed rate	itemized deductions	State Unemployment Tax Act (SUTA)
assessed value	levied	tax
assessor	market value	tax credits
earned income tax credit	mill	tax rate
escrow account	personal property	taxable income
estimated tax payments		total income
exemptions		

CONCEPTS	EXAMPLES
6.1 Calculate the tax levied on property based on the assessed value.	
Dollars per $100	Assessed value is 60% of market value; Tax rate is $3.80 per $100; Market value is $130,000.
1. Multiply the market value of the property by the assessed rate.	$130,000 × 60% = $78,000 assessed value
2. Determine the number of $100s in the assessed value.	$78,000 ÷ $100 = 780
3. Multiply the number of $100s by the tax rate to determine the amount of tax due.	780 × $3.80 = $2,964 property tax due
Dollars per $1,000	Dollars per $1,000 works the same, except determine the number of $1,000s in the market value instead of the number of $100s and then follow the steps above.
Mills per dollar of assessed value	Assessed value is $126,000; Tax rate is 32 mills.
1. Convert mills to dollars.	32 mills ÷ $1,000 = $0.032
2. Multiply the assessed value by the tax rate in dollars.	$126,000 × $0.032 = $4,032 property tax due
6.1 Calculate the tax rate levied on property based on the assessed value.	
1. Determine the amount of money needed.	$50,000,000
2. Divide the amount of money needed by the total assessed value.	Assessed value: $5,000,000,000 $50 million ÷ $5 billion = 0.01 or 1%

Key Terms are listed for ready reference.

Concepts provide specific steps and examples for easy review.

Review Exercises focus on each objective.

Quiz is a quick meaningful review for the chapter test.

Chapter 6 Review Exercises

Name   *Date*

Directions   Write your answers in the blanks provided. Round dollar amounts to the nearest hundredth.

A. Determine the amount of tax due in the following problems.   6.1 OBJECTIVE 2

	Market Value	Assessed Value	Tax Rate	Tax Due
1.	$80,000	75%	$2.95 per $1,000	_____
2.	$110,000	60%	$5.45 per $100	_____
3.	$200,000	100%	12 mills	_____

B. Complete the following problems to compute the tax rates. Round your answers to the nearest whole percent.   6.1 OBJECTIVE 3

	Money Needed	Assessed Value	Tax Rate
4.	$5,500,000	$225,000,000	_____
5.	$946,245	$19,050,000	_____

C. Complete the following problems to compute state unemployment tax for one employee. Assume a tax rate of 3% on the first $9,000.   6.2 OBJECTIVE 2

6. $4,300 gross wages _____ tax due	7. $12,000 gross wages _____ tax due	
8. $15,825 gross wages _____ tax due	9. $8,900 gross wages _____ tax due	

D. Compute federal unemployment tax. Use 0.8% as the tax rate. Assume all wages subject to tax.   6.2 OBJECTIVE 3

10. $42,000 gross earnings _____ tax due	11. $58,942 gross earnings _____ tax due
12. $18,296 gross earnings _____ tax due	13. $96,500 gross earnings _____ tax due

E. Compute federal income tax as you would on Form 1040EZ.   6.3 OBJECTIVES 2, 3

JoAnn White is single and earned $19,500 in wages and $560 in interest from her savings account. JoAnn has no exemptions other than herself. Compute JoAnn's tax.

Total income		$19,500
Plus interest income (savings account)		$ 560
14. Adjusted gross income		
Less standard deduction (single)		$ 5,450
Less exemptions (1)		$ 3,500
15. Taxable income		_____
16. Federal income tax (single, from tax table)		
Income tax withheld		$ 1,005
17. Federal income tax due		_____

QUIZ

Name   *Date*   *Score*

Directions   Solve the following problems. Place your answers in the blanks provided.

A. Compute the amount of property tax due. Round dollar amounts to the nearest hundredth.   6.1 OBJECTIVE 2

	Market Value	Assessed Value	Tax Rate	Tax Due
1.	$145,000	65%	$2.35 per $1,000 =	_____
2.	$90,000	80%	$3.35 per $100 =	_____
3.	$365,000	100%	9 mills per dollar =	_____

B. Compute the property tax rate.   6.1 OBJECTIVE 3

	Money Needed	Assessed Value	Tax Rate
4.	$240,000	$1,500,000 =	_____
5.	$7,500,000	$250,000,000 =	_____

C. Complete the following problems to compute state unemployment tax for one employee. Assume a tax rate of 3% on the first $9,000.   6.2 OBJECTIVE 2

6. $10,356 gross wages = _____ tax due	7. $6,555 gross wages = _____ tax due

D. Compute federal unemployment tax. Use 0.8% as the tax rate. Assume all wages subject to tax. Round dollar amounts to the nearest hundredth.   6.2 OBJECTIVE 3

8. $6,123 gross wages = _____ tax due	9. $18,752 gross wages = _____ tax due

E. Compute federal income tax as you would on Form 1040EZ. Kristen is single. Her total income was $21,000 in wages and $350 in interest from her savings account. Kristen has no exemptions other than herself. Compute her tax.   6.3 OBJECTIVES 2, 3

Total income		$21,000
Plus interest income (savings account)		$350
10. Adjusted gross income		_____
Less standard deduction (single)		_____
Less exemptions (1)		_____
11. Taxable income		_____
12. Federal income tax (single, from tax table)		_____
Income tax withheld		$1,709
13. Federal income tax due/Refund due		_____

Special Features Make Real-World Connections

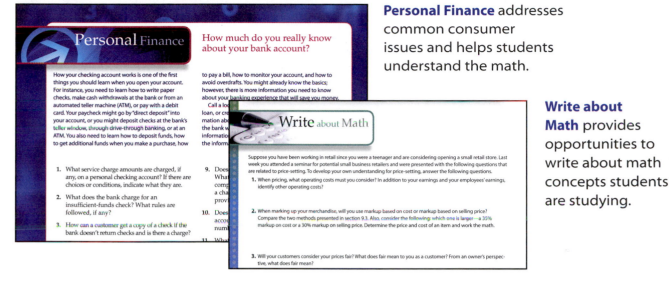

Personal Finance addresses common consumer issues and helps students understand the math.

Write about Math provides opportunities to write about math concepts students are studying.

Connect Student Learning to Assignable Content

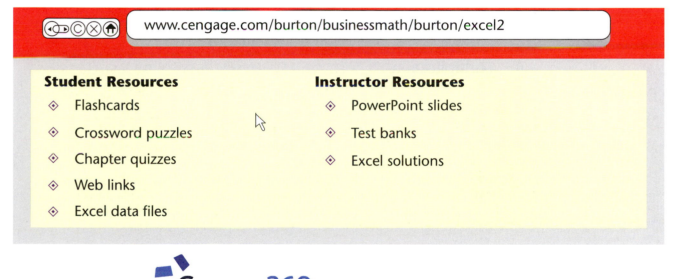

www.cengage.com/burton/businessmath/burton/excel2

Student Resources

- ◈ Flashcards
- ◈ Crossword puzzles
- ◈ Chapter quizzes
- ◈ Web links
- ◈ Excel data files

Instructor Resources

- ◈ PowerPoint slides
- ◈ Test banks
- ◈ Excel solutions

Course 360 Online Learning to the Next Degree. **Business Math CNOW**

Cengage Learning's BUSINESS MATH USING EXCEL®, 2E CNOW connects students to assignable, key text content for outcomes-based, complete learning solutions. CengageNOW™ provides homework tools with automatic grading features. Interactive, easy-to-use resources help students focus on what they need to learn.

For more information visit www.cengage.com/cengagecourse.

www.cengagebrain.com

On CengageBrain.com students will be able to save up to 60% on their course materials through our full spectrum of options. Students will have the option to rent their textbooks, purchase print textbooks, e-textbooks, or individual e-chapters and audio books, all for substantial savings over average retail prices. CengageBrain.com also includes access to Cengage Learning's broad range of homework and study tools, and features a selection of free content.

Contents

x

Chapter 3   Percent   112

Chapter 6   **Taxes**   222

Chapter 7   **Insurance**   260

Chapter 11	**Consumer Credit and Mortgages** 400

Chapter 14 Financial Statements 510

Chapter 15 Business Statistics 554

About the Authors

Sharon Burton is a professor in the Business Studies Division at Brookhaven College, Dallas (Texas) Community College District (DCCCD). She has 25+ years experience in community college teaching. Recently, she has been coordinating the medical office program at Brookhaven College. Sharon teaches Microsoft software, communications, and medical office classes on campus as well as online. She has a BBA from Lamar University and an MBE from University of North Texas.

Nelda Shelton received her BS and MBE degrees from the University of North Texas, Denton, Texas. She is an associate professor at Tarrant County College, South Campus, Fort Worth, Texas, in the Business and Office Administration Departments. Her teaching experience includes business math, business communications, office procedures, and introduction to accounting both in the classroom and distance learning via the Internet. She has worked part time for the U.S. Office of Personnel Management as a trainer and as an independent contractor and for Dallas County Community College District as a part-time instructor. She has coauthored several textbooks in the business and office administration areas.

The study of business math is a practical approach to learning math. In studying business math, you learn basic math skills that will be useful throughout your life. Checking a sales slip, balancing a checking account, and understanding the various ways interest is charged on loans are just a few of the many practical skills you will learn in the coming chapters. You will begin your study of business math with an explanation of the decimal number system—the number system most used in the United States.

HEALTH SCIENCES

Medical assistant Audra Puckett is the ultimate multi-tasker. A typical day in her doctor's office job includes answering the phone, scheduling appointments, filing medical records, and communicating with insurance companies. And those are just her administrative duties. She also checks patients' files to discern the reason for their visits, greets them, and guides them from the waiting room into the examination area. "I measure each patient's height and weight and show each into an examining room," Audra says. "There, I measure their pulse and respirations and ask about any new medications. I prepare the vials and needles for injections. I also prepare prescriptions and administer medications as instructed by the doctor, and I direct the patients to the front desk after their visits for payment and rescheduling."

People skills are a must. "I interact one-on-one with every patient," Audra says. "When I make time to start a conversation and show interest in each individual, the patients feel more comfortable, and it reflects well on the whole office. This job can be exhausting, both physically and mentally, and you can tell who is in it just for the money—their work suffers, and the patients notice. But the workers who are in it to care for people and who are driven to help the doctor make an accurate diagnosis—they're the ones who truly succeed."

How Math is Used in Health Sciences

Audra uses multiplication when she converts drug dosages from milliliters to liters and when she calculates how many blood vials are required for the particular test a patient is undergoing. She also uses multiplication when taking vital signs. "A person's pulse rate is measured in beats per minute, but I only track the pulse for 15 seconds. Then I multiply the number of heartbeats by four to get the pulse rate," she explains. "This is a huge timesaver. I'd be lost without this skill because it would take four times as long to take each pulse, which would slow down everything else in the office!"

What Do You Think?

What skills do you need to improve for a career in health sciences?

jsmith/iStockphoto.com

Math Skills Used

Addition

Subtraction

Multiplication

Division

Other Skills Needed

Communication

Organization

Multitasking

Problem Solving

OBJECTIVES

1. Identify terms used with the decimal number system.
2. Convert numbers to or from amounts in word forms.
3. Round numbers.
4. Use Excel to round numbers.

1.1 Numbers

OBJECTIVE 1 Identify terms used with the decimal number system.

The **decimal number system** (also called the Hindu-Arabic system) is a number system using base 10. It is the most universally used number system today. It is based on ten **digits**. A digit is a **numeral**. The ten digits used in this system are as follows:

1, 2, 3, 4, 5, 6, 7, 8, 9, and 0

In the decimal number system, a dot (.), which is called the **decimal point**, separates the whole number part from the decimal part. Figure 1-1 shows the names of the digits to the left and right of the decimal point—sometimes called **positions** or **places**.

Notice that commas are used to the left of the decimal point to separate each group of three digits. Digits to the left of the decimal point form the **whole number part**. Digits to the right of the decimal point form the **decimal part**.

To read a decimal number, begin by reading the whole-number part, say "and" to indicate the decimal point, and then read the decimal part.

Figure 1-1

Decimal Number System

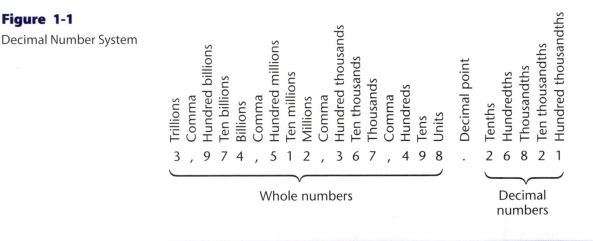

OBJECTIVE 2 Convert numbers to or from amounts in word forms.

Numbers or amounts may be written using numerals or spelled out in **word form** as shown on the next page. When an amount is written in word form, the decimal point is represented by the word *and*. For example, 15.78 is written fifteen and seventy-eight hundredths.

CHAPTER 1 BASIC MATH FUNCTIONS

Numbers	Word Forms
28	twenty-eight
39.06	thirty-nine and six hundredths
837	eight hundred thirty-seven
4,169	four thousand one hundred sixty-nine
72.1	seventy-two and one tenth
283.512	two hundred eighty-three and five hundred twelve thousandths

A common use for word forms is in writing checks. The bank requires a payer to write the amount in both number and word form, as shown in Figure 1-2. Notice that the fraction of a dollar 50/100 is written as a fraction along with the word form.

Figure 1-2

Check Showing Number and Word Form

To say aloud a number such as 0.98765, pretend it is a whole number (98,765) and notice the final position (place) that is given (hundred thousandths). Then say "ninety-eight thousand, seven hundred sixty-five hundred thousandths."

Occasionally it is helpful to come near to, or to **approximate**, an amount rather than give an exact amount. For example, suppose you purchased a portable DVD player and a digital photo frame for $219.95. If a friend asks what you paid for them, you might say $220.

You rounded up the amount to the nearest whole dollar (unit position) rather than saying the actual dollars and cents. If you had paid $219.05, you might have rounded down to the nearest whole dollar and said $219. Study the following examples.

EXAMPLES

Portable DVD player and digital photo frame cost $219.95, or approximately $220.	Portable DVD player and digital photo frame cost $219.05, or approximately $219.

If you understand approximation and positions (places), you will understand **rounding** numbers. Here are the rules for rounding numbers.

Rules for Rounding

1 Determine the position (place) being rounded.

2 If the digit to the right of the position (place) is 5 *or more*, round up by 1.

   Example 6.8 rounds up to 7 (8 is more than 5)

3 If the digit to the right of the position is *less than* 5, do not round up. Drop all digits from that position to the right.

   Example 6.4 rounds to 6 (4 is less than 5)

You can easily round to any position by looking at the number to its right and applying Rule 2 or Rule 3 given above.

EXAMPLES

5.35	rounded to the nearest tenth is 5.4	5 is equal to 5.
0.981	rounded to the nearest hundredth is 0.98	1 is less than 5.

When a number in the round-off position is 9, as in 0.98, and the digit to the right is 5 or more, round up by adding 1 to the 9 even though a decimal number may change to a whole number.

EXAMPLES

0.99	rounded to the nearest tenth is 1.0	9 is more than 5.
358.8599	rounded to the nearest thousandth is 358.860	9 is more than 5.
2,976.8	rounded to the nearest hundred is 3,000 Notice that all digits to the right of the hundreds place are changed to zeros.	7 is more than 5.

It is likely that you will be using Excel on the job to complete math calculations. Excel provides commands that make calculations quick and easy. The commands in Excel 2010 are organized on the Ribbon. You will see tabs on the Ribbon that relate to various activities. To help you find the needed command, the path to the command is shown.

Using the Increase Decimal or Decrease Decimal Commands

Home/Number/Increase Decimal

On the Home tab, in the Number group, notice the Increase Decimal and Decrease Decimal commands. When you click Increase Decimal, Excel adds a decimal place to the selected cell. When you click Decrease Decimal, Excel removes a decimal place from the selected cell. You can increase or decrease a single cell or a group of cells. You can only increase and decrease decimals. This feature will not round whole numbers to the left of the decimal place.

Excel follows the rules you just learned for rounding. If the number to the right of the desired place is 5 or greater, Excel rounds up. If the number to the right of the desired place is 4 or less, Excel rounds down.

Figure 1-3

Rounding Using Increase Decimal or Decrease Decimal

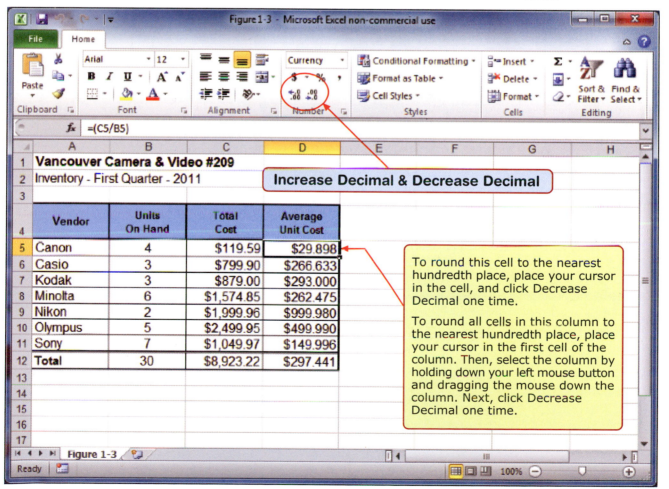

STEPS

1. To round a single cell, place your cursor in the cell to be rounded. Click Increase Decimal or Decrease Decimal the desired number of times.

2. To round a column to a certain number of decimal places, select the column by clicking on the first cell in the column. Then while holding down your left mouse button, drag the cursor down to the last cell in the column. The column will be highlighted. Click Increase Decimal or Decrease Decimal the desired number of times.

   Notice in Cell D5 in Figure 1-3, the spreadsheet for Vancouver Camera & Video, that to round 29.898 to the nearest cent (or hundredths place), you click Decrease Decimal one time. The number changes to 29.90.

3. Open the file *ch01pr01.xlsx*. Complete Practices 1 and 2. Leave this file on your screen. Should you need to stop working, save the file as *ch01pr01a.xlsx*.

Figure 1-4

Using Currency Style

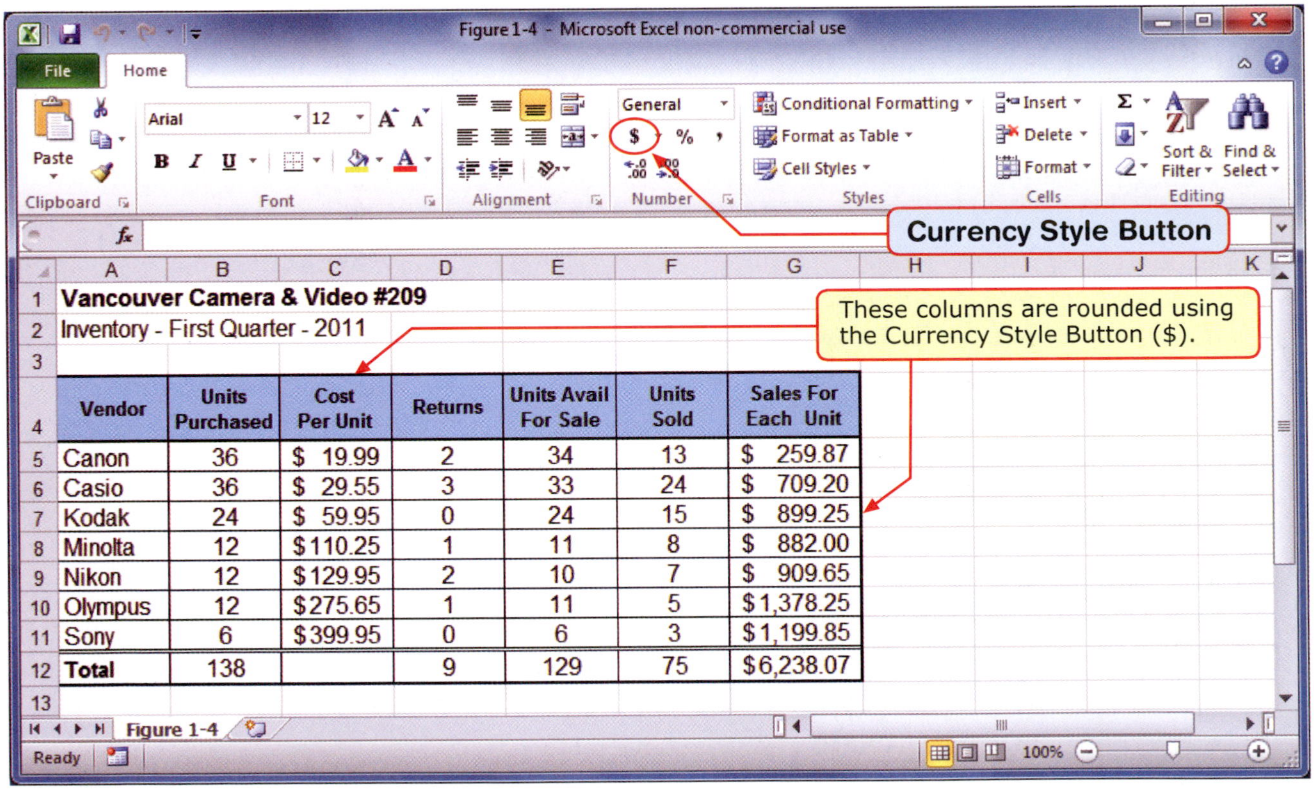

Vendor	Units Purchased	Cost Per Unit	Returns	Units Avail For Sale	Units Sold	Sales For Each Unit
Canon	36	$ 19.99	2	34	13	$ 259.87
Casio	36	$ 29.55	3	33	24	$ 709.20
Kodak	24	$ 59.95	0	24	15	$ 899.25
Minolta	12	$110.25	1	11	8	$ 882.00
Nikon	12	$129.95	2	10	7	$ 909.65
Olympus	12	$275.65	1	11	5	$1,378.25
Sony	6	$399.95	0	6	3	$1,199.85
Total	138		9	129	75	$6,238.07

Vancouver Camera & Video #209
Inventory - First Quarter - 2011

Currency Style Button

These columns are rounded using the Currency Style Button ($).

Using the Currency Style Command

Home/Number/$

Another quick way to round a number to two decimal places when working with currency is to use the **Currency Style command** [$]. Notice in Figure 1-4 on the previous page that the Cost per Unit and Sales For Each Unit columns have been formatted using the Currency Style command.

STEPS

1. Click on the first cell in the column you want to format using the Currency Style command. If you want the entire column to be formatted, hold down the left mouse button and drag the mouse down the column to highlight it.

2. Click on the Currency Style button [$].

3. The *ch01pr01.xlsx* file should still be on your screen. Scroll down the screen and complete Practice 3. Leave this file on your screen to use in the next practice. Should you need to stop working, save the file as *ch01pr01a.xlsx*.

> **TIPS**
>
> *To correct any entry error, use the delete key or the backspace to clear the contents of a cell.*

Using the Format Cells Command

Home/Number

A third way to round numbers to a specific decimal place is to use Format Cells. On the Home tab, in the Number group, click the Dialog Box Launcher next to Number to launch the Format Cells dialog box. You can specify the desired number of decimal places here. See Figure 1-5 on the next page.

STEPS

1. Select the cells you want to round.

2. On the Home tab, in the Number group, click the Dialog Box Launcher next to Number to launch the Format Cells dialog box. You may choose:

   - General for no specific cell format.

   - Number to be able to set the number of desired decimal places and the way negative numbers appear.

   - Currency to be able to set the number of desired decimal places, add or delete the dollar sign, and set the way negative numbers appear.

   - Accounting to be able to set the number of desired decimal places and add or delete the dollar sign.

3. Click on Currency.

4. In the Decimal places box, key the number that represents the number of decimal places desired. In the Symbol box, choose the dollar sign ($). In the Negative numbers box, choose the number with the negative sign.

5. Click on OK. The dollar sign is placed next to the whole number without spaces between it and the number.

6. The *ch01pr01.xlsx* file should still be on your screen. Scroll down the screen and complete Practice 4. When you have finished with this practice, save the file as *ch01pr01a.xlsx*. Close the file.

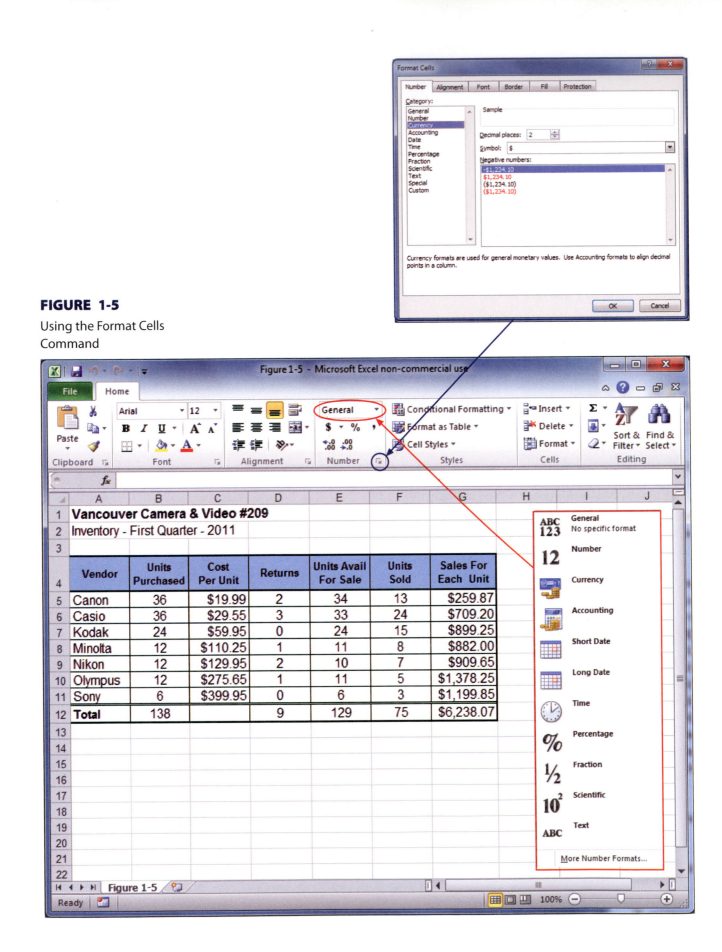

FIGURE 1-5

Using the Format Cells Command

CHAPTER 1 BASIC MATH FUNCTIONS

Name _____ Date _____

Directions Complete the following problems.

A. Write the numeral and the position the underlined digits represent. `OBJECTIVE 1`

1. 6<u>4</u>5   _____

2. 42,<u>3</u>49   _____

3. 27.0<u>2</u>   _____

4. <u>6</u>7,256.1   _____

5. <u>2</u>,765,437   _____

6. 95.54<u>9</u>   _____

7. 8<u>4</u>   _____

8. 232.<u>2</u>65   _____

9. 1,00<u>7</u>.1   _____

10. 1.9795<u>1</u>   _____

11. <u>3</u>00,511   _____

12. 0.4<u>3</u>8   _____

13. 0.0005<u>9</u>   _____

14. <u>7</u>,811   _____

B. Write numerals for the following word forms. `OBJECTIVE 2`

15. One hundred thirty   _____

16. Ninety-five thousand two hundred twenty   _____

17. Seventy-three and sixty-five hundredths   _____

18. Six million three thousand twenty-one   _____

19. Five thousand six hundred and thirty-four thousandths   _____

20. One thousand two   _____

21. Twenty-six hundredths   _____

22. Three billion, thirty-four million, six thousand forty   _____

23. Fifty-one and six thousandths   _____

24. One hundred nine and four tenths   _____

25. Seven thousand, four hundred, sixty-two and three hundredths   _____

26. Five hundred and eighteen hundredths   _____

C. Write word forms for the following numerals. `OBJECTIVE 2`

27. 595   _____

28. 3,721.2   _____

29. 500,465,602   _____

30. 3,942,001   _____

31. 2.469   _____

32. 3.24 _____

33. 3,452,000.042 _____

34. 0.94265 _____

35. 9,090.99 _____

36. 0.3795 _____

D. Round the following numbers to the nearest dollar. OBJECTIVE **3**

37. $585.25 _____

38. $9,049.87 _____

39. $802.10 _____

40. $12.75 _____

41. $1.49 _____

42. $27.95 _____

43. $110.99 _____

44. $720.01 _____

45. $49.99 _____

46. $399.71 _____

E. Round the following numbers to the place indicated. OBJECTIVE **3**

47. Round $5,267.82 to the nearest ten. _____

48. Round 269.5 to the nearest hundred. _____

49. Round 422.35 to the nearest unit. _____

50. Round 9,742 to the nearest thousand. _____

51. Round 4.2354 to the nearest tenth. _____

52. Round 9.4603 to the nearest hundredth. _____

53. Round 249.9573 to the nearest thousandth. _____

54. Round 7.2468901 to the nearest ten thousandth. _____

55. Round 4.006 to the nearest tenth. _____

56. Round 19,999 to the nearest thousand. _____

57. Round 3,611.875 to the nearest ten. _____

F. Use Excel to round numbers. OBJECTIVE **4**

58. Retrieve the file *ch01ex01.xlsx*. Follow the directions. Save the file as *ch01ex01a.xlsx*.

59. Retrieve the file *ch01ex02.xlsx*. Follow the directions. Save the file as *ch01ex2a.xlsx*.

1.2 Addition

OBJECTIVES

1. Identify terms used with addition.
2. Align numbers correctly for adding.
3. Align decimal points in addition.
4. Add mentally.
5. Add by tens mentally.
6. Add horizontally.
7. Use the Four Step Problem Solving Plan.
8. Use Excel to solve problems involving addition.

OBJECTIVE 1 Identify terms used with addition.

Quick, correct addition of numbers is a useful math skill you can acquire. Like any other skill, addition requires practice. Some everyday uses of addition are counting money, keeping score in a game, and making purchases. You must be familiar with the terms used in addition.

1,086
992
750
223

$3,051

topshotUK/iStockphoto.com

Addition is the process of combining two or more numbers and arriving at a larger number. Each number is called an **addend**. The solution is called the **sum**, **total**, or **amount**.

$$
\begin{array}{r}
931 \quad \leftarrow \text{addend} \\
\text{plus sign} \rightarrow \underline{+\ 27} \quad \leftarrow \text{addend} \\
958 \quad \leftarrow \text{sum, total, or amount}
\end{array}
$$

OBJECTIVE 2 Align numbers correctly for adding.

To prevent errors in adding, it is necessary to align the digits in columns so units are above units, tens are above tens, hundreds are above hundreds, and so on.

EXAMPLE

Incorrectly written	Correctly written
8,712	8,712
256	256
3,421	3,421
+ 951	+ 951
13,340	13,340

OBJECTIVE **3** Align decimal points in addition.

When adding numbers with decimals, it is important that you align the decimal points. This will ensure the proper placement of digits in the appropriate column. The number of decimal places in the answer is determined by the addend with the largest number of decimal places.

EXAMPLE

```
   5,146.11
      61.044
      10.07
     694.081
 + 1,237.0548     ← addend with the largest number of decimal places
   7,148.3598     ← Answer has 4 decimal places.
```

OBJECTIVE **4** Add mentally.

The more skillful you become at adding any two or more combinations of numbers in columns, the more accurately and rapidly you will be able to add. To add a column of numbers, think subtotals only. A **subtotal** is the total of two or more numbers within the column being added. Follow these steps when adding a column mentally.

STEPS

1. Add down the right column (units position) by thinking

    10, 16, 19, 22, 23

    (7 + 3 is <u>10</u>, + 6 is <u>16</u>, + 3 is <u>19</u>, + 3 is <u>22</u>, + 1 is <u>23</u>)

2. Write the number 3 in the units position of the answer. Write the number 2, which is to be carried, over the 9 in the tens column.

3. Add down the middle column (tens position) by thinking

    11, 15, 16, 24, 28

    (2 + 9 is <u>11</u>, + 4 is <u>15</u>, + 1 is <u>16</u>, + 8 is <u>24</u>, + 4 is <u>28</u>)

4. Write the number 8 in the tens position in the answer. Write the number 2, which is to be carried, over the 3 in the hundreds column.

5. Add down the left column (hundreds position) by thinking

    5, 14, 17, 21, 23, 32

    (2 + 3 is <u>5</u>, + 9 is <u>14</u>, + 3 is <u>17</u>, + 4 is <u>21</u>, + 2 is <u>23</u>, + 9 is <u>32</u>)

6. Write the number 32 with a comma after the 3 to make it easier to distinguish the thousands position from the hundreds position in the answer.

    3,283

```
  22
 397  ⎤
   +  ⎥
 943  ⎦ 10
   +  ⎤
 306  ⎦ 16
   +  ⎤
 413  ⎦ 19
   +  ⎤
 283  ⎦ 22
   +  ⎤
 941  ⎦ 23
─────
3,283
```

To add more accurately and rapidly, you can memorize the number combinations that total 10.

EXAMPLES

Two digits:	1	2	3	4	5
	+9	+8	+7	+6	+5
	10	10	10	10	10

Three digits:	1	1	1	1
	1	2	3	4
	+8	+7	+6	+5
	10	10	10	10

2	2	2	3
2	3	4	3
+6	+5	+4	+4
10	10	10	10

In the combinations shown, these numbers may appear in any sequence.

EXAMPLE

2	2	6
2	6	2
+6	+2	+2
10	10	10

Instead of adding down a column, learn to recognize these groups of tens to increase your speed in adding. At first, this method may appear to take too much time. However, with practice, you will gain speed.

CALCULATOR TIP

Check how your calculator works by adding a problem you can mentally add. For instance, add 5 + 6. Enter the 5, enter the + sign, enter the 6, enter the + again. The answer is shown in the display.

EXAMPLE

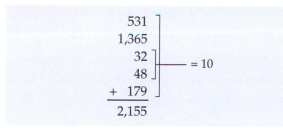

$$\left.\begin{array}{r} 531 \\ 1{,}365 \\ 32 \\ 48 \\ +\ 179 \\ \hline 2{,}155 \end{array}\right.$$

531
1,365
32 ⎤
48 ⎦ = 10
+ 179

TIPS

Add horizontally by adding the positions from right to left.

In business, it is common for numbers to be written horizontally across a page rather than in vertical columns. Examples are invoices, checkbooks, and inventory reports. You could rewrite the numbers in a column and add vertically, but it is more efficient to add horizontally.

EXAMPLE

$698.11 + $47.88

STEPS

1. Add the hundredths column, 1 + 8, and write the answer, 9, at the far right as shown.   9

2. Add the tenths column, 1 + 8, and write the answer, 9, to the left of the first 9 as shown.   99

3. Place the decimal point next to the 9 as shown.   .99

4. Add the units, tens, and hundreds columns following the same procedure given in steps 1 and 2. $745.99

OBJECTIVE **7** Use the Four Step Problem Solving Plan.

Solving problems is a critical skill. Knowing what to look for and what procedures to apply are very important. To identify what procedures to use, you should be familiar with the problem situation, be able to collect the appropriate information, identify an action plan, perform the action plan, and draw conclusions.

Four Step Problem Solving Plan

1. Clues

- Read the problem slowly and carefully. Reading aloud may help.
- Ask yourself if you've seen a problem similar to the one you are reading.
- What facts are relevant or what facts are you expected to know?
- What is the problem asking or what are you trying to find?
- Underline clue words, such as the ones shown in the following table.

Sample Clue Words

Addition	Subtraction	Multiplication	Division
sum	difference	product	share
total	how much more	total	distribute
in addition, in all	remainder	area	quotient
whole	minus	times	average

2. Action Plan

- Visualize the problem by drawing pictures, charts, diagrams, or other illustrations.
- Determine how the known and unknown facts are related.
- Identify the steps to take in the appropriate sequence.

3. Solve

Perform the steps in the action plan.

4. Conclusion

- Look over your solution.
- Does it seem reasonable?
- Did you answer the question the problem is asking?
- Did you answer using the language in the question?

Use the Four Step Problem Solving Plan to solve a word problem involving addition.

EXAMPLE

As a member of a frequent flyer program, you receive one mile for each mile you fly, miles for staying in certain hotels, and miles for shopping at certain stores. When you have accumulated enough miles, you can obtain a free airline ticket. You have a balance on your frequent flyer statement of 16,452 miles. You have earned the following miles this month that have not been posted on your monthly statement: 345, 280, 500, 190, 310. You want to know how many miles you now have to see if you have enough for a free ticket. You need 20,000 miles for the free ticket.

Problem Solving Plan

Clues	Action Plan	Solve
You have 16,452 miles. You have earned extra miles since your statement. You need 20,000 miles for a free ticket.	To determine total miles, add the recently earned miles to the balance on your statement.	16,452 345 280 500 190 + 310 18,077

Conclusion

You need 20,000 miles and only have 18,077 miles. You do not have enough for a free ticket at this time.

OBJECTIVE 8 Use Excel to solve problems involving addition.

Excel offers an **AutoSum** shortcut that makes adding quick and easy. You can also create a **formula** (also called **function**) to add a column or row of numbers. You can do this using the keyboard or by using the Pointing Method.

Using the AutoSum Command

home/editing/Σ

Excel's AutoSum button [Σ] is on the Home tab in the Editing group (see Figure 1-6). It is used to add an entire column or row of numbers. Notice the formula in the formula bar does not have any spaces.

FIGURE 1-6

Excel's AutoSum Button

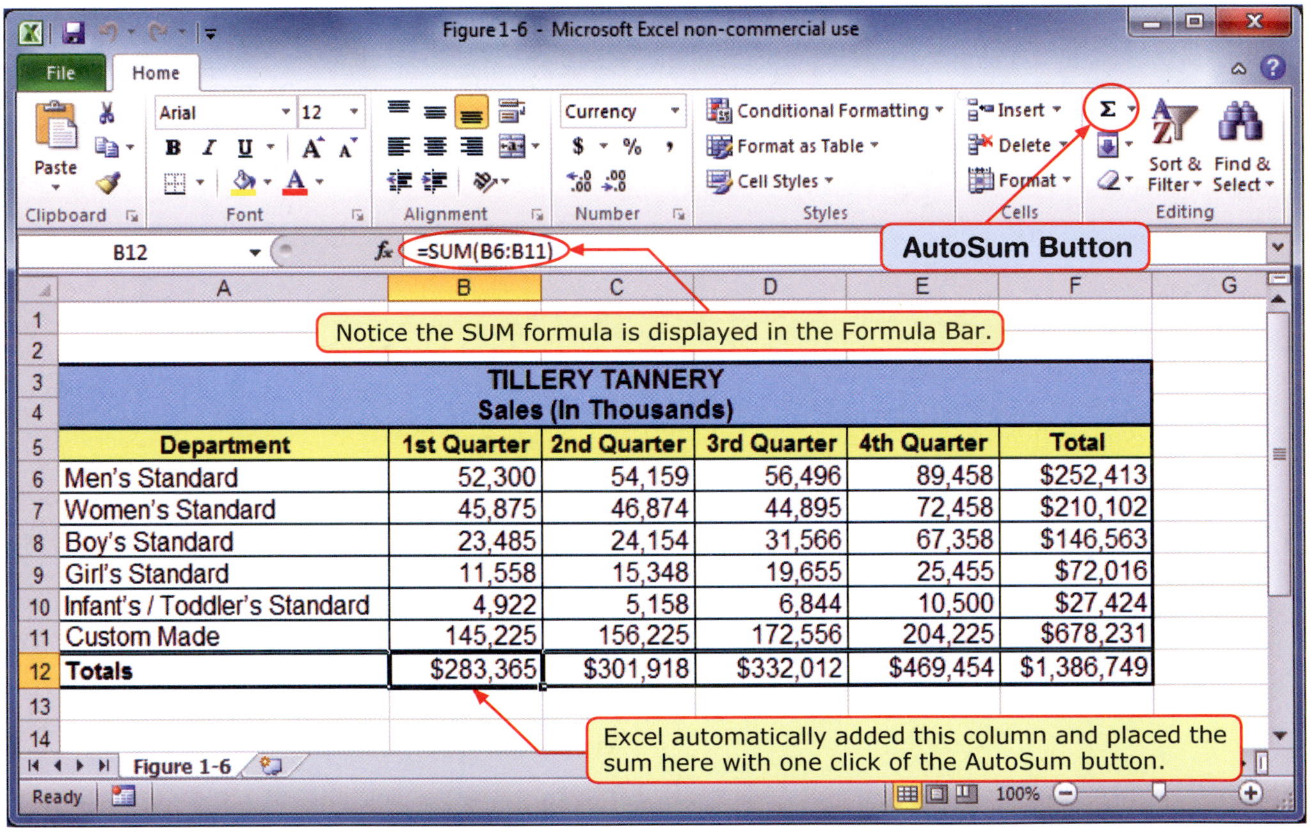

Figure 1-6 - Microsoft Excel non-commercial use
File
Home
AutoSum Button
=SUM(B6:B11)
Notice the SUM formula is displayed in the Formula Bar.
TILLERY TANNERY
Sales (In Thousands)
Department | 1st Quarter | 2nd Quarter | 3rd Quarter | 4th Quarter | Total
Men's Standard | 52,300 | 54,159 | 56,496 | 89,458 | $252,413
Women's Standard | 45,875 | 46,874 | 44,895 | 72,458 | $210,102
Boy's Standard | 23,485 | 24,154 | 31,566 | 67,358 | $146,563
Girl's Standard | 11,558 | 15,348 | 19,655 | 25,455 | $72,016
Infant's / Toddler's Standard | 4,922 | 5,158 | 6,844 | 10,500 | $27,424
Custom Made | 145,225 | 156,225 | 172,556 | 204,225 | $678,231
Totals | $283,365 | $301,918 | $332,012 | $469,454 | $1,386,749
Excel automatically added this column and placed the sum here with one click of the AutoSum button.

STEPS

Retrieve the file *ch01pr02.xlsx*.

1. Add Column B, 1st Quarter Sales, vertically by selecting the entire column, including Cell B12, where the total is to appear. Click the AutoSum button. The total appears in Cell B12.
2. Add Row 6 horizontally, by selecting the entire row, including Total. Click the AutoSum button. The total appears in Cell F6.
3. Total the rest of the spreadsheet vertically and horizontally. Format all answers for Currency. Set Decimal places to zero. Set Currency symbol to $.
4. Save the file as *ch01pr02a.xlsx*.

Using the Keyboard to Enter an Addition Formula

Begin by keying the equals symbol (=) which alerts Excel that you are entering a formula, not text. You can also start a formula with a plus sign (+) or a minus sign (–). If you do not begin your formula with one of these symbols, Excel will assume you are entering text and will not calculate the results.

STEPS

Retrieve the file *ch01pr03.xlsx*.

Using the keyboard, enter a formula in Cell F6 to calculate the Total Sales for the Men's Standard Department.

Total Sales = 1Q Sales + 2Q Sales + 3Q Sales + 4Q Sales
= B6 + C6 + D6 + E6

1. Click in Cell F6.   2. Key the equals symbol (=).

3. Key the cell address (B6) of the first number to be added.

4. Key the plus sign (+) to tell Excel to add.

5. Key C6.   6. Key +.   7. Key D6.   8. Key +.

9. Key E6.   10. Press Enter.

11. Repeat this process in Cells F7 through F11.

12. Using the AutoSum button, total all columns vertically.

13. Format all column totals and row totals for Currency. Set Decimal places to zero. Set Currency symbol to $.

14. Save the file as *ch01pr03a.xlsx*.

Using the Pointing Method to Enter an Addition Formula

A quicker method (called the **Pointing Method**) eliminates keyboarding by using the mouse to point to the cells that should be added.

STEPS

Retrieve the file *ch01pr04.xlsx*.

Using the Pointing Method, enter a formula in Cell F6 to calculate the Total Sales for the Men's Standard Department.

Total Sales = 1Q Sales + 2Q Sales + 3Q Sales + 4Q Sales
= B6 + C6 + D6 + E6

1. Click in Cell F6 where the results of the formula will appear.

2. Key =.   3. Click on Cell B6.   4. Key +.

5. Click on Cell C6.   6. Key +.   7. Click on Cell D6.

8. Key +.   9. Click on Cell E6.   10. Press Enter.

11. Repeat this process in Cells F7 through F11 to find the Total Sales for each of the other Departments.

12. Using the AutoSum button, total all columns vertically.

13. Format all column totals and row totals for Currency. Set Decimal places to zero. Set Currency symbol to $.

14. Save the file as *ch01pr04a.xlsx*.

TIPS

To display your formulas, hold down the Ctrl button then press the ~ (tilde—found to the left of the 1 key). Displaying formulas is similar to a toggle switch. Repeating Ctrl~ turns viewing the formulas on and off.

TIPS

If you click the wrong cell by mistake, click the correct cell. If you start keying in the wrong cell, press Esc. Then click the correct cell.

Name _____ *Date* _____

Directions   Complete the following problems.

A.   **Rewrite and add the following problems in the space provided to**   OBJECTIVES **2, 3**
practice aligning and adding columns of numbers. Show maximum
decimals.

1.	**2.**	**3.**	**4.**	**5.**
14	1,419	387	0.1932	829.2
890	429	6,780	837.64	270.2968
1,092	906	1,000.1	5.001	8.00
+ 1,463	+ 1,489	+ 9,046	+ 5,196.3	+ 110.43

Rewrite and add your problems below.

1.   **2.**   **3.**   **4.**   **5.**

B.   **Fill in the blanks with the numbers you think as you mentally add**   OBJECTIVE **4**
down each column of figures.

6. 5	**7.** 9	**8.** 8	**9.** 5	**10.** 4
4 a. _____	2 a. _____	1 a. _____	7 a. _____	3 a. _____
9 b. _____	3 b. _____	7 b. _____	3 b. _____	7 b. _____
2 c. _____	8 c. _____	6 c. _____	2 c. _____	6 c. _____
7 d. _____	5 d. _____	7 d. _____	7 d. _____	8 d. _____
6 e. _____	6 e. _____	9 e. _____	5 e. _____	5 e. _____
5 f. _____	5 f. _____	8 f. _____	6 f. _____	4 f. _____
+ 1 g. _____	+ 2 g. _____	+ 9 g. _____	+ 3 g. _____	+ 2 g. _____

C.   **Fill in the blanks with the numbers you think as you mentally add**   OBJECTIVE **5**
down each column of figures by tens.

11. 5	**12.** 6	**13.** 8	**14.** 9	**15.** 7
8 a. _____	4 a. _____	9 a. _____	6 a. _____	3 a. _____
5 b. _____	2 b. _____	2 b. _____	1 b. _____	1 b. _____
+ 2 c. _____	+ 8 c. _____	+ 1 c. _____	+ 4 c. _____	+ 9 c. _____

16. 6	**17.** 9	**18.** 6	**19.** 2	**20.** 4
9 a. _____	3 a. _____	7 a. _____	2 a. _____	4 a. _____
4 b. _____	4 b. _____	4 b. _____	6 b. _____	7 b. _____
3 c. _____	7 c. _____	3 c. _____	7 c. _____	2 c. _____
1 d. _____	1 d. _____	5 d. _____	2 d. _____	3 d. _____
+ 7 e. _____	+ 6 e. _____	+ 5 e. _____	+ 1 e. _____	+ 5 e. _____

D. Complete the following problems. OBJECTIVE **5**

21.	22.	23.	24.
3,226	45,112	70,001	398
231	3,785	3,223	4,567
50	221	75	197
+ 1,257	+ 9,353	+ 15,280	+ 8,199

25.	26.	27.	28.
33,423	98.000	0.455	1.223
37	7.455	0.23	0.6
1,445	0.290	1.096	0.9855
+ 25,256	+ 14.230	+ 0.905	+ 2.0505

29.	30.	31.	32.
77.44	9.99	7.222	4.9123
2.9	5.32	0.579	0.288
36.97	0.355	0.166	0.76
+ 85.31	+ 6.999	+ 1.02	+ 7.987

33.	34.	35.	36.
$27.50	$1.98	$98.88	$0.50
15.95	3.01	7.27	35.35
1.99	7.55	90.10	4.83
+ 83.11	+ 5.05	+ 27.01	+ 19.90

37.	38.	39.	40.
$270.33	$1,887.50	$27,994.22	3,007
98.50	228.11	3,097.45	15,097
452.66	5.50	329.90	2,493
+ 28.75	+ 3,322.57	+ 98,203.97	+ 45

E. Complete the following problems by adding horizontally. Write your answers, showing maximum decimals, in the blanks provided. OBJECTIVE **6**

41. $7,320 + 5,921 =$ _____

42. $334.50 + 9.78 =$ _____

43. $131 + 439 + 874 =$ _____

44. $3.95 + 4.95 + 3.25 + 6.15 =$ _____

45. $2,106 + 973 + 229 + 14 =$ _____

46. $19.16 + 0.99 + 1.66 =$ _____

47. $8,695,030 + 46,788 =$ _____

48. $312.35 + 345.09 + 0.22 =$ _____

49. $169 + 25 + 198 + 37 =$ _____

50. $6.4 + 3.75 + 9.2 + 12 =$ _____

F. Solve the following word problems. Write your answers in the blanks provided. Place commas and dollar signs where appropriate. OBJECTIVE 7

51. Carlota played 9 holes of golf. She scored the following on each hole: 5, 5, 4, 6, 4, 4, 3, 5, and 4. Total all 9 scores and determine her total score for 9 holes of golf. _____

52. Maria checked her grocery receipt to determine whether the amounts paid for each of her ten purchases had been added correctly. The following numbers appeared on her slip: $1.98, $0.89, $3.29, $2.76, $4.11, $1.19, $0.79, $0.84, $1.00, $3.25. Add the numbers and determine the total. _____

53. Rafael Molina decided to increase his investment portfolio to include small cap technology stocks. He purchased 100 shares each of Robotic Visions, Inc., costing $298; DSL.net, Inc., costing $320; and Secure Blue, costing $225. What was Rafael's total investment? _____

54. Roscoe purchased four new CDs for his blues collection. He paid $15.00, $14.95, $12.95, and $15.00. Tax on the purchase was $4.56. How much was Roscoe's purchase? _____

55. Bryan, the office manager for Bailey & Gorman law firm, decided to redecorate the firm's client waiting area. He purchased a library table for $375, a lamp for $99, a picture for $24.95, a flower arrangement for $69.95, and a mantel clock for $389. How much money did Bryan spend? _____

56. Khan decided to carpet his house. He wanted to estimate the amount of carpet he would need before he went shopping. The square footage for each room in the house was 205, 90, 900, 300, 250, 275, and 200. How many square feet of carpet must Khan buy in order to carpet his entire house? _____

57. For Memorial Day, Dos Rios Campgrounds rented these campsites: 39 tent-only campsistes, 86 water and electricity campsites, and 110 full-hookup campsites. Forty-five campsites were not rented. How many total campsites at Dos Rios were available for rental? _____

58. Johnson's Gourmet Sandwich Shop sold 86 Cucumber and Apricot sandwiches, 63 Focaccia Turkey Club sandwiches, 110 South of the Border sandwiches, 120 Monte Cristo sandwiches, 75 Grilled Tofu sandwiches, and 91 Eggplant sandwiches. How many sandwiches were sold? _____

G. Use Excel to solve problems involving addition. OBJECTIVE 8

59. Retrieve the file *ch01ex03.xlsx*. Follow the directions. Save the file as *ch01ex03a.xlsx*.

60. Retrieve the file *ch01ex04.xlsx*. Follow the directions. Save the file as *ch01ex04a.xlsx*.

1.3 Subtraction

OBJECTIVE 1 Identify terms used with subtraction.

Subtraction, like addition, is a basic math skill used in business. **Subtraction** is the process of determining the difference between two numbers. The **difference** is obtained by subtracting the **subtrahend** from the **minuend**, as shown.

EXAMPLE

$$\begin{array}{rl} \$95.66 & \leftarrow \text{minuend} \\ \text{minus sign} \rightarrow \quad -\ 36.12 & \leftarrow \text{subtrahend} \\ \hline \$59.54 & \leftarrow \text{difference} \end{array}$$

In subtraction, as in addition, it is important that you align numbers and decimals. The terminology used in stating a subtraction problem varies. You might say, "9 minus 5," "9 take away 5," "9 subtract 5," "5 subtracted from 9," or "the difference between 9 and 5."

A **negative number** results when you subtract a larger number from a smaller number. Negative numbers are often expressed by enclosing the number within angle brackets, such as ⟨29⟩. They may also be enclosed within parentheses, expressed with a minus sign before the number (–29), or printed in red.

OBJECTIVE 2 Subtract vertically.

To subtract vertically, work from right to left, subtracting the bottom number from the top.

EXAMPLE

$$\begin{array}{r} 36 \\ -\ 15 \\ \hline \end{array}$$

STEPS

1. Align the minuend, 36, over the subtrahend, 15.

2. Working from right to left, subtract the units position, $6 - 5 = 1$. Write the difference, 1, beneath the 5 in the units position.

3. Subtract the tens position, $3 - 1 = 2$. Write the difference, 2, under the 1 in the tens position.

4. The solution is 21.

Subtraction is based on addition. Therefore, you can check your solutions to problems by adding the difference and the subtrahend. The result is the minuend. Study the following problem and check the answer.

$$
\begin{array}{r}
447 \quad \leftarrow \text{minuend} \\
- 138 \quad \leftarrow \text{subtrahend} \\
\hline
309 \quad \leftarrow \text{difference}
\end{array}
$$

Because you can check subtraction problems by adding, your calculations should be accurate.

$$
\text{add:} \quad
\begin{array}{r}
138 \quad \leftarrow \text{subtrahend} \\
+ 309 \quad \leftarrow \text{difference} \\
\hline
447 \quad \leftarrow \text{minuend}
\end{array}
$$

OBJECTIVE **4** Regroup in subtraction.

Regrouping, or **borrowing** as it is sometimes called, should not be difficult for you. In the example below, the number has been rewritten to show the positions or places to help you learn how to borrow.

EXAMPLE

$$
\begin{array}{r}
75 \\
- 39
\end{array}
\quad \text{or} \quad
\begin{array}{r}
7 \text{ tens} + 5 \text{ units} \\
- 3 \text{ tens} + 9 \text{ units}
\end{array}
$$

STEPS

1. Working from right to left, subtract the units position. Because the 9 cannot be subtracted from the 5, you must borrow 10 from the tens position and add it to the 5 to make 15. In doing so, you are reducing the tens position by 1, leaving 6 tens. Draw a line through the 7 and write a 6 above it to help you remember that you have reduced the 7 to a 6 when you begin subtracting the tens position. You can now subtract the units position, $15 - 9 = 6$.

2. Subtract the tens position, $6 - 3 = 3$.

$$
\begin{array}{r}
\overset{6\ 15}{\cancel{75}} = \quad 6 \text{ tens} \quad 15 \text{ units} \\
- 39 = - 3 \text{ tens} - 9 \text{ units} \\
\hline
3 \text{ tens} \quad 6 \text{ units}
\end{array}
$$

3. The solution is 36.

Anytime you cannot subtract a number, regroup by borrowing ten from the place value column(s) to the left of the column in which you are working. Always check your answer by adding the subtrahend and the difference.

OBJECTIVE 5 Solve problems with zeros in regrouping in subtraction.

Many students have difficulty with borrowing when subtraction problems contain zeros. The following steps will be helpful to you.

EXAMPLE

$$
\begin{array}{rll}
900 & \text{or} & \text{9 hundreds} + \text{0 tens} + \text{0 units} \\
-\ 18 & & \qquad\qquad\ \ \text{1 ten}\ + \text{8 units} \\
\hline
\end{array}
$$

STEPS

1. Subtract the units position. Because 8 cannot be subtracted from 0, borrow 1 from the tens position. Because the tens position is 0, you must borrow 1 from the hundreds position, reducing it by 1. Study how the numbers are now regrouped.

8 hundreds + 10 tens + 0 units

$$
\begin{array}{r}
{\scriptstyle 8\ 10} \\
\cancel{9}\,\cancel{0}\ 0 \\
-\,1\ 8 \\
\end{array}
\quad \leftarrow \text{1 hundred} = \text{10 tens}
$$

Now you can borrow 1 from the tens position, as shown here.

8 hundreds + 9 tens + 10 units

$$
\begin{array}{r}
{\scriptstyle 9} \\
{\scriptstyle 8\ 10\,10} \\
\cancel{9}\,\cancel{0}\,\cancel{0} \\
-\,1\ 8 \\
\hline
2 \\
\end{array}
\quad \leftarrow \text{1 ten} = \text{10 units}
$$

Subtract the units position, $10 - 8 = 2$.

2. Remember, the tens position has been reduced by 1 because you borrowed 1. It is now 9. Subtract the tens position.

$$
\begin{array}{r}
{\scriptstyle 9} \\
{\scriptstyle 8\ 10\,10} \\
\cancel{9}\,\cancel{0}\,\cancel{0} \\
-\,1\ 8 \\
\hline
8\ 2 \\
\end{array}
$$

3. Subtract the hundreds position, $8 - 0 = 8$.

$$
\begin{array}{r}
{\scriptstyle 9} \\
{\scriptstyle 8\ 10\,10} \\
\cancel{9}\,\cancel{0}\,\cancel{0} \\
-\,1\ 8 \\
\hline
8\ 8\ 2 \\
\end{array}
$$

OBJECTIVE 6 Subtract horizontally.

In business it often becomes necessary to subtract a problem that is written across the page horizontally rather than vertically. You should learn to subtract horizontally rather than take the time to rewrite the problem. Follow these steps to subtract horizontally.

EXAMPLE

$$\$334.92 - \$12.41$$

STEPS

1. Subtract the hundredths position, 2 – 1, and write the answer, 1, at the far right in the blank.

        1

2. Subtract the tenths position, 9 – 4, and write the answer, 5, next to the 1 in the blank.

        51

> **TIPS**
>
> *Remember, always check your answer by adding the subtrahend and the difference.*

3. Place the decimal point next to the 5. Subtract the units position, 4 – 2, and write the answer, 2, next to the decimal point.

        2.51

4. Subtract the tens position, 3 – 1, and write the answer, 2, next to the 2 in the blank.

        22.51

5. There is no number to subtract from the hundreds position. Write the number 3 to the left of the 2 that is in the tens position in the blank. Add the dollar sign beside the 3.

        $322.51

OBJECTIVE 7 Express negative numbers.

A negative number results when a larger number is subtracted from a smaller number. To subtract a larger number from a smaller number, reverse the numbers and subtract. You must remember to place a negative sign before the answer, or the answer will be incorrect.

EXAMPLE

$$
\begin{array}{r}
31 \\
- \ 48 \\
\end{array}
\qquad
\begin{array}{l}
\text{minuend (smaller)} \\
\text{subtrahend (larger)}
\end{array}
$$

$$
\begin{array}{r}
48 \\
- \ 31 \\
\hline
17 \\
\end{array}
\qquad
\text{Difference is a negative number.}
$$

The difference is –17.

Negative numbers are sometimes used to express degrees of temperature, such as –2 degrees Fahrenheit or –18.8 degrees Celsius. Think of a thermometer. When the temperature drops below zero, negative numbers are used to describe the temperature in degrees. Numbers above zero are positive numbers. Notice that the negative sign often resembles a minus sign, which indicates subtraction.

Another example of negative numbers is when you write a check for more money than you have deposited in the bank. If the bank honors the check, it will notify you that you have a negative balance.

OBJECTIVE 8 Add negative numbers.

You may be required to add a column of negative numbers, as in the following example.

EXAMPLE

$$
\begin{array}{r}
-47 \\
-83 \\
-23 \\
\underline{-15} \\
-168
\end{array}
$$

You add as if they are positive numbers, placing the negative sign before the answer.

OBJECTIVE 9 Combine addition and subtraction.

You may be required to complete calculations on the job that combine positive and negative numbers, resulting in a negative or a positive number.

EXAMPLE

$$
\begin{array}{r}
+25 \\
+13 \\
-88 \\
+07 \\
\underline{-26}
\end{array}
$$

Total the positive numbers (+) 25, 13, 7. Total the negative numbers (–) 88, 26. Then subtract the two sums. If the total of the positive numbers is the greater of the two, the answer is a positive number. If the total of the negative numbers is the greater of the two, the answer is a negative number.

Total positive numbers →	$+ 25 + 13 + 7 = +45$	
Total negative numbers →	$- 88 - 26$	$= -114$
Subtract →	-114	
	$\underline{+45}$	
Solution →	-69	

OBJECTIVE 10 Use Excel to solve problems involving subtraction.

As you learn more and more about Excel's formulas, you will see the need to use subtraction in the formulas. An example is a payroll register that has been created showing the gross earnings for each employee minus all the deductions, resulting in the net pay each employee will earn.

Formulas that contain subtraction follow the rules you learned about formulas in addition. The hyphen on the keyboard represents the minus sign (–) in subtraction. You may enter the formula from the keyboard or use the Pointing Method. An example of a formula that contains subtraction operations is used in Cell F6 to calculate Net Pay.

= D6 – E6

The following spreadsheet (see Figure 1-7) shows the formula in the Formula bar. Notice that you do not use spaces when you key formulas in Excel.

FIGURE 1-7

Subtraction Formula in Excel

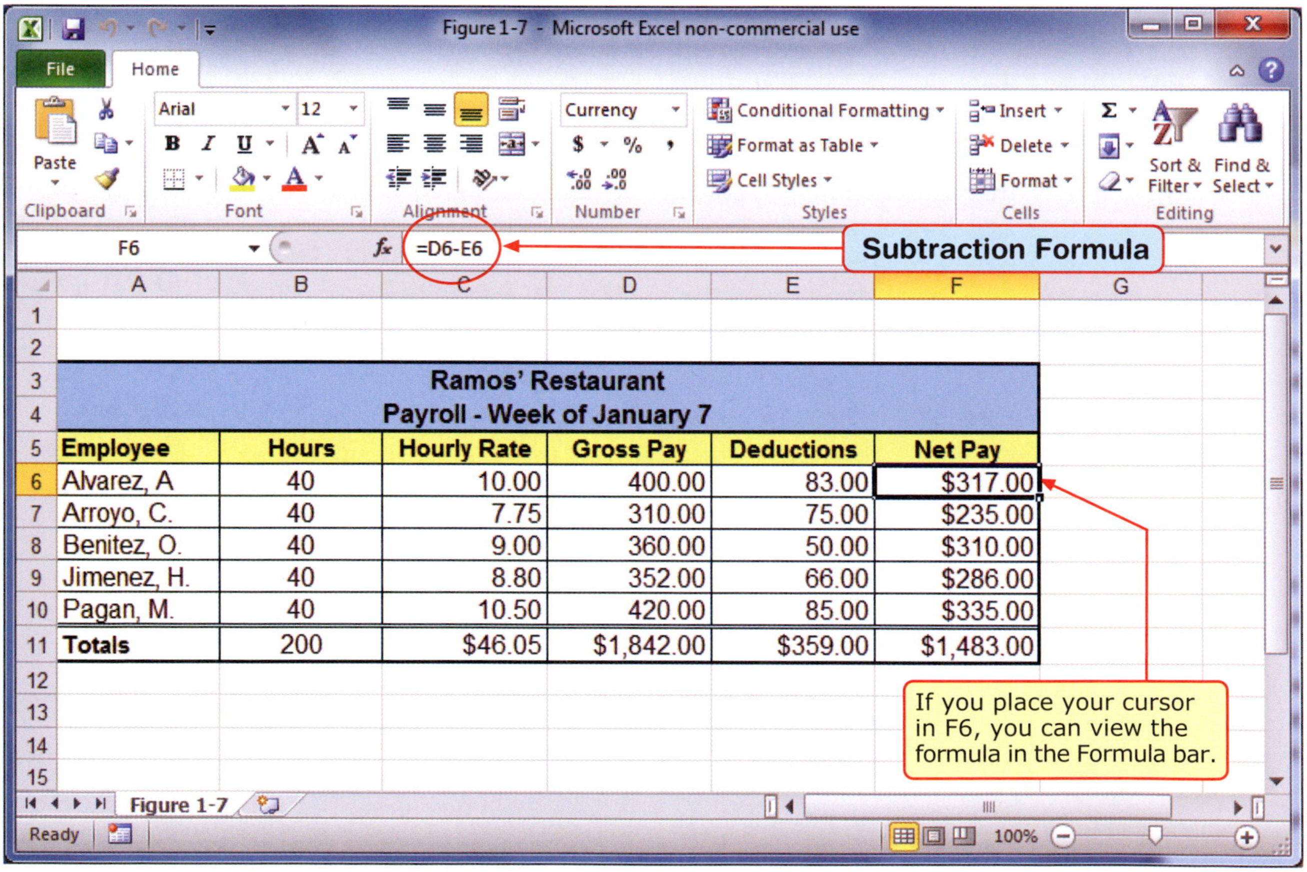

	A	B	C	D	E	F
3	Ramos' Restaurant					
4	Payroll - Week of January 7					
5	**Employee**	**Hours**	**Hourly Rate**	**Gross Pay**	**Deductions**	**Net Pay**
6	Alvarez, A	40	10.00	400.00	83.00	$317.00
7	Arroyo, C.	40	7.75	310.00	75.00	$235.00
8	Benitez, O.	40	9.00	360.00	50.00	$310.00
9	Jimenez, H.	40	8.80	352.00	66.00	$286.00
10	Pagan, M.	40	10.50	420.00	85.00	$335.00
11	**Totals**	200	$46.05	$1,842.00	$359.00	$1,483.00

Retrieve the file *ch01pr05.xlsx*.

Using the Pointing Method, enter a formula in Cell F6 to calculate the Net Pay for A. Alvarez.

Net Pay = Gross Pay – Deductions

= D6 – E6

1. Click in Cell F6 to activate the cell where the results of the formula will appear.

2. Key =.

3. Click the cell to be subtracted from (minuend).

4. Key the minus sign (-) to tell Excel to subtract.

5. Click in the cell to be subtracted (the subtrahend).

6. Press Enter to enter the formula.

7. Repeat steps 2 through 6 in each of the other cells in Column F in order to calculate Net Pay for each of the other Employees.

8. Use AutoSum to total each column.

9. Format all Totals (except for Total Hours) for Currency. Set Decimal places to 2. Set Currency symbol to $.

10. Save the file as *ch01pr05a.xlsx*.

TIPS

When the minuend is smaller than the subtrahend, the result is a negative number. Excel will place a minus sign (–) in front of the number. If you have formatted the cell for Accounting, Excel will place parentheses around the number to show it is negative.

Olly/Shutterstock.com

Name   Date

Directions   Solve the following problems. Write your answers in the blanks provided. Place commas and dollar signs in answers where appropriate.

A. Subtract the numbers vertically; regroup. Then check your subtraction by adding.   OBJECTIVES **2, 3, 4, 5**

1. 700
    − 234

2. 8,090
    − 3,156

3. $500.00
    − 436.48

4. 1,000,000
    − 90,768

5. 10,908
    − 9,090

6. 8,006
    − 5,970

7. 380.00
    − 198.07

8. 30,080,114
    − 29,090,009

9. $400.05
    − 10.09

10. $80.90
     − 70.60

11. $569,487
     − 10,807

12. $1,000,100
     − 99,999

13. 2,080.109
     − 359.090

14. 80.900
     − 6.999

15. 7,000.10
     − 458.72

16. 33.0008
     − 9.0810

17. 4.6795
     − 0.0039

18. 30.007
     − 5.199

19. 195.167
     − 96.180

20. 79.108
     − 12.090

B. Subtract the following numbers horizontally.   OBJECTIVE **6**

21. 345 − 29   _____

22. $49.50 − $5.07   _____

23. 1,200 − 387   _____

24. 1,489 − 379   _____

25. $14.69 − $3.02   _____

26. 1,467,902 − 9,999   _____

27. 3.167 − 3.159   _____

28. $99.95 − $49.95   _____

29. $139.50 − $89.75   _____

30. $9.98 − $3.75   _____

31. 47,580 − 37,642   _____

32. 89,900 − 25,000   _____

33. 35,689 − 4,119   _____

34. $75.75 − $32.41   _____

35. $117.15 − $109.26   _____

36. $829.50 − $27.60   _____

37. 1.463 − 0.095   _____

38. 15.182 − 0.380   _____

39. 16.190 − 0.145   _____

40. 105.156 − 18.940   _____

C. Find negative numbers for the following problems.   OBJECTIVE 7

41.
479
− 999

42.
9,881
− 15,887

43.
10,320
− 50,321

44.
$49.50
− 87.75

45.
1.898
− 23.443

46.
$7.90
− 8.75

47.
$77.48
− 95.02

48.
84,410
− 100,966

49.
$3,691
− 4,707

50.
$595.23
− 779.32

51.
19,337
− 22,447

52.
14.978
− 27.650

D. Combine addition and subtraction for the following problems.   OBJECTIVES 8, 9

53.
+79
−33
+45
−99
+25
−56

54.
+53
−106
−464
+768
−101
−221

55.
+12.10
−47.50
−25.00
+88.65
−23.25
−18.17

56.
−8.99
+22.118
+1.98
−75.007
+10.009
−11.111

57.
−71
−23
+12
−57
+12
−88

58.
+87.90
−108.01
+2.61
−98.76
−48.75
−2.95
+1.11

59.
+186.90
+143.20
−196.50
−190.90
−29.48
−38.29
+96.50

60.
−169.77
−67.90
+1.71
−8.50
+27.33
−150.49
−88.22

E. Solve the following word problems.   OBJECTIVES 2-9

61. Chien purchased 3 CDs totaling $42.97. When he arrived home, he realized one of the CDs was not one he wanted. He returned it, and the store refunded him $14.99. How much did he pay for the 2 CDs he kept?

62. A local office supply store is having a sale on copy paper—buy two cases of copy paper for $67.50 and get a third case free. If the normal price for copy paper is $24.50 a case, how much would you save by purchasing at the sale price?

63. Margaret purchased electronics costing $94.50. The department store allowed a 25% discount as a sales promotion. Margaret received a $23.63 discount. What did Margaret pay for the electronics?

64. Kreiger Grocery Store ordered $1,492.88 worth of merchandise from Grant Manufacturing Company. There was $346.92 of the goods damaged that had to be returned. How much is due on the order?

65. Janet earned $372.80 after taxes last week and decided to save $95.50 toward her car payment. How much money did she have to live on after saving? _____

66. Kha's living expenses each month are as follows: $650 for rent, $450 for car payment, $25 for VISA payment, and $28 for furniture payment. Kha makes $2,300 net pay a month. How much money does she have after paying her expenses? _____

67. Robert spent $500 on a new mountain bike. He also had to buy a spare tire for $39. He had a coupon for $50 off. How much did Robert spend? _____

68. Levita shopped at the 5-7-9 Shop. She found a blouse priced at $24 but marked $8.00 off. How much did the blouse cost? _____

69. Because of the poor economy, Kim's union agreed to a $0.38 decrease in pay per hour, per employee. Kim's previous hourly wage was $10.50. How much per hour will Kim now make? _____

70. Keshinda decided to pay off her automobile loan. Her balance is $459.80. Her payoff amount is $432.90. How much will Keshinda save by paying off the loan early? _____

71. Annith bought a 1967 Pontiac Firebird that had been in an accident and the motor would not run. She and her father restored the Firebird to like-new condition. Annith paid $5,580 for the car and sold it for $24,000 after spending $8,500 for parts and having it painted. How much did Annith make on the car? _____

72. Ms. Starling decided to have her carpets cleaned. A-1 Carpet Cleaners offered to clean four rooms and one hallway for $99. If she had all her rooms cleaned, the cost would be $149. How much more would it cost to have all her carpets cleaned? _____

73. Jacob balanced his checkbook. The bank reported he had $18 in ATM charges and a $12 service charge that had to be deducted from his checkbook. The balance in his checkbook before deducting these charges was $1,709.88. What was the balance after these charges were deducted? _____

F. Use Excel to solve problems involving subtraction. `OBJECTIVE 10`

74. Retrieve the file *ch01ex05.xlsx*. Follow the directions. Save the file as *ch01ex05a.xlsx*.

75. Retrieve the file *ch01ex06.xlsx*. Follow the directions. Save the file as *ch01ex06a.xlsx*.

1.4 Multiplication

OBJECTIVES

1. Identify terms used with multiplication.
2. Multiply whole numbers.
3. Multiply with decimals.
4. Solve problems with zeros in multiplication.
5. Check multiplication.
6. Accumulate products.
7. Use Excel to solve problems involving multiplication.

OBJECTIVE 1 Identify terms used with multiplication.

Multiplication is one of the basic math concepts that will enable you to calculate more quickly. It is a shortcut for repeated addition. One of the uses of multiplication is determining the total amount owed when you purchase more than one item costing the same amount, such as 6 CDs at $9.95 each. You can add $9.95 six times, but it is quicker to multiply $9.95 by 6. Through the use of multiplication, you will be able to determine if your paycheck has been computed correctly and if the charges on your monthly bills are correct.

Multiplication is the mathematical procedure for finding the product of two numbers. The number to be multiplied is called the **multiplicand**, and the number that indicates how many times to multiply is the **multiplier**. The result, or the answer, is known as the **product**. Sometimes the multiplicand and multiplier are referred to as **factors**. Study the following example.

EXAMPLE

$$
\begin{array}{r}
273 \\
\times\ 28 \\
\hline
7{,}644
\end{array}
$$

multiplication sign →
← multiplicand
← multiplier } factors
← product

© Losevsky Pavel, 2010/Used under license from Shutterstock.com

To find the product of two numbers, follow these steps.

STEPS

1. Align the numbers as you would for addition and subtraction. Note the alignment of the example above.

2. Multiply the multiplicand by the first digit on the right in the multiplier (8 in the example below). Place the partial product below the line.

Written:	273	
	× 28	
partial product →	2,184	← 273 × 8 = 2,184

3. Multiply the multiplicand by the next digit to the left (2 in the example), placing the partial product on a separate line one place to the left under the first product.

Written:	273	
	× 28	
	2,184	
partial product →	5 46	← 273 × 2 = 546

4. Draw a horizontal line. Then add.

	273
	× 28
	2,184
	5 46
	7,644

Note: Each time a number is multiplied, the product is written under the previous product one place to the left.

When multiplying decimals, multiply as previously explained. Then count the number of decimal places in the multiplicand and the multiplier. Mark off that many places in the product, counting from right to left.

EXAMPLES

1.9201	← 4 decimal places
× 0.6	←1 decimal place
1.15206	←5 decimal places

$17.95	←2 decimal places
× 15	←0 decimal places
$269.25	←2 decimal places

Two instances where zeros occur in multiplication need explanation: (1) where zeros appear at the end of a number and (2) where they appear in the middle of a multiplier.

Zeros at the End of a Number

Follow these steps.

EXAMPLE

$$
\begin{array}{r}
2{,}150 \\
\times\ 1{,}300
\end{array}
\quad \text{zeros at end of numbers}
$$

STEPS

1. When multiplying numbers ending in zero, ignore the zeros, as shown below.

$$
\begin{array}{r}
215 \\
\times\ 13 \\
\hline
645 \\
215 \\
\hline
2{,}795
\end{array}
$$

2. Count the number of zeros ignored (1 in the multiplicand and 2 in the multiplier = 3) and add three zeros to the right of the product.

$$2{,}795{,}000$$

This procedure is called **annexing** or **appending** zeros.

Zero in Multiplier

When the multiplier contains a zero, use the following steps to multiply.

EXAMPLE

$$
\begin{array}{r}
136 \\
\times\ 206
\end{array}
\quad \text{multiplier contains zero}
$$

STEPS

1. Apply the rules learned in multiplication until you get to the zero in the multiplier. Ignore it and multiply by the next number, 2.

2. When you write the second product, move one extra place to the left for every zero in the multiplier. Study the following example.

$$
\begin{array}{r}
136 \\
\times\ 206 \\
\hline
816 \\
272 \\
\hline
28{,}016
\end{array}
$$

First product is 136×6. Ignore 0.
Second product is 136×2.
Instead of moving one position to the left (under the 1), move two positions (under the 8).

> **CALCULATOR TIP**
>
> *In addition and subtraction you must clear your register between problems; when you use the = key, you don't.*

To check an answer in multiplication, reverse the multiplier and multiplicand and multiply. You will obtain the same product. To practice, check the preceding practice problem by multiplying 206 by 136. Another example is shown below.

EXAMPLE

$$61 \times 37 = 2{,}257$$
$$37 \times 61 = 2{,}257$$

In business, it is often necessary to accumulate the totals of several products. An example is when you place an order for office supplies.

EXAMPLE

4 boxes colored binders @ $24.99 box	=	_____
3 packs sticky pop-up notes @ $29.99 pack	=	_____
2 heavy-duty storage boxes @ $26.99 12/pack each	=	_____
Subtotal	=	_____

Four Step Problem Solving Plan

Clues	Action Plan	Solve
Prices:	To find the subtotal, multiply each quantity by the price of the item.	4 × $24.99 = $99.96
4 boxes colored binders @ $24.99		3 × $29.99 = $89.97
3 packs sticky pop-up notes @ $29.99	Then, add the products.	2 × $26.99 = + $53.98
2 heavy-duty storage boxes @ $26.99		Subtotal $243.91

Conclusion

The subtotal for the office supplies is $243.91.

TIPS

In multiplication you can multiply 61 × 37 or multiply 37 × 61 and get the same product.

TIPS

When accumulating products, @ always means multiply.

CALCULATOR TIP

To accumulate products, you can use the memory plus key (M+) and the memory recall key (MRC) to obtain the total of all products. After each product press M+. When all products have been calculated, press the MRC key for the answer. To clear the MRC memory, press MRC then press the memory minus (M−) key. The clear (C or CE) key will not clear MRC memory.

Use Excel to solve problems involving multiplication.

Formulas using multiplication are real time-savers that provide many helpful calculations, such as calculating payroll, sales tax, and invoice amounts. Just as you created formulas for addition and subtraction, you can create formulas for multiplication using the keyboard or the Pointing Method. The asterisk (*) is the operator that signals Excel to multiply. Here is an example of a formula that contains a multiplication operation.

$$= B6 * C6$$

The following spreadsheet (see Figure 1-8) shows the formula in Cell D6.

Figure 1-8

Multiplication Formula in Excel

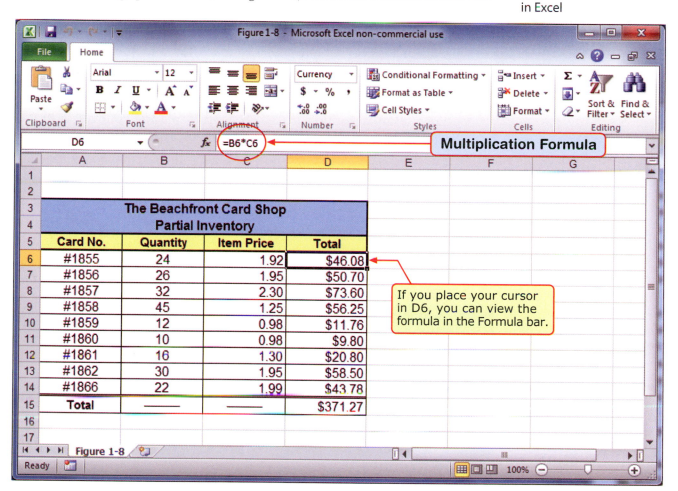

Retrieve the file ***ch01pr06.xlsx***.

Using the Pointing Method, enter a formula in Cell D6 to find the sales for Card #1855.

$$\text{Sales} = \text{Quantity} \times \text{Item Price}$$
$$= B6 * C6$$

1. Click in Cell D6 to activate the cell where the results of the formula will appear.

2. Key =.

3. Click in the cell to be multiplied (multiplicand). In this case, this is the Quantity.

4. Key the asterisk (*) to tell Excel to multiply.

5. Click in the cell that indicates how many times to multiply (multiplier). In this case, this is the Item Price.

6. Press Enter.

7. Enter a similar formula in Cell D7. Start by placing your cursor in Cell D7 to activate the cell and repeat steps 2 through 6.

8. Continue in this manner until you reach Cell D14, which will be the total for the last card in the list.

9. Total Column D using AutoSum.

10. Format Column D for Currency. Set Decimal places to 2. Set Currency symbol to $.

11. Save the file as ***ch01pr06a.xlsx***.

Rick Lewis/Shutterstock.com

Name _____ Date _____

Directions   Solve the following problems. Write your answers in the blanks provided. Place commas and dollar signs in answers where appropriate.

A. Multiply the following whole numbers.   OBJECTIVE 2

1. $233 \times 793 =$ _____
2. $1{,}298 \times 333 =$ _____
3. $45 \times 106 =$ _____
4. $132 \times 855 =$ _____
5. $92 \times 82 =$ _____
6. $2{,}521 \times 1{,}459 =$ _____
7. $\$998 \times 21 =$ _____
8. $987 \times 19{,}151 =$ _____
9. $8{,}201 \times 653 =$ _____
10. $\$1{,}448 \times 188 =$ _____
11. $1{,}995 \times 249 =$ _____
12. $144 \times 144 =$ _____
13. $12{,}557 \times 77 =$ _____
14. $57 \times 897 =$ _____
15. $2{,}855 \times 98 =$ _____
16. $1{,}992 \times 123 =$ _____
17. $46 \times 144 =$ _____
18. $1{,}899 \times 82 =$ _____
19. $566 \times 38 =$ _____
20. $521 \times 476 =$ _____

21.	22.	23.	24.	25.
1,958	472	148	397	769
× 46	× 326	× 47	× 26	× 595

B. Multiply the following decimals. Show maximum decimals.   OBJECTIVE 3

26.	27.	28.	29.	30.
0.3952	76.9	1.111	$86.92	$12.37
× 0.4834	× 48.2	× 1.3	× 0.05	× 0.0008

C. Multiply the following decimals and money amounts. Round your answers to the nearest cent.   OBJECTIVE 3

31. $\$2.46 \times 2.7 =$ _____
32. $\$1.76 \times 8.21 =$ _____
33. $\$1.98 \times 15 =$ _____
34. $\$8.54 \times 122 =$ _____
35. $\$109.98 \times 2.91 =$ _____
36. $\$2.29 \times 24 =$ _____
37. $\$5.06 \times 1.06 =$ _____
38. $\$0.21 \times 0.47 =$ _____
39. $\$4.50 \times 892 =$ _____
40. $\$45.75 \times 1.95 =$ _____
41. $\$3.75 \times 4.68 =$ _____
42. $\$0.02 \times 321.4 =$ _____

D. Multiply the following numbers containing zeros. OBJECTIVES **4, 5**

43. $3,009 \times 50 =$ _____

44. $\$5,090 \times 75 =$ _____

45. $1,800 \times 206 =$ _____

46. $20,000 \times 10 =$ _____

47. $\$400 \times 202 =$ _____

48. $8.008 \times 0.07 =$ _____

49. $\$1,708 \times 105 =$ _____

50. $6,005 \times 9.007 =$ _____

51. $1,040 \times 20 =$ _____

52. $\$27 \times 304 =$ _____

53. $701 \times 22 =$ _____

54. $\$104.05 \times 101 =$ _____

E. Find the following accumulations of products. For money amounts, round to the nearest cent. OBJECTIVE **6**

55. $31 \times 54 =$ _____

56. $1.87 \times 0.15 =$ _____

$47 \times 67 =$ _____

$5.43 \times 3.01 =$ _____

$90 \times 28 =$ _____

$0.32 \times 2.95 =$ _____

Total = _____

Total = _____

57. $\$0.59 \times 18 =$ _____

58. $\$25.40 \times 12.98 =$ _____

$\$0.29 \times 68 =$ _____

$\$98.99 \times 31.50 =$ _____

$\$0.99 \times 72 =$ _____

$\$17.49 \times 25.88 =$ _____

Total = _____

Total = _____

F. Solve the following word problems. OBJECTIVES **2-6**

59. Madison Furniture Company ordered 4 sofa sleepers at $599 each, 3 love seats at $199 each, and 3 ottomans at $79 each. What was the total purchase price of all the furniture ordered? _____

60. Meredith worked part-time sacking groceries and checking at the cash register for a local food store. When she sacked groceries, she was paid $7.25 per hour. When she checked, she was paid $8.50 per hour. Monday she checked and worked 8 hours, Tuesday she sacked and worked 4 hours, Wednesday she did not work, Thursday she checked and worked 8 hours, and Friday and Saturday she sacked and worked 8 hours each day. What were Meredith's total wages earned before taxes for the week? _____

61. Jesse Morton sold 3 cars he had restored to like-new condition. He received $18,000 each for the cars. What was the total price he received for the 3 cars? _____

62. An accident occurred causing damage to 2 cars. Each owner took his car to Carlos' Repair Shop for estimates. Carlos estimated each car needed a new fender at $1,990, a new bumper at $850, and a new headlight assembly at $250. What was the total estimate for 1 car? for 2 cars? _____

63. Erin went to Best Burgers and bought 5 hamburgers at $2.79 each, 5 small soft drinks at $0.89 each, and 5 large orders of French fries at $1.29 each. What did the purchase cost Erin before tax?

_____

64. Fuji Moore paid $467 per month for 48 months on her automobile. What did the car cost her?

_____

65. Dale works for Very-Clean Carpet Cleaners. He is paid a bonus for each additional service he sells during the week. This week he sold 5 heavy-duty treatments and received a $25 bonus for each, sold 6 extra rooms and received a $10 bonus per room, and sold 10 poly-care protective coatings and received an $8 bonus for each. How much money did he make in bonuses this week?

_____

66. Kim received a raise of $0.70 per hour. Her old hourly wage was $10.80. How much per 40-hour week was Kim making before her raise? after her raise?

_____

67. Winston has paid $268.34 for 60 months on his furniture purchase. What did the furniture cost Winston?

_____

68. Machine A runs for 6 hours and produces 6.45 widgets per hour. Machine B runs for 4 hours and produces 7.81 widgets per hour. Machine C runs for 5.5 hours and produces 7.21 widgets per hour. How many widgets can be produced in all?

_____

69. Zachary pays his car insurance 4 times per year. Each payment is $103.05. How much does Zachary pay for car insurance in one year?

_____

70. Rosita ordered several pieces of lumber. The order included 12 one-by-fours at $6.98 each, 9 one-by-twos at $1.22 each, and 12 sheets of plywood at $7.32 each. What was Rosita's total bill?

_____

71. Carter's Quick Copy charges $0.10 a copy. Nina needed to make 237 copies of one page and 438 copies of the second page. How much will she be charged for copies?

_____

72. Montel ordered 5 cases of copy paper at $24 per case, 3 boxes of pens at $5.95 per box, 2 software programs at $9 each, and 4 software programs at $39 each. Before taxes, what did Montel's order amount to?

_____

73. Randy sells bread to the local grocery stores. He sells daily 144 loaves of wheat at $0.75 each and 35 loaves of French bread at $0.55 each. What are Randy's daily total sales?

_____

G. Use Excel to solve problems involving multiplication. OBJECTIVE 7

74. Retrieve the file *ch01ex07.xlsx*. Follow the directions. Save the file as *ch01ex07a.xlsx*.

75. Retrieve the file *ch01ex08.xlsx*. Follow the directions. Save the file as *ch01ex08a.xlsx*.

1.5 Division

OBJECTIVE 1 Identify terms used with division.

Division is the process of determining how many times one number is contained in another. The **dividend** is the number that is to be divided by another number. The **divisor** is the number by which to divide. The **quotient** is the solution, or answer, to a division problem.

One way to indicate that you are to divide is to draw the symbol $\overline{)}$ over the dividend. For example, if you want to indicate that 6 is to be divided by 2, you write $2\overline{)6}$.

You can also use the symbol ÷ to indicate division. For example, if 6 is to be divided by 2, you write 6 ÷ 2. If a dividend cannot be divided evenly, the number left over is the **remainder** and is often placed over the divisor making a fraction, such as $\frac{5}{7}$. Study this example.

EXAMPLE

$$
\begin{array}{r}
\text{quotient} \rightarrow \quad 13 \\
\text{divisor} \rightarrow \quad 6\overline{)79} \quad \leftarrow \text{dividend} \\
\underline{6} \\
\text{partial dividend} \rightarrow \quad 19 \\
\underline{18} \\
\text{remainder} \rightarrow \quad 1
\end{array}
$$

The quotient is 13 with a remainder of 1 or $13\frac{1}{6}$.

OBJECTIVE 2 Divide whole numbers.

Division, like multiplication, is one of the basic math concepts that will enable you to calculate more rapidly. In your everyday life, you might use division to *average* your grade in this course or to split a sandwich to share with a friend at lunch.

Assume you made the following grades on 5 tests: 80, 92, 78, 91, and 84. To determine your overall grade, add the 5 grades (425) and divide the total by 5 (85). This procedure is called **averaging**. Use the example at the top of the next page to learn to divide.

$$5)\overline{425}$$

STEPS

1. Look at the dividend and determine what part is greater than the divisor (4 is not greater than 5, but 42 is). Determine the number of times this part can be divided by the divisor. Since $8 \times 5 = 40$, it is 8. Write this number, 8, over the partial dividend, 42, and write the product, 40, under the partial dividend, 42, as shown. Subtract the product from the partial dividend.

$$\begin{array}{r} 8 \\ 5)\overline{425} \\ \underline{40} \\ 2 \end{array}$$ ← 42 is the partial dividend

2. Bring down the next number in the dividend, 5, and place it beside the remainder, 2, creating a second partial dividend, 25. Determine the number of times the second partial dividend can be divided by the divisor. In this case 5, since $5 \times 5 = 25$. Write this number, 5, next to the 8 and write the product, 25, under the partial dividend, as shown.

$$\begin{array}{r} 85 \\ 5)\overline{425} \\ \underline{40} \\ 25 \\ \underline{25} \end{array}$$ ← partial dividend

Notice that the divisor, 5, divides evenly into the dividend, 425, with no remainder. The solution is 85.

Use the following four step problem solving plan to solve a word problem involving averaging.

EXAMPLE

Assume you did the following number of sit-ups during eight workouts: 42, 44, 51, 35, 60, 38, 54, and 52. What is the average number of sit-ups you did during the workouts?

Four Step Problem Solving Plan

Clues	Action Plan	Solve
Sit-ups completed: 42, 44, 51, 35, 60, 38, 54, and 52. There were 8 workouts.	To determine the average number of sit-ups you did, add the 8 amounts and divide the total by 8.	$42 + 44 + 51 + 35 + 60 + 38 + 54 + 52 = 376$ $$\begin{array}{r} 47 \\ 8)\overline{376} \\ \underline{32} \\ 56 \\ \underline{56} \\ 0 \end{array}$$

Conclusion
The average number of sit-ups you did was 47.

In the previous example, $425 \div 5$, the divisor, 5, divides the dividend, 425, evenly; that is, without a remainder. In the following example, study the division process and note how the remainder is shown as a fraction.

EXAMPLE

$$
\begin{array}{r}
124\frac{7}{12} \leftarrow \text{remainder as a fraction} \\
12\overline{)1{,}495} \\
\underline{1\ 2} \\
29 \\
\underline{24} \\
55 \\
\underline{48} \\
7
\end{array}
$$

A remainder may be shown as a decimal. To do this, you add one zero to the dividend for each decimal place desired. For example, assume 3 decimal places are needed. You carry out the answer 4 places and round the answer to 3 places.

EXAMPLE

$$
\begin{array}{r}
97.0666 = 97.067 \quad \text{rounded to the thousandths position} \\
15\overline{)1{,}456.0000} \quad \leftarrow 145 \text{ is the first partial dividend.} \\
\underline{135} \\
106 \quad \leftarrow \text{second partial dividend} \\
\underline{105} \\
100 \quad \leftarrow \text{third partial dividend} \\
\underline{90} \\
100 \quad \leftarrow \text{fourth partial dividend}
\end{array}
$$

As shown in the third partial dividend, a zero was brought down, but the partial dividend, 10, was still smaller than the divisor, 15. Therefore, a zero was placed in the quotient and another zero was brought down from the dividend to the third partial dividend.

OBJECTIVE **4** Divide numbers with decimals.

When the dividend contains decimal places, place a decimal point in the quotient at the point above the decimal point in the dividend.

EXAMPLE

$$
\begin{array}{r}
2.02 \\
5\overline{)10.10} \\
\underline{10} \\
10 \\
\underline{10}
\end{array}
$$

When the divisor has a decimal, however, it must be changed to a whole number. Therefore, in the example below, the divisor, 1.95, must be changed to a whole number. To do this, you move the decimal point over two places to the right, changing the divisor to 195. When you move the decimal in the divisor, you must also move the decimal in the dividend the same number of places. You then divide as usual.

EXAMPLE

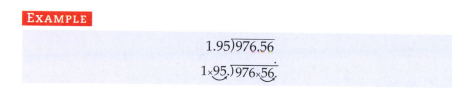

Because the decimal point in the divisor was moved two places to the right, the decimal point in the dividend was moved two places to the right.

OBJECTIVE 5 Check division by multiplying.

Division can be checked by multiplying the quotient by the divisor and adding any remainder to the product. The result will be the dividend. Study this example.

EXAMPLE

$$49 \overline{)1{,}372} \quad \overset{28}{} \qquad \text{Check:} \quad 49 \times 28 = 1{,}372$$

OBJECTIVE 6 Check division by estimation.

Estimation is another useful way of checking division. It allows you to determine whether your quotient is close enough to the correct answer without working through the entire division process. To do this, round the divisor and the dividend to positions you can divide mentally. Study the following examples.

EXAMPLES

$$984 \div 53 \text{ rounded to } 1{,}000 \div 50 = 20$$
$$2.98 \div 30 \text{ rounded to } 3 \div 30 = 0.1$$
$$1{,}525 \div 52 \text{ rounded to } 1{,}500 \div 50 = 30$$

By using estimation, you can determine whether a quotient is reasonable. In the example $1{,}525 \div 52$, you rounded to $1{,}500 \div 50$. When you divide, you find the answer is 30. The exact answer is 29.33 rounded to 2 decimal places. By using this method of estimating your quotient, you find that your estimated answer is close enough to the exact answer that you are probably correct. Should the problem not divide evenly, carry your answer to at least one decimal place.

OBJECTIVE 7 Use Excel to solve problems involving division.

You use the slash symbol (/) to alert Excel when you want to divide. An example of a formula using division is =C11/B10 (see Figure 1-9).

FIGURE 1-9

Division Formula in Excel

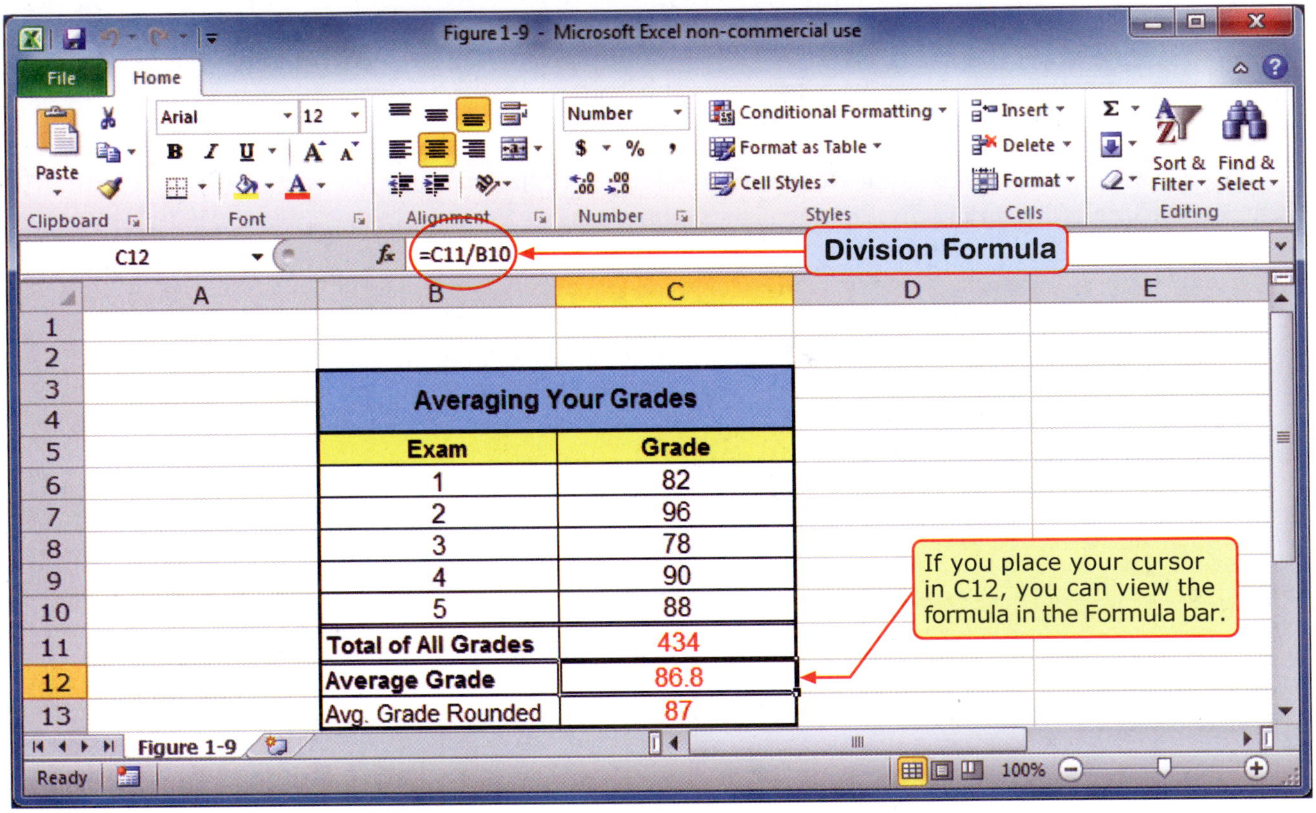

STEPS

Retrieve the file ***ch01pr07.xlsx***.

Enter a formula in Cell C12 to calculate the average grade.

Average Grade = Total of All Grades ÷ Number of Grades
= C11/B10

1. Use AutoSum to enter a formula in Cell C11 to total the grades.
2. Click in Cell C12 and key =.
3. Click C11 the cell to be divided (dividend).
4. Key slash (/) to tell Excel to divide.
5. Click B10 the cell to be divided by (divisor).
6. Press Enter.
7. Format Cell C12 for Number. Set Decimal places to 1. Set Use 1000 Separator (,) to off.
8. Key the answer in Cell C12 into Cell C13. Round your answer to the nearest whole number using Decrease Decimal.
9. Save the file as ***ch01pr07a.xlsx***.

TIPS

The average is the sum of all the data divided by the number of items in the data.

Name _____ Date _____

Directions   Solve the following problems. Write your answers in the blanks provided. Place commas and dollar signs in answers where appropriate.

A. Divide. Round decimal answers to the hundredth position.   OBJECTIVES **2, 3**

1. $12,118 \div 73 =$ _____

2. $\$4,536 \div 45 =$ _____

3. $110,754 \div 378 =$ _____

4. $\$30,478 \div 106 =$ _____

5. $43,372 \div 14 =$ _____

6. $26,257 \div 27 =$ _____

7. $2,756 \div 26 =$ _____

8. $133,632 \div 39 =$ _____

9. $7,104 \div 37 =$ _____

10. $\$4,032 \div 19 =$ _____

11. $497\overline{)43,736}$

12. $25\overline{)9,400}$

13. $264\overline{)26,664}$

14. $461\overline{)17,518}$

B. Divide. Carry all answers to 3 places and round to 2 places.   OBJECTIVES **4, 5**

15. $1.9\overline{)8.695}$

16. $14.3\overline{)1.09}$

17. $6.37\overline{)96.48}$

C. Divide. Round all answers to 3 places. Round dollar amounts to the nearest cent. Check by multiplying the divisor by the quotient.   OBJECTIVES **4, 5**

18. $1.1 \div 0.38 =$ _____

19. $601 \div 2.22 =$ _____

20. $0.25 \div 0.41 =$ _____

21. $33.87 \div 256 =$ _____

22. $\$75.40 \div 0.39 =$ _____

23. $0.8543 \div 0.131 =$ _____

24. $\$1.99 \div 0.50 =$ _____

25. $2,997 \div 0.7 =$ _____

D. Divide the following decimals. Round all answers to 2 places.   OBJECTIVES **4, 5**

26. $11.1 \div 0.38 =$ _____

27. $601 \div 2.221 =$ _____

28. $\$75.40 \div 1.40 =$ _____

29. $1.85 \div 0.131 =$ _____

30. $450.10 \div 1.80 =$ _____

31. $2,211.39 \div 25.44 =$ _____

32. $608.56 \div 74.99 =$ _____

33. $300.80 \div 4.05 =$ _____

E. Show estimated and exact quotients for the following problems. Round OBJECTIVE 6
answers to 2 decimal places.

	Estimated Quotient	Exact Quotient
34. $235 \div 791 =$	_____	_____
35. $333 \div 64 =$	_____	_____
36. $789 \div 52 =$	_____	_____
37. $896 \div 188 =$	_____	_____

F. Solve the following word problems. OBJECTIVES 2-6

38. Rick, Dave, Bryan, and John decided to purchase a used bass boat for $4,550 and share the cost equally. How much would each person pay? _____

39. Julio played all three courses at the miniature golf course. His scores were 42, 36, and 48. What was the average of all three scores? (Hint: To average, add all the scores and divide by the number of scores.) _____

40. Bill bowled in a league every Monday night. He bowled 4 games with the following scores: 237, 222, 190, and 256. What was his average score for the night? Carry your answer to the nearest hundredth. _____

41. Redmond Brick Company delivered 14,368 bricks to a new home under construction. There are 4 bricklayers ready to begin. If each bricklayer lays the same number of bricks, how many bricks will each worker use? _____

42. Ruth and Merri ate lunch together at Berries Restaurant. Since Berries serves such large lunch portions, they decided to buy one order and split the cost. Their lunch came to $12.74, and they left a $2.00 tip. How much did lunch (with tip) cost each person? _____

43. The Navajo National Bank loaned John Morgan $150,000 including interest for a new business he and his wife were starting. The loan is to be paid over a period of 25 years. How much would John's monthly payments be? _____

G. Use Excel to solve problems involving division. OBJECTIVE 7

44. Retrieve the file *ch01ex09.xlsx*. Follow the directions. Save the file as *ch01ex09a.xlsx*.

45. Retrieve the file *ch01ex10.xlsx*. Follow the directions. Save the file as *ch01ex10a.xlsx*.

1.6 Basic Math Operations and Excel

OBJECTIVE

1. Combine basic math operations in Excel.

OBJECTIVE 1 Combine basic math operations in Excel.

Often you may create a **multimath formula** that includes more than one of the basic math operations you have learned. The following is such a formula written for Excel with no spaces.

=(B8*C8)+(1.5*B8*D8)

This formula calculates gross earnings in a payroll problem. Regular pay is calculated by multiplying the hourly rate times regular hours. Overtime pay is calculated by multiplying 1.5 times the hourly rate times the overtime hours. The 1.5 represents time-and-one-half. To calculate the gross earnings, the regular pay and the overtime pay are added together. The parentheses tell Excel to multiply the numbers within each set of parentheses before adding.

Look at the spreadsheet in Figure 1-10.

TIPS

Excel follows the same basic Order of Operations that is used in algebra.

Figure 1-10

Spreadsheet Showing Multiple Math Operations in One Formula

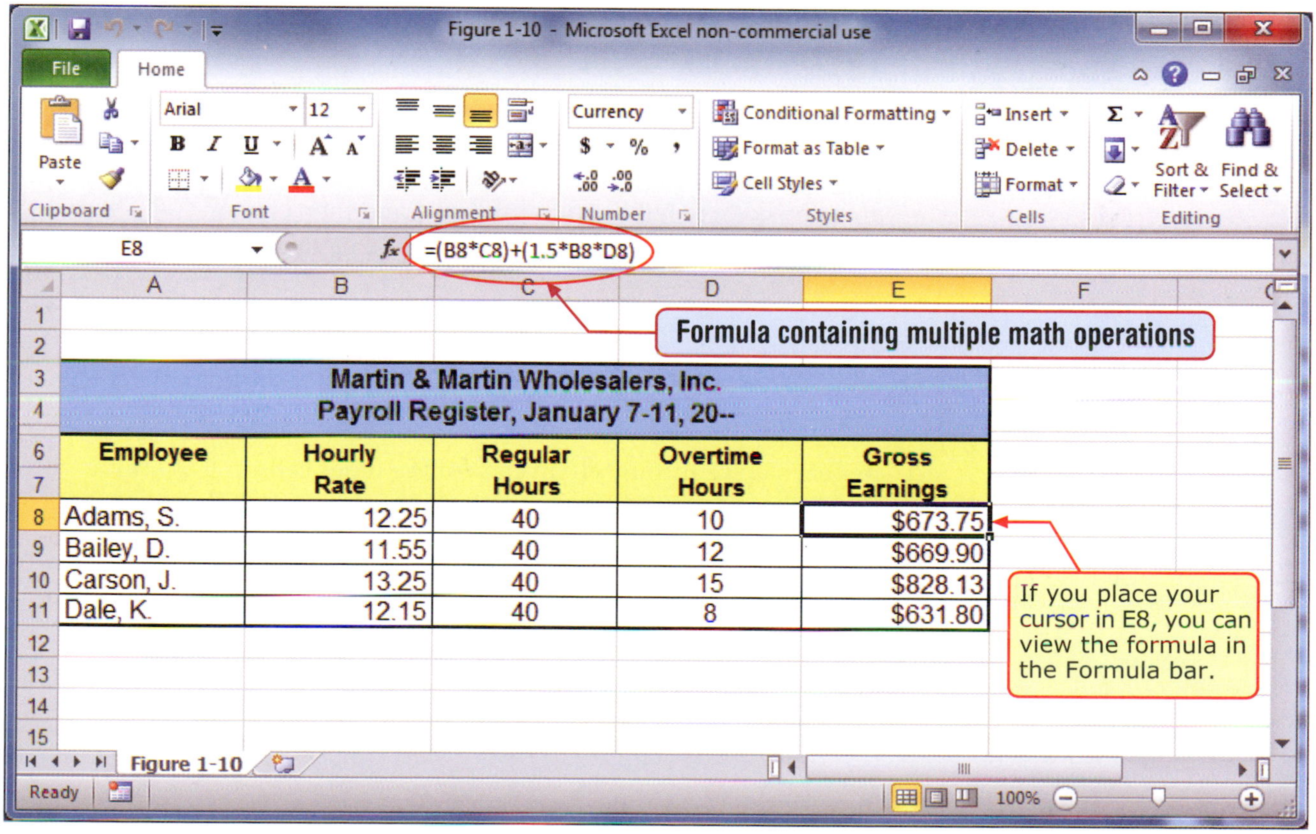
Figure 1-10 - Microsoft Excel non-commercial use
E8
=(B8*C8)+(1.5*B8*D8)
Formula containing multiple math operations
Martin & Martin Wholesalers, Inc.
Payroll Register, January 7-11, 20--
Employee
Hourly Rate
Regular Hours
Overtime Hours
Gross Earnings
Adams, S. 12.25 40 10 $673.75
Bailey, D. 11.55 40 12 $669.90
Carson, J. 13.25 40 15 $828.13
Dale, K. 12.15 40 8 $631.80
If you place your cursor in E8, you can view the formula in the Formula bar.
Figure 1-10
Ready

You must first understand how to calculate gross earnings on paper before you can begin to create the formula for it. The following display shows the order in which the computations are to be done.

(Hourly Rate * Regular Hours) + (1.5 * Hourly Rate * Overtime Hours)

STEPS

Retrieve the file *ch01pr08.xlsx*.

Using the Pointing Method, enter a multimath formula in Cell E8 to calculate the Gross Earnings for S. Adams.

Regular Earnings = Hourly Rate × Regular Hours
Overtime Earnings = 1.5 × Hourly Rate × Overtime Hours
Gross Earnings = Regular Earnings + Overtime Earnings
=(B8*C8)+(1.5*B8*D8)

1. Click in Cell E8 to activate the cell where the results of the formula will appear.

2. Key =.

3. Key a left parenthesis.

4. Calculate the Regular Earnings. To multiply Hourly Rate times Regular Hours, click in Cell B8 (the Hourly Rate), key an asterisk (*) to tell Excel to multiply, and then click in Cell C8 (the Regular Hours). Excel automatically places each cell address in the formula.

5. Key a right parenthesis.

6. Key the plus sign (+) to tell Excel to add.

7. Key a left parenthesis.

8. Calculate the Overtime Earnings. To multiply 1.5 (time-and-onehalf) times Hourly Rate times Overtime Hours, key 1.5, key an asterisk (*) to tell Excel to multiply, click in Cell B8 (the Hourly Rate), key an asterisk (*) to tell Excel to multiply, and then click in Cell D8 (the Overtime Hours). Excel automatically places each cell address in the formula.

9. Key a right parenthesis.

10. Press Enter to enter the formula. Your formula should look like this: =(B8*C8)+(1.5*B8*D8). Your answer should be 673.75.

11. Repeat steps 2 through 10 in each of the other cells in Column E in order to calculate the Gross Earnings for each of the other employees.

12. Format Column E for Currency. Set Decimal places to 2. Set Currency symbol to $.

13. Save the file as *ch01pr08a.xlsx*.

Name _____   Date _____

Directions   Complete the following problems.

A. Use Excel to solve problems involving basic math operations.

1.   Retrieve the file *ch01ex11.xlsx*.

   a.   Enter a multimath formula in each cell of Column E to calculate the 3-week average for each player.

   b.   Enter a multimath formula in each cell of Row 11 to calculate the 5-member team average for each week.

   c.   Format for Number. Set Decimal places to 1. Set Use 1000 Separator (,) to off.

   d.   Save the file as *ch01ex11a.xlsx*.

2.   Retrieve the file *ch01ex12.xlsx*.

   a.   Follow the instructions in the file and complete all exercises.

   b.   Save the file as *ch01ex12a.xlsx*.

3.   Retrieve the file *ch01ex13.xlsx*.

   a.   Enter a formula in Cell E8 to calculate the Balance in the escrow fund for January. Start with the beginning Balance, then add the January Deposit and subtract any January Payments. (In this case, the January Payment is zero.)

   b.   Copy the formula in Cell E8 down through all of the cells in Column E.

   c.   Format Column E for Currency. Set Decimal places to 2. Set Currency symbol to None.

   d.   Save the file as *ch01ex13a.xlsx*.

4.   Retrieve the file *ch01ex14.xlsx*.

   a.   Enter the multimath formula in each cell of Column F to determine the Ending Balance for each of the accounts. Format for Currency. Set Decimal places to 2. Set Currency symbol to None.

   b.   Total the Beginning Balance and the Ending Balance columns. Format for Currency. Set decimal places to 2. Set Currency symbol to $.

   c.   Save the file as *ch01ex14a.xlsx*.

5.   Retrieve the file *ch01ex15.xlsx*. Follow the directions. Save the file as *ch01ex15a.xlsx*.

6.   Retrieve the file *ch01ex16.xlsx*. Follow the directions. Save the file as *ch01ex16a.xlsx*.

Chapter Review and Assessment

KEY TERMS

addend	dividend	place
addition	division	Pointing Method
amount	divisor	position
annexing	estimation	product
appending	factors	quotient
approximate	Format Cells command	regrouping
AutoSum command	formula	remainder
averaging	function	rounding
borrowing	Increase Decimal command	subtotal
Currency Style command	minuend	subtraction
decimal number system	multimath formula	subtrahend
decimal part	multiplicand	sum
decimal point	multiplication	total
Decrease Decimal command	multiplier	whole number part
difference	negative number	word form
digit	numeral	

CONCEPTS	EXAMPLES
1.1 Read and round numbers. Trillions, Comma, Hundred billions, Ten billions, Billions, Comma, Hundred millions, Ten millions, Millions, Comma, Hundred thousands, Ten thousands, Thousands, Comma, Hundreds, Tens, Units, Decimal point, Tenths, Hundredths, Thousandths, Ten thousandths, Hundred thousandths 3 , 9 7 4 , 5 1 2 , 3 6 7 , 4 9 8 . 2 6 8 2 1 Whole numbers Decimal numbers	The whole number part is to the left of the decimal point and the decimal part is to the right of the decimal point.
	Numbers can be written in word forms; for example, 452.7 is written as four hundred fifty-two and seven tenths.
1.1 Round numbers to approximate an answer.	If a gaming console cost $197.95, you might say it cost approximately $200.
1.1 Use rounding rules. **Step 1** Determine the position (place) being rounded.	0.99 rounded to the nearest tenth is 1.0 (9 is more than 5)
Step 2 If the digit to the right of the position (place) is 5 *or more*, round up by 1. **Example** 6.8 rounds up to 7 (8 is more than 5)	0.43 rounded to the nearest tenth is 0.4 (3 is less than 5) 26.0169 rounded to the nearest thousandth is 26.017 (9 is more than 5)

CONCEPTS	EXAMPLES
Step 3 If the digit to the right of the position is *less than 5*, do not round up. Drop all digits from that position to the right. **Example** 6.4 rounds to 6 (4 is less than 5)	1982.4 rounded to the nearest hundred is 2000 (8 is more than 5) Notice that all digits to the right of the hundreds place are changed to zeros.
1.2 Align numbers in addition. Align units above units, tens above tens, hundreds above hundreds, and so on. If addends have decimals, it is important to align the decimal points.	$\begin{array}{r} 23.981 \\ 14.2334 \\ 2.14 \\ +3{,}999.24566 \\ \hline 4{,}039.60006 \end{array}$
1.2 Add mentally. Adding mentally can increase your speed in addition.	Add 8, 2, 5, 5, and 4. Add the units position by thinking: 10, 15, 20, 24 8 + 2 is <u>10</u>, + 5 is <u>15</u>, + 5 is <u>20</u>, + 4 is <u>24</u>
1.2 Add by tens mentally. To add more accurately and rapidly, memorize the number combinations that total 10.	$\begin{array}{r} 2 \\ 6 \\ +2 \\ \hline 10 \end{array} \qquad \begin{array}{r} 6 \\ 2 \\ +2 \\ \hline 10 \end{array}$
1.2 Add horizontally.	Add the positions moving from right to left.
1.2 Use the four step problem solving plan. 1. Clues 2. Action Plan 3. Solve 4. Conclusion	1. Identify all clues. 2. Prepare your action plan—visualize the problem, determine the known and unknown facts. 3. Perform the steps in the action plan. 4. Draw the appropriate conclusion.
1.3 Subtract vertically. Subtract the subtrahend from the minuend to get the difference, borrowing when necessary. To check, add the difference to the subtrahend to get the minuend.	$\begin{array}{r} 987 \\ -503 \\ \hline 484 \end{array}$ minuend subtrahend difference add: $\begin{array}{r} 503 \\ +484 \\ \hline 987 \end{array}$ subtrahend difference minuend
1.3 Regroup in subtraction. When a number cannot be subtracted from a smaller number, you must borrow 10 from the position to its left. This process is called regrouping or borrowing.	$\begin{array}{r} \overset{1\ 9\ 13}{2037} \\ -982 \\ \hline 1055 \end{array}$
1.3 Subtract horizontally.	Subtract the positions from left to right.
1.3 Express negative numbers. To subtract a larger number from a smaller number, reverse the numbers and subtract.	$\begin{array}{r} 31 \\ -48 \end{array} \qquad \begin{array}{r} -48 \\ 31 \\ \hline -17 \end{array}$

CONCEPTS	EXAMPLES
1.3 Add negative numbers. Add the numbers as if they are positive numbers, placing the negative sign before the answer.	$\begin{aligned} -47 \\ \underline{-13} \\ -60 \end{aligned}$
1.3 Combine addition and subtraction. Total the positive numbers. Total the negative numbers. Subtract the results.	$\begin{aligned} +37 \\ -23 \\ +25 \\ \underline{-28} \\ -50 \end{aligned}$ $\quad$ $\begin{aligned} +37 \\ \underline{+25} \\ +62 \end{aligned}$ $\quad$ $\begin{aligned} -23 \\ \underline{-28} \\ -51 \end{aligned}$ $\quad$ $\begin{aligned} +62 \\ \underline{-51} \\ +11 \end{aligned}$
1.4 Multiply whole numbers. The multiplicand is multiplied by the multiplier, resulting in the product. When the multiplier has more than one digit, partial products must be used.	$\begin{aligned} 54 \quad &\text{multiplicand} \\ \underline{\times\,32} \quad &\text{multiplier} \\ 108 \quad &\text{partial product} \\ \underline{162} \quad &\text{partial product} \\ 1{,}728 \quad &\text{product} \end{aligned}$
1.4 Multiply with decimals. Multiply as if decimals were whole numbers. Then count the number of decimal places in the multiplicand and the multiplier and mark off that many places in the product, counting from right to left. Multiplication can be checked by reversing the multiplicand and multiplier and multiplying again.	$\begin{aligned} 0.17 \quad &\text{multiplicand} \\ \underline{\times\,0.29} \quad &\text{multiplier} \\ 153 \quad &\text{partial product} \\ \underline{34} \quad &\text{partial product} \\ 0.0493 \quad &\text{product} \end{aligned}$
1.4 Solve problems with zeros in multiplication. When numbers end in zeros, ignore the zeros and multiply. Count the zeros ignored and add that many zeros to the right of the product.	$\begin{aligned} 40 \\ \underline{\times\,5} \end{aligned}$ $\qquad$ $\begin{aligned} 4 \\ \underline{\times\,5} \\ 20 \end{aligned}$ Add 1 zero to answer = 200
1.4 Accumulate products. Multiply to obtain each product, and then total the products.	$\begin{aligned} 4 \times \$24.99 = \quad \$99.90 \\ 3 \times \$29.99 = \quad \$89.97 \\ 2 \times \$26.99 = \underline{+\$53.98} \\ \$243.91 \end{aligned}$
1.5 Divide whole numbers. $\overline{)}$ and ÷ mean divide. Division is the process of determining how many times one number is contained in another. The dividend is the number that is to be divided by another number. The divisor is the number by which to divide. The quotient is the solution, or answer, to a division problem. Division can be checked by multiplying and estimation.	$\begin{array}{r} 45\frac{5}{8} \\ 8\overline{)365} \\ \underline{32} \\ 45 \\ \underline{40} \\ 5 \end{array}$
1.5 Divide numbers with decimals. When the divisor has a decimal, it must be changed to a whole number. When you move the decimal in the divisor, you must also move the decimal in the dividend the same number of places. You then divide as usual.	$7{\scriptstyle\times}62.\overline{)421{\scriptstyle\times}98.}$

Chapter 1 Review Exercises

A. Write the numeral and the position the underlined digits represent. 1.1 OBJECTIVE 1

   1. 8,975,000 _____

   2. 55.65 _____

   3. 539,921 _____

   4. 3.747 _____

   5. 63.785 _____

   6. 93.67 _____

B. Write numerals for the following word forms. 1.1 OBJECTIVE 2

   7. Eighty-nine and sixty-five hundredths _____

   8. One million seven thousand twenty-one _____

   9. Four thousand six hundred and twenty-six thousandths _____

  10. Two thousand eight _____

  11. Six trillion _____

C. Write word forms for the following numerals. 1.1 OBJECTIVE 2

  12. 7,728.4 _____

  13. 1,800,001 _____

  14. 11,792.7 _____

  15. 6,429,001,019 _____

  16. 88.982 _____

D. Round the following numbers to the place indicated. 1.1 OBJECTIVE 3

  17. 35.427 to the nearest ten _____

  18. 642,497.4 to the nearest hundred _____

  19. $426.48 to the nearest hundred dollars _____

  20. 42,962.854 to the nearest unit _____

  21. 9,700 to the nearest thousand _____

  22. 59,012,345 to the nearest thousand _____

  23. 0.974526 to the nearest tenth _____

  24. 469.2465 to the nearest hundredth _____

  25. 9.4603 to the nearest hundredth _____

  26. 0.56792 to the nearest thousandth _____

  27. 7.6490035 to the nearest thousandth _____

E. Add the following whole numbers and decimals. 1.2 OBJECTIVES 2, 3

28.	29.	30.	31.
6.94	3.21	9.89	7.75
2.38	6.76	8.13	8.98
+ 4.14	+ 3.02	+ 5.38	+ 5.00

32.	33.	34.	35.
6,758	35	12.009	16.25
1,001	678	3.105	9.9
89	1,250	9.287	17.33
325	124	6.532	1.59
+ 34	+ 89	+ 1.008	+ 0.86

F. Add the following numbers mentally and horizontally by tens. 1.2 OBJECTIVES 5, 6

36. $56 + 64 =$ _____

37. $923 + 77 =$ _____

38. $854 + 246 =$ _____

39. $225 + 775 =$ _____

40. $311 + 689 =$ _____

41. $751 + 849 =$ _____

G. Subtract the following numbers and then check using addition. 1.3 OBJECTIVES 2, 3

42.	43.	44.	45.
1,258	758	5,294	999
– 137	– 647	– 2,381	– 762

H. Regroup to subtract the following numbers. 1.3 OBJECTIVES 4, 5

46.	47.	48.	49.
$200.05	$769,487	3,080.109	43.0008
– 10.09	– 10,807	– 359.090	– 9.0810

I. Subtract the following numbers horizontally. 1.3 OBJECTIVE 6

50. $345 - 290 =$ _____

51. $59.50 - $5.07 =$ _____

52. $4,200 - 339 =$ _____

53. $4,489 - 609 =$ _____

J. Calculate the following negative numbers. 1.3 OBJECTIVE 7

54. $348 - 466 =$ _____

55. $759 - 826 =$ _____

56. $82.7 - 230.1 =$ _____

57. $8.25 - 15.26 =$ _____

58. $71.2 - 94.5 =$ _____

59. $55.21 - 73.88 =$ _____

K. Multiply the following whole numbers, decimal numbers, and **1.4 OBJECTIVES 2, 3, 4**
numbers with zeros. Show maximum decimals.

60. $3,132 \times 0.855 =$ _____

61. $42,521 \times 1,459 =$ _____

62. $\$5,090 \times 751 =$ _____

63. $\$1.76 \times 8.216 =$ _____

L. Accumulate products for the following. **1.4 OBJECTIVE 6**

64. $131 \times 54 =$ _____

$247 \times 67 =$ _____

$390 \times 28 =$ _____

Total = _____

65. $3.95 \times 66 =$ _____

$1.85 \times 2 =$ _____

$3.98 \times 12 =$ _____

Total = _____

M. Divide the following whole numbers with remainders and **1.5 OBJECTIVES 2, 3, 4, 5**
decimals. Carry answers to 2 decimal places.

66. $10,754 \div 415 =$ _____

67. $\$30,478 \div 10 =$ _____

68. $21.998 \div 0.77 =$ _____

69. $7.865 \div 0.65 =$ _____

N. Show estimated and exact quotients for the following problems. **1.5 OBJECTIVE 6**
Carry answers to 2 decimal places.

	Estimated Quotient	Exact Quotient			Estimated Quotient	Exact Quotient
70. $235 \div 79 =$	_____	_____	71.	$320 \div 69 =$	_____	_____
72. $549 \div 41 =$	_____	_____	73.	$785 \div 188 =$	_____	_____

O. Solve the following word problems.

74. Gloria went shopping and bought 4 dresses at $49.99 each, 5 pairs of jeans at $35.00 each, and 3 pairs of shoes at $29.99 each. How much did Gloria spend before sales tax? _____

75. Judith planned to purchase a new game console on sale for $279.00. She wondered how much it would cost her since sales tax would be an additional 8.75% (0.875). How much is the sales tax? _____

76. The Practical Investment Club has 13 members with equal shares. Their total investment to date is $24,689.55. How much is the value of each member's share in the club? _____

P. Use Excel to solve the following problems. **1.5 OBJECTIVE 7, 1.6 OBJECTIVE 1**

77. Retrieve the file *ch01ex17.xlsx*. Follow the directions. Save the file as *ch01ex17a.xlsx*.

78. Retrieve the file *ch01ex18.xlsx*. Follow the directions. Save the file as *ch01ex18a.xlsx*.

APPLY   Math@Work   HEALTH SCIENCES

EXAMPLE   A medical assistant working for a large hospital often is involved in checking budget figures related to the department for which he or she works.

TRY IT...

1. In the following medical supply report, add total amounts horizontally for each week and then total amounts vertically for each month. The total amount in the lower right-hand corner (h) should be the same both horizontally and vertically. The process of verifying totals is called *footing* (or *crossfooting*).

Harris Regional Hospital Medical Supply Report

Week	January	February	March	Total Sales
1	$110,198	$117,533	$117,633	a.
2	111,467	116,922	115,171	b.
3	100,186	113,867	114,116	c.
4	115,863	119,730	101,169	d.
Totals	e.	f.	g.	h.

2. Twenty-four employees attended a 3-hour class on diversity. At the end of the class, they were tested. Total the scores and obtain an average grade for the class by dividing the total by the number of students taking the test. Round the average to the tenths position.

99	72	52	77	98	88	82	76	55	71	77	90
100	60	89	65	88	86	97	100	96	65	82	77

Total of All Scores: _____   Average: _____

Write about Math

1. Give one example of how decimal places (tenths, hundredths, thousandths, ten thousandths, hundred thousandths) are used in your personal life.

2. Discuss which two basic math functions—addition, subtraction, multiplication, or division—you think is used most often in business and why.

Personal Finance

Will you have to take a math-related employment test when seeking employment?

Knowing what to expect from prospective employers when applying for positions can give you an advantage over those competing for the job with you. The following project will help you improve your knowledge about math-related employment tests you might be required to take as part of your interview process. Employment tests are usually administered by the human resources department. Today more and more employers are testing applicants prior to hiring because they want to screen the applicants. You do not have to take the test, but you are not likely to get the job if you refuse. The company has a purpose for asking you to take a test. Some tests are designed to find if you really do have the skills you say you do on your application or resume. Other tests measure whether you possess the right fit for the job or if you will fit in with the culture of the organization. If you agree to take the test, do the best you can.

Juanmoninoi/iStockphoto.com

1. Look in the newspaper or on the Internet to see if math tests are mentioned for employment. Temporary agencies and private employment agencies are good sources for you to contact. Your local state workforce commission and large industries in your area are excellent sources of information. Contact five businesses, temporary agencies, or employment agencies in your area and ask whether the company or agency administers a math test for employment. If so, ask the following questions about the test.

   a. What types of problems are on the test?

   b. How many problems are on the test?

   c. What percent of problems are word problems?

   d. Are there problems where the applicant is required to count money?

   e. Is the test timed?

   f. Is the applicant allowed to use a calculator?

   g. Does the test include other parts such as personality or grammar?

   h. Is information about the test posted online with sample problems?

   i. Can you obtain a copy of the test or a sample from which to study?

   j. How are the tests graded? Are there a minimum number of points required to pass the test?

   k. What industries are more likely to require math tests based on your research?

2. Prepare a report of your findings.

3. Describe in a short paragraph how this project will help you bridge the gap between the classroom and the workplace.

Name _____ Date _____ Score _____

Directions Complete the following problems.

A. Write the numeral and the position each underlined digit represents. 1.1 OBJECTIVE 1

1. 8<u>9</u>0 _____

2. <u>5</u>00,001.2 _____

3. 1.87<u>3</u> _____

4. 12.<u>3</u>22 _____

B. Write the following in numbers. 1.1 OBJECTIVE 2

5. ninety-three and eleven hundredths _____

6. nine and thirty-seven thousandths _____

C. Write the following numerals in word form. 1.1 OBJECTIVE 2

7. 672 _____

8. 6,889 _____

9. 3.111 _____

10. 5,079.53 _____

D. Round the following numbers to the place indicated. 1.1 OBJECTIVE 3

11. _____ $87.56 to the nearest ten

12. _____ 0.98356 to the nearest ten thousandth

13. _____ 0.65901 to the nearest tenth

14. _____ 25,530,752 to the nearest million

E. Add. 1.2 OBJECTIVES 2-6

15.	**16.**	**17.**	**18.**
$27.50	1,990	10,332	1.822
13.44	18,975	2,110	0.28
122.25	6,800	15,332	0.2114
8.95	221	480	10.922
21.75	56,830	2,890	4.00066
+ 252.88	+ 88,555	+ 12	+ 0.12543

19. $689.00 + 25.86 + 4,007.10 = $ _____

20. $82.11 + 32.49 + 379.84 = $ _____

21. $104.00 + 50.87 + 756.99 = $ _____

22. $369.34 + 33.22 + 3,165.05 = $ _____

F. Subtract. 1.3 OBJECTIVES 2-8

23.	**24.**	**25.**	**26.**
2.898	$6.90	$67.48	54,410
− 23.492	− 9.01	− 97.67	− 111,360

27. $21,479 − 16,952 = $ _____

28. $800 − $756.82 = $ _____

29. $112.99 − 45.99 = $ _____

30. $2.118 − 0.0988 = $ _____

G. Combine subtraction and addition. 1.3 OBJECTIVE 9

31.	32.	33.	34.
−27	+89	+ 32.10	−8.99
+48	−33	−47.50	+22.118
−38	+45	−25.00	−1.98
−38	+99	+88.65	+75.007
+40	−25	+23.25	+10.009
+50	−56	−18.17	−11.111

H. Multiply. Show maximum decimals. 1.4 OBJECTIVES 2-5

35. $77.7 × 0.076 = _____

36. $19.95 × 180 = _____

37. 124.333 × 0.0321 = _____

38. 1,799 × 9.901 = _____

I. Accumulate products. 1.4 OBJECTIVE 6

39. 23.88 × 3 = _____
    15.98 × 6 = _____
    12.05 × 5 = _____
    Subtotal = _____

40. 115.80 × 4 = _____
    231.25 × 9 = _____
    38.50 × 10 = _____
    Subtotal = _____

J. Divide the following whole numbers, numbers with decimals, and remainders. Check division. Round answers to 3 places. 1.5 OBJECTIVES 1-4

41. 8.990 ÷ 0.228 = _____

42. 0.9097 ÷ 0.213 = _____

43. $2,889 ÷ 0.50 = _____

44. 4.2 ÷ 3.9 = _____

45. 89.777 ÷ 32.33 = _____

46. 10.00009 ÷ 0.10 = _____

K. Solve the following word problems.

47. Jude ran in place for 6 minutes in the morning and for 4 minutes in the evening. How many minutes did he run in place over a 7-day period? _____

48. Julie worked during the summer in the fields picking lettuce to earn extra money for college expenses. She picked 24 bushels each day for five days each week that she worked. How many bushels did she pick during the 12 weeks she worked picking lettuce? _____

49. In one week, Convenient Copy made 15,296 copies from self-service copy machines @ 10 cents a copy, 385 transparency masters @ $1.50 cents per copy, designed and created 36 PowerPoint presentations at a cost of $5,206.50. What were the total sales for the week? _____

L. Use Excel to solve the following problems. 1.3 OBJECTIVE 10, 1.4 OBJECTIVE 7

50. Retrieve the file *ch01qz01*. Follow the directions. Save the file as *ch01qz01a.xlsx*.

51. Retrieve the file *ch01qz02*. Follow the directions. Save the file as *ch01qz02a.xlsx*.

CHAPTER 2 Fractions

2.1 FRACTIONS AND MIXED NUMBERS

2.2 ADD AND SUBTRACT FRACTIONS AND MIXED NUMBERS

2.3 MULTIPLY AND DIVIDE FRACTIONS AND MIXED NUMBERS

You probably are familiar with common fractions and decimal fractions because they are used every day. Here are some ways you might use common fractions: $\frac{3}{4}$ hour overtime worked last night, $1\frac{1}{2}$ cups of milk in a recipe, and $3\frac{2}{3}$ yards of fabric to upholster a chair. Some examples of decimal fractions would be: 7.9 gallons of gas, 1.23 pounds of hamburger, and wages of $31.50 per hour. Decimal fractions are used in this manner: eggs cost $1.05 per dozen and a monthly storage rental fee is $129.60. To be successful in business transactions, you must have a clear understanding of fractions.

CHEF

Executive Chef Mark Khoury works in a small, trendy upscale restaurant. It is his responsibility to create the menu. In doing so, he must take food costs into consideration and also must choose the right side items to complement his main dishes. Mark manages the inventory for the kitchen, keeps a close eye on seasonal food costs, and helps his team prep and cook the food. Organizing a menu and creating unique dishes for his restaurant means Mark has to be on top of dining trends, be aware of fresh ingredients available at the local market, and teach his crew to make his creations the same way every time so diners know they will get exactly what they ordered.

Being a chef is hard work. Most days are long and physically demanding. "Recently the title 'chef' has become associated with more glamour than it has had in the past," Mark says. Chefs often are called out to the table to be congratulated by content diners and may sometimes rub elbows with the rich and famous people who enjoy their creations. "Due to the explosion of TV shows featuring amateur and professional chefs competing on television, chefs are being viewed in a more glamorous light," he says. "The heat of the kitchen is very real, but in real life chefs don't usually enjoy the type of glamour you see on television."

Courtesy of Mark Khoury

Math Skills Used

Addition

Subtraction

Multiplication

Fractions

Other Skills Needed

Communication

Interpersonal

Organization

Physical endurance

How Math Is Used in Cooking

Mark says, "Math is primary, and almost has to be an instinctive part of any chef's work day." When prepping for the day shift, a chef has to multiply the original recipe for what is projected to be sold for the night or the next two nights, and that always changes based on the season and how busy the restaurant gets. He says, "If a recipe requires 4 ounces of flour, 12 eggs, and 2 teaspoons of nutmeg, we need to use multiplication or division to maintain the same recipe but for a bigger or smaller volume."

What Do You Think?

What skills do you need to improve in order to be able to become a chef?

2.1 Fractions and Mixed Numbers

OBJECTIVES

1. Identify terms used with fractions.
2. Distinguish between fractions and mixed numbers.
3. Convert improper fractions to whole numbers.
4. Convert improper fractions to mixed numbers.
5. Convert mixed numbers to improper fractions.
6. Reduce fractions to lowest terms.
7. Raise fractions to higher terms.
8. Convert fractions to decimals.
9. Convert decimals to fractions.
10. Use Excel to enter fractions and mixed numbers.

OBJECTIVE 1 Identify terms used with fractions.

A **fraction** represents part of a whole. A fraction contains one number written above another number separated by a bar, as shown below.

$$\frac{1}{3}, \frac{2}{3}, \frac{5}{4}$$

The top number is the **numerator**. It expresses the number of equal parts of the whole number. The bottom number is the **denominator**. It expresses the number of equal parts the whole number is divided into. The line or bar that separates the numerator from the denominator means "divided by." For example,

fraction bar → $\frac{1}{4}$ ← numerator ← denominator

One-fourth means one part of four equal parts, as shown in Figure 2-1.

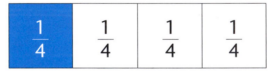

Figure 2-1
One-fourth Means One Part of Four Equal Parts

OBJECTIVE 2 Distinguish between fractions and mixed numbers.

There are three types of fractions: proper, improper, and mixed. A **proper fraction** is one in which the numerator is less than the denominator. Therefore, a proper fraction expresses less than one whole number, such as $\frac{1}{2}$, $\frac{3}{4}$, or $\frac{1}{8}$.

$\frac{1}{2}$ Numerator is smaller than denominator.

Proper fractions are used in the workplace. For example, an employee may have to spend three-fourths of his or her workday on a particular project.

Figure 2-2 represents the proper fraction $\frac{3}{4}$, or three parts of the whole.

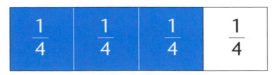

Figure 2-2
Three-fourths is a Proper Fraction

An **improper fraction** is one in which the numerator is equal to or greater than the denominator and expresses one or more whole numbers, such as $\frac{8}{5}$, $\frac{5}{3}$, or $\frac{12}{6}$.

$\frac{8}{5}$ Numerator is greater than denominator.

Figure 2-3 shows the improper fraction $\frac{8}{5}$ is more than one whole.

| $\frac{1}{5}$ | $\frac{1}{5}$ | $\frac{1}{5}$ | $\frac{1}{5}$ | $\frac{1}{5}$ | | $\frac{1}{5}$ | $\frac{1}{5}$ | $\frac{1}{5}$ |

Figure 2-3

Eight-fifths is an Improper Fraction

A **mixed number** consists of a whole number and a fraction, such as $3\frac{2}{5}$, $2\frac{1}{3}$, or $6\frac{7}{8}$.

whole number part → $3\frac{2}{5}$ ← fraction part

An example of a mixed number is found in home building. For instance, the length of a post may be shown as $17\frac{3}{4}$ feet.

jhorrocks/iStockphoto.com

OBJECTIVE **3** **Convert improper fractions to whole numbers.**

To convert an improper fraction to a whole number, divide the numerator by the denominator.

EXAMPLE

Convert $\frac{180}{30}$ to a whole number.

STEPS

Convert $\frac{180}{30}$ to a whole number by dividing 180 by 30.

$$\frac{180}{30} = 30\overline{)\begin{matrix}6\\180\end{matrix}}$$
$$\underline{180}$$
$$0$$

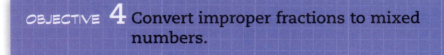

OBJECTIVE 4 Convert improper fractions to mixed numbers.

An improper fraction can be converted to a mixed number by dividing the numerator by the denominator. The result will be a number with a whole number part and a fraction part.

EXAMPLE

Convert $\frac{35}{6}$ to a mixed number.

STEPS

1. Divide the numerator by the denominator.

$$
\begin{array}{r}
5 \\
6\overline{)35} \\
\underline{30} \\
5
\end{array}
$$

2. Place the remainder over the divisor.

$$\frac{5}{6} \quad \begin{array}{l} \leftarrow \text{ remainder from divisor} \\ \leftarrow \text{ original denominator (divisor)} \end{array}$$

3. Write the mixed number as $5\frac{5}{6}$.

   The whole number part is the quotient 5. The remainder 5 is used as the numerator of the fraction part. Keep 6 as the denominator.

EXAMPLE

Convert $\frac{19}{6}$ to a mixed number.

STEPS

Divide 19 by 6.

$$\frac{19}{6} = 6\overline{)19}^{\,3\frac{1}{6}}$$
$$\underline{18}$$
$$1$$

OBJECTIVE 5 Convert mixed numbers to improper fractions.

To convert a mixed number to an improper fraction, multiply the denominator by the whole number, add the numerator to that product, and place the sum over the original denominator.

EXAMPLE

Convert $9\frac{1}{4}$ to an improper fraction.

1. Multiply the denominator by the whole number.

$$4 \times 9 = 36$$

2. Add the product and the numerator.

$$36 + 1 = 37$$

3. Place the sum over the original denominator.

$$\frac{37}{4}$$

EXAMPLES

Convert the following mixed numbers to improper fractions.

1. $24\frac{7}{8}$

2. $4\frac{8}{12}$

STEPS

1. $24\frac{7}{8} = \frac{(8 \times 24) + 7}{8} = \frac{199}{8}$

2. $4\frac{8}{12} = \frac{(12 \times 4) + 8}{12} = \frac{56}{12}$

OBJECTIVE **6** Reduce fractions to lowest terms.

Sometimes proper fractions, such as $\frac{88}{100}$ and $\frac{75}{125}$, are too large to work with in solving math problems. Therefore, it is helpful to reduce them to lowest terms. Reducing a fraction to **lowest terms** means you must find the smallest numerator and denominator possible without changing the original value of the fraction. To do this, you must find a number or divisor that will divide evenly into both the numerator and the denominator.

Trial-and-Error Method

In many cases, you can use a trial-and-error method to reduce fractions. Always look for a common divisor that will divide evenly into both the numerator and the denominator. The largest number that will divide evenly into both the numerator and denominator is the **greatest common divisor**.

EXAMPLE

Reduce $\frac{18}{36}$ to lowest terms.

STEPS

$$\frac{18}{36} = \frac{18}{36} \qquad \begin{array}{l} \leftarrow \text{divided by } 18 = 1 \\ \leftarrow \text{divided by } 18 = 2 \end{array}$$

$$\frac{18}{36} = \frac{1}{2} \qquad \text{lowest terms}$$

Trial-and-Error Methods

- If the numerator will divide the denominator evenly, the numerator is the *greatest common divisor*, as shown below.

$$\frac{9 \div 9}{36 \div 9} = \frac{1}{4}$$

- If the numerator and denominator are both even numbers, they can be divided by 2. Study this example.

$$\frac{18 \div 2}{32 \div 2} = \frac{9}{16}$$

- If both the numerator and denominator end in 0, they can be divided by 10, as shown below.

$$\frac{40 \div 10}{50 \div 10} = \frac{4}{5}$$

- If both the numerator and denominator end in 5 or 0, they can be divided by 5. Study this example.

$$\frac{25 \div 5}{35 \div 5} = \frac{5}{7}$$

- If the numerator and denominator are multiples of 3—such as 3, 6, 9, 12, 15, and so on, they can be divided by 3. Study this example.

$$\frac{18 \div 3}{33 \div 3} = \frac{6}{11}$$

EXAMPLES

Write the following fractions in lowest terms.

1. $\dfrac{135}{275}$ 2. $\dfrac{80}{270}$

STEPS

1. Both 135 and 275 can be divided by 5.

$$\frac{135}{275} = \frac{135}{275} \qquad \leftarrow \text{divided by } 5 = 27$$
$$\qquad\qquad \leftarrow \text{divided by } 5 = 55$$

$$\frac{135}{275} = \frac{27}{55} \qquad \text{lowest terms}$$

2. For $\frac{80}{270}$, divide both 80 and 270 by 10.

$$\frac{80}{270} = \frac{80}{270} \qquad \leftarrow \text{divided by } 10 = 8$$
$$\qquad\qquad \leftarrow \text{divided by } 10 = 27$$

$$\frac{80}{270} = \frac{8}{27} \qquad \text{lowest terms}$$

Greatest-Common-Divisor Method

If none of the trial-and-error methods apply, use the following steps to determine the greatest common divisor.

STEPS

1. Divide the denominator by the numerator.

2. If there is a remainder, divide the original divisor by the remainder.

3. Continue to divide the last divisor by the remainder until there is no remainder, if possible.

4. If there is no remainder, the last divisor used in this process is the greatest common divisor.

5. Divide both the numerator and denominator by the greatest common divisor. The answer will be the lowest terms to which the fraction can be reduced.

6. If there is a remainder of 1, the fraction is already at its lowest terms.

EXAMPLE

Reduce $\frac{268}{460}$ to lowest terms using the greatest-common-divisor method.

STEPS

1. Divide the denominator by the numerator.

$$\begin{array}{r} 1 \\ 268 \overline{)460} \\ \underline{268} \\ 192 \end{array}$$

2. Divide the original divisor by the remainder.

$$\begin{array}{r} 1 \\ 192 \overline{)268} \\ \underline{192} \\ 76 \end{array}$$

3. Continue the division process until there is no remainder, as shown in (d).

(a) $\begin{array}{r} 2 \\ 76 \overline{)192} \\ \underline{152} \\ 40 \end{array}$ (b) $\begin{array}{r} 1 \\ 40 \overline{)76} \\ \underline{40} \\ 36 \end{array}$ (c) $\begin{array}{r} 1 \\ 36 \overline{)40} \\ \underline{36} \\ 4 \end{array}$ (d) $\begin{array}{r} 9 \\ 4 \overline{)36} \\ \underline{36} \\ 0 \end{array}$

4. The last divisor 4 is the greatest common divisor and is used to divide 268 and 460.

$$\frac{268 \div 4}{460 \div 4} = \frac{67}{115}$$

EXAMPLE

The fraction $\frac{278}{455}$ is already reduced to lowest terms because the last divisor 1 in the last division step (f) is the greatest common divisor.

STEPS

(a) $\begin{array}{r} 1 \\ 278 \overline{)455} \\ \underline{278} \\ 177 \end{array}$ (b) $\begin{array}{r} 1 \\ 177 \overline{)278} \\ \underline{177} \\ 101 \end{array}$ (c) $\begin{array}{r} 1 \\ 101 \overline{)177} \\ \underline{101} \\ 76 \end{array}$

(d) $\begin{array}{r} 1 \\ 76 \overline{)101} \\ \underline{76} \\ 25 \end{array}$ (e) $\begin{array}{r} 3 \\ 25 \overline{)76} \\ \underline{75} \\ 1 \end{array}$ (f) $\begin{array}{r} 25 \\ 1 \overline{)25} \\ \underline{2} \\ 5 \\ \underline{5} \\ 0 \end{array}$

Just as fractions can be reduced to lowest terms, they can also be raised to higher terms by multiplying the numerator and denominator by the same number. Raising fractions to higher terms is important in addition and subtraction of fractions.

EXAMPLE

Raise $\frac{2}{3}$ to a fraction with a denominator of 12.

$$\frac{2}{3} = \frac{?}{12}$$

STEPS

1. Divide the new denominator, 12, by the original denominator, 3, to find the quotient, the common multiplier. That number is 4.

$$12 \div 3 = 4$$

2. Multiply both the numerator and denominator by the quotient from Step 1 to get the new fraction with a denominator of 12.

$$2 \times 4 = 8 \text{ and } 3 \times 4 = 12$$

3. Write the new numerator over the desired denominator.

$$\frac{8}{12}$$

The result, $\frac{8}{12}$, is sometimes referred to as an **equivalent fraction** because it is equal to the original fraction, $\frac{2}{3}$.

EXAMPLES

Write the following fractions with the denominators shown.

1. $\frac{7}{9} = \frac{?}{45}$

2. $\frac{11}{12} = \frac{?}{72}$

STEPS

1. $\frac{7 \times 5}{9 \times 5} = \frac{35}{45}$

2. $\frac{11 \times 6}{12 \times 6} = \frac{66}{72}$

OBJECTIVE **8** Convert fractions to decimals.

Because both fractions and decimals represent parts of a whole number, a fraction can be converted to a decimal and a decimal can be converted to a fraction. For example, $\frac{5}{10}$ is equivalent to 0.5, and the decimal 0.25 represents the fraction $\frac{25}{100}$. The conversion may simplify some calculations when you are solving a particular math problem. To convert a common fraction to a decimal, divide the numerator by the denominator.

Convert $\frac{7}{8}$ to a decimal, carrying the answer to three decimal places (thousandths position).

STEPS

Divide the numerator by the denominator, placing a decimal point after the numerator and adding one zero at a time to the right of the decimal point. Carry the answer to the desired number of decimal places.

$$
\begin{array}{r}
0.875 \\
8)\overline{7.000} \\
\underline{6\,4} \\
60 \\
\underline{56} \\
40 \\
\underline{40} \\
0
\end{array}
$$

TIPS

The result, 0.875, is read as "eight hundred seventy-five thousandths."

Sometimes a denominator may not evenly divide a numerator, as shown below.

EXAMPLE

Convert $\frac{5}{12}$ to a decimal.

STEPS

$$
\begin{array}{r}
0.4166 \\
12)\overline{5.0000} \\
\underline{4\,8} \\
20 \\
\underline{12} \\
80 \\
\underline{72} \\
80 \\
\underline{72} \\
8
\end{array}
$$

TIPS

To convert a common fraction to a decimal, divide the numerator by the denominator. To convert fractions to decimal fractions, decide on a desired number of decimal places. Set the decimal indicator on your calculator.

Decimal places have been added to continue the division process. However, in this particular problem, there will always be a remainder because the denominator, 12, will not evenly divide the numerator, 5. You can round your answer to any desired number of places. In this example, the decimal equivalent 0.4166 is shown rounded to 2 and 3 decimal places. You can also place a line above the last digit to indicate that this digit will always repeat. In division, when one or more numbers repeat in a pattern, it is called a **repeating decimal**.

$\frac{5}{12} = 0.42$ rounded to the nearest hundredth (2 decimal places)

$\frac{5}{12} = 0.417$ rounded to the nearest thousandth (3 decimal places)

$\frac{5}{12} = 0.41\overline{6}$ repeating decimal

TIPS

Depending on the degree of accuracy required, decimals may be rounded to tenths or hundredths, or they may be carried out as far as needed.

Decimal Equivalents Chart

Rather than taking time to convert a fraction to its decimal equivalent, you should become familiar with common decimal equivalents, as shown in Figure 2-4.

Figure 2-4

Decimal Equivalents Chart

Fraction		Decimal Equivalent
$\frac{1}{5}$	=	0.2
$\frac{1}{4}$	=	0.25
$\frac{1}{3}$	=	0.3333 (rounded)
$\frac{1}{2}$	=	0.5
$\frac{5}{8}$	=	0.625
$\frac{2}{3}$	=	0.6667 (rounded)
$\frac{3}{4}$	=	0.75
$\frac{7}{8}$	=	0.875

A mixed number is converted to a decimal using the same method to convert a fraction to a decimal.

EXAMPLE

Convert $5\frac{5}{8}$ to a decimal.

STEPS

1. Convert the fractional part by dividing the numerator by the denominator.

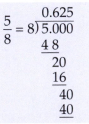

$$\frac{5}{8} = 8\overline{)5.000}$$

2. Write the whole number 5 with the decimal equivalent 0.625.

5.625

EXAMPLES

Convert the following fractions to decimals.

1. $\frac{1}{6}$ 2. $\frac{1}{3}$ 3. $8\frac{5}{12}$

1. Convert $\frac{1}{6}$ to a decimal by dividing 1 by 6.

$$\frac{1}{6} = 6\overline{)1.0000}^{\,0.1666} = 0.167$$

$$\begin{array}{r} \underline{0} \\ 10 \\ \underline{6} \\ 40 \\ \underline{36} \\ 40 \\ \underline{36} \\ 40 \\ \underline{36} \\ 4 \end{array}$$

Since 6 will not divide into 1, place a 0 to the left of the decimal point. Now 6 can divide into 10 once with a remainder of 4. Continue placing zeros to the right of the decimal point and continue dividing to the nearest desired decimal point. Therefore, the result is 0.17 (nearest hundredth), 0.167 (nearest thousandth), or $0.1\overline{6}$.

2. Divide 1 by 3 and keep adding zeros to the nearest desired decimal point. The result is written as 0.3 (nearest tenth) or 0.33 (nearest hundredth), 0.333 (nearest thousandth), or $0.\overline{3}$.

$$\frac{1}{3} = 3\overline{)1.000}^{\,0.333} = 0.333$$

$$\begin{array}{r} \underline{0} \\ 10 \\ \underline{9} \\ 10 \\ \underline{9} \\ 10 \\ \underline{9} \\ 1 \end{array}$$

3. Change the fractional part by dividing the numerator by the denominator.

$$\frac{5}{12} = 12\overline{)5.000}^{\,0.416} = 0.42$$

$$\begin{array}{r} \underline{48} \\ 20 \\ \underline{12} \\ 80 \\ \underline{72} \\ 8 \end{array}$$

Write the whole number 8 with the decimal equivalent 0.42.

$$8.42$$

There are several methods of converting a decimal to a fraction. One method is to think of the decimal in its word form. For example: 0.3, which is read three tenths, is $\frac{3}{10}$ and 0.25, which is read twenty-five hundredths, is $\frac{25}{100}$.

EXAMPLE

Convert 1.35 to a fraction.

STEPS

1. Write the decimal part in its fractional form.

$$\frac{35}{100}$$

2. Reduce to its lowest terms, if necessary.

$$\frac{35}{100} = \frac{7}{20}$$

Therefore, the fractional equivalent of 1.35 is $1\frac{7}{20}$.

EXAMPLES

Convert the following decimals to fractions.

1. 0.45   2. 0.105   3. 2.583

STEPS

1. Write the decimal in its fractional form as $\frac{45}{100}$. Reduce to its lowest terms: $\frac{45}{100} = \frac{9}{20}$. Therefore, the fractional equivalent of 0.45 is $\frac{9}{20}$.

2. Write the decimal in its fractional form and reduce to lowest terms.

$$0.105 = \frac{105}{1,000} = \frac{21}{200}$$

3. $2.583 = 2\frac{583}{1,000}$

©iofoto, 2010/ Used under license from Shutterstock.com

OBJECTIVE 10 Use Excel to enter fractions and mixed numbers.

Excel has a fraction format that displays numbers as fractions. When using this format, be careful entering your fractions. If you enter 1/2 in a cell, for example, Excel interprets it as 2-Jan (or 1-Feb depending on your setup) instead of a fraction. Figure 2-5 shows a fraction that has a value of less than one.

STEPS

To enter a fraction:

1. Open a new workbook in Excel.
2. Click on Cell A3 where the results will appear.
3. Enter a zero followed by a space followed by the fraction in x/y format (where x is the numerator and y is the denominator). For example, if you want to enter two-thirds, key 0[space]2/3.
4. Press Enter. The fraction appears in the cell. When you place the cursor on the cell containing 2/3, the decimal equivalent is shown in the formula bar, as shown in Figure 2-5.
5. Leave this screen open to use in the next steps.

Figure 2-5
Entering Fractions in Excel

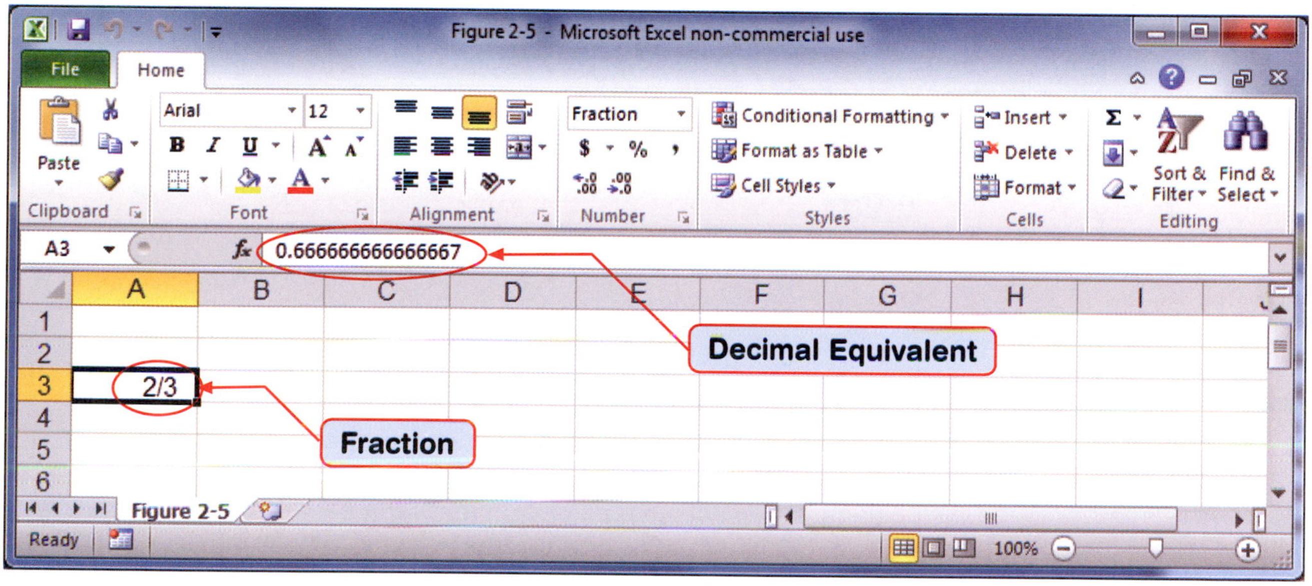

STEPS

To enter a mixed number:

1. Key the whole number followed by a space followed by the fraction in x/y format. For example, click Cell A6, then key 2[space]2/3[enter] to enter 2 2/3. When you place the cursor on the cell containing 2 2/3, the mixed number appears in the cell. The decimal equivalent appears in the formula bar as shown in Figure 2-6.
2. Leave this screen open to use in the next steps.

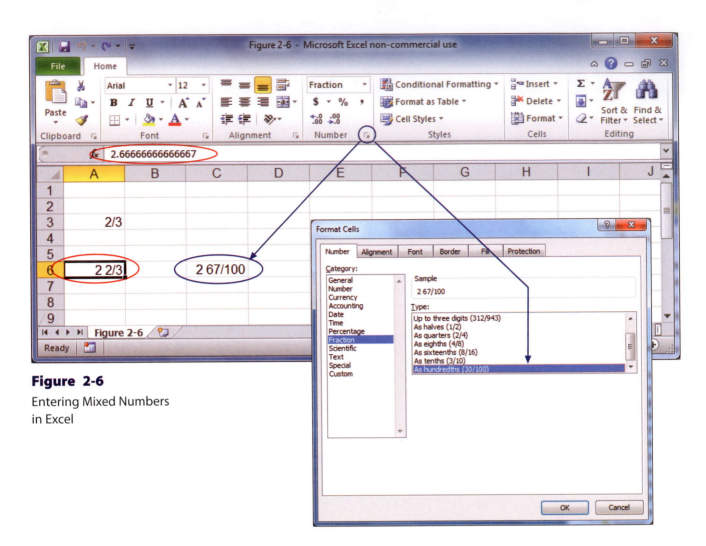

Figure 2-6

Entering Mixed Numbers
in Excel

STEPS

To see the available fraction formats:

1. Enter 2 2/3 in Cell C6.

2. Click Cell C6. Open the Format cells dialog box (Home/Cells/ Format/Format Cells). Click on the Number tab.

3. Click Fraction in the Category list shown on the left side. You can format fractions up to three digits and perform calculations using them. If you enter a fraction and the result needs to be shown in hundredths, select As hundredths from the Type list. Click OK to accept the format. The result 2 67/100 appears in Cell C6.

4. Do not save this screen.

The Practice below will guide you in entering fractions in hundredths and their decimal equivalents.

PRACTICE

Retrieve the file *ch02pr01.xlsx*. Follow the directions. Save the file as *ch02pr01a.xlsx*.

Name _____   Date _____

Directions   Complete the following problems. Write your answers in the blanks provided.

A. Identify each of the following numbers as a proper fraction, an improper fraction, or a mixed number. Indicate your answer with P for a proper fraction, I for an improper fraction, or M for a mixed number.   **OBJECTIVE 2**

1. $\frac{33}{6}$ _____

2. $\frac{5}{13}$ _____

3. $2\frac{1}{6}$ _____

4. $\frac{3}{5}$ _____

5. $\frac{8}{3}$ _____

6. $1\frac{2}{3}$ _____

7. $\frac{5}{8}$ _____

8. $\frac{7}{8}$ _____

B. Convert the following improper fractions to whole numbers.   **OBJECTIVE 3**

9. $\frac{12}{3}$ _____

10. $\frac{120}{40}$ _____

11. $\frac{60}{12}$ _____

12. $\frac{88}{8}$ _____

13. $\frac{36}{6}$ _____

14. $\frac{132}{4}$ _____

15. $\frac{168}{8}$ _____

16. $\frac{210}{5}$ _____

C. Convert the following improper fractions to mixed numbers or whole numbers. Reduce to lowest terms where necessary.   **OBJECTIVES 3, 4**

17. $\frac{75}{8}$ _____

18. $\frac{8}{3}$ _____

19. $\frac{7}{5}$ _____

20. $\frac{110}{89}$ _____

21. $\frac{99}{3}$ _____

22. $\frac{59}{12}$ _____

23. $\frac{128}{16}$ _____

24. $\frac{145}{120}$ _____

D. Change the following mixed numbers to improper fractions.   **OBJECTIVE 5**

25. $6\frac{1}{4}$ _____

26. $36\frac{3}{4}$ _____

27. $5\frac{1}{3}$ _____

28. $4\frac{3}{8}$ _____

29. $75\frac{3}{8}$ _____

30. $37\frac{1}{2}$ _____

31. $4\frac{3}{4}$ _____

32. $12\frac{2}{3}$ _____

E. Reduce the following fractions to lowest terms. OBJECTIVE **6**

33. $\frac{9}{18}$ _____

34. $\frac{36}{124}$ _____

35. $\frac{8}{48}$ _____

36. $\frac{228}{314}$ _____

37. $\frac{12}{28}$ _____

38. $\frac{6}{9}$ _____

39. $\frac{183}{366}$ _____

40. $\frac{150}{365}$ _____

41. $\frac{6}{8}$ _____

42. $\frac{72}{148}$ _____

F. Raise the following fractions to higher terms using the indicated denominators. OBJECTIVE **7**

43. $\frac{10}{25} = \frac{?}{125}$ _____

44. $\frac{11}{18} = \frac{?}{36}$ _____

45. $\frac{5}{24} = \frac{?}{96}$ _____

46. $\frac{5}{8} = \frac{?}{72}$ _____

47. $\frac{4}{19} = \frac{?}{57}$ _____

48. $\frac{7}{17} = \frac{?}{51}$ _____

49. $\frac{7}{10} = \frac{?}{50}$ _____

50. $\frac{7}{8} = \frac{?}{24}$ _____

51. $\frac{5}{8} = \frac{?}{48}$ _____

52. $\frac{9}{13} = \frac{?}{182}$ _____

G. Convert the following fractions to decimals and round your answers to the nearest hundredth. OBJECTIVE **8**

53. $\frac{8}{50}$ _____

54. $5\frac{5}{7}$ _____

55. $9\frac{5}{12}$ _____

56. $8\frac{12}{100}$ _____

57. $\frac{4}{9}$ _____

58. $\frac{9}{20}$ _____

59. $7\frac{1}{7}$ _____

60. $\frac{7}{12}$ _____

61. $\frac{3}{5}$ _____

62. $\frac{9}{42}$ _____

H. Convert the following decimals to fractions and reduce to lowest terms. OBJECTIVES **6, 9**

63. 0.75 _____

64. 0.8 _____

65. 0.03 _____

66. 0.2482 _____

67. 0.68 _____

68. 0.36 _____

69. 0.86 _____

70. 0.125 _____

71. 0.24 _____

72. 0.18 _____

I. Use Excel to format cells for fractions and mixed numbers, to enter fractions and mixed numbers, and to find decimal equivalents. OBJECTIVE **10**

73. Retrieve the file *ch02ex01.xlsx*. Follow the directions. Save the file as *ch02ex01a.xlsx*.

74. Retrieve the file *ch02ex02.xlsx*. Follow the directions. Save the file as *ch02ex02a.xlsx*.

2.2 Add and Subtract Fractions and Mixed Numbers

OBJECTIVE 1 Identify terms used with adding and subtracting fractions.

Fractions such as $\frac{1}{4}$ and $\frac{3}{4}$ are **like fractions** because they have a common denominator, in this case, 4. Fractions such as $\frac{1}{4}$ and $\frac{1}{8}$ are **unlike fractions** because they have different denominators, in this case, 4 and 8.

OBJECTIVE 2 Add and subtract like fractions.

Not only should you be able to convert fractions to decimals and decimals to fractions, you should also be able to add and subtract fractions. Suppose you want to order a custom blind to fit a window opening that is $48\frac{1}{2}$ inches wide, leaving a $\frac{3}{8}$-inch space on either side of the blind (between it and the window frame) for clearance. What width should you specify when ordering your custom blind? You must be able to add and subtract fractions in order to deal with everyday problems such as this one.

stevecoleccs/iStockphoto.com

Add or subtract like fractions (those with common denominators) and place the result over the common denominator to form a new fraction. When needed, reduce the answer to its lowest terms.

EXAMPLES

1. $\dfrac{5}{9} + \dfrac{2}{9}$

2. $\dfrac{11}{12} - \dfrac{7}{12}$

STEPS

1. Add the numerators and place the result over the common denominator.

$$5 + 2 = 7 \qquad \frac{7}{9}$$

2. Subtract the numerators, place the result over the common denominator, and reduce to lowest terms.

$$11 - 7 = 4 \qquad \frac{4}{12} = \frac{1}{3} \quad \text{reduced}$$

When like fractions are added, the sum may be an improper fraction, as shown below.

Add and convert the following improper fractions to mixed numbers. Then convert the mixed number to a decimal.

1. $\dfrac{3}{5} + \dfrac{4}{5}$

2. $\dfrac{1}{5} + \dfrac{2}{5} + \dfrac{3}{5}$

STEPS

1. Add the like fractions and convert the sum to a mixed number and then a decimal.

$$\frac{3}{5} + \frac{4}{5} = \frac{7}{5} = 1\frac{2}{5}, \text{ or } 1.4$$

2. Add the like fractions and convert the sum to a mixed number and then a decimal.

$$\frac{1}{5} + \frac{2}{5} + \frac{3}{5} = \frac{6}{5} = 1\frac{1}{5}, \text{ or } 1.2$$

OBJECTIVE **3** Find the least common denominator.

Fractions such as $\frac{1}{4}$ and $\frac{3}{4}$ are like fractions and can be added as they appear because they have a common denominator. Fractions such as $\frac{1}{4}$ and $\frac{1}{2}$ are called unlike fractions because they have different denominators. Because unlike fractions have different denominators, they cannot be added as they appear. The denominators must be changed so they are the same. To add unlike fractions or mixed numbers, you must first find a common denominator. A **common denominator** is a number that can be divided evenly by all the unlike denominators.

The **least common denominator**, sometimes referred to as the **LCD**, is the smallest number that can be divided evenly by all the unlike denominators. For example, the least common denominator of the fractions $\frac{1}{2}$ and $\frac{1}{5}$ is 10, since 10 can be divided evenly by both 2 and 5.

Two methods of finding the least common denominator are the inspection method and prime number method.

The **inspection method** is quick and easy when the denominators involved are small. By simple observation, you should be able to determine the least common denominator. The inspection method may be difficult to use when fractions have large denominators or when many fractions are to be added.

EXAMPLES

Find the least common denominator.

1. $\dfrac{1}{2}, \dfrac{3}{4}, \dfrac{1}{3}$

2. $\dfrac{1}{4}, \dfrac{2}{3}, \dfrac{5}{12}$

CHAPTER 2 FRACTIONS

STEPS

1. By simple observation, the smallest common number that all the unlike denominators 2, 4, and 3 will evenly divide is 12.

$$12 \div 2 = 6 \qquad \frac{1}{2} = \frac{6}{12}$$
$$12 \div 4 = 3 \qquad \frac{3}{4} = \frac{9}{12}$$
$$12 \div 3 = 4 \qquad \frac{1}{3} = \frac{4}{12}$$

2. By simple observation, the least common denominator is 12 because 12 is the smallest number the denominators 4, 3, and 12 will evenly divide.

$$12 \div 4 = 3 \qquad \frac{1}{4} = \frac{3}{12}$$
$$12 \div 3 = 4 \qquad \frac{2}{3} = \frac{8}{12}$$
$$12 \div 12 = 1 \qquad \frac{5}{12} = \frac{5}{12}$$

The second method of determining the least common denominator is the **prime number method**. A **prime number** is a whole number larger than 1 that can be divided evenly only by itself and by 1. The six smallest prime numbers are 2, 3, 5, 7, 11, and 13. The **prime factorization** of a number is the number written as a product of primes. Study the following example.

EXAMPLE

Find the least common denominator of $\frac{3}{8}$, $\frac{7}{12}$, and $\frac{11}{20}$.

STEPS

1. Write the denominators horizontally across the page.

$$8 \qquad 12 \qquad 20$$

2. Divide each denominator by a prime number common to two or more of the numbers. Write the quotient above each denominator.

$$\begin{array}{c} 4 \quad 6 \quad 10 \\ \hline 2)\overline{8 \quad 12 \quad 20} \end{array}$$

3. Each of the new quotients, 4, 6, and 10, can still be divided by 2. Therefore, continue the division process using the same prime number 2.

$$\begin{array}{c} 2 \quad 3 \quad 5 \\ \hline 2)\overline{4 \quad 6 \quad 10} \\ \hline 2)\overline{8 \quad 12 \quad 20} \end{array}$$

4. Continue to divide by the prime number 2. The new quotient 2 can still be divided by the prime number 2, but the quotients 3 and 5 cannot be evenly divided by 2. Because 3 and 5 cannot be evenly divided by 2, write these amounts in the row of answers. Continue to divide by the prime number 2.

$$\begin{array}{c} 1 \quad 3 \quad 5 \\ \hline 2)\overline{2 \quad 3 \quad 5} \\ \hline 2)\overline{4 \quad 6 \quad 10} \\ \hline 2)\overline{8 \quad 12 \quad 20} \end{array}$$

5. Because the prime number 2 will not evenly divide these last quotients in the row, try the next prime number, which is 3. Because 1 and 5 are not divisible by 3, write these amounts in the row of answers.

$$
\begin{array}{c}
1\quad 1\quad 5 \\
\overline{3)\,1\quad 3\quad 5} \\
\overline{2)\,2\quad 3\quad 5} \\
\overline{2)\,4\quad 6\quad 10} \\
\overline{2)\,8\quad 12\quad 20}
\end{array}
$$

6. Because the prime number 3 will not evenly divide these last quotients, try the next prime number, 5. The last quotient can be divided once by 5. Divide until all quotients are 1.

$$
\begin{array}{c}
1\quad 1\quad 1 \\
\overline{5)\,1\quad 1\quad 5} \\
\overline{3)\,1\quad 3\quad 5} \\
\overline{2)\,2\quad 3\quad 5} \\
\overline{2)\,4\quad 6\quad 10} \\
\overline{2)\,8\quad 12\quad 20}
\end{array}
$$

7. Because no prime number can evenly divide these last quotients, you can now determine the least common denominator by multiplying the five divisors 2, 2, 2, 3, and 5—the prime numbers used in this example.

$$2 \times 2 \times 2 \times 3 \times 5 = 120$$

120 is the least common denominator of $\frac{3}{8}$, $\frac{7}{12}$, and $\frac{11}{20}$.

OBJECTIVE **4** Add and subtract unlike fractions.

Now that you have determined the least common denominator, you can add the fractions in the last example by raising each fraction to 120ths and then adding.

EXAMPLE

$$
\begin{array}{ll}
\dfrac{3}{8} = \dfrac{45}{120} & 120 \div 8 = 15;\ 15 \times 3 = 45 \\[2mm]
\dfrac{7}{12} = \dfrac{70}{120} & 120 \div 12 = 10;\ 10 \times 7 = 70 \\[2mm]
+\dfrac{11}{20} = +\dfrac{66}{120} & 120 \div 20 = 6;\ 6 \times 11 = 66 \\[2mm]
\hline
\dfrac{181}{120} = 1\dfrac{61}{120} &
\end{array}
$$

The sum $\frac{181}{120}$ is converted to a mixed number $1\frac{61}{120}$.

$$\frac{5}{18} + \frac{7}{20} - \frac{11}{24}$$

STEPS

1. Find the least common denominator for 18, 20, and 24. Write the three denominators using the prime number method. When the prime numbers 2 and 3 won't divide, use the next prime number 5.

```
              1    1    1
         5)   1    5    1
         3)   3    5    1
         3)   9    5    3
         2)   9    5    6
         2)   9   10   12
         2)  18   20   24
```

2. Find the least common denominator by multiplying the prime numbers in the left column.

$$2 \times 2 \times 2 \times 3 \times 3 \times 5 = 360$$

3. Raise each fraction to 360ths and then add or subtract.

$$\frac{5}{18} + \frac{7}{20} - \frac{11}{24}$$

$$= \frac{5 \times 20}{360} + \frac{7 \times 18}{360} - \frac{11 \times 15}{360}$$

$$= \frac{100}{360} + \frac{126}{360} - \frac{165}{360}$$

$$= \frac{61}{360}$$

OBJECTIVE 5 Add mixed numbers.

To add mixed numbers with like fractions, follow these steps.

Adding Mixed Numbers with Like Fractions

1. Add the fractional parts.
2. Add the whole numbers.
3. Add the sum of the fractional parts and the sum of the whole numbers together.
4. Reduce answer to lowest terms as needed.

EXAMPLE

Suppose you are a sales clerk in a fabric store who cut two pieces of trimming for a customer. One piece measured $12\frac{4}{7}$ inches, and the other measured $15\frac{2}{7}$ inches. Add the two pieces together to get the total measurement for the order.

Problem Solving Plan

Clues	Action Plan	Solve
Two pieces of trimming were cut. First piece is $12\frac{4}{7}$ inches. Second piece is $15\frac{2}{7}$ inches.	Add the fractional parts. Add the whole numbers. Add the two sums.	$\frac{4}{7} + \frac{2}{7} = \frac{6}{7}$ $12 + 15 = 27$ $27 + \frac{6}{7} = 27\frac{6}{7}$

Conclusion

Although the customer may pay a different price for each trim, he or she will pay for a total of $27\frac{6}{7}$ inches of trimming.

In some cases, the sum of the fractional parts of the mixed number is greater than 1, making it an improper fraction. Convert the improper fraction to a mixed number. Study the next example.

EXAMPLE

$$11\frac{9}{12} + 3\frac{7}{12}$$

STEPS

1. Add the fractional parts and convert the improper fraction to a mixed number. Reduce to lowest terms, if necessary.

$$\frac{9}{12}$$
$$+\frac{7}{12}$$
$$\frac{16}{12} = 1\frac{4}{12} = 1\frac{1}{3}$$

2. Add the whole numbers.

$$11$$
$$+\ 3$$
$$14$$

3. Add the mixed number and the sum of the whole numbers.

$$1\frac{1}{3}$$
$$+\ 14$$
$$15\frac{1}{3}$$

To add mixed numbers with unlike fractions, follow the same steps for adding mixed numbers with like fractions. Remember to determine the least common denominator.

CHAPTER 2 FRACTIONS

$$13\frac{3}{5} + 2\frac{3}{10}$$

STEPS

1. Determine the least common denominator.

$$10$$

2. Add the fractional parts.

$$\frac{3}{5} = \frac{6}{10} \text{ and } \frac{3}{10} = \frac{3}{10}$$

$$\frac{6}{10} + \frac{3}{10} = \frac{9}{10}$$

3. Add the whole numbers.

$$13 + 2 = 15$$

4. Add the whole numbers and the fractional parts.

$$15 + \frac{9}{10} = 15\frac{9}{10}$$

OBJECTIVE **6** Subtract mixed numbers.

As with addition of fractions, subtraction of fractions can occur only when there is a common denominator. The basic steps for subtracting fractions are as follows.

> **Subtracting Fractions**
> 1. **Find the least common denominator as necessary.**
> 2. **Subtract the numerators and place the difference over the common denominator.**
> 3. **Reduce to lowest terms as necessary.**

EXAMPLES

1. $\frac{5}{8} - \frac{3}{8}$
2. $\frac{3}{5} - \frac{1}{2}$

STEPS

1. Subtract $\frac{3}{8}$ from $\frac{5}{8}$ and reduce to lowest terms.

$$\begin{array}{r} \frac{5}{8} \\ -\frac{3}{8} \\ \hline \frac{2}{8} = \frac{1}{4} \end{array}$$

2. To subtract $\frac{1}{2}$ from $\frac{3}{5}$, determine the least common denominator and then subtract the two fractions.

$$
\begin{array}{rcl}
\frac{3}{5} & = & \frac{6}{10} \\
-\frac{1}{2} & = & -\frac{5}{10} \\
\hline
& & \frac{1}{10}
\end{array}
$$

You may need to borrow to do subtraction with mixed numbers. Subtract one from the whole number, convert it to a fraction with the same denominator as the fractional part, and add it to the fraction.

EXAMPLES

Subtract the following using borrowing.

1. $9 - \frac{1}{6}$ 2. $12\frac{3}{10} - 4\frac{1}{5}$ 3. $3 - 1\frac{2}{3}$

STEPS

1. To subtract $\frac{1}{6}$ from the whole number 9, borrow or subtract 1 from the 9, the whole number in the minuend, and express it in sixths, as in $\frac{6}{6}$. The 9 reduced by 1 is 8 because you borrowed 1 from it. Place the 8 beside the $\frac{6}{6}$. Then subtract the fractions. The fraction is already in lowest terms, so you do not need to reduce it.

$$
\begin{array}{rcl}
9 & = & 8\frac{6}{6} \\
-\frac{1}{6} & = & -\frac{1}{6} \\
\hline
& & 8\frac{5}{6}
\end{array}
$$

2. Determine a common denominator and change the fractions to equivalent fractions. Subtract the fractional parts and the whole numbers. Since the fraction is already in lowest terms, you do not need to reduce it.

$$
\begin{array}{rcl}
12\frac{3}{10} & = & 12\frac{3}{10} \\
-4\frac{1}{5} & = & -4\frac{2}{10} \\
\hline
& & 8\frac{1}{10}
\end{array}
$$

3. To subtract $1\frac{2}{3}$ from 3, borrow 1 from 3, leaving $2\frac{3}{3}$. Then, subtract $1\frac{2}{3}$ from $2\frac{3}{3}$.

$$
\begin{array}{rcl}
3 & = & 2\frac{3}{3} \\
-1\frac{2}{3} & = & -1\frac{2}{3} \\
\hline
& & 1\frac{1}{3}
\end{array}
$$

CHAPTER 2 FRACTIONS

OBJECTIVE 7 Use Excel to add and subtract fractions and mixed numbers.

As you learned earlier in this chapter, to enter a single fraction instead of a date in Excel, enter a zero and a space before the fraction. For instance, to enter $\frac{1}{5}$, enter 0 1/5. The cell will display 1/5, and the formula bar will display 0.2 instead of 5-Jan.

Cells can also be formatted in advance to recognize fractions without the leading zero.

STEPS

1. Open Excel with a blank screen.
2. In Cell A3, key 0[space]3/4.
3. Press Enter. If the fraction appears in the worksheet and its decimal equivalent appears in the formula bar, you know the cell has been formatted to display fractions. See Figure 2-7.

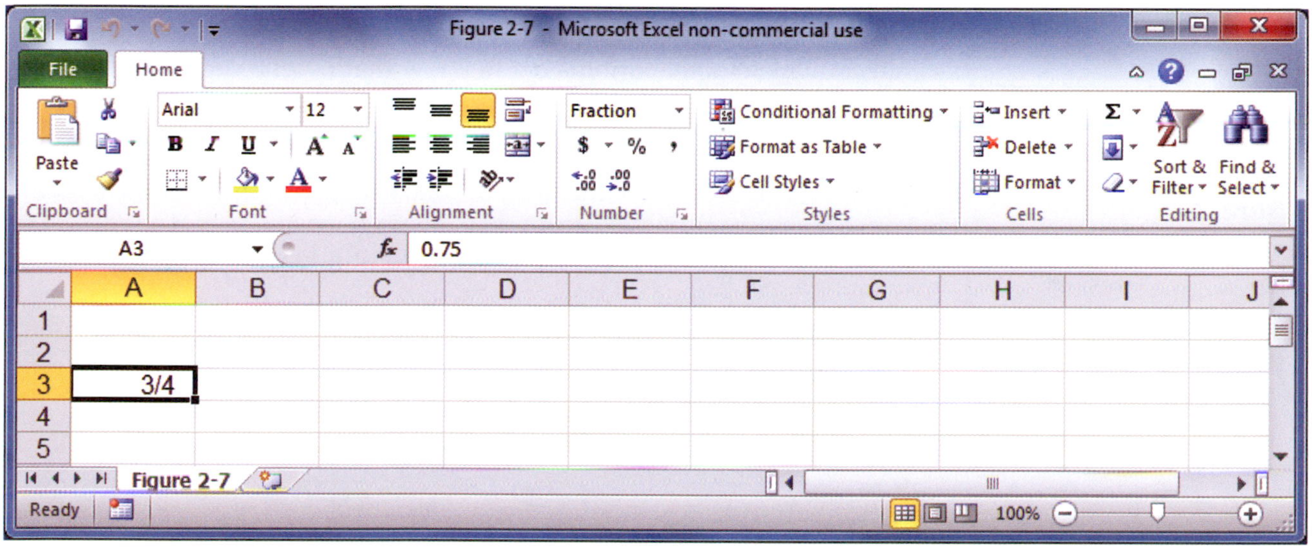

Figure 2-7
Entering Fractions in Excel

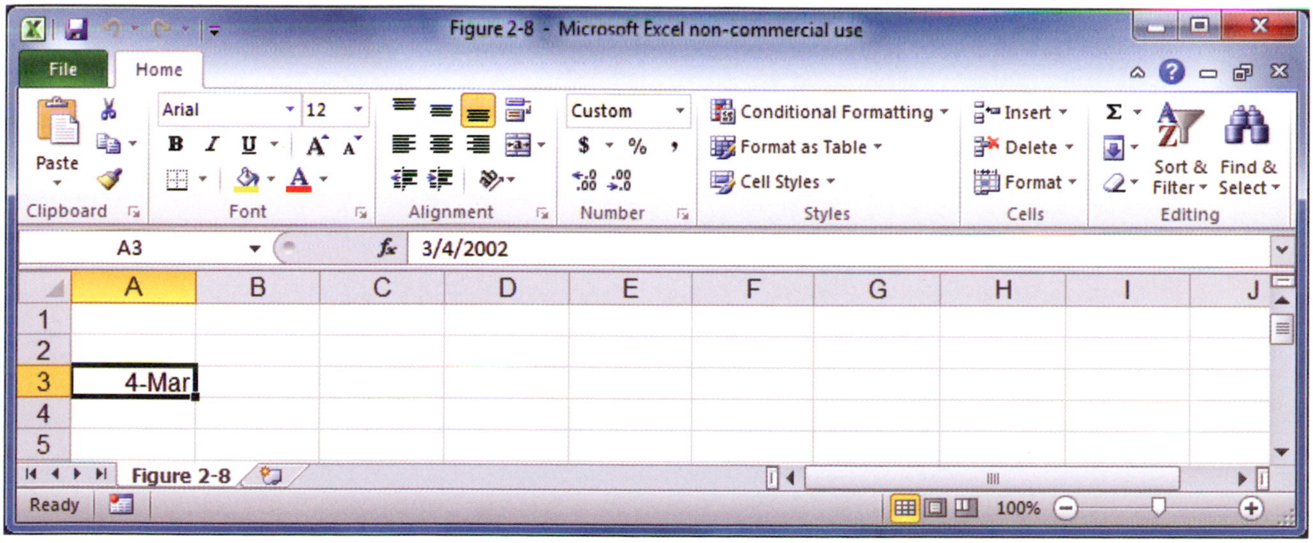

Figure 2-8
Displaying a Date in a Cell

If Excel displays a date as shown in the formula bar in Figure 2-8, and not as a fraction, format the desired cell to display fractions before keying the fractions.

STEPS

1. Delete the contents of Cell A3.
2. Click Cell A3. Open the Format cells dialog box (Home/Cells/Format/Format Cells).
3. Click on the Number tab.
4. Select Fraction in the Category list on the left side.
5. From the Type list, select Up to two digits.
6. Click OK to apply the formatting feature.
7. In Cell A3, key 3/4.
8. Press Enter. The fraction rather than a date will now be displayed.
9. Do not save this screen.

TIPS

If you will be using a lot of fractions in a worksheet, a quick way to format cells is to select the whole document by clicking the blank square in the top left corner of the worksheet and then format all cells for fractions.

If the cells are formatted to appear as fractions, the formula bar will display 3/4 as 0.75, its decimal equivalent. Excel recognizes that the information in Cell A3 is a fraction. You must see a fraction in the worksheet and its decimal equivalent in the formula bar to know that Excel recognizes a fraction.

Add Fractions and Mixed Numbers in Excel

You can also add fractions with Excel. In Chapter 1, you learned how to use the AutoSum shortcut (Σ). You also learned how to create your own formula to add numbers using the keyboard and the Pointing Method.

Figure 2-9
Adding Fractions and Mixed Numbers in Excel

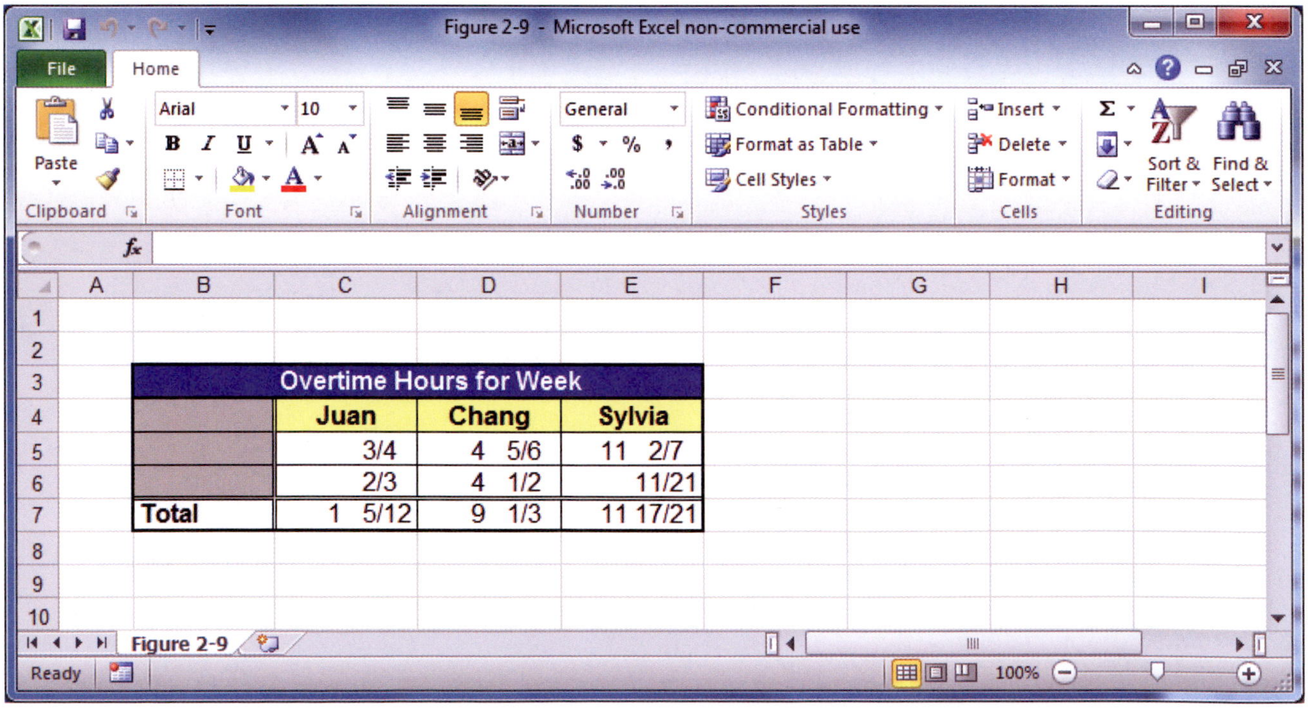

Enter each fraction in individual cells. Use AutoSum to add the fractions. The results are shown in Cells C7, D7, and E7 in Figure 2-9. In the cells showing single fractions, zeros and spaces were added before entering the fractions.

The cells with totals were formatted for fractions up to two digits. You must format fractions correctly to avoid rounding errors.

Subtract Fractions and Mixed Numbers in Excel

In Chapter 1, you learned that formulas for subtraction follow the rules you learned about formulas for addition.

Enter each fraction in individual cells. To subtract, position the cursor in the cell where the difference is to be shown. Enter a formula. For example, in Cell D4 enter the formula =B4–C4. Figure 2-10 shows the result of Excel subtracting the fractions entered in Cells B4 and C4, B5 and C5, and B6 and C6. The cells with totals were formatted for fractions up to two digits.

Figure 2-10

Subtracting Fractions and Mixed Numbers in Excel

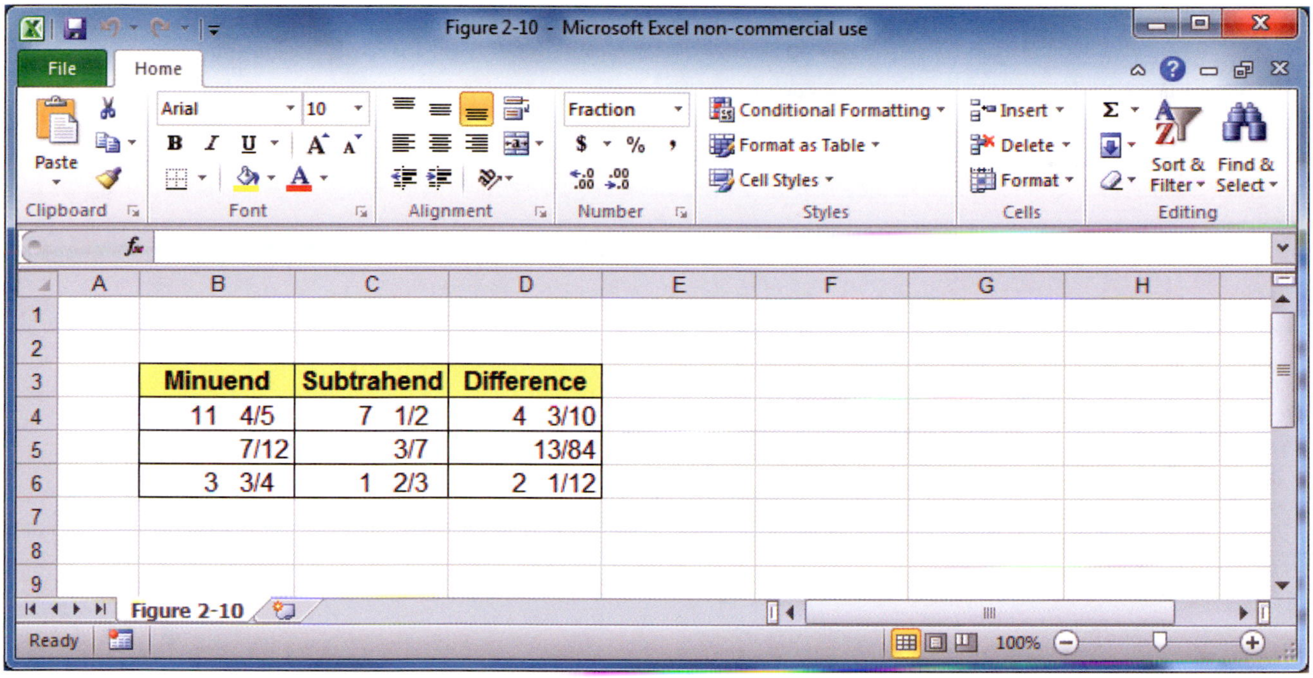

Copying Formulas

A quick way to copy a formula down a column or across a row is to use the Copy and Paste commands on the Home tab (See Figure 2-11). In the following practice, you will copy the formulas for addition and subtraction.

STEPS

1. To copy a formula to other cells, click on the cell where the formula is located.

2. Click the Copy button on the Home tab in the Clipboard group. (The active cell begins to blink). Highlight the cells where you want to copy the formula. Click Paste on the Home tab in the Clipboard group. The correct cells will be referenced in the copied formula.

3. Do not save this file.

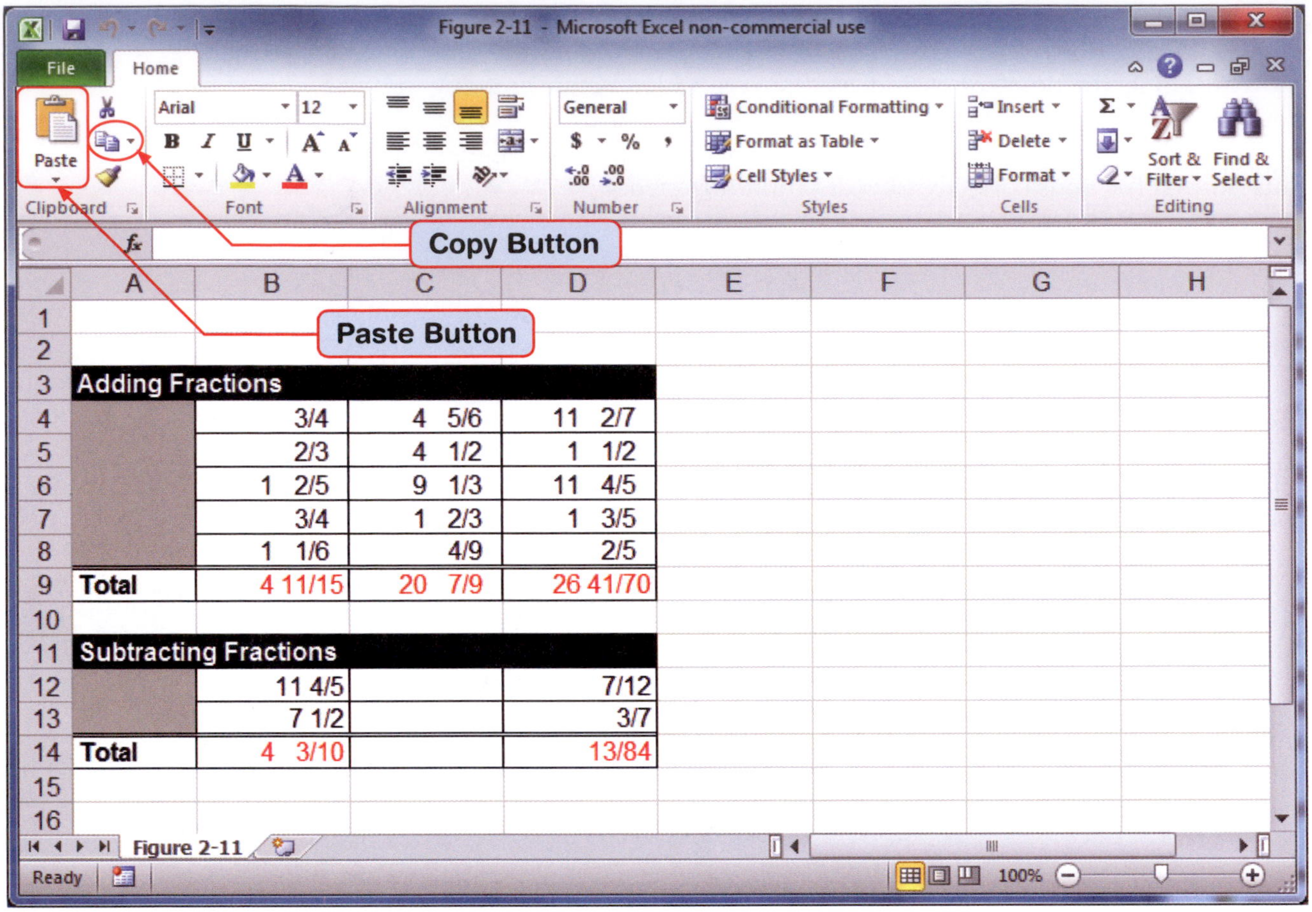

Figure 2-11

Excel's Copy and Paste Buttons

TIPS

You may see ######## appear in a column after you have copied a formula. If so, widen the column. You can widen the column by clicking on Format/Format Column Width and changing the width of the column. You can also select the Format command and choose AutoFit Column Width on the submenu.

STEPS

Retrieve the file *ch02pr02.xlsx*

1. Use the AutoSum button to enter the formula in Cell B9 to add Column B.
2. Format Cell B9 for Fraction. Set Type to Up to two digits.
3. Click on Cell B9.
4. Click the Copy button. The selected cell blinks.
5. Highlight Cells C9 and D9.
6. Click Paste or press Enter. The results appear in Cells C9 and D9.
7. Click on Cell B14. Use the Pointing Method to enter the formula to subtract Cell B13 from Cell B12.
8. Enter = and point to Cell B12.
9. Key - and point to Cell B13.
10. Press Enter to subtract the two cells.
11. Format Cell B14 for Fraction. Set Type to Up to two digits.
12. Click on Cell B14.
13. Click the Copy button.
14. Highlight Cell D14.
15. Click Paste or press Enter. The result appears in Cell D14.
16. Save the file as *ch02pr02a.xlsx*.

Name _____ Date _____

Directions Complete the following problems. Write your answers in the blanks provided. Express your answers in lowest terms.

A. Add the following fractions with like denominators. OBJECTIVE 2

1. $\frac{6}{8} + \frac{5}{8} + \frac{3}{8}$ _____
2. $\frac{4}{5} + \frac{3}{5} + \frac{2}{5}$ _____
3. $\frac{11}{25} + \frac{8}{25}$ _____
4. $\frac{15}{30} + \frac{12}{30}$ _____
5. $\frac{1}{5} + \frac{2}{5} + \frac{4}{5}$ _____
6. $\frac{3}{7} + \frac{6}{7}$ _____
7. $\frac{1}{3} + \frac{2}{3} + \frac{1}{3}$ _____
8. $\frac{15}{32} + \frac{27}{32}$ _____

B. Subtract the following fractions with like denominators. OBJECTIVE 2

9. $\frac{11}{12} - \frac{5}{12}$ _____
10. $\frac{5}{9} - \frac{2}{9}$ _____
11. $\frac{11}{15} - \frac{8}{15}$ _____
12. $\frac{19}{30} - \frac{7}{30}$ _____
13. $\frac{7}{8} - \frac{3}{8}$ _____
14. $\frac{17}{25} - \frac{12}{25}$ _____
15. $\frac{11}{16} - \frac{7}{16}$ _____
16. $\frac{13}{24} - \frac{7}{24}$ _____

C. Find the least common denominator of the following fractions. OBJECTIVE 3

17. $\frac{2}{15}, \frac{3}{5}, \frac{6}{25}$ _____
18. $\frac{5}{12}, \frac{3}{5}, \frac{1}{2}$ _____
19. $\frac{3}{5}, \frac{1}{2}, \frac{3}{4}$ _____
20. $\frac{2}{3}, \frac{6}{7}, \frac{10}{21}$ _____
21. $\frac{3}{4}, \frac{5}{6}, \frac{2}{3}$ _____
22. $\frac{5}{18}, \frac{4}{9}, \frac{5}{36}$ _____
23. $\frac{2}{5}, \frac{1}{15}, \frac{5}{9}$ _____
24. $\frac{1}{3}, \frac{1}{2}, \frac{2}{9}$ _____

D. Add the following unlike fractions. OBJECTIVE 4

25. $\frac{1}{4} + \frac{5}{8}$ _____
26. $\frac{3}{4} + \frac{6}{7} + \frac{4}{28}$ _____
27. $\frac{7}{12} + \frac{3}{7}$ _____
28. $\frac{5}{18} + \frac{19}{24}$ _____
29. $\frac{5}{6} + \frac{1}{3}$ _____
30. $\frac{4}{9} + \frac{3}{8}$ _____
31. $\frac{9}{8} + \frac{15}{16}$ _____
32. $\frac{3}{25} + \frac{1}{50} + \frac{19}{30}$ _____

E. Subtract the following unlike fractions. OBJECTIVE 4

33. $\frac{3}{4} - \frac{1}{3}$ _____

34. $\frac{5}{15} - \frac{7}{25}$ _____

35. $\frac{3}{4} - \frac{3}{8}$ _____

36. $\frac{6}{7} - \frac{11}{21}$ _____

37. $\frac{1}{2} - \frac{2}{5}$ _____

38. $\frac{5}{8} - \frac{5}{12}$ _____

39. $\frac{4}{5} - \frac{2}{3}$ _____

40. $\frac{5}{6} - \frac{7}{9}$ _____

F. Add the following mixed numbers with like denominators. OBJECTIVE 5

41. $71\frac{2}{8}$
$3\frac{5}{8}$
$+4\frac{3}{8}$

42. $13\frac{4}{5}$
$+18\frac{3}{5}$

43. $12\frac{3}{8}$
$+9\frac{1}{8}$

44. $15\frac{4}{25}$
$\pm 17\frac{11}{25}$

45. $5\frac{6}{35}$
$+7\frac{8}{35}$

46. $17\frac{5}{12}$
$13\frac{7}{12}$
$+4\frac{5}{12}$

47. $2\frac{12}{13}$
$5\frac{9}{13}$
$+3\frac{6}{13}$

48. $11\frac{9}{16}$
$7\frac{5}{16}$
$+2\frac{7}{16}$

G. Add the following mixed numbers with unlike denominators. OBJECTIVE 5

49. $44\frac{5}{8}$
$+3\frac{5}{12}$

50. $16\frac{5}{6}$
$+10\frac{6}{7}$

51. $13\frac{4}{9}$
$+11\frac{3}{8}$

52. $12\frac{5}{8}$
$+16\frac{1}{7}$

53. $9\frac{5}{8}$
$+13\frac{4}{7}$

54. $71\frac{2}{3}$
$54\frac{5}{8}$
$+3\frac{5}{12}$

55. $27\frac{1}{2}$
$84\frac{3}{5}$
$+10\frac{2}{10}$

56. $17\frac{3}{8}$
$1\frac{1}{4}$
$+5\frac{5}{16}$

H. Subtract the following mixed numbers with like denominators. OBJECTIVE 6

57. $11\frac{11}{16}$
$-5\frac{9}{16}$

58. $6\frac{3}{4}$
$-4\frac{1}{4}$

59. $10\frac{16}{21}$
$-6\frac{5}{21}$

60. $14\frac{4}{5}$
$-6\frac{1}{5}$

61. $18\frac{7}{8}$
$-9\frac{3}{8}$

62. $12\frac{15}{32}$
$-10\frac{7}{32}$

63. $112\frac{5}{8}$
$-10\frac{3}{8}$

64. $35\frac{11}{13}$
$-27\frac{3}{13}$

CHAPTER 2 FRACTIONS

I. Subtract the following mixed numbers with unlike denominators. OBJECTIVE 6

65. $23\frac{3}{5}$ **66.** $9\frac{5}{8}$ **67.** $15\frac{5}{7}$ **68.** $37\frac{4}{7}$

    $-11\frac{2}{7}$ $-7\frac{7}{12}$ $-10\frac{1}{3}$ $-21\frac{5}{9}$

69. $2\frac{3}{4}$ **70.** $12\frac{5}{8}$ **71.** $25\frac{5}{6}$ **72.** $7\frac{5}{6}$

    $-1\frac{2}{3}$ $-9\frac{1}{2}$ $-19\frac{5}{9}$ $-4\frac{2}{3}$

J. Subtract the following whole and mixed numbers. OBJECTIVE 6

73. $5 - \frac{1}{4}$ _____   **74.** $23 - 11\frac{2}{5}$ _____

75. $26 - 11\frac{1}{6}$ _____   **76.** $35 - 22\frac{1}{3}$ _____

77. $112 - 15\frac{1}{3}$ _____   **78.** $8 - 4\frac{3}{5}$ _____

79. $3 - 1\frac{1}{2}$ _____   **80.** $27 - 13\frac{2}{7}$ _____

K. Solve the following word problems.

81. In her running log, Sylvia Valdez recorded the following miles: $4\frac{1}{4}$, 5, $3\frac{3}{4}$, $2\frac{7}{8}$. What is Sylvia's total mileage for the 4 days? _____

82. At a fabric store, you bought $3\frac{3}{4}$ yards of silk, $7\frac{1}{2}$ yards of gauze, $4\frac{1}{8}$ yards of denim, and $2\frac{1}{4}$ yards of lining. How many total yards of fabric did you buy? _____

83. Leticia made $6\frac{3}{4}$ gallons of peach iced tea for the class party. Of the total amount, only $4\frac{2}{3}$ gallons were consumed. How much iced tea will need to be stored? _____

84. In a survey, one in five students responded that they preferred a power drink over a particular brand of cola. What is the decimal equivalent? _____

85. Rani bought a computer for her at-home office on sale at $\frac{1}{3}$ off the original price. What is the decimal equivalent of $\frac{1}{3}$ to the nearest hundredth? _____

86. Susan's recipe uses $5\frac{1}{2}$ cups of white flour and $3\frac{3}{4}$ cups of whole wheat flour. How many cups of flour does the recipe need? _____

87. Last week Tom Macrino worked the following number of hours: 9, $2\frac{2}{3}$, $6\frac{1}{4}$, 8, $3\frac{1}{3}$. How many hours did Tom work last week? _____

L. Use Excel to add and subtract the following fractions. OBJECTIVE 7

88. Retrieve the file *ch02ex03.xlsx*. Follow the directions. Save the file as *ch02ex03a.xlsx*.

89. Retrieve the file *ch02ex04.xlsx*. Follow the directions. Save the file as *ch02ex04a.xlsx*.

2.3 Multiply and Divide Fractions and Mixed Numbers

OBJECTIVE 1 Multiply fractions.

You may have already encountered multiplying and dividing fractions in some of your day-to-day activities. For example, suppose you were asked to deliver 30 gallons of popcorn for the annual company picnic. Your committee decided to have several $2\frac{1}{2}$-gallon cans placed at different points on the picnic grounds. This situation would require that you know how many $2\frac{1}{2}$-gallon cans to bring to fill with popcorn from the 30-gallon supply.

pagadesign/iStockphoto.com

Mario has $\frac{2}{3}$ yard of fabric. He used $\frac{7}{8}$ of it to cover an office seat cushion. How much fabric did he use? To calculate the yardage needed, you need to find $\frac{7}{8}$ yard of $\frac{2}{3}$ yard, so multiply $\frac{2}{3} \times \frac{7}{8}$. To multiply fractions, multiply the numerators and the denominators. Then reduce to lowest terms.

$$\frac{2}{3} \times \frac{7}{8} = \frac{2 \times 7}{3 \times 8} = \frac{14}{24}$$

$$\frac{14}{24} = \frac{7}{12} \qquad \text{in lowest terms}$$

EXAMPLE

$$\frac{5}{8} \times \frac{3}{5} \times \frac{1}{3}$$

STEPS

1. Multiply the numerators of the first two fractions. Then multiply that product by the numerator of the third fraction.

   $$5 \times 3 \times 1 = 15$$

2. Multiply the denominators of the first two fractions. Then multiply that product by the denominator of the third fraction.

   $$8 \times 5 \times 3 = 120$$

3. Rewrite the fraction.

$$\frac{15}{120}$$

4. Reduce to lowest terms as needed.

$$\frac{15}{120} = \frac{1}{8} \quad \text{in lowest terms}$$

OBJECTIVE **2** Use cancellation.

Multiplying fractions can be simplified by using cancellation. **Cancellation** is the process of determining a common number that will evenly divide any one of the numerators and any one of the denominators in the fractions being multiplied. Repeat this process as much as you can.

EXAMPLES

1. $\frac{2}{7} \times \frac{5}{8}$

2. $\frac{1}{2} \times \frac{6}{15} \times \frac{5}{12}$

STEPS

1. Determine the common factor that will evenly divide any one of the numerators and any one of the denominators. The numbers 2 and 8 are divisible by 2. The original numerator and denominator are marked with diagonal lines to cancel them, as shown.

$$\frac{\cancel{2}}{7} \times \frac{5}{\cancel{8}}$$

2. Divide the numerator 2 and the denominator 8 by the common factor 2. The quotients become the new numerator and denominator.

$$\overset{1}{\cancel{2}} \times \frac{5}{\cancel{8}} \qquad \text{Divide by 2.}$$

$$\frac{1}{7} \times \frac{\overset{4}{5}}{4} = \frac{5}{28} \qquad \text{in lowest terms}$$

3. Cancel.

Divide by 2.
Then divide by 3
and then by 5.

4. Multiply the numerators and the denominators.

$$1 \times 1 \times 1 = 1$$
$$1 \times 3 \times 4 = 12$$
$$\frac{1}{12} \qquad \text{in lowest terms}$$

TIPS

Canceling is a method of "lowering" any numerator and/or denominator before multiplying. Canceling is simply a shortcut.

To multiply whole numbers and fractions, convert the whole number to an improper fraction and cancel any numerators and denominators, if possible.

EXAMPLE

$$5 \times \frac{2}{3} \times \frac{7}{8}$$

STEPS

1. Convert the whole number to an improper fraction and cancel any numerators and denominators, if possible.

$$\frac{5}{1} \times \frac{\overset{1}{\cancel{2}}}{3} \times \frac{7}{\underset{4}{\cancel{8}}}$$

2. Multiply the numerators and then the denominators.

$$\frac{5}{1} \times \frac{1}{3} \times \frac{7}{4} = \frac{35}{12}$$

3. Convert the improper fraction to a mixed number. Make sure the fractional part of the mixed number is in lowest terms.

$$2\frac{11}{12}$$

EXAMPLE

Phillip Fontano earns $2,345 a month. He spends one-fifth of his monthly salary for rent. How much does he pay each month for rent?

STEPS

When a math problem uses the word *of*, as in "He spends one-fifth of his monthy salary," the word *of* means to multiply.

Problem Solving Plan		
Clues	**Action Plan**	**Solve**
Phillip earns $2,345 a month. Phillip spends $\frac{1}{5}$ of his salary.	To determine the rent, multiply $\frac{1}{5} \times 2,345$.	$\frac{1}{5} \times \$2,345 =$ $\frac{1}{\cancel{5}} \times \frac{\overset{469}{\cancel{2,345}}}{1}$ $\frac{1}{1} \times \frac{469}{1} = \$469$
Conclusion		
Phillip's rent for each month is $469.		

The steps for multiplying mixed numbers are basically the same as those used for multiplying whole numbers and fractions.

$$6\frac{2}{7} \times 3\frac{1}{8}$$

1. Convert the mixed numbers to improper fractions.

$$6\frac{2}{7} = \frac{44}{7} \qquad\qquad 3\frac{1}{8} = \frac{25}{8}$$

2. Rewrite the problem and cancel any numerators and denominators, if possible.

$$\frac{\overset{11}{\cancel{44}}}{7} \times \frac{25}{\underset{2}{\cancel{8}}}$$

3. Multiply the numerators and then the denominators.

$$\frac{11}{7} \times \frac{25}{2} = \frac{275}{14}$$

4. Convert the improper fraction to a mixed number.

$$\frac{275}{14} = 19\frac{9}{14}$$

You are already familiar with the steps used for multiplying mixed numbers. The same basic steps are used here for multiplying mixed numbers and whole numbers.

$$12 \times 2\frac{7}{8}$$

1. Change the whole number to a fraction and convert the mixed number to an improper fraction.

$$\frac{12}{1} \times \frac{23}{8}$$

2. Cancel any numerators and denominators and multiply.

$$\frac{\overset{3}{\cancel{12}}}{1} \times \frac{23}{\underset{2}{\cancel{8}}} = \frac{69}{2}$$

3. Convert the improper fraction to a mixed number.

$$\frac{69}{2} = 34\frac{1}{2}$$

TIPS

When a whole number is multiplied by a proper fraction, the answer is smaller than the whole number.

A common method of dividing fractions is to invert the divisor, change the division symbol to a multiplication symbol, and then multiply. The fraction is inverted, or turned upside down, because division is the inverse, or opposite, of multiplication. For example, a divisor such as $\frac{2}{3}$ is inverted to $\frac{3}{2}$.

EXAMPLE

$$\frac{5}{6} \div \frac{2}{3}$$

STEPS

1. Invert the divisor and then multiply. (The dividend $\frac{5}{6}$ remains the same.)

$$\frac{5}{\cancel{6}_{2}} \times \frac{\cancel{3}^{1}}{2} = \frac{5}{4}$$

2. Convert the improper fraction to a mixed number and reduce.

$$\frac{5}{4} = 1\frac{1}{4}$$

To divide whole numbers and fractions, express the whole number as a fraction by placing it over the denominator 1 and inverting the divisor. Then multiply.

EXAMPLE

$$6 \div \frac{3}{4}$$

STEPS

1. Express the whole number as a fraction by placing it over the denominator 1 and inverting the divisor.

$$\frac{6}{1} \times \frac{4}{3}$$

2. Cancel, if necessary, and multiply.

$$\frac{\cancel{6}^{2}}{1} \times \frac{4}{\cancel{3}_{1}} = \frac{8}{1} = 8$$

TIPS

When a whole number is divided by a proper fraction, the answer is larger than the whole number because this is the same as multiplying by an improper fraction.

To divide mixed numbers, convert all mixed numbers to improper fractions, as shown in the following example.

EXAMPLE

$$14\frac{4}{5} \div 9\frac{1}{3}$$

STEPS

1. Convert each mixed number to an improper fraction.

$$14\frac{4}{5} = \frac{74}{5} \qquad\qquad 9\frac{1}{3} = \frac{28}{3}$$

2. Invert the divisor, cancel, if necessary, and multiply. Both 74 and 28 can be divided evenly by 2.

$$\overset{37}{\cancel{\frac{74}{5}}} \times \frac{3}{\underset{14}{\cancel{28}}} = \frac{111}{70} = 1\frac{41}{70} \qquad \text{in lowest terms}$$

To divide a whole number by a mixed number, write the whole number as a fraction over 1 and convert the mixed number to an improper fraction. Then invert the divisor and multiply.

EXAMPLE

$$9 \div 3\frac{3}{4}$$

STEPS

1. Express the whole number as a fraction by placing it over the denominator 1 and convert the mixed number to an improper fraction.

$$\frac{9}{1} \div \frac{15}{4}$$

2. Invert the divisor and multiply. Then convert to a mixed number and reduce.

$$\frac{9}{1} \times \frac{4}{15} = \frac{36}{15} = 2\frac{6}{15} = 2\frac{2}{5}$$

To divide a mixed number by a whole number, write the whole number as a fraction over 1. Then multiply.

EXAMPLE

$$2\frac{1}{8} \div 5$$

STEPS

1. Multiply the whole number 2 by the denominator 8 and add 1. Convert the whole number 5 to a fraction.

$$\frac{17}{8} \div \frac{5}{1}$$

2. Invert the divisor, multiply the two fractions, and reduce.

$$\frac{17}{8} \times \frac{1}{5} = \frac{17}{40}$$

2.3 Multiply and Divide Fractions and Mixed Numbers

icongenic/iStockphoto.com

EXAMPLE

In Crystal's clothing shop, each vest takes $1\frac{1}{2}$ yards of material. Find the number of vests that can be cut from a piece of linen fabric that is 8 yards in length.

Problem Solving Plan	
Clue	**Action Plan**
Total length of fabric is 8 yards. Length of fabric needed for each vest is $1\frac{1}{2}$ yards.	To determine the number of vests that can be made from 8 yards, divide the total length of fabric by the yard requirement to make one vest.
Solve	
1. Number of possible vests equals the total fabric available divided by the fabric in one vest.	$8 \div 1\frac{1}{2}$
2. Convert the mixed number to an improper fraction.	$\frac{8}{1} \times \frac{3}{2}$
3. Invert the divisor.	$\frac{8}{1} \times \frac{2}{3}$
4. Multiply.	$\frac{16}{3}$
5. Change the improper fraction to a mixed number.	$5\frac{1}{3}$
Conclusion	
Crystal can make five vests from 8 yards of linen fabric. There will be $\frac{1}{3}$ yard left.	

OBJECTIVE 6 Use Excel to multiply and divide fractions and mixed numbers.

In Chapter 1, you learned how to create formulas for multiplication. The asterisk (*) signals Excel to multiply. An example of a formula that contains a multiplication operation is =A6*B6.

PRACTICE

✎ Retrieve the file *ch02pr03.xlsx*. Follow the directions. Save the file as *ch02pr03a.xlsx*.

To tell Excel you want to divide, use the slash symbol (/). In Chapter 1, you learned how to use the /in solving problems involving division. An example of a formula to divide Cell G16 by Cell F16 is =G16/F16.

PRACTICE

✎ Retrieve the file *ch02pr04.xlsx*. Follow the directions. Save the file as *ch02pr04a.xlsx*.

Name _____   Date _____

Directions   Complete the following problems. Write your answers in the space provided. Reduce your answers to lowest terms as needed.

A. Multiply the following fractions, whole numbers, and mixed numbers. OBJECTIVES 1, 2, 3

1. $\frac{2}{3} \times \frac{5}{6} \times \frac{1}{4} =$

2. $\frac{4}{5} \times \frac{3}{8} =$

3. $\frac{2}{4} \times \frac{2}{3} =$

4. $\frac{5}{6} \times \frac{7}{8} =$

5. $\frac{6}{9} \times \frac{5}{8} =$

6. $6\frac{4}{9} \times \frac{5}{7} =$

7. $2 \times \frac{5}{6} =$

8. $\frac{2}{3} \times 6 =$

9. $\frac{5}{9} \times 2\frac{2}{3} =$

10. $4 \times \frac{7}{8} =$

11. $\frac{5}{9} \times 5 =$

12. $7\frac{5}{6} \times 2\frac{5}{8} =$

13. $2\frac{7}{8} \times 4\frac{1}{3} =$

14. $4\frac{2}{3} \times 4\frac{1}{3} =$

15. $2\frac{7}{8} \times 2\frac{1}{2} =$

16. $\frac{6}{7} \times \frac{3}{8} =$

B. Divide the following fractions, whole numbers, and mixed numbers. OBJECTIVES 2, 4, 5

17. $2 \div \frac{3}{4} =$

18. $\frac{1}{9} \div \frac{1}{3} =$

19. $\frac{2}{8} \div \frac{2}{7} =$

20. $\frac{3}{8} \div \frac{1}{4} =$

21. $\frac{4}{9} \div \frac{1}{4} =$

22. $\frac{1}{2} \div \frac{3}{8} =$

23. $5 \div 3\frac{1}{6} =$

24. $6\frac{1}{4} \div 3 =$

25. $4 \div 1\frac{2}{3} =$

26. $8\frac{3}{8} \div 4 =$

27. $6\frac{2}{3} \div 2\frac{3}{5} =$

28. $6\frac{1}{4} \div 7\frac{2}{5} =$

29. $2\frac{1}{3} \div 3\frac{1}{8} =$

30. $3\frac{1}{3} \div 1\frac{5}{8} =$

31. $\frac{1}{9} \div \frac{1}{7} =$

32. $\frac{3}{11} \div \frac{4}{7} =$

C. Solve the following word problems.

33. Gail owns a small linen shop and makes pillows for her clients. She bought $\frac{4}{5}$ yard of fabric to make a pillow and used $\frac{2}{3}$ of it. How much fabric did she use?

34. Sandpiper Sightseeing Tours purchased a new van for the business. On the first trip, Jesse drove $2\frac{1}{5}$ hours at an average speed of 55 mph. How far did Jesse travel?

35. Wayne served 30 pizzas at the office party, all of which were eaten. Each person ate $\frac{1}{4}$ of a pizza. How many people did Wayne serve at the party?

36. A tract of land containing $288\frac{3}{4}$ acres was divided into lots $4\frac{1}{8}$ acres in size. How many building lots were formed from this tract of land?

D. Use Excel to multiply and divide fractions and mixed numbers. OBJECTIVE 6

37. Retrieve the file **ch02ex05.xlsx**. Follow the directions. Save the file as **ch02ex05a.xlsx**.

38. Retrieve the file **ch02ex06.xlsx**. Follow the directions. Save the file as **ch02ex06a.xlsx**.

Chapter Review and Assessment

KEY TERMS

cancellation
common denominator
Copy command
decimal equivalent
denominator
equivalent fraction
Format Cells dialog box
fraction

greatest common divisor
greatest-common-divisor method
improper fraction
inspection method
least common denominator (LCD)
like fractions
lowest terms
mixed number

numerator
Paste command
prime factorization
prime number
prime number method
proper fraction
repeating decimal
unlike fractions

CONCEPTS	EXAMPLES
2.1 Types of fractions	
Proper fraction	$\dfrac{2}{3}, \dfrac{7}{8}, \dfrac{5}{6}$
Improper fraction	$\dfrac{12}{10}, \dfrac{21}{7}, \dfrac{15}{9}$
Mixed number	$2\dfrac{9}{10}, 5\dfrac{6}{10}$
2.1 Convert fractions.	
Improper fraction to whole number Divide numerator by denominator.	$\dfrac{15}{3} = 5$
Improper fraction to mixed number Divide numerator by denominator. Place remainder over divisor.	$\dfrac{121}{7} = 17\dfrac{2}{7}$
Mixed number to improper fraction Multiply whole number by denominator. Add numerator and product. Place sum over denominator.	$8\dfrac{5}{6} = \dfrac{53}{6}$
2.1 Reduce fractions to lowest terms.	
Find the smallest numerator and denominator possible without changing the original value of the fraction being reduced.	$\dfrac{125}{505} = \dfrac{125 \div 5}{505 \div 5} = \dfrac{25}{101}$
2.1 Raise fractions to higher terms.	
Multiply numerator and denominator by the same number.	$\dfrac{7}{8} = \dfrac{7 \times 2}{8 \times 2} = \dfrac{14}{16}$
2.1 Convert fractions to decimals.	
Divide the numerator by the denominator. Round if necessary.	Convert $\frac{5}{8}$ to a decimal. 5 divided by 8 = 0.625

CONCEPTS	EXAMPLES
2.1 Convert decimals to fractions. Convert the decimal as it would be read. Reduce to lowest terms.	Convert 0.25 to a fraction. $\dfrac{25}{100} = \dfrac{1}{4}$

2.2 Add and subtract like fractions.

Add – Add numerators and reduce to lowest terms.

Subtract – Subtract numerators and reduce to lowest terms.

$\dfrac{4}{9} + \dfrac{1}{9} = \dfrac{5}{9}$

$\dfrac{7}{8} - \dfrac{1}{8} = \dfrac{6}{8} = \dfrac{3}{4}$

2.2 Find the least common denominator.

Inspection method

Prime number method

$\dfrac{5}{15} - \dfrac{4}{12}$ LCD is 60.

2.2 Add and subtract unlike fractions.

Step 1 Find the least common denominator.

Step 2 Change each fraction to an equivalent fraction with like denominators.

Step 3 Add (or subtract) the new fractions with like denominators.

Step 4 Reduce to lowest terms.

$\dfrac{3}{5} + \dfrac{3}{4}$ LCD is 20.

$\dfrac{3 \times 4}{5 \times 4} + \dfrac{3 \times 5}{4 \times 5}$

$\dfrac{12}{20} + \dfrac{15}{20}$

$\dfrac{27}{20} = 1\dfrac{7}{20}$

$\dfrac{7}{12} - \dfrac{1}{3}$ LCD is 12.

$\dfrac{7}{12} - \dfrac{1 \times 4}{3 \times 4}$

$\dfrac{7}{12} - \dfrac{4}{12}$

$\dfrac{3}{12} = \dfrac{1}{4}$

2.2 Add and subtract mixed numbers.

Step 1 If fractions have different denominators, find the LCD and change the fractions to equivalent fractions using the LCD.

Step 2 Add or subtract the fractions and whole numbers.

Step 3 Reduce to lowest terms.

$8\dfrac{1}{5} + 7\dfrac{2}{3}$ LCD is 15.

$8\dfrac{3}{15} + 7\dfrac{10}{15}$

$15\dfrac{13}{15}$

$7\dfrac{5}{6} - 4\dfrac{1}{2}$ LCD is 6.

$7\dfrac{5}{6} - 4\dfrac{3}{6}$

$3\dfrac{2}{6} = 3\dfrac{1}{3}$

2.3 Multiply fractions.

Step 1 Cancel if possible.

Step 2 Multiply the numerators.

Step 3 Multiply the denominators.

Step 4 Write the new numerator and new denominator as a fraction.

$\dfrac{4 \times 2}{5 \times 3}$

$4 \times 2 = 8$

$5 \times 3 = 15$

$\dfrac{8}{5}$

$\dfrac{\overset{1}{\cancel{5}}}{\underset{4}{\cancel{12}}} \times \dfrac{\overset{3}{\cancel{9}}}{\underset{2}{\cancel{10}}}$

$\dfrac{1 \times 3}{4 \times 2}$

$\dfrac{3}{8}$

CONCEPTS	EXAMPLES

2.3 Use cancellation.

Step 1 Determine the common factor that will evenly divide any one of the numerators and any one of the denominators. The original numerator and denominator are marked with diagonal lines to show the cancellation.

Step 2 Divide the numerator and the denominator by the common factor. The quotients become the new numerator and denominator.

Step 3 Repeat the process until there are no more common factors.

Step 4 Multiply the numerators and the denominators to find the product in lowest terms.

$$\frac{5}{12} \times \frac{9}{10}$$

The common factor that can divide evenly into 5 and 10 is 5. The common factor that can divide evenly into 12 and 9 is 3.

$$\frac{\overset{1}{\cancel{5}}}{\underset{4}{\cancel{12}}} \times \frac{\overset{3}{\cancel{9}}}{\underset{2}{\cancel{10}}}$$

$$\frac{1 \times 3}{4 \times 2}$$

$$\frac{3}{8}$$

2.3 Multiply whole numbers and fractions.

Step 1 Convert the whole number to an improper fraction.

Step 2 Multiply the numerators and then the denominators.

Step 3 Convert the improper fraction to a mixed number.

$$8 \times \frac{2}{5} = \frac{8}{1} \times \frac{2}{5}$$

$$\frac{8 \times 2}{1 \times 5} = \frac{16}{5}$$

$$3\frac{1}{5}$$

2.3 Multiply mixed numbers and whole numbers.

Step 1 Convert whole numbers to fractions and convert mixed numbers to improper fractions.

Step 2 Cancel any numerators and denominators and multiply.

Step 3 Convert the improper fraction to a mixed number, reducing to lowest terms if necessary.

$$3\frac{1}{3} \times 10 = \frac{10}{3} \times \frac{10}{1}$$

$$\frac{100}{3}$$

$$33\frac{1}{3}$$

2.3 Divide fractions and whole numbers.

Step 1 Invert the divisor and multiply.

Step 2 Convert an improper fraction to a mixed number or reduce if necessary.

$$\frac{7}{8} \div \frac{1}{3} = \frac{7}{8} \times \frac{3}{1} \qquad \frac{2}{3} \div 6 = \frac{2}{3} \times \frac{1}{6}$$

$$\frac{21}{8} = 2\frac{5}{8} \qquad \frac{2}{18} = \frac{1}{9}$$

2.3 Divide mixed numbers.

Step 1 Convert each mixed number to an improper fraction.

Step 2 Invert the divisor, cancel if possible, and multiply.

$$7\frac{1}{2} \div 5\frac{1}{3} = \frac{15}{2} \div \frac{16}{3}$$

$$\frac{15}{2} \times \frac{3}{16} = \frac{45}{32} = 1\frac{13}{32}$$

Chapter 2 Review Exercises

Name _____   Date _____

Directions   Complete the following problems. Write your answers in the blanks provided. Be sure to place commas and dollar signs where needed. Express fractional parts in lowest terms. Round decimals to the nearest hundredth.

A. **Convert the following improper fractions to mixed or whole**   **2.1 OBJECTIVES 3, 4**
   numbers. Reduce to lowest terms where necessary.

1. $\frac{59}{12}$ _____

2. $\frac{5}{2}$ _____

3. $\frac{132}{12}$ _____

4. $\frac{31}{10}$ _____

5. $\frac{25}{4}$ _____

6. $\frac{141}{6}$ _____

7. $\frac{39}{9}$ _____

8. $\frac{45}{8}$ _____

B. **Change the following mixed numbers to improper fractions.**   **2.1 OBJECTIVE 5**
   Do not reduce to lowest terms.

9. $4\frac{15}{30}$ _____

10. $70\frac{3}{5}$ _____

11. $4\frac{9}{16}$ _____

12. $11\frac{5}{16}$ _____

13. $3\frac{5}{16}$ _____

14. $8\frac{5}{10}$ _____

15. $2\frac{20}{5}$ _____

16. $6\frac{2}{3}$ _____

C. **Write the following fractions as decimals. Round your answers**   **2.1 OBJECTIVE 8**
   to the nearest hundredth.

17. $\frac{4}{5}$ _____

18. $\frac{3}{18}$ _____

19. $2\frac{2}{7}$ _____

20. $5\frac{5}{8}$ _____

21. $4\frac{3}{8}$ _____

22. $\frac{7}{8}$ _____

23. $15\frac{2}{3}$ _____

24. $1\frac{8}{9}$ _____

D. **Find the fractional equivalents of the following decimals.**   **2.1 OBJECTIVE 9**
   Reduce to lowest terms where necessary.

25. 3.6 _____

26. 2.08 _____

27. 8.039 _____

28. 1.206 _____

29. 9.469 _____

30. 7.5 _____

31. 3.66 _____

32. 0.54 _____

E. Add the following like and unlike fractions. **2.2** OBJECTIVES **2, 4**

33. $\frac{1}{4} + \frac{11}{12} + \frac{7}{16}$ _____

34. $\frac{7}{8} + \frac{3}{4}$ _____

35. $\frac{1}{2} + \frac{7}{8}$ _____

36. $\frac{2}{5} + \frac{5}{6}$ _____

37. $\frac{4}{5} + \frac{3}{4}$ _____

38. $\frac{1}{3} + \frac{3}{4}$ _____

F. Add the following mixed numbers. **2.2** OBJECTIVE **5**

39. $2\frac{4}{6} + 2\frac{3}{6}$ _____

40. $3\frac{4}{7} + 2\frac{6}{7}$ _____

41. $4\frac{3}{8} + 2\frac{7}{8}$ _____

42. $7\frac{4}{16} + 2\frac{14}{16}$ _____

43. $8\frac{2}{8} + 2\frac{2}{8}$ _____

44. $4\frac{3}{7} + 1\frac{1}{2}$ _____

G. Subtract the following fractions and mixed numbers. **2.2** OBJECTIVE **6**

45. $\frac{7}{8} - \frac{3}{8}$ _____

46. $\frac{7}{8} - \frac{1}{8}$ _____

47. $\frac{1}{8} - \frac{1}{32}$ _____

48. $\frac{3}{4} - \frac{1}{5}$ _____

49. $4\frac{1}{3} - 1\frac{1}{4}$ _____

50. $12\frac{3}{5} - 3\frac{6}{7}$ _____

H. Multiply the following fractions, whole numbers, and mixed numbers. **2.3** OBJECTIVES **1, 3**

51. $\frac{5}{6} \times \frac{2}{5}$ _____

52. $\frac{3}{8} \times \frac{4}{6}$ _____

53. $\frac{5}{8} \times 2$ _____

54. $2 \times \frac{6}{7}$ _____

55. $4 \times \frac{11}{12}$ _____

56. $\frac{1}{9} \times 12$ _____

57. $2\frac{2}{3} \times 1\frac{3}{4}$ _____

58. $3\frac{2}{3} \times 3\frac{5}{6}$ _____

59. $1\frac{1}{3} \times 2\frac{1}{8}$ _____

60. $7\frac{8}{9} \times 2\frac{1}{12}$ _____

I. Divide the following whole numbers, fractions, and mixed numbers. **2.3** OBJECTIVE **5**

61. $\frac{3}{4} \div \frac{2}{3}$ _____

62. $\frac{8}{9} \div \frac{3}{5}$ _____

63. $\frac{3}{5} \div \frac{4}{6}$ _____

64. $2 \div 1\frac{1}{3}$ _____

65. $8 \div 3\frac{2}{5}$ _____

66. $6 \div 1\frac{5}{8}$ _____

67. $2\frac{2}{3} \div 1\frac{3}{4}$ _____

68. $2\frac{1}{5} \div 2\frac{1}{3}$ _____

69. $2\frac{1}{3} \div 1\frac{1}{2}$ _____

70. $1\frac{1}{3} \div 2\frac{1}{4}$ _____

J. Solve the following word problems. Be sure to place dollar signs as needed. Express fractional parts in lowest terms.

71. Hector Perez purchased a total of 22 yards of fabric to upholster his office couch but only needs $19\frac{5}{8}$ yards. In addition to upholstering his couch, he wants to cover 3 pillows. How many total yards of fabric will be left for making pillows after he upholsters the couch? _____

72. Last week John Barton worked the following number of hours: 8, $6\frac{3}{4}$, $9\frac{1}{4}$, $5\frac{1}{2}$, and 6. How many total hours did John work last week? _____

73. Last week part-time student workers restocked the college bookstore and worked a total of 50 hours. They worked $10\frac{1}{2}$ hours on Monday, $8\frac{1}{4}$ hours on Tuesday, $9\frac{3}{4}$ hours on Wednesday, and $11\frac{1}{4}$ hours on Thursday. Calculate the hours the students worked on Friday. _____

74. On Thursday morning, Sutton's Produce delivered the following produce to your catering shop: $6\frac{1}{2}$ pounds of green leafy lettuce, 4 pounds of tomatoes, $2\frac{1}{4}$ pounds of cucumbers, $3\frac{3}{4}$ pounds of white onions, 3 pounds of fresh mushrooms, and $1\frac{3}{4}$ pounds of parsley. Total the weight of the produce order. _____

75. Smith and Williams Construction Company owns a $514\frac{1}{2}$-acre tract of land. The company wants to divide the land into 5-acre lots. How many lots can the company form from this tract of land? _____

76. Anita owns and operates Martinez Landscape Company. She has been contracted to put in a sprinkler system. She cut a piece of pipe into 5 lengths of $1\frac{1}{2}$ feet each. How long was the original piece of pipe? _____

77. Carswell Concrete Company doubled its orders for concrete this month over last month's figure of $75\frac{3}{4}$ loads. How many loads did Carswell deliver this month? _____

78. Winona inherited $\frac{2}{3}$ of her grandmother's estate. The estate amounted to $78,000. How much money did Winona receive? _____

79. Grady sold $\frac{1}{2}$ of his interest of $50,000 in the Randolph Manufacturing Company to one of his 6 partners. How much did that partner receive? _____

80. How far can Diedre travel in her car on $14\frac{5}{8}$ gallons of gasoline if the car averages $22\frac{1}{2}$ miles per gallon? _____

81. If office space is renting for $1.25 per square foot, how much would it cost you to rent an office with $900\frac{2}{3}$ square feet? _____

82. If you drove your car 65 miles an hour for $3\frac{3}{4}$ hours, how many miles would you drive? _____

K. Use Excel to solve the following problems. `2.1 OBJECTIVE 10, 2.2 OBJECTIVE 7, 2.3 OBJECTIVE 6`

83. Retrieve the file *ch02ex07.xlsx*. Follow the directions. Save the file as *ch02ex07a.xlsx*.

84. Retrieve the file *ch02ex08.xlsx*. Follow the directions. Save the file as *ch02ex08a.xlsx*.

EXAMPLE A chef often has to adjust recipes based on the amount of people being served or other constraints.

TRY IT...

1. A baker received a special order for a white wedding cake. The white cake recipe makes 12 cups of batter. Because of the particular baking pans being used, 16 cups of batter are needed. How should the baker adjust the recipe?

2. Apply your understanding of fractions by increasing or decreasing the following measurements. Complete the table.

Original	Double	Triple	One-Half	One-Third
2 pints				
$\frac{1}{2}$ ounce				
$\frac{2}{3}$ gallon				
$\frac{3}{4}$ cup				

Write about Math

1. What does reducing a fraction to lowest terms mean?

2. Distinguish between reducing and cancelling fractions.

Personal Finance

Do you use your budget to manage your money?

Understanding how your budget affects your expenses, savings, and debt is important for creating a solid foundation for you. Not having a budget can lead to overspending, debt problems, or even the inability to plan for your future. Using a budget allows you to compare your financial resources with your financial *needs* and your financial *wants*.

In everyday life people must live according to their means. That is, they must live by a budget in order to survive. The purpose of a budget is to plan how you will spend or save money. Use what you have learned in this chapter to understand the relationship among fractions, decimals, and percents and the budget shown at the right.

Chan tracks her expenses every month. She uses percents to see how much is spent for each expense item. To figure what fraction of Chan's rent is of her

Chan Peterson's Monthly Budget for March 20--					
Category	Amount	Fraction	Decimal	Percent
Income					
Paycheck	A	$2,500			
Stock Dividend	A	$ 150			
Additional Support	A	$1,000			
Total Income		$3,650			
Expenses					
Rent	B	$ 950	$\frac{19}{73}$	0.26	26%
Utilities	D	$ 242			
Credit card debt	E	$ 332			
Food	E	$ 560			
Entertainment	E	$ 50			
Savings	C	$ 100			
Car/Insurance	C	$ 880			
Car/Gasoline	E	$ 200			
Other	E	$ 336			
Total Expenses		$3,650			

A = Income
C = Fixed Personal Expenses
E = Variable Personal Expenses
B = Fixed/Household Expenses
D = Variable/Household Expenses

total expenses, reduce $\frac{950}{3,650} = \frac{19}{73}$, which is 0.26 shown as a decimal. By converting the decimal to a percent, you can see that Chan's rent equals 26% of her expenses. Once you figure the fractions, complete the budget by converting them into decimals and percents.

1. What percent of Chan's total income is her paycheck? Express as a percent, decimal, and fraction.

2. If Chan wanted to increase her savings to $300, she could move $200 from Other to Savings. What would be the revised monthly percent of her total expenses?

3. Suppose that Chan had an emergency, such as tire replacement for her car. What would be her options to adjust her budget?

4. Calculate the total for the Variable Personal Expenses (E). What is the percent of the total expenses?

5. How do you view variable personal expenses in managing your personal budget?

6. If you had an emergency, how would you adjust your budget to accommodate the emergency?

Name   Date   Score

Directions Complete the following problems. Write your answers in the blanks provided. Reduce to lowest terms, if necessary.

A. Convert the improper fractions to mixed numbers or whole numbers. `2.1 OBJECTIVES 3, 4`

1. $\frac{31}{5}$ _____   2. $\frac{69}{2}$ _____

3. $\frac{181}{9}$ _____   4. $\frac{43}{8}$ _____

B. Change the following mixed numbers to improper fractions. `2.1 OBJECTIVE 5`

5. $21\frac{3}{4}$ _____   6. $6\frac{4}{9}$ _____

7. $2\frac{5}{8}$ _____   8. $13\frac{4}{9}$ _____

C. Reduce the following fractions to lowest terms. `2.1 OBJECTIVE 6`

9. $\frac{50}{200}$ _____   10. $\frac{144}{288}$ _____

11. $\frac{36}{39}$ _____   12. $\frac{16}{98}$ _____

D. Raise the following fractions to higher terms using the indicated denominators. `2.1 OBJECTIVE 7`

13. $\frac{20}{60} = \frac{?}{180}$ _____   14. $\frac{6}{13} = \frac{?}{52}$ _____

15. $\frac{8}{9} = \frac{?}{72}$ _____   16. $\frac{2}{6} = \frac{?}{96}$ _____

E. Find the decimal equivalents of the following fractions. Carry your answers to three decimal places. `2.1 OBJECTIVE 8`

17. $\frac{6}{20}$ _____   18. $3\frac{9}{36}$ _____

19. $6\frac{1}{2}$ _____   20. $\frac{3}{50}$ _____

F. Convert the following decimals to fractions. `2.1 OBJECTIVE 9`

21. 0.61 _____   22. 0.045 _____

23. 0.30 _____   24. 0.2986 _____

G. Add the following fractions. 2.2 OBJECTIVES 2, 4

25. $\frac{2}{4} + \frac{6}{8} + \frac{1}{3}$ _____

26. $6\frac{4}{5} + 7\frac{2}{9}$ _____

27. $2\frac{3}{4} + 3\frac{7}{8}$ _____

28. $\frac{8}{9} + \frac{4}{7}$ _____

H. Find the least common denominator. 2.2 OBJECTIVE 3

29. $\frac{3}{20}, \frac{9}{40}, \frac{30}{60}$ _____

30. $\frac{8}{4}, \frac{12}{16}, \frac{3}{32}$ _____

31. $\frac{6}{9}, \frac{1}{4}, \frac{8}{12}$ _____

32. $\frac{2}{5}, \frac{4}{6}, \frac{7}{8}$ _____

I. Subtract the following fractions. 2.2 OBJECTIVES 2, 4

33. $\frac{9}{12} - \frac{3}{12}$ _____

34. $\frac{32}{40} - \frac{2}{4}$ _____

35. $\frac{2}{5} - \frac{1}{3}$ _____

36. $5 - \frac{2}{3}$ _____

J. Multiply the following fractions. 2.3 OBJECTIVES 1, 2, 3

37. $2\frac{2}{3} \times 4$ _____

38. $9\frac{1}{2} \times \frac{3}{4}$ _____

39. $\frac{1}{3} \times \frac{3}{5} \times \frac{4}{10}$ _____

40. $\frac{2}{9} \times \frac{6}{8} \times \frac{1}{2}$ _____

K. Divide the following fractions. 2.3 OBJECTIVES 4, 5

41. $\frac{5}{6} \div \frac{5}{6}$ _____

42. $12 \div \frac{3}{4}$ _____

43. $2\frac{2}{3} \div 1\frac{1}{3}$ _____

44. $2\frac{6}{7} \div \frac{4}{5}$ _____

L. Solve the following word problems. Write your answers in the blanks provided. Be sure to place dollar signs as needed. Express fractional parts in lowest terms.

45. Showoff Fabrics is having a sale on decorator fabric. Yesterday they sold 10 yards of blue, $3\frac{1}{3}$ yards of red, $8\frac{1}{2}$ yards of green, and $6\frac{3}{8}$ yards of yellow. Calculate the total yardage sold. _____

46. If tin is selling for $7.50 per pound, what is the cost of $15\frac{1}{3}$ pounds of tin? _____

47. The city has 120 garden plots to resod. If each plot is $4\frac{1}{2}$ feet wide and $8\frac{1}{2}$ feet long, how many square feet of sod will it take to resod each plot individually? _____

48. If the sod used in Exercise 47 costs $1.63 per square foot at Orr's Garden Supplies, what is the cost to resod all the plots? _____

M. Use Excel to solving the following problems. 2.1 OBJECTIVE 10, 2.2 OBJECTIVE 7, 2.3 OBJECTIVE 6

49. Retrieve the file *ch02qz01*. Follow the directions. Save the file as *ch02qz01a.xlsx*.

50. Retrieve the file *ch02qz02*. Follow the directions. Save the file as *ch02qz02a.xlsx*.

A lot of information used in business and in everyday life contains values expressed in percents. Percents are used in reporting the cost of living, unemployment, discounts, tax rates, and interest rates. For example, you may have heard or read that sales in the housing industry increased by 4.2% or the price of coats has been reduced by 70%. You should fully understand the concepts associated with percents to work with their many business and personal applications.

REAL ESTATE AGENT

As a real estate agent, Jigna Shah is both a small business owner and a subcontractor under a larger real estate corporation. She is responsible for all aspects of her business including marketing, accounting, working with referrals, and advertising to find clients. Jigna works hard to present her skills and qualifications to potential clients. Once a client is secured, she must aid them in preparing their home for sale. If the client is a buyer, she assists them in preparing a "wants and needs" list so she can help them find exactly what they're looking for. Jigna only gets paid when she sells a property. She says, "A happy client is a satisfied client which is the best form of advertising."

Jigna knows that working for herself, even under the umbrella of a larger corporation, is a double-edged sword. "You can either work yourself to death or not work enough. You think you can control your time, but you're wrong. Your clients control your time. This is where creating a balance between your work life and personal life is very important."

Courtesy Jigna Shah

How Math is Used in the Real Estate Business

Jigna helps buyers calculate mortgage payments. When a home is sold, she calculates net proceeds by subtracting commission, interest, remaining loan balance, and any other cost from the sales price. She must also calculate home appreciation based on the current appreciation rate in the neighborhood, create budgets, and project future costs based on past expenses. Jigna manages her expenses with expense sheets and a profit and loss statement. She calculates distances between properties and carefully watches her profit margin. She says, "This will give me the needed guidelines to know how much I can spend on clients, how much I need to spend in terms of license renewals and continuing education, and how much I would have left for my bottom line and at the same time be competitive."

What Do You Think?

What math skills do you need to improve in order to be a real estate agent?

Math Skills Used

Decimals

Fractions

Percents

Multiplication

Division

Subtraction

Compound Interest

Other Skills Needed

Computer and Internet skills

Communication

Organization

Map Reading

3.1 Introduction to Percents

OBJECTIVE 1 Identify terms used with percents.

A **percent**, like a fraction or a decimal, represents a part of a whole. Percent means per hundred, or parts per 100. The symbol for percent is %. For example, 25% means 25 parts of 100 parts, or $\frac{25}{100}$ expressed as a fraction. Expressed as a decimal, 25% is 0.25. As another example, thirty-three hundredths written as a percent is 33%, as a fraction is $\frac{33}{100}$, and as a decimal is 0.33. Percents are often converted to decimals or fractions so calculations can be completed.

OBJECTIVE 2 Write a percent as a decimal.

The easiest way to write a percent as a decimal is to drop the percent symbol and divide the number by 100.

EXAMPLE

Write the decimal equivalent for 35% using this method.

$$100\overline{)35.00} \qquad \begin{array}{c} 0.35 \end{array} \qquad\qquad 35\% = 0.35$$

A shortcut for dividing the number by 100 is to drop the percent symbol and move the decimal point 2 places to the left, adding zeros as needed.

EXAMPLE

Write 42% as its decimal equivalent using this method.

Percent				Decimal Equivalent
42%	=	0.42×	=	0.42

In the preceding example, it is understood that there is a decimal point to the right of the whole number 42, although it may not appear.

Many businesses use mixed number percents, such as an interest rate of $8\frac{1}{4}\%$ or a price increase of $7\frac{3}{4}\%$. To write a mixed number percent as its decimal equivalent, use the steps in the next example.

EXAMPLE

Write $8\frac{1}{4}\%$ as a decimal.

STEPS

1. Convert the fractional part of the mixed number to a decimal.

$$8\tfrac{1}{4}\% = 8.25\%$$

2. Convert the resulting percent to its decimal equivalent.

$$8.25\% = 0.08\underset{\frown}{2}5 = 0.0825$$

You can see that one zero has been added to the right of the decimal point to express the decimal equivalent, 0.0825.

OBJECTIVE 3 Write a decimal as a percent.

Writing a decimal as a percent does not change the value of either number. To write a decimal as a percent, multiply the decimal number by 100 and add the percent symbol.

EXAMPLE

Write 0.157 as a percent.

$$0.157 \times 100 = 15.7\%$$

A shortcut for multiplying the decimal number by 100 is to move the decimal point 2 places to the right, adding zeros as needed. Then add a percent symbol.

TIPS

A shortcut for multiplying a decimal number by 100 is to move the decimal point 2 places to the right, adding zeros as needed. Then add a percent symbol.

EXAMPLE

Convert 0.05 to a percent using this method.

Decimal				Percent
0.05	=	$0\underset{\frown}{05}.\%$	=	5%

These examples illustrate the conversion of decimals to percents.

EXAMPLES

Decimal				Percent
0.6	=	$0\underset{\frown}{60}.\%$	=	60%
0.08	=	$0\underset{\frown}{08}.\%$	=	8%
2.10	=	$2\underset{\frown}{10}.\%$	=	210%
0.825	=	$0\underset{\frown}{82}.5\%$	=	82.5%
0.0034	=	$0\underset{\frown}{00}.34\%$	=	0.34%
1.1250	=	$1\underset{\frown}{12}.50\%$	=	112.50%

To write a percent as a fraction, drop the percent symbol and write a fraction, placing the percent as the numerator and 100 as the denominator. Reduce the fraction to lowest terms.

kr7ysztof/iStockphoto.com

EXAMPLE

5% is converted to a fraction in the following manner.

$$5\% = \frac{5}{100} = \frac{1}{20}$$

The following examples illustrate writing percents as fractions.

EXAMPLES

Percent				Fraction
13%	=	$\frac{13}{100}$	=	$\frac{13}{100}$
14%	=	$\frac{14}{100}$	=	$\frac{7}{50}$
45%	=	$\frac{45}{100}$	=	$\frac{9}{20}$
130%	=	$\frac{130}{100}$	=	$1\frac{3}{10}$

Frequently, a percent appears with a decimal. To write the percent as a fraction, follow the steps in the example.

EXAMPLE

Write 12.5% as a fraction.

STEPS

1. Change the percent to a decimal.

$$12.5\% = 0.125$$

2. Change the decimal to a fraction and reduce.

$$0.125 = \frac{125}{1,000} = \frac{1}{8}$$

To convert a percent containing a fraction, such as $8\frac{2}{3}\%$, to a fraction, follow the steps in the following example.

EXAMPLE

Write $8\frac{2}{3}\%$ as a fraction.

STEPS

Drop the percent symbol and divide the percent by 100. Remember to invert the divisor and multiply.

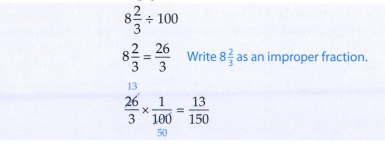

$$8\frac{2}{3} \div 100$$

$$8\frac{2}{3} = \frac{26}{3} \qquad \text{Write } 8\frac{2}{3} \text{ as an improper fraction.}$$

$$\frac{\overset{13}{\cancel{26}}}{3} \times \frac{1}{\underset{50}{\cancel{100}}} = \frac{13}{150}$$

OBJECTIVE 5 Write a fraction as a percent.

One method for changing a fraction to a percent is to change the fraction to a decimal and then change the decimal to a percent. To convert a fraction to a percent, use these steps.

EXAMPLE

Write $\frac{1}{5}$ as a percent.

STEPS

1. Convert the fraction to its decimal equivalent.

$$\frac{1}{5} = 0.20 \qquad 1 \div 5 = 0.20$$

2. Convert the decimal to a percent.

$$0.20 = 0\underset{\smile}{.20.}\% = 20\%$$

Study these examples illustrating writing fractions as percents.

EXAMPLES

Fraction		Decimal		Percent
$\frac{1}{4}$	=	0.25	=	25%
$\frac{5}{8}$	=	0.625	=	62.5%
$\frac{6}{8}$	=	0.75	=	75%

OBJECTIVE **6** Use Excel to format a percent, decimal, or fraction.

When you enter a number in a cell, Excel automatically applies the General format. The General format displays integers, decimals, date, time, and other options. To change to a different number format, open the Format cells dialog box (Home/Cells/Format/Format Cells). Click on the Number tab. In the Category list on the left, you can choose to format the cell as a number (decimal), percentage, or fraction. When you select a format from the Category list, additional options specific to the format appear in the right part of the dialog box, as shown in Figure 3-1. Formatting a number does not change calculations. It only affects the appearance of a number.

Figure 3-1

Format Cells Dialog Box

Format Cells	? X
Number Alignment Font Border Fill Protection	

Category:

General
Number
Currency
Accounting
Date
Time
Percentage
Fraction
Scientific
Text
Special
Custom

Sample

Decimal places: 2

Percentage formats multiply the cell value by 100 and displays the result with a percent symbol.

OK   Cancel

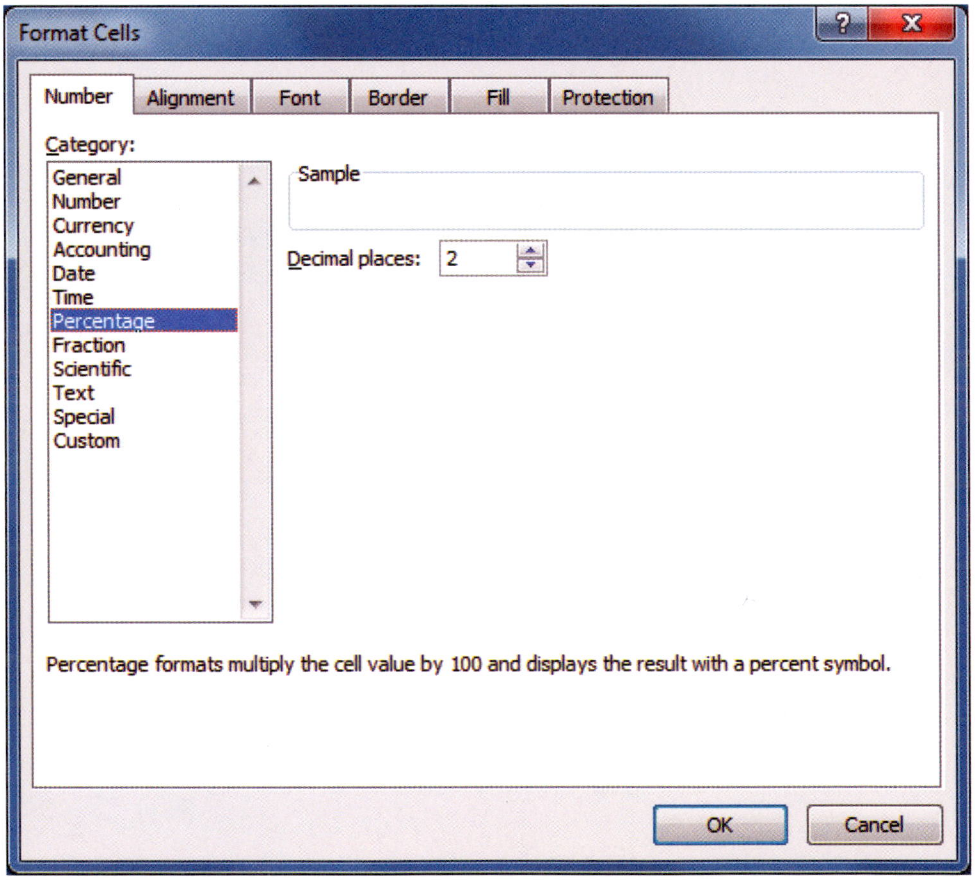

You can apply formatting to empty cells. When you enter the data in those cells, Excel will format the data according to the selection you specified.

Cells in a row can be formatted at the same time by selecting the cells before proceeding with the formatting steps. To select the cells in a row, hold down the left mouse button and drag the mouse across the row to highlight the cells. Open the Format Cells dialog box to proceed with the formatting.

PRACTICE

 Retrieve the file **ch03pr01.xlsx**. Follow the directions. Save the file as **ch03pr01a.xlsx**.

CHAPTER 3 PERCENT

Name _____   Date _____

Directions Solve the following problems. Write your answers in the blanks provided.

A. Write the following percents as decimals. OBJECTIVE **2**

1. 3%   = _____   2. 2.7%   = _____

3. 15.2%   = _____   4. 57%   = _____

5. 31.2%   = _____   6. 6.5%   = _____

7. 2.54%   = _____   8. 128%   = _____

B. Write the following decimals as percents. OBJECTIVE **3**

9. 6.3   = _____   10. 0.861   = _____

11. 0.07   = _____   12. 4.00   = _____

13. 0.43   = _____   14. 0.8   = _____

15. 0.897   = _____   16. 0.62   = _____

C. Write the following percents as fractions and reduce to lowest terms. OBJECTIVE **4**

17. 8%   = _____   18. 58%   = _____

19. 0.1%   = _____   20. 175%   = _____

21. $6\frac{2}{3}\%$ = _____   22. 10.6%   = _____

23. 0.15%   = _____   24. 112%   = _____

D. Write the following fractions as percents. Round to the nearest tenth, if necessary. OBJECTIVE **5**

25. $2\frac{3}{4}$ = _____   26. $\frac{3}{8}$ = _____

27. $\frac{6}{10}$ = _____   28. $\frac{10}{12}$ = _____

29. $\frac{11}{12}$ = _____   30. $\frac{5}{8}$ = _____

31. $8\frac{5}{9}$ = _____   32. $1\frac{8}{9}$ = _____

E. Format percents, decimals, and fractions in Excel. OBJECTIVE **6**

33. Retrieve the file *ch03ex01.xlsx*. Follow the directions. Save the file as *ch03ex01a.xlsx*.

34. Retrieve the file *ch03ex02.xlsx*. Follow the directions. Save the file as *ch03ex02a.xlsx*.

OBJECTIVES

1. Identify the terms part, rate, and base.
2. Find the part.
3. Find the rate.
4. Find the base.
5. Identify the elements of percent problems.
6. Use Excel to find the part, rate, and base.

3.2 Part, Rate, and Base

OBJECTIVE **1** Identify the terms part, rate, and base.

The ability to compare numbers is necessary in both business and personal activities. For example, it is essential to know how to figure the percent of return on an investment to determine whether you should make the investment. Also, you might want to figure the dollar amount of your 5% pay raise.

Percents are commonly used to determine interest, sales, taxes, commissions, discounts, and to make comparisons. Study the terminology and concepts presented in this chapter carefully because these fundamentals are crucial to the development of your business math skills. Learning these concepts will help you solve business and personal math problems involving percents.

The computations involved in working with percent problems require that you be able to identify the following elements: *base*, *rate*, and *part*. The **base** represents 100%, or the whole of something. The **part** is a selected piece of the base. The **rate** is the percentage or fraction the part is of the base. In the illustration, the *base* is 60 squares. The *part* is the 12 shaded squares. The *rate* is $\frac{12}{60} = \frac{1}{5} = 20\%$.

When the rate is expressed as a percent, it is called a **percentage**. When the rate is expressed as a fraction, it is called a **ratio**. For example, if each square above represented a student in a class, and the shaded squares represented the number who got A's, the ratio of A students to the total number of students would be $\frac{1}{5}$ and would be stated as "one of five," "one in five," or "one to five." The percentage of students who got A's would be 20%.

Whenever you need to know the amount of a commission, discount, or finance charge, you must find the part. To find the part (or number) when the base and rate are known, change the rate (percent) to a decimal and multiply it by the base. The formula is expressed as follows:

$$\text{Part} = \text{Base} \times \text{Rate}$$

Study this illustration for an easy way to determine the formula for part.

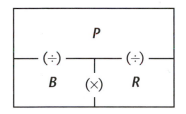

Locate the element in the square to be determined. In this case, locate the letter *P* for part. Cover the *P* with your finger. You can see that *B* and *R* remain. Think of this as *B* times *R*, as in the formula:

$$P = B \times R$$

EXAMPLE

What is a 30% discount on a $150 jacket?

Problem Solving Plan		
Clues	**Action Plan**	**Solve**
Base is $150. Rate is 30%. Part is unknown.	Change the decimal to a percent. To determine the part, *P*, multiply the base, *B*, by the rate, *R*.	30% = 0.30 $P = B \times R$ $P = \$150 \times 0.30$ $P = \$45$
Conclusion		
A 30% discount on a $150 jacket is $45.		

Part Shown With Decimals

To find a part when the rate is shown as a percent with or without a decimal, change the percent to a decimal and then calculate the part.

EXAMPLE

What is 6.5% of 130?

1. Identify each element. Base is 130. Rate is 6.5%. Part is unknown.

2. Change the percent to a decimal by dividing it by 100, or moving the decimal point 2 places to the left.

$$6.5\% = 0.065$$

3. Apply the formula: Part = Base × Rate

4. Part = 130 × 0.065

5. Part = 8.45   So, 8.45 (part) is 6.5% (rate) of 130 (base).

Part Shown With Fractions

To find a part when the rate is shown in fractional form, change the fractional form to a decimal and then calculate the part.

EXAMPLE

Suppose you had a gain of $6\frac{1}{4}\%$ on $400. What was the gain?

STEPS

1. Change the percent to a decimal. First change the fractional part to a decimal. Then move the decimal point 2 places to the left, adding a zero.

$$6\frac{1}{4}\% = 6.25\% \qquad\qquad 1 \div 4 = 0.25$$
$$6.25\% = 0.06{\scriptstyle\smile}25$$

2. Apply the formula: Part = Base × Rate

    Base = $400   Rate = 0.0625   Part = unknown

3. Part = $400 × 0.0625

4. Part = $25.00   The gain was $25.

OBJECTIVE **3 Find the rate.**

TIPS

Notice how rate problems are stated. Usually, the base is preceded by the word of. The part is the number that is part of the base. You must determine the rate or percent because it is the element that is missing.

When you need to determine a percent as a return on an investment or as an increase or decrease in sales, you find the rate. You find the rate, or what percent one number is of another, by dividing the part by the base. This formula is expressed as follows:

Rate = Part ÷ Base

Use the illustration to determine the rate.

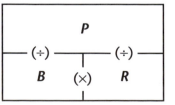

Locate the elements in the square to be calculated. In this case, locate the letter R. Cover the R with your finger. You can see that P and B remain and that P is shown over B as a fraction. Think of this as P divided by B, as in the formula:

$$R = \frac{P}{B} \quad \text{or} \quad R = P \div B$$

EXAMPLE

Find what percent $15 is of $139.

STEPS

1. Identify the elements.

   $15 is what percent of $139? or What percent of $139 is $15?

   part   base   base part

   Base is $139. Part is $15. What is the rate?

2. Apply the formula: Rate = Part ÷ Base

3. Rate = 15 ÷ 139 = 0.108   rounded

4. Rate = 0.108   Change the decimal to a percent.

5. Rate = 0.108 × 100 = 10.8% Move the decimal point 2 places to the right and add the percent symbol.

OBJECTIVE 4 Find the base.

When you need to determine the selling price of an item or the total amount of sales for the month, you find the base. You find the base when the part and rate are known. To figure the base, change the rate (percent) to a decimal and divide the part by the rate. This formula is expressed as follows:

$$\text{Base} = \text{Part} \div \text{Rate}$$

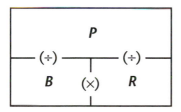

Locate the element in the square to be calculated. In this case, locate the letter B for base. Cover the B with your finger. You can see that P and R remain and that P is shown over R as a fraction. Think of this as P divided by R, as in the formula:

$$B = \frac{P}{R} \quad \text{or} \quad B = P \div R$$

EXAMPLE

$1,325 is 9.5% of what amount?

STEPS

1. Identify the elements.

   Part is $1,325. Rate is 9.5%. What is the base?

2. Apply the formula: Base = Part ÷ Rate

3. Base = $1,325 ÷ 0.095   Change rate to its decimal equivalent.

4. Base = $13,947.37   Round to the nearest dollar.

OBJECTIVE **5** Identify the elements of percent problems.

The key to working with the three formulas just discussed is being able to identify the elements: base, rate, and part (or percentage). It is important that you know what values or elements you have and which value is missing. Whenever two values or elements of a problem are known, the third value can be found by using the base, rate, and part formulas.

The rate is easy to identify because it is written with the percent symbol or with the word *percent*. However, it may be more difficult to distinguish between the base and part. To help you distinguish between the base and the part, notice how the problems are written. For example, where the base refers to total sales, the part may refer to commission. Where the base refers to savings, the part may refer to the interest earned. Where the base refers to gross income, the part may refer to net income. Study the table below to become familiar with the terms.

Usually is the Base	Usually is the Part
Sales	Sales Tax
Value of Bonds	Dividends
Retail Price	Discount
Old Salary	Raise
Value of Real Estate	Appreciation
Savings	Interest
Total Sales	Commission

OBJECTIVE 6 Use Excel to find the part, rate, and base.

You can use an Excel worksheet to perform calculations to find part, rate, and base. Figure 3-2 shows data from Johnson and Brown, Inc.'s, sales summary, which is used to illustrate how to calculate the rate.

Figure 3-2

A Sales Summary

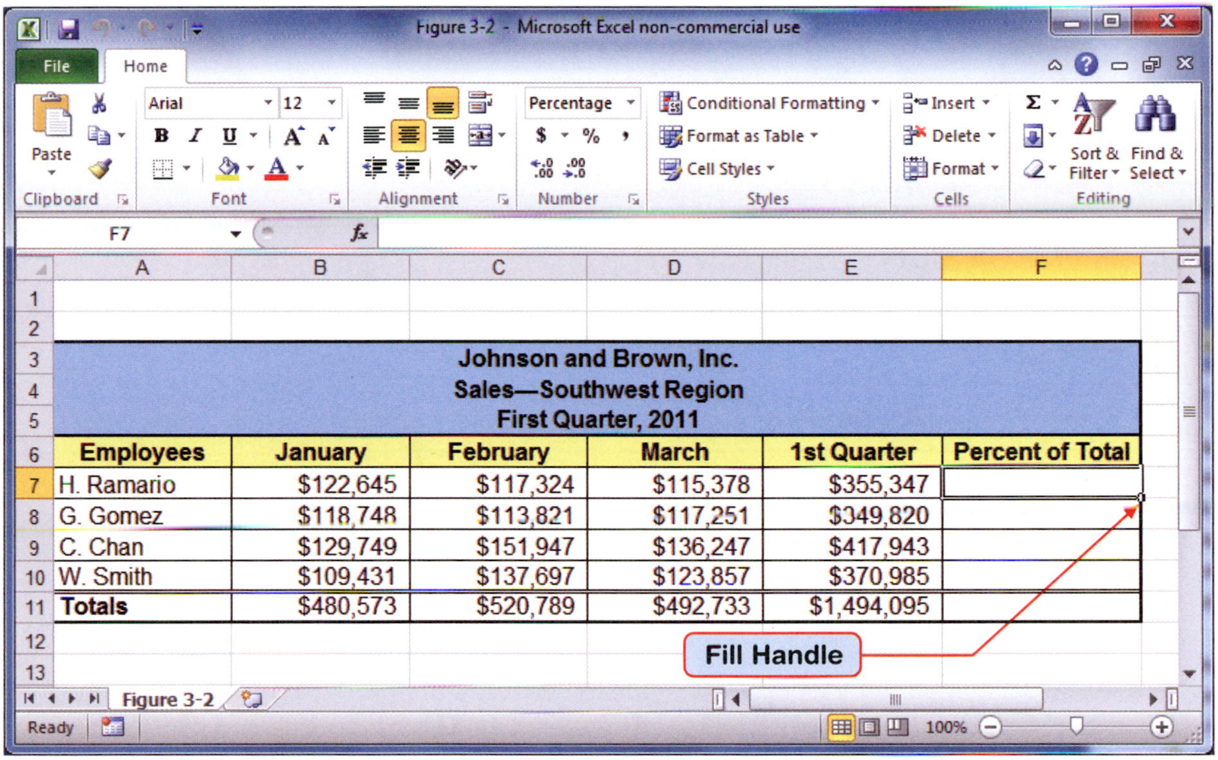

Employees	January	February	March	1st Quarter	Percent of Total
Johnson and Brown, Inc. Sales—Southwest Region First Quarter, 2011					
H. Ramario	$122,645	$117,324	$115,378	$355,347	
G. Gomez	$118,748	$113,821	$117,251	$349,820	
C. Chan	$129,749	$151,947	$136,247	$417,943	
W. Smith	$109,431	$137,697	$123,857	$370,985	
Totals	$480,573	$520,789	$492,733	$1,494,095	

The *base*, $1,494,095, is the total of all the sales. The *part* is shown as individual first-quarter totals. For instance, Ramario's $355,347 is part of the total sales. Remember, if you know the total of all sales and individual sales, you can calculate the unknown, or the percent (rate) of the total sales.

A quick way to copy a formula down a column or across a row is to drag the **fill handle** of the cell you want to copy. See Figure 3-2.

EXAMPLE

What percent of $1,494,095 total sales is $355,347, the first quarter sales total for H. Ramario?

STEPS

Retrieve the file ***ch03pr02.xlsx***.

1. Format Percent of Total column for Percentage with 2 decimal places.
2. Enter the formula =E7/E11 in Cell F7 to calculate what percent of the total of 1st Quarter Sales were for H. Ramario (R = P/B).
3. Copy the formula in Cell F7 by clicking on the fill handle in Cell F7. Drag it down to Cell F11 and release. An error occurs as shown in Figure 3-3 on the next page.

Figure 3-3

Error in Cell Reference

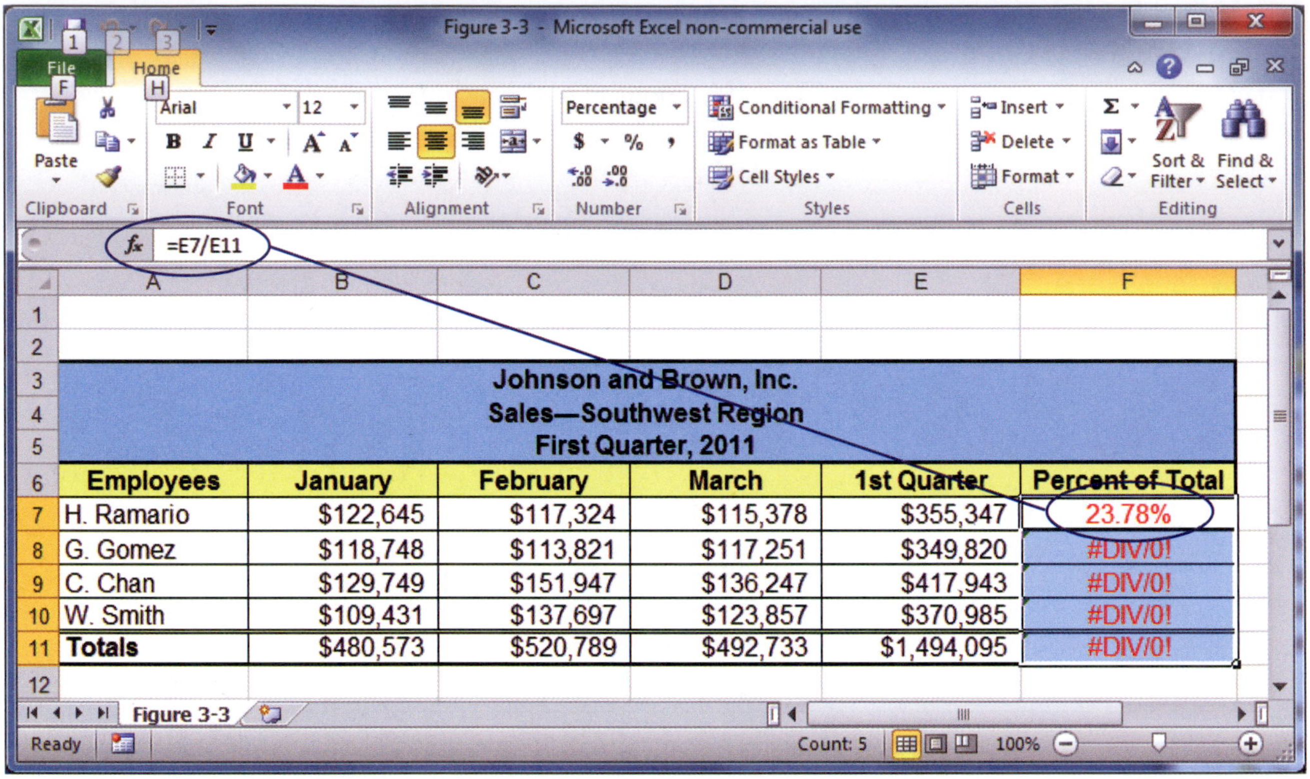

Excel's reference to a cell is a **relative cell reference**, which is a reference to a cell relative to the position of the formula. An error occurred because the equation tells Excel to divide by the cell four spaces below, which is empty. You need to tell Excel to always use Cell E11.

Signaling Excel to refer to one specific cell is an **absolute cell reference**. Using absolute cell references, you tell Excel it must return to the same cell to find part of a formula. If a dollar sign precedes the letter and number of a cell address, such as $E$11, the reference is absolute.

4. To correct this situation, you must create an absolute cell reference. Click in Cell F7 to activate the cell.

5. Key = and click in Cell E7.

6. Key / to tell Excel to divide.

7. Key $E$11 to alert Excel the cell reference is absolute.

8. Press Enter to complete the formula. See Figure 3-4 on the next page.

9. Using the fill handle, copy the formula in F7 into Cells F8 through F11. The correct formulas are entered. See Figure 3-5 on the next page.

10. Save the file as *ch03pr02a.xlsx*.

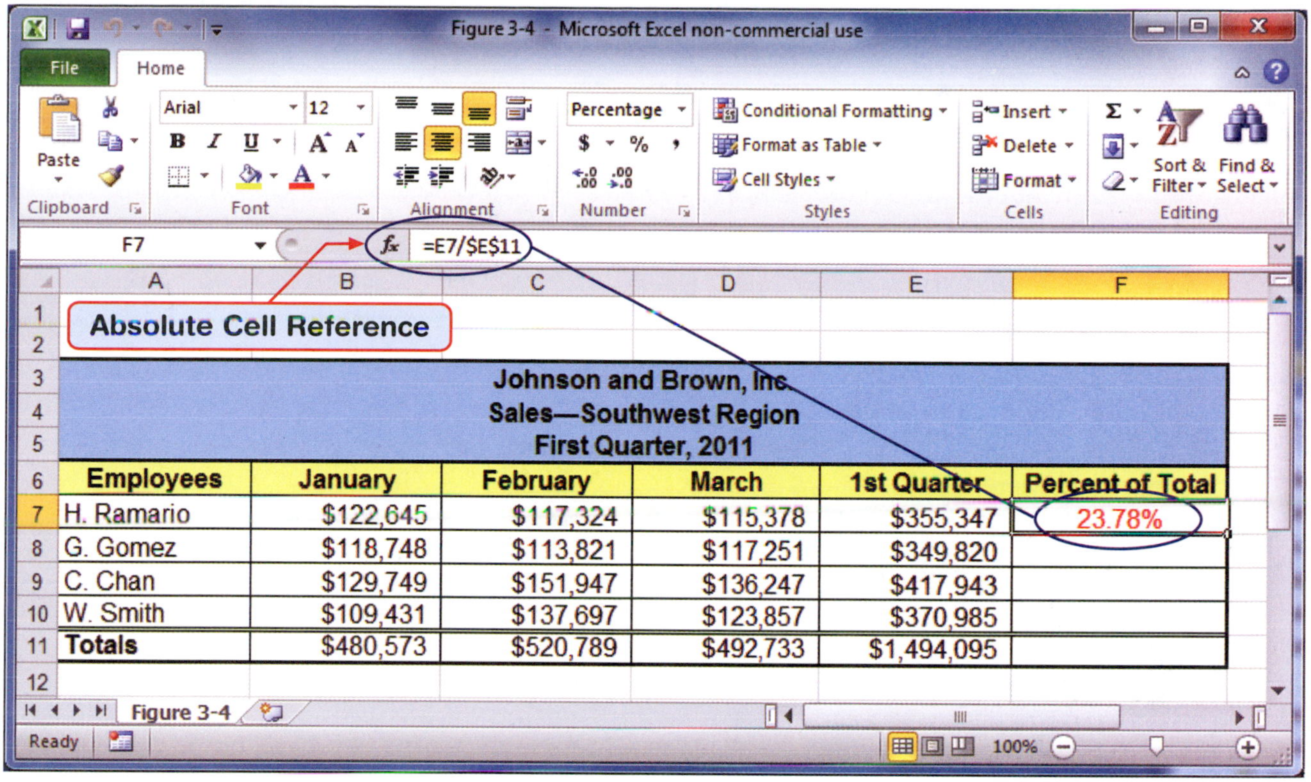

Figure 3-4

Absolute Cell Reference

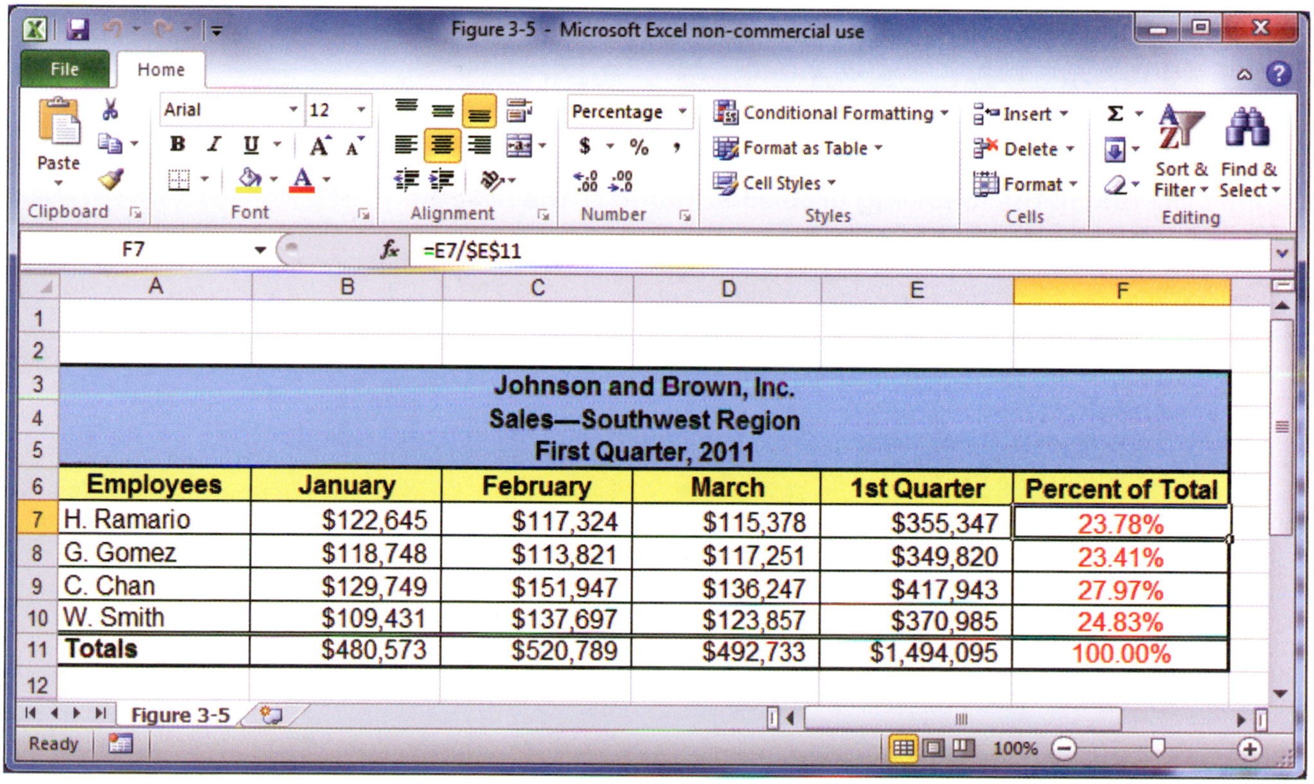

Figure 3-5

Formula Copied Into Cells F8–F11

Now you can answer the question: What percent of $1,494,095 (base) is $355,347 (part)? It is 23.78% of $1,494,095. You know all three parts of the percent problem—part, rate, and base.

Name _____   Date _____

Directions   Solve the following problems. Write your answers in the blanks provided. Place commas, dollar signs, and percent symbols as needed.

A. Identify the elements of the following problems. Do not calculate.   OBJECTIVES **1, 5**

   1.   What number is 34% of 65?   P _____   R _____   B _____

   2.   4 is what percent of 1,265?   P _____   R _____   B _____

   3.   100% of what amount is 108.3?   P _____   R _____   B _____

   4.   What percent of 29 is 99?   P _____   R _____   B _____

   5.   85.7 is 56% of what amount?   P _____   R _____   B _____

   6.   20% of 16.25 is what number?   P _____   R _____   B _____

B. Find the part in the following problems. Round to the nearest hundredth.   OBJECTIVE **2**

   7.   0.6% of 125   = _____   **8.**   42% of $3,324   = _____

   9.   3.3% of 631   = _____   **10.**   20% of 201   = _____

 11.   3% of 96   = _____   **12.**   110% of 388   = _____

 13.   Find 45% of 600.   = _____   **14.**   Find 0.75% of 172. = _____

 15.   What is 27.4% of 80? = _____   **16.**   5.61% of 120   = _____

C. Find the rate in the following problems. Round to the nearest hundredth of a percent.   OBJECTIVE **3**

 17.   What percent of 40 is 19?   _____

 18.   5.7 is what percent of 135?   _____

 19.   What percent of 75 is 13?   _____

 20.   45 is what percent of 215?   _____

 21.   31.27 is what percent of 313?   _____

 22.   61 is what percent of 462?   _____

 23.   What percent of 100 is 125?   _____

 24.   What percent of 12 is 7?   _____

D. Find the base—the total amount—in these problems. OBJECTIVE **4**
Round to the nearest hundredth.

25. 7 is 31% of what total amount? _____

26. 125% of what total amount is 62? _____

27. 44 is 27% of what total amount? _____

28. 80% of what total amount is 60? _____

29. 16 is 80% of what total amount? _____

30. 9.1 is 32% of what total? _____

31. 5.7% of what total is 92? _____

32. 32.4% of what total is 120? _____

33. 6% of what total is 48? _____

34. 2% of what total is 7? _____

E. Find the part, rate, or base in the following problems. OBJECTIVES **2, 3, 4**
Round part and base to the nearest hundredth. Round rate to the nearest
tenth of a percent. For each problem, write the formula you use to solve it.

35. Steve DeJong receives a commission of 3% of the total amount of his sales. He sold $13,895 worth of goods last week. How much was his commission?

_____ = _____

36. An item was priced at $145.50. If the discount was 20%, what was the amount of the discount?

_____ = _____

37. This month, Gloria Hutchin's electric bill is $14.58 lower than last month. If this month's bill was 8% lower, how much was last month's electric bill?

_____ = _____

38. You took a test containing 60 questions. If you correctly answered 46 questions, what percent did you answer correctly?

_____ = _____

39. You have been asked to make a down payment of $180, which represents 15% of the purchase price, on a laptop computer. What is the total purchase price?

_____ = _____

40. An auto repair shop added $6.60 to your repair bill for "shop supplies." The cost of the repairs was $330.00. What was the rate charged?

_____ = _____

41. A real estate agent receives 7% of the selling price as compensation for her work. What amount of money would she receive for selling a house for $136,400?

    _____ = _____

42. When finished, a highway will be 54 miles long. Only 24.3 miles have been completed. What percentage of the highway has been built?

    _____ = _____

43. Jody Wiesenthal, a salesperson in a specialty shop, is paid a salary of $500 per month plus a 4% commission on all sales. Last month she sold $25,210 worth of goods. What was her commission?

    _____ = _____

44. A sofa you want to buy is priced at $895. If the sale is 25% off, what is the amount of the discount?

    _____ = _____

45. If you pay 8.25% sales tax on the purchase of computer software that costs $328, how much tax will you pay?

    _____ = _____

46. If $150 commission was paid on $6,000 of sales, what was the rate of commission?

    _____ = _____

47. You have made a down payment of $14,000 on a new home, which represents 10% of the purchase price. What is the price of the home?

    _____ = _____

48. Evan completed about 75% of a jigsaw puzzle. The puzzle contained 1,500 pieces. About how many pieces were in the partially-completed jigsaw puzzle?

    _____ = _____

49. Laura bought a new sweater for $36. She also paid $2.16 in sales tax. What was the sales tax rate charged by the store?

    _____ = _____

50. Sunoj practiced piano for 40 minutes on Monday. This represented 32% of the entire time he spent practicing for the entire week. How long did Sunoj practice piano during the week?

    _____ = _____

F. Calculate percents in Excel. OBJECTIVE 6

51. Retrieve the file *ch03ex03.xlsx*. Follow the directions. Save the file as *ch03ex03a.xlsx*.

52. Retrieve the file *ch03ex04.xlsx*. Follow the directions. Save the file as *ch03ex04a.xlsx*.

3.3 Percent of Increase and Decrease

OBJECTIVES

1. Identify terms used with percent of increase and percent of decrease.
2. Find the increase and the percent of increase.
3. Find the increase and the total when the percent is given.
4. Find the decrease and the percent of decrease.
5. Find the decrease and the total when the percent is given.
6. Determine percentage distribution.
7. Use Excel to calculate increase and decrease and percentage distribution.

OBJECTIVE 1 Identify terms used with percent of increase and percent of decrease.

In business it is often necessary to compare current expenses, costs, sales, and profits with amounts from previous months or years. Businesses must analyze their statements and reports from any number of years to make comparisons and identify trends. These trends can be used as a basis for sound business decisions. For example, you might need to compare this year's sales for a particular department with last year's sales.

As an employee, you should be able to figure the percent of increase in your salary when you receive a pay raise. As a consumer, you may want to figure the amount or percent of increase in the price of a product. It is important to be able to figure these types of basic math problems because they occur often in both business and your personal life.

An *increase* or *decrease* is the difference between two numbers being compared. There is an increase when the current amount is larger than the amount for the previous period. There is a decrease when the current amount is smaller than the amount for the previous period. A **rate of increase** or **rate of decrease** is the percent obtained when the amount of increase or decrease is divided by the base or previous amount. A **percentage distribution** shows the percent each part is of the total.

OBJECTIVE 2 Find the increase and the percent of increase.

To find the increase, you must determine the amount of change that has occurred. You can find the amount of change by subtracting the smaller number from the larger number. Look at how the amount of change is calculated in the following example.

EXAMPLE

Sales this year:	$800,120
Sales last year:	− 620,125
Amount of change:	$179,995

You can quickly determine that $179,995 is an increase because the amount from the previous period is smaller than the current amount.

You can find the percent of increase using the following formula.

Percent of Increase = Amount of Increase ÷ Previous Amount

Percent of increase, amount of increase, and previous amount relate to rate, part, and base in the following formula:

$$\text{Rate} = \text{Part} \div \text{Base}$$
$$R = P \div B$$

EXAMPLE

Use the preceding example—sales this year, $800,120; sales last year, $620,125; amount of increase, $179,995—to find the percent of increase by applying the formula: percent of increase = amount of increase ÷ previous amount or $R = \frac{P}{B}$.

$$\text{Part} \div \text{Base} = \text{Rate}$$
$$\$179,995 \div \$620,125 = 0.29$$
$$100 \times 0.29 = 29\% \text{ increase}$$

OBJECTIVE 3 Find the increase and the total when the percent is given.

In the following example, the percent of increase is given but the amount of increase and the total earnings must be calculated. Use the following formula to calculate the amount of the increase.

$$\text{Amount of Increase} = \text{Previous Amount} \times \text{Percent of Increase}$$
$$\text{Part} = \text{Base} \times \text{Rate}$$
$$P = B \times R$$

Find the total earnings by adding the amount of increase to the base.

EXAMPLE

Ally Dazai earned 15% more this year than last. If her earnings last year were $24,600, find her earnings for this year.

STEPS

1. Before you can find this year's total earnings, identify each element of the problem. In this example, the base is $24,600 and the rate is 15%. To solve the problem, you must calculate the part (the amount of the increase).

2. Calculate the increase by using the formula.

$$P = B \times R$$
$$= \$24,600 \times 15\%$$
$$= \$24,600 \times 0.15 \quad \text{Change percent to decimal.}$$
$$= \$3,690 \quad \text{amount of increase}$$

3. Calculate the total earnings for this year by adding the amount of increase to the base.

$24,600	base
+ 3,690	amount of increase
$28,290	total earnings for this year

TIPS

When calculating percent of increase or percent of decrease problems, always divide by the base (last or previous year in this example).

TIPS

A quick method for calculating total earnings is to add 100% to the rate and multiply the sum by the base.

You can calculate this year's earnings another way. Using the same example, follow these steps to calculate this year's earnings.

STEPS

1. Add 100% to rate.

$$15\% + 100\% = 115\%$$

2. Multiply the sum by the base.

$$\$24,600 \times 115\% = \$24,600 \times 1.15 = \$28,290 \quad \text{total earnings}$$

OBJECTIVE 4 Find the decrease and the percent of decrease.

In the following example, you need to find the percent of decrease when amounts for this year and last year are given. Study the following example and steps to determine how to figure the percent of decrease. First, calculate the decrease by subtracting the current amount from the previous amount. Then use the following formula to calculate the percent of the decrease.

Percent of Decrease = Amount of Decrease ÷ Previous Amount

Rate = Part ÷ Base

$$R = P \div B$$

You should recognize that this is the same formula as the one used to find the rate in problems presented earlier: $R = P \div B$. Last year's sales is the base of comparison, and the amount of decrease is the part.

EXAMPLE

Sales this year were $127,430. Sales last year were $145,507. Find the percent of decrease in sales.

STEPS

1. Find the decrease by subtracting the current amount from the previous amount.

$$\$145,507 - 127,430 = \$18,077 \quad \text{decrease}$$

2. After calculating the decrease, use the formula to find the percent of decrease.

$$R = P \div B$$
$$= \$18,077 \div \$145,507$$
$$= 0.1242 \quad \text{rounded}$$

$$0.1242 \times 100 = 12.4\% \quad \text{percent of decrease}$$

TIPS

This formula is the same one used to find the percent of increase except the word **increase** *has been replaced by the word* **decrease.**

The amount (or part) is calculated and then subtracted from the base.

EXAMPLE

Greene College's enrollment of 8,425 declined by 8%. What was the total college enrollment after the decline?

STEPS

1. Determine the decrease by using the formula $P = B \times R$.

$$8{,}425 \times 8\% = 8{,}425 \times 0.08 = 674 \quad \text{decrease}$$

2. To calculate the total enrollment after the decline, subtract the decrease from the base.

$$8{,}425 - 674 = 7{,}751 \quad \text{total enrollment after 8\% decline}$$

A quick method for calculating the total amount after the decrease is to first determine the *complement* of the percent. To find the complement of the percent, change the percent to its decimal equivalent and subtract from 1.00. Then, multiply the complement of the percent by the base.

STEPS

1. Change the percent to its decimal equivalent and subtract from 1.00.

$$1.00 - 0.08 = 0.92$$

2. Multiply the base by the complement.

$$8{,}425 \times 0.92 = 7{,}751 \quad \text{total enrollment after the 8\% decline}$$

EXAMPLE

First Electronic laid off 15% of its 580 employees. How many people are currently employed by First Electronic?

TIPS

The following phrases might help you identify an increase or decrease problem.

Increase—greater than, more than, an increase of, were up, exceeded

Decrease—less than, a decrease of, a reduction of, marked down, down from

Problem Solving Plan

Clues	Action Plan	Solve
Base is 580.	Change the percent to a decimal.	$15\% = 0.15$
Rate is 15%.	Subtract the result from 1.00.	$1.00 - 0.15 = 0.85$
People laid off is the part.	Multiply the base by the result.	$P = 580 \times 0.85$
People currently employed is complement of the part.		$P = 493$

Conclusion

493 people are currently employed by First Electronic.

A *percentage distribution* shows the percent each component is of the total. In the following example, the sales amount for each department is a component of the total sales. To determine the percent for each department, divide each department's sales amount by the total amount. This is the same basic formula used to determine rate: $R = P \div B$. Because you must determine a percent for each department, you should recognize that the base is $17,293 and the part is each department's amount. Study the following steps.

EXAMPLE

Departments	Sales	Percent
Hosiery	$2,937	_____
China	5,845	_____
Stationery	2,432	_____
Boys' Wear	6,079	_____
Total Sales	$17,293	100%

STEPS

↓ Total the column.

Departments	Sales	Percent	
Hosiery	$2,937	17.0	$2,937 \div 17,293 = 0.1698 = 17.0\%$
China	5,845	33.8	$5,845 \div 17,293 = 0.3379 = 33.8\%$
Stationery	2,432	14.1	$2,432 \div 17,293 = 0.1406 = 14.1\%$
Boys' Wear	6,079	35.1	$6,079 \div 17,293 = 0.3515 = 35.2\%$*
Total Sales	$17,293	100%	

↑ Divide each department amount by the total sales.

* Note: Because of rounding, many times you will need to adjust a percent by a tenth of a percent to make the total add up to 100%.

Being able to determine what percent each amount is of the total is important in your personal budgeting. For instance, to make comparisons in your own budget, you need to know what percent of your net income is spent for food, clothing, rent, entertainment, and so on. After making these comparisons, you might discover areas to adjust your spending.

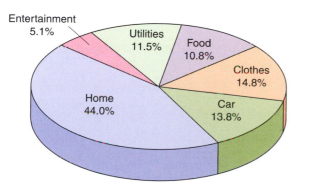

Entertainment 5.1%
Utilities 11.5%
Food 10.8%
Clothes 14.8%
Home 44.0%
Car 13.8%

OBJECTIVE 7 Use Excel to calculate increase and decrease and percentage distribution.

Figure 3-6 shows first- and second-quarter data, including columns for increase and decrease and percent of increase and decrease of certain expenses.

STEPS

Retrieve the file *ch03pr03.xlsx*

1. Format Column D for Currency. Set Decimal places to 2. Set Currency symbol to $.
2. Enter a formula in Cell D6 to calculate the Dollar Increase or Decrease in the amount of income from Consulting Fees between the 1st and 2nd Quarters. (Find the amount of change by subtracting the 1st Quarter amount from 2nd Quarter amount. In Excel, the formula is =C6-B6. A decrease will be displayed as a negative number.)
3. Copy the formula into the other cells of Column D to determine the Dollar Increase or Decrease for each of the expense categories, the Total Expenses, and the Net Income.
4. Format Column E for Percentage. Set Decimal places to 2.
5. Enter a formula in Cell E6 to calculate the Percent or Rate of Increase or Decrease. (Use the percentage formula, $R = P/B$, to calculate the rate. In Excel, the formula is =D6/B6.)

Figure 3-6
First- and Second-Quarter Worksheet

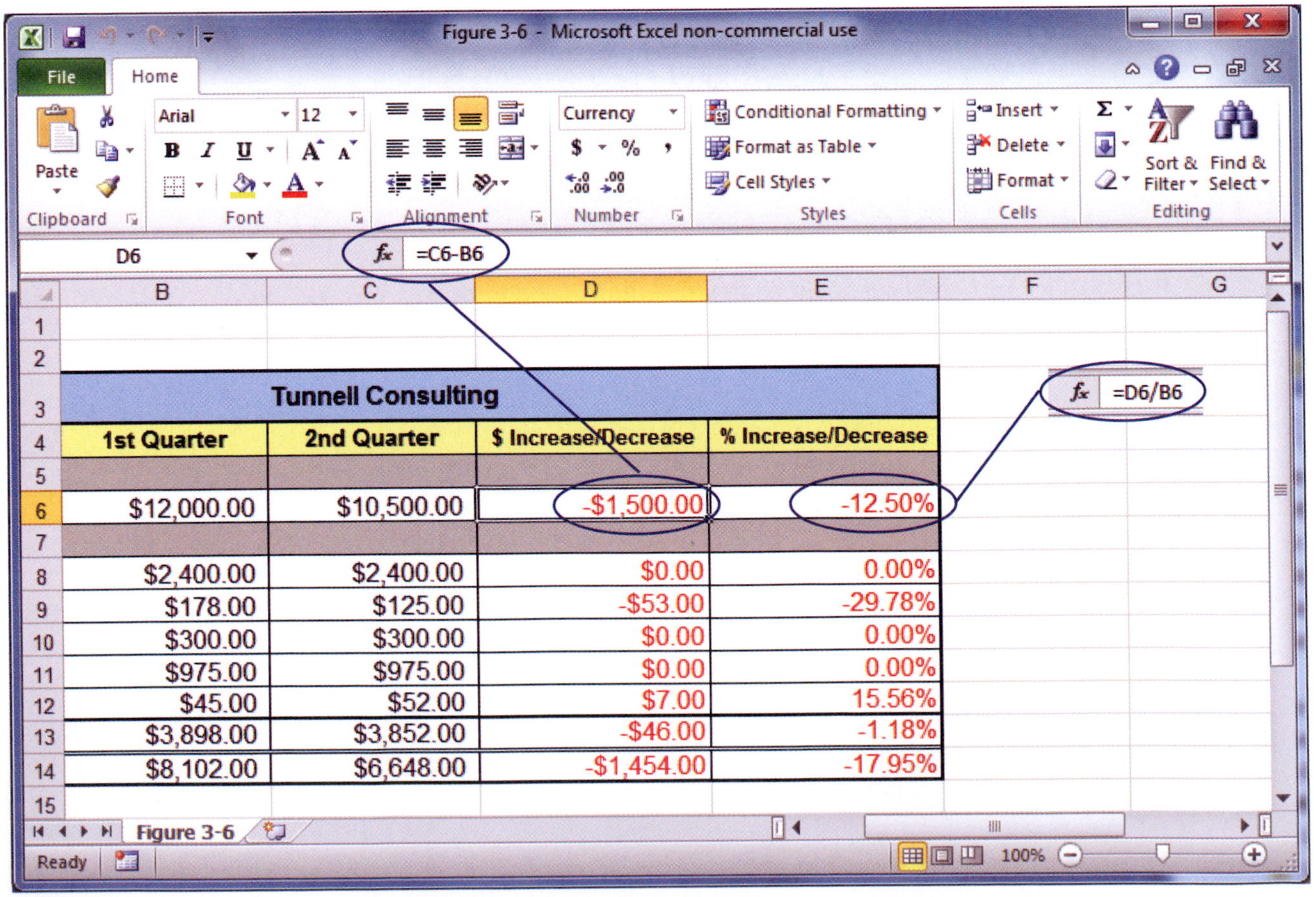

	B	C	D	E
3	Tunnell Consulting			
4	1st Quarter	2nd Quarter	$ Increase/Decrease	% Increase/Decrease
5				
6	$12,000.00	$10,500.00	-$1,500.00	-12.50%
7				
8	$2,400.00	$2,400.00	$0.00	0.00%
9	$178.00	$125.00	-$53.00	-29.78%
10	$300.00	$300.00	$0.00	0.00%
11	$975.00	$975.00	$0.00	0.00%
12	$45.00	$52.00	$7.00	15.56%
13	$3,898.00	$3,852.00	-$46.00	-1.18%
14	$8,102.00	$6,648.00	-$1,454.00	-17.95%

6. Copy the formula into the other cells of Column D to determine the Percent of Increase or Decrease for each of the expense categories, the Total Expenses, and the Net Income.

7. Save the file as **ch03pr03a.xlsx**.

As you know, a percentage distribution shows the percent each component is of the total, or base. Figure 3-7 shows the sales amount for each department as a percent of the total sales.

Figure 3-7

Sales as a Percent of Total Sales

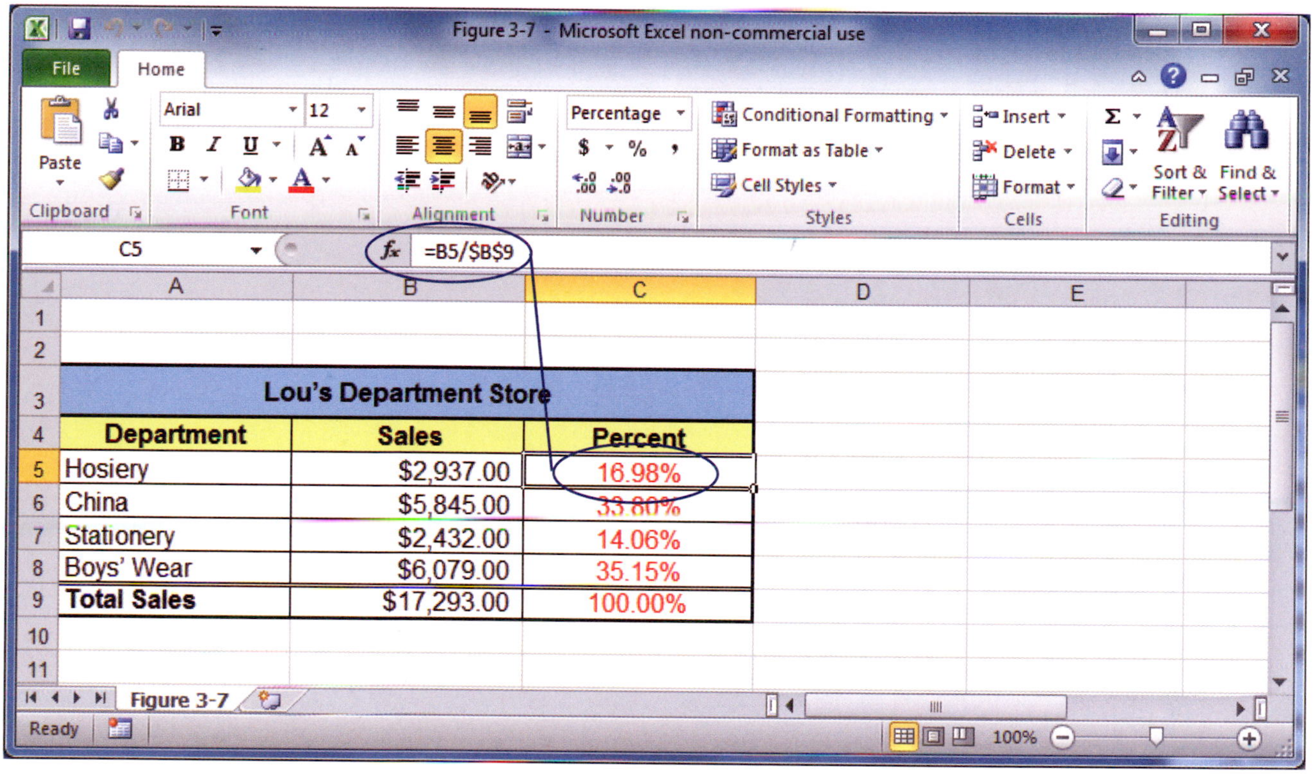

To determine the percent of each department, use the same basic formula you used to determine the rate: $R = \frac{P}{B}$. Remember to make the cell address absolute so it will not be modified as it is copied from cell to cell. In Cell C5, the formula includes the absolute cell reference with the addition of $ before the letter and the number of the the cell address in the divisor of the formula.

STEPS

⊗ Retrieve the file **ch03pr04.xlsx** and find the percent for each department.

1. Format Column C for Percentage. Set Decimal places to 2.

2. In Cell C5, key = and point to Cell B5. Key / and click on Cell B9. The formula will be shown as =B5/B9. However, B9 in the formula is not absolute.

3. To make B9 in the formula absolute, select Cell C5. In the Formula box, after the /, insert $ before B and before 9. Press Enter to complete the formula. The formula will read =B5/$B$9.

4. Copy the formula into the other cells of Column C.

5. Save the file as **ch03pr04a.xlsx**.

TIPS

To make a cell absolute you can use the F4 key. For example, in step 3, select Cell C5. Then click B9 in the formula bar and press F4. Press Enter to complete the formula.

Name _____   Date _____

Directions   Solve the following problems. Write your answers in the blanks provided. Place commas, dollar signs, and percent symbols as needed. For rate answers, round to the nearest tenth of a percent.

A. Find the increase and the rate of increase in salaries.   OBJECTIVE **2**

	Salary Last Year	Salary Present Year	Increase	Rate of Increase
1.	$25,680	$27,250	_____	_____
2.	$24,370	$25,290	_____	_____

B. Find the increase and the new salary.   OBJECTIVE **3**

	Salary Last Year	Rate of Increase	Increase	Salary Present Year
3.	$35,574	5%	_____	_____
4.	$49,888	8.5%	_____	_____

C. Find the decrease and the rate of decrease in prices.   OBJECTIVE **4**

	Price Last Year	Price Present Year	Decrease	Rate of Decrease
5.	$1.10	$1.07	_____	_____
6.	$1.12	$1.05	_____	_____

D. Find the decrease and the new price.   OBJECTIVE **5**

	Price Last Year	Rate of Decrease	Decrease	Price Present Year
7.	$495	20%	_____	_____
8.	$874	12.5%	_____	_____

E. Find the the rate of increase or decrease in the following enrollments.   OBJECTIVES **2, 4**

	Enrollment Last Year	Enrollment Present Year	Rate of Increase (+) or Decrease (−)
9.	605	703	_____
10.	585	553	_____
11.	725	690	_____
12.	590	623	_____
13.	390	420	_____

F. Determine the percentage distribution for the following types of cars on Bob's Used Car lot. OBJECTIVE 6

	Categories	Vehicles	Percent
14.	Sedans	21	_____
15.	Sport Coupes	6	_____
16.	SUV's	45	_____
17.	Minivans	25	_____
18.	Pickup Trucks	33	_____
19.	Totals	_____	_____

G. Solve the following word problems. Round all percents to one decimal place. OBJECTIVES 2, 3, 4, 5

20. Cheng Card & Gift Shop's total sales last year were $152,198. The shop sold 9% more this year. Find the total sales for this year. _____

21. Adam Pike will earn 6% more this year than last. If his earnings last year were $35,750, what will his earnings be for this year? _____

22. Manny Espino's stock market investment of $5,320 has declined 5% in value. Determine the worth of the investment now. _____

23. The price of a smartphone last year was $295. The price has dropped 33%. What is the price this year? _____

24. The printing costs in Chen Ding's department have increased from $1,340 to $1,608. Calculate the rate of increase. _____

25. Advertising revenue for *The Campus News* increased from $21,911 to $22,472. Find the increase and the rate of increase. _____

26. Your stock dropped from $23.50 per share to $21.75. What was the rate of decrease? _____

27. At Musicland, sales of CDs have decreased from 512 to 338 per month. Find the rate of decrease. _____

28. Enrollment at your school last year was 875. This year's enrollment is 930. How many students are new to your school? What is the rate of increase? _____

H. Use Excel to solve problems involving percent of increase or percent of decrease. OBJECTIVE 7

29. Retrieve the file *ch03ex05.xlsx*. Follow the directions. Save the file as *ch03ex05a.xlsx*.

30. Retrieve the file *ch03ex06.xlsx*. Follow the directions. Save the file as *ch03ex06a.xlsx*.

Chapter Review and Assessment

KEY TERMS

absolute cell reference	percent	rate of decrease
base	percentage	rate of increase
fill handle	percentage distribution	ratio
part	rate	relative cell reference

CONCEPTS	EXAMPLES
3.1 Write a percent as a decimal. Drop the percent symbol and divide the number by 100. Drop the percent symbol and move the decimal point 2 places to the left.	$17\% = \dfrac{17}{100} = 0.17$ $\quad 100\overline{)17.00}\,^{0.17}$ $29\% = 0.29_x = 0.29$
3.1 Write a decimal as a percent. Multiply the decimal number by 100 and add a percent symbol. Move the decimal point 2 places to the right and add a percent symbol.	$0.297 \times 100 = 29.7\%$ $0.03 = 0_x 03. = 3\%$
3.1 Write a percent as a fraction. Drop the percent symbol and write the fraction, placing the percent as the numerator and 100 as the denominator. Reduce to lowest terms.	$12\% = \dfrac{12}{100} = \dfrac{3}{25}$
3.1 Write a fraction as a percent. Convert the fraction to its decimal equivalent. Convert the decimal to a percent.	$\dfrac{3}{5} = 0.60$ $0.6 = 60\%$
3.2 Find the part. When the base and rate are known, change the rate to a decimal and multiply it by the base. $P = B \times R$	40% of $120 is what number? $\$120 \times 0.40 = \$48.00$ What is 1.8% of 210? $210 \times 0.018 = 3.78$ If $10\frac{1}{4}\%$ is the gain on $600, what is the amount? $\$600 \times 0.1025 = \$61.50$

CONCEPTS	EXAMPLES
3.2 Find the rate. Divide the part by the base. $R = P \div B$	$14 is what percent of $560? $14 \div 560 = 0.025 = 2.5\%$
3.2 Find the base. Change the rate to a decimal and divide the part by the rate. $B = P \div R$	$2,450 is 3.5% of what amount? $2{,}450 \div 0.035 = \$70{,}000$

3.2 Identify the elements of percent problems.

If two parts of a problem are known, the third part can be found by using the base, rate, and part formulas.

The rate is easy to identify because it has the percent symbol or the word *percent*. However, it may be more difficult to distinguish between the base and the part. To help you distinguish between base and part, notice how the problems are written. For example, where the base refers to total sales, the part may refer to commission. Where the base refers to savings, the part may refer to interest earned. Where the base refers to gross income, the part may refer to net income.

Examples of the base include total sales, value of bonds, retail price, previous salary, value of real estate, and total expenses.

Examples of the part include sales tax, dividends, discount, salary raise or increase, and rent.

3.3 Find the increase and the percent of increase.

Subtract the smaller number from the larger number to find the amount of increase.

Divide the increase amount by the previous amount to find the percent of increase.

$R = P \div B$

$354,012   sales last year

$391,020   sales current year

$391{,}020 - 354{,}012 = \$37{,}008$ increase amount

$6,570   sales this year

$- \$4,230   sales last year

$2,340   amount of increase

$2{,}340 \div \$4{,}230 = 0.55$ or 55%   percent of increase

CONCEPTS	EXAMPLES

3.3 Find the increase and the total when the percent is given.

Multiply the base by the rate to find the increase amount.

$P = B \times R$

Add the increase to the original amount to find the new total.

Alternate method: Add 100% to the rate and multiply the sum by the base.

Jordan Ann earned 15% more this year than last. If her earnings last year were $32,580, what would her earnings be for this year?

$32,580 \times 0.15 = \$4,887$ increase amount

$32,580 + \$4,887 = \$37,467$ new total

$32,580 \times 1.15 = \$37,467$ alternate method

3.3 Find the decrease and the percent of decrease.

Find the decrease by subtracting the current amount from the previous amount.

Divide the decrease by the previous amount to find the percent of decrease.

$R = P \div B$

$32,600$ cash this year

$47,640$ cash last year

$47,640 - \$32,600 = \$15,040$

$15,040 \div \$47,640 = 31.6\%$

3.3 Find the decrease and the total when the percent is given.

Multiply the base by the rate to find the decrease amount.

$P = B \times R$

Subtract the decrease from the base to find the new total.

Alternate method: Multiply the base by the complement of the rate.

The base is $1,240 and the rate is 9%.

$1,240 \times 0.09 = \$111.60$ decrease amount

$1,240 - \$111.60 = \$1,128.40$ new total

$1,240 \times 0.91 = \$1,128.40$ alternate method

3.3 Determine percentage distribution.

Obtain a total, if needed. Divide each part by the base.

$R = P \div B$

Dept A = $13,468   sales

Dept B = $15,298   sales

Total Depts sales = $28,766

Dept A = 46.8% $13,468 \div \$28,766$

Dept B = 53.2% $15,298 \div \$28,766$

Chapter 3 Review Exercises

Name _____   Date _____

Directions   Solve the following problems. Write your answers in the blanks provided.

A. Change the following percents to decimals.   **3.1** OBJECTIVE **2**

1. 15.5%   = _____   2. 17.2%   = _____

3. 30%   = _____   4. 7.6%   = _____

5. 72%   = _____   6. 1.35%   = _____

7. $\frac{5}{8}$%   = _____   8. $6\frac{1}{4}$%   = _____

9. $\frac{7}{10}$% = _____   10. 72.45%   = _____

B. Change the following decimals to percents.   **3.1** OBJECTIVE **3**

11. 0.667   = _____   12. 0.375   = _____

13. 0.47   = _____   14. 0.391   = _____

15. 1.45   = _____   16. 0.05   = _____

17. 0.417   = _____   18. 5.01   = _____

19. 0.003   = _____   20. 0.516   = _____

C. Write the following percents as fractions and reduce to lowest terms.   **3.1** OBJECTIVE **4**

21. 9%   = _____   22. 12%   = _____

23. 65%   = _____   24. $\frac{1}{4}$%   = _____

25. 56%   = _____   26. 12.5%   = _____

27. 125%   = _____   28. $83\frac{1}{3}$% = _____

D. Write the following fractions as percents.   **3.1** OBJECTIVE **5**

29. $2\frac{1}{2}$ = _____   30. $\frac{57}{100}$ = _____

31. $\frac{1}{4}$ = _____   32. $4\frac{1}{2}$ = _____

33. $\frac{7}{4}$ = _____   34. $\frac{1}{5}$ = _____

E. Find the rate, the base, or the part. Round rates to the nearest tenth of a percent. 3.2 OBJECTIVES 2, 3, 4

35. 42% of $3,324 is what? _____

36. 17.3% of $1,163 is what? _____

37. $21 is what percent of $139? _____

38. $28 is what percent of $275? _____

39. $30 is 15% of what? _____

40. $57 is 5% of what? _____

41. 20% of $879 is what? _____

42. $163 is what percent of $3,310? _____

43. $16 is 19.5% of what? _____

F. Solve the following problems. 3.3 OBJECTIVES 2, 3, 4, 5

44. Ian Batting sold a computer for $255 that originally cost him $1,200. What was Ian's percent of decrease based on the cost of the computer? _____

45. The price of a Delta Airlines ticket to Houston, Texas, decreased 12%. The original fare was $662. What is the price of the new fare? _____

46. Diane Reed had office supply sales of $3,285 this month. This was 78% of last month's sales. What was the amount of last month's sales? _____

47. The price of a software program at Computer Warehouse dropped from $299 to $245. What was the percent of decrease in price? _____

48. Paula Pruitt invested $4,334 in the stock market. The investment has declined 7% in value. Determine the worth of the investment now. _____

49. An office furniture store has an inventory of $547,912.34. This is a 22% increase from last year's ending figure. Determine last year's amount of closing inventory. _____

50. Last year Direct Marketing had $122,222 in sales. This year Direct Marketing's sales are down by 9%. What are Direct Marketing's sales this year? _____

51. Luisa paid $45 for a business math text at the college bookstore. The price increased by 4% from last year. What was the old selling price of the textbook? _____

52. A cell phone priced at $298 is marked down 25%. Find the amount the phone was discounted. Calculate the new price. _____

53. Yolanda Hammond sold an original painting for $2,400. If she originally paid $1,400 for the art, find her percent of increase. _____

54. Last year Gaston Company had sales of $450,450. This year sales are up 76%. What were the sales this year? _____

55. Trey Griffith receives an annual salary of $31,000 from J.C. Reddings, Inc. Today his supervisor informs him that he will be getting a $2,300 raise. What percent of his old salary is the $2,300 raise? _____

56. The price of a calculator at Vizquel Office Supply dropped from $49.95 to $38.95. What was the percent of decrease in price? _____

57. This year the enrollment for Eastfield Junior College was 5,323. This was a 14% increase from the enrollment last year. What was the enrollment for Eastfield Junior College last year? (Round to the nearest unit.) _____

58. Jackie Morgan found an antique chair in her attic. It was originally purchased for $2.50. The chair is now worth $1,250. What is the percent of increase? _____

59. The price of a personal computer dropped from $1,800 to $1,200. What was the percent of decrease? _____

60. This year the price of an inkjet printer rose to $359. This is an increase of 15% more than last year's price. What was the old selling price? (Round to the nearest cent.) _____

61. Marble Creamery pays Ted O'Reilley an annual salary of $46,000. Today Ted's manager informs him that he will receive a $5,000 raise. What percent of Ted's salary is the $5,000 raise? _____

62. The price of an airline ticket to New York increased 12%. The ticket price is now $456. What is the old selling price? (Round to the nearest cent.) _____

63. Last year Kari Flores earned $34,800, an increase of 13.4% over the previous year. What were Kari's earnings in the previous year? (Round to the nearest cent.) _____

G. Determine what percent the following amounts are of the total sales. 　`3.3 OBJECTIVE 6`
Round percents to the nearest tenth.

64. Neil is a department manager for Hoover's Hardware. Each week he computes a breakdown of his sales. Given the following figures for sales, determine what percent each amount is of the total sales.

Power Tools	Sales	Percent
Sanders	$1,345.45	_____
Drills	986.77	_____
Saws	1,188.92	_____
Screwdrivers	1,444.65	_____
Routers	762.33	_____
Total Sales	$5,728.12	100.0%

H. Use Excel to solve the following problems. 　`3.1 OBJECTIVE 6, 3.2 OBJECTIVE 6, 3.3 OBJECTIVE 7`

65. Retrieve the file *ch03ex07.xlsx*. Follow the directions. Save the file as *ch03ex07a.xlsx*.

66. Retrieve the file *ch03ex08.xlsx*. Follow the directions. Save the file as *ch03ex08a.xlsx*.

APPLY Math@Work REAL ESTATE AGENT

EXAMPLE   Real estate agents have to learn basic real estate law, the ins and outs of mortgages, zoning regulations, and much more. Compared to these areas, working real estate math problems can be easy. Real estate agents must be able to use percentages to make calculations for commissions, percents of income on purchase prices, and interest. Complete the following typical real estate math problems.

TRY IT...

1. The net income from a property is $18,000 per year. What percentage of income is this on a purchase price of $200,000?

2. A piece of property was owned for 10 years, then it sold for $154,000 with a 10% profit. What did the owner pay for the property originally?

3. An agent earns $7,875 on the sale of a $315,000 house. What is the agent's rate of commission?

4. An agent earns 3% commission on the sale of a $150,000 house. What is the amount of commission the agent earns?

Write about Math

1. You can write a decimal as a fraction or a fraction as a decimal. Why is that?

2. Is dividing by 100 the same as multiplying by $\frac{1}{100}$? Explain your answer using 60 as an example and showing your calculations.

3. Is 0.97% the same as 97%? Explain.

4. Describe the three components of a percent problem.

5. A common error in working with percent problems is to confuse the base and the part. Describe how you will be able to distinguish between the two components.

Personal Finance

How much are higher prices costing you?

Feeling the pinch? As American families are seeing balances in their bank accounts shrinking much faster these days, they are facing increasing costs of household categories, such as gasoline, groceries, and energy.

Families are exposed on a daily basis to cost increases. Almost daily you read or hear about increases in grocery prices, such as a 2.5 percent to 3.5 percent increase in grocery prices within a year's time. At local gas stations, the cost of regular unleaded fuel increases anywhere from 5 percent to 8 percent every few days, not to mention the increases in energy/electricity cost. It's enough to make everyone more interested in learning how to stretch their paychecks!

The following project will help you improve your knowledge about your personal finances regarding energy/electricity costs.

With energy costs fluctuating, you should understand how your home or apartment uses energy and where you could be saving energy and money. Become

morganl/iStockphoto.com

power smart to help you reduce your energy costs. The following instructions provide steps to calculate your electricity costs and percent of change. If you heat with natural gas, follow the same steps by using your monthly usage per 100 cubic feet (Ccf) as shown on your bill.

1. Obtain your monthly usage per Kilowatt-hour shown on two or three statements.

2. Obtain the current price per kilowatt hour (kWh).

3. Multiply your usage by the current price per kWh.

4. Determine the amount of change.

5. Calculate the percent of increase.

The amount you pay per month fluctuates for several reasons. For example, daily temperatures and high usage of particular appliances, such as irons, clothes washer and dryer, and television will increase the kilowatt-hours because family or friends are visiting you.

6. If your electricity costs have increased as a whole, what adjustments, if any, have you made to your monthly budget? What adjustments will you need to make to your monthly budget if electricity costs continue to rise?

7. List at least five tips to save on your energy costs. Be prepared to share your tips with other class members.

QUIZ

Directions Complete the following problems.

A. Convert the following percents to decimals. `3.1 OBJECTIVE 2`

1. 0.0235% = _____
2. 63% = _____
3. 8.5% = _____
4. 7% = _____

B. Convert the following decimals to percents. `3.1 OBJECTIVE 3`

5. 0.41 = _____
6. 0.0651 = _____
7. 0.1115 = _____
8. 4.63 = _____

C. Change the following percents to fractions. Reduce each fraction to `3.1 OBJECTIVE 4` lowest terms when possible.

9. 65% = _____
10. 50% = _____
11. 111% = _____
12. 5% = _____

D. Change the following fractions to percents. Round to the nearest tenth. `3.2 OBJECTIVE 1`

13. $\frac{1}{5}$ = _____
14. $\frac{3}{8}$ = _____
15. $\frac{5}{10}$ = _____
16. $\frac{2}{3}$ = _____

E. Find the part in the following problems. `3.2 OBJECTIVE 3`

17. 80% of 300 = _____
18. 6% of 2 = _____
19. 15% of 50 = _____
20. 40% of 111 = _____

F. Find the rate in the following problems. Round to the nearest tenth. `3.2 OBJECTIVE 3`

21. 20 is what percent of 100? _____

22. 90 is what percent of 175? _____

G. Determine the part, rate, or base for the following problems. Round `3.2 OBJECTIVES 2, 3, 4` percents to the nearest hundredth and dollar amounts to the nearest cent.

23. 25% of $360 is ____?____. _____

24. $86 is what percent of $2,500? _____

25. $58 is 15% of ____?____. _____

H. Find the rate of increase or decrease for the following problems. Round to the nearest hundredth. 3.3 OBJECTIVES 2, 4

	Sales Last Year	Sales Current Year	Rate of Increase or Decrease
26.	$245,321	$294,678	_____
27.	35,123	65,888	_____
28.	111,111	95,000	_____
29.	21,050	30,050	_____
30.	650,066	400,000	_____

I. Determine percentage distribution for the following problems. Round to the nearest hundredth. 3.3 OBJECTIVE 6

	Departments	Sales	Percent
31.	Linens	$45,900	_____
32.	Men's Wear	68,600	_____
33.	Women's Wear	135,000	_____
34.	Children's	210,500	_____
		$460,000	100.00%

J. Solve the following word problems. Round rates to the nearest tenth of a percent.

35. Suppose you bought something that was priced at $6.95, and the total bill was $7.61. What is the sales tax rate? _____

36. Gasoline at your local service station sold for $2.48 per gallon last week, and this week it is selling for $2.97. What is the percent increase? _____

37. A local manufacturing company will lay off 15% of its 3,500 employees. How many employees will lose their jobs? _____

38. A small retail shop must collect $8\frac{1}{2}$% of the amount of each sale for sales tax. If sales for the week are $13,987, calculate the amount of sales tax collected. _____

39. If 32 shipments, or 8% of all shipments, arrived with damaged containers, how many shipments were received? _____

40. If $12\frac{1}{2}$%, or 135, of the employees at an international law firm are going to be reassigned positions, how many employees does the law firm have? _____

K. Use Excel to solve the following problems. 3.1 OBJECTIVE 6, 3.2 OBJECTIVE 6, 3.3 OBJECTIVE 7

41. Retrieve the file *ch03qz01.xlsx*. Follow the directions. Save the file as *ch03qz01a.xlsx*.

42. Retrieve the file *ch03qz02.xlsx*. Follow the directions. Save the file as *ch03qz02a.xlsx*.

Bank Services

Most people think of cash when they think of money. Many people, however, still pay with checks. According to the Federal Reserve Bank fewer checks are being written due to the increasing use of credit cards, debit cards, and electronic funds transfers. However, checks still are the most commonly used and widely accepted method of payment.

In this chapter, you will be introduced to one very important bank service—the checking account. Because almost all business and personal financial transactions involve manual and electronic checking, it is important that you have a good understanding of the terminology and procedures associated with checking accounts.

BANK SERVICES

Courtesy of Christie Miller

Bank teller Christie Miller begins each day with an allotment of cash and is held accountable for its safe handling. She processes deposits and withdrawals, cashes checks, and accepts loan payments. As you can imagine, her job demands accuracy at all times. "I get a lot of satisfaction from handling people's money responsibly," Christie says. "When my cash balances correctly at the end of the day, I know I did my job well."

Christie's first priority is to meet customer needs. She does this by being familiar with the bank's financial products and services while exuding friendliness. "In some ways, this is almost a sales position. I contribute to the success of the branch by attracting new customers and opening new accounts," she explains. "If I think a customer may benefit from a CD or some other savings option, I tell them about it."

Christie spends much of her day verifying dollar amounts, customer identity, and account information. Of equal importance are computer and keyboarding skills. "Everything at my bank, from transactions to customer information, is computerized," Christie says. She specifically recommends learning how to type numbers quickly and accurately.

How Math is Used in Bank Services

On a daily basis, Christie makes change and counts money in both coin and bill form. She uses addition to verify dollar amounts on deposit slips and subtraction to determine deposit amounts when customers want cash back. She also uses multiplication in calculating exchange rates when she issues foreign currency. "Without math skills, my job would be impossible," says Christie. "There is no way around it."

What Do You Think?

What skills do you need to improve for a career in bank services?

Math Skills Used

Counting

Addition

Subtraction

Multiplication

Other Skills Needed

Trustworthiness

Discretion

Attention to Detail

Customer Service

OBJECTIVES

1. Identify terms used with checking accounts.

2. Identify checking account services.

3. Maintain a checkbook and a check register.

4. Use Excel to complete a deposit slip and a check register.

4.1 The Checking Account

OBJECTIVE 1 Identify terms used with checking accounts.

Banks (including credit unions and savings and loan institutions) offer both personal and business checking accounts. A checking account provides a convenient method of paying for purchases, services rendered, and other monetary obligations.

A **check** is a written order (also called a *draft*) used to tell a bank to pay money (transfer funds) from an account to the check holder. A **checking account** is an account opened at a bank for the purpose of making payments from funds on deposit in that account. A checking account is a *demand deposit account.* The money in the account is available to the account holder on demand—by writing a check, using a debit card, making a withdrawal, or transferring funds. Most banks offer interest-bearing checking accounts.

A **checkbook** includes blank checks and deposit slips, along with a check register or check stubs for recording checks written on the account and deposits made into the account. A **bank statement** is a report showing the activity in a checking account including paid checks, deposits, charges against the account, and the balance on the date of the statement. **Reconciliation** is the process of making adjustments and corrections to the check register or check stubs so that the balance agrees with the bank statement balance.

OBJECTIVE 2 Identify checking account services.

Most banks provide a wide range of financial services related to checking accounts. These are the most common.

- **Electronic funds transfer (EFT)** using the **Automated Clearing House (ACH)** The Automated Clearing House is an electronic network that enables banks (and other financial institutions) to transfer funds among themselves. Electronic funds transfer (EFT) is the process of moving funds electronically from an account in one bank to an account in another bank. This system enables a number of financial services for businesses and individuals. The terms EFT and ACH are often used interchangeably.
- **Automatic payments** Using ACH, banks enable customers to set up automatic payments, which are bill payments made directly from your checking account on a regularly scheduled basis. For example, a landlord might get a tenant's authorization to draw an automatic payment of rent from the tenant's bank account each month or a loan company might arrange for you to make your loan payments automatically each month.

TIPS

Although money handling is becoming more electronic, paper copies of checks are still necessary when no electronic means are available.

Automatic payments offer convenience, reliability, and cost savings. If you use automatic payments, be careful to deduct the payments from your check register or you might think you have more money in your account than you actually have, which could lead to overdrafts.

- **Direct deposit** This is a payment made by a deposit directly to the receiver's bank account rather than by mailing a check. It is the other end of an automatic payment. For example, paychecks can be automatically paid to employees and social security payments automatically paid to retirees by making direct deposits to their bank accounts.
- **Deposit insurance** The Federal Deposit Insurance Corporation (FDIC) insures depositors' accounts up to $250,000 per person per institution, except for some retirement accounts.
- **Overdraft protection** Writing a check for more money than you have in your checking account results in an overdraft. Banks offer overdraft protection in several ways. For example, your checking account can be linked to a savings account, home equity line (a line of credit secured by your home equity), or credit card. If you overdraw your checking account, the excess funds are transferred from your savings account or charged as a loan against your equity line or credit card. Banks usually charge a fee for covering an overdraft in this way.

Brad Killer/iStockphoto.com

- **Returned** or **dishonored check** If you overdraw your account without overdraft protection, the bank either loans you the funds and charges you a penalty fee or it returns (bounces) your check. Returned check charges by your bank are high. Also, you will probably have to pay a dishonored check charge to the business you originally wrote the check to. Deliberately issuing a check with nonsufficient funds is a crime.
- **Stop payment** You might issue a check to a business or individual for a product or service and find out later that the service was not performed, or the product was defective or not delivered. If your bank is notified before the check is cashed, it can stop payment on the check. Banks don't guarantee that they can stop a payment, and they charge a fee for the service. A common reason for stopping a payment is when a check has been lost. If you are asked to reissue a check that has been lost, you should always stop payment on the original check.
- **Converted check** When you write a check to a business, your check is likely to be converted to an EFT. This process speeds payment to the company and reduces their costs. Your bank statement may list converted checks under a heading called "electronic payments" instead of with your other cleared checks.
- **Digital check images** Banks used to return your canceled checks with your bank statement. The *Check Clearing for the 21st Century Act* (Check 21), which took effect in October 2004, empowers banks to substitute a digital image of a check (both front and back) and to destroy the paper check. This eliminates the cost of handling and mailing checks through clearing houses and back to your bank, and it speeds processing. Banks usually offer you the option (for a fee) of receiving a monthly printout of your cleared checks.

- **Debit card** A debit card can be thought of as an electronic checkbook. It is a plastic card, like a credit card, that is linked to your checking account with a personal identification number or PIN. The bank assigns the PIN number, or you can choose your own. For your security, the PIN should *never* be written on the card in case it is lost or stolen. When you make a purchase with a debit card, the money is immediately deducted from your checking account. Always keep your purchase receipts to compare to your monthly bank statement.
- **Automated teller machine (ATM)** ATM machines are located outside of banks and in supermarkets, convenience stores, and shopping malls. They allow 24-hour access to your accounts. To withdraw funds, you insert a debit card into the ATM, enter your PIN, and enter the amount you wish to withdraw (usually in multiples of $20). The code and amount are verified, the cash is dispensed, and your debit card is returned with a printed receipt. To make a deposit, the same procedure is followed except you insert an envelope containing the money and/or checks along with a deposit slip into the ATM. You can also use ATMs to check your account balances and transfer funds between accounts. Usually, there is no charge if you use an ATM owned by your bank. If you access your funds through a commercial ATM, you are charged a fee by the ATM owner and probably by your bank as well.
- **Online banking** Most brick and mortar banks allow online access to your accounts, and there are e-banks that operate only over the Internet. You can make almost any transaction online that you could make at a bank branch or at home with your checkbook. You can see all the activity in your account and see images of your checks.
- **Electronic bill paying** A popular feature of online banking is online bill paying. From your computer, virtually anywhere or anytime, you can conveniently pay all your bills without writing a single check. Payees are set up in advance. To make a payment, you simply select a payee, enter the amount you are paying along with the date of payment, and click submit. With electronic bill paying you initiate each payment from your computer, while with automatic payments the money is taken out automatically based on your prior approval.
- **Other bank services** Banks offer several services that are not directly related to your checking account. Examples include the purchase of certified or cashier's checks, money orders, traveler's checks, notary service, and foreign currency exchange.

Commercial Banking

Business expenses and income must be kept separate from personal income and reported to the IRS separately. Bank fees can sometimes be higher than for personal checking accounts because of the number of deposits made and checks written. While free business checking is not as common as it is for personal accounts, some banks do offer it. Businesses often maintain separate accounts for specific purposes. Payroll is always paid from a special account.

EXAMPLE

For her small retail shop, Esmeralda Saenz accesses the Internet and logs on to her bank's website to view her business checking account online. She checks her balance and a list of her debit and credit transactions, transfers funds electronically, pays bills, and views past statements—virtually anything she could do if she were in a physical bank branch (without, of course, having to stand in line).

Esmeralda enjoys the following benefits of online banking:

- Company checks and free endorsement stamps (allowing her to endorse checks with a company stamp)
- Free debit card
- Credit card and payment processing (allowing her customers to use charge cards such as MasterCard, VISA, or Discover)
- Business credit card (in her business name)
- Unlimited online and telephone account access

OBJECTIVE 3 Maintain a checkbook and a check register.

A check authorizes a bank to pay a certain sum from the checking account to an individual or a business known as a **payee**. The person or business who writes the check is the **drawer** (the person who pays). The drawer's bank is the **drawee**.

The check in Figure 4-1 has been completed by Phillip Rochelle, the drawer. It includes the following parts:

a. Drawer's name and address
b. Check number
c. Date of check
d. Name of party to whom the check is written (payee)
e. Amount of check written in numbers and words
f. From left to right along the bottom of the check the bank's routing number, the drawer's account number, drawer's check number
g. Drawer's signature
h. Bank's name and address
i. ABA (American Bankers Association) transit number

TIPS

ATM and debit card transactions and fees, withdrawals, and purchases should be recorded in your check register and deducted from your balance in order to maintain an accurate balance at all times. This prevents overdrafts.

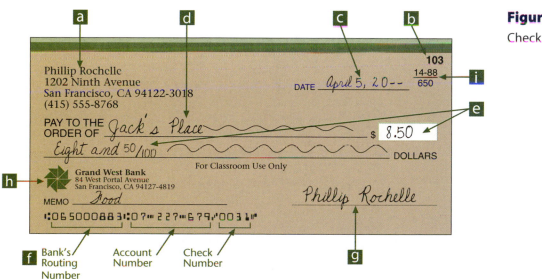

Figure 4-1

Check

The handwritten information on the check can also be completed on a check writer or a computer. Even the signature, which is usually written by hand, can be affixed with a signature machine or when printing checks using a computer. Such a signature is called a *facsimile*, and companies that use facsimile signatures place strict controls on their use to prevent misuse and theft.

Check-Writing Tips

- A check is a form of money and should be protected. Fill in all information clearly so it cannot be altered.
- Use a pen when writing a check. Black ink is best. Do not use a pencil, felt-tip marker, or pen with colored ink (such as red). Ink from a pen cannot be easily erased or smeared.
- Use the current date on a check. To avoid alteration, write out the date instead of using numerical abbreviations.
- Be sure to write clearly.
- Make certain the written amount is exactly the same as the numerical amount. If the two amounts differ, the written amount is considered legally binding.
- Sign your name neatly. Your signature should match the one on file at the bank. Illegible handwriting is easy to forge.

Deposit Slip

A **deposit slip** is completed when cash (currency or coin) and/or checks are deposited to a checking account. The **depositor** fills in the form. The depositor, Phillip Rochelle, has prepared the deposit slip shown in Figure 4-2.

The deposit slip contains the following information:

a. Depositor's name and address, which are usually preprinted
b. Date of deposit
c. Depositor's signature for any cash received
d. Bank's name and address
e. Bank's routing number and depositor's account number
f. ABA (American Bankers Association) transit number
g. Amount of currency and coin
h. Amount of each check
i. Subtotal amount deposited
j. Amount of cash depositor receives
k. Net deposit, which is the actual amount being deposited

Figure 4-2

Deposit Slip

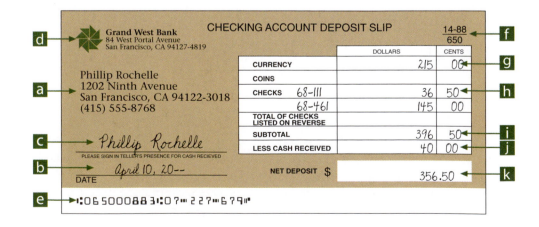

CHAPTER 4 BANK SERVICES

To help identify each deposited check, Mr. Rochelle listed each check's **American Bankers Association (ABA)** transit number on the deposit slip. As you see in Figure 4-2, the ABA number is located in the upper right corner of the check somewhere below the check number. It may appear as a fraction, such as Mr. Rochelle's ABA number, or as 14-88/650. The first two numbers (or top numbers) identify the city or state in which the bank is located and the specific bank on which the check is drawn. The second number (or bottom number) identifies the Federal Reserve District where the check will be cleared and is the routing number used by the Federal Reserve Bank. These numbers allow the check to be traced more easily should it become lost.

Endorsements

In order for Mr. Rochelle to deposit the two checks to his account, he must sign the backs of the checks. His signature is known as a blank endorsement. An example of a **blank endorsement** is shown in Figure 4-3.

A blank endorsement would allow anyone to cash a check if it were lost or stolen. For this reason, be cautious when you use a blank endorsement, as the check becomes a negotiable instrument.

To ensure protection should the checks be lost or stolen before being deposited, the words *for deposit only* are written on the checks above the signature. This type of endorsement, known as a **restrictive endorsement**, allows the payee only to deposit a check into his or her account. If a check is endorsed "for deposit only," cash cannot be received from the bank. The check can only be deposited. Figure 4-4 illustrates this type of endorsement.

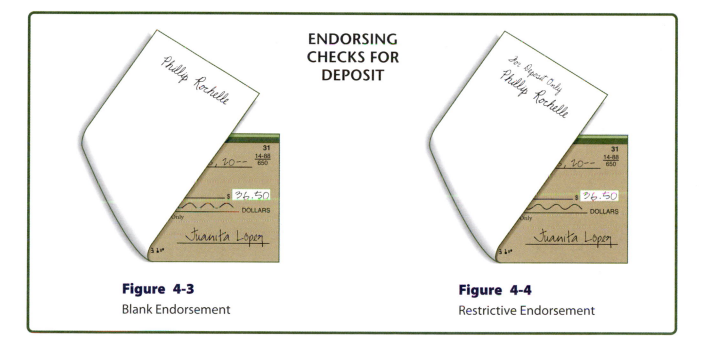

ENDORSING CHECKS FOR DEPOSIT

Figure 4-3
Blank Endorsement

Figure 4-4
Restrictive Endorsement

A **full endorsement** is used when the payee wants to transfer a check to another party. For example, a check may be passed on to someone else to pay a bill. The endorsement would be written as "pay to the order of" and the name of the third party.

Check Register or Check Stub

> **TIPS**
>
> *Keep your receipts and make it a practice to record all checking transactions, including deposits and cash withdrawals, as they occur.*

A check register or check stub is used to help the depositor keep track of checks written. The **check register** or **check stub** provides a record of each check number and date, the amount of each check, the deposits made, and the balance in the checking account. Examples of a check register and a check stub are shown in Figures 4-5 and 4-6. The forms provide the following information:

- **a.** Check number
- **b.** Date
- **c.** Individual or business to whom the check is written and a brief description of the transaction
- **d.** Amount of check
- **e.** Amount of deposit made
- **f.** Balance brought forward, which is the balance in the account after the last check was written or the last deposit was made
- **g.** **Running balance**, which is determined after each check has been subtracted from or a deposit has been added to the account (notice the lines with the balances are shaded slightly)

Figure 4-5
Check Register

a CHECK NUMBER	b DATE	c DESCRIPTION OF TRANSACTION	d AMOUNT OF CHECK		✓	e AMOUNT OF DEPOSIT		g f BALANCE BROUGHT FORWARD $ 1062	37
101	4/2/--	South Realty Co	800	00				800	00
		Rent						262	37
102	4/4/--	Butler Pharmacy	51	88				51	88
		Prescription						210	49
103	4/5/--	Jack's Place	8	50				8	50
		Ticket						201	99
	4/8/--	Deposit				50	00	50	00
								253	33

Figure 4-6
Check and Check Stub

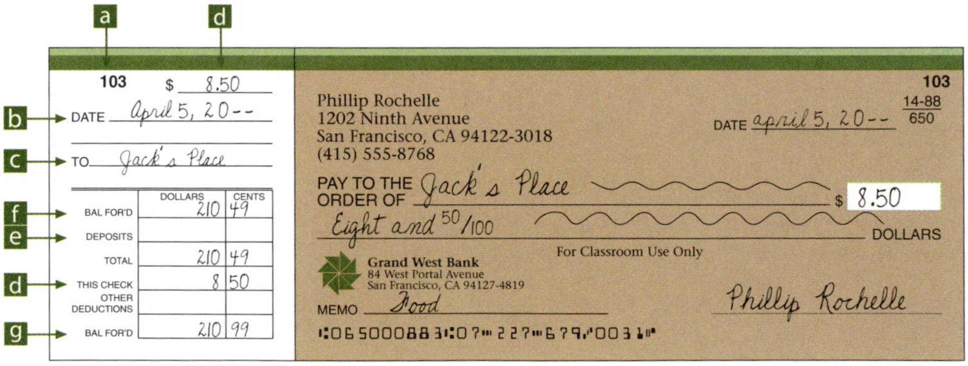

> **TIPS**
>
> *Use the + key to add deposits and – and = keys to deduct checks to keep a running balance in your calculator.*

EXAMPLE

Suppose you need to write Check 121 to McNally Garage for car repair, dated April 20, in the amount of $127.50 and a deposit of $100.00.

Study Figures 4-7, 4-8, and 4-9 illustrating the steps involved in completing a check register or check stub.

1. Write the check number (the number will already be printed on a check stub).

2. Write the current date.

3. Write to whom the check is written or a description of the transaction. Indicate the purpose of the check.

4. Write the amount of the check twice—once under *Amount of Check* and once under the balance column on the same line. Some check registers have only one line and require the amount to be written only once. An example of a single line check register is shown in Figure 4-8.

5. Subtract the amount of the check from the previous balance and record the new balance.

6. Add the deposit (if one has been made) for the new balance.

7. Complete the check stub as shown in Figure 4-9.

CHECK NUMBER	DATE	DESCRIPTION OF TRANSACTION	AMOUNT OF CHECK	✓	AMOUNT OF DEPOSIT	BALANCE BROUGHT FORWARD $ 1,021 00
121	4/20/--	McNally Garage	127 50			127 50
		Car repair				893 50
	4/20/--	Deposit			100 00	100 00
						993 50

Figure 4-7

Check Register Using Two Lines

CHECK NUMBER	DATE	DESCRIPTION OF TRANSACTION	AMOUNT OF CHECK	✓	AMOUNT OF DEPOSIT	BALANCE BROUGHT FORWARD $ 1,021 00
121	4/20/--	McNally Garage Car repair	127 50			893 50
	4/20/--	Deposit			100 00	993 50

Figure 4-8

Check Register Using Single Line

121 $ __27.50__

DATE _April 20, 20--_
TO _McNally Garage_
FOR _Car repair_

	DOLLARS	CENTS
BAL FOR'D	1,021	00
DEPOSITS	100	00
TOTAL	1,121	00
THIS CHECK	127	50
OTHER DEDUCTIONS		
BAL FOR'D	993	50

Figure 4-9

Check Stub

TIPS

Make it a practice to record all checking transactions, including deposits and cash withdrawals, as they occur.

OBJECTIVE 4 Use Excel to complete a deposit slip and a check register.

A deposit slip wouldn't necessarily be created in a worksheet. However, one was created in Excel, as shown in Figure 4-10, to give you additional practice using the worksheet. To calculate the net deposit requires basic math skills—addition and subtraction—and Excel's basic formulas.

Completing a Deposit Slip

As shown in Figure 4-10, Phillip Rochelle had $215 in currency and two checks and wanted to withdraw $40 in cash. Using Excel, complete the deposit slip for Phillip Rochelle.

Figure 4-10
Deposit Slip

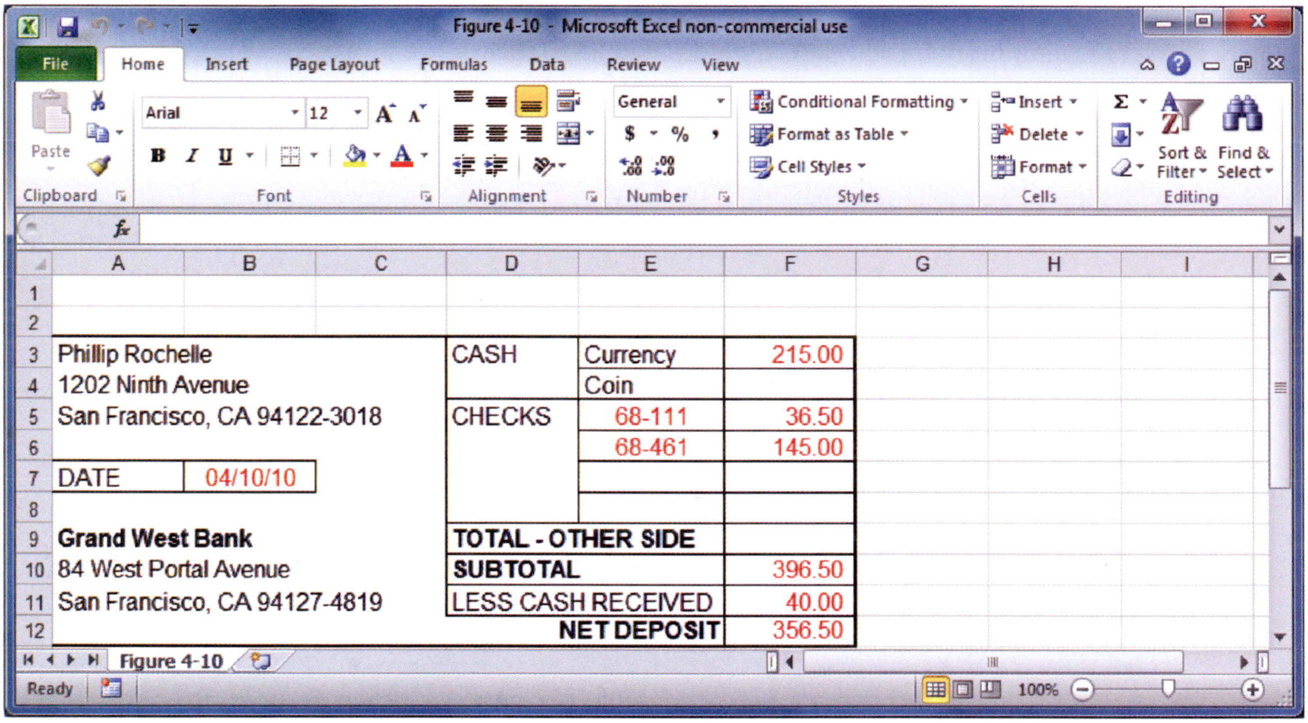

	A–B		D	E	F
3	Phillip Rochelle		CASH	Currency	215.00
4	1202 Ninth Avenue			Coin	
5	San Francisco, CA 94122-3018		CHECKS	68-111	36.50
6				68-461	145.00
7	DATE	04/10/10			
8					
9	Grand West Bank		TOTAL - OTHER SIDE		
10	84 West Portal Avenue		SUBTOTAL		396.50
11	San Francisco, CA 94127-4819		LESS CASH RECEIVED		40.00
12				NET DEPOSIT	356.50

STEPS

Retrieve the file *ch04pr01.xlsx*.

1. Enter the date April 10, 2010 in Cell B7. Format for Date, Type x/xx/xx.
2. Format Column F for Currency. Set Decimal places to 2 and Currency symbol to None.
3. Enter Currency: 215.00.
4. Enter check numbers in Column E: 68-111; 68-461.
5. Enter check amounts: for 68-111, 36.50; for 68-461, 145.00.
6. Use AutoSum to calculate the Subtotal of cash and checks.
7. Enter Less Cash Received: 40.00.

8. Enter the formula =F10-F11 in Cell F12 to calculate the Net Deposit.

9. Save the file as *ch04pr01a.xlsx*.

Filling In a Check Register

A check register is often included in software applications to keep track of activities. Figure 4-11 shows a check register created in Excel.

Figure 4-11

Check Register

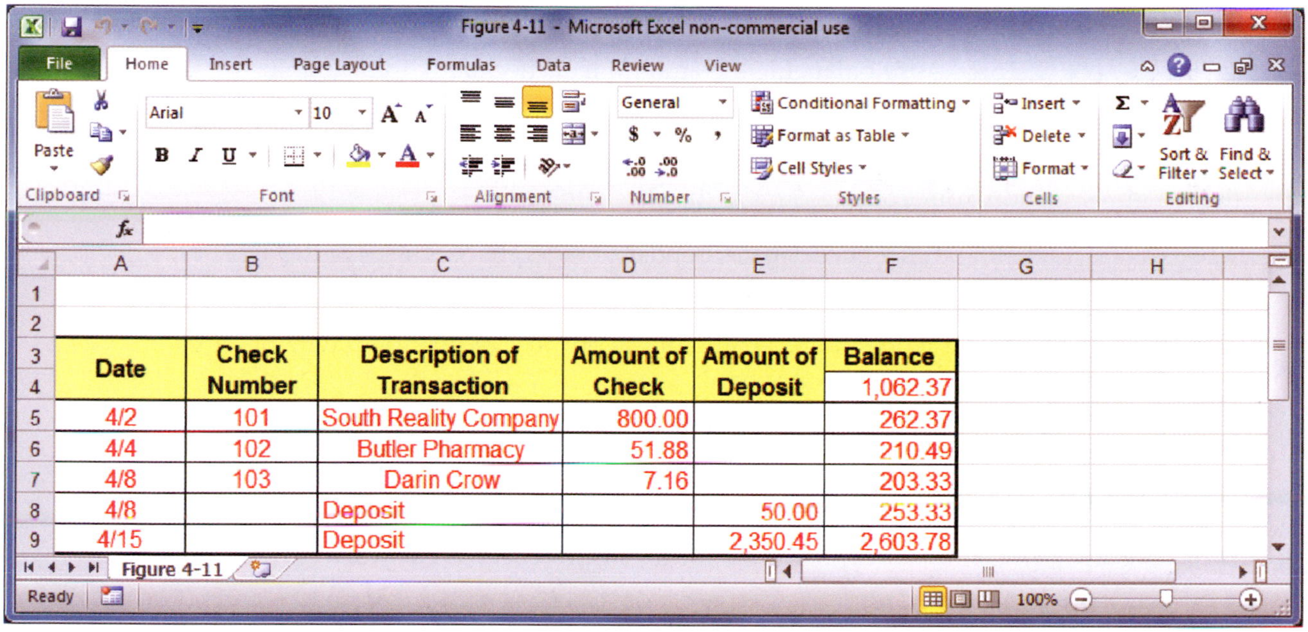

Date	Check Number	Description of Transaction	Amount of Check	Amount of Deposit	Balance
					1,062.37
4/2	101	South Reality Company	800.00		262.37
4/4	102	Butler Pharmacy	51.88		210.49
4/8	103	Darin Crow	7.16		203.33
4/8		Deposit		50.00	253.33
4/15		Deposit		2,350.45	2,603.78

Use the following steps in Excel to fill in a check register.

STEPS

Retrieve the file *ch04pr02.xlsx*.

1. Enter the beginning Balance 1062.37 in Cell F4.

2. Format cells in Column A for Date, Type x/xx.

3. Format Columns D, E, and F for Currency. Set Decimal places to 2 and Currency symbol to None.

4. For Row 5, enter 4/2; 101; South Realty Company; 800.00.

5. Enter the formula =F4-D5+E5 to calculate the new balance in Cell F5.

6. For Row 6, enter 4/4; 102; Butler Pharmacy; 51.88.

7. For Row 7, enter 4/8; 103; Darin Crow; 7.16.

8. For Row 8, enter 4/8; Deposit; 50.00.

9. For Row 9, enter 4/15; Deposit; 2350.45.

10. Copy the formula in Cell F5 to the remaining cells in Column F.

11. Save the file as *ch04pr02a.xlsx*.

Name _____   Date _____

Directions   Complete the following problems. Write your answers in the blanks provided.

A. Match the statements with the correct terms.   OBJECTIVE 1

   a. bank statement   **b.** check   **c.** checkbook

   d. checking account   **e.** reconciliation

   1. _____ The process of balancing the amount in a checkbook to the bank statement so the balances agree.

   2. _____ A written order that authorizes your bank to pay money or to transfer funds from your account to the check holder.

   3. _____ A listing of the checks paid, deposits made, charges against the account, and the balance on a specific date.

   4. _____ An account opened at a bank for the purpose of making payments from funds on deposit in that bank.

   5. _____ Includes checks and a record of checks written and deposits made into an account.

B. Complete the following statements by filling in the correct terms.   OBJECTIVE 2

   6. A bill payment made directly from your checking account on a regularly scheduled basis is a(n) _____.

   7. _____ is a line of credit to write checks for more than the actual balance.

   8. _____ is an electronic network that enables banks to transfer funds.

   9. _____ allows customers to access their checking account funds immediately.

  10. _____ is the process of moving funds electronically from an account in one bank to an account in another bank.

  11. A payment made by a deposit directly to the receiver's bank account rather than by mailing a check is a _____.

  12. _____ allows you to pay bills using the Internet.

  13. Bank accounts are insured by FDIC for _____ for each depositor per institution.

  14. A(n) _____ is used by banks to show cleared checks online or with your statement.

C. Complete the following statements by filling in the correct terms. OBJECTIVE 2

15. The person who receives the sum written on the check is the _____.

16. The person who writes the check is the _____.

17. The bank of the person who writes the check is known as the _____.

18. The _____ is completed when cash and/or checks are deposited to a checking account.

19. The _____ is usually located in the upper right corner of the check somewhere below the check number.

20. A(n) _____ endorsement allows anyone who comes into possession of a check to cash it or to deposit it into the holder's account.

21. A(n) _____ endorsement limits the transactions that can be performed with a check.

D. Complete the following check register by filling in the cash balances for each transaction. OBJECTIVE 3

CHECK NUMBER	DATE	DESCRIPTION OF TRANSACTION	AMOUNT OF CHECK	✓	AMOUNT OF DEPOSIT	BALANCE BROUGHT FORWARD $	0 00	
	6/15/--	Deposit			950 00			
								22.
846	6/16/--	McCray Mgmt Corp Fee	350 00					23.
847	6/16/--	Money Saver Drug Store Prescription	72 40					24.
848	6/16/--	Citco Oil Co. Gasoline bill	36 90					25.
849	6/17/--	The Telephone Co. Phone bill	30 30					26.
	6/20/--	Deposit			127 75			27.
850	6/22/--	Delhi Dept. Store Sweaters	42 20					28.
851	6/22/--	Bruce Johnston Mowing Lawn	12 70					29.
852	6/23/--	Robert's Florist Roses	9 60					30.

E. Complete the following word problems. OBJECTIVE 3

31. On Check stub 510, Dallas Johnson found he had transposed the check amount as $32.10 when it should have been $23.10. His checkbook balance was $677.80. What should it have been? _____

32. Amalia Herrera wrote a check for $39.50, but she recorded it in her checkbook register as $31.50. Will her running balance show more or less money than she actually has? _____

    How much more or less? _____

F. **Fill in the check stubs using the information given. Carry the balance** OBJECTIVE **3**
forward from the first check stub to the next numbered check stub.

33. Balance forward: $2,793.00
Date: April 20, 20--
Check number: 130
To: R&R Tax Service
For: Consultation
Amount of check: $175

| No. _____ $ _____ |
| DATE _____ |
| TO _____ |
| FOR _____ |

	DOLLARS	CENTS
BAL FOR'D		
DEPOSITS		
TOTAL		
THIS CHECK		
OTHER DEDUCTIONS		
BAL FOR'D		

34. Date: April 20, 20--
Check number: 131
To: Bruce's Office Supply
For: Folders
Amount of check: $27.50
Deposit: $360.90

| No. _____ $ _____ |
| DATE _____ |
| TO _____ |
| FOR _____ |

	DOLLARS	CENTS
BAL FOR'D		
DEPOSITS		
TOTAL		
THIS CHECK		
OTHER DEDUCTIONS		
BAL FOR'D		

G. **Complete the check register by filling in the information given.** OBJECTIVE **3**
Carry the balance down the right-hand column.

35. Balance: $1,968.80
Date: 6/10/–
Check no.: 321
To: June's Deli
For: Lunch
Amount: $9.95

36. Date: 6/10/–
Check no.: 322
To: S & S Cleaners
For: Dry cleaning
Amount: $20.40

37. Deposit: $814
Date: 6/10/–

CHECK NUMBER	DATE	DESCRIPTION OF TRANSACTION	AMOUNT OF CHECK	✓	AMOUNT OF DEPOSIT	BALANCE BROUGHT FORWARD	
						$	

H. **Use Excel to complete a deposit slip and check register.** OBJECTIVE **4**

38. Retrieve the file *ch04ex01.xlsx*. Follow the directions. Save the file as *ch04ex01a.xlsx*.

39. Retrieve the file *ch04ex02.xlsx*. Follow the directions. Save the file as *ch04ex02a.xlsx*.

4.2 Bank Statement Reconciliation

OBJECTIVES

1. Understand why a checking account must be reconciled.

2. Interpret a bank statement.

3. Reconcile a bank statement.

4. Use Excel to reconcile a bank statement.

OBJECTIVE 1 Understand why a checking account must be reconciled.

The first rule in managing a checking account is to keep good records. If you know the amount of money remaining in your account, you will be less likely to overdraw your account. Balancing your checkbook with your bank statement allows you to keep track of your money and the activity in your account. By making a habit of balancing your checkbook every month, you will always know how much money is *really* in your account. This will also help you avoid overdrawn funds for which there is a charge, not to mention a potential credit issue. Balancing your account will also help you become aware of any unauthorized use of your debit card or checkbook.

OBJECTIVE 2 Interpret a bank statement.

Each month the bank sends its checking account customers a statement of his or her account. If you bank online, you might not get a statement by mail; but you can access it online. Although the statement covers a month's transactions, it may begin and end on any day. For example, a statement may cover September 15 through October 16. A **bank statement** is a list of all the account activity processed through the bank during the statement period. The information on this statement helps the customer verify the check register or check stubs.

toddmedia/iStockphoto.com

Study the statement sent to Phillip Rochelle that is illustrated in Figure 4-12. It shows:

a. Customer's account number
b. Account summary
c. Total amounts of transactions by type, including number and bank statement beginning and ending balances
d. Detail of deposits
e. Detail of checks paid—Note that check number 403 is a converted check, and the utility company converted it to an EFT.
f. Detail of ATM withdrawals and debit card charges—Note that these ATM withdrawals were made at this bank's ATM. If any had been made at a commercial ATM, additional fees would have been assessed.
g. Detail of bank charges and fees

Figure 4-12

Bank Statement

GRAND WEST BANK
84 West Portal Avenue
San Francisco, CA 94127-4819

CUSTOMER SERVICE INFORMATION
Web site: www.grandwestbank.com
Phone No.:   (415) 555-2378

CHECKING ACCOUNT STATEMENT   April 15, 20-- through May 14, 20--
Phillip Rochelle   Acct. No. 1210-730-661942 ← **a**
1202 Ninth Avenue
San Francisco, CA 94122-3018

ACCOUNT SUMMARY ←——————————————————— **b**

	NO.	AMOUNT
Beginning Balance		$528.70
Deposits and Additions	2	420.17
Checks Paid	7	323.41 ←——— **c**
ATM & Debit Card Withdrawals	3	180.00
Other Withdrawals, Fees & Charges	1	10.00
Ending Balance		**$435.46**

DEPOSITS AND ADDITIONS ←——————————————— **d**

DATE	DESCRIPTION		AMOUNT
4/15	Employer	ACH 1000022	$210.09
4/30	Employer	ACH 1000126	210.08
Total Deposits & Additions			**$420.17**

CHECKS PAID ←——————————————— **e**

CHECK NO.	DESCRIPTION	DATE PAID	AMOUNT
399		4/16	$7.16
402		4/20	51.80
403	Utility Company Arc Arc ID:40880001	4/27	200.00
404		5/1	16.20
405		5/4	19.53
406		5/11	20.00
408		5/13	8.72
Total Checks Paid			**$323.41**

ATM & DEBIT CARD WITHDRAWALS ←——————————————— **f**

DATE	DESCRIPTION		AMOUNT
9/10	ATM Withdrawal	Grand West Bank	$60.00
9/17	Debit Card Withdrawal	Middletown IGA	40.00
9/22	ATM Withdrawal	Grand West Bank	80.00
Total ATM & Debit Card Withdrawals			**$180.00**

OTHER WITHDRAWALS, FEES & CHARGES ←——————————————— **g**

DATE	DESCRIPTION	AMOUNT
9/6	Service Charge	$10.00
Total Other Withdrawals, Fees & Charges		**$10.00**

Use reverse side to reconcile account

The statement balance may not agree with the depositor's checkbook balance for the following reasons:

1. *Outstanding checks* Checks that have been written and deducted by the depositor from the check register or check stubs but do not appear on this month's bank statement are called **outstanding checks**. These might be checks that were written during the statement period, but have not cleared yet, or checks you have written since the statement closing date. Checks that have cleared the bank are called **canceled checks**.

2. *Outstanding deposits* Deposits that have been made by the depositor but do not appear on this month's bank statement are called **outstanding deposits**. Usually, these will be deposits you have made since the statement closing date.

3. *Debits to the depositor's account* These charges may include **service charges (SC)**, sometimes called bank charges, which are monthly fees charged to the depositor for providing a checking account. Other charges may include ATM fees, stop payment fees, overdraft fees, or returned check charges. When checks are drawn against an account that does not contain sufficient funds to cover the amount of the checks, they might be marked **nonsufficient funds (NSF)** and be returned to the holder—usually the payee.

4. *Credits to the depositor's account* This would usually be earned interest added to the depositor's checking account balance when a minimum balance is maintained. A checking account that pays interest is called an **interest-bearing checking account**.

5. *Errors made by either the depositor or the bank* Bank errors today are extremely rare (one out of tens or hundreds of millions of transactions). Most errors occur as a result of addition or subtraction errors or transpositions, such as $21.45 for $12.45. Forgetting to record transactions—deposits, checks, ATM withdrawals, or debit card charges—will also cause your check register or check stub balance to be incorrect.

For these reasons, it is important that you compare the check register or check stub balance with the bank statement. If you are still unable to clear up the discrepancy, you may want to contact a customer service representative at your bank for additional help. A fee may be involved with this service, but it is important that you keep your account up to date.

OBJECTIVE **3** Reconcile a bank statement.

When the check register or check stub balance and the statement balance do not agree, the depositor must **reconcile** the balances; that is, find out what is causing the difference and make the necessary corrections. This procedure is usually completed on a **reconciliation form**. After the adjustments have been made, the balances should agree.

Mandy Rankin received her statement, and the balance was $831.74. She noted the following items on the bank statement (see Figure 4-13):

a. Deposits include two direct deposits of her earnings from her employer.

b. Her ATM and debit card withdrawals included a $3.00 charge by the ATM owner for her $80.00 withdrawal on September 22.

c. Other withdrawals included an automatic payment on her loan to Speedy Loan Co., a transfer to her savings account she made online, a $3.00 charge by her own bank for using a non-bank ATM, and her regular $10.00 service charge for maintaining the account.

Figure 4-13

Mandy Rankin's Bank Statement

CITIZEN'S BANK
6628 Avenue P
Houston, TX 77011-4739

CUSTOMER SERVICE INFORMATION

Web site:	www.citbankco.com
Phone No.:	(713) 555-2225

CHECKING ACCOUNT STATEMENT
Mandy Rankin
1121 Country Place Circle
Houston, TX 77079-2945

August 31, 20-- through September 30, 20--
Acct. No. **01170258**

ACCOUNT SUMMARY

	NO.	AMOUNT
Beginning Balance		$1,016.18
Deposits and Additions	4	1,184.24
Checks Paid	12	946.37
ATM & Debit Card Withdrawals	3	229.31
Other Withdrawals, Fees & Charges	4	193.00
Ending Balance		**$831.74**

DEPOSITS AND ADDITIONS

DATE	DESCRIPTION		AMOUNT
9/8	Employer	ACH 10001019	$330.40
9/15			362.95
9/22	Employer	ACH 10002178	330.40
9/23			160.49
Total Deposits & Additions			**$1,184.24**

CHECKS PAID

CHECK NO. DESCRIPTION	DATE PAID	AMOUNT
4549	9/4	$24.35
4551	9/9	138.20
4552	9/10	42.50
4553	9/10	284.15
4554	9/12	52.15
4555	9/13	36.88
4556	9/15	20.00
4557	9/17	159.26
4558	9/17	92.40
4559	9/18	24.50
4560	9/22	31.67
4561	9/25	40.31
Total Checks Paid		**$946.37**

ATM & DEBIT CARD WITHDRAWALS

DATE	DESCRIPTION		AMOUNT
9/10	ATM Withdrawal	Citizen's Bank	$100.00
9/17	Debit Card Withdrawal	Trace Hardware	46.31
9/22	Non-bank ATM Withdrawal	14878 Mall Rd., Houston, TX	83.00
Total ATM & Debit Card Withdrawals			**$229.31**

OTHER WITHDRAWALS, FEES & CHARGES

DATE	DESCRIPTION	AMOUNT
9/6	Speedy Loan Co. ACH 10000972	$80.00
9/16	Online transfer to Sav xxxxxx747 No. 230001471	100.00
9/22	Non-bank ATM fee	3.00
9/30	Service Charge	10.00
Total Other Withdrawals, Fees & Charges		**$193.00**

Use reverse side to reconcile account

In comparing the bank statement with her check register, Mandy noted that Check 4562, in the amount of $34.35, had not been paid by the bank and she had forgotten to record the September 17 debit card purchase for $46.31 in her check register. Her final checkbook balance was $859.70.

The reconciliation form is usually printed on the back of the bank statement. The form contains the following parts, as shown in Figure 4-14.

a. Bank balance on statement

b. Less outstanding checks

c. Plus outstanding deposits

d. Adjusted bank balance

e. Checkbook balance

f. Less unrecorded bank charges (debits)

g. Plus unrecorded deposits (credits)

h. Adjusted checkbook balance

Reconciliation of Bank Statement

a →	Bank balance on statement	$831.74
b →	Less outstanding checks	
	_____ $34.35	
	_____ _____	
	_____ _____	$34.35
		$797.39
c →	Plus outstanding deposits	_____
d →	ADJUSTED BANK BALANCE	$797.39
e →	Checkbook balance	$859.70
f →	Less unrecorded debits	$46.31
		$10.00
		$6.00 $62.31
		$797.39
g →	Plus unrecorded credits	_____
h →	ADJUSTED CHECKBOOK BALANCE	$797.39

Figure 4-14

Reconciliation Form

TIPS

Use the M+ key to store the bank statement balance and outstanding deposits, use the M– key to enter the outstanding checks, and use the MRC key to obtain the adjusted bank balance.

STEPS

1. Write in the ending bank statement balance.

2. Subtract outstanding checks and add outstanding deposits.

3. Record the adjusted bank balance.

4. Write in the checkbook balance from your check register or check stub. You can reconcile your account to any date in your check register following the closing date of the statement, but since you probably would have continued writing checks, making deposits, and making ATM and debit card charges, choosing the last balance in your check register will mean you'll have to account for several more items than if you reconcile to a balance on a date near the statement closing date.

5. Subtract unrecorded debits. Note that, since she was unaware of the $3.00 charge made by the ATM owner, she only recorded $80.00 in her check register for the September 22 ATM withdrawal. The $6.00 debit is for both her bank's $3.00 fee and the ATM owner's fee.

6. Write in the adjusted checkbook balance, which should match the adjusted bank balance.

To reconcile her checkbook with her monthly bank statement, Mandy created a form in Excel, as shown in Figure 4-15 on the next page. She entered the titles and subtitles for the categories needed on a reconciliation form. Then she entered the formulas needed to automatically calculate the balances.

Each month Mandy enters her outstanding checks, deposits, and bank charges, and the balances are automatically calculated for her. If a discrepancy shows between the bank statement and her checkbook, she reviews all the records to determine the difference. Mandy Rankin reconciled her checkbook with her bank statement by following the steps below.

You can create a bank reconciliation form as a template—a document that can be retrieved each month to reconcile your bank statement.

STEPS

Retrieve the file *ch04pr03.xlsx*

1. Enter Today's Date in Cell F4. Format for Date, Type x/xx/xx.

2. Enter the Bank Statement Date 9/30 in Cell F5. Format for Date, Type x/xx/xx.

3. Enter the Bank Balance on Statement 734.62 in Cell H6.

4. Enter the Outstanding Check Number 4563 in Cell B9 and the Check Amount 34.35 in Cell C9.

5. Enter a formula to total Outstanding Checks in Cell H12.

6. Enter a formula to calculate the Subtotal in Cell H13.

7. Enter a formula to total Outstanding Deposits in Cell H19.

8. Enter a formula to calculate the ADJUSTED BANK BALANCE in Cell H20.

9. Enter the Checkbook Balance 459.87 in Cell H21.

10. Enter the date of the transfer 9/6 in Cell B24. Format for Date, Type x/xx.

11. Enter the transfer amount 80.00 in Cell C24.

12. Enter the date of the next charge 9/7 in Cell B25. Format for Date, Type x/xx.

13. Enter the next charge 10.00 in Cell C25.

14. Enter a formula to calculate the total Unrecorded Debits in Cell H27.

15. Enter a formula to calculate the Subtotal in Cell H28.

16. Enter the Date of the unrecorded credit 9/08 in Cell B31. Format for Date, Type x/xx.

17. Enter the Amount of the unrecorded credit 330.40 in Cell C31.

18. Enter a formula to calculate the Total Unrecorded Credits in Cell H34.

19. Enter a formula to calculate the ADJUSTED CHECKBOOK BALANCE in Cell H35.

TIPS

When formatting multiple cells (that may or may not be near one another), you can hold down the CTRL key while clicking in each cell you wish to format. Then, when you choose your formatting style, all selected cells will be formatted.

20. Format dollar entries for Currency. Set Decimal places to 2 and Currency symbol to $.

21. Save the file as *ch04pr03a.xlsx*.

Figure 4-15

Excel Reconciliation Form

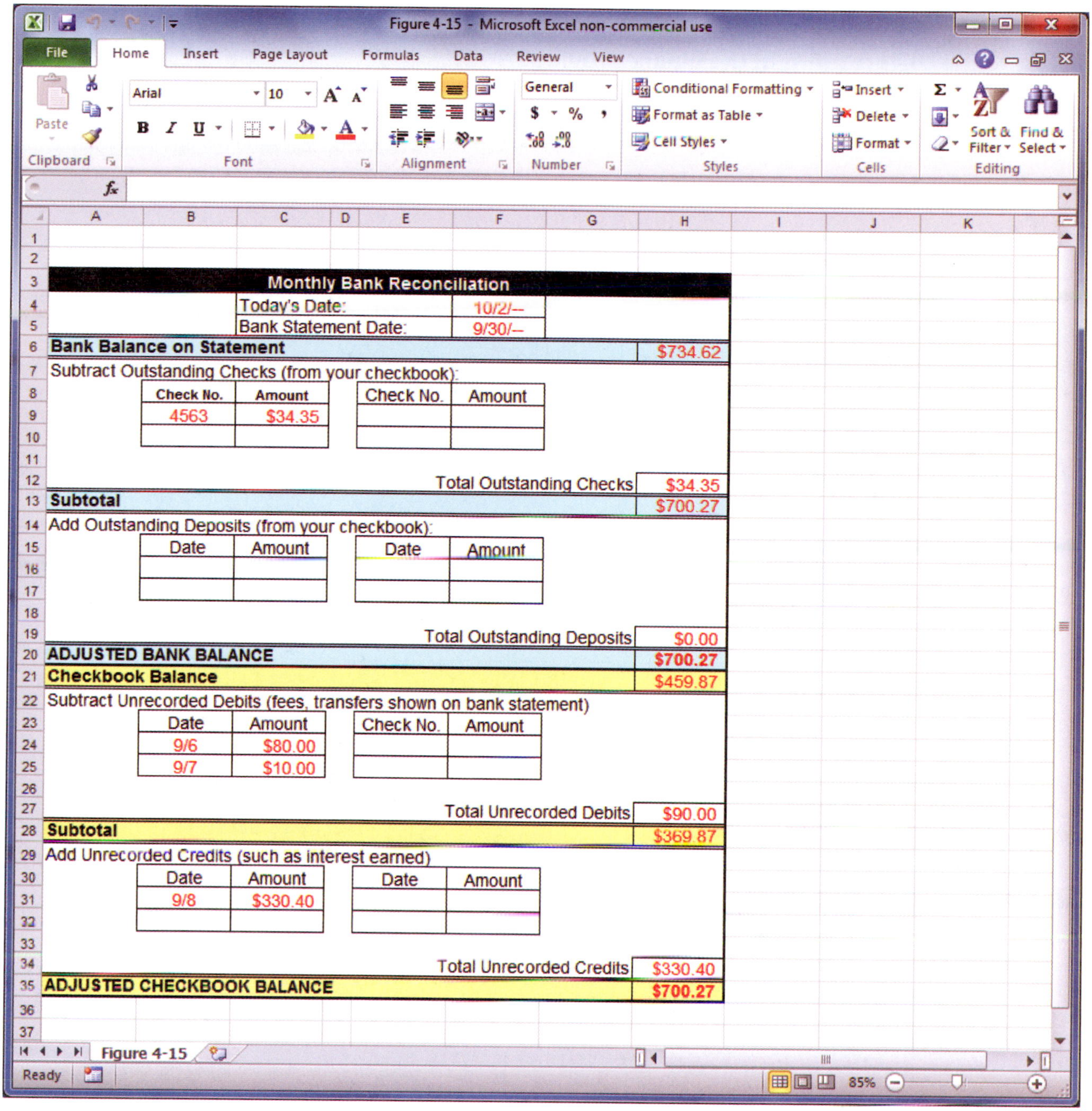

	Monthly Bank Reconciliation						
	Today's Date:			10/2/--			
	Bank Statement Date:			9/30/--			
Bank Balance on Statement						$734.62	
Subtract Outstanding Checks (from your checkbook):							
	Check No.	Amount		Check No.	Amount		
	4563	$34.35					
				Total Outstanding Checks		$34.35	
Subtotal						$700.27	
Add Outstanding Deposits (from your checkbook):							
	Date	Amount		Date	Amount		
				Total Outstanding Deposits		$0.00	
ADJUSTED BANK BALANCE						$700.27	
Checkbook Balance						$459.87	
Subtract Unrecorded Debits (fees, transfers shown on bank statement)							
	Date	Amount		Check No.	Amount		
	9/6	$80.00					
	9/7	$10.00					
				Total Unrecorded Debits		$90.00	
Subtotal						$369.87	
Add Unrecorded Credits (such as interest earned)							
	Date	Amount		Date	Amount		
	9/8	$330.40					
				Total Unrecorded Credits		$330.40	
ADJUSTED CHECKBOOK BALANCE						$700.27	

Name _____ Date _____

Directions   Complete the following problems.

A. Write the correct terms in the blanks provided.

1. _____ are checks that have been written and deducted by the depositor from the check register or stub but do not appear on the bank statement.

2. _____ are funds that have been deposited but do not appear on the bank statement.

3. _____ are regular monthly bank charges for providing a checking account.

4. _____ is the process of making adjustments and corrections to your check register or stubs so that your balance agrees with the bank statement balance.

B. Interpret and reconcile the following bank statement.   OBJECTIVES 2, 3

Benito Moya received his bank statement from First Junction Bank. His check register balance was $792.37. The outstanding checks were:

| **273** | $21.47 | **278** | $31.15 | **282** | $62.00 |
| **275** | $18.22 | **281** | $2.19 | **283** | $75.00 |

A $300 deposit had not been recorded by the bank.

```
First Junction Bank
67 West Ridgeway, P.O. Box 9511                       ACCOUNT NO.
Los Alamos, NM 89544-9511                             92-118-20
                                                   STATEMENT DATE
          BENITO MOYA                                 12/17/--
          82 CLARK RD.                                PAGE NO.
          LOS ALAMOS, NM 87544                           1
                                                   CYCLE   SC CODE
   ()******()   PERSONAL (PLUS)                      12      04

  CHECKING STATEMENT SUMMARY ........................................
     PREVIOUS STATEMENT 11/19/--, BALANCE OF ..............$1,010.08
       1 DEPOSITS OR OTHER CREDITS TOTALING ----(1 ITEMS)    472.50
       6 CHECKS OR OTHER DEBITS TOTALING ....(6 ITEMS)       307.68
          SERVICE CHARGE AMOUNT .............................  7.00
  CURRENT BALANCE AS OF 12/17/-- .....................$1,167.90

  MISCELLANEOUS DEBITS .............................................
     DATE       AMOUNT   TRANSACTION DESCRIPTION
     12/17      $7.00    REGULAR SERVICE CHARGE

  MISCELLANEOUS CREDITS ............................................
     DATE       AMOUNT   TRANSACTION DESCRIPTION
     12/31      $472.50

  DAILY BALANCE SUMMARY ............................................
  DATE...CHECK NO....AMOUNT          DATE...CHECK NO....AMOUNT
  11/18    272     $29.49            12/05    277      $12.99
  11/21    274     $19.25            12/12    279      $92.00
  11/26    276     $38.15            12/20    280     $115.80
```

5. What is the date of the statement?

_____

6. What is the previous balance?

_____

7. What is the current balance?

_____

8. List and identify the service charges.

_____

Reconciliation of Bank Statement

Bank balance on statement _____ **9.**

Less outstanding checks

_____   _____

_____   _____

_____   _____   _____ **10.**

_____ **11.**

Plus outstanding deposits _____

_____   _____ **12.**

ADJUSTED BANK BALANCE _____ **13.**

Checkbook balance _____ **14.**

Less unrecorded debits _____   **15.**

_____   _____ **16.**

SUBTOTAL CHECKBOOK BALANCE _____ **17.**

Plus unrecorded credits _____   **18.**

_____   _____ **19.**

ADJUSTED CHECKBOOK BALANCE _____ **20.**

C. Solve the following word problems. OBJECTIVE 3

21. Marta Fuentes had a balance of $1,200.50 in her checking account. The bank issued her a credit of $505 and charged her $12 for new checks. There were no outstanding checks or deposits. What should her checkbook balance be? _____

22. After comparing her check register to her bank statement, Judy Weeman had not checked off Checks 112 for $42.50, 115 for $13.75, and 121 for $142.33. What was the total of her outstanding checks? _____

23. The bank statement shows a balance of $4,772.12, and Carmen Cruz's checkbook balance shows $4,793.84. What is the difference between the two? _____

D. Use Excel to complete the following reconciliation forms. OBJECTIVE 4

24. Retrieve the file *ch04ex03.xlsx*. Follow the directions. Save the file as *ch04ex03a.xlsx*.

25. Retrieve the file *ch04ex04.xlsx*. Follow the directions. Save the file as *ch04ex04a.xlsx*.

Chapter Review and Assessment

KEY TERMS

American Bankers Association (ABA)

Automated Clearing House (ACH)

automated teller machine (ATM)

automatic payments

bank statement

blank endorsement

canceled checks

check

check register

check stub

checkbook

checking account

converted check

debit card

deposits

deposit insurance

deposit slip

depositor

digital check image

direct deposit

dishonored check

drawee

drawer

electronic bill paying

electronic funds transfer (EFT)

full endorsement

interest-bearing checking account

nonsufficient funds (NSF)

online banking

outstanding checks

outstanding deposits

overdraft protection

payee

reconcile

reconciliation

reconciliation form

restrictive endorsement

returned check

running balance

service charges

stop payment

CONCEPTS	EXAMPLES
4.1 Maintain a checkbook and a check register. Institutions offer different types of checking accounts. To deposit checks into an account, you must have the appropriate endorsements on the back side of the checks.	Demand deposit account Interest-bearing checking account The depositor fills out the deposit slip. Three types of endorsements are blank, restrictive, and full.
4.2 Reconcile a bank statement. Step 1 Add ending bank balance. Step 2 Subtract outstanding checks. Step 3 Add outstanding deposits. This is the adjusted bank balance. Step 4 Add checkbook balance. Step 5 Subtract unrecorded debits. Step 6 Add unrecorded bank credits. This is the adjusted checkbook balance.	Reconciling or balancing your checkbook with your bank statement allows you to accurately keep track of your money and the activity in your account. To balance your checkbook, check off items in your register, update your checkbook register, and use the reconciliation form.

Chapter 4 Review Exercises

Name _____ Date _____

Directions   Complete the following problems.

A.   Complete the following check register by filling in the cash balances for each transaction.   `4.1 OBJECTIVE 3`

CHECK NUMBER	DATE	DESCRIPTION OF TRANSACTION	AMOUNT OF CHECK	✓	AMOUNT OF DEPOSIT	BALANCE BROUGHT FORWARD $ 523 65	
853	6/23/--	Julie Anderson Child care	164 20				1.
854	6/24/--	Money Saver Drugstore Prescriptions	29 46				2.
	6/24/--	Deposit			303 14		3.
855	6/25/--	XYZ Corporation Magazines	37 40				4.
856	6/25/--	Spring Valley Church Donation	75 00				5.
857	6/26/--	Our Neighborhood Grocery Groceries	82 40				6.
	6/27/--	Deposit			303 14		7.
858	6/27/--	Triple A Cleaners Dry cleaning	27 60				8.

B.   Calculate the totals and balances on the check stubs. Carry each balance forward to the next numbered check stub.   `4.1 OBJECTIVE 2`

No. 107 $ 33.10
DATE July 15, 20--
TO Zarif
FOR Lawn Care

	DOLLARS	CENTS
BAL FOR'D	800	90
DEPOSITS		
TOTAL		
THIS CHECK		
OTHER DEDUCTIONS		
BAL FOR'D		

9.
10.
11.

No. 108 $ 6.55
DATE July 16, 20--
TO S.M. Cooper
FOR Weekly Paper

	DOLLARS	CENTS
BAL FOR'D		
DEPOSITS		
TOTAL		
THIS CHECK		
OTHER DEDUCTIONS		
BAL FOR'D		

12.
13.
14.
15.

No. 109 $ 31.50
DATE July 18, 20--
TO The Dress-R
FOR Skirt

	DOLLARS	CENTS
BAL FOR'D		
DEPOSITS		
TOTAL		
THIS CHECK		
OTHER DEDUCTIONS		
BAL FOR'D		

16.
17.
18.
19.

No. __110__ $ __13.45__			
DATE July 20, 20--			
TO Sun Cleaners			
FOR Dry Cleaning			

	DOLLARS	CENTS	
BAL FOR'D			**20.**
DEPOSITS			
TOTAL			**21.**
THIS CHECK			**22.**
OTHER DEDUCTIONS			
BAL FOR'D			**23.**

No. __111__ $ __22.70__			
DATE July 21, 20--			
TO Dr. Garcia			
FOR Eye Exam			

	DOLLARS	CENTS	
BAL FOR'D			**24.**
DEPOSITS			
TOTAL			**25.**
THIS CHECK			**26.**
OTHER DEDUCTIONS			
BAL FOR'D			**27.**

No. __112__ $ __97.20__			
DATE July 22, 20--			
TO Trent's			
FOR Tune Up			

	DOLLARS	CENTS	
BAL FOR'D			**28.**
DEPOSITS	750	00	
TOTAL			**29.**
THIS CHECK			**30.**
OTHER DEDUCTIONS			
BAL FOR'D			**31.**

C. Identify the effect of the following items to either the bank statement or the check register balance. To indicate the correct action, select the appropriate letter from the following.

4.2 OBJECTIVE 3

a. Add to bank statement balance **b.** Subtract from bank statement balance

c. Add to checkbook balance **d.** Subtract from checkbook balance

32. ____ Services charges and fees   **33.** ____ Error. Check not recorded in check register.

34. ____ Interest on the checking account   **35.** ____ Outstanding checks

36. ____ Outstanding deposits   **37.** ____ Deposited check returned for nonsufficient funds

D. Solve the following word problems. Write your answers in the blanks provided.

4.2 OBJECTIVE 3

38. Roshida Cowling has a $1,181.11 checkbook balance. The bank statement shows a $2,111.46 balance and a $10.00 service charge. Outstanding checks total $940.35. What is Roshida's adjusted checkbook balance? Does it balance with the bank statement?   _____

39. Paul Hastings had a checkbook balance of $1,345.00. His bank statement showed a deposit of $423 that he hadn't recorded and a $15 service fee. What should his checkbook balance be?   _____

40. Julie Marsh has a checkbook balance of $565.67. She has not recorded these checks: check 123 for $23.34, check 124 for $45.88, and check 125 for $76.05. Julie also needs to record a deposit of $125. What is her checkbook balance now?   _____

41. On check stub 988, Hattie Kaufman found she had transposed $67.54 when it should have been $65.74. Her checkbook balance was $234.11. What is the corrected balance?   _____

42. Richard Umberling has a checkbook balance of $323.19. The bank statement shows a balance of $503.66. The outstanding checks total $75.44. The bank deducted $12.50 for an order of new checks. The service charge is $10.00. The difference in the balances is a deposit not recorded in the checkbook. What is the amount?   _____

43. Penny Schwartz has a balance of $2,668.77 in her checkbook. There were direct deposits totaling $235.11 that she hadn't recorded and a service charge of $25.00. There were no outstanding checks or deposits. What should her reconciled checkbook balance be?

44. State National Bank sent Jeff Satterwhite his bank statement showing a $1,018.34 balance. Jeff's checkbook showed a $651.09 balance. The following checks were outstanding: Check 867 for $23.98, Check 869 for $11.11, Check 870 for $122.98, and Check 871 for $58.80. The monthly service charge was $12.50. Jeff had forgotten to record a deposit in his checkbook for $162.88. What is the adjusted checkbook balance? Does it balance with the bank statement?

45. Mary Wong had a balance of $1,754.03 in her checking account. Her statement showed a direct deposit of $623.12 by her employer that she hadn't expected yet and $15 in ATM fees. There were no outstanding checks or deposits. What should her checkbook balance be?

46. Javier Sanchez added the following deposits to his company account: 5/1, $55.76; 5/2, $67.99; 5/3, $128.11; 5/4, $298.04; and 5/5, $96.43. His beginning checkbook balance was $349.09. What is his current balance after these deposits?

47. On December 31, the checkbook balance of Huffman Company was $45,980.65. The bank statement showed $78,452.10. Checks outstanding totaled $12,878.03. The statement revealed an unrecorded deposit in Huffman's checking account of $19,617.27 as well as a service charge of $23.85. What is the bank statement balance after the checks are included?

What is the corrected checkbook balance?

48. Tito Bates' bank statement showed a balance of $920.51. He had the following outstanding checks: Check 556 for $23.09, Check 559 for $86.44, Check 560 for $11.25, and Check 561 for $161.59. The bank deducted a $13.50 service charge. Tito's balance in his checkbook was $661.64. What was the checkbook balance after reconciliation? Did it agree with his adjusted statement balance?

49. The Southside Company's checkbook balance was $1,854.39. The bank charged the company $34 for service fees and a customer paid off a note for $505.22 with an ACH deposit. The interest earned for the month was $7.86. What is the current checkbook balance after these items?

50. Reneé Terrace received her bank statement showing a balance of $1,475.98. The outstanding checks totaled $586.21. The deposits in transit were $758.03. There was no service charge. Her checkbook balance was $1,647.80. What was her adjusted bank statement balance?

E. Use Excel to solve the following problems.

4.1 OBJECTIVE **4**
4.2 OBJECTIVE **4**

51. Retrieve the file *ch04ex05.xlsx*. Follow the directions. Save the file as *ch04ex05a.xlsx*.

52. Retrieve the file *ch04ex06.xlsx*. Follow the directions. Save the file as *ch04ex06a.xlsx*.

EXAMPLE   A bank teller is the person most people associate with a bank. Tellers make up about one-third of most banks' employees and conduct most of a bank's routine transactions.

TRY IT...

Mark Whitley, head teller for City of Hamilton Credit Union, is ready to balance for the day. He must run a report of the activity for the day. Complete the following report by adding or subtracting according to the symbols shown to the left of each amount.

```
                    CITY OF HAMILTON CREDIT UNION
                  END OF DAY HEAD TELLER TRIAL BALANCE
                            FOR 3/16/20—
     RUN ON:   3/16/20—                          01 – MAIN OFFICE

     BEGINNING OF DAY      BEGINNING TELLER'S CASH    +      30,559.55
                           BEGINNING VAULT CASH       +      70,210.42
                                                          ----------
                           BEGINNING CHANGE FUND      =      _____     1.

     DAILY ACTIVITY        CASH FROM BANK+ / TO BANK –              .00
                           CASH FROM VAULTS+ / TO VAULTS –          .00
                           TCD DISPENSES TO MEMBERS–   +            .00
                           OUTSIDE CHECKS             –      62,954.32
                           CASH DISBURSED             –      23,405.10
                           IN-HOUSE DRAFTS            –         600.00
                           CASH SHORT                 –            .00
                           ADVANCE VOUCHERS           –            .00
                           RECEIPT VOUCHERS           +      59,350.25
                           CASH OVER                  +            .00
                                                          ----------
                           NET DAILY ACTIVITY         =      _____     2.

     END OF DAY            ENDING TELLER'S CASH       +      42,875.45
                           ENDING VAULT CASH          +      30,285.35
                                                          ----------
                           ENDING CHANGE FUND         =      _____     3.
```

Write about Math

1. Explain the various types of endorsements for checks.

2. Describe the importance of reconciling a bank statement. Include the benefits gained from keeping an accurate checking account.

Personal Finance

How much do you really know about your bank account?

How your checking account works is one of the first things you should learn when you open your account. For instance, you need to learn how to write paper checks, make cash withdrawals at the bank or from an automated teller machine (ATM), or pay with a debit card. Your paycheck might go by "direct deposit" into your account, or you might deposit checks at the bank's teller window, through drive-through banking, or at an ATM. You also need to learn how to deposit funds, how to get additional funds when you make a purchase, how to pay a bill, how to monitor your account, and how to avoid overdrafts. You might already know the basics; however, there is more information you need to know about your banking experience that will save you money.

Call a local bank (main bank or any branch), savings & loan, or credit union and obtain the following information about their checking accounts. You may find the bank will mail you a brochure that has most of the information in it, or you may visit the bank and pick up the information. Answer the following questions.

1. What service charge amounts are charged, if any, on a personal checking account? If there are choices or conditions, indicate what they are.

2. What does the bank charge for an insufficient-funds check? What rules are followed, if any?

3. How can a customer get a copy of a check if the bank doesn't return checks and is there a charge?

4. Does the bank offer overdraft protection? What are the conditions?

5. What is the charge for a stop-payment on a check? What is the procedure?

6. Does the bank charge for cashier's checks, money orders, traveler's checks, non-customer check-cashing privilege, notary service, or any other services?

7. Can a computer be used to transfer funds between accounts at the bank such as between checking and savings accounts?

8. Does the bank charge for personal assistance with an account?

9. Does the bank provide online bill paying? What is the procedure? What are the computer equipment requirements? Is there a charge? If so, how much? Is tech support provided for setting up online bill paying?

10. Does the bank have a hotline to call to get account information? What is the phone number? Is a password needed?

11. What is the procedure for closing an account?

12. Does the bank offer ATM card privileges? Can the ATM card be used at other banks' ATMs? What are the charges? Can the ATM card be used like a credit card and what are the benefits of using it as a credit card versus a debit card?

13. What is the minimum amount of money to deposit before opening an account?

14. What is the service charge for a business account? Is there a service charge for deposits for a business account?

15. What information did you find by completing this project that you believe to be the most helpful to you in the future?

Name _____   Date _____   Score _____

Directions   Complete the following problems.

A. Complete the check register below by filling in the cash balances for each transaction.   `4.1 OBJECTIVE 3`

CHECK NUMBER	DATE	DESCRIPTION OF TRANSACTION	AMOUNT OF CHECK	✓	AMOUNT OF DEPOSIT	BALANCE BROUGHT FORWARD $ 814 65	
1046	8/11/--	The Telephone Company Phone bill	51 47				1.
	8/11/--	Deposit From Paycheck			861 66		2.
1047	8/12/--	Lo-Price Oil Car Service	73 21				3.
1048	8/13/--	Smithson Cleaners Cleaning	11 75				4.
1049	8/13/--	White's Dept. Store Shirt	42 00				5.
	8/13/--	Deposit			115 98		6.

B. Calculate the totals and balances on the following check stubs, carrying the balance forward to the next numbered check.   `4.1 OBJECTIVE 3`

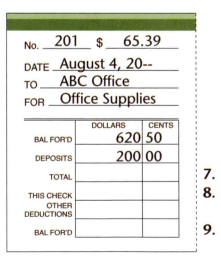

No. _201_ $ _65.39_

DATE _August 4, 20--_

TO _ABC Office_

FOR _Office Supplies_

	DOLLARS	CENTS
BAL FOR'D	620	50
DEPOSITS	200	00
TOTAL		
THIS CHECK		
OTHER DEDUCTIONS		
BAL FOR'D		

7.
8.
9.

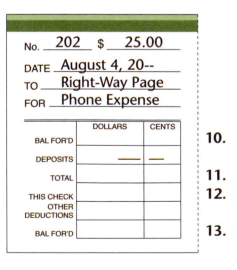

No. _202_ $ _25.00_

DATE _August 4, 20--_

TO _Right-Way Page_

FOR _Phone Expense_

	DOLLARS	CENTS
BAL FOR'D		
DEPOSITS	—	—
TOTAL		
THIS CHECK		
OTHER DEDUCTIONS		
BAL FOR'D		

10.
11.
12.
13.

No.	203	$	39.45

DATE __August 5, 20--__
TO __Big Deals Furniture__
FOR __Office Furniture__

	DOLLARS	CENTS
BAL FOR'D		
DEPOSITS	——	—
TOTAL		
THIS CHECK		
OTHER DEDUCTIONS		
BAL FOR'D		

14.

15.
16.

17.

No.	204	$	6.21

DATE __August 6, 20--__
TO __U.S. Post Office__
FOR __Postage Expense__

	DOLLARS	CENTS
BAL FOR'D		
DEPOSITS	——	—
TOTAL		
THIS CHECK		
OTHER DEDUCTIONS		
BAL FOR'D		

18.

19.
20.

21.

C. Solve the following word problems. 4.2 OBJECTIVE 3

22. If a check was written for $92.01 and recorded in the check register as $29.01, the checkbook balance would be "off" by what amount? _____

23. On December 31, Bill's company checkbook showed a $587.98 balance. Bill's bank statement showed a $687.99 balance. Check 590 for $123.09 and Check 592 for $33.44 were outstanding. A $200 deposit was in transit. The bank charged a $15 service fee. The statement showed $2.55 in interest earned and an unrecorded $150 deposit. Does his account balance match the statement? _____

    If not, what is the difference in the balances? _____

24. Teresa Quitman wrote a check for $176.65, but she recorded it in her checkbook register as $716.65. What is the difference? Is the checkbook balance affected? If so, by how much? _____

25. Wanda received a bank statement that showed her balance to be $458.92. There were three outstanding checks: Check 111 for $56.43, Check 115 for $12.22, and Check 118 for $39.30. There was an ACH deposit for $125 and a bank service charge of $15. Wanda had a checkbook balance of $190.97. She had forgotten to record a $50 deposit in her checkbook. What was the checkbook and bank balance after reconciliation? _____

26. Katherine Santos had a balance of $764.83 in her checking account. The bank deducted $235.11 due to a returned customer check. The bank also credited her account $5.45 in interest earned and deducted a $13 service charge. There were no outstanding checks or deposits. What should her checkbook balance be? _____

27. If the checkbook balance is $511.40 and a deposit of $601.08 was not recorded, what is the correct balance in the checkbook? _____

D. Use Excel to solving the following problems. 4.1 OBJECTIVE 4 / 4.2 OBJECTIVE 4

28. Retrieve the file *ch04qz01.xlsx*. Follow the directions. Save the file as *ch04qz01a.xlsx*.

29. Retrieve the file *ch04qz02.xlsx*. Follow the directions. Save the file as *ch04qz02a.xlsx*.

Payroll is usually one of the largest operating expenses a company has. Employers must maintain accurate payroll records for three reasons. First, the company must keep accurate records because wages and salaries are income tax deductions for the employer. Second, data must be collected in order to compute earnings for each employee for each payroll period. Third, information must be provided to complete federal and state payroll reports that employers are required by law to file. Payroll, like most other accounting functions, is most often computerized. In this chapter you will manually complete the payroll functions the software would do in order to gain an overall understanding of the payroll process.

EMPLOYMENT AGENCY SITE MANAGER

Rebekah Hasting works as a site manager for an employment placement firm. It is her responsibility to recruit, interview, and hire employees for her client companies. Once the employees begin their new jobs, she is responsible for managing the client account and the payroll process for the employees working with the client. She says, "I complete their payroll every Monday and then deal with any issues that arise with the employees. These issues range from benefits, employee relations, payroll, and terminations." Rebekah spends half of her day completing administrative work and the other half interacting with employees.

Rebekah knows that people often view employment placement firms as companies that provide only temporary labor. However, she says, "Our firm actually places long-term, permanent employees with organizations that often contract out their human resource processes."

Courtesy of Rebekah Hasting

How Math Is Used in Employment Placement Firms

Rebekah uses math on a daily basis to complete payroll. Employees must turn in a timesheet with the amount of hours they worked. She says, "Most of the time, there are a handful of timesheets that do not have the hours added up correctly, if at all." She must then add all the hours they worked. Rebekah also uses math to determine deductions that need to be taken from a paycheck. For example, she subtracts amounts from gross income for state income tax, federal income tax, Social Security, and Medicare taxes.

What Do You Think?

What skills do you need to improve in order to be able to complete a payroll?

Math Skills Used

Addition

Decimals

Division

Percent

Multiplication

Subtraction

Other Skills Needed

Accuracy

Communication

Interpersonal

Organization

OBJECTIVES

1. Identify terms used for computing gross earnings.

2. Calculate gross pay for common pay periods.

3. Calculate gross earnings for straight time, overtime, and double time.

4. Use Excel to calculate straight time, overtime, and double time.

OBJECTIVE 1 Identify terms used for computing gross earnings.

Here are some common terms used in working with payroll information.

Compensation   Salary, wages, pay, or benefits received for the performance of a service.

Double Time   Twice an employee's hourly rate. There is no requirement under the wage and hour laws to pay more than time and one-half.

Fair Labor Standards Act (FLSA)   An act of law (sometimes called the Wage and Hour Law) establishing minimum wages and requiring employers whose firms are involved in interstate commerce (sale of goods from state to state) to pay their employees time and one-half for all hours worked in excess of 40 hours per week. There is no requirement that time and one-half be paid for weekends or holidays. The act also provides that certain employees (management and supervisory) are exempt from its regulations.

Gross Earnings   The total amount of an employee's pay before deductions.

Hourly Wage (Hourly Rate)   Wages paid according to the number of hours worked.

Overtime   All time worked in excess of straight time.

Straight Time   Hours paid at an employee's regular wage, usually the first 40 hours worked per week. However, this number may vary from company to company. In this chapter, 40 hours is used to represent straight time. Straight time is often referred to as **regular time**.

Time and One-Half   One and one-half times an employee's hourly rate.

OBJECTIVE 2 Calculate gross pay for common pay periods.

Employees receive compensation as salary, wages, pay, or benefits for the performance of a service. In your work experience or when searching for employment, you may have found employers that pay their employees at different times. The following table shows the common pay periods.

COMMON PAY PERIODS		
Salary Paid	**Period**	**Number of Paychecks**
Weekly	Once per week	52 paychecks each year
Biweekly	Every 2 weeks	26 paychecks each year
Semimonthly	Twice a month	24 paychecks each year
Monthly	Once a month	12 paychecks each year

Assume you are paid $24,960 per year. The following table shows what you would earn for each of the common pay periods.

Weekly	$24,960 ÷ 52 = $480
Biweekly	$24,960 ÷ 26 = $960
Semimonthly	$24,960 ÷ 24 = $1,040
Monthly	$24,960 ÷ 12 = $2,080

TIPS

If you work 52 weeks per year, you work 2,080 hours, since 40 × 52 = 2,080. To calculate the hourly rate, divide the annual salary by 2,080 hours, for example: $24,960 ÷ 2,080 = $12.00 per hour.

OBJECTIVE 3 Calculate gross earnings for straight time, overtime, and double time.

The calculations for gross earnings (the total amount of an employee's pay before deductions) vary depending on several factors. Examples of these factors include how many hours an employee works or whether the company is required to pay time and one-half for all hours over a regular time. In all computations dealing with money amounts, round to the nearest cent.

Compensation by Hourly Wage: Straight Time

The wage paid for each hour worked is the hourly wage or hourly rate. As previously mentioned, straight time (also called regular time or regular earnings) in most companies is 40 hours per week. However, some companies are experimenting with shorter work hours.

EXAMPLE

To compute Juan Olivar's weekly salary (gross earnings) at $9.50 per hour, multiply the number of hours worked by the hourly rate.

40 × $9.50 = $380 per week   gross earnings

Compensation by Hourly Wage: Overtime

When a company is engaged in interstate commerce where its products move from state to state, it is required by the Fair Labor Standards Act (FLSA) to pay its employees time and one-half for all hours worked over 40 hours. All hours over 40 hours are considered overtime.

naphtalina, 2010/iStockphoto.com

EXAMPLE

Tomoki Ryomoto worked 48 hours this week operating a press for ZIP Printing Company. Tomoki receives $16 per hour straight time. What does he earn for 8 hours of overtime? Determine Tomoki's gross earnings.

Four Step Problem Solving Plan

Clue	Action Plan	Solve
Tomoki worked 40 straight-time hours at a regular hourly rate of $16.	Multiply straight-time hours by hourly rate.	$40 \times \$16 = \$640$
Overtime is paid at time and one-half.	Multiply hourly rate by 1.5 to find time and one-half rate.	$\$16 \times 1.5 = \$24$
Tomoki worked 8 overtime hours.	Multiply time and one-half rate by overtime hours worked.	$\$24 \times 8 = \$192$
Gross earnings is the sum of straight-time and overtime earnings.	Add straight-time and overtime earnings to calculate gross earning.	$\$640 + \$192 = \$832$

Conclusion

Tomoki earned $192 for 8 hours of overtime. Tomoki had $832 gross earnings for the week.

Compensation by Hourly Wage: Double Time

Many companies offer additional compensation to employees who work on Sundays and holidays in the form of double time; that is, double the hourly wage.

EXAMPLE

Shawn Williams worked 52 hours in one week—8 hours each weekday, 8 hours overtime on Saturday, and 4 hours double time on Sunday, which was New Year's Day (a holiday). His hourly rate is $17.50. Compute Shawn's gross earnings.

STEPS

1. Multiply the straight-time hours by the hourly rate.

   Straight time: $40 \times \$17.50 = \$700$

2. Compute overtime by multiplying the number of overtime hours by the hourly rate and by 1.5.

   Overtime: $8 \times \$17.50 \times 1.5 = \$210$

3. Compute double time by multiplying the number of hours by the hourly rate and by 2.

   Double time: $4 \times \$17.50 \times 2 = \$140$

4. Determine total earnings (gross earnings) by adding straight-time, overtime, and double-time amounts.

   $\$700 + \$210 + \$140 = \$1,050$ total earnings

Calculating payroll is one of the many accounting functions Excel has made simple to do. Usually, companies create a **template file** (a file that has the design, layout, and formulas that can be used over and over) with each employee's name, Social Security number, hourly wage, regular hours, and any other information needed to calculate net pay. A template is especially useful if you plan to use a similar worksheet over and over, such as a payroll register.

Calculating Straight Time, Overtime, and Double Time in Excel

You will now use Excel to calculate the earnings for Juan Oliver, Tomoki Ryomoto, and Shawn Williams.

STEPS

Retrieve the file *ch05pr01.xlsx*.

1. Enter a formula in Cell D6 to calculate Juan Oliver's Regular Earnings—40 hours × $9.50 per hour.

2. Enter a formula in Cell F6 to calculate Juan Oliver's Overtime Earnings—Overtime Hours × Pay Rate × 1.5.

3. Enter a formula in Cell H6 to calculate Juan Oliver's Double Time Earnings—Double Time Hours × Pay Rate × 2.

4. Enter a formula in Cell I6 to calculate Juan Oliver's Gross Earnings—Regular Earnings + Overtime Earnings + Double Time Earnings.

5. Enter formulas to calculate the earnings for Ryomoto and Williams. Format all answers to Currency. Set Decimal places to 2. Set Currency symbol to None.

6. Total the four earnings columns. Format for Currency. Set Decimal places to 2. Set Currency symbol to $.

7. Save the file as *ch05pr01a.xlsx*.

TIPS

To create a template, follow the same basic steps you would to create a spreadsheet. The only difference is the way you save the file. From the Save As dialog box, select Excel Template in the Save as Type box.

TIPS

Some templates are available in Excel that provide solutions to common business problems. To choose a template, click New. Choose a sample template from the list on the left. You can download many other templates from Microsoft Office Online.

Name _____   Date _____

Directions   Solve the following problems. Write your answers in the blanks provided. Place commas and dollar signs in answers as needed. Round answers to the nearest cent unless otherwise noted.

A. **For each annual amount of pay, calculate what you would earn for the given pay period.**   OBJECTIVE **2**

1. $42,800   = _____ weekly

2. $36,300   = _____ monthly

3. $59,400   = _____ biweekly

4. $18,900   = _____ semimonthly

5. $29,700   = _____ monthly

6. $42,100   = _____ semimonthly

7. $19,500   = _____ weekly

8. $10,900   = _____ monthly

B. Calculate straight time.   OBJECTIVE **3**

9.   40 hours @ $12.50 per hour   = _____

10. 35 hours @ $7.75 per hour   = _____

11. 26 hours @ $11.30 per hour   = _____

12. 40 hours @ $18.00 per hour   = _____

C. Calculate overtime at time and one-half.   OBJECTIVE **3**

13. 17 hours @ $18.50 straight-time rate   = _____

14. 12 hours @ $17.10 straight-time rate   = _____

15. 10 hours @ $12.90 straight-time rate   = _____

16. 9 hours @ $10.50 straight-time rate   = _____

D. Calculate double time.   OBJECTIVE **3**

17. 6 hours @ $9.90 straight-time rate   = _____

18. 8 hours @ $8.75 straight-time rate   = _____

19. 10 hours @ $10.60 straight-time rate   = _____

20. 5 hours @ $16.60 straight-time rate   = _____

E. Calculate straight time plus overtime. Round all answers to the nearest cent. OBJECTIVE 3

Neal Sloan worked 40 hours straight time and 12 hours overtime at an hourly rate of $24.10. Compute the following:

21. Straight-time earnings   = _____

22. Overtime earnings   = _____

23. Gross earnings   = _____

Rosa Martinez worked 40 hours straight time and 15 hours overtime at an hourly rate of $9.10. Compute the following:

24. Straight-time earnings   = _____

25. Overtime earnings   = _____

26. Gross earnings   = _____

Lee Kashieta worked 40 hours straight time and 8 hours overtime at an hourly rate of $17.50. Compute the following:

27. Straight-time earnings   = _____

28. Overtime earnings   = _____

29. Gross earnings   = _____

Leticia Alvarez worked 40 hours straight time and 20 hours overtime at an hourly rate of $10.50. Of the 20 hours overtime, 8 hours were at double time. Compute the following:

30. Straight-time earnings   = _____

31. Overtime earnings   = _____

32. Gross earnings   = _____

Maria Olivas worked 40 hours straight time and 10 hours overtime at an hourly rate of $12.10. Compute the following:

33. Straight-time earnings   = _____

34. Overtime earnings   = _____

35. Gross earnings   = _____

F. Use Excel to complete an employee's earnings record. OBJECTIVE 4

36. Retrieve the file *ch05ex01.xlsx*. Follow the directions. Save the file as *ch05ex01a.xlsx*.

37. Retrieve the file *ch05ex02.xlsx*. Follow the directions. Save the file as *ch05ex02a.xlsx*.

OBJECTIVES

1. Identify terms used for various compensation methods.
2. Calculate compensation by salary.
3. Calculate compensation by salary plus commission.
4. Calculate compensation by piecework.
5. Use Excel to calculate various methods of compensation.

5.2 Gross Pay for Various Compensation Methods

OBJECTIVE 1 Identify terms used for various compensation methods.

Commission   Compensation in the form of a percentage of total sales.

Piecework   Compensation based on the number of pieces completed.

Piece Rate   The amount paid for each piece produced.

Returned Merchandise   Goods returned due to defects, errors, or other reasons.

Salaried   An employee who is paid an annual amount which is divided over a given number of pay periods. Salaried employees usually do not receive overtime pay.

OBJECTIVE 2 Calculate compensation by salary.

Compensation is salary, wages, pay, or benefits for the performance of a service. When an employee is salaried, pay is usually based on a yearly amount. Most salaried employees do not receive compensation for time worked over 40 hours.

EXAMPLE

Nadia Manez is an elementary school teacher working for the Lakemont Independent School District (LISD). Nadia signed a contract with LISD for an annual salary of $29,800, to be paid in 12 equal payments. What are Nadia's monthly gross earnings?

STEPS

To compute Nadia's monthly salary (gross earnings), divide the annual salary by 12 (months). Round the answer to the nearest dollar.

$29,800 ÷ 12 = $2,483   per month gross earnings, rounded

OBJECTIVE 3 Calculate compensation by salary plus commission.

Often, sales personnel receive compensation in the form of a salary plus a percentage of their total sales. This compensation is, a *commission*. Usually, the commission is paid for **net sales**, which is total sales less returned merchandise over a set quota. Follow these steps to determine this week's gross earnings for Gary Parsons.

Gary's salary is $500 per week. This week his total sales were $2,500, and $75 in merchandise was returned. His quota is set at $1,700. His commission is based on 6% of sales minus returned merchandise after he has met his quota. Calculate Gary's gross earnings for the week.

Four Step Problem Solving Plan

Clues	Action Plan	Solve
Gary's sales were $2,500, and returns were $75.	Subtract returns from total sales to determine net sales.	$2,500 − $75 = $2,425
His quota is $1,700.	Subtract quota from net sales.	$2,425 − $1,700 = $725
He is paid 6% commission for net sales over $1,700.	Multiply sales above quota by 6% to determine commission.	$725 × 0.06 = $43.50
Gross earnings is the sum of salary and commission.	Add weekly salary to sales commission.	$500 + $43.50 = $543.50

Conclusion

Gary's gross earnings were $543.50.

OBJECTIVE **4** Calculate compensation by piecework.

Compensation based on piecework (a wage earned based on the number of units or pieces produced) is common among manufacturing companies, especially in the garment industry. An employee is paid for the number of pieces completed during the pay period. Usually, a quota is set that each employee must meet, but compensation is calculated on total pieces completed. Another example is compensation paid on the number of orders a warehouse employee fills. To compute gross earnings, multiply the total pieces completed or lines of an order filled during the pay period by the amount per piece or line. Study this example.

EXAMPLE

Toby Jennings works for a wholesale drug warehouse. He is compensated based on the number of lines he fills from an order form. His job is to read each order and, for each line, go to the proper bin in the warehouse and pull the number of items ordered on that line. He is paid a piece rate of $0.04 for each line he fills. Toby filled 15,193 line items this pay period.

STEP

Multiply total lines completed by piece rate per line.

$$15{,}193 \times \$0.04 = \$607.72 \quad \text{gross earnings}$$

Most large companies use specialized software that has a payroll component, such as Peachtree First Accounting for payroll management. Smaller companies use less sophisticated software, such as Quicken to track and calculate payroll. Excel, however, provides payroll functions found in these software programs that meet many company's needs. The fact that Excel is one of Microsoft's products means it is easier to learn because of the similarity of the commands in all of Microsoft's products.

Use Excel to calculate the examples you just did.

STEPS

Retrieve the file *ch05pr02.xlsx*.

A. Calculate monthly salary. Nadia Manez, an elementary school teacher, earns $29,800 annually.

1. Create a formula in Cell C7 to compute Nadia's monthly salary by dividing her annual salary by 12.

2. Format for Currency. Set Decimal places to 0. Set Currency symbol to $.

B. Calculate salary plus commission. Gary Parsons earns a salary plus commission. His straight-time salary is $500 per week. This week his total sales were $2,500 and he had $75 in returned merchandise. His quota is set at $1,700. His commission is based on 6% of sales minus returned merchandise after he has met his quota.

1. Create a multimath formula in Cell F22 to calculate Gary's weekly earnings.

2. Subtract the Returned Merchandise and the Quota required from Total Sales to calculate actual sales. Then multiply his actual sales by his 6% Commission. Lastly, add his Salary to his Commission to determine his Weekly Earnings. Your formula should be =(B22–C22–D22)*E22+A22.

3. Format for Currency. Set Decimal places to 2. Set Currency symbol to $.

C. Calculate compensation based on piecework. Toby Jennings works for a wholesale drug warehouse. He is compensated based on the number of lines he fills from an order form. He is paid $0.04 for each line he fills. He filled 15,193 lines this pay period.

1. Create a formula in Cell C37 to calculate Toby's Gross Earnings. Multiply Lines Filled by Rate per Line.

2. Format for Currency. Set Decimal places to 2. Set Currency symbol to $.

3. Save the file as *ch05pr02a.xlsx*.

Name _____   Date _____

Directions   Solve the following problems. Write your answers in the blanks provided. Place commas and dollar signs in answers as needed. Round all answers to the nearest cent.

A. Calculate compensation by salary.   OBJECTIVE 2

1. Hillary Morgan is an associate professor of economics at Hillsboro State University. Hillary is paid an annual salary of $48,300. What is her monthly salary?   _____

2. Dr. Reed Walker teaches at Tyler Community College and receives an annual salary of $52,800. Dr. Walker prefers to have his salary paid over nine months. What is his monthly salary?   _____

B. Calculate salary plus commission.   OBJECTIVE 3

Gene Jordan receives a salary of $440 per week plus 18% commission on all net sales over $2,800. Gene's total sales last week were $5,500. Returned sales were $1,250. What were Gene's gross earnings for the week?

3. Gross earnings: _____

What would Gene's gross earnings have been if there were no returned sales?

4. Gross earnings: _____

Dimetria Farnsworth has been making $395 per week plus a 20% commission on all sales over $2,500. Dimetria received a $25 a week raise in her salary. Her commission rate and amount stayed the same. Her total sales this week were $3,800. She also had $430 in returned sales. What were Dimetria's gross earnings for the week?

5. Gross earnings: _____

Delbert Easterling agreed to work on straight commission earning 10% of his total sales. He had been making a salary of $295 per week plus a 10% commission on all sales over $3,500. Delbert's total sales for this week were $6,700. What were Delbert's gross earnings this week under the new arrangement of 10% of all sales?

6. Gross earnings: _____

What would Delbert have earned if he had not changed to a straight commission of 10%?

7. Gross earnings: _____

Johnny Haas receives a salary of $450 per week plus a 7% commission on all sales over $1,500. Johnny's total sales last week were $2,159. He had $471 in returned sales. What were his gross earnings for the week?

8. Gross earnings: _____

C. Calculate compensation by piecework. OBJECTIVE 4

Retha Davidson works in a custom assembly plant. On one project, she was paid $4.50 for each item she assembled, but earned a guaranteed minimum of $100 per day. During the 4-day project she assembled 24, 20, 25, and 21 items, respectively. What are her gross earnings for each day? What are her gross earnings for the total project?

9. Total number of items assembled: _____

10. Gross earnings for each day:

    _____

11. Gross earnings for the project: _____

Fruitgrowers, Inc. pays $4 per bushel of fruit picked. The five members of the Littleton family pick fruit for Fruitgrowers, Inc. Three of them can pick 1.5 bushels per hour, and two can pick 2.3 bushels per hour. How many bushels does the family pick in one 8-hour day? What are the gross earnings for one day for a member of the family who can pick 1.5 bushels per hour per day? What are the gross earnings for one day for a member who can pick 2.3 bushels per hour per day? What are the gross earnings for the entire family for a 5-day week if they met their average each day?

12. Total number of bushels the family can pick in one day: _____

13. Gross earnings for one day for one member that can pick 1.5 bushels per hour per day: _____

14. Gross earnings for one day for one member that can pick 2.3 bushels per hour per day: _____

15. Gross earnings for the entire family for the week: _____

Evan Jurrens writes test items for an online science educational software company. He gets paid $20 per chapter plus $0.75 per test item. For chapter 1, Evan wrote 32 test items. For chapter 2, he wrote 40 test items, and for chapter 3, he wrote 36 test items. What are Evan's gross earnings for each chapter? What are his gross earnings for the three-chapter unit?

16. Total number of chapters: _____

17. Total number of questions written: _____

18. Gross earnings for each chapter: _____

19. Gross earnings for the unit: _____

D. Use Excel to calculate compensation by salary, salary plus commission, and piecework. OBJECTIVE 5

20. Retrieve the file *ch05ex03.xlsx*. Follow the directions. Save the file as *ch05ex03a.xlsx*.

21. Retrieve the file *ch05ex04.xlsx*. Follow the directions. Save the file as *ch05ex04a.xlsx*.

5.3 Payroll Deductions

OBJECTIVES
1. Identify terms used for payroll deductions.
2. Calculate Social Security and Medicare withholding.
3. Find the federal income tax withholding using the wage bracket method.
4. Find the federal income tax withholding using the percentage method.
5. Find the state income tax withholding.
6. Find the amount paid to the Internal Revenue Service (IRS) each payroll tax period.
7. Use Excel to calculate Social Security, Medicare, federal income tax, and state income tax.

OBJECTIVE 1 Identify terms used for payroll deductions.

Earlier in this chapter, you learned how to compute gross earnings. The various deductions that are taken from your paycheck were not mentioned. You will now learn about these deductions. Some are required by federal law. Others may be deducted from your pay at your request.

To understand the procedure for computing your paycheck, you must know the terminology related to the various deductions, forms, and laws involved in payroll deductions. Here are some of the terms you will use.

Accumulated Earnings   The accumulation or collection of earnings each pay period for an employee.

Employee's Earnings Record   A record showing an employee's personal payroll information, yearly earnings, and deductions.

Employee's Withholding Allowance Certificate   This is *Form W-4*, which specifies the number of withholding allowances claimed by an employee for tax purposes.

Federal Income Tax (FIT)   Under federal law, the Internal Revenue Service (IRS) requires employers to withhold federal income taxes from employees' wages and to submit the withheld taxes to the IRS. Employers must also keep records of the names and addresses of people employed, their exemptions, earnings, and withholdings, and the amounts and dates of payments. Employers must submit reports to the IRS on a quarterly (every three months) basis (*Form 941 Employer's Quarterly Federal Tax Return*) and to employees on an annual (yearly) basis (*Form W-2 Wage and Tax Statement*). With few exceptions, employers must meet these requirements if they employ one or more people.

Federal Insurance Contributions Act (FICA)   This law, originally passed in 1935, provides for retirement income after an employee reaches a minimum age of 62, disability benefits for any employee who becomes disabled (and for his or her dependents), and a health insurance program after an employee reaches the age of 65. The funds (taxes) to support these programs are provided by workers through deductions withheld from their paychecks, with equal amounts also paid by employers. These taxes are shown on your payroll stub as **Social Security** and **Medicare**. In the examples and problems in this book, the tax rate for Social Security is 6.2% on the first $106,800 earned (as of 2010) and 1.45% for Medicare on all earnings, for a combined FICA tax rate of 7.65%. Social Security and Medicare taxes are calculated on gross earnings.

Net Pay   The total amount of an employee's pay after deductions; that is, gross pay minus deductions.

Payroll Register   A summary of payroll information for a particular pay period.

Percentage Method   A method to calculate federal income tax withholding using tables in publication *Circular E, Employer's Tax Guide* (Publication 15).

Pre-Tax Deductions   Some deductions are made from gross earnings before calculating *taxable earnings*. These include (but are not limited to) medical, dental, and vision insurance premiums; flexible spending account (FSA) contributions; 401(k) and 403(b) retirement plan contributions; and some prepaid parking fees.

State and Local Income Tax Withholding   The amount withheld from earnings for taxes imposed by some states and local governments on gross earnings.

Taxable Earnings   The tax base on which the income tax withholding is calculated.

Wage Bracket Method   A method to look up federal income tax withholding using tables provided in publication *Circular E, Employer's Tax Guide*.

OBJECTIVE 2 Calculate Social Security and Medicare withholding.

The federal government has established by law the percentage of total earnings that will be withheld from your paycheck for FICA taxes. The Social Security wage base as of January 2010 is $106,800. The maximum Social Security an employee would pay in 2010 is $6,622 ($106,800 × 6.2%). Medicare has no wage base (all wages are subject to the 1.45% tax). Employers must match the amount of FICA tax (Social Security and Medicare) deducted from each employee's wages.

The 2010 FICA rates are used in this chapter. To compute the amount of Social Security and Medicare to be withheld from an employee's gross earnings per pay period, use the following procedure.

> **TIPS**
>
> *Social Security and Medicare are often referred to collectively as FICA (Federal Insurance Contributions Act).*

> **TIPS**
>
> *When the maximum earnings are reached, no additional Social Security is withheld that year.*

STEPS

1. For Social Security tax, multiply gross earnings per pay period times 6.2% on the first $106,800 earned. Carry answers to 4 decimal places. Then round to 2 places. If you use 2 or 3 places, your answer can be off by a penny.

2. For Medicare tax, multiply gross earnings per pay period times 1.45%. Carry answers to 4 decimal places. Then round to 2 places. If you use 2 or 3 places, your answer can be off by a penny.

3. Social Security tax plus Medicare tax equals total FICA withheld.

OBJECTIVE 3 Find the federal income tax withholding using the wage bracket method.

The amount of federal income tax withheld is based on a person's total gross earnings, marital status, and number of allowances claimed. Each employee must complete *Form W-4*, which states the number of allowances claimed.

Employers are required to have on file an Employee's Withholding Allowance Certificate (Form W-4) for each employee. Employees are encouraged to file an updated Form W-4, especially if they owed taxes or received a large refund when filing their federal income tax return for the prior year. Form W-4, includes a worksheet designed to help employees calculate the number of withholding allowances they could claim. An employee may also use the Withholding Calculator on the IRS website at www.irs.gov/individuals for help in determining how many withholding allowances to claim on Form W-4.

Taxpayers may be subject to a penalty if they have not met minimum withholding requirements. Taxpayers must have had enough tax withheld to equal at least 90% of their tax for the current year, or 100% of the amount of their prior year income tax (whichever is smaller), or they must owe less than $1,000 in tax for the current year. Thus, computing the correct number of withholding allowances is essential to ensure that enough is withheld to meet the 90% required by law by year end.

Study the worksheet and Form W-4 in Figure 5-1. The employee provides his or her name, address, Social Security number, marital status, and number of allowances claimed. An employee may have additional money withheld, especially if he or she owed additional taxes for the prior year.

Figure 5-1

Worksheet and Form W-4

Personal Allowances Worksheet (Keep for your records.)

A Enter "1" for **yourself** if no one else can claim you as a dependent . . . . **A** __1__

B Enter "1" if: { • You are single and have only one job; or
• You are married, have only one job, and your spouse does not work; or
• Your wages from a second job or your spouse's wages (or the total of both) are $1,500 or less. } . . **B** _____

C Enter "1" for your **spouse**. But, you may choose to enter "-0-" if you are married and have either a working spouse or more than one job. (Entering "-0-" may help you avoid having too little tax withheld.) . . . . . . **C** _____

D Enter number of **dependents** (other than your spouse or yourself) you will claim on your tax return . . . . **D** _____

E Enter "1" if you will file as **head of household** on your tax return (see conditions under **Head of household** above) . **E** _____

F Enter "1" if you have at least $1,800 of **child or dependent care expenses** for which you plan to claim a credit . . **F** _____
(**Note.** Do **not** include child support payments. See Pub. 503, Child and Dependent Care Expenses, for details.)

G **Child Tax Credit** (including additional child tax credit). See Pub. 972, Child Tax Credit, for more information.
• If your total income will be less than $61,000 ($90,000 if married), enter "2" for each eligible child; then **less** "1" if you have three or more eligible children.
• If your total income will be between $61,000 and $84,000 ($90,000 and $119,000 if married), enter "1" for each eligible child plus "1" **additional** if you have six or more eligible children. . . . . **G** _____

H Add lines A through G and enter total here. (**Note.** This may be different from the number of exemptions you claim on your tax return.) ▶ **H** __1__

| For accuracy, complete all worksheets that apply. | { | • If you plan to **itemize or claim adjustments to income** and want to reduce your withholding, see the **Deductions and Adjustments Worksheet** on page 2.
• If you have **more than one job** or are **married and you and your spouse both work** and the combined earnings from all jobs exceed $18,000 ($32,000 if married), see the **Two-Earners/Multiple Jobs Worksheet** on page 2 to avoid having too little tax withheld.
• If **neither** of the above situations applies, **stop here** and enter the number from line H on line 5 of Form W-4 below. |

------- Cut here and give Form W-4 to your employer. Keep the top part for your records. -------

Form **W-4**
Department of the Treasury
Internal Revenue Service

Employee's Withholding Allowance Certificate

▶ Whether you are entitled to claim a certain number of allowances or exemption from withholding is subject to review by the IRS. Your employer may be required to send a copy of this form to the IRS.

OMB No. 1545-0074

20**10**

| 1 Type or print your first name and middle initial. **Courtney** | Last name **Langford** | 2 Your social security number **900 16 9123** |

| Home address (number and street or rural route) **16 Jasmine Lane** | 3 ☐ Single ☒ Married ☐ Married, but withhold at higher Single rate.
Note. If married, but legally separated, or spouse is a nonresident alien, check the "Single" box. |

| City or town, state, and ZIP code **Texarkana, TX 75503-6603** | 4 If your last name differs from that shown on your social security card, check here. You must call 1-800-772-1213 for a replacement card. ▶ ☐ |

5 Total number of allowances you are claiming (from line **H** above **or** from the applicable worksheet on page 2)   **5** | __1__

6 Additional amount, if any, you want withheld from each paycheck . . . . **6** $

7 I claim exemption from withholding for 2010, and I certify that I meet **both** of the following conditions for exemption.
• Last year I had a right to a refund of **all** federal income tax withheld because I had **no tax liability and**
• This year I expect a refund of **all** federal income tax withheld because I expect to have **no tax liability.**
If you meet both conditions, write "Exempt" here . . . . ▶ **7**

Under penalties of perjury, I declare that I have examined this certificate and to the best of my knowledge and belief, it is true, correct, and complete.

Employee's signature
(Form is not valid unless you sign it.) ▶ *Courtney Langford*   Date ▶ 1/5/10

| 8 Employer's name and address (Employer: Complete lines 8 and 10 only if sending to the IRS.) | 9 Office code (optional) | 10 Employer identification number (EIN) |

For Privacy Act and Paperwork Reduction Act Notice, see page 2.   Cat. No. 10220Q   Form **W-4** (2010)

Figure 5-2

Withholding Tax Table • Wage Bracket Method

SINGLE Persons— WEEKLY Payroll Period
(For Wages Paid Through December 2010)

And the wages are–		And the number of withholding allowances claimed is										
At least	But less than	0	1	2	3	4	5	6	7	8	9	10
		The amount of income tax to be withheld is										
$0	$120	$0	$0	$0	$0	$0	$0	$0	$0	$0	$0	$0
120	125	1	0	0	0	0	0	0	0	0	0	0
125	130	1	0	0	0	0	0	0	0	0	0	0
130	135	2	0	0	0	0	0	0	0	0	0	0
135	140	2	0	0	0	0	0	0	0	0	0	0
140	145	3	0	0	0	0	0	0	0	0	0	0
145	150	3	0	0	0	0	0	0	0	0	0	0
150	155	4	0	0	0	0	0	0	0	0	0	0
155	160	4	0	0	0	0	0	0	0	0	0	0
160	165	5	0	0	0	0	0	0	0	0	0	0
165	170	5	0	0	0	0	0	0	0	0	0	0
170	175	6	0	0	0	0	0	0	0	0	0	0
175	180	6	0	0	0	0	0	0	0	0	0	0
180	185	7	0	0	0	0	0	0	0	0	0	0
185	190	7	0	0	0	0	0	0	0	0	0	0
190	195	8	1	0	0	0	0	0	0	0	0	0
195	200	8	1	0	0	0	0	0	0	0	0	0
200	210	9	2	0	0	0	0	0	0	0	0	0
210	220	11	3	0	0	0	0	0	0	0	0	0
220	230	12	4	0	0	0	0	0	0	0	0	0
230	240	14	5	0	0	0	0	0	0	0	0	0
240	250	15	6	0	0	0	0	0	0	0	0	0
250	260	17	7	0	0	0	0	0	0	0	0	0
260	270	18	8	1	0	0	0	0	0	0	0	0
270	280	20	9	2	0	0	0	0	0	0	0	0
280	290	21	11	3	0	0	0	0	0	0	0	0
290	300	23	12	4	0	0	0	0	0	0	0	0
300	310	24	14	5	0	0	0	0	0	0	0	0
310	320	26	15	6	0	0	0	0	0	0	0	0
320	330	27	17	7	0	0	0	0	0	0	0	0
330	340	29	18	8	1	0	0	0	0	0	0	0
340	350	30	20	9	2	0	0	0	0	0	0	0
350	360	32	21	11	3	0	0	0	0	0	0	0
360	370	33	23	12	4	0	0	0	0	0	0	0
370	380	35	24	14	5	0	0	0	0	0	0	0
380	390	36	26	15	6	0	0	0	0	0	0	0
390	400	38	27	17	7	0	0	0	0	0	0	0
400	410	39	29	18	8	1	0	0	0	0	0	0
410	420	41	30	20	9	2	0	0	0	0	0	0
420	430	42	32	21	11	3	0	0	0	0	0	0
430	440	44	33	23	12	4	0	0	0	0	0	0
440	450	45	35	24	14	5	0	0	0	0	0	0
450	460	47	36	26	15	6	0	0	0	0	0	0
460	470	48	38	27	17	7	0	0	0	0	0	0
470	480	50	39	29	18	8	1	0	0	0	0	0
480	490	51	41	30	20	9	2	0	0	0	0	0
490	500	53	42	32	21	10	3	0	0	0	0	0
500	510	54	44	33	23	12	4	0	0	0	0	0
510	520	56	45	35	24	13	5	0	0	0	0	0
520	530	57	47	36	26	15	6	0	0	0	0	0
530	540	59	48	38	27	16	7	0	0	0	0	0
540	550	60	50	39	29	18	8	1	0	0	0	0
550	560	62	51	41	30	19	9	2	0	0	0	0
560	570	63	53	42	32	21	10	3	0	0	0	0
570	580	65	54	44	33	22	12	4	0	0	0	0
580	590	66	56	45	35	24	13	5	0	0	0	0
590	600	68	57	47	36	25	15	6	0	0	0	0
600	610	69	59	48	38	27	16	7	0	0	0	0
610	620	71	60	50	39	28	18	8	1	0	0	0
620	630	72	62	51	41	30	19	9	2	0	0	0
630	640	74	63	53	42	31	21	10	3	0	0	0
640	650	75	65	54	44	33	22	12	4	0	0	0
650	660	77	66	56	45	34	24	13	5	0	0	0
660	670	78	68	57	47	36	25	15	6	0	0	0
670	680	80	69	59	48	37	27	16	7	0	0	0
680	690	81	71	60	50	39	28	18	8	1	0	0
690	700	83	72	62	51	40	30	19	9	2	0	0
700	710	85	74	63	53	42	31	21	10	3	0	0
710	720	88	75	65	54	43	33	22	12	4	0	0
720	730	90	77	66	56	45	34	24	13	5	0	0
730	740	93	78	68	57	46	36	25	15	6	0	0
740	750	95	80	69	59	48	37	27	16	7	0	0
750	760	98	81	71	60	49	39	28	18	8	1	0
760	770	100	83	72	62	51	40	30	19	9	2	0
770	780	103	85	74	63	52	42	31	21	10	3	0
780	790	105	88	75	65	54	43	33	22	12	4	0
790	800	108	90	77	66	55	45	34	24	13	5	0
800	810	110	93	78	68	57	46	36	25	15	6	0
810	820	113	95	80	69	58	48	37	27	16	7	0
820	830	115	98	81	71	60	49	39	28	18	8	1
830	840	118	100	83	72	61	51	40	30	19	9	2
840	850	120	103	85	74	63	52	42	31	21	10	3
850	860	123	105	88	75	64	54	43	33	22	12	4
860	870	125	108	90	77	66	55	45	34	24	13	5
870	880	128	110	93	78	67	57	46	36	25	15	6

Figure 5-2
Withholding Tax Table • Wage Bracket Method

MARRIED Persons— WEEKLY Payroll Period
(For Wages Paid Through December 2010)

And the wages are—		And the number of withholding allowances claimed is										
At least	But less than	0	1	2	3	4	5	6	7	8	9	10
		The amount of income tax to be withheld is—										
$0	$270	$0	$0	$0	$0	$0	$0	$0	$0	$0	$0	$0
270	280	1	0	0	0	0	0	0	0	0	0	0
280	290	2	0	0	0	0	0	0	0	0	0	0
290	300	3	0	0	0	0	0	0	0	0	0	0
300	310	4	0	0	0	0	0	0	0	0	0	0
310	320	5	0	0	0	0	0	0	0	0	0	0
320	330	6	0	0	0	0	0	0	0	0	0	0
330	340	7	0	0	0	0	0	0	0	0	0	0
340	350	8	1	0	0	0	0	0	0	0	0	0
350	360	9	2	0	0	0	0	0	0	0	0	0
360	370	10	3	0	0	0	0	0	0	0	0	0
370	380	11	4	0	0	0	0	0	0	0	0	0
380	390	12	5	0	0	0	0	0	0	0	0	0
390	400	13	6	0	0	0	0	0	0	0	0	0
400	410	14	7	0	0	0	0	0	0	0	0	0
410	420	15	8	1	0	0	0	0	0	0	0	0
420	430	16	9	2	0	0	0	0	0	0	0	0
430	440	17	10	3	0	0	0	0	0	0	0	0
440	450	18	11	4	0	0	0	0	0	0	0	0
450	460	19	12	5	0	0	0	0	0	0	0	0
460	470	20	13	6	0	0	0	0	0	0	0	0
470	480	21	14	7	0	0	0	0	0	0	0	0
480	490	23	15	8	1	0	0	0	0	0	0	0
490	500	24	16	9	2	0	0	0	0	0	0	0
500	510	26	17	10	3	0	0	0	0	0	0	0
510	520	27	18	11	4	0	0	0	0	0	0	0
520	530	29	19	12	5	0	0	0	0	0	0	0
530	540	30	20	13	6	0	0	0	0	0	0	0
540	550	32	21	14	7	0	0	0	0	0	0	0
550	560	33	23	15	8	1	0	0	0	0	0	0
560	570	35	24	16	9	2	0	0	0	0	0	0
570	580	36	26	17	10	3	0	0	0	0	0	0
580	590	38	27	18	11	4	0	0	0	0	0	0
590	600	39	29	19	12	5	0	0	0	0	0	0
600	610	41	30	20	13	6	0	0	0	0	0	0
610	620	42	32	21	14	7	0	0	0	0	0	0
620	630	44	33	23	15	8	1	0	0	0	0	0
630	640	45	35	24	16	9	2	0	0	0	0	0
640	650	47	36	26	17	10	3	0	0	0	0	0
650	660	48	38	27	18	11	4	0	0	0	0	0
660	670	50	39	29	19	12	5	0	0	0	0	0
670	680	51	41	30	20	13	6	0	0	0	0	0
680	690	53	42	32	21	14	7	0	0	0	0	0
690	700	54	44	33	23	15	8	1	0	0	0	0
700	710	56	45	35	24	16	9	2	0	0	0	0
710	720	57	47	36	26	17	10	3	0	0	0	0
720	730	59	48	38	27	18	11	4	0	0	0	0
730	740	60	50	39	29	19	12	5	0	0	0	0
740	750	62	51	41	30	20	13	6	0	0	0	0
750	760	63	53	42	32	21	14	7	0	0	0	0
760	770	65	54	44	33	23	15	8	1	0	0	0
770	780	66	56	45	35	24	16	9	2	0	0	0
780	790	68	57	47	36	26	17	10	3	0	0	0
790	800	69	59	48	38	27	18	11	4	0	0	0
800	810	71	60	50	39	29	19	12	5	0	0	0
810	820	72	62	51	41	30	20	13	6	0	0	0
820	830	74	63	53	42	32	21	14	7	0	0	0
830	840	75	65	54	44	33	23	15	8	1	0	0
840	850	77	66	56	45	35	24	16	9	2	0	0
850	860	78	68	57	47	36	26	17	10	3	0	0
860	870	80	69	59	48	38	27	18	11	4	0	0
870	880	81	71	60	50	39	29	19	12	5	0	0
880	890	83	72	62	51	41	30	20	13	6	0	0
890	900	84	74	63	53	42	32	21	14	7	0	0
900	910	86	75	65	54	44	33	23	15	8	1	0
910	920	87	77	66	56	45	35	24	16	9	2	0
920	930	89	78	68	57	47	36	26	17	10	3	0
930	940	90	80	69	59	48	38	27	18	11	4	0
940	950	92	81	71	60	50	39	29	19	12	5	0
950	960	93	83	72	62	51	41	30	20	13	6	0
960	970	95	84	74	63	53	42	32	21	14	7	0
970	980	96	86	75	65	54	44	33	23	15	8	1
980	990	98	87	77	66	56	45	35	24	16	9	2
990	1000	99	89	78	68	57	47	36	26	17	10	3
1000	1010	101	90	80	69	59	48	38	27	18	11	4
1010	1020	102	92	81	71	60	50	39	29	19	12	5
1020	1030	104	93	83	72	62	51	41	30	20	13	6
1030	1040	105	95	84	74	63	53	42	32	21	14	7
1040	1050	107	96	86	75	65	54	44	33	23	15	8
1050	1060	108	98	87	77	66	56	45	35	24	16	9
1060	1070	110	99	89	78	68	57	47	36	26	17	10
1070	1080	111	101	90	80	69	59	48	38	27	18	11
1080	1090	113	102	92	81	71	60	50	39	29	19	12
1090	1100	114	104	93	83	72	62	51	41	30	20	13
1100	1110	116	105	95	84	74	63	53	42	32	21	14

Once the payroll clerk knows an employee's gross earnings, number of withholding allowances, and marital status, he or she can determine the amount of federal income tax to be withheld. To determine the tax to be withheld from an employee's gross earnings, most payroll clerks use the wage and bracket withholding tables contained in the IRS publication *Circular E, Employer's Tax Guide*. These tables are subdivided on the basis of marital status and cover payroll periods for monthly, semimonthly, biweekly, weekly, and daily or miscellaneous payroll. The figures used in this text are taken from the *Circular E, Employer's Tax guide: For use in 2010*. Note that no computations are necessary to determine the amount of federal income tax to withhold using this method. You simply look up the amount on the proper tax table.

EXAMPLE

Assume Paula Russell's gross earnings are $534.25 per week, she is married and has claimed one withholding allowance. Follow these steps to use the federal income tax table shown in Figure 5-2 on page 175.

STEPS

1. Beginning at the upper left column entitled "At least," move down that column until you find the amount $530, then read across and note the number $540 in the "But less than" column. This entry says that Paula Russell made "at least" $530 "but less than" $540. Her gross earnings of $534.25 fall between these two numbers.

2. Continue moving to the right across the same line until you find the number of withholding allowances claimed, 1. The amount of money shown in this column headed by the number 1 is the amount of federal income tax to be withheld from gross earnings: $20.

OBJECTIVE 4 Find the federal income tax withholding using the percentage method.

Many companies prefer to use the percentage method to calculate federal withholding tax. The percentage method requires fewer tables than those needed with the wage bracket method, and it is more easily adapted to computerized payroll systems. Notice in Figure 5-3, the withholding table for allowances, and in Figure 5-4, the withholding table for the weekly payroll period.

STEPS

1. Using the Percentage Method Table in Figure 5-3, choose the employee's payroll period. Multiply the amount for one withholding allowance for the payroll period by the number of allowances the employee claims.

2. Subtract that amount from the employee's gross wages.

3. Determine the amount to withhold from the appropriate table. (See Table for Percentage Method of Withholding in Figure 5-4.)

TIPS

The amount of withholding tax found using the wage bracket method may vary somewhat from the percentage method. Any difference is adjusted when the income tax return is filed.

CHAPTER 5 PAYROLL

Calculate the amount of income tax to be withheld for Frank Rodriguez. Frank is married, claims four withholding allowances, and has weekly gross earnings of $1,230.

Four Step Problem Solving Plan

Clues	Action Plan	Solve
Frank is paid weekly.	Locate the withholding allowance for one person from Figure 5-3.	$70.19
Frank claims 4 withholding allowances.	Multiply the single withholding allowance by the number of allowances.	$70.19 × 4 = $280.76
Frank's gross earnings are $1,230.	Subtract the amount allowed for withholding allowances from Frank's gross earnings.	$1,230 − $280.76 = $949.24
Frank is married.	Find the MARRIED person section in Figure 5-4. Notice that $949.24 is over $471, but not over $1,457.	$20.70 + 15% over $471
	Subtract $471 from Frank's net gross earnings of $949.24.	$949.24 − $471 = $478.24
	Multiply 15% times the amount over $471. Round to the nearest cent.	$478.24 × 15% = $71.74
	Add the base withholding, $20.70, to the 15%.	$20.70 + $71.74 = $92.44

Conclusion

Frank will have $92.44 deducted weekly from his gross earnings for federal income tax.

Percentage Method— 2010 Amount for One Withholding Allowance

Payroll Period	One Withholding Allowance
Weekly	$70.19
Biweekly	140.38
Semimonthly	152.08
Monthly	304.17
Quarterly	912.50
Semiannually	1,825.00
Annually	3,650.00
Daily or miscellaneous (each day of the payroll period)	14.04

Figure 5-3

Withholding Table for Allowances (Percentage Method)

Figure 5-4
Percentage Method Withholding Tables

Tables for Percentage Method of Withholding
(For Wages Paid in 2010)

TABLE 1 — WEEKLY Payroll Period

(a) SINGLE person (including head of household)—

If the amount of wages (after subtracting withholding allowances) is: The amount of income tax to withhold is:

Not over $116 . . . .$0

Over —	But not over —		of excess over —
$116	— $200	. . .10%	— $116
$200	— $693	. . .$8.40 plus 15%	— $200
$693	— $1,302	. . .$82.35 plus 25%	— $693
$1,302	— $1,624	. . .$234.60 plus 27%	— $1,302
$1,624	— $1,687	. . .$321.54 plus 30%	— $1,624
$1,687	— $3,344	. . .$340.44 plus 28%	— $1,687
$3,344	— $7,225	. . .$804.40 plus 33%	— $3,344
$7,225	. . . .	.$2,085.13 plus 35%	— $7,225

(b) MARRIED person—

If the amount of wages (after subtracting withholding allowances) is: The amount of income tax to withhold is:

Not over $264 . . . .$0

Over —	But not over —		of excess over—
$264	— $471	. . .10%	— $264
$471	— $1,457	. . .$20.70 plus 15%	— $471
$1,457	— $1,809	. . .$168.60 plus 25%	— $1,457
$1,809	— $2,386	. . .$256.60 plus 27%	— $1,809
$2,386	— $2,789	. . .$412.39 plus 25%	— $2,386
$2,789	— $4,173	. . .$513.14 plus 28%	— $2,789
$4,173	— $7,335	. . .$900.66 plus 33%	— $4,173
$7,335	. . . .	.$1,944.12 plus 35%	— $7,335

OBJECTIVE 5 Find the state income tax withholding.

State income tax is collected by withholding. Seven states do not have state income tax—Alaska, Florida, Nevada, South Dakota, Texas, Washington, and Wyoming. State income tax is paid in addition to federal income tax.

EXAMPLE

Terri Adams has gross earnings for the month of $3,100. If her state has a 4.5% income tax rate, find the state withholding tax.

STEP

To calculate state withholding tax, multiply the amount of gross earnings by the state withholding tax rate.

$$\$3,100 \times 0.045 = \$139.50$$

OBJECTIVE 6 Find the amount paid to the Internal Revenue Service (IRS) each payroll tax period.

Each payroll period employers send to the IRS the amount of employees' Social Security withheld, a matching amount, and the amount of federal income tax withheld from employees' gross pay. As an example, if an employee paid $76.12 in Social Security and Medicare taxes, and $85.00 in federal income tax, the employer would send the IRS the following amount.

$ 76.12	employee Social Security and Medicare withheld
$ 76.12	employer matching Social Security and Medicare
+ $ 85.00	employee federal income tax withheld
$237.24	total sent to the IRS (money is actually deposited into the Federal Treasury)

CHAPTER 5 PAYROLL

OBJECTIVE **7** Use Excel to calculate Social Security, Medicare, federal income tax, and state income tax.

Excel can be used to calculate Social Security, Medicare, federal income tax, and state income tax. These deductions are all part of an employee's earnings record and a payroll register. Here you will create a partial payroll register—those columns related only to Social Security, Medicare, federal income tax, and state income tax. Study the partial payroll register in Figure 5-5.

Figure 5-5

Partial Payroll Register

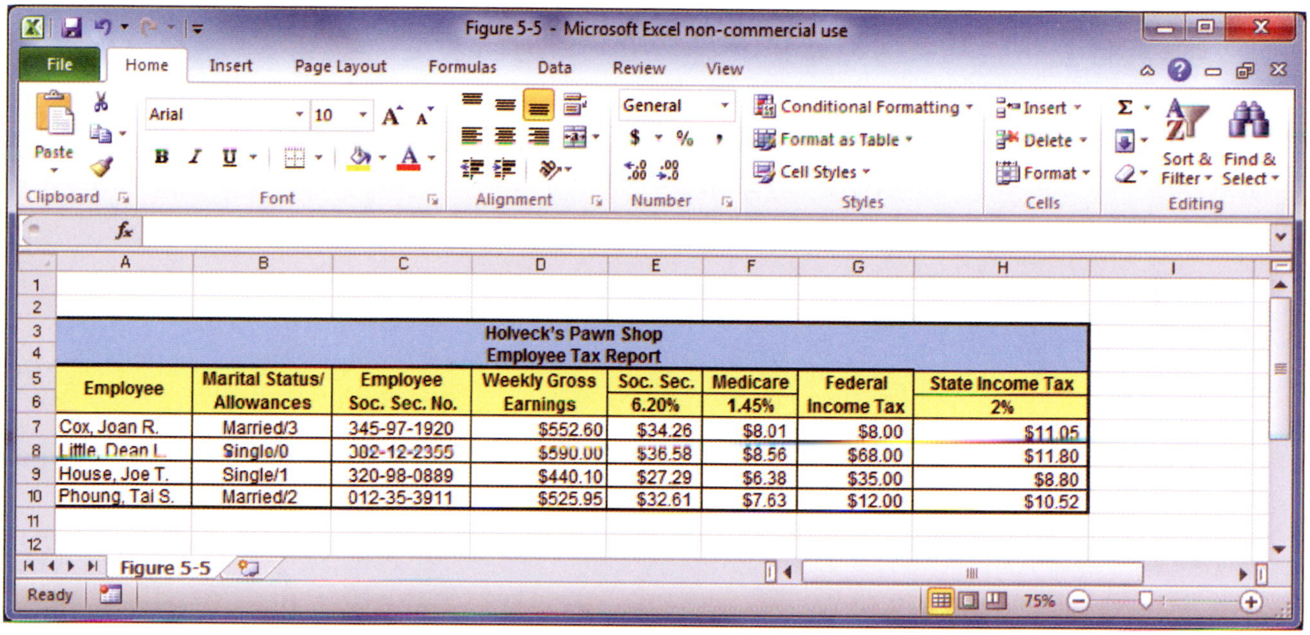

Employee	Marital Status/ Allowances	Employee Soc. Sec. No.	Weekly Gross Earnings	Soc. Sec. 6.20%	Medicare 1.45%	Federal Income Tax	State Income Tax 2%
		Holveck's Pawn Shop Employee Tax Report					
Cox, Joan R.	Married/3	345-97-1920	$552.60	$34.26	$8.01	$8.00	$11.05
Little, Dean L.	Single/0	302-12-2355	$590.00	$36.58	$8.56	$68.00	$11.80
House, Joe T.	Single/1	320-98-0889	$440.10	$27.29	$6.38	$35.00	$8.80
Phoung, Tai S.	Married/2	012-35-3911	$525.95	$32.61	$7.63	$12.00	$10.52

Absolute Cell Referencing

Recall that to keep the cell reference constant when a formula or function is copied, Excel uses an absolute cell reference. When a dollar sign precedes the letter and number of a cell address, such as $D$5, the reference is absolute.

STEPS

Retrieve the file *ch05pr03.xlsx*.

1. Enter the formula –D7*$E$6 in Cell E7 to calculate Social Security. Copy the formula to the remaining cells of Column E.

2. Enter formulas to calculate Medicare in Column F.

3. Use the (weekly) wage bracket method and enter Federal Income Tax withheld in Column G.

4. Enter formulas to calculate State Income Tax at 2% of gross earnings in Column H.

5. Format Columns E through H for Currency. Set Decimal places to 2. Set Currency symbol to $.

6. Save the file as *ch05pr03a.xlsx*.

Name _____ Date _____

Directions Solve the following problems. Write your answers in the blanks provided. Place commas and dollar signs in answers as needed. Round answers to the nearest cent.

A. Compute Social Security using 6.2% and Medicare using 1.45%. OBJECTIVE 2

Gross Earnings	Social Security	Medicare
$408.11	1. _____	2. _____
$516.10	3. _____	4. _____
$332.90	5. _____	6. _____
$708.15	7. _____	8. _____
$90.60	9. _____	10. _____
$256.55	11. _____	12. _____
$121.75	13. _____	14. _____
$880.90	15. _____	16. _____
$611.75	17. _____	18. _____
$397.20	19. _____	20. _____

B. Determine the amount of weekly federal income tax to be withheld using the wage bracket method. (Use the tax tables on pages 198–199.) OBJECTIVE 3

	Gross Earnings	Marital Status	Allowances	Amount
21.	$389.40	Single	2	_____
22.	$469.90	Single	3	_____
23.	$371.20	Married	4	_____
24.	$586.97	Married	3	_____
25.	$411.60	Single	1	_____
26.	$772.80	Married	4	_____
27.	$590.00	Single	0	_____
28.	$955.81	Married	2	_____
29.	$300.05	Single	0	_____

C. Determine the amount of weekly federal income tax to be withheld using the percentage method. (Use the tax tables on pages 201–202.) OBJECTIVE 4

	Gross Earnings	Allowances	Marital Status	Amount
30.	$610.00	4	Single	_____
31.	$825.18	0	Married	_____
32.	$322.40	1	Married	_____
33.	$760.95	0	Single	_____
34.	$469.21	2	Married	_____

D. Calculate the state income tax for the following employees using a 4.5% state income tax rate. OBJECTIVE 5

	Employee	Earnings This Pay Period	State Income Tax Withheld
35.	James Kwah	$1,450.25	_____
36.	Leroy Washington	$980.85	_____
37.	Janet Moore	$1,010.50	_____
38.	Teri Rodriguez	$1,225.80	_____
39.	Tai Kwan	$875.75	_____

E. Calculate the amount the employer must send to the IRS. OBJECTIVE 6

40. Employee's Federal Income Tax: $505.00
Employee's Social Security: $202.69
Employee's Medicare: $47.40 _____

41. Employee's Federal Income Tax: $1,212.00
Employee's Social Security: $486.46
Employee's Medicare: $113.77 _____

42. Employee's Federal Income Tax: $4,848.00
Employee's Social Security: $1,945.86
Employee's Medicare: $455.08 _____

F. Use Excel to calculate Social Security, Medicare, federal income tax, and state income tax. OBJECTIVE 7

43. Retrieve the file *ch05ex05.xlsx*. Follow the directions. Save the file as *ch05ex05a.xlsx*.

44. Retrieve the file *ch05ex06.xlsx*. Follow the directions. Save the file as *ch05ex06a.xlsx*.

OBJECTIVES

1. Create an employee's earnings record.
2. Create a payroll register.
3. Use Excel to create a payroll register.

5.4 Employee's Earnings Record and Payroll Register

OBJECTIVE 1 Create an employee's earnings record.

An employee may have additional deductions such as deductions for medical insurance (pre-tax), life insurance, union dues, savings bonds, and credit union savings or payments. The payroll clerk keeps an earnings record on file for each employee that summarizes all necessary information, including that required by the federal government. An example of a portion of a record for Courtney Langford is shown in Figure 5-6.

Figure 5-6
Employee's Earnings Record

Employee's Earnings Record

Name: Courtney Langford — Employee No.: 6 — Allowances: 1

Address: 16 Jasmine Lane — S.S. No.: 900-16-9123

Texarkana, TX 75503-6603 — Male: ___ Female: X

Married: X Single: ___ — Pay Rate: $15.00 — Per Hour: X

Date Employed: 1/2/-- — Per Day: ___

Date Terminated: ___ — Job Class.: Accounts Payable Clerk

Date	Reg. Hrs.	O.T. Hrs.	Wages per Hour	Earnings			Deductions				Total Deductions	Net Pay	Accumulated Gross Earnings
				Regular	Overtime	Gross	FICA Soc. Sec.	FICA Medicare	Federal Inc. Tax	Medical Ins.			
2/07/--	40	2	15.00	600.00	45.00	645.00	39.99	9.35	33.00	17.50	99.84	545.16	3,214.00
2/14/--	40	8	15.00	600.00	180.00	780.00	48.36	11.31	54.00	17.50	131.17	648.83	3,994.00

EXAMPLE

To complete an employee's earnings record for Courtney Langford for the week ending February 14, follow these steps. Courtney lives in Texas, where there is no state income tax. She pays $17.50 medical insurance weekly, which is deducted from her gross earnings before determining her federal income tax deduction using the Wage Bracket Method.

STEPS

1. Compute straight time: 40 × $15 = $600
2. Compute overtime: $15 × 1.5 = $22.50 × 8 = $180
3. Compute total earnings: $600 + $180 = $780

4. Compute Social Security: $780 × 6.2% = $48.36

5. Compute Medicare: $780 × 1.45% = $11.31

6. Determine taxable earnings, then find the federal income tax withholding using the table on page 175. Remember that medical insurance is a pre-tax deduction and should be deducted from gross earnings before computing federal income tax. Taxable earning: $780.00 − $17.50 = $762.50. Federal income tax withheld: $54.00

7. Add all deductions: $48.36 + $11.31 + $54.00 + $17.50 = $131.17

8. Compute net pay: $780 − $131.17 = $648.83

Accumulated Earnings Column

The accumulated earnings column, often labeled as YTD (year to date) earnings, of the employee's earnings record is a listing of gross wages the employee has earned to date. Each week the gross earnings amount is added to the previous gross earnings amount to show the current total earnings. The employee's Form W-2 is completed from this information and reported to the employee and the IRS at the end of the year. To compute accumulated earnings to date for the week ending February 14, add as follows:

$3,214.00	accumulated earnings as of 2/7
+ 780.00	this week's gross earnings, 2/14
$3,994.00	accumulated earnings to date

OBJECTIVE 2 Create a payroll register.

A payroll register (see Figure 5-7) is a summary record of the payroll information for a particular pay period. Study the payroll register on the next page and compare it to the employee's earnings record for Courtney Langford. Notice that Courtney's payroll information from the week ending 2/14 has been added to the payroll register. Notice that all computations completed in the payroll register were also completed in the employee's earnings record.

After the information is transferred to the payroll register, you must total each column in the register, checking to make sure:

1. Regular pay plus overtime pay equals gross earnings.
2. Gross earnings minus total deductions equal the total of the Net Pay column. Remember to deduct medical insurance premiums before determining the amount of federal income tax withheld.

This method of checking amounts is called **footing**. Your payroll register must balance. If it doesn't, check for errors in your calculations if done manually, or in formulas if done in a spreadsheet.

After the payroll register is complete and net pay is calculated, the payroll checks are printed. On the check stub, the employee will see all the information needed to understand how their wages are computed: their pay rate, their hours worked, a detailed listing of their deductions, and their year-to-date totals. See Figure 5-8.

TIPS

Remember, each pay period employers deduct Social Security, Medicare, and federal income tax from employees' gross earnings. Employers also must match the employees' Social Security and Medicare. To do this, employers make a federal deposit that is twice the amount of the employees' Social Security and twice the amount of the employees' Medicare, plus the amount withheld for the employees' federal income tax.

TIPS

When checking totals for Social Security and Medicare on the payroll register, you cannot verify the total of each column by multiplying total gross earnings by 6.2% or 1.45%. The amounts may not match due to rounding in the individual calculations. This is true for state income tax as well when it is shown. The IRS requires the employer to deposit the exact amount (to the penny) withheld from employees' gross earnings.

Figure 5-7 Payroll Register

					Earnings		Gross Earnings	Deductions				Total Deductions	Net Pay
Employee Name	Allow.	Status	Hours Worked	Pay Rate	Regular	Overtime 1.5		Fed. Inc. Tax	Social Security 6.2%	Medicare 1.45%	Medical Ins. Pre-tax		
Jones, J.	1	M	44	18.70	748.00	112.20	860.20	65.00	53.33	12.47	21.00	151.80	708.40
Hart, B.	3	S	40	16.60	664.00	0.00	664.00	44.00	41.17	9.63	21.00	115.80	548.20
Davis, L.	0	M	48	17.40	696.00	208.80	904.80	83.00	56.10	13.12	21.00	173.22	731.58
Ely, K.	2	M	42	18.60	744.00	55.80	799.80	45.00	49.59	11.60	21.00	127.19	672.61
Langford, C.	1	M	48	15.00	600.00	180.00	780.00	54.00	48.36	11.31	17.50	131.17	648.83
				Totals	3,452.00	556.80	4,008.80	291.00	248.55	58.13	101.50	699.18	3,309.62

Figure 5-8 Payroll Check

Jones Excavating, Inc.
12637 Industrial Parkway
Texarkana, TX 77057

Pay Date: 2/21/20-- **10473**
Period Beginning: 2/07/20--
Period Ending: 2/14/20--

Courtney Langford
16 Jasmine Lane
Texarkana, TX 75503-6603

Marital Status: Married
Allowances: 1

Employee Number: 6   Social Security Number: 900-16-9123

Earnings	Rate	Hours	This Period	YTD
Regular	15.00	40.00	600.00	3,472.00
Time and one-half		8.00	180.00	522.00
Double time				
Gross Earnings			**$780.00**	$3,994.00

Deductions				
Federal Income Tax			54.00	395.00
Social Security Tax			48.36	305.15
Medicare Tax			11.31	67.86
Medical Insurance			17.50*	105.00
401K Contribution			0.00	0.00
Total Deductions			**$131.17**	$873.01

| Net Pay | | | $648.83 | $3,120.99 |

*Excluded from federal taxable earnings

- -

Jones Excavating, Inc.   **10473**
12637 Industrial Parkway   15-88
Texarkana, TX 77057   1110
(903) 555-6400   DATE   2/21/20--

PAY TO THE
ORDER OF   Courtney Langford $648.83

Six hundred forty-eight and 83/100   **Dollars**

First Texarkana Bank
100 Main Street
Texarkana, TX 75501-0045

Constance Patterson

|:111000885|:02"59736114/10473

OBJECTIVE 3 Use Excel to create a payroll register.

Some payroll registers contain more information than others, but basically they all summarize payroll information for a pay period. Study the payroll register shown in Figure 5-9.

Figure 5-9

Payroll Register

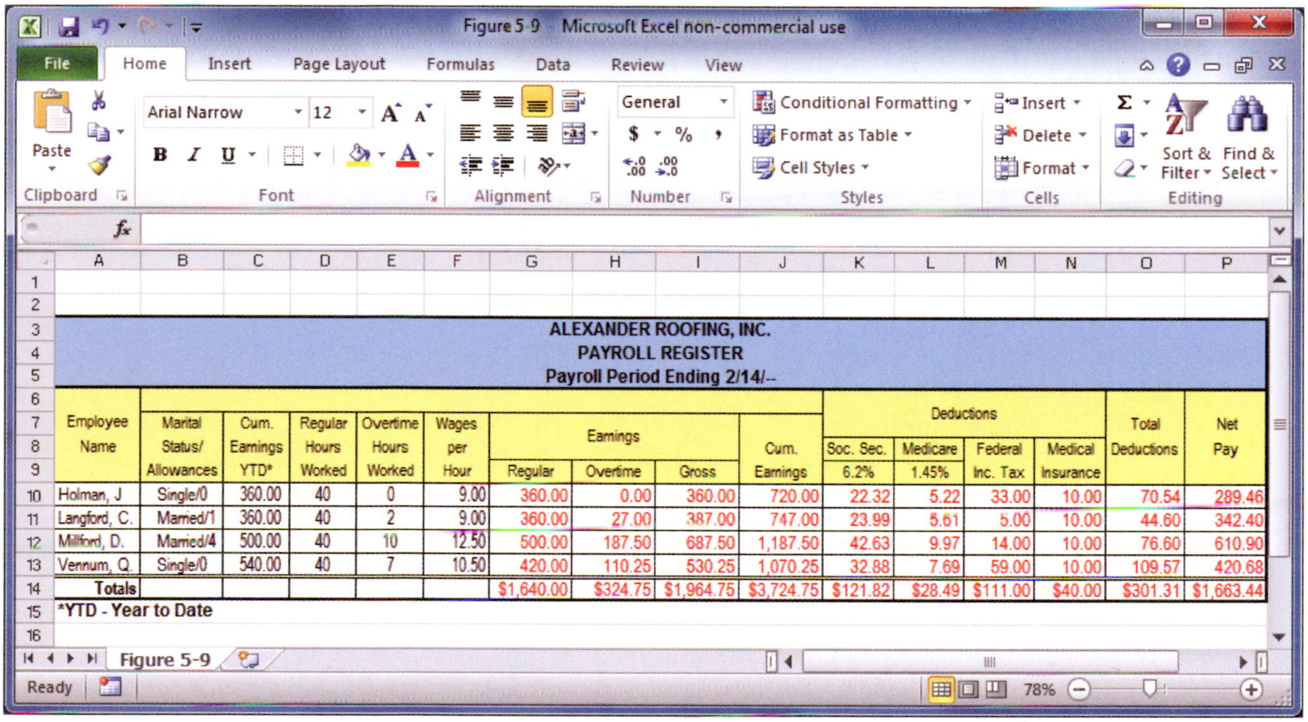

ALEXANDER ROOFING, INC.
PAYROLL REGISTER
Payroll Period Ending 2/14/--

Employee Name	Marital Status/ Allowances	Cum. Earnings YTD*	Regular Hours Worked	Overtime Hours Worked	Wages per Hour	Earnings: Regular	Earnings: Overtime	Earnings: Gross	Cum. Earnings	Deductions: Soc. Sec. 6.2%	Deductions: Medicare 1.45%	Deductions: Federal Inc. Tax	Deductions: Medical Insurance	Total Deductions	Net Pay
Holman, J	Single/0	360.00	40	0	9.00	360.00	0.00	360.00	720.00	22.32	5.22	33.00	10.00	70.54	289.46
Langford, C.	Married/1	360.00	40	2	9.00	360.00	27.00	387.00	747.00	23.99	5.61	5.00	10.00	44.60	342.40
Millford, D.	Married/4	500.00	40	10	12.50	500.00	187.50	687.50	1,187.50	42.63	9.97	14.00	10.00	76.60	610.90
Vennum, Q.	Single/0	540.00	40	7	10.50	420.00	110.25	530.25	1,070.25	32.88	7.69	59.00	10.00	109.57	420.68
Totals						$1,640.00	$324.75	$1,964.75	$3,724.75	$121.82	$28.49	$111.00	$40.00	$301.31	$1,663.44

*YTD - Year to Date

ROUND Function

When working with currency, the totals may be a penny or so off when multiplications and divisions result in numbers with many decimal places. To avoid this problem, use the =ROUND function, which rounds a number to a specific number of digits. The format for the function is =ROUND(number, num_digits). For example, if Cell A5 contains 12.758 and you want to round that value to two decimal places, you enter =ROUND(A5,2). Then the number in Cell A5 is 12.76.

You may calculate the number before you round it. For example, in the worksheet above =ROUND((I10*$K$9),2)) is entered in Cell K10 to calculate Social Security rounded to 2 decimal places. Notice that parentheses are needed around the multiplication. Also an absolute cell reference is used for Cell K9 so 6.2% will always be used in the calculation.

TIPS

You can create a payroll template that contains information that is repeated each pay period, such as employee information and formulas.

PRACTICE

Retrieve the file *ch05pr04.xlsx*. Follow the directions. Save the file as *ch05pr04a.xlsx*.

Name _____ Date _____

Directions Complete the following problems. Write your answers in the blanks provided. Round answers to the nearest hundredth.

A. Complete a partial 5-week earnings record for Christina Morales. OBJECTIVES 2, 3

Compute the deductions, net pay, and accumulated gross earnings. Assume that Christina is married and that $40.50 (pre-tax) was withheld for medical insurance and $15 for union dues each week. Use the wage bracket method (Figure 5-2) to determine federal income tax.

	Gross Earnings	Allow.	Fed. Inc. Tax	Social Security	Medicare	Medical Insurance	Union Dues	Total Deductions	Net Pay	Accum. Gross Earnings
				6.2%	1.45%	Pre-tax				$4,296.11
1.	759.60	2								
2.	786.95	2								
3.	799.90	3								
4.	759.60	3								
5.	791.60	3								

B. Complete a partial 5-week employee earnings record for Joseph Craig. OBJECTIVES 2, 3

Compute the deductions, net pay, and accumulated gross earnings for each weekly pay period. Assume that Joseph is single and that $28.25 was withheld for medical insurance (pre-tax) and $20 for his United Way contribution. Use the wage bracket method to determine federal income tax.

	Gross Earnings	Allow.	Fed. Inc. Tax	Social Security	Medicare	Medical Insurance	United Way	Total Deductions	Net Pay	Accum. Gross Earnings
				6.2%	1.45%	Pre-tax				$1,558.90
6.	650.95	1								
7.	688.10	1								
8.	700.25	1								
9.	610.40	0								
10.	685.50	0								

C. Complete a payroll register. OBJECTIVES 2, 3

Complete the following payroll register for Thorndike Manufacturing Company. All workers receive time and one-half for hours worked in excess of 40 hours per week. Compute Social Security using 6.2% and Medicare using 1.45%. Medical insurance and union dues deductions are shown in the payroll register. Use the wage bracket method to determine federal income tax. Total each column and verify the total net pay amount.

Register

	Employee Name	Allow.	Status	Hours Worked	Pay Rate	Earnings Regular	Earnings Overtime 1.5	Gross Earnings	Fed. Inc. Tax	Social Security 6.2%	Medicare 1.45%	Medical Ins. Pre-tax	Union Dues	Total Deductions	Net Pay
11.	Allman, M.	1	M	49	12.90							21.00	12.00		
12.	Bell, L.	0	S	40	10.80							14.00			
13.	Cardino, J.	3	M	48	17.40							21.00			
14.	Fiero, N.	2	M	52	13.50							21.00	12.00		
15.	Ivy, E.	1	S	50	10.70							14.00	12.00		
16.	Jones, I.	1	S	46	15.50							14.00	12.00		
17.	Mulligan, J.	3	M	40	22.20							14.00			
18.	Neels, N.	3	M	50	15.50							21.00	12.00		
19.	Rodriguez, P.	5	M	40	20.00							21.00			
20.	Smith, R.	2	M	49	17.40							21.00	12.00		
21.	Sutton, B.	3	S	42	11.30							21.00	12.00		
22.	Talbot, A.	3	M	40	21.60							14.00			
23.	Ussery, D.	4	M	44	19.40							21.00	12.00		
24.	Vickery, C.	0	S	40	12.90							14.00			
	Totals											252.00	96.00		

D. Complete a payroll register. OBJECTIVES 2, 3

Complete the following weekly payroll register for Mexican Imports International. All workers receive time and one-half for hours worked in excess of 40 hours per week. Compute Social Security using 6.2% and Medicare using 1.45%. Medical insurance and credit union savings deductions are shown in the payroll register. Use the percentage method to determine federal income tax.

	Gross Earnings	Allow.	Marital Status	Fed. Inc. Tax	Social Security 6.2%	Medicare 1.45%	Medical Ins. (Pre-tax)	Cr. Union Savings	Total Deductions	Net Pay
25.	775.80	1	M				35.00	20.00		
26.	690.20	3	M				35.00	20.00		
27.	740.38	2	S				35.00	20.00		
28.	710.50	0	M				35.00	20.00		
29.	695.90	2	S				35.00	20.00		
30.	705.55	1	S				35.00	20.00		

E. Use Excel to complete a payroll register. OBJECTIVE 3

31. Retrieve the file *ch05ex07.xlsx*. Follow the directions. Save the file as *ch05ex07a.xlsx*.

32. Retrieve the file *ch05ex08.xlsx*. Follow the directions. Save the file as *ch05ex08a.xlsx*.

Chapter Review and Assessment

KEY TERMS

accumulated earnings

commission

compensation

double time

employee's earnings record

Employee's Withholding Allowance Certificate (Form W-4)

Fair Labor Standards Act (FLSA)

federal income tax (FIT)

Federal Insurance Contributions Act (FICA)

footing

gross earnings

hourly wage (hourly rate)

Medicare

net pay

net sales

overtime

payroll register

percentage method

piece rate

piecework

pre-tax deductions

regular time

returned merchandise

Round function

salaried

Social Security

state and local income tax withholding

straight time (regular time)

taxable earnings

template file

time and one-half

wage bracket method

CONCEPTS	EXAMPLES
5.1 Calculate gross pay for common pay periods.	
Weekly: Divide the annual salary by 52.	$44,928 \div 52 = $864
Biweekly: Divide the annual salary by 26.	$44,928 \div 26 = $1,728
Semimonthly: Divide the annual salary by 24.	$44,928 \div 24 = $1,872
Monthly: Divide the annual salary by 12.	$44,928 \div 12 = $3,744
5.1 Calculate gross earnings.	
Straight time: Multiply hourly rate by regular hours.	$40 \times 15.00 hourly rate = $600
Overtime	
Time and one-half: Multiply hours worked at time and one-half by hourly rate and by 1.5.	$8 \times $15 \times 1.5 = $180
Double time: Multiply double time hours worked by hourly rate and by 2.	$8 \times $15 \times 2 = $240
5.2 Calculate compensation by salary.	Annual Salary = $32,400
Divide annual salary by 12 months if paid monthly.	Monthly Salary = $32,400 \div 12 = $2,700
5.2 Calculate compensation by salary plus commission.	Salary, $500 per week; commission rate, 3%; find gross earnings on sales of $5,500.
Gross Earnings = Salary + Commission	Gross Earnings = $500 + (0.03 \times $5,500)$ $= $500 + $165 = $665

CONCEPTS	EXAMPLES
5.2 Calculate compensation by piecework. Gross Earnings = Number of items × Piece rate	Items produced, 180; piece rate, $1.75; find gross earnings. Gross earnings = 180 × $1.75 = $315
5.3 Calculate Social Security withholding. Gross earnings are multiplied by the tax rate. When the maximum earnings are reached, no additional Social Security is withheld that year.	Gross earnings: $550; Social Security tax rate 6.2%; find Social Security tax. Social Security tax = $550 × 0.062 = $34.10
5.3 Calculate Medicare withholding. Gross earnings are multiplied by the Medicare tax rate. All earnings are subject to Medicare tax.	Gross earnings: $550; Medicare tax rate: 1.45%; find Medicare tax. Medicare tax = $550 × 0.0145 = $7.98
5.3 Calculate taxable earnings. Subtract pre-tax deductions from gross earnings to determine taxable earnings.	Gross earnings—Medical insurance premium = Taxable earnings $45,000 gross earnings – $1,920 medical insurance premiums = $43,080 taxable earnings
5.3 Find the federal income tax withholding using the wage bracket method. 1. Find the proper table (*Circular E, Employer's Tax Guide*) for your payroll period (weekly, biweekly, semimonthly, monthly) and the employee's marital status, as shown on his or her Form W-4. 2. Then, using the appropriate table, search down the left column to find the bracket containing the correct taxable earnings and across to the column for the number of allowances claimed to find the amount to withhold for FIT.	Single, 1 allowance, weekly payroll period: $595.10 = $57.00 FIT Married, 3 allowances, weekly payroll period: $728.40 = $27.00 FIT
5.3 Find the federal income tax withholding using the percentage method. 1. Multiply the amount for one withholding allowance for the payroll period (weekly, biweekly, semimonthly, monthly, etc.) by the number of allowances the employee claims. 2. Subtract the answer in No. 1 from gross earnings. 3. Determine the amount to withhold from the Tables for Percentage Method of Withholding found in *Circular E, Employer's Tax Guide.*	Single, 2 allowances, weekly payroll period, $466.50 gross earnings: 1. 2 × $70.19 = $140.38 2. $466.50 – $140.38 = $326.12 3. $8.40 plus 15% of excess over $200. $326.12 – $200.00 × 15% = $18.92 $8.40 + $18.92 = $27.32 FIT

CONCEPTS	EXAMPLES
5.3 Find the state income tax withholding.	Married employee with weekly earnings of $495; find the state income tax withholding given a state tax rate of 3.5%. $$\$495 \times 0.035 = \$17.33$$
5.4 Create an employee's earnings record.	Details of compensation paid to employees including their date of employment, marital status, allowances, hourly wage, hours worked, gross earnings, deductions, and net pay. Much of the information is the same as would appear on paycheck stubs and payroll register. This information is used to prepare W-2 Forms for the IRS, state and local governments, and employees.
5.4 Create a payroll register. 1. Calculate Regular Earnings (Regular hours times hourly rate).	Sharita, who is married and claims 3 allowances, earns $12.30 per hour plus time-and-a-half overtime. She pays $29.85 in medical insurance per weekly paycheck. Her paycheck shows $506.71 for 45 hours worked. Is her paycheck correct? Regular Earnings = 40 hours straight time × $12.30 hourly rate = $492.00
2. Determine Overtime Wages (Time and one-half: hourly rate x 1.5; Double time: hourly rate x 2).	
3. Calculate Overtime Earnings (Multiply overtime hours by appropriate overtime rate, time and one-half or double-time rate).	Overtime Earnings = $12.30 hourly rate × 5 overtime hours × 1.5 = $92.25
4. Calculate Gross Earnings (Add Regular and Overtime earnings).	Gross Earnings = $492.00 + $92.25 = $584.25
5. Calculate Social Security Withholding. (Multiply Gross Earnings by 6.2%, subject to maximum).	Social Security Withholding = $584.25 × 6.2% = $36.22
6. Calculate Medicare Withholding (Multiply Gross Earnings by 1.45%).	Medicare Withholding = $584.25 × 1.45% = $8.47
7. Subtract pre-tax deductions from gross earnings.	$584.25 − ($36.22 + $8.47 + $29.85) = $509.71
8. Find or calculate Federal Income Tax Withholding (Use the Federal Tax Bracket method to look up withholding amounts from the tables or calculate withholding using the percentage method).	Federal Income Tax Withholding for Married, 3 allowances, $509.71 taxable earnings = $3
9. Calculate Total Deductions (Add FIT, social security, Medicare, and other deductions such as medical insurance and union dues).	Total Deductions = $29.85 + $36.22 + $8.47 + $3 = $77.54
10. Calculate Net Pay (Subtract total deductions from gross earnings).	Net Pay = $584.25 − $77.54 = $506.71
11. Verify Total Net Earnings (Verify that the gross earnings minus the total deductions equals the net earnings).	Her paycheck is correct.

Chapter 5 Review Exercises

Name _____   Date _____

Directions Complete the following problems. Write your answers in the blanks provided. Round all amounts to the nearest cent. Place commas and dollar signs in money amount answers.

A. Solve the following problems.   `5.1 OBJECTIVE 2`

1. Patricia Holmes earns a salary of $625 a week. In one week, she worked 60 hours. Find her gross earnings for the week. _____

2. Jan Lupinacci makes $39,300 annually. What is her monthly salary before taxes? _____

3. Seng Onnarath makes $29,700 annually. What is his semimonthly salary? _____

B. Solve the following problems. Both employees receive time and one-half for hours over 40 and double time on national holidays.   `5.1 OBJECTIVE 3`

From Monday through Friday, Cameron Halai worked 30 hours. She worked an additional 16 hours on Saturday and Sunday. Her regular hourly rate is $19.80.

4. Straight-time earnings = _____

5. Time and one-half earnings = _____

6. Double-time earnings = _____

7. Gross earnings = _____

Cara Hemingway worked 40 hours straight time at an hourly rate of $15.50. She worked 13 hours overtime; 5 of those hours on Labor Day.

8. Straight-time earnings = _____

9. Time and one-half earnings = _____

10. Double-time earnings = _____

11. Gross earnings = _____

C. Calculate gross earnings based on salary, salary plus commission, and compensation by piecework.   `5.2 OBJECTIVES 2, 3`

12. Julian Alonso earns $72,000 annually at Howard University. Julian has elected to have his salary paid over 9 months. What is his monthly salary? _____

13. Deloris Smith works as a clerk in a jewelry store. She earns $200 per week straight time, plus 10% on all sales over $2,000. This week she sold $8,990 worth of jewelry. What are her gross earnings this week? _____

14. Juan Martinez finishes cabinet doors and is paid $10.50 per door. On Monday he finished 10 doors, on Tuesday he finished 12 doors, on Wednesday he finished 11 doors, on Thursday he finished 15 doors, and on Friday he finished 8 doors. What were his gross earnings for the week? _____

D. Calculate Social Security (6.2%) and Medicare (1.45%). 5.3 OBJECTIVE 2

Gross earnings are $655.84.

15. Social Security = _____   16. Medicare = _____

Gross earnings are $1,432.50

17. Social Security = _____   18. Medicare = _____

Gross earnings are $903.72

19. Social Security = _____   20. Medicare = _____

E. Calculate federal income tax withholding using the wage bracket method. 5.3 OBJECTIVE 3

	Taxable Earnings	Marital Status	Allowances	Pay Period	
21.	$561.10	Single	0	Weekly	_____
22.	$701.95	Married	5	Weekly	_____
23.	$328.25	Single	3	Weekly	_____

F. Calculate federal income tax using the percentage method. 5.3 OBJECTIVE 4

	Taxable Earnings	Marital Status	Allowances	Pay Period	
24.	$1,382.50	Single	1	Weekly	_____
25.	$775.00	Married	2	Weekly	_____
26.	$2,109.45	Married	2	Weekly	_____

G. Calculate state income tax. 5.3 OBJECTIVE 5

27. Gross earnings are $644.23; state income tax rate is 4.5%. _____

28. Gross earnings are $715.05; state income tax rate is 2.5%. _____

29. Gross earnings are $1,258.41; state income tax rate is 1.8%. _____

H. Calculate the amount paid to the Internal Revenue Service each payroll period. 5.3 OBJECTIVE 6

30. Employee's federal income tax = $4,231.10

    Employee's Social Security tax = $1,748.81

    Employee's medicare = $ 409.00

    Amount paid to IRS =   _____

31. Employee's federal income tax = $5,178.21

    Employee's Social Security tax = $2,006.56

    Employee's Medicare = $ 469.28

    Amount paid to IRS =   _____

32. Amelia Ramos is a marketing representative with weekly earnings of $789. She is married and claims three withholding allowances. Her deductions include Social Security (6.2%), Medicare (1.45%), federal withholding tax (use the Percentage Method), state income tax of 1%, union dues of $20.20, and credit union savings of $100. Find Amelia's net pay for a week in March.

Social Security: _____

Medicare: _____

Federal Income Tax: _____

State Income Tax: _____

Union Dues: _____

Credit Union: _____

Total Deductions: _____

Net Pay: _____

33. Neal Dover is an instructor at a community college. He earns $3,072 monthly. He is married and claims two withholding allowances. His deductions include Social Security (6.2%), Medicare (1.45%), federal withholding tax, state income tax of 1.6%, and disability insurance of $38.25. What is Neal's net pay for one month?

Social Security: _____

Medicare: _____

Federal Income Tax: ___$422.36___

State Income Tax: _____

Disability Insurance: _____

Net Pay: _____

34. Lorenzo Sanchez works on a roofing crew and is paid $18.70 per hour. He is single and claims one withholding allowance. His deductions include Social Security (6.2%), Medicare (1.45%), federal withholding tax (use the wage bracket method), and state income tax of 2%. Find Lorenzo's net pay for a week in which he works 38 hours.

Gross wages: _____

Social Security: _____

Medicare: _____

Federal Income Tax: _____

State Income Tax: _____

Net Pay: _____

I. **Use Excel to complete an employee's earnings record.**

5.1 OBJECTIVE **4**, 5.3 OBJECTIVE **7**
5.4 OBJECTIVE **3**

35. Retrieve the file *ch05ex09.xlsx*. Follow the directions. Save the file as *ch05ex09a.xlsx*.

36. Retrieve the file *ch05ex10.xlsx*. Follow the directions. Save the file as *ch05ex10a.xlsx*.

EXAMPLE Payroll clerks perform a vital function by computing and recording earnings owed to each company employee by hand or on a computer to ensure employees are always paid on time.

TRY IT...

1. You are the payroll clerk for Jason's Video Store. Compute the gross earnings for each employee. Overtime is paid at time and one-half.

	Employee	Hours Worked Straight	Hours Worked Overtime	Hours Worked Total	Hourly Rate	Earnings Straight	Earnings Overtime	Earnings Total
a.	Johnson, L.	40	3	43	$9.60			
b.	Nuygen, A.	40	4.5	44.5	$8.80			
c.	Brown, B.	40	0	40	$9.60			
d.	Weaver, G.	40	6	46	$10.00			

2. Compute the earnings for each employee of Devlin Manufacturing Company to complete the following payroll register. All workers receive overtime pay for hours worked in excess of 40 hours per week at a rate of time and one-half. Use the tax tables in this chapter for federal income tax withholding.

	Emp. No.	Allow.	Status	Hours Worked	Pay Rate	Earnings Regular	Earnings Overtime 1.5	Gross Earnings	Fed. Inc. Tax	Social Security 6.2%	Medicare 1.45%	Medical Ins. Pre-tax	Union Dues	Total Deductions	Net Pay
a.	1	3	M	44	22.00							21.00	12.00		
b.	2	2	S	40	15.60							21.00			
c.	3	5	M	48	19.20							21.00	12.00		
d.	4	1	S	42	17.10							14.00	12.00		
e.	5	3	M	40	13.60							21.00			
	Totals											98.00	36.00		

Write about Math

1. Why do some companies pay double time? Give two or three examples of companies that pay double time and explain why they pay it.

2. Give two or three examples of the types of companies that pay a salary plus a commission, that pay compensation by piecework, or that use other compensation methods.

Personal Finance

Do you have savings goals?

Saving money can be exciting! Is there something you really want: a new(er) car, college education, a vacation, a boat, a remodeled home, or a long-lasting retirement? In this chapter, savings was one of the deductions withheld from gross earnings and transferred to a savings account in a bank, credit union, or other financial institution. A weekly or monthly deduction from your paycheck makes saving easier and allows you to reach short- or long-term savings goals. Also, having a savings account helps you financially when you have an emergency such as a sudden illness or accident, vehicle breakdown, or job loss.

© Michael Shake, 2010/Used under license from Shutterstock.com

For some people saving money is easy, and for others it is difficult. Don't think of saving as doing without something; think of saving as paying a bill—a bill you owe yourself so you may have those extras that make working worthwhile. First, establish a savings plan. You should review your finances and get them in order. That means analyzing your checking account, budget, and monthly expenses. Next you can determine what amount you can save. Make the following calculations and answer the questions concerning savings.

1. If you authorized the payroll department to deduct $5.00 per week from your paycheck, what amount would you have had deducted in one year?

2. How much would you have had deducted in three years?

3. What if you increased your savings to $10.00 per week the fourth year?

4. Should an emergency fund have enough money to cover your expenses for a full year?

5. Would saving build your self-confidence and make you feel better about your finances?

6. Is buying items using a credit card more expensive than paying cash?

7. Should you wait until you are out of college and in a high-paying job before you begin saving?

8. What is meant by "A penny saved is a penny earned?"

9. Is it true that only the wealthy can save?

10. If you estimated a vacation trip you wanted to take would cost $1,050.00, how much payroll deduction would you have deducted each week if the trip was six months from now to cover the cost of the trip?

Name _____ Date _____ Score _____

Directions Solve the following problems. Write your answers in the blanks provided. Round all amounts to the nearest cent.

A. Calculate indicated earnings. Round the amounts to the nearest dollar. 5.1 OBJECTIVE 2

1. Amy Shaw makes $39,500 annually = _____ biweekly

2. Chris Mace makes $21,300 annually = _____ weekly

3. Tony Dawn makes $13,900 annually = _____ monthly

4. Jerry Todd makes $18,450 annually = _____ semimonthly

5. Sheila Smith makes $55,000 annually = _____ monthly

B. Calculate straight time plus overtime (overtime = time and one-half). 5.1 OBJECTIVE 3

Theresa Minter worked 40 hours straight time and 10 hours overtime at an hourly rate of $8.50. Compute the following:

6. Straight-time earnings = _____

7. Time and one-half earnings = _____

8. Gross earnings = _____

C. Calculate straight time and overtime (time and one-half and double time) and add to get gross earnings. 5.1 OBJECTIVE 3

Carrie Harris worked 40 hours straight time and 16 hours overtime, 8 hours of which were double time. Her hourly rate is $14.20. Compute the following:

9. Straight-time earnings = _____

10. Time and one-half earnings = _____

11. Double time earnings = _____

12. Gross earnings = _____

D. Calculate compensation by salary plus commission. 5.2 OBJECTIVE 3

Maria Nolan receives a salary of $400 per week plus a 7% commission on all net sales over $2,000. Maria's total sales were $6,422. Sales returned were $496. Compute the following:

13. Commission amount = _____

14. Gross earnings = _____

Seth Tyson earns a salary of $325 per week plus a 13% commission on all sales over $3,000. His total sales were $12,986. No sales were returned. Compute the following:

15. Commission amount = _____

16. Gross earnings = _____

E. Calculate compensation by piecework. 5.2 OBJECTIVE 4

17. Maddie Marshall is a machine operator in a metal fabrication shop. On her current project, she earns $2.15 for each part she makes. During the current pay period, she fabricated 410 parts. What are her gross earnings? _____

18. Ezra Adler works in a manufacturing plant that makes cardigan sweaters. He is paid $7.85 per sweater completed, but is guaranteed to earn $75 each day. During one 5-day work week, he made 9, 11, 13, 8, and 10 sweaters. What were his gross earnings for that week? _____

19. Candace Johnston assembles parts for washing machines. She earns $1.85 per part. She makes, on average, 25 parts each day Monday through Friday. How much, on average, does she earn in a week? _____

F. Compute Social Security at 6.2% and Medicare at 1.45%. 5.3 OBJECTIVE 2

Gross Earnings	Social Security Withholding	Medicare Withholding
$874.99	20. _____	21. _____
$620.44	22. _____	23. _____
$365.12	24. _____	25. _____
$281.73	26. _____	27. _____
$413.01	28. _____	29. _____
$1,390.45	30. _____	31. _____
$972.88	32. _____	33. _____

G. Complete an employee's weekly earnings record. 5.3 OBJECTIVES 2, 4 5.4 OBJECTIVES 1, 2

Use the percentage method tax tables in this chapter of the text to calculate federal income tax withholding. Compute Social Security tax and Medicare. Martha's gross earnings to date are $4,150.67. Assume she pays $13.75 for medical insurance and $3.00 for union dues each week. Even though Martha is married, she claims only 1 allowance. Her rate of pay is $9.50 per hour. Any hours worked over 40 are paid at time and one-half.

	Hrs. Wkd		Earnings			Deductions							
Date	Reg.	O.T.	Reg.	O.T.	Gross Earnings	Federal Income Tax	Social Security 6.20%	Medi-care 1.45%	Med. Ins.	Union Dues	Total Ded.	Net Pay	Accum. Earnings
34. 4/1	40	12											
35. 4/8	40	1											
36. 4/15	40	6											

Employee's Weekly Earnings Record — Name: Vester, Martha

H. Use Excel to complete an employee's weekly earnings record. 5.1 OBJECTIVE 4, 5.3 OBJECTIVE 7 5.4 OBJECTIVE 3

37. Retrieve the file *ch05qz01.xlsx*. Follow the directions. Save the file as *ch05qz01a.xlsx*.

38. Retrieve the file *ch05qz02.xlsx*. Follow the directions. Save the file as *ch05qz02a.xlsx*.

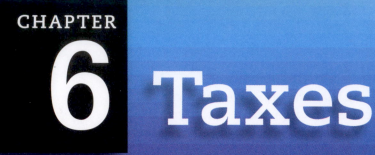

CHAPTER 6 Taxes

The payment of taxes, whether they are local, state, or federal, is necessary so your public officials have the money needed to run various programs, agencies, and public offices. Some payroll taxes, such as state and federal unemployment taxes, are imposed only on employers while Social Security, Medicare, and federal income taxes are imposed on both employers and their employees.

The amount and types of taxes you are required to pay are determined by the various governing bodies in your city, state, and federal governments, based on the tax laws. You, as a voter, help determine the tax laws, either directly by voting on tax issues or indirectly by electing the officials who make the laws. This chapter presents some of these taxes and how they are computed.

TAX ASSOCIATE

Courtesy of Catherine Albers

Tax associate Catherine Albers works with clients to help them calculate their income taxes. She asks her clients about their sources of income and family situations in order to determine what kind of taxes they may owe, what type of deductions they may be permitted to take, and what tax benefits they may be entitled to receive. After Catherine determines what the client owes to the Internal Revenue Service (IRS), she compares that figure with the money that was withheld from all paychecks and determines if the client owes more money or if he or she is entitled to receive a refund from the government for overpayment. Once all the tax forms are filled out she then sends them electronically or manually to the IRS and/or state.

Catherine admits, "A lot of people think that doing taxes is not very exciting and that you are just calculating figures all day." However, she knows that her job is important and requires a lot of interpersonal interaction and attention to detail. She says, "I really enjoy helping people with their taxes because it feels as if I am helping them with an important part of their financial lives."

How Math is Used in Tax Preparation

Catherine uses math to calculate people's incomes and deductions. Many people have several different sources of income which must be added together. She also uses math in determining the amount of money the individual owes to the IRS. Catherine acknowledges, "Math is used in every component of the tax process. In fact, the tax form is like one long math problem with multiple additions and subtractions that must be accurate."

What Do You Think?

What skills do you need to improve in order to be able to become a tax associate?

Math Skills Used

Percents

Addition

Subtraction

Other Skills Needed

Communication

Interpersonal skills

Organization

OBJECTIVES

1. Identify terms used with property tax and property tax rates.
2. Calculate the tax levied on property based on the assessed value.
3. Calculate the tax rate levied on property based on the assessed value.
4. Use Excel to calculate property taxes.

6.1 Property Tax and Property Tax Rate

OBJECTIVE 1 Identify terms used with property tax and property tax rates.

You will need to learn the following terms related to property tax and property tax rates.

Assessed Rate   An arbitrary rate set by the taxing body.

Assessed Value   The amount of money for which property is listed in the public tax records for tax purposes.

Assessor   The elected or appointed public official responsible for the collection of property tax.

Levied   Assessed or collected, as with a tax.

Market Value   The amount of money property would sell for in a competitive open market.

Mill   A unit in which tax rate is expressed; 1/10 of a cent (0.1¢) or 1/1,000 of a dollar ($0.001).

Personal Property   Possessions such as jewelry, autos, boats, and furniture.

Property Tax   A tax imposed on a property owner to help fund public services such as fire and police protection, schools, and parks.

Real Property   Property such as land and buildings.

Tax   The amount of money paid by a property owner.

Tax Rate   The percent set by the taxing body that is used to calculate tax owed.

OBJECTIVE 2 Calculate the tax levied on property based on the assessed value.

Property taxes may be imposed by townships, cities, counties, states, or school districts on the owner of any type of real property to raise funds for such services as police and fire protection, roads, parks, school districts, or street repairs. This tax is levied quarterly, semiannually, or annually. Property taxes are calculated on a value. This value is the amount for which property is listed in the tax records for tax purposes. It is the *assessed value*—as opposed to *market value*, which is the amount the property would bring in a competitive and open market. The tax usually is not shown as a percentage but is stated in dollar amounts, such as $1.80 per $100 (1.8%) of assessed value, $18.00 per $1,000 (1.8%) of assessed value, or 52 mills per dollar ($0.052) of assessed value.

The property in Miller County is assessed at 50% of market value with a tax rate of $5.95 per $100 valuation. Mr. Jones owns a farm with a market value of $400,000. Determine the amount of property tax he is required to pay annually.

STEPS

1. Multiply the market value of the property by the assessed rate.

$400,000 × 50% = $200,000   assessed value

2. Determine the number of $100s in the assessed value.

$200,000 ÷ $100 = 2,000

3. Multiply the number of $100s by the tax rate per $100 to determine the amount of tax due.

2,000 × $5.95 = $11,900   property tax due

Often, property taxes are not paid directly by the property owner, but by the mortgage company for the owner from an escrow account. An **escrow account** is an account created by the lender to hold money, collected monthly along with the property owner's mortgage payment, to insure that property taxes get paid. The owner receives a statement when the lender pays the tax.

EXAMPLE

In some areas, the tax rate is levied as the number of dollars per $1,000. If the tax rate is $3.80 per $1,000, determine the amount of annual tax for a property having an assessed value of $149,000.

STEPS

1. Divide the market value of the property by $1,000 to determine the number of thousands.

$149,000 ÷ $1,000 = 149

2. Multiply the tax rate per thousand ($3.80) by the number of 1,000s to determine the amount of tax due.

149 × $3.80 = $566.20   property tax due

EXAMPLE

In other areas, the tax rate is levied in mills. A mill is one-thousandth of a dollar. If the tax rate is 22 mills, divide 22 by 1,000 then multiply that answer by the assessed value. Determine the amount of annual tax for a property having an assessed value of $118,000.

STEPS

1. Convert the tax rate in mills to dollars.

22 mills ÷ 1,000 = $0.022   tax rate in dollars

2. Multiply the assessed value of the property by the tax rate in dollars.

$118,000 × $0.022 = $2,596   property tax due

TIPS

Always convert tax rates expressed in mills to dollars in decimal form by dividing mills by 1,000, then multiplying the rate in dollars by the assessed value of the property.

EXAMPLE

If the tax rate is 35 mills per dollar, determine the amount of annual tax for a property having an assessed value of $230,000.

Problem Solving Plan		
Clues	**Action Plan**	**Solve**
The tax rate is 35 mills.	Since the assessed value is in dollars and the mill is 1,000 of a dollar, divide the mills by 1,000 to determine the tax rate in dollars.	$35 \div 1,000 = 0.035$
The assessed value is $230,000.	Multiply the assessed value by the tax rate in dollars.	$230,000 \times 0.035 = \$8,050$
Conclusion		
The annual property tax is $8,050.		

OBJECTIVE 3 Calculate the tax rate levied on property based on the assessed value.

The tax assessor's office collects the budget information necessary to compute the tax rates and assesses the value of property in the county.

EXAMPLE

Suppose Bowie County needs $50 million to complete repairs on all county roads. All the real property (buildings and land) in the county has been assessed at $1,000,000,000. Find the property tax rate needed to raise $50 million.

STEPS

Divide the amount of money needed by the total assessed value of all the property.

$50,000,000 \div \$1,000,000,000 = 0.05$ or 5%   tax rate

To calculate property taxes using Excel, you can create simple spreadsheets using simple formulas. Property tax offices do not use Excel to calculate taxes. Most property tax collection agencies use specialized software. The software tracks and calculates property value; exemptions; any changes in individual accounts; and, of course, taxes owed.

Calculate Property Tax Due Based on Each $100 of Assessed Valuation.

Figure 6-1

Property Tax Assessment per $100 of Assessed Value

	A	B	C	D	E	F	G
1							
2							
3	Property Assessment:		80%	of Fair Market Value			
4		Tax Rate:	$1.55	per $100 of Assessed Value			
5	Fair Market	Assessed		Tax Rate		Tax	
6	Value	Value	$1.55	per	$100	Due	
7	$39,000	$31,200			312.00	$483.60	
8	$88,500	$70,800			708.00	$1,097.40	
9	$110,200	$88,160			881.60	$1,366.48	
10							
11							

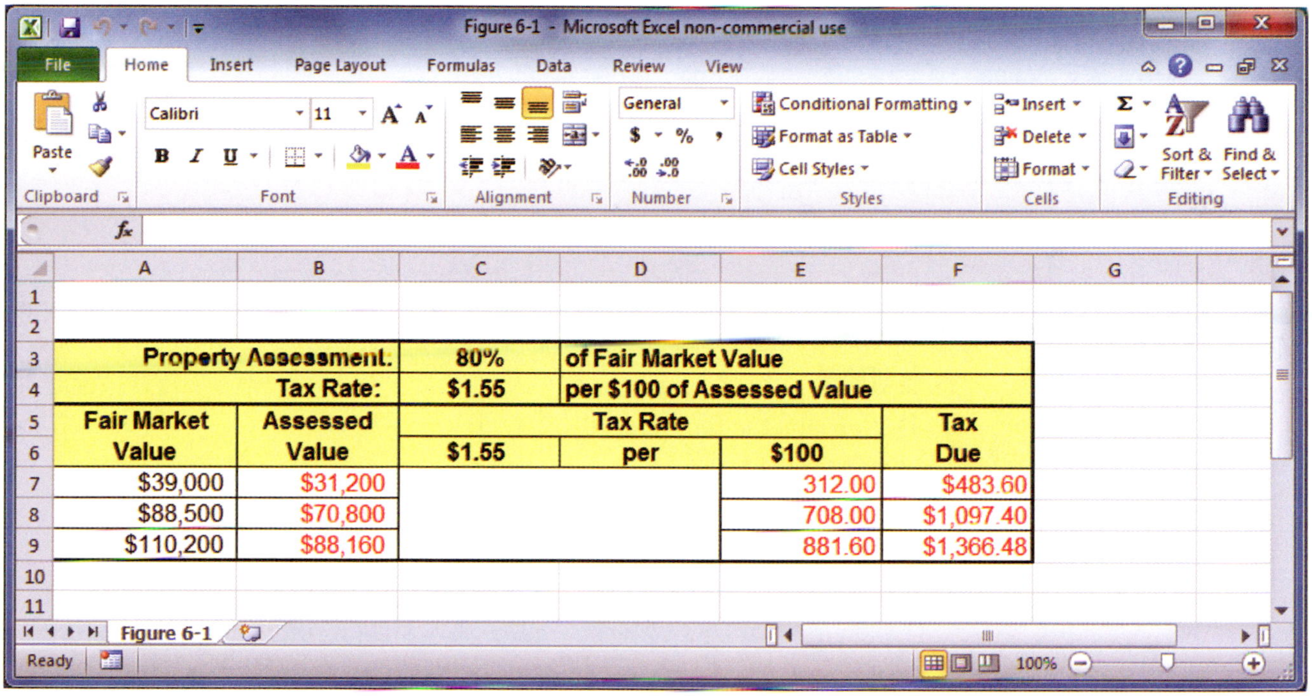

STEPS

Retrieve the file *ch06pr01.xlsx*.

1. Enter the formula =A7*$C$3 in Cell B7 to calculate the Assessed Value. (Assessed Value is 80% times the Fair Market Value.) Copy the formula down the column.

2. Enter the formula =B7/$E$6 in Cell E7 to calculate the number of 100s. (Divide Assessed Value by the amount in Cell E6.) Copy the formula down the column.

3. Enter the formula =E7*$C$6 in Cell F7 to calculate the Tax Due. (Multiply the number of 100s by the tax rate.) Copy the formula down the column.

4. Format Column B for Currency, 0 Decimal places, and $. Format Column E for Number and 2 Decimal places. Format Column F for Currency, 2 Decimal places, and $.

5. Save the file as *ch06pr01a.xlsx*.

Calculate Property Tax Due Based on Each $1,000 of Assessed Valuation.

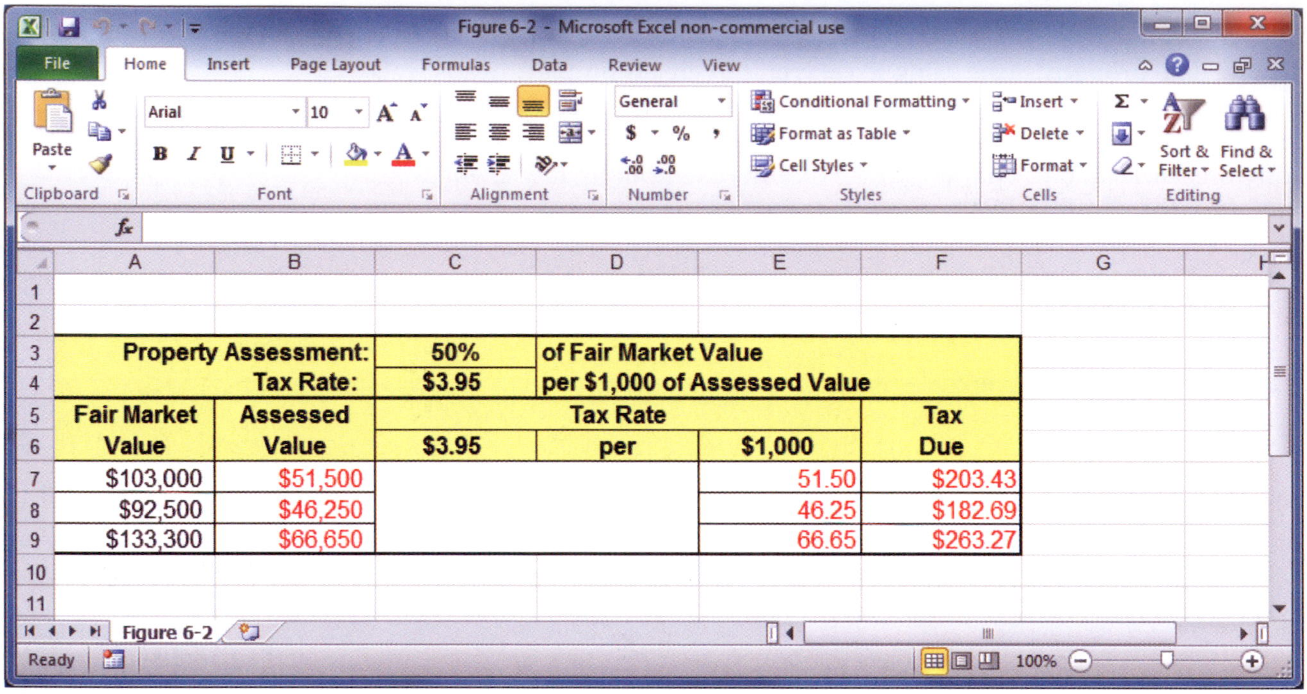

	A	B	C	D	E	F
3	Property Assessment:		50%	of Fair Market Value		
4	Tax Rate:		$3.95	per $1,000 of Assessed Value		
5	Fair Market	Assessed	Tax Rate			Tax
6	Value	Value	$3.95	per	$1,000	Due
7	$103,000	$51,500			51.50	$203.43
8	$92,500	$46,250			46.25	$182.69
9	$133,300	$66,650			66.65	$263.27

Figure 6-2

Property Tax Assessment per $1,000 of Assessed Value

STEPS

Retrieve the file *ch06pr02.xlsx*.

1. Enter the formula =A7*$C$3 in Cell B7 to calculate the Assessed Value. (Assessed Value is 50% times the Fair Market Value.) Copy the formula down the column.
2. Enter the formula =B7/$E$6 in Cell E7 to calculate the number of 1000s. (Divide Assessed Value by Cell E6.) Copy the formula down the column.
3. Enter the formula =E7*$C$6 in Cell F7 to calculate the Tax Due. (Multiply the number of 1000s by the Tax Rate.) Copy the formula down the column.
4. Format Column B for Currency, 0 Decimal places, and $. Format Column E for Number and 2 Decimal places. Format Column F for Currency, 2 Decimal places, and $.
5. Save the file as *ch06pr02a.xlsx*.

TIPS

Remember, to calculate assessed value based on mills, first determine the amount of assessed value on the property. Next divide the mills by 1,000 to determine the price per mill. Finally, multiply the price per mill by the assessed value.

Calculate Property Tax Due Based on Mills per Dollar of Assessed Valuation.

Create formulas to calculate the property tax due based on mills similar to the formulas in the spreadsheets shown above.

PRACTICE

Retrieve the file *ch06pr03.xlsx*. Follow the directions. Save the file as *ch06pr03a.xlsx*.

Name _____   Date _____

Directions   Solve the following problems. Place commas and dollar signs in answers as needed.

A. Calculate the tax levied on property based on assessed value. Round to the nearest hundredth.   OBJECTIVE 2

	Market Value	Assessed Value	Tax Rate	Tax Due
1.	$51,000	80%	$1.50 per $1,000 =	_____
2.	$65,000	60%	$2.05 per $1,000 =	_____
3.	$150,000	50%	$3.95 per $10,000 =	_____
4.	$49,000	65%	46 mills per dollar =	_____
5.	$900,000	80%	$50 per $10,000 =	_____
6.	$75,000	80%	$1.75 per $1,000 =	_____
7.	$108,000	50%	32 mills per dollar =	_____
8.	$86,000	65%	$2.75 per $1,000 =	_____
9.	$1,000,000	80%	$1.95 per $10,000 =	_____
10.	$92,000	30%	45 mills per dollar =	_____

B. Calculate the tax rate levied on property based on the assessed value. Round to the nearest whole percent.   OBJECTIVE 3

	Money Needed	Assessed Value	Tax Rate
11.	$800,000	$10,000,000 =	_____
12.	$62,000	$900,000 =	_____
13.	$45,000	$775,000 =	_____
14.	$208,000	$1,000,000 =	_____
15.	$139,000	$3,500,000 =	_____
16.	$80,000	$800,000 =	_____
17.	$149,000	$21,000,000 =	_____
18.	$500,000	$1,000,000 =	_____
19.	$200,000	$3,000,000 =	_____
20.	$1 billion	$6 billion =	_____

C. **The Carson County School District has placed a tax issue on the ballot requesting 8 mills. A previous school levy of 4.5 mills is due to expire.** OBJECTIVES **2, 3**

Assessment rate	40%
Current Carson County property tax rate	49.708 mills
Total assessed value in Carson County	$1,200,000,000

21. How much additional funding will the new levy provide the schools if it is approved by voters?

_____

22. How much will it increase the property tax on Wayne Pritchard's home that has a market value of $180,000?

_____

23. If Mr. Pritchard's home reappraises at a market value of $190,800, and the school levy passes, how much will his annual property tax be?

_____

D. Solve the following word problems. OBJECTIVES **2, 3**

24. Madison County Tax Assessor, Robert Graves, received the budget requests from the various county districts for the coming year. The total budget amount needed is $775,000,000. The total assessed property valuation is $5,000,000,000. What will the tax rate be? Round to the nearest whole percent. _____

25. Elidio Marcelino purchased a home with a market value of $156,000 in Dallas County. The assessment rate in Dallas County is $5.40 per $1,000 based on 100% market value. What is the amount of property tax? _____

26. Chico County's tax rate for last year was 51.550 mills. This year it is 54.116 mills. What is the percent of increase in the tax rate? Carry your answer to the hundredths position. _____

27. Caroline Benton purchased a home in Bakers County with a market value of $183,000. The assessment rate in Bakers County is $4.87 per $1,000 based on 90% market value. What is the amount of property tax on Caroline's home? _____

28. The Padaluga County School District recently passed a tax levy requesting 6.5 mills. Pierce Chesterton owns a home with a market value of $176,000. If the assessment rate is 60%, how much will Pierce pay in taxes for the levy? _____

E. Use Excel to calculate assessed value, tax rate, and property tax. OBJECTIVE **4**

29. Retrieve the file *ch06ex01.xlsx*. Follow the directions. Save the file as *ch06ex01a.xlsx*.

30. Retrieve the file *ch06ex02.xlsx*. Follow the directions. Save the file as *ch06ex02a.xlsx*.

6.2 State and Federal Unemployment Tax

OBJECTIVES

1. Identify terms used with state unemployment tax (SUTA) and federal unemployment tax (FUTA).

2. Calculate state unemployment tax.

3. Calculate federal unemployment tax.

4. Use Excel to calculate state unemployment tax (SUTA), and federal unemployment tax (FUTA).

OBJECTIVE 1 Identify terms used with state unemployment tax (SUTA) and federal unemployment tax (FUTA).

The following terms are related to state and federal unemployment tax.

Federal Unemployment Tax Act (FUTA) This tax authorizes the IRS to collect a tax on each employer's payroll to fund state workforce agencies. FUTA covers the costs of administering the Unemployment Insurance (UI) and Job Service programs in all states. In addition, FUTA pays one-half of the cost of extended unemployment benefits (during periods of unemployment) and provides funds from which states may borrow, if necessary, to pay benefits. The rate is set by Congress at 6.2% on the first $7,000 earnings per year for each employee. Assume 0.8% on the first $7,000 for all problems in this chapter.

State Unemployment Tax Act (SUTA) SUTA, collected by state governments to fund state workforce agencies, is used solely for the payment of benefits to eligible unemployed workers. The rates vary by state based upon their individual needs. Assume 3% on the first $9,000 for all problems in this chapter.

While Congress has set the federal rate at 6.2%, they allow the states to offset the federal rate up to 5.4% against their own rates. So, if a state sets its SUTA rate at 6%, the FUTA rate in that state would be 0.8% (6.2% − 5.4%). If the state rate is 3%, the federal rate drops to 3.2% (6.2% − 3% = 3.2%).

OBJECTIVE 2 Calculate state unemployment tax.

State unemployment tax is levied on a certain portion of an employer's payroll on the basis of the gross wages paid to the employees. Like property taxes, these taxes are an expense to a business. They are paid by the employer only. The rate of the state unemployment tax varies considerably from state to state. However, most states adopt a base amount of earnings on which the employer must pay tax.

EXAMPLE

Carter Wholesale Drug Company had total wages of $219,300 for the first quarter. All wages were subject to the state unemployment tax of 3% because no employee had earned the maximum of $9,000 by the end of the quarter. Find the amount of state unemployment tax owed.

$$\$219,300 \times 3\% = \$6,579 \quad \text{tax due}$$

The following chart shows the first and second quarter earnings of Madison Trucking Company's six employees and the SUTA tax owed for each at the end of each quarter. Once each employee's earnings reach $9,000, the employer stops paying the 3% state unemployment tax for that employee. Notice that Brown, Jones, and Green reached the $9,000 maximum in the first quarter, while Moore, Bixby, and Jordan did not reach the $9,000 mark until sometime in the second quarter. The total amount of SUTA tax that the employer must pay is $1,512.00 at the end of the first quarter and $108.00 at the end of the second quarter for a total of $1,620.00.

Employee	First Quarter Earnings	Amt. Subject to SUTA Tax	First Quarter SUTA Tax	Second Quarter Earnings	Amt. Subject to SUTA Tax	Second Quarter SUTA Tax
Brown, C.	$9,800	$9,000	$270.00	$9,800	– 0 –	– 0 –
Moore, T.	$8,890	$8,890	$266.70	$8,890	$110[*]	$3.30
Jones, M.	$12,600	$9,000	$270.00	$12,600	– 0 –	– 0 –
Green, J.	$9,050	$9,000	$270.00	$9,050	– 0 –	– 0 –
Bixby, L.	$7,710	$7,710	$231.30	$7,710	$1,290[**]	$38.70
Jordan, S.	$6,800	$6,800	$204.00	$6,800	$2,200[***]	$66.00
Totals		**$50,400**	**$1,512.00**		**$3,600**	**$108.00**

[*] Notice $110 of Moore's pay this quarter is needed to reach $9,000; therefore, the employer only pays SUTA on $110.

[**] Notice $1,290 of Bixby's pay this quarter is needed to reach $9,000; therefore, the employer only pays SUTA on $1,290.

[***] Notice $2,200 of Jordan's pay this quarter is needed to reach $9,000; therefore, the employer only pays SUTA on $2,200.

OBJECTIVE 3 Calculate federal unemployment tax.

Federal unemployment tax (FUTA) is similar to state unemployment tax and is levied on the employer only. Generally, this tax applies to every employer who, during the last or present year, paid wages of $1,500 or more in any calendar quarter or had one or more employees at any time in each of 20 calendar weeks. If during any calendar quarter, the amount of FUTA tax equals or exceeds $500, the employer must deposit it with the IRS. To compute federal unemployment tax, multiply gross earnings subject to tax by the tax rate.

EXAMPLE

Mario Riveria earned $6,450 during the first quarter. By the end of the second quarter, his total earnings were $15,200. How much federal unemployment tax will Mario's employer owe for his second quarter earnings if the FUTA rate in his state is 0.8%?

STEPS

1. Subtract Mario's first quarter earnings from the $7,000 maximum.

   $7,000 – $6,450 = $550   quarter earnings subject to tax

2. Multiply the amount of second quarter earnings subject to the tax by the FUTA rate.

   $550 × 0.008 = $4.40   FUTA tax for second quarter

Use Excel to calculate state unemployment tax (SUTA), and federal unemployment tax (FUTA).

As with property taxes, Excel is usually not used to calculate SUTA, FUTA, or federal income tax. Specialized software programs are used. However, tax information is calculated in Excel that aids in inputting information in the specialized software. For instance, a schedule of expenses might be kept to aid in itemizing deductions for income tax. Since Excel is so widely used, many software programs allow information from Excel to be imported into the programs, thus eliminating having to enter the information.

SUTA and FUTA

SUTA and FUTA are calculated based on payroll information. Most payroll functions are attached to an accounting software, which allows you to make journal entries and post to ledger accounts that track amounts owed to SUTA and FUTA. This accounting software also allows you to write checks, based on the information in the ledger, to pay SUTA and FUTA. Study Figure 6-3, then follow the steps to calculate SUTA and FUTA using Excel.

Figure 6-3

SUTA and FUTA Calculations

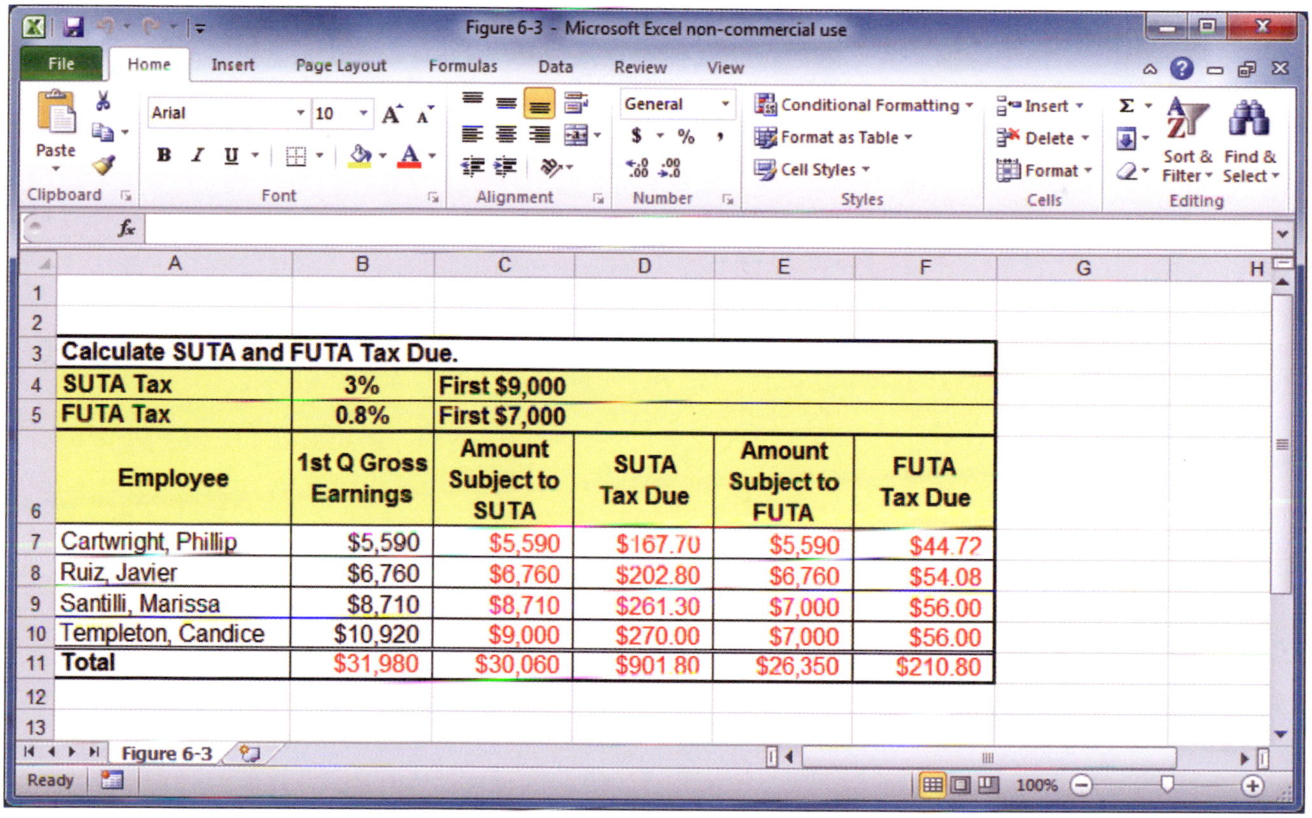

Calculate SUTA and FUTA Tax Due.

SUTA Tax	3%	First $9,000			
FUTA Tax	0.8%	First $7,000			
Employee	1st Q Gross Earnings	Amount Subject to SUTA	SUTA Tax Due	Amount Subject to FUTA	FUTA Tax Due
Cartwright, Phillip	$5,590	$5,590	$167.70	$5,590	$44.72
Ruiz, Javier	$6,760	$6,760	$202.80	$6,760	$54.08
Santilli, Marissa	$8,710	$8,710	$261.30	$7,000	$56.00
Templeton, Candice	$10,920	$9,000	$270.00	$7,000	$56.00
Total	$31,980	$30,060	$901.80	$26,350	$210.80

PRACTICE

Retrieve the file *ch06pr04.xlsx*. Follow the directions. Save the file as *ch06pr04a.xlsx*.

Name _____   Date _____

Directions   Write your answers in the blanks provided. Round all dollar amounts to the hundredth position.

A. Calculate the state unemployment tax due for one employee. Use 3% up to and including $9,000.   OBJECTIVE **2**

1. $15,600 gross wages   _____ tax due

2. $8,150 gross wages   _____ tax due

3. $8,990 gross wages   _____ tax due

4. $9,000 gross wages   _____ tax due

5. $15,142 gross wages   _____ tax due

6. $10,250 gross wages   _____ tax due

7. $7,850 gross wages   _____ tax due

8. $15,950 gross wages   _____ tax due

9. $8,800 gross wages   _____ tax due

B. Calculate the federal unemployment tax due for one employee. Use 0.8% up to and including $7,000.   OBJECTIVE **3**

10. $5,990 gross wages   _____ tax due

11. $9,560 gross wages   _____ tax due

12. $10,200 gross wages   _____ tax due

13. $7,800 gross wages   _____ tax due

14. $5,000 gross wages   _____ tax due

15. $4,225 gross wages   _____ tax due

16. $3,333 gross wages   _____ tax due

17. $2,059 gross wages   _____ tax due

18. $15,615 gross wages   _____ tax due

C. Use Excel to calculate SUTA and FUTA.   OBJECTIVE **4**

19. Retrieve the file *ch06ex03.xlsx*. Follow the directions. Save the file as *ch06ex03a.xlsx*.

20. Retrieve the file *ch06ex04.xlsx*. Follow the directions. Save the file as *ch06ex04a.xlsx*.

6.3 Federal Income Tax

> **OBJECTIVE 1 Identify terms used with federal income tax.**

Some cities, most states, and the federal government use income tax as a source of revenue. Individual income tax provides the largest single source of revenue for federal government operations. For most people, federal income tax is their largest tax expense.

An individual has three choices when filing his or her federal income tax: Form 1040EZ, Form 1040A, or Form 1040. You can find these forms on the IRS web site (www.irs.gov). Calculating income tax for some tax payers can be very complicated. This section introduces only the basic concepts.

The following terms are used with federal income tax.

Adjusted Gross Income The amount of income remaining after adjustments.

Adjustments to Income Allowable deductions from income include certain business expenses, contributions to a health savings account, moving expenses, alimony, IRA contributions, student loan interest, and tuition and fees.

Earned Income Tax Credit A federal program for low- to moderate-income workers who meet certain requirements that offers a refund of federal income taxes withheld. In some cases, the earned income credit can exceed the amount of taxes withheld. The maximum benefit in 2009 was $5,028 for those with incomes not exceeding $43,415.

Estimated Tax Payments Quarterly tax payments to the IRS that are required if you expect to owe at least $1,000 in tax (2009) after subtracting your withholding and credits. Other qualifications apply based on the amount of withholding and credits and prior year taxes or estimated payments.

Exemptions The taxpayer is allowed one exemption per dependent. In 2009, for example, you could deduct $3,500 from your taxable income for each dependent.

Health Savings Account (HSA) A qualifying employer-sponsored plan allowing employees to have pre-tax deductions from their paychecks deposited into a savings account that can be used only for medical expenses.

Individual Retirement Account (IRA) With some restrictions set by the IRS, employed individuals can set aside pre-tax funds for their retirement years in a traditional IRA or a Roth IRA. Contributions to a traditional IRA are deducted from earnings as a tax savings. The money is taxed when it is withdrawn. There are penalties for early withdrawal.

Itemized Deductions Amounts subtracted from adjusted gross income before tax is computed. Deductions are listed on Schedule A. Some examples include the following.

- Medical and dental expenses that are more than 7.5% of your adjusted gross income
- State and local income taxes, real estate and property taxes, and sales taxes

Note

Each year, the IRS makes available an instruction booklet that explains how to calculate that year's income tax. Changes are made from year to year, such as in the standard deduction allowed for each person. However, the process used to calculate your income tax is basically the same.

TIPS

Special rules may apply concerning deductions available to taxpayers who live in a location that has been declared a disaster area during the tax year.

- Home mortgage interest (includes qualifying interest paid on home equity loans)
- Contributions or gifts made to qualifying charities
- Part or all of each loss caused by theft, vandalism, fire, storm, or similar causes
- Unreimbursed employee expenses such as job travel, union dues, job education, and so on
- Tax preparation fees

Standard Deduction   The standard deduction is a dollar amount that reduces the amount of income on which you are taxed. You cannot take the standard deduction if you claim itemized deductions. For example, if you do not itemize your deductions, you take a standard deduction. The standard deductions in 2009 were:

Single or married filing separately	$5,450
Head of household	$8,000
Married filing jointly or qualifying widow(er)	$10,900

Additional amounts are allowed if you or your spouse is blind and/or over the age of 65.

Tax Credits   Items that reduce your calculated income tax; for example, credit for child and dependent care expenses.

Taxable Income   The amount of income subject to tax after adjustments, deductions, and exemptions.

Total Income   Includes all the income you receive, such as wages, salaries, tips, dependent care benefits, employer-provided adoption benefits, interest income, ordinary dividend income, taxable refunds, credits or offsets of state and local income tax, alimony, business income, capital gain distributions, pensions, IRA distributions, annuities, rents, royalties, partnerships, certain scholarships and fellowship grants, prizes and awards, gambling winnings, jury fees, rental income, unemployment compensation, and Social Security benefits.

InkkStudios/iStockphoto.com

OBJECTIVE 2 Collect information to prepare federal income tax.

Several forms are essential for organizing records and filing annual income tax returns. Keeping your records up to date and accurate is a must for filing correct information and avoiding being audited by the IRS. The IRS recommends you keep a copy of your tax return, worksheets used, and all records that verify information. Generally, the IRS may audit your records within 3 years of your filing date.

Social Security Number

Katherine M. Grayson is single and is in her first year of college. Katherine works part-time as a receptionist for Morgan Reynolds, a local attorney. When Katherine was hired by Reynolds and Associates, she was asked for her Social Security number, shown in Figure 6-4. This number is her taxpayer's identification number, and it will appear on all tax forms that Katherine files.

Figure 6-4
Social Security Card

Employee's Withholding Allowance Certificate (Form W-4)

Katherine was also asked to complete an Employee's Withholding Allowance Certificate (Form W-4). Refer to Chapter 5 for more information about this form. Katherine claims one allowance for herself. Study the form she completed, shown in Figure 6-5.

Figure 6-5
Employee's Withholding Allowance Certificate (Form W-4)

Form **W-4**
Department of the Treasury
Internal Revenue Service

Employee's Withholding Allowance Certificate

► **Whether you are entitled to claim a certain number of allowances or exemption from withholding is subject to review by the IRS. Your employer may be required to send a copy of this form to the IRS.**

OMB No. 1545-0074
20--

1 Type or print your first name and middle initial Katherine M.	Last name Grayson	2 Your social security number 900 43 4750
Home address (number and street or rural route) 4611 Valley Lane		3 ☒ Single ☐ Married ☐ Married, but withhold at higher Single rate. **Note:** *If married, but legally separated, or spouse is a nonresident alien, check the "Single" box.*
City or town, state, and ZIP code Texarkana, TX 75503		4 **If your last name differs from that on your social security card, check here. You must call 1-800-772-1213 for a new card.** ► ☐

5 Total number of allowances you are claiming (from line **H** above **or** from the applicable worksheet on page 2) . . . 5 | 1

6 Additional amount, if any, you want withheld from each paycheck . . . 6 | $

7 I claim exemption from withholding for 2009, and I certify that I meet **both** of the following conditions for exemption:
- Last year I had a right to a refund of **all** Federal income tax withheld because I had **no** tax liability **and**
- This year I expect a refund of **all** Federal income tax withheld because I expect to have **no** tax liability.

If you meet both conditions, write "Exempt" here . . . ► 7

Under penalties of perjury, I declare that I have examined this certificate and to the best of my knowledge and belief, it is true, correct, and complete.

Employee's signature
(Form is not valid unless you sign it.) ► Katherine M. Grayson **Date ►** 3/1/--

8 Employer's name and address (Employer: Complete lines 8 and 10 only if sending to the IRS.)	9 Office code (optional)	10 Employer identification number (EIN)

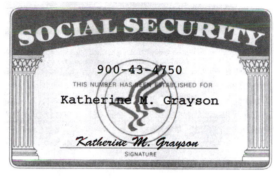

sjlocke/iStockphoto.com

Wage and Tax Statement (Form W-2)

At the end of the year, Katherine received a copy of her Wage and Tax Statement (Form W-2). This form shows Katherine's gross earnings ($18,950), total federal income tax withheld ($950.00), total Social Security tax withheld ($1,174.90), and Medicare tax withheld ($274.78). This Wage and Tax Statement must accompany the federal income tax return she files. Also, Katherine will retain a copy of her W-2 form for her personal files. Study the W-2 form she received shown in Figure 6-6.

The Wage and Tax Statement is completed by the employer. The employer would have this information compiled from the employee's records. The IRS requires employers to provide W-2 forms by January 31 following the year the income was earned. An employee who has had an address change should contact the employer prior to the January 31 deadline.

Figure 6-6

Wage and Tax Statement
(Form W-2)

a Control number		OMB No. 1545-0008	Safe, accurate, FAST! Use	IRS e~file	Visit the IRS Web Site at www.irs.gov/efile

b Employer identification number **75-546-1978**	1 Wages, tips, other compensation **$18,950.00**	2 Federal income tax withheld **$950.00**
c Employer's name, address, and ZIP code **Morgan Reynolds 29 Professional Plaza Texarkana, TX 75503**	3 Social security wages **$18,950.00**	4 Social security tax withheld **$1,174.90**
	5 Medicare wages and tips **$18,950.00**	6 Medicare tax withheld **$274.78**
	7 Social security tips	8 Allocated tips
d Employee's social security number **900-43-4750**	9 Advance EIC payment	10 Dependent care benefits
e Employee's first name and initial Last name Suff. **Katherine M. Grayson 4611 Valley Lane Texarkana, TX 75503**	11 Nonqualified plans	12a See instructions for box 12
	13 Statutory employee ☐ Retirement plan ☐ Third-party sick pay ☐	12b
	14 Other	12c
		12d
f Employee's address and ZIP code		

15 State Employer's state ID number **TX**	16 State wages, tips, etc. **$18,950.00**	17 State income tax	18 Local wages, tips, etc.	19 Local income tax	20 Locality name

Form **W-2** Wage and Tax Statement   **20 - -**   Department of the Treasury—Internal Revenue Service

Copy B—To Be Filed with Employee's **FEDERAL** Tax Return.
This information is being furnished to the Internal Revenue Service.

Annual 1099 form

Katherine has a savings account at National First Bank. At the end of the year, Katherine received from the bank a Form 1099-INT to notify her of the amount of interest ($752.05) her money earned during the year. Study the form she received, shown in Figure 6-7.

Form 1099-INT is completed by your bank. A copy is sent to you and one is sent to the IRS. There is no form for you to complete.

Figure 6-7

Form 1099-INT

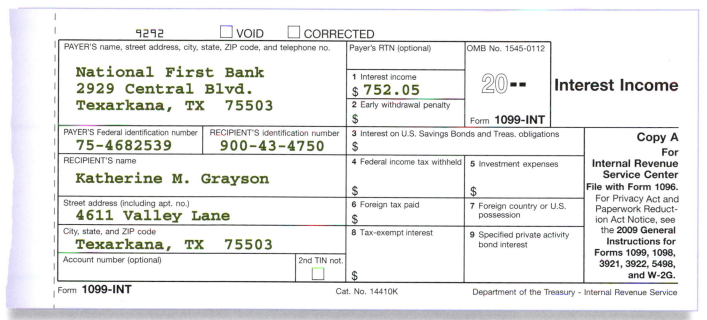

OBJECTIVE 3 Calculate federal income tax using Form 1040EZ.

Your filing status, age, and gross income determine whether you must file a tax return. Gross income means money, goods, and property you received on which you must pay taxes. It does not include nontaxable benefits.

You may use Form 1040EZ if you meet all of the following requirements: (1) Filing status is single or married filing jointly. (2) You do not claim any dependents. (3) You do not claim IRAs, alimony paid, bad debt deduction, moving expenses, the educator expense deduction, a student loan interest deduction or the tuition and fees deduction. (4) You can claim only the earned income credit. (5) You (and your spouse if married and filing a joint return) were under age 65 at the end of the taxable year and not blind. (6) Your taxable income is less than $100,000. (7) You had only wages, salaries, tips, and taxable scholarship or fellowship grants; unemployment compensation; or Alaska Permanent Fund dividends, and your taxable interest was not over $1,500. (8) You did not receive any advance earned income credit payments. (9) You do not owe any household employment taxes on wages you paid a

Figure 6-8

Form 1040EZ

Department of the Treasury—Internal Revenue Service

Income Tax Return for Single and Joint Filers With No Dependents (99) **20--**

OMB No. 1545-0074

Label
(See page 9.)

Use the IRS label.

Otherwise, please print or type.

Presidential Election Campaign (page 9)

L A B E L H E R E	

Your first name and initial
Bryan

Last name
Phillips

Your social security number
130 : 32 : 8955

If a joint return, spouse's first name and initial

Last name

Spouse's social security number

Home address (number and street). If you have a P.O. box, see page 9.
1015 Madison Road

Apt. no.

▲ You **must** enter your SSN(s) above. ▲

City, town or post office, state, and ZIP code. If you have a foreign address, see page 9.
Cincinnati, OH 45242

Checking a box below will not change your tax or refund.

Check here if you, or your spouse if a joint return, want $3 to go to this fund . . . ▶ ☐ **You**   ☐ **Spouse**

Income

Attach Form(s) W-2 here.

Enclose, but do not attach, any payment.

1	Wages, salaries, and tips. This should be shown in box 1 of your Form(s) W-2. Attach your Form(s) W-2.	**1** **12,550**
2	Taxable interest. If the total is over $1,500, you cannot use Form 1040EZ.	**2** **780**
3	Unemployment compensation and Alaska Permanent Fund dividends (see page 11).	**3**
4	Add lines 1, 2, and 3. This is your **adjusted gross income.**	**4** **13,330**
5	If someone can claim you (or your spouse if a joint return) as a dependent, check the applicable box(es) below and enter the amount from the worksheet on back. ☐ **You** ☐ **Spouse** If no one can claim you (or your spouse if a joint return), enter $8,950 if **single;** $17,900 if **married filing jointly.** See back for explanation.	**5** **8,950**
6	Subtract line 5 from line 4. If line 5 is larger than line 4, enter -0-. This is your **taxable income.** ▶	**6** **4380**

Payments and tax

7	Federal income tax withheld from box 2 of your Form(s) W-2.	**7** **1,005**
8a	**Earned income credit (EIC)** (see page 12).	**8a**
b	Nontaxable combat pay election. 8b	
9	Recovery rebate credit (see worksheet on pages 17 and 18).	**9**
10	Add lines 7, 8a, and 9. These are your **total payments.** ▶	**10** **1,005**
11	**Tax.** Use the amount on **line 6 above** to find your tax in the tax table on pages 28–36 of the booklet. Then, enter the tax from the table on this line.	**11** **4380**

Refund

Have it directly deposited! See page 18 and fill in 12b, 12c, and 12d or Form 8888.

12a	If line 10 is larger than line 11, subtract line 11 from line 10. This is your **refund.** If Form 8888 is attached, check here ▶ ☐	**12a** **567**
▶ **b**	Routing number	▶ **c** Type: ☐ Checking ☐ Savings
▶ **d**	Account number	

Amount you owe

13	If line 11 is larger than line 10, subtract line 10 from line 11. This is the **amount you owe.** For details on how to pay, see page 19. ▶	**13**

Third party designee

Do you want to allow another person to discuss this return with the IRS (see page 20)? ☐ **Yes.** Complete the following. ☒ **No**

Designee's name ▶	Phone no. ▶ ( )	Personal identification number (PIN)

Sign here

Joint return? See page 6.

Keep a copy for your records.

Under penalties of perjury, I declare that I have examined this return, and to the best of my knowledge and belief, it is true, correct, and accurately lists all amounts and sources of income I received during the tax year. Declaration of preparer (other than the taxpayer) is based on all information of which the preparer has any knowledge.

Your signature *Bryan Phillips*	Date 4/11	Your occupation **Student**	Daytime phone number **(555) 555-0199**
Spouse's signature. If a joint return, **both** must sign.	Date	Spouse's occupation	

Paid preparer's use only

Preparer's signature ▶	Date	Check if self-employed ☐	Preparer's SSN or PTIN
Firm's name (or yours if self-employed), address, and ZIP code ▶		EIN	
		Phone no. ( )	

household employee. (10) You are not a debtor in a Chapter 11 bankruptcy case filed after October 16, 2005. (11) You are not claiming the additional standard deduction for real estate taxes or disaster losses.

To complete the 1040EZ short form and compute taxable income, the following formula is used.

Taxable Income = Total Income – Standard Deduction – Exemptions

The Internal Revenue Service provides tax tables that cover four categories of taxpayers: single, married filing jointly, married filing separately, and head of household. Those who file declaring they are unmarried heads of households must meet qualifications having to do with support of children, parents, or relatives. Also, these tables read similarly to the tax table you used in Chapter 5. Look at the tax table in Figure 6-10 on pages 246 and 220. Notice its headings. There are three columns of taxable amounts. In the first column at the upper left corner, it reads "If line 40 (taxable income) is At least _____ But less than _____." Follow this column until you find the applicable taxable amount. Use the taxable income amount from line 27 on the Form 1040A.

EXAMPLE

Calculate Brian Phillips' income tax and the amount due or the amount of his refund. Brian is single and a student with only part-time wages and a small amount of interest income. Note on line 5, because Brian is single, he combines the standard deduction of $5,450 and the single exemption of $3,500 for a total of $8,950.

STEPS

1. Calculate the adjusted gross income.

$$\$12,550 + \$780 = \$13,330$$

2. Calculate the taxable income.

$$\$13,330 - \$8,950 = \$4,380$$

3. Find the income tax in tax tables (see Figure 6-10 Tax Table on pages 246–247).

$$\$438 \qquad \text{tax}$$

4. Subtract to find the difference between the tax and the amount of taxes paid (withheld) to see if additional tax or a refund is due.

$$\$1,005 - \$438 = \$567 \quad \text{refund due}$$

OBJECTIVE 4 Calculate federal income tax using Form 1040A.

Form 1040A is used when: (1) You only had income from wages, tips, salaries, interest and ordinary dividends, capital gain distributions, taxable scholarship and fellowship grants, pensions, annuities, IRAs, unemployment compensation, taxable social security and railroad retirement benefits, Alaska Permanent Fund Dividend; (2) The only adjustments to income you can claim are educator expenses, IRA deduction, student loan interest deduction, or tuition and fees deduction; (3) You do not itemize deductions; (4) Your taxable income is less than $100,000; (5) The only tax credits you can claim are child tax credit, additional child tax credit, education credits, earned income credit, credit for child and dependent care expenses, credit for the elderly or the disabled, retirement savings contributions credit; (6) You did not have an alternative minimum tax adjustment on stock you acquired from the exercise of an incentive stock option.

An exemption is taken for the head of the household and for each of his or her dependents, including spouse and children. If a married person had two children, he or she can claim four exemptions—one for himself or herself, one for his or her spouse, and one each for the two children. The taxpayer is allowed a deduction of $3,500 for each exemption.

Income is wages, salaries, tips, taxable interest, ordinary dividends, capital gains distributions (gain on property when sold), IRA distributions (money withdrawn from IRA), pensions and annuities, unemployment compensation, social security benefits, and any other income reported to the IRS.

EXAMPLE

Katherine Grayson is single. Complete Form 1040A for Katherine Grayson using her Form W-2 (Figure 6-6) and her Form 1099-INT (Figure 6-7). Katherine also has a $2,000 IRA contribution.

STEPS

1. Determine the personal exemptions.

Katherine is single, so she has one exemption.

2. Calculate the total income.
$$\$18{,}950 + \$752 = \$19{,}702$$

3. Calculate the adjusted gross income by subtracting $2,000 IRA contribution from the total income.
$$\$19{,}702 - \$2{,}000 = \$17{,}702$$

4. Subtract the standard deduction from the adjusted gross income.
$$\$17{,}702 - \$5{,}450 = \$12{,}252$$

5. Subtract any exemptions to find taxable income.
$$\$12{,}252 - \$3{,}500 = \$8{,}752 \qquad \text{taxable income}$$

6. Find the income tax in the tax tables (see Figure 6-10 Tax Table on pages 246–247).
$$\$899 \qquad \text{tax}$$

7. Subtract the tax from the amount of taxes paid (withheld) to find the amount of tax due or refund due.
$$\$950 - \$899 = \$51 \qquad \text{refund due}$$

TIPS

You may round off cents to whole dollars on your return and schedules. To round, drop amounts under 50 cents and increase amounts from 50 to 99 cents to the next dollar.

Figure 6-9

Form 1040A

Form **1040A**	Department of the Treasury—Internal Revenue Service		

U.S. Individual Income Tax Return (99) **2008** IRS Use Only—Do not write or staple in this space.

Label (See page 17.)

Use the IRS label. Otherwise, please print or type.

Your first name and initial: **Katherine M.** Last name: **Grayson**

If a joint return, spouse's first name and initial: _____ Last name: _____

Home address (number and street). If you have a P.O. box, see page 17: **4611 Valley Lane** Apt. no. _____

City, town or post office, state, and ZIP code. If you have a foreign address, see page 17: **Texarkana, TX 75503**

OMB No. 1545-0074

Your social security number 900 43 4750

Spouse's social security number _____

▲ You **must** enter your SSN(s) above. ▲

Checking a box below will not change your tax or refund.

Presidential Election Campaign ▶ Check here if you, or your spouse if filing jointly, want $3 to go to this fund (see page 17) ▶ ☐ You ☐ Spouse

Filing status
Check only one box.

1. ☒ Single
2. ☐ Married filing jointly (even if only one had income)
3. ☐ Married filing separately. Enter spouse's SSN above and full name here. ▶
4. ☐ Head of household (with qualifying person). (See page 18.) If the qualifying person is a child but not your dependent, enter this child's name here. ▶
5. ☐ Qualifying widow(er) with dependent child (see page 19)

Exemptions

6a ☒ **Yourself.** If someone can claim you as a dependent, **do not** check box 6a.

b ☐ **Spouse**

If more than six dependents, see page 20.

c **Dependents:**

(1) First name Last name	(2) Dependent's social security number	(3) Dependent's relationship to you	(4) ✓ if qualifying child for child tax credit (see page 20)
			☐
			☐
			☐
			☐
			☐
			☐

Boxes checked on 6a and 6b: **1**

No. of children on 6c who:
- lived with you: _____
- did not live with you due to divorce or separation (see page 21): _____

Dependents on 6c not entered above: _____

d Total number of exemptions claimed.

Add numbers on lines above ▶ **1**

Income

Attach Form(s) W-2 here. Also attach Form(s) 1099-R if tax was withheld.

If you did not get a W-2, see page 23.

Enclose, but do not attach, any payment.

7 Wages, salaries, tips, etc. Attach Form(s) W-2. **7 18,950**

8a **Taxable** interest. Attach Schedule 1 if required. **8a 752**
b **Tax-exempt** interest. **Do not** include on line 8a. 8b

9a Ordinary dividends. Attach Schedule 1 if required. 9a
b Qualified dividends (see page 24). 9b

10 Capital gain distributions (see page 24). 10

11a IRA distributions. 11a | 11b Taxable amount (see page 24). 11b

12a Pensions and annuities. 12a | 12b Taxable amount (see page 25). 12b

13 Unemployment compensation and Alaska Permanent Fund dividends. 13

14a Social security benefits. 14a | 14b Taxable amount (see page 27). 14b

15 Add lines 7 through 14b (far right column). This is your **total income.** ▶ **15 19,702**

Adjusted gross income

16 Educator expenses (see page 29). 16
17 IRA deduction (see page 29). 17 **2,000**
18 Student loan interest deduction (see page 31). 18

19 Tuition and fees deduction. Attach Form 8917. 19
20 Add lines 16 through 19. These are your **total adjustments.** 20 **2,000**

21 Subtract line 20 from line 15. This is your **adjusted gross income.** ▶ **21 17,702**

For Disclosure, Privacy Act, and Paperwork Reduction Act Notice, see page 78. Cat. No. 11327A Form **1040A** (2008)

Figure 6-9

Form 1040A

	22	Enter the amount from line 21 (adjusted gross income).		22	**17,702**
Tax, credits, and payments	23a	Check if: { ☐ **You** were born before January 2, 1944, ☐ Blind } **Total boxes** { ☐ **Spouse** was born before January 2, 1944, ☐ Blind } **checked** ▶ 23a			☐
	b	If you are married filing separately and your spouse itemizes deductions, see page 32 and check here ▶ 23b			☐
Standard Deduction for—	c	Check if standard deduction includes real estate taxes (see page 32) ▶ 23c			☐
	24	Enter your **standard deduction** (see left margin).		24	**5,450**
● People who checked any box on line 23a, 23b, or 23c **or** who can be claimed as a dependent, see page 32.	25	Subtract line 24 from line 22. If line 24 is more than line 22, enter -0-.		25	**12,252**
	26	If line 22 is over $119,975, or you provided housing to a Midwestern displaced individual, see page 32. Otherwise, multiply $3,500 by the total number of exemptions claimed on line 6d.		26	**3,500**
● All others:	27	Subtract line 26 from line 25. If line 26 is more than line 25, enter -0-. This is your **taxable income.** ▶		27	**8,752**
Single or Married filing separately, $5,450	28	**Tax,** including any alternative minimum tax (see page 33).		28	**899**
	29	Credit for child and dependent care expenses. Attach Schedule 2.	29		
Married filing jointly or Qualifying widow(er), $10,900	30	Credit for the elderly or the disabled. Attach Schedule 3.	30		
	31	Education credits. Attach Form 8863.	31		
Head of household, $8,000	32	Retirement savings contributions credit. Attach Form 8880.	32		
	33	Child tax credit (see page 37). Attach Form 8901 if required.	33		
	34	Add lines 29 through 33. These are your **total credits.**		34	
	35	Subtract line 34 from line 28. If line 34 is more than line 28, enter -0-.		35	
	36	Advance earned income credit payments from Form(s) W-2, box 9.		36	
	37	Add lines 35 and 36. This is your **total tax.** ▶		37	**899**
	38	Federal income tax withheld from Forms W-2 and 1099.	38	**950**	
	39	2008 estimated tax payments and amount applied from 2007 return.	39		
If you have a qualifying child, attach Schedule EIC.	40a	**Earned income credit (EIC).**	40a		
	b	Nontaxable combat pay election. 40b			
	41	Additional child tax credit. Attach Form 8812.	41		
	42	Recovery rebate credit (see worksheet on pages 53 and 54).	42		
	43	Add lines 38, 39, 40a, 41, and 42. These are your **total payments.** ▶		43	**950**
Refund	44	If line 43 is more than line 37, subtract line 37 from line 43. This is the amount you **overpaid.**		44	**51**
Direct deposit? See page 55 and fill in 45b, 45c, and 45d or Form 8888.	45a	Amount of line 44 you want **refunded to you.** If Form 8888 is attached, check here ▶ ☐		45a	**51**
	▶ b	Routing number ▷ ☐☐☐☐☐☐☐☐☐ ▶ c Type: ☐ Checking ☐ Savings			
	▶ d	Account number ☐☐☐☐☐☐☐☐☐☐☐☐☐☐☐☐☐			
	46	Amount of line 44 you want **applied to your 2009 estimated tax.**	46		
Amount you owe	47	**Amount you owe.** Subtract line 43 from line 37. For details on how to pay, see page 56. ▶		47	
	48	Estimated tax penalty (see page 57).	48		

Third party designee	Do you want to allow another person to discuss this return with the IRS (see page 57)? ☐ **Yes.** Complete the following. ☐ **No**
	Designee's name ▶ _____ Phone no. ▶ (___) _____ Personal identification number (PIN) ▶ ☐☐☐☐☐

Sign here	Under penalties of perjury, I declare that I have examined this return and accompanying schedules and statements, and to the best of my knowledge and belief, they are true, correct, and accurately list all amounts and sources of income I received during the tax year. Declaration of preparer (other than the taxpayer) is based on all information of which the preparer has any knowledge.
Joint return? See page 17. Keep a copy for your records.	Your signature **Kathryn Grayson** Date 4/3/-- Your occupation **Receptionist** Daytime phone number **(555) 555-0123**
	Spouse's signature. If a joint return, **both** must sign. Date Spouse's occupation

Paid preparer's use only	Preparer's signature ▶ Date Check if self-employed ☐ Preparer's SSN or PTIN
	Firm's name (or yours if self-employed), address, and ZIP code ▶ EIN _____ Phone no. (___)

Form **1040A** (2008)

For those who have types of income, adjustments, deductions, or credits not allowed on either of Forms 1040EZ or 1040A, there is Form 1040 with its many schedules and forms. Schedule A allows you to itemize your deductions. While the scope of Form 1040 reaches beyond what can be illustrated here, the example of the Winters family will give you some idea of how reporting on Form 1040 is different from 1040EZ and 1040A.

EXAMPLE

Thomas Winters and his wife Ann file a joint return. Thomas made $20,380 in wages, and Ann made $10,329 working part time. They have one child, age 8. Thomas contributed $2,000 to an IRA during the year. Their itemized deductions are $5,600 for medical and dental expenses, $1,230 for real estate tax, $480 for personal property tax, $3,910 for home mortgage interest, and $2,800 for charitable contributions. They had $5,177 in income taxes withheld during the year.

STEPS

1. Calculate the total income.
$$\$20,380 + \$10,329 = \$30,709$$

2. Calculate the adjusted gross income by subtracting the $2000 IRA contribution from the total income.
$$\$30,709 - \$2,000 = \$28,709$$

3. For medical expenses, only the amount exceeding 7.5% of adjusted gross income can be deducted.
$$7.5\% \times \$28,709 = \$2,153 \text{ (rounded)}$$
$$\$5,600 - \$2,153 = \$3,447$$

4. Find the total itemized deductions.

Medical expenses + Real estate tax + Personal property tax + Home mortgage interest + Charitable deductions = $3,447 + 1,230 + 480 + 3,910 + 2,800 = $11,867

5. Subtract the itemized deductions from the adjusted gross income.
$$\$28,709 - \$11,867 = \$16,842$$

6. Find the amount for 3 exemptions.
$$\$3,500 \times 3 = \$10,500$$

7. Subtract the amount for exemptions from the total in Step 5 to find the taxable income.
$$\$16,842 - \$10,500 = \$6,342 \quad \text{taxable income}$$

8. Find the income tax in the tax tables (see Figure 6-10 Tax Table).
$$\$633 \qquad \text{tax}$$

9. Subtract the tax from the amount of taxes paid (withheld) to find the amount of tax due or refund due.
$$\$5,177 - \$633 = \$4,544 \quad \text{refund due}$$

TIPS

When you itemize your deductions (married filing jointly) and the amount is over $10,900, you use your itemized figure. If your deductions are less than $10,900, you are allowed by law the standard deduction.

TIPS

You can file electronically, sign electronically, and get your refund or even pay electronically. IRS e-file offers accurate, safe, and fast alternatives to filing on paper.

Figure 6-10

Tax Table

20--
Tax Table

⚠️ **CAUTION**

See the instructions for line 44 that begin on page 37 to see if you must use the Tax Table below to figure your tax.

Example. Mr. and Mrs. Brown are filing a joint return. Their taxable income on Form 1040, line 43, is $25,300. First, they find the $25,300–25,350 taxable income line. Next, they find the column for married filing jointly and read down the column. The amount shown where the taxable income line and filing status column meet is $2,964. This is the tax amount they should enter on Form 1040, line 44.

Sample Table

At least	But less than	Single	Married filing jointly *	Married filing separately	Head of a household
			Your tax is—		
25,200	25,250	3,366	2,949	3,366	3,186
25,250	25,300	3,374	2,956	3,374	3,194
25,300	25,350	3,381	(2,964)	3,381	3,201
25,350	25,400	3,389	2,971	3,389	3,209

If line 43 (taxable income) is— At least	But less than	Single	Married filing jointly *	Married filing separately	Head of a house-hold
			Your tax is—		
0	5	0	0	0	0
5	15	1	1	1	1
15	25	2	2	2	2
25	50	4	4	4	4
50	75	6	6	6	6
75	100	9	9	9	9
100	125	11	11	11	11
125	150	14	14	14	14
150	175	16	16	16	16
175	200	19	19	19	19
200	225	21	21	21	21
225	250	24	24	24	24
250	275	26	26	26	26
275	300	29	29	29	29
300	325	31	31	31	31
325	350	34	34	34	34
350	375	36	36	36	36
375	400	39	39	39	39
400	425	41	41	41	41
425	450	44	44	44	44
450	475	46	46	46	46
475	500	49	49	49	49
500	525	51	51	51	51
525	550	54	54	54	54
550	575	56	56	56	56
575	600	59	59	59	59
600	625	61	61	61	61
625	650	64	64	64	64
650	675	66	66	66	66
675	700	69	69	69	69
700	725	71	71	71	71
725	750	74	74	74	74
750	775	76	76	76	76
775	800	79	79	79	79
800	825	81	81	81	81
825	850	84	84	84	84
850	875	86	86	86	86
875	900	89	89	89	89
900	925	91	91	91	91
925	950	94	94	94	94
950	975	96	96	96	96
975	1,000	99	99	99	99

1,000

At least	But less than	Single	Married filing jointly	Married filing separately	Head of a house-hold
1,000	1,025	101	101	101	101
1,025	1,050	104	104	104	104
1,050	1,075	106	106	106	106
1,075	1,100	109	109	109	109
1,100	1,125	111	111	111	111
1,125	1,150	114	114	114	114
1,150	1,175	116	116	116	116
1,175	1,200	119	119	119	119
1,200	1,225	121	121	121	121
1,225	1,250	124	124	124	124
1,250	1,275	126	126	126	126
1,275	1,300	129	129	129	129

If line 43 (taxable income) is— At least	But less than	Single	Married filing jointly *	Married filing separately	Head of a house-hold
			Your tax is—		
1,300	1,325	131	131	131	131
1,325	1,350	134	134	134	134
1,350	1,375	136	136	136	136
1,375	1,400	139	139	139	139
1,400	1,425	141	141	141	141
1,425	1,450	144	144	144	144
1,450	1,475	146	146	146	146
1,475	1,500	149	149	149	149
1,500	1,525	151	151	151	151
1,525	1,550	154	154	154	154
1,550	1,575	156	156	156	156
1,575	1,600	159	159	159	159
1,600	1,625	161	161	161	161
1,625	1,650	164	164	164	164
1,650	1,675	166	166	166	166
1,675	1,700	169	169	169	169
1,700	1,725	171	171	171	171
1,725	1,750	174	174	174	174
1,750	1,775	176	176	176	176
1,775	1,800	179	179	179	179
1,800	1,825	181	181	181	181
1,825	1,850	184	184	184	184
1,850	1,875	186	186	186	186
1,875	1,900	189	189	189	189
1,900	1,925	191	191	191	191
1,925	1,950	194	194	194	194
1,950	1,975	196	196	196	196
1,975	2,000	199	199	199	199

2,000

At least	But less than	Single	Married filing jointly	Married filing separately	Head of a house-hold
2,000	2,025	201	201	201	201
2,025	2,050	204	204	204	204
2,050	2,075	206	206	206	206
2,075	2,100	209	209	209	209
2,100	2,125	211	211	211	211
2,125	2,150	214	214	214	214
2,150	2,175	216	216	216	216
2,175	2,200	219	219	219	219
2,200	2,225	221	221	221	221
2,225	2,250	224	224	224	224
2,250	2,275	226	226	226	226
2,275	2,300	229	229	229	229
2,300	2,325	231	231	231	231
2,325	2,350	234	234	234	234
2,350	2,375	236	236	236	236
2,375	2,400	239	239	239	239
2,400	2,425	241	241	241	241
2,425	2,450	244	244	244	244
2,450	2,475	246	246	246	246
2,475	2,500	249	249	249	249
2,500	2,525	251	251	251	251
2,525	2,550	254	254	254	254
2,550	2,575	256	256	256	256
2,575	2,600	259	259	259	259
2,600	2,625	261	261	261	261
2,625	2,650	264	264	264	264
2,650	2,675	266	266	266	266
2,675	2,700	269	269	269	269

If line 43 (taxable income) is— At least	But less than	Single	Married filing jointly *	Married filing separately	Head of a house-hold
			Your tax is—		
2,700	2,725	271	271	271	271
2,725	2,750	274	274	274	274
2,750	2,775	276	276	276	276
2,775	2,800	279	279	279	279
2,800	2,825	281	281	281	281
2,825	2,850	284	284	284	284
2,850	2,875	286	286	286	286
2,875	2,900	289	289	289	289
2,900	2,925	291	291	291	291
2,925	2,950	294	294	294	294
2,950	2,975	296	296	296	296
2,975	3,000	299	299	299	299

3,000

At least	But less than	Single	Married filing jointly	Married filing separately	Head of a house-hold
3,000	3,050	303	303	303	303
3,050	3,100	308	308	308	308
3,100	3,150	313	313	313	313
3,150	3,200	318	318	318	318
3,200	3,250	323	323	323	323
3,250	3,300	328	328	328	328
3,300	3,350	333	333	333	333
3,350	3,400	338	338	338	338
3,400	3,450	343	343	343	343
3,450	3,500	348	348	348	348
3,500	3,550	353	353	353	353
3,550	3,600	358	358	358	358
3,600	3,650	363	363	363	363
3,650	3,700	368	368	368	368
3,700	3,750	373	373	373	373
3,750	3,800	378	378	378	378
3,800	3,850	383	383	383	383
3,850	3,900	388	388	388	388
3,900	3,950	393	393	393	393
3,950	4,000	398	398	398	398

4,000

At least	But less than	Single	Married filing jointly	Married filing separately	Head of a house-hold
4,000	4,050	403	403	403	403
4,050	4,100	408	408	408	408
4,100	4,150	413	413	413	413
4,150	4,200	418	418	418	418
4,200	4,250	423	423	423	423
4,250	4,300	428	428	428	428
4,300	4,350	433	433	433	433
4,350	4,400	438	438	438	438
4,400	4,450	443	443	443	443
4,450	4,500	448	448	448	448
4,500	4,550	453	453	453	453
4,550	4,600	458	458	458	458
4,600	4,650	463	463	463	463
4,650	4,700	468	468	468	468
4,700	4,750	473	473	473	473
4,750	4,800	478	478	478	478
4,800	4,850	483	483	483	483
4,850	4,900	488	488	488	488
4,900	4,950	493	493	493	493
4,950	5,000	498	498	498	498

---

* This column must also be used by a qualifying widow(er).

Figure 6-10

Tax Table

20-- Tax Table–Continued

If line 43 (taxable income) is—		And you are—			
At least	But less than	Single	Married filing jointly *	Married filing separately	Head of a household
		Your tax is—			

5,000

At least	But less than	Single	Married filing jointly	Married filing separately	Head of a household
5,000	5,050	503	503	503	503
5,050	5,100	508	508	508	508
5,100	5,150	513	513	513	513
5,150	5,200	518	518	518	518
5,200	5,250	523	523	523	523
5,250	5,300	528	528	528	528
5,300	5,350	533	533	533	533
5,350	5,400	538	538	538	538
5,400	5,450	543	543	543	543
5,450	5,500	548	548	548	548
5,500	5,550	553	553	553	553
5,550	5,600	558	558	558	558
5,600	5,650	563	563	563	563
5,650	5,700	568	568	568	568
5,700	5,750	573	573	573	573
5,750	5,800	578	578	578	578
5,800	5,850	583	583	583	583
5,850	5,900	588	588	588	588
5,900	5,950	593	593	593	593
5,950	6,000	598	598	598	598

6,000

At least	But less than	Single	Married filing jointly	Married filing separately	Head of a household
6,000	6,050	603	603	603	603
6,050	6,100	608	608	608	608
6,100	6,150	613	613	613	613
6,150	6,200	618	618	618	618
6,200	6,250	623	623	623	623
6,250	6,300	628	628	628	628
6,300	6,350	633	633	633	633
6,350	6,400	638	638	638	638
6,400	6,450	643	643	643	643
6,450	6,500	648	648	648	648
6,500	6,550	653	653	653	653
6,550	6,600	658	658	658	658
6,600	6,650	663	663	663	663
6,650	6,700	668	668	668	668
6,700	6,750	673	673	673	673
6,750	6,800	678	678	678	678
6,800	6,850	683	683	683	683
6,850	6,900	688	688	688	688
6,900	6,950	693	693	693	693
6,950	7,000	698	698	698	698

7,000

At least	But less than	Single	Married filing jointly	Married filing separately	Head of a household
7,000	7,050	703	703	703	703
7,050	7,100	708	708	708	708
7,100	7,150	713	713	713	713
7,150	7,200	718	718	718	718
7,200	7,250	723	723	723	723
7,250	7,300	728	728	728	728
7,300	7,350	733	733	733	733
7,350	7,400	738	738	738	738
7,400	7,450	743	743	743	743
7,450	7,500	748	748	748	748
7,500	7,550	753	753	753	753
7,550	7,600	758	758	758	758
7,600	7,650	763	763	763	763
7,650	7,700	768	768	768	768
7,700	7,750	773	773	773	773
7,750	7,800	778	778	778	778
7,800	7,850	783	783	783	783
7,850	7,900	788	788	788	788
7,900	7,950	793	793	793	793
7,950	8,000	798	798	798	798

8,000

At least	But less than	Single	Married filing jointly	Married filing separately	Head of a household
8,000	8,050	803	803	803	803
8,050	8,100	808	808	808	808
8,100	8,150	813	813	813	813
8,150	8,200	818	818	818	818
8,200	8,250	823	823	823	823
8,250	8,300	828	828	828	828
8,300	8,350	833	833	833	833
8,350	8,400	839	838	839	838
8,400	8,450	846	843	846	843
8,450	8,500	854	848	854	848
8,500	8,550	861	853	861	853
8,550	8,600	869	858	869	858
8,600	8,650	876	863	876	863
8,650	8,700	884	868	884	868
8,700	8,750	891	873	891	873
8,750	8,800	899	878	899	878
8,800	8,850	906	883	906	883
8,850	8,900	914	888	914	888
8,900	8,950	921	893	921	893
8,950	9,000	929	898	929	898

9,000

At least	But less than	Single	Married filing jointly	Married filing separately	Head of a household
9,000	9,050	936	903	936	903
9,050	9,100	944	908	944	908
9,100	9,150	951	913	951	913
9,150	9,200	959	918	959	918
9,200	9,250	966	923	966	923
9,250	9,300	974	928	974	928
9,300	9,350	981	933	981	933
9,350	9,400	989	938	989	938
9,400	9,450	996	943	996	943
9,450	9,500	1,004	948	1,004	948
9,500	9,550	1,011	953	1,011	953
9,550	9,600	1,019	958	1,019	958
9,600	9,650	1,026	963	1,026	963
9,650	9,700	1,034	968	1,034	968
9,700	9,750	1,041	973	1,041	973
9,750	9,800	1,049	978	1,049	978
9,800	9,850	1,056	983	1,056	983
9,850	9,900	1,064	988	1,064	988
9,900	9,950	1,071	993	1,071	993
9,950	10,000	1,079	998	1,079	998

10,000

At least	But less than	Single	Married filing jointly	Married filing separately	Head of a household
10,000	10,050	1,086	1,003	1,086	1,003
10,050	10,100	1,094	1,008	1,094	1,008
10,100	10,150	1,101	1,013	1,101	1,013
10,150	10,200	1,109	1,018	1,109	1,018
10,200	10,250	1,116	1,023	1,116	1,023
10,250	10,300	1,124	1,028	1,124	1,028
10,300	10,350	1,131	1,033	1,131	1,033
10,350	10,400	1,139	1,038	1,139	1,038
10,400	10,450	1,146	1,043	1,146	1,043
10,450	10,500	1,154	1,048	1,154	1,048
10,500	10,550	1,161	1,053	1,161	1,053
10,550	10,600	1,169	1,058	1,169	1,058
10,600	10,650	1,176	1,063	1,176	1,063
10,650	10,700	1,184	1,068	1,184	1,068
10,700	10,750	1,191	1,073	1,191	1,073
10,750	10,800	1,199	1,078	1,199	1,078
10,800	10,850	1,206	1,083	1,206	1,083
10,850	10,900	1,214	1,088	1,214	1,088
10,900	10,950	1,221	1,093	1,221	1,093
10,950	11,000	1,229	1,098	1,229	1,098

11,000

At least	But less than	Single	Married filing jointly	Married filing separately	Head of a household
11,000	11,050	1,236	1,103	1,236	1,103
11,050	11,100	1,244	1,108	1,244	1,108
11,100	11,150	1,251	1,113	1,251	1,113
11,150	11,200	1,259	1,118	1,259	1,118
11,200	11,250	1,266	1,123	1,266	1,123
11,250	11,300	1,274	1,128	1,274	1,128
11,300	11,350	1,281	1,133	1,281	1,133
11,350	11,400	1,289	1,138	1,289	1,138
11,400	11,450	1,296	1,143	1,296	1,143
11,450	11,500	1,304	1,148	1,304	1,148
11,500	11,550	1,311	1,153	1,311	1,153
11,550	11,600	1,319	1,158	1,319	1,158
11,600	11,650	1,326	1,163	1,326	1,163
11,650	11,700	1,334	1,168	1,334	1,168
11,700	11,750	1,341	1,173	1,341	1,173
11,750	11,800	1,349	1,178	1,349	1,178
11,800	11,850	1,356	1,183	1,356	1,183
11,850	11,900	1,364	1,188	1,364	1,188
11,900	11,950	1,371	1,193	1,371	1,193
11,950	12,000	1,379	1,198	1,379	1,199

12,000

At least	But less than	Single	Married filing jointly	Married filing separately	Head of a household
12,000	12,050	1,386	1,203	1,386	1,206
12,050	12,100	1,394	1,208	1,394	1,214
12,100	12,150	1,401	1,213	1,401	1,221
12,150	12,200	1,409	1,218	1,409	1,229
12,200	12,250	1,416	1,223	1,416	1,236
12,250	12,300	1,424	1,228	1,424	1,244
12,300	12,350	1,431	1,233	1,431	1,251
12,350	12,400	1,439	1,238	1,439	1,259
12,400	12,450	1,446	1,243	1,446	1,266
12,450	12,500	1,454	1,248	1,454	1,274
12,500	12,550	1,461	1,253	1,461	1,281
12,550	12,600	1,469	1,258	1,469	1,289
12,600	12,650	1,476	1,263	1,476	1,296
12,650	12,700	1,484	1,268	1,484	1,304
12,700	12,750	1,491	1,273	1,491	1,311
12,750	12,800	1,499	1,278	1,499	1,319
12,800	12,850	1,506	1,283	1,506	1,326
12,850	12,900	1,514	1,288	1,514	1,334
12,900	12,950	1,521	1,293	1,521	1,341
12,950	13,000	1,529	1,298	1,529	1,349

13,000

At least	But less than	Single	Married filing jointly	Married filing separately	Head of a household
13,000	13,050	1,536	1,303	1,536	1,356
13,050	13,100	1,544	1,308	1,544	1,364
13,100	13,150	1,551	1,313	1,551	1,371
13,150	13,200	1,559	1,318	1,559	1,379
13,200	13,250	1,566	1,323	1,566	1,386
13,250	13,300	1,574	1,328	1,574	1,394
13,300	13,350	1,581	1,333	1,581	1,401
13,350	13,400	1,589	1,338	1,589	1,409
13,400	13,450	1,596	1,343	1,596	1,416
13,450	13,500	1,604	1,348	1,604	1,424
13,500	13,550	1,611	1,353	1,611	1,431
13,550	13,600	1,619	1,358	1,619	1,439
13,600	13,650	1,626	1,363	1,626	1,446
13,650	13,700	1,634	1,368	1,634	1,454
13,700	13,750	1,641	1,373	1,641	1,461
13,750	13,800	1,649	1,378	1,649	1,469
13,800	13,850	1,656	1,383	1,656	1,476
13,850	13,900	1,664	1,388	1,664	1,484
13,900	13,950	1,671	1,393	1,671	1,491
13,950	14,000	1,679	1,398	1,679	1,499

* This column must also be used by a qualifying widow(er).

OBJECTIVE 6 Use Excel to calculate taxable income.

Federal Income Tax

Accounting offices that calculate federal income tax for individuals, partnerships, and corporations also use specialized software. Tax information is input on the various schedules along with a 1040 form designed and required by the IRS. The software automatically calculates the tax owed or refund due. The tax forms are reviewed and signed by the tax preparer and the taxpayer and either mailed to the IRS or filed electronically through the Internet. You can use a spreadsheet such as the one in Figure 6-11 to calculate taxable income.

PRACTICE

Retrieve the file *ch06pr05.xlsx*. Follow the directions. Save the file as *ch06pr05a.xlsx*.

Figure 6-11
Calculate Taxable Income

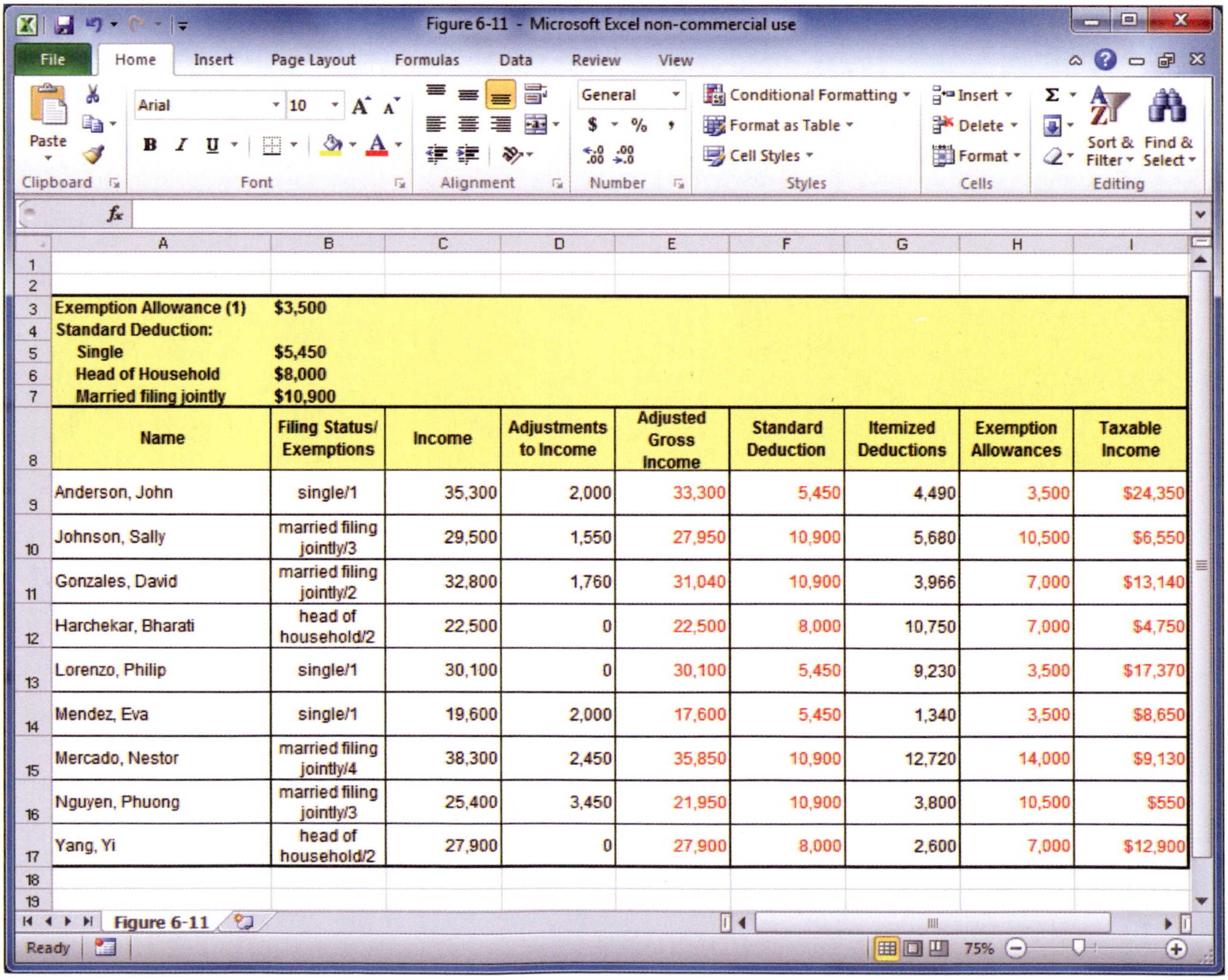

Exemption Allowance (1)	$3,500
Standard Deduction:	
Single	$5,450
Head of Household	$8,000
Married filing jointly	$10,900

Name	Filing Status/ Exemptions	Income	Adjustments to Income	Adjusted Gross Income	Standard Deduction	Itemized Deductions	Exemption Allowances	Taxable Income
Anderson, John	single/1	35,300	2,000	33,300	5,450	4,490	3,500	$24,350
Johnson, Sally	married filing jointly/3	29,500	1,550	27,950	10,900	5,680	10,500	$6,550
Gonzales, David	married filing jointly/2	32,800	1,760	31,040	10,900	3,966	7,000	$13,140
Harchekar, Bharati	head of household/2	22,500	0	22,500	8,000	10,750	7,000	$4,750
Lorenzo, Philip	single/1	30,100	0	30,100	5,450	9,230	3,500	$17,370
Mendez, Eva	single/1	19,600	2,000	17,600	5,450	1,340	3,500	$8,650
Mercado, Nestor	married filing jointly/4	38,300	2,450	35,850	10,900	12,720	14,000	$9,130
Nguyen, Phuong	married filing jointly/3	25,400	3,450	21,950	10,900	3,800	10,500	$550
Yang, Yi	head of household/2	27,900	0	27,900	8,000	2,600	7,000	$12,900

Name _____ Date _____

Directions   Solve the following problems. Write your answers in the blanks provided.

A. Use the income tax tables on pages 219 and 220 to determine the   OBJECTIVE **3**
amount of tax due.

Taxable Income (Married Filing Jointly)	Tax Due		Taxable Income (Single)	Tax Due
1. $6,775	_____	2. $12,950		_____
3. $12,054	_____	4. $13,800		_____
5. $9,211	_____	6. $10,990		_____
7. $11,335	_____	8. $7,805		_____
9. $8,510	_____	10. $11,215		_____
11. $7,890	_____	12. $4,350		_____
13. $10,360	_____	14. $2,975		_____

B. Compute taxable income, federal income tax due, and amount owed or   OBJECTIVE **3**
refund using Form 1040EZ.

Mary Bailey is single. Her total wages for the year were $16,000. She claims no dependents other than herself. Her W-2 shows she had $1,995 in federal income tax withheld.

15.   Taxable income: _____   **16.**   Tax due: _____   **17.**   refund/owe: _____

Rachel Greenwood is single. Her total wages for the year were $20,000. She claims no dependents other than herself. Rachel's W-2 shows she had $1,028 in federal income tax withheld.

18.   Taxable income: _____   **19.**   Tax due: _____   **20.**   refund/owe: _____

Rosa Martinez is single. Her total wages were $19,500, and her interest earned from a savings account was $350. She claimed herself as a dependent. Rosa had $1,140 withheld for federal taxes.

21.   Taxable income: _____   **22.**   Tax due: _____   **23.**   refund/owe: _____

Danny Roberts attends college, lives at home, and works part-time at a local grocery store chain. Danny's total wages were $10,710, and he had $1,150 in federal income tax withheld during the year. He is single and claims 0 exemptions because his father claims him.

24.   Taxable income: _____   **25.**   Tax due: _____   **26.**   refund/owe: _____

C. Compute taxable income, federal income tax due, and amount owed or refund using Form 1040A. OBJECTIVE 4

Kyle O'Nealy is single and earned $18,500 at Hillside Manufacturing. He contributed $2,000 to an IRA and earned interest amounting to $110. He had $1,946 in federal taxes withheld.

27. Taxable income: _____ **28.** Tax due: _____ **29.** refund/owe: _____

Les Pittman is single and earned $13,600 as a machine operator. He had $1,100 in earned interest. His income tax withholding was $1,565. How much additional tax does he owe, or what is his refund?

30. Taxable income: _____ **31.** Tax due: _____ **32.** refund/owe: _____

D. Compute federal income tax for Form 1040. OBJECTIVE 5

33. Jamie and Viviana Carrazco are married and filed a joint return. Jamie made $45,500. Viviana made $12,600 working part time. They have four minor children. Jamie contributed $3,500 to an IRA for himself. Viviana contributed $3,000 to her IRA. Their itemized deductions are: $4,450 for medical and dental expenses; $13,200 for home mortgage interest; $540 for personal property tax; and $10,800 for charitable contributions. Together, they had $1,515 withheld for income tax during the year. Compute the federal income tax refund/owed if they itemize their deductions using Form 1040.

Jamie's income   _____
Viviana's income   _____
Total income   _____
Minus adjustments to income (IRAs)   _____
Adjusted Gross Income   _____

Less itemized deductions (Schedule A)
    Medical expense
        Total medical expenses   _____
        Adjusted gross income times 7.5% _____
    Total deductible medical expense   _____

    Other deductions
        Home mortgage interest   _____
        Personal property tax   _____
        Charitable contributions   _____
    Total other deductions   _____
Total all deductions   _____
Less exemptions (6 @ $3,500 each)   _____
Taxable income   _____
Federal income tax (married filing jointly)   _____
Federal income tax withheld   _____
Amount due/Refund due   _____

34. Albert and Debra O'Donnell are married and filed a joint return; they are still working and not retired. Albert made $42,300, and Debra made $35,600. They have three minor children. Albert contributed $2,000 to an IRA for himself and $2,000 to an IRA for Debra. Their itemized deductions are $18,450 for medical and dental expenses; $12,100 for real estate tax; $14,200 for home mortgage interest; $580 for personal property tax; and $9,800 for charitable contributions. Together they had $6,685 in income taxes withheld during the year. Compute the federal income tax refund/owed if they itemize their deductions using Form 1040.

Albert's income   _____
Debra's income   _____
Total income   _____
Minus adjustments to income (IRAs)   _____
Adjusted Gross Income   _____

Less itemized deductions (Schedule A)
     Medical expense
         Total medical expenses   _____
         Adjusted gross income times 7.5%   _____
     Total deductible medical expense   _____

     Other
     deductions
         Real estate tax   _____
         Home mortgage interest   _____
         Personal property tax   _____
         Charitable contributions   _____
         Total other deductions   _____
     Total all deductions   _____
     Less exemptions (5 @ $3,500 each)   _____
     Taxable income   _____
     Federal income tax (married filing jointly)   _____
     Federal income tax withheld   _____
     Amount due/Refund due   _____

E. Use Excel to calculate taxable income.   OBJECTIVE 6

35. Retrieve the file *ch06ex05.xlsx*. Follow the directions. Save the file as *ch06ex05u.xlsx*.

Chapter Review and Assessment

KEY TERMS

adjusted gross income

adjustments to income

alternative minimum tax

assessed rate

assessed value

assessor

earned income tax credit

escrow account

estimated tax payments

exemptions

Federal Unemployment Tax Act (FUTA)

Health Savings Account (HSA)

individual retirement account (IRA)

itemized deductions

levied

market value

mill

personal property

property tax

real property

standard deduction

State Unemployment Tax Act (SUTA)

tax

tax credits

tax rate

taxable income

total income

CONCEPTS	EXAMPLES
6.1 Calculate the tax levied on property based on the assessed value.	
Dollars per $100	Assessed value is 60% of market value; Tax rate is $3.80 per $100; Market value is $130,000.
1. Multiply the market value of the property by the assessed rate.	$130,000 × 60% = $78,000 assessed value
2. Determine the number of $100s in the assessed value.	$78,000 ÷ $100 = 780
3. Multiply the number of $100s by the tax rate to determine the amount of tax due.	780 × $3.80 = $2,964 property tax due
Dollars per $1,000	Dollars per $1,000 works the same, except determine the number of $1,000s in the market value instead of the number of $100s and then follow the steps above.
Mills per dollar of assessed value	Assessed value is $126,000; Tax rate is 32 mills.
1. Convert mills to dollars.	32 mills ÷ $1,000 = $0.032
2. Multiply the assessed value by the tax rate in dollars.	$126,000 × $0.032 = $4,032 property tax due
6.1 Calculate the tax rate levied on property based on the assessed value.	
1. Determine the amount of money needed.	$50,000,000
2. Divide the amount of money needed by the total assessed value.	Assessed value: $5,000,000,000 $50 million ÷ $5 billion = 0.01 or 1%

CONCEPTS	EXAMPLES
6.2 Calculate state unemployment tax.	SUTA tax rate is 3.0% on first $9,000 of wages; First quarter wages are $6,900; Total wages at end of second quarter are $13,800. Find first and second quarter SUTA taxes. Find maximum SUTA tax.
1. Multiply first quarter wages subject to tax by the tax rate.	$6,900 × 3% = $207.00
2. Subtract first quarter wages from maximum wages subject to tax.	$9,000 − $6,900 = $2,100
3. Multiply second quarter wages subject to tax by the tax rate.	$2,100 × 3% = $63.00
4. Add first and second quarter taxes, or multiply the tax rate times the maximum wages.	$207.00 + $63.00 = $270.00 total SUTA tax Or $9,000 × 3% = $270.00
6.2 Calculate federal unemployment tax.	Find FUTA tax rate. First quarter wages are $6,900; Total wages at end of second quarter are $13,800; Find first and second quarter FUTA taxes. Find maximum FUTA tax.
1. Find FUTA rate.	6.2% − 5.4% = 0.8%
2. Multiply first quarter wages subject to tax by the tax rate.	$6,900 × 0.8% = $55.20
3. Subtract first quarter wages from maximum wages subject to tax.	$7,000 − $6,900 = $100
4. Multiply second quarter wages subject to tax by the tax rate.	$100 × 0.8% = $0.80
5. Add first and second quarter taxes, or multiply the tax rate times the maximum wages.	$55.20 + $0.80 = $56.00 total FUTA tax Or $7,000 × 0.8% = $56.00
6.3 Calculate federal income tax.	Wages are $37,348; interest earned is $372; married filing jointly; plus three exemptions; IRA contributions of $3,000; amount withheld $5,284. Reporting on Form 1040A.
Form 1040EZ Use Form 1040EZ when your return is simple.	
Form 1040A Use form 1040A when you do not plan to itemize your deductions.	
Form 1040 Use Form 1040 when you want to itemize your deductions.	
1. Find total income.	$37,348 + $372 = $37,720 total income
2. Subtract adjustments to find adjusted gross income.	$37,720 − $3,000 = $34,720 adjusted gross income
3. Subtract standard deductions.	$34,720 − $10,900 = $23,820 standard deduction taken
4. Find total exemptions.	5 × $3,500 = $17,500 exemptions allowed
5. Subtract exemptions to find taxable income.	$23,820 − $17,500 = $6,320 taxable income
6. Find income tax from tax table or use tax worksheet to compute tax.	$633 tax due
7. Subtract credits and add other taxes, if any, to find total tax.	None
8. Subtract tax payments (withholding) to find amount of tax due or refund due.	$5,284 − $633 = $4,651 refund due

Chapter 6 Review Exercises

Name _____   Date _____

Directions   Write your answers in the blanks provided. Round dollar amounts to the nearest hundredth.

A. Determine the amount of tax due in the following problems.   `6.1 OBJECTIVE 2`

	Market Value	Assessed Value	Tax Rate	Tax Due
1.	$80,000	75%	$2.95 per $1,000	_____
2.	$110,000	60%	$5.45 per $100	_____
3.	$200,000	100%	12 mills	_____

B. Complete the following problems to compute the tax rates. Round your answers to the nearest whole percent.   `6.1 OBJECTIVE 3`

	Money Needed	Assessed Value	Tax Rate
4.	$5,500,000	$225,000,000	_____
5.	$946,245	$19,050,000	_____

C. Complete the following problems to compute state unemployment tax for one employee. Assume a tax rate of 3% on the first $9,000.   `6.2 OBJECTIVE 2`

6.	$4,300 gross wages	_____ tax due	7.	$12,000 gross wages	_____ tax due
8.	$15,825 gross wages	_____ tax due	9.	$8,900 gross wages	_____ tax due

D. Compute federal unemployment tax. Use 0.8% as the tax rate. Assume all wages subject to tax.   `6.2 OBJECTIVE 3`

10.	$42,000 gross earnings	_____ tax due	11.	$58,942 gross earnings	_____ tax due
12.	$18,296 gross earnings	_____ tax due	13.	$96,500 gross earnings	_____ tax due

E. Compute federal income tax as you would on Form 1040EZ.   `6.3 OBJECTIVES 2, 3`

JoAnn White is single and earned $19,500 in wages and $560 in interest from her savings account. JoAnn has no exemptions other than herself. Compute JoAnn's tax.

Total income	$19,500
Plus interest income (savings account)	$ 560

14.   Adjusted gross income .... _____
        Less standard deduction (single) .... $ 5,450
        Less exemptions (1) .... $ 3,500

15.   Taxable income .... _____

16.   Federal income tax (single, from tax table) .... _____
        Income tax withheld .... $ 1,005

17.   Federal income tax due .... _____

F. Compute federal income tax as you would on Form 1040A. 6.3 OBJECTIVE 4

18. Asad Karim is single, 55 years of age, and earned $22,300 during the year. He had a total of $1,530 withheld in income tax from his pay. He contributed $3,500 to his IRA. Calculate the tax owed or the refund for Asad. _____

19. Raquel Aguilar is single and earned $12,250 during the year. She had a total of $290 withheld in income tax. Calculate the tax owed or refund due. _____

G. Compute federal income tax as you would on Form 1040. 6.3 OBJECTIVE 5

20. Samuel and Margery Steinbach are married and plan to file a joint return. Both are still working and not retired. Samuel earned $27,200 and Margery earned $15,600 in wages for the year. They have three minor children. They earned interest of $1,033 from a savings account. Margery contributed $3,000 to her IRA during the year. Their itemized deductions are $2,950 for medical expenses; $1,050 for real estate tax; $12,400 for home mortgage interest; $1,522 for personal property tax; and $3,680 for charitable contributions. Together, their income tax withholding was $3,664. Compute Samuel and Margery's income tax owed or refund due.

Samuel's income _____
Margery's income _____
Savings interest _____
Total income _____
Minus adjustments to income (IRAs) _____
Adjusted Gross Income _____

Less itemized deductions (Schedule A)
    Medical expense
        Total medical expenses _____
        Adjusted gross income times 7.5% _____
    Total deductible medical expense _____

    Other deductions
        Real estate tax _____
        Home mortgage interest _____
        Personal property tax _____
        Charitable contributions _____
    Total other deductions _____
Total all deductions _____
Less exemptions (5@ $3,500 each) _____
Taxable income _____
Federal income tax (married filing jointly) _____
Federal income tax withheld _____
Amount due/Refund due _____

H. Use Excel to calculate property tax, SUTA, FUTA, and taxable income. 6.1 OBJECTIVE 4, 6.2 OBJECTIVE 4 6.3 OBJECTIVE 6

21. Retrieve the file *ch06ex06.xlsx*. Follow the directions. Save the file as *ch06ex06a.xlsx*.

22. Retrieve the file *ch06ex07.xlsx*. Follow the directions. Save the file as *ch06ex07a.xlsx*.

23. Retrieve the file *ch06ex08.xlsx*. Follow the directions. Save the file as *ch06ex08a.xlsx*.

24. Retrieve the file *ch06ex09.xlsx*. Follow the directions. Save the file as *ch06ex09a.xlsx*.

APPLY TAX ASSOCIATE

Many accounting firms hire part-time tax associates, especially during tax season (February through April 15). Skills may be acquired by taking a tax preparer course and successfully completing it.

Using the information below, complete the following problems using the procedure for Form 1040EZ.

Name	Marital Status	Total Income	IRA	Tax Withheld
Jacob Beauchamp	Single	$24,800	$3,000	$1,250
Tabitha Harrison	Single	$20,500	-0-	$1,495

1. What was Jacob's taxable income?

2. How much tax should Jacob pay according to the tax tables?

3. How much tax does Jacob owe or how much is his refund?

4. What was Tabitha's taxable income?

5. How much tax should Tabitha pay according to the tax tables?

6. How much tax does Tabitha owe or how much is her refund?

Write about Math

1. People may go to a tax preparer that will prepare their taxes and, for a fee, give them an immediate refund. What are the advantages and disadvantages of using such a service? Locate one of these tax preparers in your area. Call and find the fee charged for providing an immediate tax refund.

2. The IRS says they are striving to make federal income tax preparation easier by writing the 1040 Instruction Booklet in "plain English." What is your opinion of this instruction booklet? Give at least three examples from the booklet that demonstrate your opinion. Copies are online at www.irs.gov.

3. What are the advantages and disadvantages to using IRS e-file (electronic filing)?

Personal Finance

How much do you know about your property taxes and how they are assessed?

Property tax is an expense to every property owner. Whether you live in New York, Texas, California, or any other state, you must pay property taxes on real property. Real property is usually buildings and land. As a homeowner you pay property taxes on your residence. Your assessor may be appointed or elected depending on where you live. In New York State, almost all property is assessed locally by assessors who are appointed or elected at the municipal level. In Texas the county tax assessor is elected through public elections.

Counties, cities, towns, villages, school districts, and special districts each raise money through real property taxes. The money funds schools, pays for police and fire protection, maintains roads, and funds other municipal services enjoyed by residents.

1. Research about property tax in the county where you live by calling or visiting your local tax assessor's office or research online. Answer the following questions.
   a. Who is your county tax assessor, collector, or treasurer?

   b. What are the qualifications to become the tax assessor?

   c. Is the assessor appointed? If so, by whom? Or, are they elected? If so, how often?

   d. In what county are your taxes assessed?

   e. What is the website URL for your tax assessor?

   f. What is the address and phone number of your tax assessor?

   g. Who determines how much taxes are needed? What is the procedure?

   h. What kind(s) of property is taxed?

   i. Who assesses the property and how often?

   j. What method is used to determine assessed valuation of a piece of property?

   k. What is ad valorem tax?

   l. What is your tax rate? How is tax rate based—per $100, $1,000, mills?

   m. For what period is the rate in effect?

   n. To whom does the tax assessor report his or her findings about property values?

   o. When are property taxes due?

   p. What is the procedure to pay your property tax? How can you pay—check, phone, mail, or online?

   q. Do you receive a statement or bill for your property tax?

   r. What determines the amount of your property tax bill?

   s. If you don't agree with the amount of your property tax, how do you dispute it?

   t. How would you know if your property tax amount is fair?

2. Locate from your own personal records or the records of a friend or relative the property tax bill or statement for a piece of property. Make a copy of the notice. Make certain you whiteout or cover up any personal information, such as name and location of the property. Identify the counties, cities, towns, villages, school districts, and special districts that raise money through the real property tax on the bill. Turn the statement and your findings in to your instructor.

Name _____ Date _____ Score _____

Directions   Solve the following problems. Place your answers in the blanks provided.

A. **Compute the amount of property tax due. Round dollar amounts to the nearest hundredth.**   **6.1** OBJECTIVE **2**

	Market Value	Assessed Value	Tax Rate	Tax Due
1.	$145,000	65%	$2.35 per $1,000 =	_____
2.	$90,000	80%	$3.35 per $100 =	_____
3.	$365,000	100%	9 mills per dollar =	_____

B. **Compute the property tax rate.**   **6.1** OBJECTIVE **3**

	Money Needed	Assessed Value	Tax Rate
4.	$240,000	$1,500,000 =	_____
5.	$7,500,000	$250,000,000 =	_____

C. **Complete the following problems to compute state unemployment tax for one employee. Assume a tax rate of 3% on the first $9,000.**   **6.2** OBJECTIVE **2**

    6. $10,356 gross wages = _____ tax due   **7.** $6,555 gross wages = _____ tax due

D. **Compute federal unemployment tax. Use 0.8% as the tax rate. Assume all wages subject to tax. Round dollar amounts to the nearest hundredth.**   **6.2** OBJECTIVE **3**

    8. $6,123 gross wages = _____ tax due   **9.** $18,752 gross wages = _____ tax due

E. **Compute federal income tax as you would on Form 1040EZ. Kristen is single. Her total income was $21,000 in wages and $350 in interest from her savings account. Kristen has no exemptions other than herself. Compute her tax.**   **6.3** OBJECTIVES **2, 3**

	Total income	$21,000
	Plus interest income (savings account)	$350
10.	Adjusted gross income	_____
	Less standard deduction (single)	_____
	Less exemptions (1)	_____
11.	Taxable income	_____
12.	Federal income tax (single, from tax table)	_____
	Income tax withheld	$1,709
13.	Federal income tax due/Refund due	_____

F. Compute federal income tax as you would on Form 1040A. 6.3 OBJECTIVE 4

14. Bill Fritz is single, 55 years of age, and earned $24,600 during the year. He had a total of $1,476 withheld in income tax from his pay. He contributed $3,500 to his IRA. Calculate the tax owed or refund due for Bill. _____

15. Tomoko Yokozawa is single, in college, and earned $13,300 during the year. She had $798 in income tax withheld. She contributed $1,500 to her IRA. She paid $500 in student loan interest that is deductible. Calculate the tax owed or refund due for Tomoko. _____

G. Compute federal income tax as you would on Form 1040. 6.3 OBJECTIVE 5

16. Bryan and Deborah Alsup are married and plan to file a joint return. Bryan is working and Deborah is a stay-at-home mom. Bryan earned $47,600 for the year. They have four minor children. They earned interest of $950 from a savings account. Bryan contributed $3,000 to an IRA during the year. Their itemized deductions are $7,933 for medical expenses, $2,950 for real estate tax, $11,100 for home mortgage interest, $1,409 for personal property tax, and $2,640 for charitable contributions. They had $1,005 in income taxes withheld. Compute Bryan and Deborah's income tax owed or refund due.

Bryan's income _____
Savings interest _____
Total income _____
Minus adjustments to income (IRA contributions) _____
Adjusted Gross Income _____

Less itemized deductions (Schedule A)
    Medical expense
        Total medical expenses _____
        Adjusted gross income times 7.5% _____
    Total deductible medical expense _____

    Other deductions
        Real estate tax _____
        Home mortgage interest _____
        Personal property tax _____
        Charitable contributions _____
    Total other deductions _____
Total all deductions _____
Less exemptions (6 @ $3,050 each) _____
Taxable income _____
Federal income tax (married filing jointly) _____
Federal income tax withheld _____
Amount due/Refund due _____

H. Use Excel to calculate property tax, SUTA, FUTA, and taxable income. 6.1 OBJECTIVE 4, 6.2 OBJECTIVE 4 6.3 OBJECTIVE 6

17. Retrieve the file *ch06qz01.xlsx*. Follow the directions. Save the file as *ch06qz01a.xlsx*.

18. Retrieve the file *ch06qz02.xlsx*. Follow the directions. Save the file as *ch06qz02a.xlsx*.

19. Retrieve the file *ch06qz03.xlsx*. Follow the directions. Save the file as *ch06qz03a.xlsx*.

CHAPTER
7 Insurance

7.1 HEALTH AND LIFE INSURANCE

7.2 MOTOR VEHICLE AND PROPERTY INSURANCE

Businesses and individuals can purchase protection against financial loss due to an illness, an automobile accident, the death of an individual, and damage to property due to an accident, fire, or theft. This protection is insurance. Insurance is tailored to meet the individual needs of a person or business. Purchasing the best insurance for you requires knowledge about all types of insurance. Purchasing insurance is an important decision because it means balancing current costs and the possibility of loss in the future. Some individuals do not believe in purchasing large amounts of insurance, while others want the assurance that should anything happen they will have the necessary funds to cover the costs. In this chapter, you will learn about health, auto, life, and property insurance.

INSURANCE AGENT

Courtesy of Nick Bogan

Nick Bogan sells insurance policies to businesses and individuals. He also assesses companies' risk management plans. Nick manages the office and networks with clients. He says, "I deal with many different clients who have many different needs, from home builders to homeowners, and retail stores to restaurants." Nick also needs to know about construction and labor costs when dealing with home and business claims.

Insurance is more than just handing out checks for auto accidents and damage from hail storms. Nick knows that many people dread talking to their agent after receiving a ticket or having an automobile accident. "We're not 'Big Brother' keeping an eye on every person's driving record," he says. "We're here to help you recover when accidents or disasters occur."

How Math Is Used in Insurance

Insurance agents use math when developing insurance proposals and settling claims. Many insurance decisions are based on cost. Nick says, "Whether you're a business owner or an individual, the cost of your insurance plays a significant role in how you manage your budget. I use math to help find the best combination of coverage at a price the client can afford."

For example, math plays an important role when developing a proposal for property insurance for an individual homeowner. Nick must calculate what percentage of a home's exterior is made of brick, wood, stone, or vinyl. He also must calculate the ratio of different types of flooring throughout the home in order to develop a repair and/or replacement cost for the home. Also, each home has unique characteristics that must be considered to get an accurate value and to make sure the homeowner has adequate coverage in case of an accident or disaster.

What Do You Think?

What skills do you need to improve for a career in insurance?

Math Skills Used

Decimals

Geometry

Percents

Ratios

Other Skills Needed

Communication

Interpersonal skills

Multi-tasking

7.1 Health and Life Insurance

OBJECTIVE 1 Identify terms used with health and life insurance.

General terms basic to all types of insurance are discussed here. More specific terminology will be discussed as each area is covered.

Beneficiary Person or persons designated to receive the proceeds of a life insurance policy in the event of the insured's death.

Claim A form filed to request payment for losses covered in an insurance policy.

Coverage A term used to describe the type or amount of loss protected against by an insurance policy.

Deductible An amount deducted from an insurance settlement; the amount of loss the insured agrees to accept.

Face Value The amount of insurance purchased.

Health Insurance Covers a predetermined portion of the cost of health care.

Insurance Protection against cost of loss.

Insurance Agent A person who sells insurance and provides claims service to the policyholders.

Insured The individual or company receiving the insurance protection.

Life Insurance An agreement providing for the payment of a stipulated sum to one or more beneficiaries upon the death of the insured person.

Policy A written contract between the insurance company and the insured that explains the benefits and limitations of the protection purchased.

Policyholder The person or business that purchases an insurance policy.

Premium Payment to the insurance company for the insurance policy.

Settlement The amount an insurance company agrees to pay on a claim.

Term The time for which an insurance policy is in effect.

OBJECTIVE 2 Determine the type of health insurance plan and the premiums.

Health insurance provides protection against a portion of the costs incurred due to illness or accident. Most employers provide some type of health insurance coverage. Companies receive cheaper rates than individuals because they can provide coverage for their workers under group plans. Some employers pay all of the premiums, while most pay only a part or none at all.

With health insurance, there are *fee-for-service* plans and *managed care* plans. Fee-for-service plans provide the insured with complete control over health care decisions, but require high deductibles and/or co-pays. With these plans, the policyholder must file a claim for each service provided.

Managed health care organizations attempt to lower costs by negotiating discounted rates for their policyholders, focusing on preventive care, and limiting choices. There are three basic types of managed health insurance plans: **Health Maintenance Organization (HMO)**, **Preferred Provider Organization (PPO)**, and **Point of Service (POS) plan**. All three types provide access to their own network of health care professionals, hospitals, clinics, etc. They differ in the amount of control plan members have in their choice of health care providers; and they differ in the cost of premiums, *co-payments*, and *deductibles*. A **co-payment** is a fixed payment made to a care provider by a medical patient at the time of service. Co-pays and deductibles reduce the cost of medical insurance for employers and encourage patients to be more responsible about seeking medical care.

As a member of an HMO, the insured must have a **primary care physician**—a doctor who monitors their health, provides primary care, and makes referrals to specialists inside the network as needed. Access to providers outside the network will not be reimbursed by the HMO except in case of emergency treatment. Co-pays are generally low and there are no deductibles.

As a member of a PPO, the insured can choose among that organization's doctors and other care providers or go outside the network (at a higher out-of-pocket cost), giving the policyholder more control over who provides his or her health care. Premiums and co-payments are generally higher than with an HMO, and deductibles may apply.

POS plans, as with HMO's, require that the patient's health be monitored by a primary care physician; but unlike an HMO, the physician can make referrals to providers outside the network. As with a PPO, the insured can choose a provider outside the network. However, when going outside the network, deductibles and higher co-pays will apply and the insured may be required to file claims for those services.

sjlocke/iStockphoto.com

With employer-sponsored plans, employees usually are given choices as to the types and amount of coverage. For example, an employee may opt out of coverage or choose to add dental, vision, and/or disability coverage. They might also choose between individual or family plans.

EXAMPLE

Assume that Raycon Corporation has contracted with Alliance Health Care for a group plan. Raycon has agreed to pay $100 of each employee's premium per month. The employee is offered two types of coverage: 100% coverage (Plan A) or $500 deductible (Plan B). Under Plan A, the insurance covers 100% of the medical costs the employee incurs. Under Plan B, the employee pays the first $500 of medical expenses, and the insurance covers the remainder.

Determine the monthly premium for an individual and for a family under each plan.

Plan A: 100% Coverage	Plan B: $500 Deductible
Annual premium for individual: $1,950	Annual premium for individual: $1,600
Family coverage: Additional $100 per month	Family coverage: Additional $100 per month

STEPS

1. To determine the individual monthly premium, divide the annual premium by 12 months. Then subtract the amount the company will pay.

   Plan A: $1,950 ÷ 12 = $162.50   **Plan B:** $1,600 ÷ 12 = $133.33
   $162.50 − $100 = $62.50 $133.33 − $100 = $33.33

2. To determine the family monthly premium, add $100 to the individual monthly premium.

   Plan A: $62.50 + $100 = $162.50   **Plan B:** $33.33 + $100 = $133.33

   The monthly premium for Plan B is smaller, but the employee must pay the first $500 of medical expenses.

OBJECTIVE 3 Determine the premiums for life insurance.

Life insurance provides funds to your beneficiaries after your death. You may purchase any amount of life insurance coverage you desire. The basic purpose of life insurance is to give financial protection to your survivors after your death. Upon the insured's death, the insurance company pays the full amount of the policy to the *beneficiary* (person designated to receive the amount of the policy). Life insurance premiums vary from company to company. As you would with any purchase, obtain quotes from several companies before making a decision to buy life insurance. Two common types of life insurance are available—term and permanent. Several variations of these types of insurance policies are offered; however, this chapter discusses examples of two types.

- *Term life insurance* is a type of policy that is limited to a specific length of time or term. It is the least expensive type of life insurance. Term policies may be purchased with premiums increasing annually, every 5 years, or every 10 years, and so on. When the time period expires, the coverage ends or the insured may continue the coverage with increasing premiums. The policy builds up no cash value. If the death of the insured occurs during the term of the policy, the beneficiary receives the face value of the policy. Term insurance's primary use is to provide coverage of financial responsibilities for the insured in case of death. Such responsibilities may include consumer debt, dependent care, college education for dependents, funeral costs, and mortgages. (See Figure 7.1 for an example of decreasing term policy.)

Age	Amount of Life Insurance	Age	Amount of Life Insurance
Under 21	$50,000	51 – 55	$25,000
30 – 35	$45,000	56 – 60	$20,000
36 – 40	$40,000	61 – 65	$15,000
41 – 45	$35,000	66 and over	$10,000
46 – 50	$30,000		

Figure 7-1

Table for Term Life Insurance

Decreasing Term Policy

Death Benefits with Premium of $15 per Month

- *Permanent life insurance* is a type of policy that covers you for your lifetime or until maximum age as defined in the policy. Permanent life insurance has a cash value that can be paid to you before you die. Your premiums buy insurance coverage and a savings component as well. There are three main types of permanent life insurance: whole life, universal life, and variable life.

  Whole life (ordinary life) has a level premium paid annually until the insured's death, when the face value of the policy is paid to the beneficiary. A whole life policy builds cash value as the premiums are paid. This offers a consistent premium and a guaranteed cash value.

  Universal life takes advantage of high interest rates and yields higher earnings on the cash value of a policy. As the account earns money, premiums can be paid from the earnings. Universal life policies also allow consumers to permanently withdraw cash from the policy. (See Figure 7.2 on the next page showing a universal life insurance policy with cash accumulating.)

  Variable life is similar to universal life insurance. It offers more investment options and thus creates the possibility of higher rates of return on your money. Usually, the insured pays a set premium.

Premiums on any type of policy depend on age, health, gender, height, weight, and tobacco usage.

Figure 7-2

Universal Life Table

UNIVERSAL LIFE ANNUAL REPORT (6 mos.)

POLICYHOLDER: AGENT: 75GMO35

JENNY WARDLAW
4452 HILLSIDE DRIVE
GRAND PRAIRIE, TX 75052

GEORGIA GOODING
58 PECAN CLUSTER CT.
SPRING, TX 77381

INSURED: JENNY WARDLAW

POLICY NUMBER:	2300123443	PLANNED ANNUAL PREMIUM:	$333.24
POLICY ISSUE DATE:	05/14/20-	FREQUENCY OF PREMIUM:	MONTHLY
POLICY ISSUE AGE:	25	PLANNED PREMIUM:	$27.77
DEATH BENEFIT OPTION:	A – LEVEL	CURRENT SPECIFIED AMOUNT:	$100,000

SUMMARY OF ACTIVITY

DATE	PREMIUMS RECEIVED	PREMIUM LOADS	EXPENSE CHARGES	COST OF INSURANCE	INTEREST CREDITED	RATE	CHARGES/ WITHDRAWALS	ACCUMULATED VALUE
05/14	0.0	0.00	5.00	16.92	0.00	4.00%*	0.00	540.87
06/14	27.77	0.42	5.00	16.92	1.93	4.00%	0.00	548.23
07/14	27.77	0.42	5.00	16.92	1.89	4.00%	0.00	555.55
08/14	27.77	0.42	5.00	16.92	1.98	4.00%	0.00	562.96
09/14	27.77	0.42	5.00	16.91	2.01	4.00%	0.00	570.41
10/14	27.77	0.42	5.00	16.91	1.97	4.00%	0.00	577.82

Calculations:

$27.77 – 0.42 – 5.00 – 16.92 + 1.93 = $7.36
$540.87 + 7.36 = $548.23

*Calculations not given for interest credited

Premiums

Premiums are usually set as a number of dollars per $1,000 of insurance coverage desired based on age, health of the insured, and type of insurance. If at age 45, the purchaser of a term insurance policy wants $200,000 worth of coverage, the rate might be quoted at $3.75 per $1,000 worth of coverage. To determine the annual premium amount, use the following formula.

$$\frac{\text{Amount of Coverage}}{\$1{,}000} \times \text{Cost per } \$1{,}000 = \text{Annual Premium}$$

TIPS

You can quickly divide the amount of coverage by 1,000 by moving the decimal 3 places to the left. Your answer is the number of 1,000s. Then multiply this number by the rate per $1,000 to obtain the annual premium.

EXAMPLE

Determine the annual premium for $200,000 worth of coverage quoted at $3.75 per $1,000.

STEPS

1. Divide the amount of coverage by $1,000 to determine the number of $1,000s in $200,000.

$200,000 ÷ $1,000 = 200

2. Multiply the number of $1,000s by the cost per $1,000.

200 × $3.75 = $750 cost of 1 year's premium

OBJECTIVE **4** Use Excel to calculate health insurance premiums.

Insurance uses specialized software to calculate insurance premiums. Insurance companies use computer underwriting software that automatically analyzes rates and insurance applications. Technology plays an important role in an underwriter's job. Underwriters use computer applications called "smart systems" to manage risks more efficiently and accurately. These systems automatically analyze and rate insurance applications, recommend acceptance or denial of the risk, and adjust the premium rate in accordance with the risk.

Health Insurance

A spreadsheet can be used to set up the options available to employees and then can be distributed for verification. Follow the steps below to calculate monthly health insurance premiums. Study Figure 7-3.

Figure 7-3

Health Insurance Premiums

	Figure 7-3 - Microsoft Excel non-commercial use	
A Calculate Plan A and B monthly health insurance premium.		

Calculate Plan A and B monthly health insurance premium.

Plan A: 100% coverage	Plan B: $100 Deductible
Individual: $1,950	Individual: $1,600
Family: $75 monthly	Family: $75 monthly
Company: $75 monthly for employee	Company: $75 monthly for employee

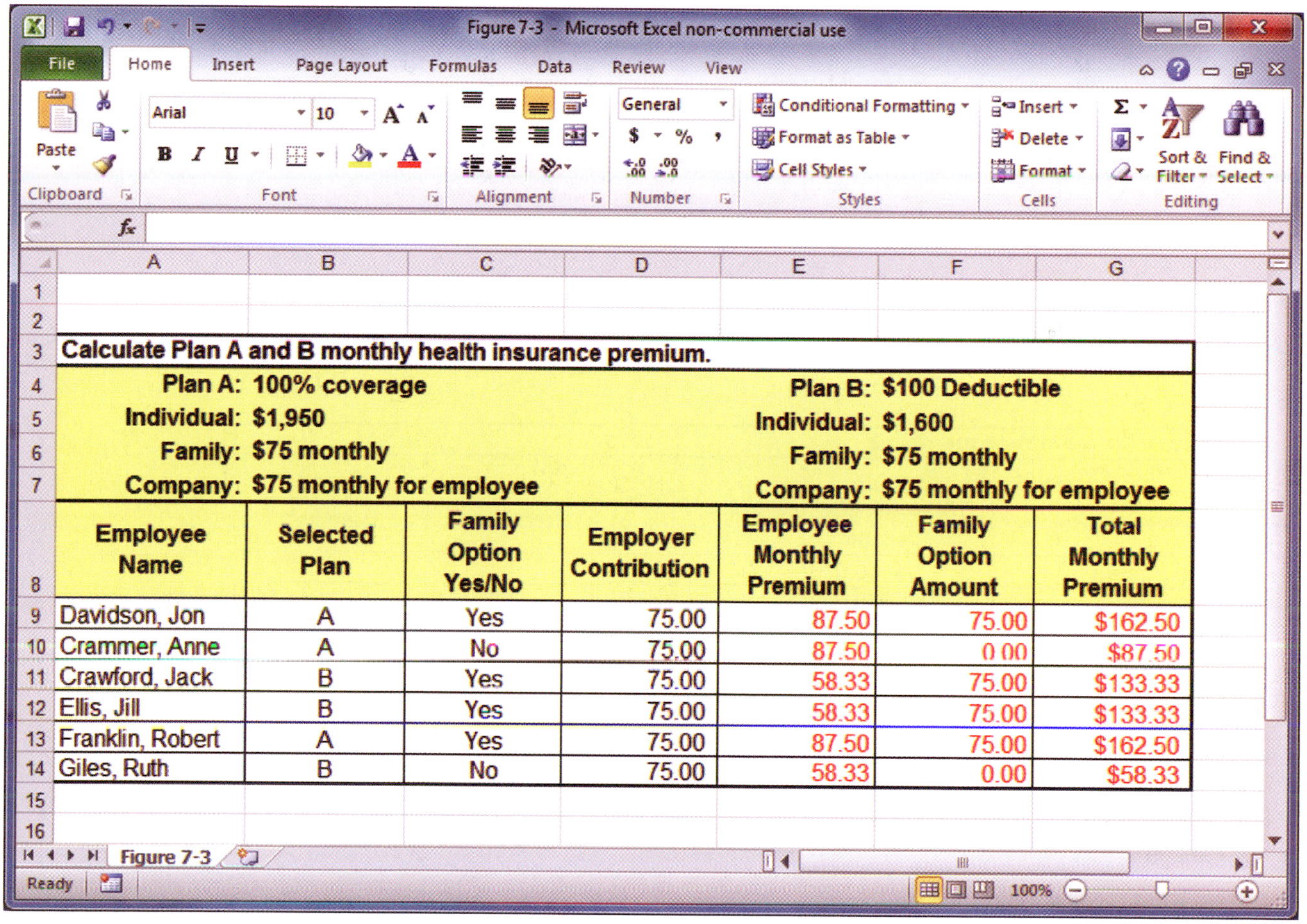

Employee Name	Selected Plan	Family Option Yes/No	Employer Contribution	Employee Monthly Premium	Family Option Amount	Total Monthly Premium
Davidson, Jon	A	Yes	75.00	87.50	75.00	$162.50
Crammer, Anne	A	No	75.00	87.50	0.00	$87.50
Crawford, Jack	B	Yes	75.00	58.33	75.00	$133.33
Ellis, Jill	B	Yes	75.00	58.33	75.00	$133.33
Franklin, Robert	A	Yes	75.00	87.50	75.00	$162.50
Giles, Ruth	B	No	75.00	58.33	0.00	$58.33

STEPS

Retrieve the file **ch07pr01.xlsx**.

1. Enter multimath formulas in Column E to calculate the Employee's Monthly Premium (Plan A or B divided by 12 minus Employer Contribution).

2. Enter the amount in Column F for each employee that elects the Family Option (Column C—Yes only).

3. Enter formulas in Column G to calculate the Total Monthly Premium (Employee Monthly Premium + Family Option Amount).

4. Format Columns E and F for Currency, 2 Decimal places, and no $. Format Column G for Currency, 2 Decimal places, and $.

5. Save the file as *ch07pr01a.xlsx*.

OBJECTIVE 5 Use Excel to calculate life insurance premiums.

Life Insurance

Insurance agents might find an Excel spreadsheet helpful to track their policyholders and the amount of coverage, cost, annual premium, and monthly premium. Additional information could be added, such as telephone numbers and addresses. Study Figure 7-4.

Figure 7-4

Life Insurance Premiums

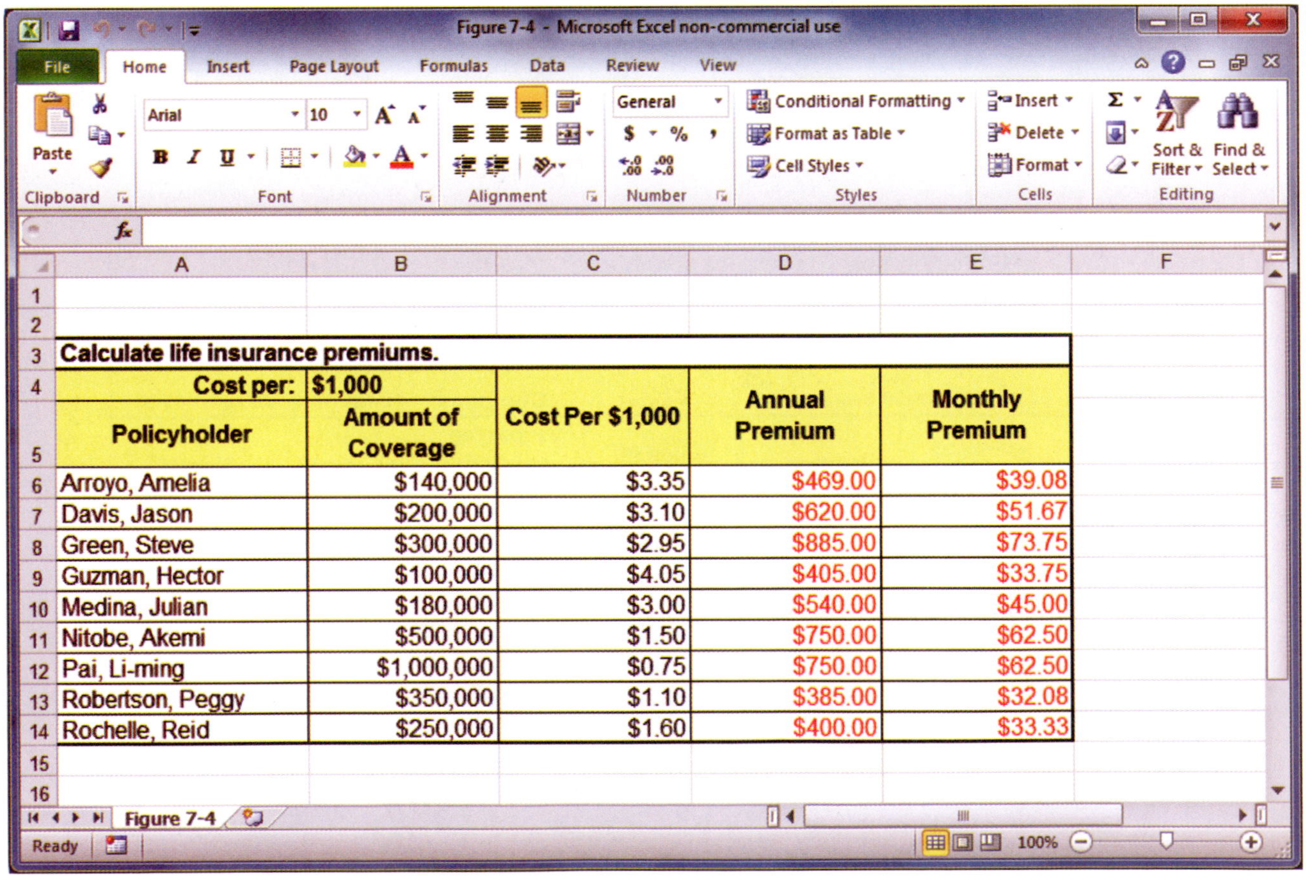

Policyholder	Amount of Coverage	Cost Per $1,000	Annual Premium	Monthly Premium
Cost per: $1,000				
Arroyo, Amelia	$140,000	$3.35	$469.00	$39.08
Davis, Jason	$200,000	$3.10	$620.00	$51.67
Green, Steve	$300,000	$2.95	$885.00	$73.75
Guzman, Hector	$100,000	$4.05	$405.00	$33.75
Medina, Julian	$180,000	$3.00	$540.00	$45.00
Nitobe, Akemi	$500,000	$1.50	$750.00	$62.50
Pai, Li-ming	$1,000,000	$0.75	$750.00	$62.50
Robertson, Peggy	$350,000	$1.10	$385.00	$32.08
Rochelle, Reid	$250,000	$1.60	$400.00	$33.33

Calculate life insurance premiums.

STEPS

Retrieve the file *ch07pr02.xlsx*. Follow the directions. Save the file as *ch07pr02a.xlsx*.

Name _____   Date _____

Directions   Solve the following problems. Write your answers in the blanks provided.

A. **Determine the monthly premium for individual and family health coverage. The employer will pay $100 of the monthly premium for each employee. An additional $80 is added to the individual monthly premium for family coverage. Round all answers to the nearest hundredth.**   `OBJECTIVE 2`

Individual annual premium: $1,500 =   1. _____ monthly premium

Family premium =   2. _____ monthly premium

Individual annual premium: $1,250 =   3. _____ monthly premium

Family premium =   4. _____ monthly premium

Individual annual premium: $990 =   5. _____ monthly premium

Family premium =   6. _____ monthly premium

Individual annual premium: $1,900 =   7. _____ monthly premium

Family premium =   8. _____ monthly premium

Individual annual premium: $2,400 =   9. _____ monthly premium

Family premium =   10. _____ monthly premium

Individual annual premium: $1,875 =   11. _____ monthly premium

Family premium =   12. _____ monthly premium

Individual annual premium: $1,210 =   13. _____ monthly premium

Family premium =   14. _____ monthly premium

Individual annual premium: $1,050 =   15. _____ monthly premium

Family premium =   16. _____ monthly premium

B. **Determine the amount of annual premium due for term life insurance.**   `OBJECTIVE 3`

17. $\dfrac{\$275,000}{\$1,000} \times \$3.25 \ = \ $ _____

18. $\dfrac{\$300,000}{\$1,000} \times \$3.95 \ = \ $ _____

19. $\dfrac{\$1,000,000}{\$1,000} \times \$5.50 \ = \ $ _____

20. $\dfrac{\$90,000}{\$1,000} \times \$3.00 \ = \ $ _____

21. $\dfrac{\$350,500}{\$1,000} \times \$4.10 \ = \ $ _____

22. $\dfrac{\$180,000}{\$1,000} \times \$4.70 \ = \ $ _____

23. $\dfrac{\$55,000}{\$1,000} \times \$3.45 \ = \ $ _____

24. $\dfrac{\$149,000}{\$1,000} \times \$3.75 \ = \ $ _____

C. Solve the following problems. OBJECTIVES 2, 3

25. Danielle Fox, a new employee at Hargrove, Estes, and Yates law firm, decided to enroll in the firm's health insurance program. The annual premium for Danielle is $1,725. The firm pays $150 of the premium per month. What does Danielle pay? _____

   After Danielle worked at Hargrove, Estes, and Yates two years, she married. To add her husband to her health insurance policy, she must pay an additional $110 per month. What annual premium does Danielle now pay? _____

   Hargrove, Estes, and Yates decided to purchase term life insurance for themselves. They purchased $200,000 for each partner, quoted at $3.78 per $1,000 for one year.

   How much will each partner pay for the coverage annually? _____

   How much will the premium be for all three partners? _____

   What would a two-year premium be for all three partners? _____

26. Denise Lieberman visited with her life insurance agent, Mark Littleton. Mark and Denise agreed that since Denise is 20 years old, she needs to purchase a $125,000 whole life insurance policy that will accumulate a cash value. Mark quoted the price of the policy at $2.77 per $1,000. What is Denise's annual premium? _____

27. Crystal Blevins purchased $300,000 of term life insurance. Because she smokes and has health problems, her premiums were quoted at $4.95 per $1,000. What is her monthly premium? _____

28. Erin Manchester is interested in purchasing a life insurance policy worth $100,000 with her daughter and three grandchildren as beneficiaries. The agent quoted $27.77 per month. What is the cost of the insurance per $1,000? Give your answer to the nearest ten-thousandth. _____

29. David and Ray's Auto Repair is owned by David and Ray Brinkman. They want to set up group health insurance for themselves and their three employees. Each policy will cost David and Ray $3,900 annually.

   What is the total premium cost annually for the company? _____

   What is the monthly premium for each employee? _____

   What would a family policy cost per month if each employee paid an additional $150 monthly for the family policy? _____

D. Use Excel to calculate health and life insurance premiums. OBJECTIVES 4, 5

30. Retrieve the file *ch07ex01.xlsx*. Follow the directions. Save the file as *ch07ex01a.xlsx*.

31. Retrieve the file *ch07ex02.xlsx*. Follow the directions. Save the file as *ch07ex02a.xlsx*.

7.2 Motor Vehicle and Property Insurance

OBJECTIVES

1. Identify terms used with motor vehicle and property insurance.

2. Determine the compensation due after a motor vehicle accident.

3. Use Excel to calculate the compensation due after a motor vehicle accident.

4. Determine the premiums for homeowner's insurance.

5. Calculate the payment when a fire insurance policy contains an 80% coinsurance clause.

6. Use Excel to calculate premiums for homeowner's insurance and the amount insurance will pay with coinsurance clause.

OBJECTIVE 1 Identify terms used with motor vehicle and property insurance.

Certain terms are basic to all types of insurance. These general terms are discussed here. More specific terminology relating to each type of insurance will be discussed as each area is covered.

Automobile Liability Insurance Covers damages for bodily injury and property damage for which an insured person becomes legally responsible because of an auto accident.

Coinsurance A coinsurance clause allows the insured to bear part of the loss when there is damage due to fire.

Homeowner's Insurance Provides coverage of property against damage or loss.

Insurance Claims Adjuster A person representing an insurance company who investigates claims and determines the amount of damage the insurance company is responsible for.

OBJECTIVE 2 Determine the compensation due after a motor vehicle accident.

Almost all states have laws that require individuals and businesses carry some type of motor vehicle insurance for every motor vehicle owned. Many kinds of coverage are available including collision, medical payment, comprehensive, uninsured motorist, and liability. **Collision coverage** pays for damage to the insured's vehicle as a result of an accident. **Medical payment coverage** protects the insured and other occupants of the insured's vehicle against the cost of bodily injury in an accident. **Comprehensive coverage** will pay to fix your vehicle less any deductible and for damage not caused by an accident, such as vandalism, theft, storm, or fire. **Uninsured motorist coverage** protects the insured and the insured's passengers against bodily/personal injuries as well as against property damage caused by another at-fault driver without liability insurance.

The cost of each coverage depends on the driver's classification according to age, sex, marital status, driver training, experience, geographic location, distance traveled to and from work, and whether the car is used for pleasure or business. An insurance policy's cost is determined by **actuaries**. An actuary is a person who works with the collection and interpretation of numerical data, for instance, someone who uses statistics to calculate insurance rates (see Figure 7-5). If a driver has a record of several accidents and/or speeding tickets, insurance is often difficult to obtain. The rates are much higher because of the increased risk for the insurance company.

Insurance companies determine premiums from tables made by actuaries. Rates vary from state to state. Financial institutions that loan money for automobile purchases require not only *liability insurance* that will fix the other person's car, but *collision insurance* that will fix your car. If an accident is your fault, your insurance company must fix the other motorist's car. If the accident is the other motorist's fault, his or her insurance must repair your car and the other motorist's car. Each accident that is your fault where you must file a claim for repair, often causes your insurance rates to increase. Too many accidents can cause your motor vehicle insurance to be cancelled.

Automobile liability insurance pays for injury or damage done to others as a result of an accident that is the fault of the insured. It will not pay for injury or damage to the insured or occupants of the insured's vehicle. Liability limits are commonly stated in abbreviated form. For example, 25/50/10 means the insurance company will pay a maximum of $25,000 for bodily injury to any one person hurt in the accident, a maximum of $50,000 for bodily injury to all persons involved in the accident, and a maximum of $10,000 for property damage. Property damage includes damage to other drivers' vehicles, road signs, guardrails, poles, trees, fences, or any other property belonging to others that is damaged in the accident.

Figure 7-5

Liability and Medical Insurance Table

LIABILITY AND MEDICAL INSURANCE (PER YEAR)					
Territory	**15/30 $5,000**	**25/50 $10,000**	**50/100 $15,000**	**100/200 $20,000**	**150/300 $25,000**
1	$210	$223	$251	$309	$345
2	$265	$310	$330	$347	$366
3	$340	$366	$389	$404	$428
4	$220	$230	$246	$261	$279

It is important to remember that the driver who is at fault in an accident (unless no-fault insurance is involved) is liable for all damages. For the protection of others, all but two states require that individuals and businesses carry automobile liability insurance. **No-fault automobile insurance** is also available. This is a form of coverage where the insured's own insurance company pays for property damage and bodily injury no matter who is at fault.

An automobile policy is usually issued for one year, and the exact amount of the premium is calculated. To decrease the cost of automobile insurance

©jcpjr, 2010/ Used under license from Shutterstock.com

premiums, the insured can purchase a policy with a deductible. For example, if a policy had a $500 deductible clause, the insured would be required to pay the first $500 of any damage claim. Depending on the agreement with the insurance company, premiums may be paid monthly, quarterly, semiannually, or annually. When an accident occurs, the insured, when determined at fault, usually must pay any expenses not covered by the insurance policy. The following is an example of payment of liability coverage.

EXAMPLE

Martin, while driving, crashes into Landers' automobile, causing injuries to Landers and Eileen (a passenger in Landers' car). Following a lawsuit, a court awarded Landers $28,000 and Eileen $22,000 for personal bodily injuries, and $8,000 to Landers for the damage to his car. Martin has 25/50/10 liability insurance. Determine how much Martin and his insurance company will pay.

STEPS

1. Bodily injury:

$$
\begin{aligned}
\text{Landers} &= \quad \$28,000 \\
\text{Eileen} &= + \ \$22,000 \\
\hline
\text{Total} &= \quad \$50,000
\end{aligned}
$$

The maximum paid to any one person is $25,000. The insurance company will pay $25,000 of Landers' $28,000 expenses and all of Eileen's expenses, which are $22,000. The maximum payment to all persons is $50,000. The total of covered expenses, $47,000, falls within the $50,000 maximum allowed for bodily injury for all persons.

$25,000 + $22,000 = $47,000   insurance pays
$28,000 − $25,000 = $3,000   Martin pays

Note that even though the total medical expenses was $47,000 and the maximum for all persons injured was $50,000, the $3,000 extra allowed for Eileen cannot be applied to Landers' expenses.

2. Property damage:

$$\text{Landers' car} = \$8,000$$

The maximum paid for any one automobile accident is $10,000. Landers' damages fall within the maximum amount. Therefore, the $8,000 will be paid in full by the insurance company.

TIPS

Uninsured motorist coverage protects you from damage or injury caused to you or the occupants of your car by an uninsured (or underinsured) driver when the other driver is at fault.

OBJECTIVE 3 **Use Excel to calculate the compensation due after a motor vehicle accident.**

Automobile insurance

A spreadsheet can be used and kept as a record to determine the amount of money the policyholder and the insurance company must pay when an accident occurs. Study Figure 7-6 on the next page.

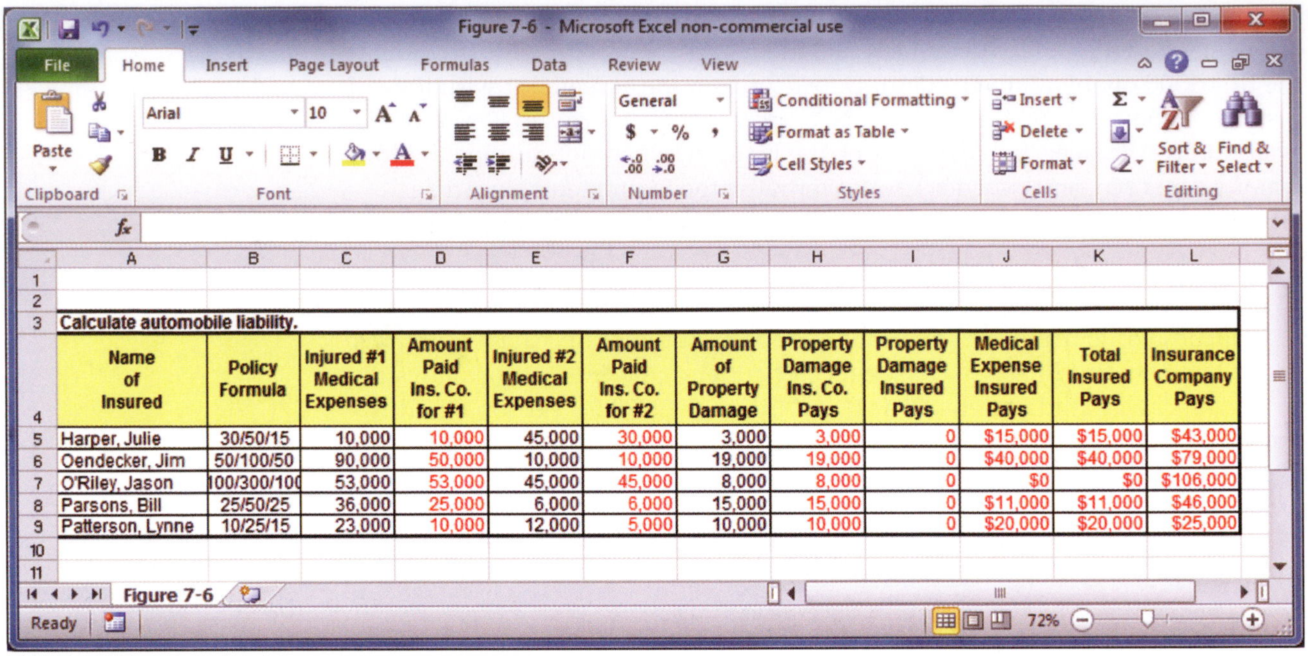

Figure 7-6

Automobile Liability

The spreadsheet shows:

Title bar: Figure 7-6 - Microsoft Excel non-commercial use

Cell A3: Calculate automobile liability.

Name of Insured	Policy Formula	Injured #1 Medical Expenses	Amount Paid Ins. Co. for #1	Injured #2 Medical Expenses	Amount Paid Ins. Co. for #2	Amount of Property Damage	Property Damage Ins. Co. Pays	Property Damage Insured Pays	Medical Expense Insured Pays	Total Insured Pays	Insurance Company Pays
Harper, Julie	30/50/15	10,000	10,000	45,000	30,000	3,000	3,000	0	$15,000	$15,000	$43,000
Oendecker, Jim	50/100/50	90,000	50,000	10,000	10,000	19,000	19,000	0	$40,000	$40,000	$79,000
O'Riley, Jason	100/300/100	53,000	53,000	45,000	45,000	8,000	8,000	0	$0	$0	$106,000
Parsons, Bill	25/50/25	36,000	25,000	6,000	6,000	15,000	15,000	0	$11,000	$11,000	$46,000
Patterson, Lynne	10/25/15	23,000	10,000	12,000	5,000	10,000	10,000	0	$20,000	$20,000	$25,000

STEPS

Retrieve the file *ch07pr03.xlsx*.

1. Compare the Policy Formula's amount for one person's injury to Injured #1's Medical Expenses and key in Column D the Amount Paid by the Insurance Company for Injured #1. (The first amount in Policy Formula is the maximum paid for any one person injured.)

2. Compare the maximum amount for one person's injuries to Injured #2's expenses and key in Column F the Amount Paid by the Insurance Company for Injured #2. (Consider what has been paid for #1 and the maximum allowable which is the second figure in the Policy Formula.) Normally an equal amount would be paid to the Injured, but here pay the second Injured the difference.

3. Compare the Policy Formula's maximum for property damage and key in Column H the amount the insurance company will pay. In Column I, calculate the amount the insured pays. (Subtract Column H from Column G.)

4. Enter multimath formulas in Column J to calculate the Amount Insured Pays. (Add Injured #1's and #2's expenses and then subtract the Amount Insurance Company Pays for each.) The difference is what the Insured must pay of the medical expenses.

5. Enter formulas in Column K to calculate Total Insured Pays of property damages and medical expenses.

6. Enter formulas to calculate the total amount the Insurance Company Pays. (Add Columns D, F and H.)

7. Format Columns D, F, H and I for Currency, 0 Decimal places, and no $. Format Columns J, K and L for Currency, 0 Decimal places, and $.

8. Save the file as *ch07pr03a.xlsx*.

Homeowner's insurance provides coverage of property against damage or loss. Premiums may be based on the nature of the risks involved, the amount of coverage purchased, the length of time owned, and the location of the property. Coverage may include damage caused by smoke, water, or chemicals, damage done by firefighters breaking into the property or by measures taken to contain the fire, riots, civil commotion, theft, hurricanes, wind, or hail.

Homeowner's insurance premiums are usually quoted based on the number of dollars per $1,000 of insurance desired. Computations are the same as for life insurance. Renters of apartments or homes may also obtain property insurance to cover damages to their household furnishings. Homeowner's insurance policies for renters are known as *tenant homeowner's policies* or *renters' insurance.*

EXAMPLE

Jan and Michael Thompson decide to purchase a tenant homeowner's insurance policy in the amount of $50,000 to cover the household furnishings in their apartment. The Royal Insurance Company quoted them a cost of $4.95 per $1,000 for the coverage. What is the cost of one year's premium?

STEPS

1. Divide the amount of coverage by $1,000 to determine the number of 1,000s in $50,000.

$$\$50,000 \div \$1,000 = 50$$

2. Multiply 50 (number of $1,000s in $50,000) by cost per $1,000 ($4.95).

$$50 \times \$4.95 = \$247.50 \quad \text{cost of 1 year's premium}$$

EscoLux/iStockphoto.com

Property is occasionally damaged by fire. If you purchase fire insurance for the full value of a property, the premiums would be expensive. Because of this expense, coinsurance may be used to help cut the costs of the premiums. A coinsurance clause allows the insured to bear part of the loss when there is damage. The insured agrees to purchase a policy for a stated percentage, usually 80% of the value of the property. Under an 80% coinsurance policy, property valued at $100,000 would be insured for $80,000. As long as the insured carries insurance covering 80% of the value of the property, the insurance company will pay for all fire damages up to $80,000.

EXAMPLE

Julie Craine is a cosmetologist. Julie purchased an 80% coinsurance policy to insure her place of business for $76,000. The business was valued at $95,000. The building caught fire and suffered $65,000 damage. Determine the amount of money Julie will collect from insurance.

STEPS

1. Multiply 80% by the value of the property.

$$0.80 \times \$95,000 = \$76,000 \quad \text{amount of insurance required}$$

2. Compare the amount of coverage to the amount required.

$$\$76,000 - \$65,000 = \$10,000$$

Julie will collect $65,000 from insurance because she had more than that amount of coverage.

Coinsurance Clause Where Fire Insurance Coverage is Not Equal to 80% of Property Value. If the insured carries less than 80% of the value of the property, the insurance company will pay damages up to whatever fractional part the actual coverage is of the required insurance. Study the following example.

EXAMPLE

Cindy Haygood's home was valued at $165,000 when she purchased a coinsurance policy. She covered the home for only $100,000. A fire occurred in Cindy's home, and the damage amounted to $90,000. Determine how much the insurance company will pay.

STEPS

1. Multiply 80% by the value of the property ($165,000).

$$0.80 \times \$165,000 = \$132,000 \quad \text{amount of insurance required}$$

2. Divide the amount of coverage by the amount required.

$$\$100,000 \div \$132,000 = 0.76 \text{ or } 76\% \quad \text{recovery (rounded)}$$

3. Multiply 0.76 by the amount of damage ($90,000).

$$0.76 \times \$90,000 = \$68,400 \quad \text{recovery}$$

TIPS

If the insured carries up to 80% of the value of the property, he or she will recover all losses up to that 80% amount. Therefore, no calculations are necessary if the amount of coverage is more than the damage.

OBJECTIVE 6 Use Excel to calculate premiums for homeowner's insurance and the amount insurance will pay with coinsurance clause.

Homeowner's Insurance

Homeowner's insurance premiums can be calculated in a spreadsheet to be kept as a record. In this practice, you will calculate the annual premium for a standard homeowner's insurance policy.

PRACTICE

Retrieve the file *ch07pr04.xlsx*. Follow the directions to calculate annual homeowner's premiums.

Then follow the steps below to calculate annual premiums for homeowner's insurance with coinsurance clauses. Study Figure 7-7.

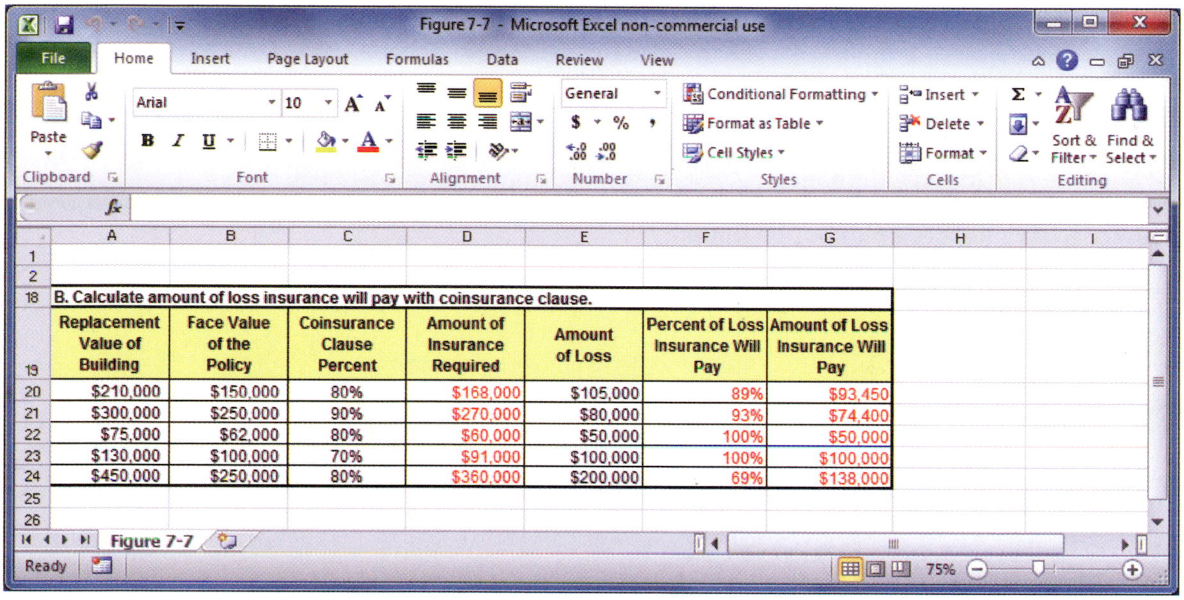

Figure 7-7

Loss with Coinsurance Clause

B. Calculate amount of loss insurance will pay with coinsurance clause.

Replacement Value of Building	Face Value of the Policy	Coinsurance Clause Percent	Amount of Insurance Required	Amount of Loss	Percent of Loss Insurance Will Pay	Amount of Loss Insurance Will Pay
$210,000	$150,000	80%	$168,000	$105,000	89%	$93,450
$300,000	$250,000	90%	$270,000	$80,000	93%	$74,400
$75,000	$62,000	80%	$60,000	$50,000	100%	$50,000
$130,000	$100,000	70%	$91,000	$100,000	100%	$100,000
$450,000	$250,000	80%	$360,000	$200,000	69%	$138,000

1. Enter a formula in Cell D20 to calculate the Amount of Insurance Required (Replacement Value of Building times Coinsurance Clause Percent). Copy the formula down Column D and format for Currency, 0 Decimal places, and $.

2. Key 100% in Cells F22 and F23 for the two buildings that meet the coinsurance requirement and need no calculation.

3. Enter a formula in Cell F20 to calculate the Percent of Loss Insurance Will Pay for each of the buildings that do not meet the Amount of Insurance Required. Round to the nearest whole percent. The formula in Cell F20 should look like this: =ROUND(B20/D20,2). Copy the formula to Cell F21 and Cell F24. Format Column F for Percentage and 0 Decimal places.

4. Enter a formula in Cell G20 to calculate the Amount of Loss the Insurance Will Pay (Percent of Loss Insurance Will Pay times Amount of Loss). Copy the formula down Column G and format for Currency, 0 Decimal places, and $.

5. Save the file as *ch07pr04a.xlsx*.

7.2 Motor Vehicle and Property Insurance

Name   Date

Directions   Solve the following problems. Write your answers in the blanks provided.

A. Determine the amount the insurance company and the individuals will pay in the following automobile accidents. All insured motorists have 25/50/10.   `OBJECTIVE 2`

Accident #1:   Personal bodily injury: Corey Kramer   = $32,000,
                               Jane Kramer   = $31,000;
            Property damage: Kramer's automobile = $15,000

1. Insurance pays for personal bodily injury: _____

2. Insurance pays for property damage: _____

3. Total paid by insurance company: _____

4. Total paid by individual causing accident: _____

Accident #2:   Personal bodily injury: Dianne Greene   = $22,000,
                               Julian Greene   = $40,000;
            Property damage: Greene's automobile = $12,000

5. Insurance pays for personal bodily injury: _____

6. Insurance pays for property damage: _____

7. Total paid by insurance company: _____

8. Total paid by individual causing accident: _____

B. Determine the annual premium due for homeowner's insurance.   `OBJECTIVE 3`

9. $110,000 coverage quoted at $6 per $1,000   = _____

10. $150,000 coverage quoted at $5.50 per $1,000   = _____

11. $45,000 coverage quoted at $1.10 per $1,000   = _____

C. Determine the amount of fire insurance coverage needed to equal 80% of property value.   `OBJECTIVE 4`

	Property Value	Needed Coverage		Property Value	Needed Coverage
12.	$75,000	_____	13.	$100,000	_____
14.	$49,000	_____	15.	$2,000,000	_____
16.	$350,000	_____	17.	$495,000	_____

D. Determine the amount paid by the insurance company on an 80% coinsurance OBJECTIVE 4
fire insurance policy for each of the following properties. Coverage is equal to
80% of property value. Round rate of recovery to the nearest whole percent
before calculating the amount of insurance paid.

	Coverage	Value	Loss	Insurance Paid
18.	$120,000	$150,000	$90,000	_____
19.	$288,000	$360,000	$200,000	_____
20.	$108,540	$135,675	$20,000	_____
21.	$184,000	$230,000	$200,000	_____

E. Solve the following problems. OBJECTIVES 2, 3, 4

22. Garvin Enterprises built and moved into a new office building valued
at $295,000. Their insurance company quoted them $3.90 per $1,000. What
would a two-year property insurance premium cost the firm if the partners
wanted full coverage? _____

23. Paula's Pets decided to purchase an 80% coinsurance property insurance
policy on their building, valued at $125,000. How much insurance do they
need to purchase to cover their building at 80%? _____

Each of three business partners is provided with an automobile owned by the
firm. While on his way to see a client, Miguel was involved in an accident that
was his fault. The firm has 50/100/25 automobile liability coverage. In the
accident, Hillary Martin incurred $5,000 of personal bodily injury. Her three
children riding in the car were also hurt. Jane had $12,000 of bodily injury; Sally,
$5,400; and Bobby, $8,300. Damage to the Martin automobile was $11,500.
Answer the following questions.

How much will the insurance pay for:

24.	Hillary?	_____	25.	Jane?	_____
26.	Sally?	_____	27.	Bobby?	_____
28.	Total bodily injury?	_____	29.	Property damage?	_____
30.	Total paid by the insurance company?				_____
31.	Total paid by Miguel over what the insurance paid?				_____

F. Use Excel to solve problems involving automobile insurance and homeowner's
insurance. OBJECTIVES 3, 6

32. Retrieve the file *ch07ex03.xlsx*. Follow the directions. Save the file as *ch07ex03a.xlsx*.

33. Retrieve the file *ch07ex04.xlsx*. Follow the directions. Save the file as *ch07ex04a.xlsx*.

Chapter Review and Assessment

KEY TERMS

actuaries
automobile liability insurance
beneficiary
claim
coinsurance
collision coverage
comprehensive coverage
coverage
co-payment
deductible
face value

health insurance
Health Maintenance Organization (HMO)
homeowner's insurance
insurance
insurance agent
insured
insurance claims adjuster
liability
life insurance
medical payments coverage

no-fault automobile insurance
Point of Service (POS) plan
policy
policyholder
Preferred Provider Organization (PPO)
premium
primary care physician
settlement
term
uninsured motorist coverage

CONCEPTS	EXAMPLES
7.1 Determine health insurance premiums.	Annual premium is $1,950; company pays $75 per month; family coverage is an additional $100 per month.
1. Divide individual annual premium by 12 months.	$1,950 ÷ 12 = $162.50 monthly premium
2. Subtract amount of premium company will pay.	$162.50 − $75.00 = $87.50 employee's share w/o family coverage
3. For family coverage, add additional amount of premium to individual's monthly payment.	$87.50 + $100 = $187.50 employee's monthly payment w/family
7.1 Determine the premiums for life insurance.	$100,000 insurance at $3.75 per $1,000
1. Determine the number of thousands in desired amount of coverage.	$100,000 ÷ $1,000 = 100
2. Multiply cost per thousand by the number of thousands in coverage.	100 × $3.75 = $375.00 premium due
7.2 Determine the compensation due after a motor vehicle accident.	In an accident, Andy's injuries were $28,000; Irene's injuries were $22,000; property damage was $8,000.
Liablity insurance of 25/50/10 means: $25,000 maximum payment for injuries to any one person $50,000 maximum payment for injuries to all persons $10,000 maximum payment for property damage	Andy = $25,000 Andy is covered for only $25,000, the Irene = $22,000 maximum for one person, while Irene Total = $47,000 is covered for all of the $22,000 because it is under the one-person maximum and the total maximum. Property = $8,000 under $10,000 maximum

Chapter 7 Review Exercises

Name _____   Date _____

Directions   Solve the following problems. Write your answers in the blanks provided.

A. Complete the following health insurance problems.   <mark>7.1 OBJECTIVE 2</mark>

Plan A: Individual annual premium is $1,410 (additional $80 a month for family coverage). The company pays nothing toward the individual's insurance premium.

1.   Individual monthly premium   = _____

2.   Family monthly premium   = _____

Plan B: Individual annual premium is $980 (additional $80 a month for family coverage). The company pays $45 of the monthly premium for each employee.

3.   Individual monthly premium   = _____

4.   Family monthly premium   = _____

5.   McNeil Manufacturing pays one-half of each employee's total health-care premium per month. The annual premium for an individual is $2,460. Family coverage can be purchased for an additional $35 monthly. Martha West is married and has two children. Compute her monthly premium for insurance that covers her and her family.   _____

B. Complete the following life insurance problems.   <mark>7.1 OBJECTIVE 3</mark>

6.   Julie Kelley wants to purchase $250,000 worth of term life insurance at a rate of $2.10 per $1,000. What is her annual premium?   _____

7.   Allyson and Rami Khayo each want to purchase $400,000 worth of term life insurance. The rate for Allyson is $2.60 per $1,000. The rate for Rami is $3.25 per $1,000. What is their total annual premium?   _____

8.   Han and Kim Nguyen each want to purchase a $200,000 term life insurance policy. The rate for Han is $3.05 per $1,000 and the rate for Kim is $2.10 per $1,000. What is their total annual premium? What is their monthly premium?   _____

9.   Mahat owns a Quick Serve One-Stop business. The business is located in a high-crime area. Therefore, Mahat feels he must carry more than the normal amount of life insurance on himself and his four employees. Mahat purchases $1,000,000 on himself at a cost of $5 per $1,000. He pays half of the premiums for each of his employees. Each employee has $200,000 coverage at a cost of $3.25 per $1,000. What is Mahat's total annual premium for himself and his employees?   _____

10. Ned Yearling, age 38, wants to purchase a $100,000 whole life insurance policy with a premium of $3.25 per $1,000. What is his annual premium?   _____

C. Complete the following automobile insurance problems. 7.2 OBJECTIVE 2

While driving to work, Po Ling Wu crashes into David Kinsley's automobile, injuring David and John Engles, a passenger in David's car. Po Ling has 20/40/10 liability coverage. David is awarded $28,000 for personal bodily injuries. John Engles is awarded $22,500. It will cost $11,450 to repair David's automobile.

11. How much will Po Ling's insurance company pay for personal bodily injuries? _____

12. How much will Po Ling's insurance company pay for property damage? _____

13. How much will Po Ling pay? _____

14. Hope Wilson has an automobile liability insurance policy with 20/40/10 coverage. She is responsible for an accident in which Rhoda Ewing is injured. Rhoda's medical expenses totaled $45,098, and damages to her car totaled $12,500. What is the total amount Hope's insurance will pay? _____

15. Scott Hanbury has an automobile liability insurance policy with 30/60/10 coverage. He is responsible for an accident in which Glen Garvin is not injured. Damages to Glen's car totaled $20,500. What is the total amount Scott's insurance will pay? _____

16. David Weber, while driving to work, crashes into a car driven by Karen Mullen. Karen's daughter Savannah is in the car with her. David has an automobile liability insurance policy with 20/40/10 coverage. Both Karen and Savannah are injured. Karen's medical expenses total $23,000, and Savannah's medical expenses total $6,700. Damages to Karen's car total $9,500. What is the total amount David's insurance will pay? _____

17. Tom Potts decides to buy a no-fault automobile insurance policy worth $30,000 and an uninsured motorist policy worth $35,000. The cost is $3.50 per $1,000 for the no-fault insurance and $2.50 per $1,000 for the uninsured motorist coverage. What is Tom's total annual premium for these coverages? _____

D. Complete the following homeowner insurance problems. 7.2 OBJECTIVE 3

18. Grace and Ramos Ramirez plan to purchase a tenant homeowner's insurance policy in the amount of $120,000 to cover their household furnishings in their new 4,000 square foot home. Their insurance company quoted them $3.20 per $1,000 for the coverage. What is the annual premium? _____

19. Jason boards his three horses outside the city by renting pasture. There is a locked tack room on the property where he keeps his saddles, blankets, harnesses, and other equipment. His homeowner's policy on his residence in the city covers both his house and the tack room. His home is valued at $140,000. What is his annual premium if quoted at $2.80 per $1,000? _____

E. Complete the following fire coinsurance problems. <mark>7.2 OBJECTIVE 4</mark>

20. The Southside Clothing Store is valued at $89,900. To satisfy the 80% coinsurance provision of the policy, for how much should the owner insure the building? _____

21. Kris Kretchen owns a building with a market value of $135,345. He has insured the building for $90,000. A fire caused $61,352 in damages. How much will the insurance company pay if his policy contains an 80% coinsurance clause? Round the percent of recovery to the nearest whole percent before calculating the insurance settlement. _____

22. Find the face value of a fire protection policy on a building worth $97,230 if it is insured for 80% of its market value. _____

23. What amount of property insurance with 80% coinsurance is necessary to insure a building valued at $3,500,000? _____

24. Pepperoni Pizza Parlor suffered smoke and water damage in the amount of $105,000. The building is valued at $210,000 and the owner has it insured for $150,000 with 80% coinsurance. How much will the insurance company settle the claim for? Round the percent of recovery to the nearest whole percent before calculating the insurance settlement. _____

F. Solve the following insurance-related word problems.

25. If an automobile insurance premium of $798 can be paid semi-annually with a 3% annual charge added, what is the amount to be paid every six months? _____

26. Lydia Morales is married and has a family. Her employer pays 60% of every employee's individual health insurance premium each month. The annual premium for this plan is $2,400 per employee. Family coverage can be purchased for an additional $55.00 per month. Compute Lydia's monthly premium for herself and her family. _____

27. While driving to work, Ben Adler crashes into Fujio Hayashi's automobile, injuring Fujio and his wife Mary. Ben has 20/40/10 liability coverage. Fujio is awarded $23,550 for personal bodily injuries. Mary is awarded $12,400. Repairs to the Hayashi's automobile will cost $12,543. How much will Ben's insurance company pay? _____

28. Richard's Body Shop had a fire which caused $55,000 in damage to its building valued at $135,000. Richard insured his building for $90,000. How much will the insurance company pay if the policy has an 70% coinsurance provision? Round the percent of recovery to the nearest whole percent before calculating the insurance settlement. _____

G. Use Excel to solve problems involving health, life, auto, and property insurance. <mark>7.1 OBJECTIVES 4, 5   7.2 OBJECTIVES 3, 6</mark>

29. Retrieve the file *ch07ex05.xlsx*. Follow the directions. Save the file as *ch07ex05a.xlsx*.

30. Retrieve the file *ch07ex06.xlsx*. Follow the directions. Save the file as *ch07ex06a.xlsx*.

31. Retrieve the file *ch07ex07.xlsx*. Follow the directions. Save the file as *ch07ex07a.xlsx*.

32. Retrieve the file *ch07ex08.xlsx*. Follow the directions. Save the file as *ch07ex08a.xlsx*.

APPLY Math@Work INSURANCE AGENT

An insurance agent must interpret information on insurance policies. Review the following portion of a renter's insurance policy and answer the questions below.

COVERAGES	LIMITS OF ANNUAL LIABILITY	PREMIUMS
Section I Property		
Coverage B. Personal Property	$30,000	
Personal Property Off Premises	$ 3,000	
Section II Liability		
Coverage C. Personal Liability	$25,000	
(Each Occurrence)		
Coverage D. Medical Payments to Others		
(Each Person)	$ 500	
Loss of Use Coverage	$ 6,000	
	Basic Premium	$ 261
Deductibles (Section I Only)	Amount of Deductible	
Deductible Clause 3 (Applies to Section I)	$ 250	$ 11
	Total Policy Premium	$ 272

1. If the renter had $36,000 damage done to his property at his residence, how much would he collect from the insurance company?

2. Suppose a guest slipped in the kitchen and incurred $4,600 in medical bills. How much would the policy pay?

3. If the renter's car was broken into and a computer valued at $4,000 was stolen, how much would the insurance pay?

Write about Math

1. Tenant homeowner's insurance covers a renter's personal property and liability. Discuss the advantages and disadvantages of purchasing tenant homeowner's insurance.

2. Discuss the ways you can help decrease the cost of automobile insurance.

Personal Finance

Are you knowledgeable enough to make decisions about buying insurance?

New employees have to decide on HMOs, PPOs, or other health plans for themselves and their families. When you purchase a new car, the financial institution that loans you money will require both liability and collision insurance. You need to be ready to make that decision and purchase. Each day the newspaper identifies someone who has had an accident or has been killed and that person's family must continue without the person's income. Who will help pay the bills? Should you purchase life insurance to avoid leaving your family without some financial security? If so, how much insurance? The mortgage company who holds the loan on your new house requires that you purchase fire insurance which is usually a homeowner's policy. These premiums are paid to the insurance company by the mortgage company who includes in your house payment an amount to make these payments. Which company should you purchase homeowner's insurance from?

Becoming knowledgeable in each of these areas will allow you to make more responsible decisions. You can improve your knowledge about each of these areas by completing the following exercises.

1. Research at least two companies that offer health insurance, such as Aetna or Anthem, about HMOs and PPOs.

   a. Explain how they differ.

   b. List the advantages and disadvantages of both.

   c. Determine your monthly premiums if you purchase health insurance privately—not through a group plan offered by an employer. Show your calculations.

2. Contact two automobile insurance agencies.

   a. Determine what the minimum requirements are for liability coverage in your state.

   b. If you do not own an automobile, describe the automobile you will most likely purchase when you do decide to buy a car.

   c. Compare motor-vehicle insurance monthly premiums for liability only and then with collision coverage. Show your calculations.

3. Contact two insurance companies who offer life insurance.

   a. Research the various kinds of life insurance policies available.

   b. Decide on one you believe to be most practical for you.

   c. Decide on the amount of insurance you need at this time in your life.

   d. Determine the monthly premiums quoted by each company. Show your calculations.

4. Contact two insurance agencies and obtain information about homeowner's insurance.

   a. Determine the policies available for your residence—renter's insurance or homeowner's insurance.

   b. Determine the monthly premiums for your residence with and then without an 80% coinsurance clause.

Name   *Date*   *Score*

Directions   Solve the following problems. Write your answers in the blanks provided.

A. **Determine the employee's monthly premium for individual and family**   **7.1 OBJECTIVE 2**
health insurance coverage. Round all answers to the nearest hundredth.
The individual annual premium is $1,728. The employer will pay $85
of the monthly premium for each employee. An additional $60 is added
to the individual monthly premium for family coverage.

    1.   Individual monthly premium   = _____

    2.   Family monthly premium   = _____

    3.   Luisa Espino is married and has two children. Her employer offers a health
insurance plan with an annual premium of $1,860 for an individual. The
employer has agreed to pay one-half of that cost. Luisa can purchase family
coverage for an additional $95 per month. Compute her monthly premium
for her and her family.   _____

B. **Determine the annual premium due for life insurance. Round**   **7.1 OBJECTIVE 3**
all answers to the nearest hundredth.

    4.   Tran Dong wants to purchase $50,000 of term life insurance at a rate of
$3.10 per $1,000. What is his annual premium?   _____

    5.   Mark Ramsey is a senior majoring in criminal justice. His advisor suggested
that he purchase life insurance before he graduates and begins working
as a policeman because once he is employed, the premiums will increase
tremendously, or he might not be able to purchase life insurance. He decides
to purchase a $250,000 life insurance policy. An insurance company quoted
him a cost of $4.10 per $1,000. What would his monthly premium be?   _____

    6.   Jake Monahans purchased a $150,000 term life insurance policy for himself
and one for his wife, Ruth. Jake's policy was quoted at $3.30 per $1,000 and
Ruth's was quoted at $3.05. What is their monthly premium for the
two policies?   _____

C. **Determine the amount of money the insurance company and the individual**   **7.2 OBJECTIVE 2**
will pay for damages in the following automobile accident:
Coverage: 20/50/10; Personal bodily injury: Sara Crown = $23,000,
Ted Crown = $16,000; Property damage: Crown's automobile = $11,050

    7.   Insurance payment for personal bodily injury   = _____

    8.   Insurance payment for property damage   = _____

    9.   Total paid by insurance company   = _____

    10.   Total paid by individual causing accident   = _____

D. Determine the annual premium due for property insurance. 7.2 OBJECTIVE 3
   Round all answers to the nearest hundredth.

11. Lilly and John Burger want to purchase tenant homeowner's insurance to cover their household furnishings valued at $29,000. Their insurance company quoted them $2.85 per $1,000. What is their annual premium for the homeowner's insurance? _____

12. Betty and Roger Morgan decide to purchase a new home valued at $155,000. The fire insurance on the home is quoted at $4.95 per $1,000. What is their monthly premium for the fire insurance? _____

E. Determine the amount paid by the insurance company on an 80% 7.2 OBJECTIVE 4
   coinsurance policy for the following properties. Round the rate of recovery to the nearest whole percent before calculating the amount of insurance paid.

	Amount of Coverage	Value	Loss	Insurance Paid
13.	$152,000	$190,000	$89,000	_____
14.	$250,000	$345,000	$155,000	_____

15. Rosa's Catering Service is in a building valued at $156,000. She insured the building against damage for $110,000. The building suffered water damage from flooding that amounted to $86,000. Her policy has an 80% coinsurance clause in it. How much will Rosa receive to cover the cost of the damage? Round the rate of recovery to the nearest whole percent before calculating the amount of insurance paid. _____

F. Solve the following insurance-related word problems.

16. Safeway Shipping pays two-thirds of each employee's individual health insurance premium each month. The annual premium for this plan is $2,700 per employee. Family coverage can be purchased for an additional $137.50 per month. As an employee of Safeway Shipping, Martha West carries the family coverage. Compute her monthly premium. _____

17. Ozzie Adams drives a car that runs into Evan Deat's automobile, injuring Evan and Mary Smith, a passenger in Evan's car. Ozzie has 25/50/10 liability coverage. Evan is awarded $32,000 for personal bodily injuries. Mary Smith is awarded $20,000. It will cost $4,309 to repair Evan's automobile. How much will Ozzie's insurance company pay? _____

18. Tasty Ice Cream Shoppe suffers fire damage of $119,000 to its building valued at $250,000. The owner has it insured for $175,000. How much will the insurance company pay if the policy has an 80% coinsurance clause? Round the rate of recovery to the nearest whole percent before calculating the amount of insurance paid. _____

G. Solve the following problems using Excel. 7.1 OBJECTIVES 4, 5
                                              7.2 OBJECTIVES 3, 6

19. Retrieve the file *ch07qz01.xlsx*. Follow the directions. Save the file as *ch07qz01a.xlsx*.

20. Retrieve the file *ch07qz02.xlsx*. Follow the directions. Save the file as *ch07qz02a.xlsx*.

Buying, or "purchasing," as it is generally called in business, is an important function. A manufacturing center buys the materials it needs for production, or a retail business buys the merchandise it needs for resale. The retail business attempts to purchase merchandise from manufacturers and wholesalers at the lowest possible cost to increase the profit they earn.

COMMERCIAL BUSINESS ANALYST

Ronald Martinez is a commercial business analyst at a multinational consumer packaged goods company. As an analyst, he is responsible for guiding and influencing strategic decisions that allow his company to grow using various quantitative methods. He works with multiple departments (for example, finance, sales, and marketing) to help them understand and solve potential business opportunities or issues. Once business questions or problems are defined—such as understanding why laundry sales are declining—he provides the data and analysis needed to make business recommendations. Then he communicates insights that will address these opportunities, for example, increasing distribution and pricing of product X versus product Y.

Ronald says, "Having average or advanced aptitude for mathematics does not ensure success as a business analyst." A business analyst must also possess the insight and ability to interpret research and the skills to put that information to work for the company. He said, "While your study or research might be extremely precise, complex, and exhaustive in scope, all this has little value unless the insights and key findings produced are turned into concrete actions that can impact the business positively. For example, although you may have produced a complex model that predicts which advertising technique will sell the most cases for a customer, it remains irrelevant because the product being sold is almost always out of stock."

How Math is Used in Business Analysis

Business is not always good, especially during periods of economic recession. Ronald says, "When our business dips, we look at all the data we have to find out what is causing the problem. From sales data to consumer research information, we uncover whether we are losing to competition, or if our consumers have just stopped buying our type of products altogether…. Math eliminates subjectivity and maintains objectivity leading to quicker management discussions and more effective solutions."

What Do You Think?

What skills do you need to become a business analyst?

Courtesy of Ronald Martinez

Math Skills Used

Algebra

Decimals

Fractions

Percents

Statistics

Other Skills Needed

Communication

Leadership

Organization

Selling skills

OBJECTIVES

1. Describe the purchasing cycle.
2. Identify terms used with purchasing.

8.1 The Purchasing Cycle

OBJECTIVE 1 Describe the purchasing cycle.

To learn about purchasing, you will study the cycle of purchasing from the point of ordering to the point of paying for the items. For example, when a small business needs office supplies, it may order directly from a retail office supply business or from a wholesaler. However, a large business may have many departments requesting supplies. It is less expensive to buy in quantity because a discount is often given. Therefore, each department may have its orders processed through a central purchasing department. This department can combine all orders and buy in quantity, thereby receiving better prices. The following example describes the route of an order for office supplies from the Human Resources Department at Elliott Steel Buildings to Low-Cost Office Supply.

Figure 8-1

Purchase Requisition

Elliott Steel Buildings
1102 Gordon Highway
Augusta, GA 30901-8155
(404) 555-3270

Purchase Requisition

Requisition No.:	12310	**Deliver To:**	Human Resources
Date Issued:	August 12, 20--	**Location:**	1st Floor
Date Required:	August 29, 20--	**Job No.:**	789
		Approved By:	C.O.S.

Quantity	Description	List Price	Total
100	Blue alphabetical sorting trays #2203	5.00	500.00
24	Calendars with holders #81F	7.25	174.00
5	Suede side chairs #81912	290.00	1450.00
1	Oak bookcase, 5 shelves #2126	839.04	839.04

Signature: _S. P. Masson_   **TOTAL:** $2,963.04

The individual or department that needs supplies prepares a purchase requisition, as shown in Figure 8-1. A **purchase requisition** is an internal order form sent to the purchasing department from another department (Human Resources in the example above) so it knows what supplies to buy. Purchase requisitions are also used to control purchases by requiring a manager's signature.

The purchasing department then prepares a purchase order that may include more items requested by other departments. A **purchase order** is a document issued by a buyer to a vendor listing products or services wanted. The purchase order authorizes the vendor to ship the items or services and bill for them at agreed prices and terms.

Elliott Steel Buildings
1102 Gordon Highway
Augusta, GA 30901-8155
(404) 555-3270

Purchase Order

To: Low-Cost Office Supply
1389 Buena Vista Road
Columbus, GA 31906-2612

Date: August 13, 20--
Order Number: 3619
Ship By: Truck
Terms: 2/10, net 30

Quantity	Cat. No.	Description	List Price	Total
100	2203	Blue alphabetical sorting trays	5.00	500.00
24	81F	Calendars with holders	7.25	174.00
5	81912	Suede side chairs	290.00	1450.00
1	2126	Oak bookcase, 5 shelves	839.04	839.04

Signature: *L. J. Troy*

TOTAL: $2,963.04

Figure 8-2
Purchase Order

After delivering the merchandise, the vendor, Low-Cost Office Supply, sends Elliott Steel Buildings an invoice or bill. An **invoice** is a record of the sales transaction showing the quantity of each item sold with its individual price, any added charges or discounts, the total price, and the payment terms. Notice the information contained in the invoice shown in Figure 8-3 closely matches the information on the purchase order.

Low-Cost Office Supply
1389 Buena Vista Road
Columbus, GA 31906-2612
(104) 555-6363

Invoice

Sold To: Elliott Steel Buildings
1102 Gordon Highway
Augusta, GA 30901-8155

Date: August 25, 20--
Our Invoice No.: 778542
Your Order No.: 3619
Shipped By: Truck
Terms: 2/10, net 30

Quantity	Description	List Price	Total
100	Blue alphabetical sorting trays #2203	5.00	500.00
24	Calendars with holders #81F	7.25	174.00
5	Suede side chairs #81912	290.00	1450.00
1	Oak bookcase, 5 shelves #2126	839.04	839.04

Checked by: *C. J.*
Salesperson: *Roby*

TOTAL: $2,963.04

Figure 8-3
Invoice

Before an invoice is approved for payment and sent to the accounting department to be paid, it is checked against the purchase order and the items that were actually received to be sure that the correct items and quantities were delivered in acceptable condition. Sometimes a **receiving report** lists each item received and is prepared by the person or department that receives the order when the merchandise arrives. It may be a copy of the purchase order.

Occasionally, it is necessary to return merchandise. For example, assume Elliott Steel Buildings returned merchandise (some of the sorting trays were the wrong color) to Low-Cost Office Supply. In this case, Low-Cost Office Supply would issue a **credit memorandum**, which notifies Elliott Steel Buildings that they have received a credit on their account for the amount of the returned merchandise. An example of a credit memorandum is shown in Figure 8-4.

Figure 8-4

Credit Memorandum

Quantity	Cat. No.	Items	Credits	Balance Due
18	2205	Red alphabetical	5.00	90.00
		sorting trays		

Low-Cost Office Supply
1389 Buena Vista Road
Columbus, GA 31906-2612
(404) 555-6363

Credit Memorandum

Sold To: Elliott Steel Buildings
1102 Gordon Highway
Augusta, GA 30901-8155

Date: September 3, 20--

No.: 909

The accounting department at Elliott Steel Buildings regularly pays invoices that have been checked and approved for payment. Like most companies, Elliott uses **voucher checks** as illustrated in Figure 8-5. The voucher is the detachable portion showing the invoice number (or numbers) being paid by the check.

Figure 8-5

Voucher Check

Elliott Steel Buildings
1102 Gordon Highway
Augusta, GA 30901-8155

No. 30667   64 - 32 / 611

September 25, 20 --

PAY TO THE ORDER OF   Low-Cost Office Supply------------------------ $ 2,873.04

Two Thousand Eight Hundred Seventy-Three and 04/100--------   DOLLARS

For Classroom Use Only

Bank Augusta
3621 Lake Shore Loop
Augusta, GA 30907-2123

Wes Peterson

⑆061100321⑆ ⑈4738596O⑈

Detach before depositing check.

Elliott Steel Buildings
1102 Gordon Highway
Augusta, GA 30901-8155

Date	Description	Gross Amount	Deductions	Net Amount
09/25/--	Invoice 778542	2,963.04	90.00 CM	2,873.04

Businesses send a monthly **statement of account** to each customer with an open account balance indicating the month's transactions, including the balance at the beginning of the month, payments made during the month, any credit from credit memorandums, and the balance owed at the end of the month. Figure 8-6 shows an example of a statement of account.

Figure 8-6

Statement of Account

Low-Cost Office Supply
1389 Buena Vista Road
Columbus, GA 31906-2612
(404) 555-6363

Statement of Account

Sold To: Elliott Steel Buildings
1102 Gordon Highway
Augusta, GA 30901-8155

Date: September 30, 20--

YOUR ACCOUNT HAS BEEN CREDITED FOR:

Date	Items	Debits	Credits	Balance Due
Aug. 25	Our Invoice 778542	2,963.04		2,963.04
Sep. 3	Credit Memo 909		90.00	2,873.04
Sep. 28	Payment, Check 30667		2,873.04	-0-

Manufacturers purchase raw materials and/or parts to make finished products. Manufacturers sell their products to other manufacturers, wholesalers, or other sales intermediaries. **Wholesalers**, often called middlemen, buy merchandise from manufacturers or other wholesalers and sell to **retailers**, who, in turn, sell directly to you, the consumer.

Manufacturers distribute their goods using a variety of carriers or transporters, such as rail, truck, ship, and plane. When goods are shipped, a **bill of lading**, a contract between the seller and the carrier, is prepared and sent with the shipment. It contains information about the origin and date of shipment, the transport vessel or vehicle and freight charges, the weight and value of the goods being shipped, and their destination. The buyer signs the bill of lading to verify delivery.

The term **free on board (FOB)**, sometimes stated as *freight on board*, is used to identify the point at which the buyer takes ownership and responsibility for the goods; that is, the point at which the shipper is *free* of responsibility for the shipment. It is also the point at which the buyer must begin paying shipping, or freight charges. The seller will state the sales terms as *FOB shipping point* (also *FOB origin*) or *FOB destination*.

With **FOB shipping point**, the buyer takes title to the goods at the seller's point of shipment and pays the freight to the buyer's business location. For example, Miller Construction, the buyer, in Dallas, Texas pays the freight cost of getting their goods to their plant using a shipper or carrier, such as Apex Transport. Ownership is passed to Miller Construction when the goods are given to the Apex Transport to be delivered to Miller Construction.

With **FOB destination**, the seller maintains ownership until the goods are delivered to the buyer and bears the cost of shipping.

Often, when the sales terms call for FOB Shipping point, the buyer will require the seller to prepay the shipping charges to the carrier, called **prepaid shipping** or **prepaid freight**, and add them to the invoice. That way, the buyer doesn't have to worry about settling freight charges with the carrier before taking delivery. Other times, the shipper will not agree to prepay the shipping costs and the goods are delivered **freight collect**, meaning that the buyer must pay freight charges to the carrier before taking delivery.

Another common term is **cash on delivery (COD)**, which means that the buyer must pay for the goods plus shipping charges upon delivery. Usually, the carrier acts as the seller's agent and collects the money for the seller.

Name _____   Date _____

Directions   Complete the following exercises.

A. Match the following terms with their definitions. Some terms may not be used.   OBJECTIVE 2

a. bill of lading   b. cash on delivery (COD)   c. credit memorandum
d. FOB shipping point   e. FOB destination   f. free on board (FOB)
g. freight collect   h. invoice   i. manufacturer
j. prepaid freight   k. purchase order   l. purchase requisition
m. receiving report   n. retailer   o. statement of account
p. voucher check   q. wholesaler

1. _____   Contract between a shipper and a carrier that accompanies a shipment of goods.

2. _____   Sales term stating that goods must be paid for when delivered.

3. _____   Notice that a business has received a credit on its account for the amount of the returned merchandise.

4. _____   A check with a detachable portion showing the invoice number(s) paid by the check.

5. _____   Form sent to the purchasing department so the purchasing staff knows what supplies to order.

6. _____   Form used to verify the item numbers and condition of the merchandise when it arrives.

7. _____   Form given to a vendor authorizing it to ship and bill for specific goods or services.

8. _____   Record of sales transaction showing each item sold and total price.

9. _____   Business that buys merchandise from a manufacturer and sells it to a retailer.

10. _____   Companies that purchase raw materials to make finished products or merchandise.

11. _____   A listing of a customer's purchases and payments showing their account balance.

12. _____   Shipping charges paid by the seller and added to the invoice.

13. _____   A business that sells directly to the consumer.

14. _____   The buyer pays for shipping merchandise to its destination.

8.2 Cash Discounts

OBJECTIVE 1 Identify terms used with cash discounts.

Many businesses offer their customers a cash discount as an incentive to pay their invoices early. Cash discounts are advantageous to both the buyer and the seller by reducing costs for both. A **cash discount** is extended to a business that pays its bill within a designated time period, usually 10 days.

A business communicates the way it will accept payment on its invoice under **terms of payment**, or *terms*. Terms of payment are shown in an abbreviated form: 2/10, n/30, for example. The figures provide the **discount rate** (2%), the **discount period** (10 days), and the **due date** (30 days from the **invoice date**). A business may not offer cash discounts. In that case, its terms might be stated as n/30, or net 30.

The discount rate is the percent the customer may deduct from the invoice total. The discount period is the number of days after the invoice date during which the seller will accept a discounted payment. In the example, if the invoice date was March 13, the discounted payment would be due by March 23. The due date is the number of days (usually 30) after the invoice date that the seller will accept the net amount (the n in n/30). In this case net means the full amount of the invoice. In the example 2/10, n/30, the full amount of the invoice would be due on April 12 (the 18 days left in March plus the first 12 days of April equals 30 days). Sometimes, businesses will charge interest or penalties for payments received after the due date.

Another type of discount is 3/10, 2/30, n/60. This means a customer can take a 3% discount if the invoice amount is paid within 10 days, 2% if paid within 30 days, or the net amount if paid within 60 days.

monkeybusinessimages/iStockphoto.com

Other payment terms that may appear on invoices are:

- **n/EOM** The net is due at the end of the month (EOM) in which the invoice is dated.
- **3/10 EOM** A 3% discount is calculated if the amount is paid during the first 10 days of the month after the month in the invoice date. For example, if the invoice is dated September 15, a 3% discount is taken as long as the invoice is paid on or before October 10.
- **n/30 ROG** The net is due 30 days after the receipt of goods (ROG) rather than the date of the invoice.

TIPS

Proxims *or* prox *means the same as* EOM.

OBJECTIVE **2** Calculate cash discounts.

To calculate the cash discount amount, multiply the total of the invoice by the percent of the cash discount allowed.

EXAMPLE

Find the cash discount and the net amount due on this invoice if paid by March 25.

Invoice date:	March 15
Terms:	2/10, n/30
Invoice total:	$945.05

STEPS

1. Multiply the invoice total by the cash discount, 2%, to obtain the cash discount.

$$\begin{array}{r} \$945.05 \\ \times \quad 0.02 \\ \hline \$18.9010 \end{array}$$ cash discount, rounded to $18.90

2. Subtract the cash discount from the invoice total to obtain the net amount due on the invoice.

$$\begin{array}{r} \$945.05 \\ - \quad 18.90 \\ \hline \$926.15 \end{array}$$ net amount due on invoice

If the invoice is not paid within 10 days, the full amount of $945.05 must be paid within 30 days after the date of the invoice. Otherwise, payment is considered past due and may be subject to a late fee and interest may be charged.

OBJECTIVE **3** Use the complement method of trade discount to find net price.

TIPS

Remember to use the formula for determining percentage, B × R = P. The total of the invoice is the base, and the percent of cash discount is the rate.

An alternate method of determining the net amount due on an invoice is to multiply the original invoice amount by the complement. A **complement** is the difference between 100% and the discount rate.

If a discount rate of 2% is given on an invoice of $425.72, what is the net amount due?

STEPS

1. Subtract the discount rate from 100%.

$$100\% - 2\% = 98\%$$

2. Multiply the invoice amount by the complement rate.

$$\$425.72 \times 98\% = \$417.21 \quad \text{net amount due}$$

$8.51

$417.21

Your answers for some problems may vary by a few cents using the complement method due to rounding.

OBJECTIVE 4 Find the net amount due after merchandise has been returned.

If merchandise has been returned, the amount of the returned merchandise is deducted from the invoice amount *before* the cash discount is calculated. Study the following example involving returned merchandise.

EXAMPLE

Invoice amount:	$3,688.00
Terms:	2/10, n/30

A credit memorandum shows that the cost of the returned merchandise was $1,175.00. Verify the invoice amount subject to the returned goods and the discount. Then find the net amount due.

TIPS

The amount of returned merchandise is subtracted from the invoice amount before a cash discount is taken.

STEPS

1. Subtract the cost of returned merchandise (shown on the credit memorandum) from the invoice amount.

$$
\begin{array}{r}
\$3,688.00 \\
-\ 1,175.00 \\
\hline
\$2,513.00 \quad \text{basis for cash discount}
\end{array}
$$

2. Obtain the cash discount by multiplying the amount subject to discount by the 2% discount rate.

$$
\begin{array}{r}
\$2,513.00 \\
\times \quad 0.02 \\
\hline
\$ \quad 50.26 \quad \text{cash discount}
\end{array}
$$

3. Subtract the cash discount from the invoice amount less the cost of returned merchandise.

$$
\begin{array}{r}
\$2,513.00 \\
-\quad 50.26 \\
\hline
\$2,462.74 \quad \text{net amount due}
\end{array}
$$

Cash discounts are not calculated on shipping or insurance charges. Therefore, to determine the total amount due on the invoice, you must remember to add shipping or insurance charges to the invoice *after* you have calculated the cash discount. If these charges already have been added to the invoice, they must be deducted from the invoice total to determine the basis on which the discount is calculated. Study the following example.

EXAMPLE

An invoice for $455.20 has terms of 2/10, n/30 with a shipping charge of $19.50. Assume the invoice is paid within the 10-day period. Determine the net amount due on the invoice.

STEPS

1. Calculate the cash discount.

$$\begin{array}{r} \$\,455.20 \\ \times \quad 0.02 \\ \hline \$\quad 9.10 \end{array} \quad \text{cash discount}$$

2. Subtract the cash discount from the invoice amount.

$$\begin{array}{r} \$455.20 \\ -\quad 9.10 \\ \hline \$446.10 \end{array} \quad \text{invoice amount minus discount}$$

3. Add shipping charges.

$$\begin{array}{r} \$446.10 \\ +\ 19.50 \\ \hline \$465.60 \end{array} \quad \text{total amount due on invoice}$$

> **TIPS**
>
> *On an invoice, charges for shipping may be shown as shipping and handling or freight.*

If the shipping charges had been added to the invoice amount, you would first subtract the shipping charges from the invoice amount, take the discount, and then add the shipping charges to the net invoice amount to obtain the total amount due on the invoice.

Remember that a cash discount is not allowed if an invoice is not paid within the discount period as defined by the terms. For example, an invoice amounting to $830.79 is dated April 29 and offers terms of 3/10, n/30 and has shipping charges of $22.29. Because the invoice was paid May 12 instead of May 10, no cash discount is allowed.

$$\begin{array}{r} \$830.79 \\ +\ 22.29 \\ \hline \$853.08 \end{array} \quad \text{total amount due on invoice}$$

> **TIPS**
>
> *Shipping and insurance charges are added to the invoice total after a discount is deducted. If these charges already have been added to the invoice, they must be deducted from the invoice total to determine the basis on which the discount is calculated.*

Occasionally a customer may not pay the full amount of the invoice but will make a partial payment. If the partial payment is made within the discount period, the customer may be allowed a cash discount on the portion of the invoice paid. If there is a 3% discount, the buyer pays 97 cents for every $1 of payment. To determine the amount of debt canceled by a partial payment, divide the partial payment by the complement of the discount percent. Remember, you find the complement by subtracting the cash discount percent from 100 percent.

EXAMPLE

Julio Rodriquez wants to pay a portion of his invoice totaling $1,657.98 with terms of 3/10, n/30. He sends a partial payment of $879 within the 10-day discount period. It was agreed he would receive a cash discount on this partial payment. Calculate the credit he should receive for this partial payment, the balance due on the invoice, and the cash discount.

Problem Solving Plan

Clues	Action Plan	Solve
Invoice total: $1,657.98 Terms: 3/10, n/30 Partial payment of $879.00 within discount period Discount allowed on partial payment	1. Find the complement of the discount rate.	100% − 3% = 97%
	2. Divide the partial payment by the complement to determine the amount of merchandise paid for.	$879 ÷ 97% (0.97) = $906.19
	3. Subtract the payment from the amount of merchandise paid for to find the cash discount.	$906.19 − $879.00 = $27.19
	4. Subtract the amount of merchandise paid for from the original total to find the balance due on the invoice.	$1,657.98 − $906.19 = $751.79

Conclusion

By making a partial payment of $879 within the discount period, a cash discount of $27.19 was earned and $906.19 worth of merchandise was paid for. This leaves a balance due of $751.79.

Creating and completing an invoice using Excel is a common business application. If an invoice form is not already available, you can create one using Excel or an Excel template.

The invoice in Figure 8-7 has been completed for three items ordered by Tracey Veloz Enterprises, Inc. You will calculate a discount (using the complement method) and add shipping charges to obtain the invoice total.

Figure 8-7

Completed Invoice

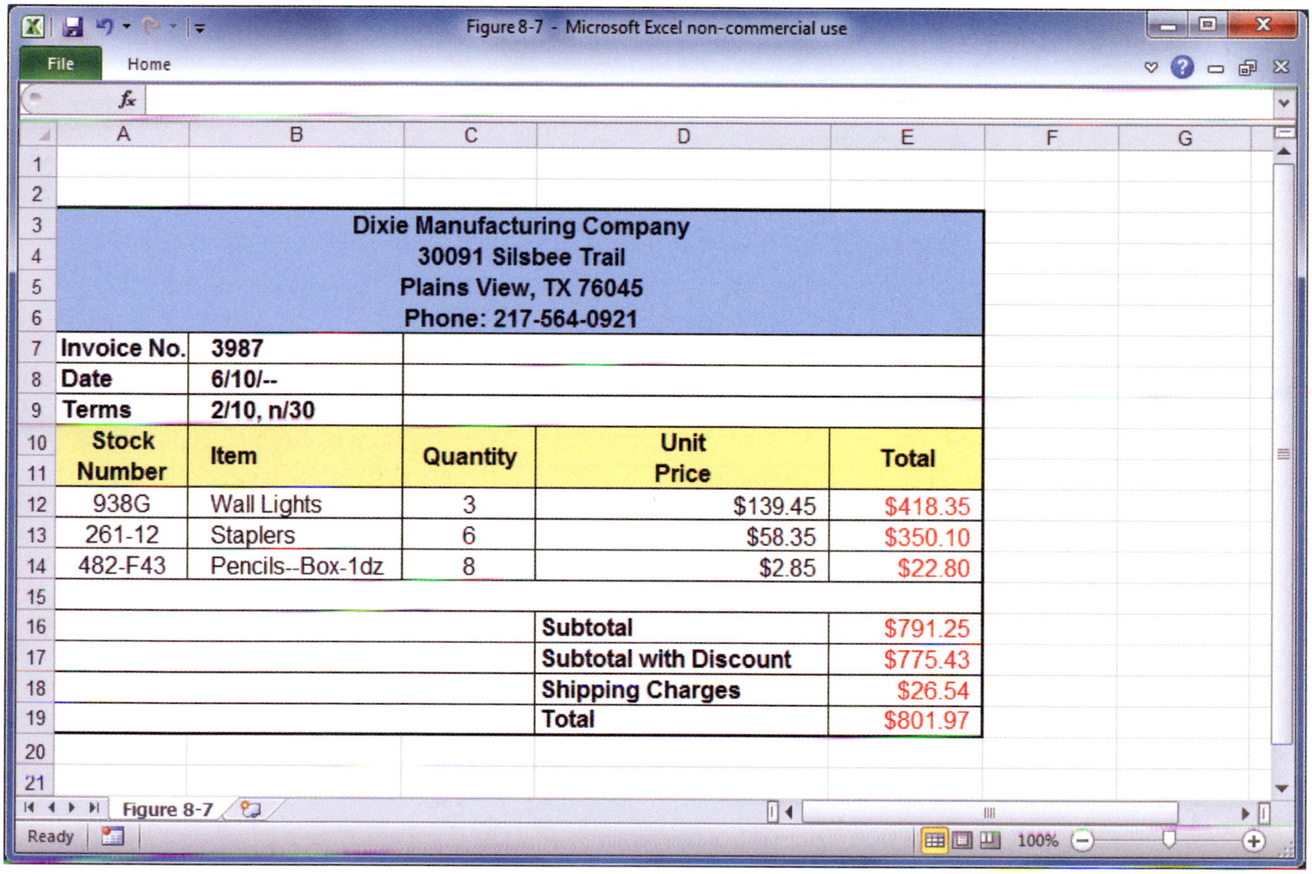

STEPS

Retrieve the file *ch08pr01.xlsx*.

1. Enter a formula in Cell E12 to multiply the Quantity by the Unit Price for the first Item. Copy the formula to Cells E13 and E14.

2. Calculate a Subtotal in Cell E16.

3. Calculate the Subtotal with Discount (of 2%) in Cell E17. The subtotal with discount is calculated at 98% of the original subtotal. The formula is =E16*98%.

4. Enter Shipping Charges of 26.54 in Cell E18.

5. Calculate the Total in Cell E19.

6. Format Column E for Currency, 2 Decimal places, and $.

7. Save the file as *ch08pr01a.xlsx*.

TIPS

You can find invoice templates in Excel by clicking on the File tab, and then click on New. On the left is a list of templates. Click on Invoices to find invoice templates.

Next you will revise the invoice. You will deduct the amount of returned merchandise, calculate the discount, and add shipping and insurance charges to obtain the invoice total. Figure 8-8 shows the revised invoice.

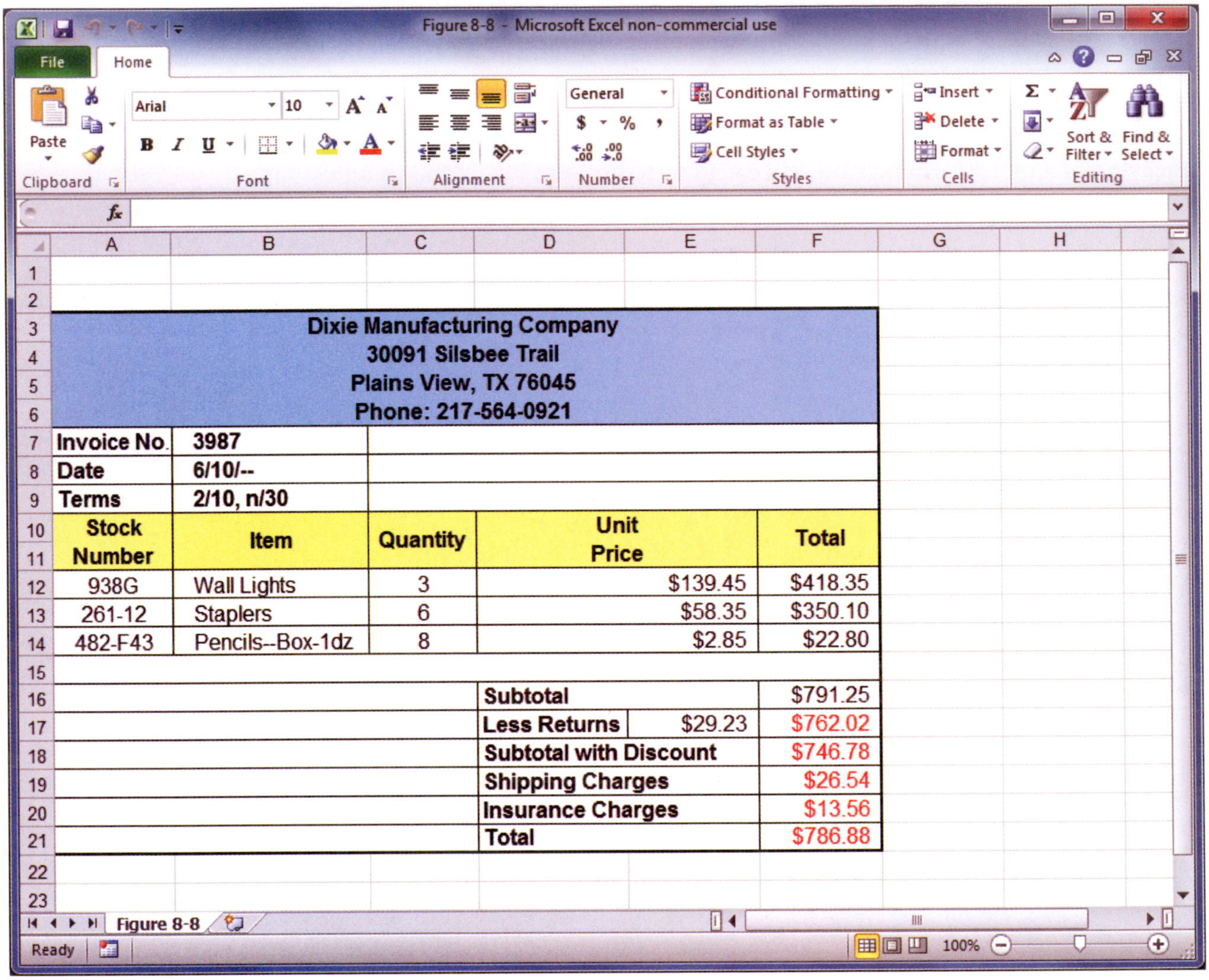

	A	B	C	D	E	F
3	Dixie Manufacturing Company					
4	30091 Silsbee Trail					
5	Plains View, TX 76045					
6	Phone: 217-564-0921					
7	Invoice No.	3987				
8	Date	6/10/--				
9	Terms	2/10, n/30				
10–11	Stock Number	Item	Quantity	Unit Price		Total
12	938G	Wall Lights	3		$139.45	$418.35
13	261-12	Staplers	6		$58.35	$350.10
14	482-F43	Pencils--Box-1dz	8		$2.85	$22.80
16				Subtotal		$791.25
17				Less Returns	$29.23	$762.02
18				Subtotal with Discount		$746.78
19				Shipping Charges		$26.54
20				Insurance Charges		$13.56
21				Total		$786.88

Figure 8-8
Invoice With Returned Merchandise, Discount, Shipping, and Insurance Charges

STEPS

Retrieve the file *ch08pr02.xlsx*.

1. Enter a formula in Cell F17 to calculate the Invoice amount less returned merchandise.
2. Enter the formula in Cell F18 to calculate the Subtotal with Discount.
3. Enter Shipping Charges of 26.54 in Cell F19.
4. Enter Insurance charges of 13.56 in Cell F20.
5. Calculate the Total in Cell F21.
6. Format Column F for Currency, 2 Decimal places, and $.
7. Save the file as *ch08pr02a.xlsx*.

Name _____   Date _____

Directions   Solve the following problems. Write your answers in the blanks provided. Place commas and dollar signs in answers as needed.

A. **Find the cash discount amount and the net amount due on these**   OBJECTIVES **2, 3**
invoices. Assume each invoice is paid within the discount period.
Round your answers to the nearest cent.

Invoice Amount	Terms	Cash Discount	Net Amount Due
$623.50	2/10, n/30	1. _____	2. _____
$4,635.65	3/10, n/60	3. _____	4. _____
$6,250.81	1/15, n/45	5. _____	6. _____

B. **Determine the cash discount and net amount due on these invoices. Round**   OBJECTIVES **4, 5**
your answers to the nearest cent.

Invoice Amount	Terms	Paid Within Discount Period	Returned Merchandise	Shipping Charges	Cash Discount	Net Amount Due
$534.78	2/10, n/45	yes	none	$13.25	7. _____	8. _____
$638.00	1/10, n/30	yes	$33.50	none	9. _____	10. _____
$213.72	2/10, n/30	no	none	$15.50	11. _____	12. _____

C. **Determine the credit given for partial payment, balance due, and cash**   OBJECTIVE **6**
discount on these invoices.

Invoice Amount	Terms	Partial Payment	Credit Given	Balance Due	Cash Discount
$1,189.40	2/10, n/30	$290.00	13. _____	14. _____	15. _____
$1,987.00	3/10, n/45	$1,400.00	16. _____	17. _____	18. _____

D. **Calculate cash discounts and net amounts due.**   OBJECTIVES **2, 3, 5, 6**

19.   Corner Grocery received an invoice for $689.30, dated October 8, with
terms 2/10, n/30. How much should they pay on October 15?   _____

20.   How much should the store pay on October 20?   _____

21.   Suppose the invoice above included shipping charges of $32.80 and was paid
on October 15. How much does the store pay on this invoice?   _____

E. **Use Excel to calculate the following invoices.**   OBJECTIVE **7**

22.   Retrieve *ch08ex01.xlsx*. Follow the directions. Save the file as *ch08ex01a.xlsx*.

23.   Retrieve *ch08ex02.xlsx*. Follow the directions. Save the file as *ch08ex02a.xlsx*.

OBJECTIVES

1. Calculate trade discounts and net prices.

2. Apply a trade discount when preparing an invoice.

3. Use Excel to calculate the net amount due after applying a trade discount.

8.3 Trade Discounts

OBJECTIVE 1 Calculate trade discounts and net prices.

A **list price** (or **suggested retail price**) is the price that the manufacturer *suggests* be charged to retail customers. (The law does not allow manufacturers to *control* their retail prices.) List prices are often marked on the packaging, but prices can be marked lower or higher by retailers.

A **trade discount** is a deduction from a list price. When trade discounts are granted to a wholesaler or retailer, the price the seller charges the customer is the **net price**, the price after trade discounts are subtracted. For example, Burnett's Home Decorator's Supply Store purchased supplies including bristle brushes for a total of $2,964.29 from a wholesaler. A trade discount rate of 12% was allowed because the supply store sells the brushes to their customers.

Trade discounts differ from cash discounts in that they are deducted on the invoice *by the seller*, while cash discounts are deducted *by the buyer* from the invoice total (before shipping is added) when payment is made within the discount period. Also, trade discounts do not change based upon the date the invoice is paid.

Businesses offer trade discounts to their customers for a variety of reasons. For example, manufacturers and wholesalers spend a great deal of time and money producing catalogs with photos, descriptions, and suggested retail prices. Market conditions can change quickly. Distributing revised discount schedules makes responding to market changes faster and cheaper than reprinting catalogs. Trade discounts are also offered to encourage customers to buy in larger quantities, or to buy discontinued items.

The discount rate is sometimes shown in the top right corner of an invoice, as shown on the top portion of the invoice in Figure 8-9. Under Terms, the trade discount is shown as a percent, 15%, which is a percent of the list price of the item.

Figure 8-9

Top Portion of an Invoice

The following example illustrates the steps to find the net price when a trade discount is given.

EXAMPLE

Find the net price of an item with a list price of $189.30 and a 15% trade discount. The base is $189.30 (list price), and the trade discount rate is 15%. The trade discount amount is the part.

STEPS

1. Multiply the list price by the trade discount rate to get the trade discount amount.

$$\begin{array}{r} \$189.30 \\ \times\ \ 0.15 \\ \hline \$\ 28.40 \quad \text{trade discount amount} \end{array}$$

2. Subtract the trade discount amount from the list price to obtain the net price.

$$\begin{array}{r} \$189.30 \\ -\ 28.40 \\ \hline \$160.90 \quad \text{net price} \end{array}$$

OBJECTIVE **2** Apply a trade discount when preparing an invoice.

When processing an order and creating an invoice, the seller computes trade discounts. Since discounts may vary between different items on an invoice, they are often calculated on each item. If the trade discounts are the same on all items purchased, it is simpler to total the invoice first and apply the discount to the total. When trade discounts are applied item by item on unit prices, the customer can quickly compare the net prices on the invoice with list prices in catalogs or on price sheets.

EXAMPLE

The list price is $2,405; the trade discount rate is 20% with terms of 3/10, n/30; and the prepaid shipping charge (FOB shipping point) is $23.00. The invoice is dated August 3, and payment will be made within the 10-day period. Find the net amount due on the invoice using the following steps.

STEPS

1. Figure the trade discount.

$2,405 \times 0.20 = \$481.00$ trade discount amount

2. Subtract the trade discount amount from the list price.

$2,405 - \$481 = \$1,924.00$ net price

Or use the complement.

$2,405 \times 80\% = \$1,924.00$ net price

TIPS

Remember to apply the $P = R \times B$ *concept to trade discounts. For example, the list price of an item is $75.50 (base), the trade discount rate is 12%, and the trade discount amount is the part.*

TIPS

When both trade and cash discounts are offered, the trade discount is always deducted first because it is a specified discount on a stated amount. A cash discount is variable because it applies to payment based on a time period. Therefore, it is deducted after the trade discount.

TIPS

In Step 3, you may use the complement method if the "actual" cash discount is needed. For example, $1,924.00 × 0.97 = $1,866.28.

3. Calculate the cash discount for paying within the discount date.

$$\$1,924 \times 0.03 = \$57.72 \qquad \text{cash discount}$$

4. Subtract the cash discount from the amount found in the net price.

$$\$1,924 - \$57.72 = \$1,866.28 \qquad \text{subtotal}$$

5. Add prepaid shipping charges (FOB shipping point).

$$\$1,866.28 + \$23 = \$1,889.28 \qquad \text{total amount due}$$

EXAMPLE

Four items in different quantities have been ordered. The trade discount is 20%, and the shipping charge of $32 is supposed to be prepaid. Complete the invoice.

STEPS

TIPS

When the terms of sale stipulate FOB shipping point, the seller is usually asked to prepay the shipping charges and add them to the invoice.

Terms: FOB Shipping Point		Trade Discount: 20%		
Qty.	Item	List Price	Net Price	Total Sale
3	WR-25-209	58.50		
10	A00004811	31.90		
24	23C787	19.20		
82	TN-994	7.60		
	Prepaid Shipping			
	Invoice Total			

Problem Solving Plan

Clues	Action Plan	Solve
Item quantities and list prices are as shown on the invoice. Trade discount is 20%. Shipping charge of $32 is prepaid.	1. Calculate the complement of 20%.	100% − 20% = 80% (0.8)
	2. Calculate the net prices by multiplying each list price by the complement percent and enter in the Net Price column.	$58.50 × 0.8 = $46.80 $31.90 × 0.8 = $25.52 $19.20 × 0.8 = $15.36 $7.60 × 0.8 = $6.08
	3. Calculate the extended sale amount for each item and enter in the Total Sale column.	$46.80 × 3 = $140.40 $25.52 × 10 = $255.20 $15.36 × 24 = $368.64 $6.08 × 82 = $498.56
	4. Enter $32.00 in the Total Sale column (there is no discount on shipping charges).	
	5. Add the numbers in the Total Sale column and put the sum on the Invoice Total line.	$140.40 + $255.20 + $368.64 + $498.56 + $32.00 = $1,294.80

Conclusion

The invoice total is $1,294.80.

Use Excel to calculate the net amount due after applying a trade discount.

Now you will calculate the net amount due after figuring the trade discount, cash discount, and additional charges that have been added to the invoice as shown in Figure 8-10.

Figure 8-10

Net Amount Due After Discounts and Additional Charges

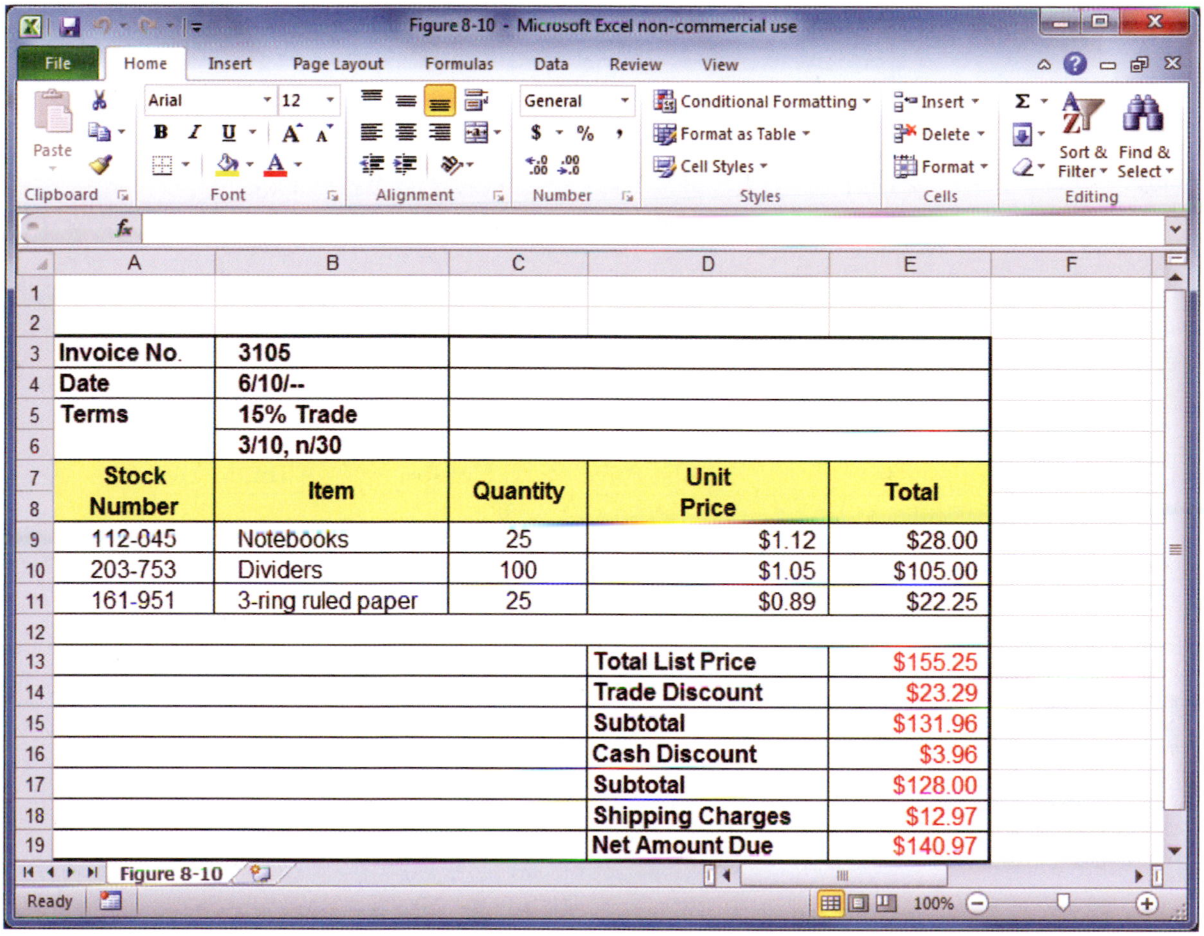

Invoice No.	3105			
Date	6/10/--			
Terms	15% Trade			
	3/10, n/30			

Stock Number	Item	Quantity	Unit Price	Total
112-045	Notebooks	25	$1.12	$28.00
203-753	Dividers	100	$1.05	$105.00
161-951	3-ring ruled paper	25	$0.89	$22.25
			Total List Price	$155.25
			Trade Discount	$23.29
			Subtotal	$131.96
			Cash Discount	$3.96
			Subtotal	$128.00
			Shipping Charges	$12.97
			Net Amount Due	$140.97

STEPS

Retrieve the file *ch08pr03.xlsx*.

1. Enter a formula in Cell E13 to calculate the Total List Price.

2. Enter a formula in Cell E14 to calculate the Trade Discount.

3. Enter a formula in Cell E15 to calculate the Subtotal.

4. Enter a formula in Cell E16 to calculate the Cash Discount.

5. Enter a formula in Cell E17 to calculate the Subtotal.

6. Enter Shipping Charges of $12.97 in Cell E18.

7. Enter a formula in Cell E19 to calculate the Net Amount Due.

8. Format Column E for Currency. Set Decimal places to 2. Set Currency symbol to $.

9. Save the file as *ch08pr03a.xlsx*.

Name _____ Date _____

Directions Solve the following problems.

A. **Determine the trade discount and the net price on the following invoices.** OBJECTIVE **1**

List Price	Trade Discount Rate		Trade Discount		Net Price
$309.80	20%	1. _____		2. _____
$1,026.80	15%	3. _____		4. _____
$1,683.50	30%	5. _____		6. _____
$240.20	25%	7. _____		8. _____

B. **Carl's Sports Shop ordered the following items from Apex Sports Products.** OBJECTIVE **2**
Apex charges $40 for delivery. Complete Apex's invoice to Carl's Sports Shop.

		FOB Destination		Trade Discount: 30%		
	Qty.	Item	List Price	Net Price	Total Sale
9.	15	Basketball	10.80		
10.	12	Football	19.90		
11.	20	Soccer ball	11.00		
12.	6	Volleyball	12.90		
13.	3	Air pump	48.50		
14.		Shipping			
15.		Invoice Total			

C. **Complete the following word problems. Round answers to hundredths.** OBJECTIVES **1, 2**

16. In Part C, assume that Apex offers Carl's Sports Shop payment terms of 2/10, n/30. If Carl pays within the discount period, how much would he pay Apex for the order? _____

17. Leo's Wholesale Cosmetics sells beauty products to salons. Leo purchases direct from the manufacturer at a 50% trade discount and sells to his retail customers at a 25% discount. One of his products is a hair color that lists for $27.95. What is Leo's net price, and what price does he charge his customers for the product? _____

18. Suppose market conditions change and the manufacturer reduces Leo's trade discount from 50% to 40%. To maintain his same profit margin, what should be his new discount to his customers? _____

D. **Use Excel to calculate net amounts due in the following invoices.** OBJECTIVE **3**

19. Retrieve *ch08ex03.xlsx*. Follow the directions. Save the file as *ch08ex03a.xlsx*.

20. Retrieve *ch08ex04.xlsx*. Follow the directions. Save the file as *ch08ex04a.xlsx*.

8.4 Series Discounts

OBJECTIVES
1. Calculate series discounts and net prices.
2. Use Excel to calculate series discounts.

OBJECTIVE 1 Calculate series discounts and net prices.

It is common for a business to offer more than one trade discount. A **series** (or chain) **discount** such as 5%, 10%, and 5% represents a 5% reduction from the list price, a 10% reduction on the remainder after the first discount has been subtracted, and another 5% reduction on the remainder after the second discount has been subtracted. A series discount may be shown with percent symbols—5%, 10%, 5%—or with slashes—5/10/5.

You can use one of the following methods to calculate a net price using a series discount.

EXAMPLE

A manufacturer offers a series discount of 20%, 10%, and 5% on building supplies that list for $795. Determine the net price.

Method 1: Calculate Series Discounts One at a Time

STEPS

1. Multiply the list price by the first discount rate.

$795 × 0.20 = $159

2. Subtract the first discount from the list price.

$795 − $159 = $636

3. Multiply the net price in Step 2 by the second discount rate.

$636 × 0.10 = $63.60

4. Subtract the second discount from the net price in Step 2.

$636.00 − $63.60 = $572.40

5. Multiply the third discount by the net price in Step 4.

$572.40 × 0.05 = $28.62

6. Subtract the third discount from the net price in Step 4.

$572.40 − $28.62 = $543.78
net price

Method 2: Calculate a Single Discount Equivalent Using Complements

An easier method to calculate a series discount and a net price is to use the complement method to find a **single discount equivalent**, one discount rate that is equal to applying the separate rates one at a time.

TIPS

Using the complement method is faster than using the actual discount method.

1. Find the complements of the individual discount rates.

$$100\% - 20\% = 80\% = 0.80 \quad \text{first discount}$$
$$100\% - 10\% = 90\% = 0.90 \quad \text{second discount}$$
$$100\% - 5\% = 95\% = 0.95 \quad \text{third discount}$$

2. Multiply the complements to get a net price equivalent.

$$0.80 \times 0.90 \times 0.95 = 0.684 \quad \text{net price equivalent}$$

3. Subtract the net price equivalent from 100% (1.00).

$$1.00 - 0.684 = 0.316 \quad \text{single discount equivalent}$$

4. Multiply the list price by the single discount equivalent.

$$\$795 \times 0.316 = \$251.22 \quad \text{dollar amount of series discount}$$

5. Subtract the dollar amount of the series discount from the list price.

$$\$795.00 - \$251.22 = \$543.78 \quad \text{net price}$$

The net price in step 5 is the same as the net price calculated in Method 1. The **net price equivalent,** when multiplied by the list price, will be the net price ($0.684 \times \$795.00 = \$543.78$). If you don't need to know the amount of the discount, you can calculate the net price by using the net price equivalent.

Method 3: Using a Series Discounts Table

A fast way to find a net price with a series discount is to use a special table with net price equivalents already calculated (Table 8-1).

1. Locate the vertical column labeled 20%.

2. Find the row labeled 10%, 5% and move right to the column headed 20%. The cell where they intersect contains 0.648.

3. Multiply the list price by 0.648.

$$\$795.00 \times 0.648 = \$543.78 \quad \text{net price}$$

As shown, the net price is determined by deducting each discount one at a time. It is important to note that the percents in the series are NEVER added. A discount of 20%, 10%, and 5% results in a different net price than a discount of 35% (20% + 10% + 5%).

Table 8-1

Net Price Equivalents for Series Discounts

Net Price Equivalents for Series Discounts											
	5%	$7\frac{1}{2}$%	10%	$12\frac{1}{2}$%	15%	$16\frac{2}{3}$%	20%	$22\frac{1}{2}$%	25%	$27\frac{1}{2}$%	30%	$32\frac{1}{2}$%
$7\frac{1}{2}$%	0.87875	0.85563	0.8325	0.80938	0.78625	0.77083	0.74	0.71688	0.69375	0.67063	0.6475	0.62438
$7\frac{1}{2}$%, $2\frac{1}{2}$%	0.85678	0.83423	0.81169	0.78914	0.76659	0.75156	0.7215	0.69895	0.67641	0.65386	0.63131	0.60877
$7\frac{1}{2}$%, 5%	0.83481	0.81284	0.79088	0.76891	0.74694	0.73229	0.703	0.68103	0.65906	0.63709	0.61513	0.59316
10%	0.855	0.8325	0.81	0.7875	0.765	0.75	0.72	0.6975	0.675	0.6525	0.63	0.6075
10%, $2\frac{1}{2}$%	0.83363	0.81169	0.78975	0.76781	0.74588	0.73125	0.702	0.68006	0.65813	0.63619	0.61425	0.59231
10%, 5%	0.81225	0.79088	0.7695	0.74813	0.72675	0.7125	0.684	0.66263	0.64125	0.61988	0.5985	0.57713
10%, 5%, $2\frac{1}{2}$%	0.79194	0.7711	0.75026	0.72942	0.70858	0.69469	0.6669	0.64606	0.62522	0.60438	0.58354	0.56270
10%, $7\frac{1}{2}$%	0.79088	0.77006	0.74925	0.72844	0.70763	0.69375	0.666	0.64519	0.62438	0.60356	0.58275	0.56194
10%, 10%	0.7695	0.74925	0.729	0.70875	0.6885	0.675	0.648	0.62775	0.6075	0.58725	0.567	0.54675

You are probably familiar with series discounts that are offered by many large department stores. For example, you may have seen an advertisement that shows "Save 50%—75% off regular-priced apparel and accessories when you take an extra 25% off." Suppose the first discount was 50% and then you received an extra 25%. The discount would be written as 50/25 or as 50%, 25%.

EXAMPLE

The regular price of a man's shirt was $60, and the sale price was $48.00—a savings of 20% off the regular price. An additional 33% discount was allowed, so the final price of the shirt was $32.00. In this situation, the series discount was 20/33.

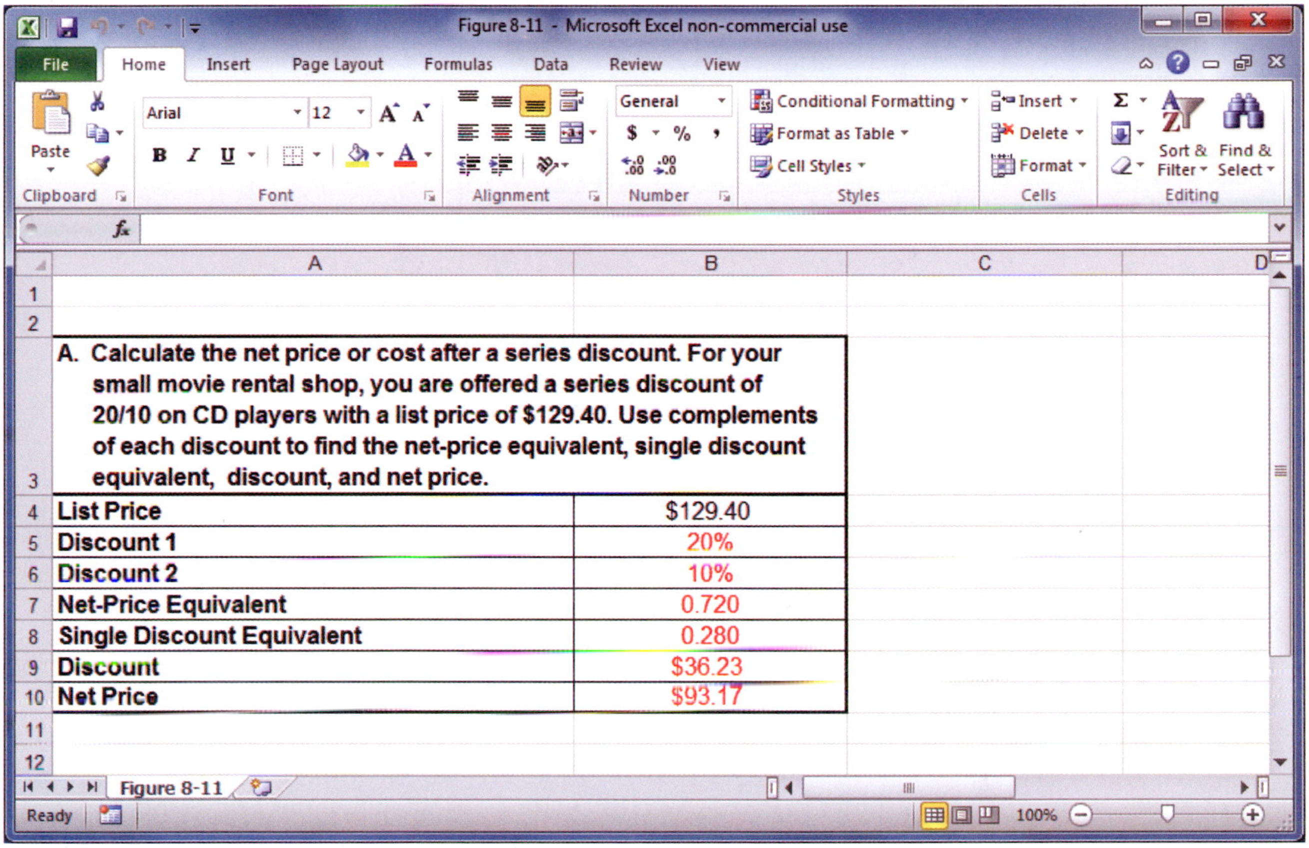

Figure 8-11

Calculate the Net Price after a Series Discount

STEPS

Retrieve the file **ch08pr04.xlsx**.

1. Enter Discount 1 for 20% in Cell B5. Format for Percentage, 0 Decimal places.

2. Enter Discount 2 for 10% in Cell B6. Format for Percentage, 0 Decimal places.

3. Enter the formula to calculate the Net-Price Equivalent in Cell B7. The formula is =(1-B5)*(1-B6). Format for Number, 3 Decimal places.

4. Enter the formula to calculate the Single Discount Equivalent in Cell B8. The formula is =1-B7. Format for Number, 3 Decimal places.
5. Enter the formula to calculate the Discount in Cell B9. Multiply the List Price by the Single Discount Equivalent.
6. Enter the formula to calculate the Net Price or cost in Cell B10. Multiply the List Price by the Net-Price Equivalent.
7. Format Cell B9 and Cell B10 for Currency, 2 Decimal places, and $.

Figure 8-12

Calculate the Net Price after a Series Discount

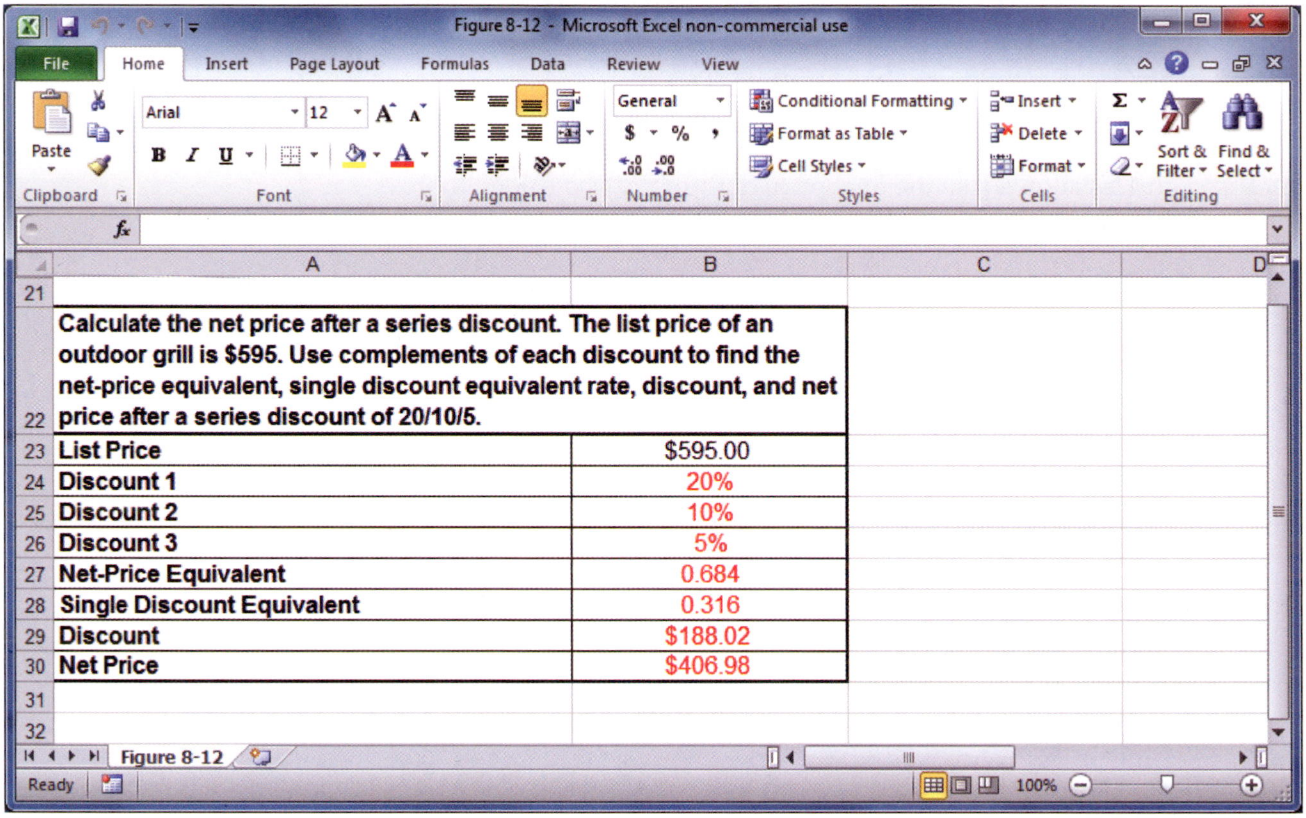

	A	B
22	**Calculate the net price after a series discount. The list price of an outdoor grill is $595. Use complements of each discount to find the net-price equivalent, single discount equivalent rate, discount, and net price after a series discount of 20/10/5.**	
23	**List Price**	$595.00
24	**Discount 1**	20%
25	**Discount 2**	10%
26	**Discount 3**	5%
27	**Net-Price Equivalent**	0.684
28	**Single Discount Equivalent**	0.316
29	**Discount**	$188.02
30	**Net Price**	$406.98

1. Enter 20% for Discount 1 in Cell B24, 10% for Discount 2 in Cell B25, and 5% for Discount 3 in Cell B26. Format for Percentage, 0 Decimal places.
2. Enter the formula to calculate the Net-Price Equivalent in Cell B27. Format for Number, 3 Decimal places.
3. Enter the formula to calculate the Single Discount Equivalent in Cell B28. Format for Number, 3 Decimal places.
4. Enter the formula to calculate the Discount in Cell B29.
5. Enter the formula to calculate the Net Price or cost in Cell B30.
6. Format Cell B29 and Cell B30 for Currency, 2 Decimal places, and $.
7. Save the file as ***ch08pr04a.xlsx***.

Name _____   Date _____

Directions   Solve the following problems.

A. Find the net price equivalents and single discount equivalents. Give single discount equivalent as a decimal and as a percent.

OBJECTIVE 1

Series Discount	Net Price Equivalent	Single Discount Equivalent
15/10/5	1. _____	2. _____
20/10/5	3. _____	4. _____

B. Use the series discount to calculate the net price and the total discount amount for each of the following items. Round answers to the nearest hundredth.

OBJECTIVE 1

List Price	Series Discount	Total Discount	Net Price
$800.25	25/15/10	5. _____	6. _____
$690.40	7/10/5	7. _____	8. _____

C. Determine the net price for each of these problems, using Table 8-1.

OBJECTIVE 1

List Price	Series Discount	Net Price
$5,440.23	20%, 10%, 5%	9. _____
$245.20	15%, 10%, $2\frac{1}{2}$%	10. _____

D. Solve each of these problems.

11. Bonnie's Boutique received a shipment for a list price of $2,394.12. They were given a series discount of 20/10. Find the net price equivalent. _____

12. For the invoice above, calculate the net price. _____

13. What is the amount of the discount? _____

14. Prepaid shipping charges of $145.75 were added to the invoice above. What is the total invoice amount? _____

15. The invoice above was dated March 25 and shows terms of 2/10, n/30. How much should Bonnie's Boutique pay, if they pay within the discount period? What is the last day they can take the discount? _____

E. Use Excel to calculate the net price and discount.

OBJECTIVE 2

16. Retrieve *ch08ex05.xlsx*. Follow the directions. Save the file as *ch08ex05a.xlsx*.

17. Retrieve *ch08ex06.xlsx*. Follow the directions. Save the file as *ch08ex06a.xlsx*.

8.5 Sales Tax

OBJECTIVE 1 Calculate sales tax.

A **sales tax** is usually a specified percent charged when certain merchandise is sold to a customer. The total of the taxable items on an invoice is called the **taxable amount** of the sale. If you live in an area requiring a sales tax, you probably know this tax is levied or set by your city, county, and/or state. Sales tax may be calculated on the basis of a unit of merchandise (*part*) rather than the total purchase price (*base*). An example of sales tax calculated on a unit of merchandise is gasoline, which is taxed by the gallon.

Calculating sales tax is simple because the process is basic multiplication and addition. Many businesses have programmed the current tax rate into their cash registers or into their software applications. Then the register or software automatically calculates the sales tax. For convenience, many city and state governments provide tax tables with the tax already computed. You can find sales tax without using tables. As sales tax is part of the base, you can find the amount of sales tax by applying the formula $P = B \times R$.

EXAMPLE

The taxable amount on an invoice is $1,589.93. The sales tax rate is 6%.

STEPS

1. Multiply the taxable amount by the sales tax rate.

$$\begin{array}{r} \$1{,}589.93 \\ \times \quad 0.06 \\ \hline \$ \quad 95.40 \end{array} \text{ sales tax}$$

2. Add the sales tax to the pretax total.

$$\begin{array}{r} \$1{,}589.93 \\ + \quad 95.40 \\ \hline \$1{,}685.33 \end{array} \text{ total due on the invoice}$$

EXAMPLE

Gloria McClelland bought a new scanner for her office for $86.98, including 8.75% sales tax. What was the purchase price before sales tax was added? What was the sales tax?

STEPS

1. Divide the actual amount paid by 1 plus the tax rate.
   (100% + 8.75% = 1 + 0.0875 = 1.0875)

   $86.98 ÷ 1.0875 = $79.98   purchase price before sales tax

2. Subtract the purchase price from the amount paid.

   $86.98 − $79.98 = $7.00   sales tax

OBJECTIVE **2** **Prepare an invoice.**

Working with invoices requires your close attention to determining and verifying the amounts before sending invoices to customers or making payments on invoices received by your company. First, you calculate the total cost for all items and deduct the amount of any trade discounts. Then you add the sales tax, if any, to determine the invoice total. Cash discounts are different. They only reduce the amount of cash you pay—not the amount of the purchase or the sales tax. Therefore, when calculating the amount of a cash discount, you apply the discount rate to the taxable amount on the invoice. The sales tax amount is not reduced.

Follow these steps when you are computing an invoice to send to a customer.

EXAMPLE

A leading educational interactive talking book lists for $29.99. A trade discount to the local software store is $8.00. The sales tax is 7.5% and neither shipping fees nor insurance charges are taxed. What is the total price?

STEPS

1. Multiply each item quantity by its unit price to obtain unit totals. Then add extended amounts.

2. Calculate any trade discounts. Subtract the discount from the list price.

   $29.99 − $8.00 = $21.99   taxable sale

3. Calculate the sales tax.

   $21.99 × 0.075 = $1.65   sales tax

4. Add the sales tax and any shipping fees and insurance charges to obtain a final total price.

   $21.99 + $1.65 = $23.64   total price with sales tax

Follow these steps to verify an invoice before paying it. Then, deduct any cash discount allowed and calculate the amount to pay.

EXAMPLE

Nathan is verifying an invoice for new telephone equipment that was purchased. He is getting ready to pay the invoice within the discount period. The invoice totals $4,087.07 including sales tax of $213.07. The sales tax rate is 5.5%; the terms are 2/10, n/30; and a taxable shipping charge of $54 was added to the invoice. Is the invoice correct? How much should be paid on the invoice after the cash discount?

STEPS

1. Subtract the sales tax from the total invoice.

   $4,087.07 − $213.07 = $3,874.00   taxable amount

2. Multiply each item quantity by its unit price to obtain unit totals, then add the extended amounts. These total $3,820.00.

   $3,820 + $54 shipping = $3,874   taxable amount is verified

3. Multiply the taxable purchase amount by 5.5% to verify the sales tax. Shipping is not deducted here because shipping is taxable.

   $3,874.00 × 0.055 = $213.07   sales tax is verified

4. Subtract the cost of shipping from the taxable amount to obtain the amount to calculate the cash discount.

   $3,874 − $54 = $3,820   cash discount price

5. Calculate the net price after the cash discount by using the complement of the discount rate.

   $3,820 × 0.98 = $3,743.60   net price

6. Add the net price, the shipping charge, and the sales tax to calculate the amount to pay.

   $3,743.60 + $54.00 + $213.07 = $4,010.67   amount to pay

OBJECTIVE 4 Use Excel to calculate sales tax.

Using Excel, sales tax can be calculated to complete an invoice.

EXAMPLE

Richardson Office Supplies sent a customer an invoice for office supplies. The customer is near the Richardson Office Supplies store, so there are no freight or shipping charges. Figure 8-13 shows the invoice sent.

Figure 8-13

Invoice With Sales Tax

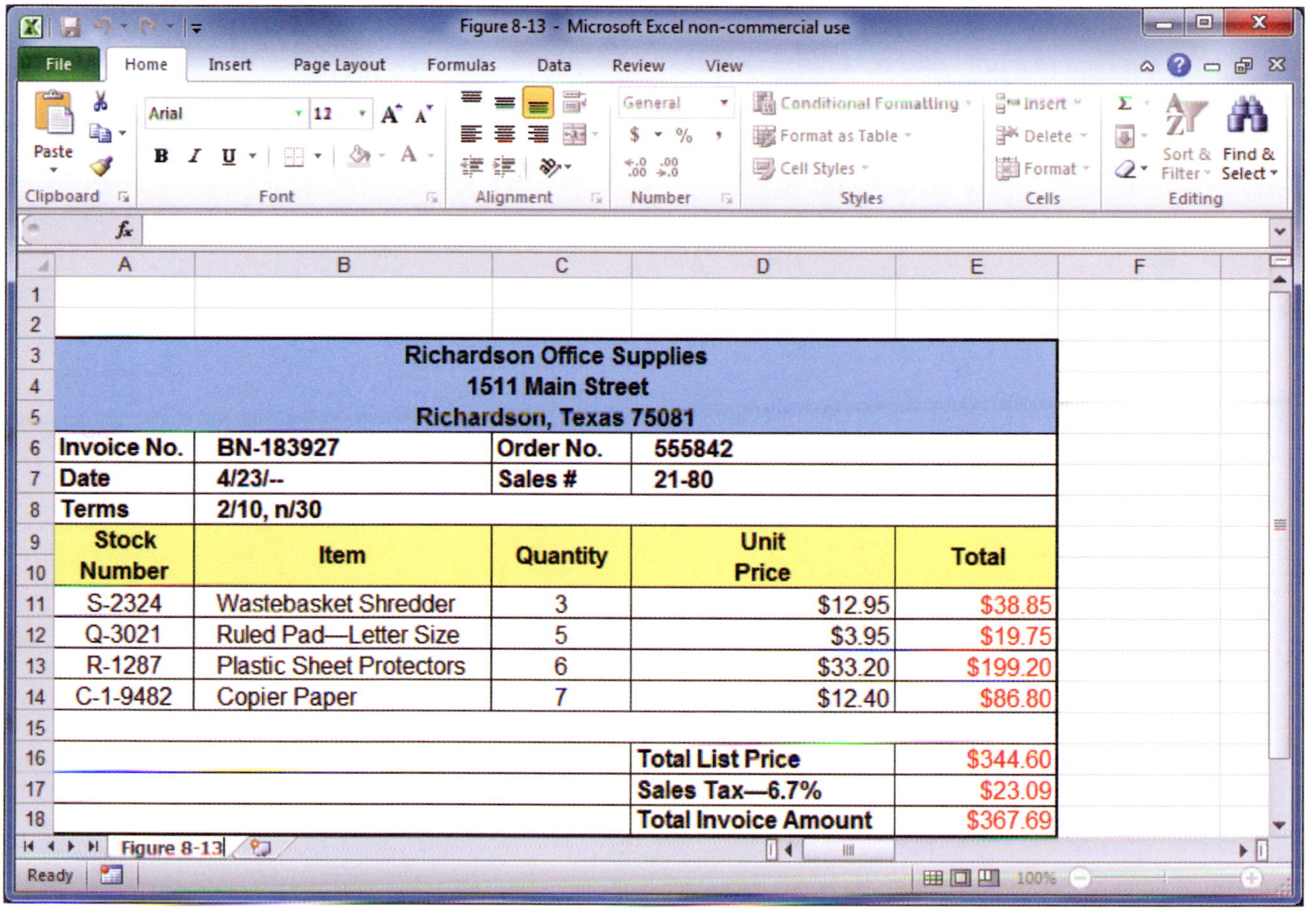

Richardson Office Supplies 1511 Main Street Richardson, Texas 75081				
Invoice No.	BN-183927	Order No.	555842	
Date	4/23/--	Sales #	21-80	
Terms	2/10, n/30			
Stock Number	Item	Quantity	Unit Price	Total
S-2324	Wastebasket Shredder	3	$12.95	$38.85
Q-3021	Ruled Pad—Letter Size	5	$3.95	$19.75
R-1287	Plastic Sheet Protectors	6	$33.20	$199.20
C-1-9482	Copier Paper	7	$12.40	$86.80
			Total List Price	$344.60
			Sales Tax—6.7%	$23.09
			Total Invoice Amount	$367.69

STEPS

Retrieve the file *ch08pr05.xlsx*.

1. Enter a formula in Cells E11 through E14 to calculate the Total for each Item. Multiply the Quantity for each item times the Unit Price for the item.
2. Enter a formula in Cell E16 to calculate the Total List Price. Add the Total for each of the four items.
3. Enter a formula in Cell E17 to calculate the Sales Tax. Multiply the Total List Price by the Sales Tax of 6.7%.
4. Enter a formula in Cell E18 to calculate the Total Invoice Amount. Add the Total List Price and the Sales Tax.
5. Format Column E for Currency, 2 Decimal places, and $.
6. Save the file as *ch08pr05a.xlsx*.

Name _____   Date _____

Directions   Solve the following problems.

A. Complete the following.   OBJECTIVE 1

1.   A sales tax is calculated on all sales. True or False?   _____

2.   When calculating a cash discount, you multiply the total amount of the
     invoice by the discount rate. True or False?   _____

B. Find the sales tax and the total amount due on these invoices.   OBJECTIVE 1
Round answers to the nearest cent.

Taxable Sale	Sales Tax Percent	Sales Tax Amount		Invoice Total	
$3,211.90	7%	3.	_____	4.	_____
$1,500.25	8%	5.	_____	6.	_____
$380.98	5.5%	7.	_____	8.	_____
$234.54	7.5%	9.	_____	10.	_____
$867.75	6%	11.	_____	12.	_____
$1,111.10	8.75%	13.	_____	14.	_____
$1,800.33	5%	15.	_____	16.	_____

C. Determine the sales tax and total amount due on these invoices. Assume   OBJECTIVE 2
shipping charges are not taxable. Round answers to the nearest cent.

Taxable Sale	Sales Tax Percent	Sales Tax Amount		Shipping Charges	Invoice Total	
$1,443.22	5%	17.	_____	$18.50	18.	_____
$550.15	7%	19.	_____	$7.75	20.	_____
$775.30	8%	21.	_____	$15.00	22.	_____
$323.12	7.5%	23.	_____	$4.50	24.	_____
$9,000.00	7%	25.	_____	$25.90	26.	_____
$7,999.00	6.5%	27.	_____	$21.98	28.	_____

D. Solve the following word problems. Round answers to the nearest cent. OBJECTIVES **1, 2, 3**

29. You are asked to verify an invoice that totals $718.12 before your company pays it. The net price of the merchandise is $635.29; the sales tax rate is 6.5%; and the shipping charge is $39.

    a. Is the invoice amount correct? _____

    b. If not, what error was made, and what should the total amount be?

    _____

    c. What was the amount of the sales tax? _____

30. In Exercise 29, the terms of payment are 2/10, n/30.

    a. What is the amount of the cash discount if paid within the discount period? _____

    b. What is the total payment amount? _____

31. You are preparing an invoice for a customer whose purchase lists for $337.50. The customer is entitled to a trade discount of 10/5; the payment terms are 3/15, n/45; and the sales tax rate is 6%. What should be the total amount of the invoice? _____

32. Marisa Tallifero bought a cordless phone priced at $49.99. It was subject to 8.75% sales tax. What was the sales tax? _____

    What was the total amount Marisa paid for the phone? _____

33. Jerry Hutchins purchased an assortment of holiday paper. His purchases amounted to $19.97, which was subject to 7.2% sales tax. How much was the sales tax? _____

34. Penny Holcomb purchased pen and pencil gift sets to give to her employees for the holidays. The total bill was $103.92, which included the sales tax of 6.5%. How much was the actual selling price? _____

    What was the amount of the sales tax? _____

35. For his party, Bobby bought 4 cans of gourmet popcorn and paid $19.96. The tax was 6.2%. How much was the actual selling price? _____

    What was the amount of the sales tax? _____

36. The amount of a sale is $479.50 and the sales tax rate is 7.25%. How much is the sales tax? _____

    What is the total selling price? _____

37. A printer is priced at $524. If a sales tax of $8\frac{1}{2}$% is charged on the printer, what is the total selling price? _____

E. Use Excel to complete the invoice. OBJECTIVE **4**

38. Retrieve *ch08ex07.xlsx*. Follow the directions. Save the file as *ch08ex07a.xlsx*.

39. Retrieve *ch08ex08.xlsx*. Follow the directions. Save the file as *ch08ex08a.xlsx*.

Chapter Review and Assessment

KEY TERMS

3/10 EOM

bill of lading

cash discount

collect on delivery (COD)

complement

credit memorandum

discount period

discount rate

due date

FOB destination

FOB shipping point

free on board

freight collect

invoice

invoice date

list price

manufacturers

net price

net price equivalent

n/EOM

n/30 ROG

prepaid freight

purchase order

purchase requisition

receiving report

retailers

sales tax

series discount

single discount equivalent

statement of account

suggested retail price

taxable amount

terms of payment

trade discount

voucher check

wholesalers

CONCEPTS	EXAMPLES
8.2 Calculate cash discounts. 1. Multiply invoice total by the cash discount. 2. Subtract cash discount from invoice total to obtain net amount due on invoice.	Invoice total: $326.45 Terms: 2/10, n/30 (paid within 10 days) $326.45 \times 0.02 = \$6.53$ cash discount $326.45 - \$6.53 = \$319.92$ net amount
8.2 Use the complement method. The complement of a percent is the difference between that percent and 100%.	List price: $825.00 Trade discount: 25% $100\% - 25\% = 75\%$ complement $0.75 \times \$825.00 = \$618.75$ net price
8.2 Find the net amount due after merchandise has been returned. 1. Subtract the cost of returned merchandise from the invoice amount. 2. Multiply the amount subject to discount by the discount rate to get the cash discount. 3. Subtract the cash discount from the invoice amount less the cost of returned merchandise.	Invoice amount: $219.78 Merchandise returned: $65.30 Terms: 2/10, n/30 $219.78 - \$65.30 = \$154.48$ basis for cash discount $154.48 \times 0.02 = \$3.09$ cash discount $154.48 - \$3.09 = \$151.39$ net amount due

CONCEPTS	EXAMPLES
8.2 Find total amount due after cash discount is subtracted and other charges are added.	Invoice amount: $966.65 Shipping charges included: $22.50 Terms: 3/10, n/60
1. Calculate the cash discount.	$966.65 × 0.03 = $29.00 cash discount
2. Subtract the cash discount from the invoice amount.	$966.65 − $29.00 = $937.65 net after cash discount
3. Add shipping charges.	$937.65 + $22.50 = $960.15 total amount due
8.2 Calculate the amount of credit for partial payments.	Merchandise total on invoice: $823.12 Terms: 2/10, n/45
1. Find the complement discount rate.	Partial payment: $500.00 100% − 2% = 98% (0.98) complement discount
2. Divide partial payment by complement to determine amount of merchandise paid for.	$500.00 ÷ 0.98 = $510.20 amount of merchandise paid for
3. Subtract payment from amount of merchandise paid for to find cash discount.	$510.20 − $500.00 = $10.20 cash discount
4. Subtract amount of merchandise paid for from original total to find balance due on invoice.	$823.12 − $510.20 = $312.92 amount still due
8.3 Calculate trade discounts and net prices.	List price: $1,115.00 Trade discount: 20%
1. Multiply the list price by the trade discount rate to get the trade discount amount.	$1,115.00 × 0.2 = $223.00 trade discount amount
2. Subtract the trade discount amount from the list price to get the net price.	$1,115.00 − $223.00 = $892.00 net price
8.3 Apply a trade discount when preparing an invoice.	List price: $3,500; trade discount rate is 15% with terms of 3/10, n/30; prepaid shipping charge (FOB shipping point) is $35. Payment made within 10-day period.
1. Figure the trade discount.	$3,500 × 0.15 = $525 trade discount amount
2. Subtract the trade discount amount from list price.	$3,500 − $525 = $2,975 net price
3. Calculate the cash discount for paying within the discount date.	$2,975 × 0.03 = $89.25 cash discount
4. Subtract the cash discount from the amount found in the net price.	$2,975 − $89.25 = $2,885.75 subtotal
5. Add prepaid shipping charges (FOB shipping point).	$2,885.75 + $35 = $2,920.75 total amount due

CONCEPTS	EXAMPLES

8.4 Calculate series discounts and net prices.

List price: $1,026.00
Trade discount: 15/10/5

Method 1 (apply one at a time)

1. Multiply list price by the first discount rate.

$1,026 \times 0.15 = $153.90   *first discount amount*

2. Subtract first discount from the list price.

$1,026.00 − $153.90 = $872.10

3. Multiply the net price in Step 2 by the second discount rate.

$872.10 \times 0.1 = $87.21   *second discount amount*

4. Subtract the second discount from the net price in Step 2.

$872.10 − $87.21 = $784.89

5. Multiply the third discount by the net price in Step 4.

$784.89 \times 0.05 = $39.25   *third discount amount*

6. Subtract the third discount from the net price in Step 4.

$784.89 − $39.25 = $745.65   *net price*

Method 2 (find single discount equivalent)

1. Find the complements of the individual discount rates.

100% − 15% = 85%; 100% − 10% = 90%;
100% − 5% = 95%   *complement percents*

2. Multiply the complements to get a net price equivalent (don't round).

0.85 \times 0.9 \times 0.95 = 0.72675   *net price equivalent*

3. Subtract the net price equivalent from 100% (1.00) to find the single discount equivalent.

1.00 − 0.72675 = 0.027325   *single discount equivalent*

4. Multiply the list price by the single discount equivalent.

$1,026.00 \times 0.27325 = $280.35   *dollar amount of series discount*

5. Subtract the dollar amount of the series discount from the list price.

$1,026.00 − $280.35 = $745.65   *net price*

8.5 Calculate sales tax.

Taxable amount of invoice: $1,128.42
Sales tax rate: 7%

1. Multiply taxable amount by the sales tax rate.

$1,128.42 \times 0.07 (7%) = $78.99   *sales tax*

2. Add the sales tax to the pretax total.

$1,128.42 + $78.99 = $1,207.41   *total invoice amount*

8.5 Prepare an invoice.

Three files at $79.99 each; Discount is $25; Sales tax 6%; Prepaid Shipping charges: $30.

1. Multiply each item quantity by its unit price to obtain unit totals, then add extended amounts.

$79.99 \times 3 = $239.97

2. Calculate any discounts. Subtract the discount from the list price.

$239.97 − $25.00 = $214.97   *net after cash discount*

3. Calculate the sales tax.

$214.97 \times 0.06 = $12.90

4. Add the sales tax, any shipping charge, and insurance fees to obtain a final total price.

$214.97 + $12.90 + $30 = $257.87   *total amount due*

Chapter 8 Review Exercises

Name _____ Date _____

Directions   Solve the following problems. Write your answers in the blanks provided. Be sure to add commas and dollar signs.

A. Find the cash discount and net amount due on the following   8.2 OBJECTIVES **2, 4**
   Assume each invoice is paid within the discount period.

Invoice Amount	Terms	Cash Discount		Net Amount Due	
$374.80	2/10, n/30	1. _____		2. _____	
$207.25	3/10, n/30	3. _____		4. _____	
$820.00	3/10, n/45	5. _____		6. _____	
$1,562.35	2/10, n/60	7. _____		8. _____	

B. Find the cash discount and net amount on the following invoices.   8.2 OBJECTIVES **2, 5**

Invoice Amount	Terms	Paid Within Discount Period	Returned Merchandise	Shipping Charges	Cash Discount		Net Amount Due	
$306.80	1/10, n/30	yes	none	$10.25	9. _____		10. _____	
$368.00	2/10, n/30	yes	$23.50	none	11. _____		12. _____	
$720.34	2/10, n/30	no	none	$25.50	13. _____		14. _____	
$3,046.10	2/10, n/45	yes	none	$38.75	15. _____		16. _____	

C. Determine the credit given for partial payment, balance due, and cash   8.2 OBJECTIVES **2, 6**
   discount on the following invoices.

Invoice Amount	Terms	Partial Payment	Credit Given		Balance Due		Cash Discount	
$1,742.50	2/10, n/30	$860.00	17. _____		18. _____		19. _____	
$894.60	3/10, n/45	$450.00	20. _____		21. _____		22. _____	
$3,963.80	2/10, n/30	$1,865.00	23. _____		24. _____		25. _____	

D. Determine the trade discount and net price on the following invoices.   8.3 OBJECTIVE **1**

List Price	Trade Discount Rate	Trade Discount		Net Price	
$965.30	20%	26. _____		27. _____	
$2,506.24	15%	28. _____		29. _____	
$1,892.82	15%	30. _____		31. _____	

E. Find the net amount due on the following invoices. All are paid by the discount date.

8.3 OBJECTIVE 2

Invoice Amount	Terms	Trade Discount Rate	Shipping Charges		Net Amount Due
$298.00	3/10, n/45	7%	$12.54	32.	_____
$4,691.50	2/10, n/30	12%	$56.10	33.	_____
$764.68	1/10, n/30	8%	$21.80	34.	_____
$735.68	2/10, n/30	15%	$13.84	35.	_____
$2,465.00	1/10, n/30	8%	$32.56	36.	_____

F. Calculate the net price and series discount on the following invoices.

8.4 OBJECTIVE 1

List Price	Series Discount		Net Price		Discount
$1,203.45	10/10/5	37.	_____	38.	_____
$688.90	5/15/10	39.	_____	40.	_____
$493.84	10/10/5	41.	_____	42.	_____

G. Determine the net price and discount for these problems using the single discount equivalent.

8.4 OBJECTIVE 1

List Price	Series Discount		Net Price		Discount
$396.78	10%, 10%, 5%	43.	_____	44.	_____
$1,497.75	10%, 5%, 5%	45.	_____	46.	_____
$537.10	10%, 5%	47.	_____	48.	_____
$601.29	10%, 5%	49.	_____	50.	_____

H. Solve the following word problems.

Trisha purchased 3 blouses at $32.50 each, 2 packages of 6 pairs of socks costing $7.50 per package, and 4 pair of hosiery costing $2.19 each. Sales tax was 6.5%.

51. How much sales tax did Trisha pay? _____

52. What was Trisha's total invoice including tax? _____

53. Carlos Mendez ordered office equipment totaling $4,320. Sale terms were 3/10, n/30, FOB shipping. The shipping charges were $23.00. If Carlos pays the invoice within the discount period, what does he pay? _____

54. Cartland Office Supply received a $1,298.33 invoice dated 6/15/--. The $1,298.33 included $120 freight. Terms were 2/10, n/60. If Cartland pays the invoice on June 21, what will it pay? _____

55. If Cartland pays the invoice on September 27, what will it pay? What is the last day of the discount period? _____

56. Tate Tool and Die ordered new equipment for its machinists. The order included 3 lathes for $529.99 each, 2 sanders for $59.99 each, and 4 scroll saws for $179.95 each. The sales tax rate is 7.25%. What will Tate Tool and Die pay after the invoice is totaled, including sales tax? _____

57. If Tate Tool and Die returns 1 lathe and 1 scroll saw, what will the total invoice amount be including sales tax? _____

I. **Complete the following invoice. Shipping is non-taxable. Calculate the cash discount and net amount due, and show the last date of the discount period.** `8.2 OBJECTIVES 2, 5` `8.5 OBJECTIVE 1`

ROCKFORD OFFICE SUPPLIES
4211 Beach Street, Beaumont, KY 42321

SOLD TO: Craig Glass & Mirror, Inc.
2366 East 114th Street
Beaumont, KY 42321

INVOICE NO.: 1255 – 2344
DATE: Jan. 25, 20--

ORDER NO. 4588	SALES ASSOCIATE A. Miller	TERMS 3/10, net 30	DATE SHIPPED Jan. 15

QTY.	STK NO.	DESCRIPTION	UNIT PRICE	TOTAL
6	L-2344	Gross, No. 2 pencil	$5.95	58.
4	P-4665	El. Pencil sharpener	$29.95	59.
3	D-1233	Executive desk	$329.95	60.
3	D-1234	Executive chair	$129.95	61.
6	W-3324	Wastebasket	$12.95	62.
5	C-5544	Computer desk	$388.00	63.
5	C-5543	Computer hutch	$99.95	64.
3	C-5542	Printer table	$149.00	65.
5	D-1235	Computer chair	$128.50	66.
5	C-5541	Computer system	$2,955.00	67.

			INVOICE TOTAL	68.
			6% SALES TAX	69.
			BALANCE	70.
			SHIPPING CHARGES	$89.00
			TOTAL AMOUNT DUE	71.

72. Cash discount _____ **73.** Net due _____ **74.** End of discount period _____

J. **Use Excel to calculate the invoice totals.** `8.2 OBJECTIVE 7` `8.5 OBJECTIVE 4`

75. Retrieve *ch08ex09.xlsx*. Follow the directions. Save the file as *ch08ex09a.xlsx*.

76. Retrieve *ch08ex10.xlsx*. Follow the directions. Save the file as *ch08ex10a.xlsx*.

Math@Work

A business analyst serves an important role in purchasing. A business analyst must be able to think beyond current demands and prepare for future needs of the organization. The analyst works closely with purchasing agents to analyze requirements, procedures, and purchasing limits. Purchasing agents are in charge of all buying. They find the best products, negotiate the prices, and make sure the right amounts are received at the right time. They study sales records and inventory levels, identify suppliers, and they stay up to date on overall market conditions and price trends that affect what they are buying.

1. Sal sells an item in his retail store for $130 less 50% which his competitor sells the same item for $100 less 20%. Find the net prices of the items for the two stores. What other discount percent must be offered by the store that sells at a higher net price in order to meet the competitor's price?

2. Sal's first invoice of the day is dated February 2 for $7,000 and was offered cash discount terms of 1/10, n/30. If the invoice was paid on February 9, what was the payment after the cash discount?

3. Sal's next invoice for the day is for $7,000, offered cash discount terms of 3/10, n/30 which includes a prepaid transport charge of $150. What is the amount needed to pay the invoice within the cash discount period?

Write about Math

1. Explain why trade discounts may change.

2. Differentiate between single discounts and series or chain discounts. Provide an example of each.

3. Distinguish between a trade discount and a cash discount.

Personal Finance

What's one way to get reluctant shoppers back into the stores?

While some states offer a sales tax-free holiday, other states do not. However, the National Retail Federation is working earnestly to persuade government to allow a national sales tax-free holiday to spur sales.

Sales tax among states vary from 2.9% to 8%, so a tax break can help consumers to purchase selected items, such as school supplies for their children or energy-efficient products, such as appliances.

If you are not familiar with sales tax-free holidays, locate information using key words such as *tax-free holidays* or *state sales tax holidays*.

©Infomages, 2010/Used under license from Shutterstock.com

Complete the following activities.

1. Describe this special holiday or time period that is offered by a number of states.

2. Determine if your state offers a sales tax-free holiday.

   a. If your state offers this holiday, identify at least five items that qualify for this tax break.

   b. What tax break would you receive on the five items?

   c. Would you still pay local sales tax?

3. What will a tax-free holiday or weekend mean to small- or medium-size retailers?

4. What impact, if any, does a tax-free holiday have on your state's economy?

5. Think about your spending habits.

   a. As a consumer, would you be purchasing these same items anyway at this time of the year?

   b. Does the tax-free holiday encourage you to save for this special time to make certain purchases?

6. Summarize pros and cons for offering this tax break.

Name _____ Date _____ Score _____

Directions   Solve the following problems. Be sure to add commas and dollar signs where needed.

A. Determine the cash discount and net amount due on these invoices. `8.2 OBJECTIVES 2, 4, 5`
Assume each invoice is paid within the discount period.

Invoice Amount	Terms	Returned Merchandise	Shipping Charges	Cash Discount	Net Amount Due
$2,566	2/10, n/30	none	none	1. _____	2. _____
$1,652	3/10, n/30	none	none	3. _____	4. _____
$600.05	2/10, n/45	none	$10.25	5. _____	6. _____
$219.45	1/10, n/30	$32.50	none	7. _____	8. _____
$123.22	3/10, n/30	$10.55	$21.50	9. _____	10. _____

B. Determine the credit given for partial payment, balance due, and cash `8.2 OBJECTIVES 2, 6`
discount on the following invoices.

Invoice Amount	Terms	Partial Payment	Credit Given	Balance Due	Cash Discount
$748.50	2/10, n/30	$360.00	11. _____	12. _____	13. _____
$1,940.60	3/10, n/45	$1,450.00	14. _____	15. _____	16. _____

C. Determine the trade discount and the net price on the following invoices. `8.3 OBJECTIVE 1`

List Price	Trade Discount Rate	Trade Discount	Net Price Due
$1,657.30	15%	17. _____	18. _____
$2,382.24	20%	19. _____	20. _____
$1,994.85	15%	21. _____	22. _____

D. Find the net amount due on the following invoices. All are paid by the `8.3 OBJECTIVE 2`
discount date.

Invoice Amount	Terms	Trade Discount Rate	Shipping Charges	Net Amount Due
$698.00	3/10, n/45	7%	$10.44	23. _____
$3,961.50	2/10, n/30	10%	$66.10	24. _____

E. Calculate the net price and series discount on the following invoices. **8.4** OBJECTIVE **1**

List Price	Series Discount	Net Price		Discount	
$2,303.48	10/5/5	25. _____		26. _____	
$888.30	5/15/10	27. _____		28. _____	

F. Determine the net price and trade discount for these problems using the single discount equivalent. **8.4** OBJECTIVE **1**

List Price	Series Discount	Net Price		Trade Discount	
$286.48	10%, 5%, 5%	29. _____		30. _____	
$979.70	10%, 10%, 5%	31. _____		32. _____	

G. Complete the following invoice. There is a $65 non-taxable shipping charge. Calculate the cash discount and net amount due, and show the last date of the discount period. **8.5** OBJECTIVE **1**

SMITH OFFICE SUPPLIES
2912 Connor Street, Dallas, TX 72225

SOLD C and E Store
TO: 1245 North Expressway
Dallas, TX 72225

INVOICE NO.: 3455
DATE: April 5, 20--

ORDER NO. 1888	SALES ASSOCIATE B. Wells	TERMS 3/10, net 30	DATE SHIPPED April 1, 20--
QTY. **STK NO.**	**DESCRIPTION**	**UNIT PRICE**	**TOTAL**

QTY.	STK NO.	DESCRIPTION	UNIT PRICE	TOTAL
5	2952	Gross, file folders	$7.85	33.
2	1919	Computer tables	$250.55	34.
6	5544	Computer desks	$388.00	35.
		INVOICE TOTAL		36.
		8% SALES TAX		37.
		BALANCE		38.
		SHIPPING CHARGES		39.
		TOTAL AMOUNT DUE		40.

41. Cash discount _____   42. Net due _____   43. End of discount period _____

H. Use Excel to complete the invoice totals. **8.2** OBJECTIVE **7**, **8.3** OBJECTIVE **3** **8.4** OBJECTIVE **2**, **8.5** OBJECTIVE **4**

44. Retrieve *ch08qz01.xlsx*. Follow the directions. Save the file as *ch08qz01a.xlsx*.

45. Retrieve *ch08qz02.xlsx*. Follow the directions. Save the file as *ch08qz02a.xlsx*.

Markup and Markdown

Retailers buy their merchandise from wholesalers for a certain price. Then they sell the merchandise at a retail, or selling, price that is high enough to cover the cost of the merchandise and the cost of business operating expenses (overhead) and still provide the desired profit for the business to be successful. For example, Southern Charm can't sell a denim shirt for the actual cost, $11.24. If it did, it would lose money, as other expenses (such as salaries, rent, utilities, and insurance) must be covered. This chapter emphasizes the mathematics required to mark up and mark down merchandise.

ACCOUNTING ASSOCIATE

Kevin Neihaus is an accounting associate in the Marketing and Communications department at a children's hospital. It is his responsibility to forecast, manage, and track the budget for that department. He also works alongside associates, directors, and vice presidents from many other departments. During a typical week, Kevin could be projecting the expenses of his department, creating new departmental policies and procedures, working with vendors, or trying to improve processes that his department uses in daily operation. He said, "It is my goal to make sure my department runs well, and we have money to do what needs to be done."

Kevin knows that hearing the term "accounting" makes people think of sitting at a desk doing the same thing over and over. He said, "My job is actually filled with changing variables. I often have to consider many different possibilities and conditions to formulate an idea of how the money will be or has been spent. Every day brings something new."

How Math is Used in Accounting

When planning a budget, Kevin uses equations to create and project the department's future expenses. This allows him to predict how much money his department will need in the coming year. Kevin also uses math to calculate exactly how much a newsletter his department is creating will cost. He said, "It is important to know how much each copy of the newsletter will cost. Adding up the costs of producing the newsletter and dividing them by the number we are producing tells me what a single print will cost. I then multiply that figure with the number of newsletters we plan on producing to estimate how much I should budget. This planning allows my department to produce great publications that patients and families want to read while staying within our budget."

What Do You Think?

What skills do you need to improve in order to work in accounting?

Math Skills Used

Addition

Subtraction

Multiplication

Statistics

Percents

Other Skills Needed

Communication

Interpersonal skills

Multi-tasking

Organizational skills

OBJECTIVES

1. Identify terms used with pricing merchandise.
2. Distinguish among basic pricing variables.
3. Calculate the selling price, markup amount, or cost when any two of the three are known.

9.1 Concepts Used in Pricing Merchandise

OBJECTIVE 1 Identify terms used with pricing merchandise.

Selling price (also *retail price*) is what the customer pays. The **cost** is what the retailer pays to the manufacturer. The difference between the cost and the selling price is **markup** (also *gross profit*). Markup is expressed both in dollars (also **markup amount**) and in percentage (also **markup rate**). For instance, an item may be marked up by $23.67 or by 30%. The markup rate can be calculated either on the selling price or on the cost.

Operating expenses are the expenses incurred by a business, such as rent, utilities, salaries, insurance, supplies, advertising, and so on. **Net profit** is the amount left over (if any) after expenses have been paid.

Markdown is a percentage of the original selling price by which the selling price is reduced. For example, a clothing store reduces its merchandise because of seasonal changes and special promotions. Markdowns are shown as percentage, such as 25% off. The selling price, once marked down, is the **reduced price** or the **discounted sale price**.

OBJECTIVE 2 Distinguish among basic pricing variables.

The fundamental purpose of a business is to make a profit. A retail business sells goods and services for an acceptable price that is sufficient to cover all expenses and to provide the company with a reasonable profit. Pricing goods is based on an equation that the selling price of an item is equal to the cost plus the markup. Study the relationship of selling price, markup, and cost.

Selling price (S)

$$\text{Selling Price} = \text{Cost} + \text{Markup}$$
$$S = C + M$$

Markup (M)

$$\text{Markup} = \text{Selling Price} - \text{Cost}$$
$$M = S - C$$

Cost (C)

$$\text{Cost} = \text{Selling Price} - \text{Markup}$$
$$C = S - M$$

Calculating Selling Price

The selling price is found by adding cost and markup.

> **EXAMPLE**
>
> Elliott's Hardware buys a tool set at a cost of $17.40 and adds $8.00 per set as markup to determine selling price. What is the selling price?

> **STEPS**
>
> Add cost and markup to obtain selling price.
>
> Cost + Markup = Selling Price
>
> $17.40 + $8.00 = $25.40   selling price

Calculating the Markup Dollar Amount

The markup amount can be determined by subtracting the cost from the selling price.

> **EXAMPLE**
>
> The selling price is $25.40 and the cost is $17.40. Determine the markup amount.

> **STEPS**
>
> Subtract cost from the selling price to determine the markup amount.
>
> Selling Price − Cost = Markup
>
> $25.40 − $17.40 = $8.00   markup amount

Calculating Cost

The cost is calculated by subtracting the markup amount from the selling price.

> **EXAMPLE**
>
> A tool set sells for $25.40 and is marked up $8.00. Calculate the cost.

> **STEPS**
>
> Subtract markup from selling price to calculate the cost.
>
> Selling Price − Markup = Cost
>
> $25.40 − $8.00 = $17.40   cost

Retailers must constantly review their decisions in marking up goods. Southern Charm, the example in the introduction, chose to mark up a special handbag. However, with local competition, the owner had to reconsider its markup. Because of the competitor's markup on the same handbag, Southern Charm's sales weren't enough to make a profit.

Name _____   Date _____

Directions   Complete the following statements and problems. Round answers to the nearest hundredth.

A. Match the following terms with the appropriate statements. A term may be used more than once.   `OBJECTIVE 1`

a. cost   **b.** markdown   **c.** markup

d. net profit   **e.** operating expenses   **f.** selling price

1. _____   Price at which merchandise is sold

2. _____   Amount manufacturer charges for merchandise

3. _____   Difference between cost to retailer and selling price

4. _____   Incurred by a business, such as rent and utilities

5. _____   Reduction from original selling price

6. Selling Price equals _____ plus _____ .

7. Markup equals _____ minus _____ .

8. Cost equals _____ minus _____ .

B. Complete the following problems.   `OBJECTIVES 2, 3`

9. If the cost is \$12.67 and the markup is \$5.00, the selling price is _____ .

10. If the selling price is \$32.99 and the cost is \$16.00, the markup is _____ .

11. If the selling price is \$125.50 and the markup is \$73.20, the cost is _____ .

12. If the markup is \$22.00 and the cost is \$15.50, the selling price is _____ .

C. Use the basic equations to determine the selling price, cost, or markup in the following problems.   `OBJECTIVES 2, 3`

	Cost	Selling Price	Markup Amount
13.	\$23.90	_____	\$15.00
14.	\$35.90	\$73.40	_____
15.	_____	\$568.95	\$126.70
16.	\$274.75	_____	\$120.30
17.	\$621.65	\$730.50	_____
18.	_____	\$44.79	\$18.80
19.	_____	\$299.00	\$242.77
20.	\$28.46	\$67.50	_____

9.2 Markup on Cost

OBJECTIVES

1. Calculate the markup amount and the rate based on cost.
2. Calculate the selling price when the markup rate is based on cost.
3. Calculate the cost when the markup amount and the markup rate based on cost are known.
4. Calculate the cost when the selling price and the markup rate based on cost are known.
5. Use Excel to calculate cost, markup, markup rate, and selling price based on cost.

OBJECTIVE 1 Calculate the markup amount and the rate based on cost.

In many business situations, the cost and selling price are known, but the markup rate is not known. In the following example, you are trying to find what percent the markup is of the cost. When the markup rate is based on cost, it can be determined by dividing the markup amount by cost. Remember that the dollar amount of markup must be determined first to find the markup rate.

EXAMPLE

Home Interior Designs, Inc. pays the wholesaler $225 for a wingback chair that is sold for $318. What is the markup rate based on cost?

STEPS

1. Obtain the amount of markup by using the basic equation.

$$\text{Selling Price} - \text{Cost} = \text{Markup}$$
$$\$318 - \$225 = \$93 \quad \textcolor{blue}{\text{markup amount}}$$

2. Obtain the markup rate by dividing the markup amount by the cost. Round to the nearest tenth of a percent. Hint: $P \div B = R$.

$$\text{Markup} \div \text{Cost} = \text{Markup Rate}$$
$$\$93 \div \$225 = 41.3\% \quad \textcolor{blue}{\text{markup rate based on cost}}$$

3. To check your answer, use

$$\text{Selling Price} = \text{Cost} + \text{Markup}$$
$$\$318 = \$225 + \$93$$

©Charles Bayerle, 2010/Used under license from Shutterstock.com

When the cost and markup rate based on cost are known, the amount of markup and the selling price can be calculated. Use the $P = B \times R$ formula to find the markup amount. First, multiply the cost (base) by the markup rate to find the amount of markup (part). Add the amount to the cost to calculate the selling price. Consider this concept as you work through the next example.

keeweeboy/iStockphoto.com

EXAMPLE

The cost of an office chair is $205. The markup rate is 25% of cost. Calculate the amount of the markup and the selling price.

STEPS

1. Calculate the amount of markup by multiplying the cost by the markup rate. Hint: $B \times R = P$.

> Cost × Markup Rate = Markup
> $205 × 0.25 = $51.25   markup amount

2. Apply the basic equation to obtain the selling price.

> Cost + Markup = Selling Price
> $205 + $51.25 = $256.25   selling price

In some instances, you may need to calculate only the selling price. If this is the case, you can add 100% to the markup rate and multiply the cost by the total markup rate as shown in the next example.

EXAMPLE

The cost of an office chair is $205. The markup rate based on cost is 25%. Calculate only the selling price.

STEPS

Multiply the cost by the markup rate plus 100%.

> Cost × (100% + Markup Rate) = Selling Price
> $205 × (100% + 25% = 125%) = Selling Price
> $205 × 1.25 = $256.25   selling price

Calculate the cost when the markup amount and the markup rate based on cost are known.

If you know both the markup amount and the markup rate based on cost, you can apply the formula $P \div R = B$, as shown in the following example.

EXAMPLE

The markup amount on Sheila's storage boxes is $13, which is a 36% markup based on cost. Find the cost. Round to the nearest cent.

STEPS

Use the formula $P \div R = B$, where markup amount = Part, markup rate = Rate, and cost = Base. Divide the markup amount by the markup rate.

$$\text{Markup} \div \text{Markup Rate} = \text{Cost}$$
$$\$13 \div 0.36 = \$36.11 \quad \text{cost}$$

OBJECTIVE **4** **Calculate the cost when the selling price and the markup rate based on cost are known.**

You can calculate cost when you know the selling price and the markup rate based on cost. Consider this concept as you work through the next example.

©Jason Keith Heydorn, 2010/Used under license from Shutterstock.com

EXAMPLE

Conn's Carpet sells 4 ft × 6 ft Oriental rugs for $179 and the markup rate is 40% of the cost. Find the cost of the rugs and the markup amount.

STEPS

1. Markup rate plus 100% = 40% + 100% = 140%

2. Divide the selling price by the markup rate.
$$\$179 \div 1.4 = \$127.86 \quad \text{cost}$$

3. Subtract the cost from the selling price to find the markup amount.
$$\text{Selling Price} - \text{Cost} = \text{Markup}$$
$$\$179.00 - \$127.86 = \$51.14 \quad \text{markup amount}$$

4. To check your answer, use the following.
$$\text{Selling Price} = \text{Cost} + \text{Markup}$$
$$\$179 = \$127.86 + \$51.14$$

OBJECTIVE 5 Use Excel to calculate cost, markup, markup rate, and selling price based on cost.

Large companies price their merchandise electronically. Small businesses may calculate their prices manually. Figure 9-1 shows selling prices calculated in Excel for selected items from Gulfstream Boutique.

Figure 9-1

Calculating Cost, Markup, Markup Rate, and Selling Price Based on Cost

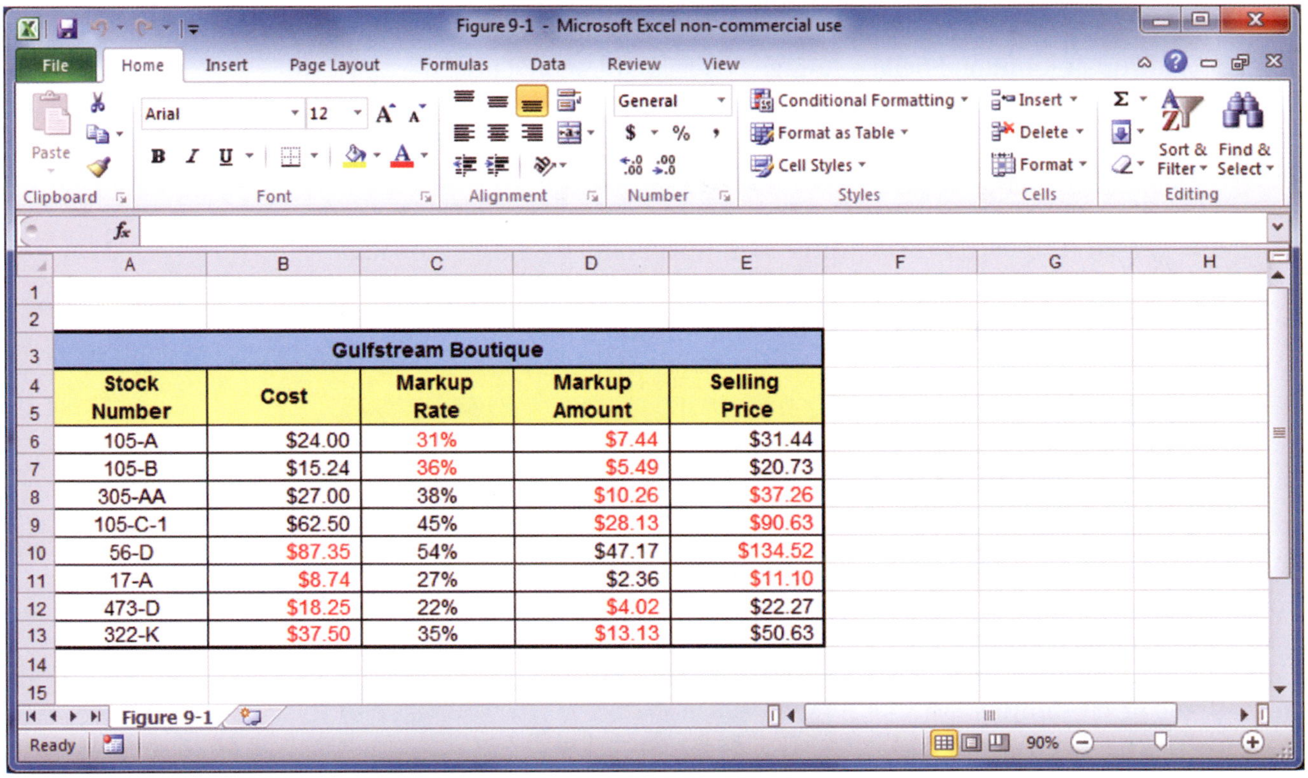

Gulfstream Boutique				
Stock Number	Cost	Markup Rate	Markup Amount	Selling Price
105-A	$24.00	31%	$7.44	$31.44
105-B	$15.24	36%	$5.49	$20.73
305-AA	$27.00	38%	$10.26	$37.26
105-C-1	$62.50	45%	$28.13	$90.63
56-D	$87.35	54%	$47.17	$134.52
17-A	$8.74	27%	$2.36	$11.10
473-D	$18.25	22%	$4.02	$22.27
322-K	$37.50	35%	$13.13	$50.63

TIPS

When Excel displays ####### because formatting prevents a number from fitting in a cell, you can widen the column by clicking on the top right edge of the column.

STEPS

Retrieve the file *ch09pr01.xlsx*.

1. Enter formulas in Rows 6 and 7 to calculate Markup Rate and Amount. Markup Amount is Selling Price minus Cost. Markup Rate is Markup Amount divided by Cost.
2. Enter formulas in Rows 8 and 9 to calculate Markup Amount and Selling Price. Markup Amount is Cost times Markup Rate. Selling Price is Cost plus Markup Amount.
3. Enter formulas in Rows 10 and 11 to calculate Cost and Selling Price. Cost is Markup Amount divided by Markup Rate. Selling Price is Cost plus Markup Amount.
4. Enter formulas in Rows 12 and 13 to calculate Cost and Markup Amount. Cost is Selling Price divided by (Markup Rate plus 100%). Markup Amount is Cost times Markup Rate.
5. Format Columns B, D, and E for currency. Set Decimal places to 2. Set Currency symbol to $. Format Column C for Percentage and 0 Decimal places.
6. Save the file as *ch09pr01a.xlsx*.

Name _____ Date _____

Directions Solve the following problems. Round dollar answers to the nearest cent.

A. Calculate the markup amount and the markup rate based on cost. OBJECTIVE 1

Cost	Selling Price	Markup Amount	Markup Rate
$38.90	$48.63	1. _____	2. _____
$53.10	$66.38	3. _____	4. _____

B. Find the selling price based on cost for the following items. OBJECTIVE 2

Cost	Markup Rate	Selling Price
$811.25	33%	5. _____
$429.60	45%	6. _____

C. Find the cost for the following items. OBJECTIVE 3

Markup Rate	Markup Amount	Cost
50%	$36.20	7. _____
33%	$17.56	8. _____

D. Calculate the cost for each of the following. OBJECTIVE 4

Selling Price	Markup Rate	Cost
$10.96	60%	9. _____
$20.41	35%	10. _____

E. Solve the following word problems, using markup on cost.

11. The Computer Corner pays $1,320.00 for a laptop computer and sells the
    computer at a markup of 25%. How much is the markup amount based on
    the cost and the selling price?   _____

12. A jewelry designer creates a bracelet that costs $18.50 to make. If she wants
    a 60% markup based on cost, what should be the selling price of the bracelet?   _____

13. Computer Accessories uses a markup of 12% on the cost of flash drives,
    which sell for $20. What is the cost?   _____

14. The desired profit of 40% based on cost is used on desk clocks, which sell for
    $18. What is the cost of the clocks? What is the markup amount?   _____

F. Use Excel to calculate cost, markup amount, markup rate, and selling price. OBJECTIVE 5

15. Retrieve the file *ch09ex01.xlsx*. Follow the directions. Save the file as *ch09ex01a.xlsx*.

16. Retrieve the file *ch09ex02.xlsx*. Follow the directions. Save the file as *ch09ex02a.xlsx*.

OBJECTIVES

1. Calculate the markup amount and rate based on selling price.

2. Calculate the selling price when cost and markup rate based on selling price are known.

3. Calculate the cost when the selling price and the markup rate based on selling price are known.

4. Compare the markup based on cost with the markup based on selling price.

5. Use Excel to calculate markup amount and rate based on selling price, and selling price and cost when the markup rate is based on selling price.

9.3 Markup on Selling Price

OBJECTIVE 1 Calculate the markup amount and rate based on selling price.

Whether retailers calculate their markup based on cost or selling price depends on several factors, such as the type and size of business and the type of merchandise sold.

In the following example, you know the cost and the selling price, and you want to find the markup rate based on the selling price. First, find the amount of the markup. Then calculate the markup rate based on selling price by dividing the markup amount by the selling price.

EXAMPLE

An iron costs $17.50 and sells for $29.95. Calculate the markup amount and rate based on the selling price.

STEPS

1. Find the amount of markup by using the basic equation.

Selling Price – Cost = Markup

$29.95 – $17.50 = $12.45   markup amount

2. Find the markup rate by dividing the markup amount by the selling price. Round to the nearest tenth of a percent. Hint: $P \div B = R$.

Markup ÷ Selling Price = Markup Rate

$12.45 ÷ $29.95 = 0.416   markup rate based

0.416 = 41.6%   on selling price

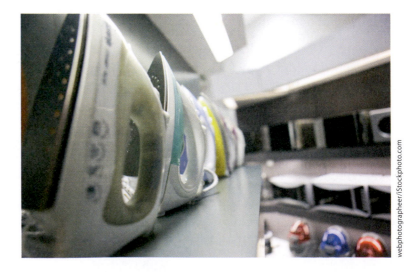

webphotographeer/iStockphoto.com

OBJECTIVE 2 Calculate the selling price when cost and markup rate based on selling price are known.

The markup rate can be based on selling price instead of cost.

EXAMPLE

The cost of a calculator is $29.30 and the markup rate is 30% of the selling price. Calculate the selling price and the markup amount.

STEPS

1. Subtract the markup rate from 100%.

$$100\% - 30\% = 70\% \qquad \text{rate}$$

2. Divide the cost by the rate.

$$\text{Cost} \div \text{Rate} = \text{Selling Price}$$
$$\$29.30 \div 0.70 = \$41.86$$

3. Subtract the cost from the selling price to find the markup amount.

$$\text{Selling Price} - \text{Cost} = \text{Markup}$$
$$\$41.86 - \$29.30 = \$12.56 \qquad \text{markup amount}$$

4. To check your answer, add the cost to the markup amount.

$$\text{Cost} + \text{Markup} = \text{Selling Price}$$
$$\$29.30 + \$12.56 = \$41.86$$

OBJECTIVE 3 Calculate the cost when the selling price and the markup rate based on selling price are known.

If you know the selling price and the markup rate based on the selling price, you can calculate the cost by applying the formula $P = B \times R$, where P is the cost to be calculated, B is the selling price, and R is the markup rate of the cost.

EXAMPLE

Bulletin boards sell for $5.99 and are marked up 20% of the selling price. Find the cost and the markup amount.

STEPS

1. Subtract the markup rate based on the selling price from 100% to obtain the cost rate.

$$100\% - 20\% = 80\% \qquad \text{cost rate}$$

2. Multiply the cost rate by the selling price to obtain the cost.

$$0.80 \times \$5.99 = \$4.79 \qquad \text{cost}$$

3. Subtract cost from selling price to obtain the markup amount.

$5.99 − $4.79 = $1.20   markup amount

4. To check your answer, add the cost plus the markup.

$4.79 + $1.20 = $5.99

OBJECTIVE **4** Compare the markup based on cost with the markup based on selling price.

Markup based on cost and markup based on selling price have been discussed. Will the markup strategies produce the same results? Compare the two strategies using the following example.

EXAMPLE

If a computer case costs $50 and a store used a 35% markup on cost, what is the selling price? How much would the store charge for the computer case if it used a 35% selling price markup?

Problem Solving Plan	
Clues	**Action Plan**
Cost is $50.	Calculate the selling price when the markup is based on cost.
Markup is 35%.	Calculate the selling price when the markup is based on selling price.
Solve	**Solve**
Markup Based on Cost	Markup Based on Selling Price
100% + Markup Rate = 100% + 35% = 135%	100% − Markup Rate = 100% − 35% = 65%
Cost × Rate = Selling Price 1.35 × $50 = $67.50 selling price	Cost ÷ Rate = Selling Price $50 ÷ 0.65 = $76.92 selling price
Conclusion	
The two markup strategies are different. The 35% markup based on cost yields a lower selling price.	

elieli/iStockphoto.com

Use Excel to calculate markup amount and rate based on selling price, and selling price and cost when the markup rate is based on selling price.

You will use formulas in Excel to calculate the markup amount and the rate based on the selling price. You will also calculate the selling price when the cost and the markup rate based on selling price are known and the cost when the selling price and the markup rate based on selling price are known. Figure 9-2 shows the markup amount and the markup rate calculated for selected items.

Figure 9-2

Calculating Markup Amount and Rate Based on Selling Price

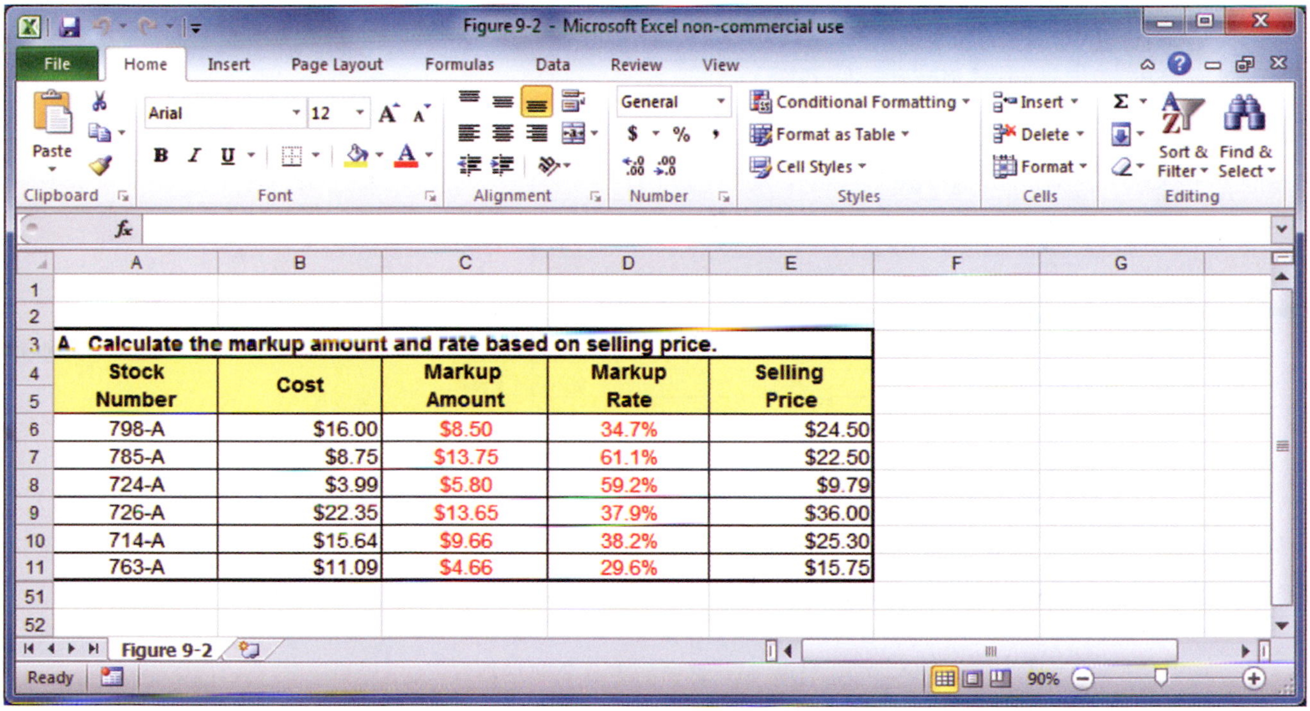

Stock Number	Cost	Markup Amount	Markup Rate	Selling Price
798-A	$16.00	$8.50	34.7%	$24.50
785-A	$8.75	$13.75	61.1%	$22.50
724-A	$3.99	$5.80	59.2%	$9.79
726-A	$22.35	$13.65	37.9%	$36.00
714-A	$15.64	$9.66	38.2%	$25.30
763-A	$11.09	$4.66	29.6%	$15.75

A. Calculate the markup amount and rate based on selling price.

STEPS

Retrieve the file *ch09pr02.xlsx*.

A. Calculate the markup amount and rate based on selling price.

1. Format Column C for Currency, 2 Decimal places, and $.

2. Enter formulas in Column C to calculate Markup Amount. The formula for Cell C6 is =E6−B6.

3. Format Column D for Percentage with 1 Decimal place.

4. Enter formulas in Column D to calculate Markup Rate based on Selling Price. The formula for Cell D6 is =C6/E6.

Figure 9-3 shows the selling price and the cost when the markup rate is based on the selling price calculated for selected items.

	Stock Number	Cost	Markup Rate	Selling Price
B. Calculate selling price when markup rate is based on selling price.				
	710-A	$18.00	30%	$25.71
	753-A	$12.75	28%	$17.71
	738-A	$4.85	16%	$5.77
	741-A	$21.78	24%	$28.66
	721-A	$25.64	12%	$29.14
	718-A	$10.91	43%	$19.14

	Stock Number	Cost	Markup Rate	Selling Price
C. Calculate cost when markup rate is based on selling price.				
	798-A	$32.50	33%	$48.50
	785-A	$24.40	15%	$28.70
	724-A	$6.24	29%	$8.79
	726-A	$20.44	37%	$32.44
	714-A	$14.01	52%	$29.18
	763-A	$13.94	17%	$16.80

Figure 9-3

Calculating Selling Price and Cost when Markup Rate is Based on Selling Price

B. Calculate the selling price when the markup rate is based on selling price.

1. Format Column D for Currency, 2 Decimal places, and $.

2. Enter formulas in Column D to calculate Selling Price when the markup is based on selling price. The formula for Cell C23 is =B23/(100%-C23).

C. Calculate the cost based when the markup rate is based on selling price.

1. Format Column B for Currency, 2 Decimal places, and $.

2. Enter formulas in Column B to calculate Cost when the markup is based on selling price. The formula for Cell B38 is =(100%-C38)*D38.

3. Save the file as *ch09pr02a.xlsx*.

Name _____   Date _____

Directions   Solve the following problems. Round percents to the nearest whole percent. Round dollar amounts to the nearest cent.

A. Calculate the markup rate based on selling price for the following items.   OBJECTIVE **1**

Cost	Selling Price	Markup Rate
$429.80	$517.00	1. _____
$151.21	$288.00	2. _____

B. Calculate the selling price when cost and markup rate are based on selling price for the following items.   OBJECTIVE **2**

Cost	Markup Rate	Selling Price
$19.95	21%	3. _____
$59.50	33%	4. _____

C. Complete the following word problems.   OBJECTIVES **1, 2**

5. A bookcase costs $35.80 and is sold for $59.99.

   a. What is the markup amount?   _____

   b. What is the markup rate based on selling price?   _____

6. A lamp sells for $125.50 and costs $59.80. What is the markup rate based on selling price?   _____

7. In Fran's Card Shop, the sales associate has marked up an item 30% on its selling price of $35. Find the markup amount.   _____

8. An item's selling price is $19.99 and the markup amount is $12.12. What is the cost?   _____

9. If the selling price is $29 and the markup amount is $22, how much is the markup rate?   _____

10. What is the cost if the markup is 55% of the selling price and the selling price is $128?   _____

11. The cost is $27.40 and the markup rate is 45% of the selling price. What is the selling price?   _____

12. What is the cost of an item that sells for $130 and 60% markup is based on selling price?   _____

13. Calculate the selling price on an item that costs $90.90 and is marked up at 22% based on its selling price.   _____

D. Use Excel to calculate cost, markup, markup rate, and selling price.   OBJECTIVE **5**

14. Retrieve the file *ch09ex03.xlsx*. Follow the directions. Save the file as *ch09ex03a.xlsx*.

15. Retrieve the file *ch09ex04.xlsx*. Follow the directions. Save the file as *ch09ex04a.xlsx*.

9.4 Markdown

OBJECTIVE 1 Determine markdown sale price.

Almost everyone wants to take advantage of special sales where merchandise has been marked down or reduced. **Markdown amount** is the difference between the original selling price of the merchandise and the reduced selling price. **Markdown rate** may be expressed as a percent, such as 20% off, or as a fraction, such as 1/3 off.

When retailers decide on their markup, they usually decide on the markdown at the same time. Merchandise is marked down from the regular selling price for many different reasons. The retailer may have purchased too much merchandise and wants to get rid of the extra, the merchandise is

sjlocke/iStockphoto.com

seasonal, the merchandise has become soiled or damaged, or the demand for the merchandise has decreased. Thus, the original selling price of the merchandise is reduced for special sales.

You can use the steps given here to determine the sale price when the original selling price and markdown rate are known.

EXAMPLE

An employee at The Crest Greeting Card Store has been asked to mark down the greeting cards 40%. One box of unique holiday cards originally sold for $27.50. Find the sale price.

STEPS

1. Find the markdown amount by multiplying the selling price by the markdown rate.

$$\$27.50 \times 0.40 = \$11.00 \quad \text{markdown amount}$$

2. Find the sale price by subtracting the markdown amount from the original selling price.

$$\$27.50 - \$11.00 = \$16.50 \quad \text{sale price}$$

EXAMPLE

The complement method may be used to determine only the sale price.

STEPS

1. Find the complement by subtracting 40% from 100%.

$$100\% - 40\% = 60\% \quad \text{complement}$$

2. Find the sale price by multiplying the original sale price by the complement.

$$\$27.50 \times 0.60 = \$16.50 \quad \text{sale price}$$

TIPS

The markdown rate is based on the original selling price. For example, if the markdown is 20%, the 20% is calculated on the original selling price (the base, or 100%).

OBJECTIVE **2** Calculate markdown rate.

You can use the steps given here to determine the markdown rate when the original selling price and sale price are known.

EXAMPLE

A sales associate has been asked to mark down several items, including a mini-lamp. It has a retail value or selling price of $24.95. The reduced price was $18.75. What is the markdown rate on the original price?

STEPS

1. Find the markdown amount by subtracting the reduced price from the selling price.

$$\$24.95 - \$18.75 = \$6.20 \quad \text{markdown amount}$$

2. Find the markdown rate by dividing the markdown amount by the original selling price.

$$\$6.20 \div 24.95 = 25\% \quad \text{markdown rate}$$

travelif/iStockphoto.com

OBJECTIVE 3 Use Excel to calculate markdown amount and sale price or markdown rate.

You can use Excel to calculate the markdown amount, the sale price, and the markdown rate as shown in Figure 9-4.

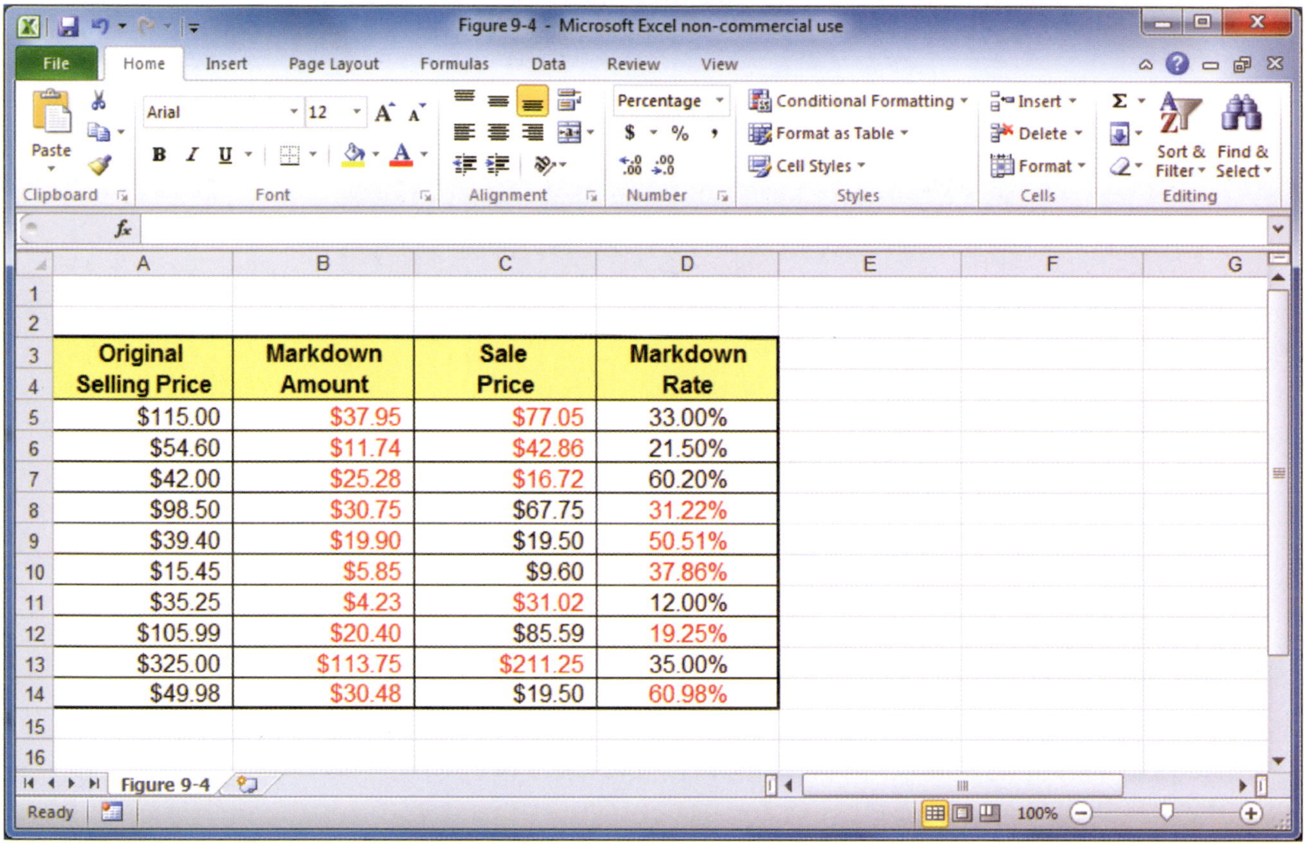

	A	B	C	D
3-4	Original Selling Price	Markdown Amount	Sale Price	Markdown Rate
5	$115.00	$37.95	$77.05	33.00%
6	$54.60	$11.74	$42.86	21.50%
7	$42.00	$25.28	$16.72	60.20%
8	$98.50	$30.75	$67.75	31.22%
9	$39.40	$19.90	$19.50	50.51%
10	$15.45	$5.85	$9.60	37.86%
11	$35.25	$4.23	$31.02	12.00%
12	$105.99	$20.40	$85.59	19.25%
13	$325.00	$113.75	$211.25	35.00%
14	$49.98	$30.48	$19.50	60.98%

Figure 9-4
Calculating Markdown Amount and Sale Price or Markdown Rate

STEPS

Retrieve the file *ch09pr03.xlsx*.

1. In Rows 5-7, enter formulas in Columns B and C to calculate the Markdown Amount and Sale Price.
2. In Rows 8-10, enter formulas in Columns B and D to calculate the Markdown Amount and Markdown Rate.
3. In Rows 11-14, enter formulas in the appropriate columns to calculate the missing information.
4. Format Columns B and C for Currency, 2 Decimal places, and $. Format Column D for Percentage with 2 Decimal places.
5. Save the file as *ch09pr03a.xlsx*.

Name _____   Date _____

Directions   Solve the following problems. Round percents to the nearest whole percent. Round dollar amounts to the nearest cent.

A. Calculate the sale price on each of the following.   `OBJECTIVE 1`

Original Selling Price	Markdown Rate	Sale Price
1. $562.56	30%	_____
2. $57.00	15%	_____
3. $32.99	35%	_____

B. Calculate the markdown rate on each of the following.   `OBJECTIVE 2`

Original Selling Price	Sale Price	Markdown Rate
4. $46.00	$32.00	_____
5. $342.50	$198.99	_____
6. $85.95	$71.00	_____

C. Calculate the markdown amount and markdown rate.   `OBJECTIVE 2`

Original Selling Price	Sale Price	Markdown Amount	Markdown Rate
$124.25	$98.40	7. _____	8. _____
$265.45	$149.99	9. _____	10. _____
$145.59	$99.99	11. _____	12. _____

D. Solve the following word problems.

13.   Gregory's Threads marked down a $315 wool suit to $225. What was the markdown amount?   _____

14.   Rafael Cardenas bought a treadmill that was on sale for $367.50. It was originallly priced at $525. What was the markdown rate?   _____

15.   A new lamp was originally priced at $148.75 and is now on sale for $119. What is the markdown amount? What is the markdown rate?   _____

16.   A DVD player originally sells for $99.99. The markdown rate is 60%. What is the sale price of the DVD player?   _____

E. Use Excel to calculate markdown sale price and rate.   `OBJECTIVE 3`

17.   Retrieve the file *ch09ex05.xlsx*. Follow the directions. Save the file as *ch09ex05a.xlsx*.

18.   Retrieve the file *ch09ex06.xlsx*. Follow the directions. Save the file as *ch09ex06a.xlsx*.

Chapter Review and Assessment

KEY TERMS

cost	markup	operating expenses
markdown	markup amount	reduced price
markdown amount	markup rate	sale price
markdown rate	net profit	selling price

CONCEPTS	EXAMPLES
9.1 Identify terms used with pricing merchandise.	Cost is $18.60 and markup amount is $4.90.
Selling Price (*S*) To calculate selling price, add cost and markup.	$18.60 + $4.90 = $23.50
Markup (*M*) To calculate markup, subtract cost from selling price.	$23.50 − $18.60 = $4.90
Cost (*C*) To calculate cost, subtract markup from selling price.	$23.50 − $4.90 = $18.60
9.2 Calculate the markup amount and the rate based on cost.	Cost is $44.90 and selling price is $69.99. Find the markup rate based on cost.
Subtract cost from selling price.	$69.99 − $44.90 = $25.09 markup amount
Divide markup amount by cost.	$25.09 ÷ $44.90 = 56% markup rate based on cost
9.2 Calculate the selling price when the markup rate is based on cost.	Cost is $57.50 and markup rate based on cost is 33%. Find selling price.
Multiply markup rate by cost.	$57.50 × 0.33 = $18.98 markup amount
Add cost and markup amount.	$57.50 + $18.98 = $76.48 selling price
9.2 Calculate the cost when the markup amount and the markup rate based on cost are known.	Markup is $8.75 and markup rate is 25%.
Divide markup amount by markup rate.	$8.75 ÷ 0.25 = $35.00 cost
9.2 Calculate the cost when the selling price and the markup rate based on cost are known.	Selling price is $106.88 and markup rate is 25%.
Add rate to cost (100%).	100% + 25% = 125%
Divide selling price by markup percent.	$106.88 ÷ 1.25 = $85.50 cost

CONCEPTS	EXAMPLES
9.3 Calculate the markup amount and rate based on selling price. Subtract cost from selling price. Divide markup by selling price.	Cost is $21.00 and selling price is $32.00. Find the markup rate based on selling price. $32.00 − $21.00 = $11.00 markup amount $11.00 ÷ $32.00 = 34% markup rate based on selling price
9.3 Calculate the selling price when cost and markup rate based on selling price are known. Subtract markup rate from 100%. Divide cost by the complement.	Cost is $4.50 and markup rate based on selling price is 25%. Find selling price. 100% − 25% = 75% complement $4.50 ÷ 0.75 = $6.00 selling price
9.3 Calculate the cost when the selling price and the markup rate based on selling price are known. Subtract markup rate from selling price base 100%. Multiply rate by selling price. Subtract cost from selling price.	Selling price is $129.00 and markup rate is 45%. 100% − 45% = 55% 0.55 × $129.00 = 70.95 cost $129.00 − $70.95 = $58.05 markup amount
9.3 Compare the markup based on cost with the markup based on selling price. **Calculate selling price using markup based on cost.** Add 100% to markup rate. Multiply rate by cost. **Calculate selling price using markup based on selling price.** Subtract markup from 100%, Divide cost by rate.	Cost = $24.90; Markup Rate = 40% 100% + 40% = 140% 1.40 × $24.90 = $34.86 selling price 100% − 40% = 60% $24.90 ÷ 0.60 = $41.50 selling price
9.4 Determine markdown sale price. Multiply selling price by markdown rate. Subtract markdown from selling price. Use complement to calculate only sale price. Subtract markdown rate from 100%. Multiply selling price by complement.	Markdown rate is 40% and original selling price is $48.00. Find the sale price. $48.00 × 0.40 = $19.20 markdown $48.00 − $19.20 = $28.80 sale price 100% − 40% = 60% complement $48.00 × 0.60 = $28.80 sale price
9.4 Calculate markdown rate. Subtract reduced price from original selling price Divide markdown amount by original selling price.	Original selling price was $112.00 and reduced price is $67.20. $112.00 − $67.20 = $44.80 $44.80 ÷ $112.00 = 40% markdown rate

Chapter Review and Assessment   **351**

Chapter 9 Review Exercises

Name _____   Date _____

Directions   Complete the following problems. Round dollar amounts to the nearest cent. Round percents to the nearest whole percent.

A. Determine the selling price, cost, or markup amount for the following items.   `9.1 OBJECTIVE 2`

	Cost	Selling Price	Markup Amount
1.	$ _____	$52.98	$15.00
2.	$112.10	$ _____	$38.90
3.	$38.00	$45.00	$ _____

B. Complete the following using markup based on cost.   `9.2 OBJECTIVES 1, 2, 3, 4`

	Cost	Markup Rate	Markup Amount	Selling Price
4.	$ _____	65%	$22.50	$ _____
5.	$76.00	35%	$ _____	$ _____
6.	$14.70	_____	$ _____	$35.25
7.	$ _____	55%	$ _____	$195.00
8.	$13.80	20%	$ _____	$ _____

C. Complete the following using markup based on selling price.   `9.3 OBJECTIVES 1, 2, 3`

	Cost	Markup Rate	Markup Amt	Selling Price
9.	$13.25	_____	$ _____	$32.50
10.	$3.50	28%	$ _____	$ _____
11.	$ _____	25%	$ _____	$16.00
12.	$9.00	32%	$ _____	$ _____

D. Complete the following using markdown.   `9.4 OBJECTIVES 1, 2`

	Markdown Rate	Markdown Amt	Original Selling Price	Sale Price
13.	33%	$ _____	$39.00	$ _____
14.	_____	$450.00	$1,320.00	$ _____
15.	25%	$ _____	$75.00	$ _____

E. Solve the following word problems.

16. A desk that originally sold for $495 was damaged at the store. To sell the desk, the store reduces the price by 40%. Determine the markdown and sale price.

   a. Markdown Amount = _____   **b.** Sale Price = _____

17. A copier costs $525 and is sold for $875. Find the markup amount and markup rate based on the cost.

   a. Markup Amount = _____   **b.** Markup Rate = _____

18. A table sells for $590. The markup was based on 28% of the selling price. Find the amount of markup and the cost.

   a. Cost = _____   **b.** Markup Amount = _____

19. If a stapler costs the retailer $13.79 and the selling price is $16.00, what is the markup rate based on selling price?   _____

20. If a case of copy paper costs $18 and it has a markup rate of 40% based on cost, what is the selling price?   _____

21. If the retailer's original selling price is $40.50 and the markdown rate is 20%, what should be the item's sale price?   _____

22. A conference table costs $285 and is sold for $385. Find the markup amount and rate based on cost.

   a. Markup Amount = _____   **b.** Markup Rate = _____

23. A bookcase was slightly damaged. The original selling price was $125. The markdown rate was 35%. What should be the sale price?   _____

24. Dorothy Williams bought a chair for $375 from her supplier. She plans to sell the chair for $650. What is Dorothy's markup amount? What is her markup rate based on cost?

   a. Markup Amount = _____   **b.** Markup Rate = _____

25. The cost of a printer is $66, and the markup rate is 40% of the selling price. Calculate the selling price.   _____

26. The cost of a set of Russian painted boxes is $12 each. To cover her costs, Lijita must mark up each box 40% on cost. What is the selling price of each box?   _____

27. Novelty Plus purchases sun visors for $1.19 and sells them for $2.98. What is the markup rate based on the selling price?   _____

28. Evelyn Ott is a weaver and sells woven shawls, ponchos, and vests. She asked her assistant to mark down her shawls from $198 to $119. What is the markdown amount? How much is the markdown rate?

   a. Markdown Amount = _____   **b.** Markdown Rate = _____

F. Use Excel to solve the following problems.   9.2 OBJECTIVE 5, 9.3 OBJECTIVE 5, 9.4 OBJECTIVE 3

29. Retrieve the file *ch09ex07.xlsx*. Follow the directions. Save the file as *ch09ex07a.xlsx*.

30. Retrieve the file *ch09ex08.xlsx*. Follow the directions. Save the file as *ch09ex08a.xlsx*.

31. Retrieve the file *ch09ex09.xlsx*. Follow the directions. Save the file as *ch09ex09a.xlsx*.

APPLY   Math@Work   ACCOUNTING ASSOCIATE

Math is used in various ways by store owners and their accountants, managers, retail buyers and other retail employees. Consider that people working in retail need to know basic skills, such as addition, subtraction, multiplication and division. However, more complex tasks in retail require more advanced math skills, such as using equations and formulas to calculate gross profit margins, cash flow, and profitability.

You are a new accounting associate and have been asked to apply markdown in the following situation. Your store received 150 vests. Toward the end of the season, 137 vests had been sold at $32.00. It has been decided to mark down the remaining vests to $24.99. Suppose that within two weeks, the remaining vests sold at $24.99, the reduced price. Calculate the percent of expected total sales the markdown cost the store.

1. Calculate the expected total sales.

2. Determine the markdown for 13 vests.

3. Calculate the percent of expected total sales the markdown cost the store.

Write about Math

Suppose you have been working in retail since you were a teenager and are considering opening a small retail store. Last week you attended a seminar for potential small business retailers and were presented with the following questions that are related to price-setting. To develop your own understanding for price-setting, answer the following questions.

1. When pricing, what operating costs must you consider? In addition to your earnings and your employees' earnings, identify other operating costs?

2. When marking up your merchandise, will you use markup based on cost or markup based on selling price? Compare the two methods presented in section 9.3. Also, consider the following: which one is larger—a 35% markup on cost or a 30% markup on selling price. Determine the price and cost of an item and work the math.

3. Will your customers consider your prices fair? What does fair mean to you as a customer? From an owner's perspective, what does fair mean?

4. Will you allow customers to bargain over the prices of any items? What if a customer brings in an ad that reads "we'll meet competitors' prices"? Will you meet competitors' prices?

Personal Finance

How are everyday markups eating away your paycheck?

If it is true that the recession is over, why are prices on some items still climbing? Because businesses continue to find ways in which they can increase their revenues. While businesses continue to raise their prices, consumers continue to purchase items with hefty markups. Why do you continue to do so? Because it is convenient -- the package is pretty, sturdy, the container can be used again, or it is the latest "thing" to have . . . or you do so because you will pay the price. Using the Internet, you can locate lists of items with unbelievable markups.

The amount you spend on high markup items may have a direct link to how much money you have left to enjoy other areas of life. Dropping $50 - $100 off your monthly food bill, beverages , or mobile devices could mean the difference in the type of car you drive, how much you can save for your children's future or where you go on vacation.

© Anton Prado PHOTO, 2010/Used under license from Shutterstock.com

1. There are variations among retails prices for prescription drugs. Become a comparison shopper. Going to the most convenient pharmacy may not offer you the best value. Make time to compare prices among your independent pharmacies and wholesale clubs located in your area. At a pharmacy, a generic capsule sells for $150.27 per 100-capsule bottle. If the pharmacy paid $10.33 per bottle, find the percent of markup on cost.

2. Will a whopping markup keep you from enjoying your next bag of popcorn? The next time you or your children want to buy popcorn at the movies, should you buy it or make another choice for another snack or wait and have a snack after the movie? When buying popcorn in a movie theater, if a medium bag of popcorn costs just 60 cents to make and retails for $6.00, find the markup rate based on cost.

3. To save money on your next restaurant trip, request tap water that already has been filtered. Before you buy the next bottled water, consider the amount of water that is filtered tap water. If a high-end restaurant sells bottled water for $8.50, while it costs them $2.80 per 16 oz, calculate the markup rate on the selling price.

4. How about a cup of tea? You might be surprised to learn about the high markup on tea. At Lady Rose Tea Room, suppose you pay $2.50 for a cup of tea that costs the shop owner 13 cents. Calculate the markup rate on the selling price.

Name _____ Date _____ Score _____

Directions   Solve the following problems. Round dollar amounts to the nearest cent. Round percents to the nearest whole percent.

A. Find the selling price, cost, or markup amount for the following items.   **9.1 OBJECTIVE 2**

	Cost	Selling Price	Markup Amount
1.	$_____	$199.95	$15.00
2.	$12.30	$_____	$32.69
3.	$75.90	$156.80	$_____

B. Complete the following using markup based on cost.   **9.2 OBJECTIVES 1, 2, 3, 4**

	Cost	Markup Rate	Markup Amount	Selling Price
4.	$_____	55%	$60.50	$_____
5.	$52.00	75%	$_____	$_____
6.	$85.00	____	$_____	$155.50
7.	$_____	45%	$_____	$1,115.00
8.	$33.40	30%	$_____	$_____

C. Complete the following using markup based on selling price.   **9.3 OBJECTIVES 1, 2, 3**

	Cost	Markup Rate	Markup Amount	Selling Price
9.	$9.25	____	$_____	$42.50
10.	$5.50	32%	$_____	$_____
11.	$_____	65%	$_____	$325.00
12.	$18.00	42%	$_____	$_____

D. Complete the following using markdown.   **9.4 OBJECTIVES 1, 2**

	Markdown Rate	Markdown Amount	Original Selling Price	Sale Price
13.	60%	$_____	$89.00	$_____
14.	____	$150.00	$900.00	$_____
15.	30%	$_____	$175.00	$_____

E. Solve the following word problems.

16. A package of stationery costs $10.50 and sells for $22.30. What is the markup amount and the markup rate based on cost?

_____

17. The cost of an office chair is $44.50. It sells for $89. What is the markup amount and the markup rate based on selling price?

_____

18. A pair of brass bookends sells for $28 and is marked up 40% based on selling price. Calculate the cost.

_____

19. A 12' × 18' area rug originally sold for $189.99 and was reduced to sell for $155.99. Find the amount of markdown and the markdown rate.

_____

20. A down comforter was originally priced at $299 and was reduced 65%. Find the amount of markdown and the sale price.

_____

21. A computer at Computer Warehouse costs $259. It is marked up 45% on the selling price. What is the selling price of the computer?

_____

22. Charlie Hoffman bought a watch at a cost of $38.75. He plans to sell the watch for $89.99. What is the amount of markup as well as the markup rate based on cost?

_____

23. A desk calculator costs $99.00. The markup based on cost is 30%. Find the selling price.

_____

24. The owner of In Your Dreams, a linen shop, purchased casual pillows for $9 each and has marked them up to $15. Carolina, the owner, reminded her assistant that the markup rate based on cost must be at least 50%. What was the markup rate based on cost of the pillows? Did the markup meet the owner's expectation?

_____

25. The selling price for a set of Brown's pottery dishes for 8 is $240 and is marked up 35% of the selling price. What is his cost?

_____

26. The markup on an item is $24.00, which is marked up 28% based on cost. Calculate the cost.

_____

27. What is the cost if the markup is 55% of the selling price and the selling price is $128?

_____

28. The cost is $27.40 and the markup rate is 45% of the selling price. What is the selling price?

_____

29. What is the cost of an item that sells for $130 and 60% mark up is based on selling price?

_____

30. Calculate the selling price on an item that cost $90.90 and is marked up at 22% based on its selling price.

_____

F. Use Excel to solve the following problems. `9.2 OBJECTIVE 5, 9.3 OBJECTIVE 5`

31. Retrieve the file *ch09qz01.xlsx*. Follow the directions. Save the file as *ch09qz01a.xlsx*.

32. Retrieve the file *ch09qz02.xlsx*. Follow the directions. Save the file as *ch09qz02a.xlsx*.

Individuals, as well as businesses, borrow money to buy a variety of goods and services. Borrowing money allows people to make purchases now rather than later. Loans are made to businesses for purchases of equipment, buildings, land, and merchandise for resale. Loans also are made to individuals. When you borrow money, an additional amount of money is added to the amount borrowed. This additional amount is interest.

Interest is also paid on invested money. For example, when you deposit money into a savings account, the bank pays you interest for the use of your money. The bank is paying you for the privilege of using your money.

SMALL BUSINESS OWNER

Rich Coleman is the owner of Next Level Transportation Services, LLC. His company provides refuse containers for large construction sites. Rich is responsible for all aspects of the business: sales, marketing, accounting, and advertising. After securing a new job, Rich must monitor its progress to ensure his company delivers its services as promised and performs to the standards he has set. He then must track payments to the company and payments to his vendors to make sure the company has sufficient cash flow. When a job is finished, he follows up with the customer to make sure they were satisfied. According to Rich, "A satisfied customer is critical in my business because word of mouth is the best advertising we could have."

"Owning your own business isn't easy," Rich says, "You have to wear many hats. In larger organizations, you'd have employees or even entire departments that handle specific jobs such as human resources, accounting, and payroll. As a small business owner, I must perform all those jobs."

Courtesy of Rich Coleman

How Math is Used in a Small Business

Rich may have containers at many different job sites at once. "Because not all job sites are the same distance from the land-fills or recycling center areas, I have to calculate the amount of time needed to drive to and from the job site, the amount of fuel needed, the cost of paying the driver for the time spent driving the route, and the cost to unload the contents of the container at the end destination. I must then add in a profit margin to ensure that we make money on the job while also making sure that our price is in line with our competitors."

What Do You Think?

What skills do you need to improve to manage a small business?

Math Skills Used

Addition

Subtraction

Division

Percents

Other Skills Needed

Communication

Employee Management

Organization

Time Management

10.1 Simple Interest

> ### OBJECTIVE 1 Identify terms used for calculating simple interest.

Interest appears in savings accounts, where a bank pays you an amount for depositing and keeping your money in an account. Interest also appears in credit cards and other loans, where you pay an organization for allowing you to use their money for a time.

The two basic types of interest are simple and compound. **Simple interest** is computed on the principal for the time of the transaction. **Compound interest** is money that builds on itself; that is, it earns money on the interest that is reinvested as well as on the original principal.

©3445128471, 2010/Used under license from Shutterstock.com

Simple interest is used when a loan is repaid in a lump sum. The borrower has use of the full amount of money for the entire period of the loan. For example, Mijoko borrows $6,500 for a new sewing machine for her business. She borrows the money for two years at 9.8% interest. Mijoko owes $1,274 in interest plus the amount she borrowed, which is $6,500 + $1,274 = $7,774. So Mijoko, the borrower, pays for the privilege of using someone's money. The lender earns the interest for providing the money.

In some situations, a small business may offer its customers a payment plan on which simple interest is calculated. For instance, Mijoko could have purchased her sewing machine from a dealer and arranged to make payments over the next two years.

The initial amount borrowed or invested for a certain period of time, sometimes called **face value**, is the **principal** (P). **Interest** (I) is the amount paid on the principal for the privilege of using someone else's money or the amount earned on investment money. The **rate** (R) is the percentage charged to lend or borrow money.

Institutions make loans using different rates based on factors such as the prime interest rate and the amount of risk involved in repayment of the loans. **Prime interest** is the interest rate that banks charge their best or most creditworthy customers.

The **time** (T) is the period of time you have to repay the loan or to earn interest on your invested money. Time is expressed in days, months, or years (called the **interest period** or the *term* of the loan) and is usually written as a number of years or a fraction of a year. If a loan is stated in a certain number of days, computing interest is based on the 360-day (ordinary simple interest) year or on the 365-day (exact simple interest) year.

Interest is based on the principal, interest rate, and amount of time. Simple interest is easily calculated. The amount of interest is determined by multiplying the principal by the interest rate by the amount of time. The following formula is used.

$$I = P \times R \times T$$

where

I = Interest
P = Principal (amount of loan)
R = Rate (percent of interest charged or earned per year)
T = Time in years

The actual amount of time for which money is being used is important in computing interest.

EXAMPLE

Suppose Natasha borrowed $900 for one year at 12% interest. Compute the simple interest.

$$I = P \times R \times T$$
$$I = \$900 \times 0.12 \times 1$$
$$I = \$108.00 \qquad \text{simple interest}$$

EXAMPLE

Suppose Natasha borrowed $900 for *two* years at 12% interest. With simple interest, if Natasha doesn't pay the loan back until the end of the second year, she will have to pay another $108 for a total of $216. Her second year of interest is based on the original principal.

$$I = P \times R \times T$$
$$I = \$900 \times 0.12 \times 2$$
$$I = \$216.00$$

When loans are for longer periods, the amount of interest is greater. Likewise, if the period is shorter than one year, the interest is less.

EXAMPLE

Suppose Natasha borrowed $900 for 8 months at 12% interest. What is the amount of interest?

Eight months is $\frac{8}{12}$ of a year.

$$I = P \times R \times T$$
$$I = \$900 \times 0.12 \times \frac{8}{12}$$
$$I = \$72.00$$

OBJECTIVE 3 Calculate ordinary simple interest, using a 360-day year.

Thus far, the amount of time for which money is borrowed has been expressed as one year, two years, and several months. Now you will learn how to calculate simple interest when time is expressed in a certain number of days—some financial organizations calculate interest using a 360-day year, called **ordinary simple interest**.

EXAMPLE

The bank loans Gricelda $4,000 at 9% for 60 days. What is the amount of interest?

Divide the number of days by 360.

$$I = P \times R \times T$$
$$I = \$4,000 \times 0.09 \times \frac{60}{360}$$
$$I = \$60.00 \qquad \text{ordinary simple interest}$$

OBJECTIVE 4 Calculate exact simple interest, using a 365-day year.

Most credit unions, federal government agencies, and the Federal Reserve Bank use a 365-day year (366 days for leap years) called **exact simple interest**.

EXAMPLE

The principal is $8,000 at 12% for 60 days. What is the amount of exact simple interest?

Divide the number of days by 365.

$$I = P \times R \times T$$
$$I = \$8,000 \times 0.12 \times \frac{60}{365}$$
$$I = \$157.81 \qquad \text{exact simple interest}$$

OBJECTIVE 5 Compare ordinary simple interest and exact simple interest.

The following example compares ordinary and exact simple interest.

EXAMPLE

Thoa began her new business with a loan of $12,000 at 12% interest for 180 days.

$$\begin{array}{ll}
\textbf{Ordinary Interest} & \textbf{Exact Interest} \\
I = P \times R \times T & I = P \times R \times T \\
\quad = \$12{,}000 \times 0.12 \times \frac{180}{360} & \quad = \$12{,}000 \times 0.12 \times \frac{180}{365} \\
\quad = \$720.00 & \quad = \$710.14
\end{array}$$

The difference is $\$720.00 - \$710.14 = \$9.86$.

The difference may not seem great to you. However, if you were discussing a business loan with your bank for hundreds of thousands of dollars, the difference would be great. You can see why lending institutions may compute simple interest using the ordinary method.

OBJECTIVE 6 Determine the maturity value of a loan.

Maturity means the length of time until the principal amount of a loan must be repaid. **Maturity value** (M) is the full amount of money that must be repaid when a loan is due; that is, the principal plus the interest.

EXAMPLE

Suppose Chan borrows $1,825 at 12% interest for one year. What is the maturity value?

STEPS

1. Calculate the interest first.
$$I = P \times R \times T$$
$$I = \$1{,}825 \times 0.12 \times 1$$
$$I = \$219 \qquad \text{simple interest}$$

2. Add the interest to the principal to find the maturity value.
$$M = P + I$$
$$M = \$1{,}825 + \$219$$
$$M = \$2{,}044 \qquad \text{maturity value}$$

To report interest as part of doing business, you calculate interest as a separate amount. However, you frequently need to calculate the maturity value as the total amount in one calculation. You can use the following formula to calculate the maturity value.

$$\text{Maturity value} = \text{Principal} \times (1 + \text{Rate} \times \text{Time})$$

For example, the maturity value, M, of a loan of $1,825 for one year at a simple interest rate of 12% per year is:

$$M = \$1{,}825 \times (1 + 0.12 \times 1)$$
$$M = \$1{,}825 \times (1.12)$$
$$M = \$2{,}044$$

You have learned to calculate the amount of interest when the principal (P), rate (R), and time (T) are given: $I = P \times R \times T$. In some cases, the interest is known, but the principal, rate, or time may not be given.

You can determine the missing part if any two of the three remaining parts are given. The illustration below will help you determine the formula needed to find the missing part.

I
$P \times R \times T$

The following summary will help you find the missing part.

To find	Use this formula
Principal	$P = \dfrac{I}{R \times T}$
Rate	$R = \dfrac{I}{P \times T}$
Time	$T = \dfrac{I}{P \times R}$

The 360-day year (ordinary simple interest) is used in the examples below.

Find the Principal

To find the principal, cover the P in the box to determine what parts remain.

EXAMPLE

Suppose you want to determine the amount of principal it will take to earn $170 interest in 120 days at 12%.

The formula is written like this:

$$P = \frac{I}{R \times T}$$

$$P = \frac{\$170}{0.12 \times \frac{120}{360}}$$

$$= \frac{\$170}{0.04} = \$4,250 \qquad \text{principal}$$

TIPS

Calculate the denominator first.

0.12 × 120 ÷ 360 = 0.04

Find the Rate

To find the interest rate, cover the *R* in the box to determine what parts remain.

EXAMPLE

Suppose you borrow $1,200 for 90 days and the interest is $35. What is the interest rate?

The formula is written like this:

$$R = \frac{I}{P \times T}$$

$$R = \frac{\$35}{\$1,200 \times \frac{90}{360}}$$

$$= \frac{\$35}{\$300} = 0.1166 = 11.7\% \qquad \text{interest rate}$$

TIPS

Use the basic simple interest formula to check your answer: $I = P \times R \times T$.

Find the Time

To find the amount of time, cover the *T* in the box to see what parts remain.

EXAMPLE

Barbara Jordon's deposit of $795 at 12% earned interest is of $110. What is the time of this deposit?

The formula is written like this:

$$T = \frac{I}{P \times R} \qquad \text{\textit{T} is in days.}$$

$$T = \frac{\$110}{\$795 \times 0.12}$$

$$= \frac{\$110}{\$95.40} = 1.153 \text{ years}$$

1.15 years × 360 days per year = 414 days

OBJECTIVE **8** Calculate the maturity date.

In some situations, the amount borrowed and the interest rate on a loan are given but an actual due date is not indicated. You often find terms of a loan expressed as "due in 90 days." When this occurs, you need to count the actual number of days to determine the date of maturity. Once you know the date the loan began, you can use the following method to determine the **maturity date**, the date on which a loan must be paid in full. The actual number of interest days is determined by totaling the number of days in each month.

Work through the example on the next page to learn how to calculate a due date. Table 10-1 shows the number of days in each month.

alexsl//iStockphoto.com

The loan date is April 15, and the loan is due in 120 days. What is the due date?

1. Determine the number of days in the specified period of time.

a.	April	15 days	30 − 15 = 15 days remaining
b.	May	31 days	
c.	June	30 days	
d.	July	31 days	

2. Add all the days.

$$15 + 31 + 30 + 31 = 107$$

3. Subtract 107 days from the 120 days due.

$$120 − 107 = 13$$

4. August has 13 days to be counted for this time period, so the maturity date is August 13.

5. To prove your answer, add all the days to be sure they total 120.

$$15 + 31 + 30 + 31 + 13 = 120$$

You can also use these steps to determine the number of interest days between two dates, such as March 20 to July 28, as follows.

March	11 days	31 − 20 = 11 days remaining
April	30 days	
May	31 days	
June	30 days	
July	28 days	end of period

$$11 + 30 + 31 + 30 + 28 = 130 \text{ days}$$

Table 10-1

Number of Days in Each Month

Number of Days in Each Month		
28 days	**30 days**	**31 days**
February (29 days in leap year)	April	January
	June	March
	September	May
	November	July
		August
		October
		December

When the time of a note is shown in months, you find the due date by counting that number of months forward from the date of the note. The due date is the same day in the month as the date of the note. A note due on the last day of the month is due on the last date of the month in which the note is due. For example, a note for one month issued on January 31 is due on February 28.

Interest

As Figure 10-1 shows, formulas in Excel can calculate simple, ordinary, and exact interest.

Figure 10-1

Using Excel to Calculate Interest

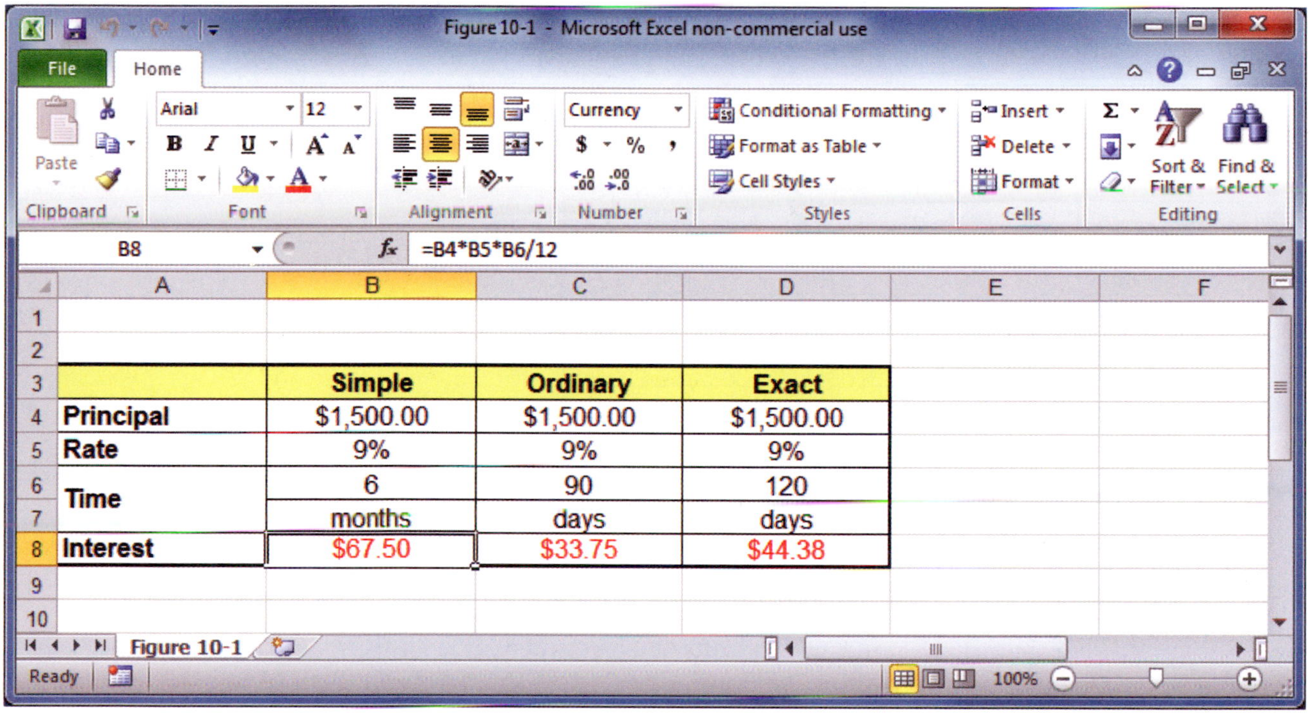

	Simple	Ordinary	Exact
Principal	$1,500.00	$1,500.00	$1,500.00
Rate	9%	9%	9%
Time	6 months	90 days	120 days
Interest	$67.50	$33.75	$44.38

B8   fx   =B4*B5*B6/12

EXAMPLE

You want to start a new home business and need to borrow $1,500 for 6 months at a rate of 9% simple interest. You calculate simple interest based on 6 months and then decide to see what the interest would be if the loan were for 90 days. A lending institution calculates your loan based on ordinary interest. After considering the amount of interest, you decide to ask for a loan based on 120 days. Another institution calculates the interest due on your loan based on exact interest. Now you can compare all three situations.

STEPS

Retrieve the file **ch10pr01.xlsx**.

1. In Cell B8, enter =B4*B5*B6/12 to calculate Simple Interest for 6 months.

2. In Cell C8, enter =C4*C5*C6/360 to calculate Ordinary Interest for 90 days.

3. In Cell D8, enter =D4*D5*D6/365 to calculate Exact Interest for 120 days.

4. Format answers for Currency, 2 Decimal places, and $.

5. Save the file as **ch10pr01a.xlsx**.

TIPS

To view the formulas: From the File tab, select the Help menu, then select the Options menu, and finally the Advanced menu. Scroll down to the section labeled Display options for this worksheet. Select Show formulas in cells instead of their calculated results.

Figure 10-2

Excel Formula to Calculate Maturity Value Using Ordinary Interest

Maturity Value

Figure 10-2 shows the Excel formula to calculate the maturity value using ordinary interest.

Figure 10-2 - Microsoft Excel non-commercial use

D5 fx =A5*(1+B5*C5/360)

	Principal	Interest Rate	Time in Days	Maturity Value
5	$25,000	11.5%	100	$25,798.61
6	$85,000	12.2%	160	$89,608.89
7	$100,000	11%	120	$103,666.67
8	$3,500	8.5%	60	$3,549.58
9	$10,000	9%	150	$10,375.00

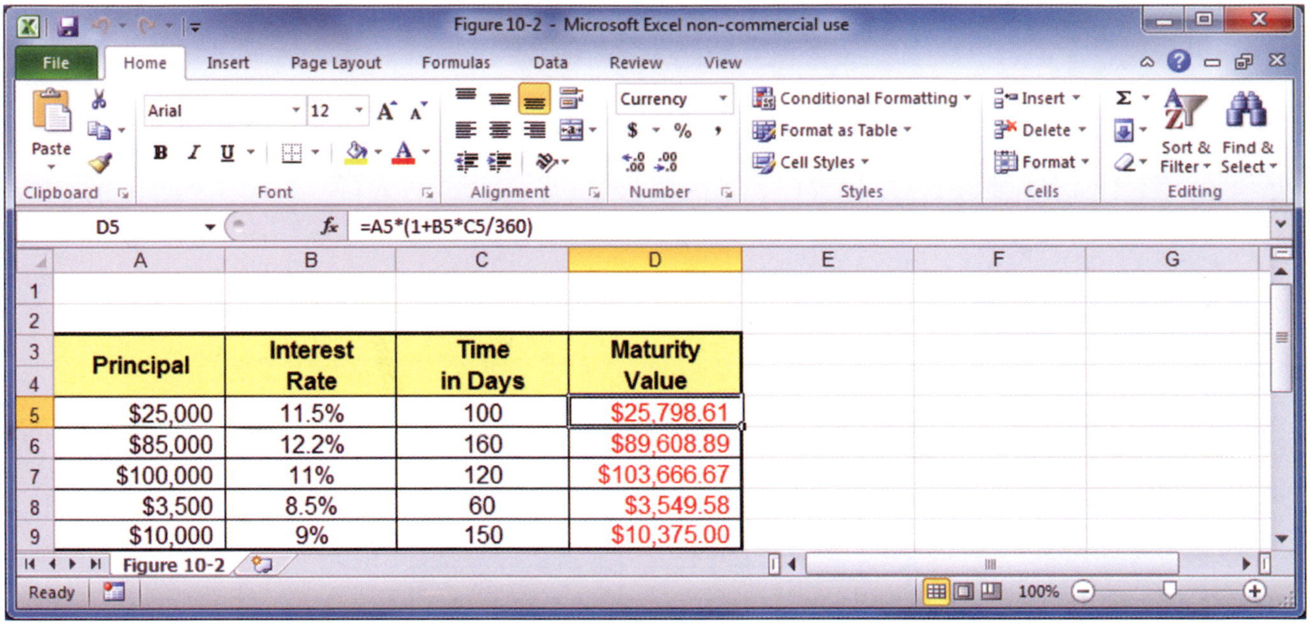

STEPS

⊗ Retrieve the file *ch10pr02.xlsx*.

1. In Cell D5, enter the formula =A5*(1+B5*C5/360) to compute Maturity Value. Copy the formula for each loan.

2. Format answers for Currency, 2 Decimal places, and $.

3. Save the file as *ch10pr02a.xlsx*.

Figure 10-3

Excel Formula to Calculate Number of Interest Days

Number of Interest Days

To calculate interest days, use the formula shown in Figure 10-3.

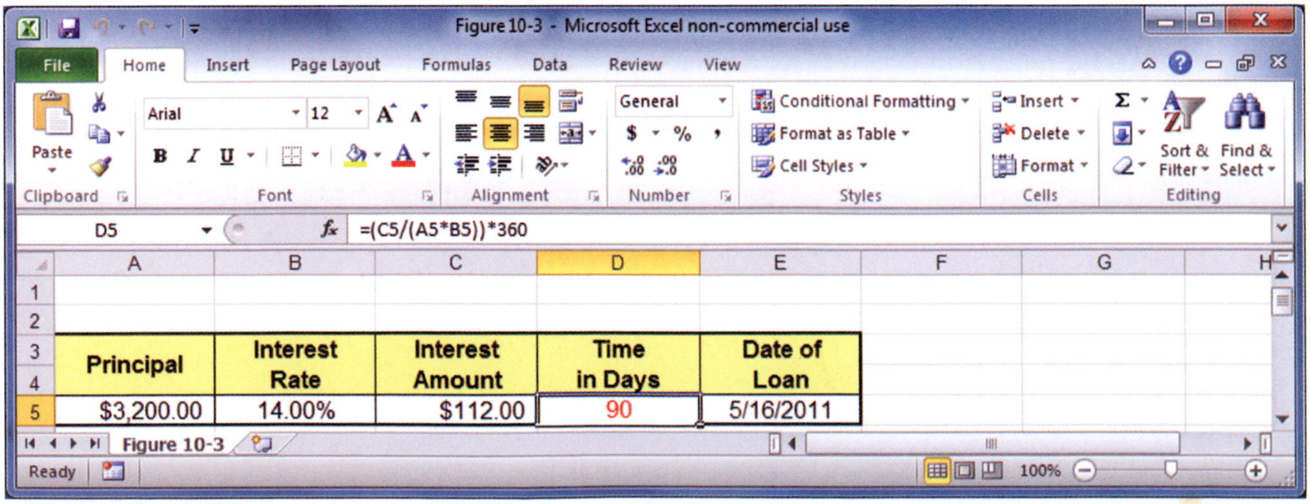

Figure 10-3 - Microsoft Excel non-commercial use

D5 fx =(C5/(A5*B5))*360

	Principal	Interest Rate	Interest Amount	Time in Days	Date of Loan
5	$3,200.00	14.00%	$112.00	90	5/16/2011

EXAMPLE

For his home business, Miguel borrowed $3,200 to purchase additional products. The interest rate was 14% using the ordinary interest method, and the interest was $112. Calculate the number of interest days.

The formula used to calculate the number of interest days is:

$$T = \frac{I}{P \times R} = \frac{\$112}{\$3,200 \times 0.14} = \frac{\$112}{\$448} = 0.25 \text{ year}$$

$$0.25 \text{ year} \times 360 \text{ days} = 90 \text{ days}$$

STEPS

Retrieve the file *ch10pr03.xlsx*.

1. In Cell D5, enter the formula =(C5/(A5*B5))*360 to compute the Time in Days.

2. Save the file as *ch10pr03a.xlsx*.

Maturity Date

Figure 10-4 shows the formula to compute the maturity date. The maturity date is computed by adding the loan date in Cell E5 to the number of interest days, which has already been calculated in Cell D5.

Figure 10-4

Maturity Date Computed by Adding Loan Date to Number of Interest Days

	Principal	Interest Rate	Interest Amount	Time in Days	Date of Loan	Maturity Date
5	$3,200.00	14.00%	$112.00	90	5/16/2011	8/14/2011

fx =E5+D5

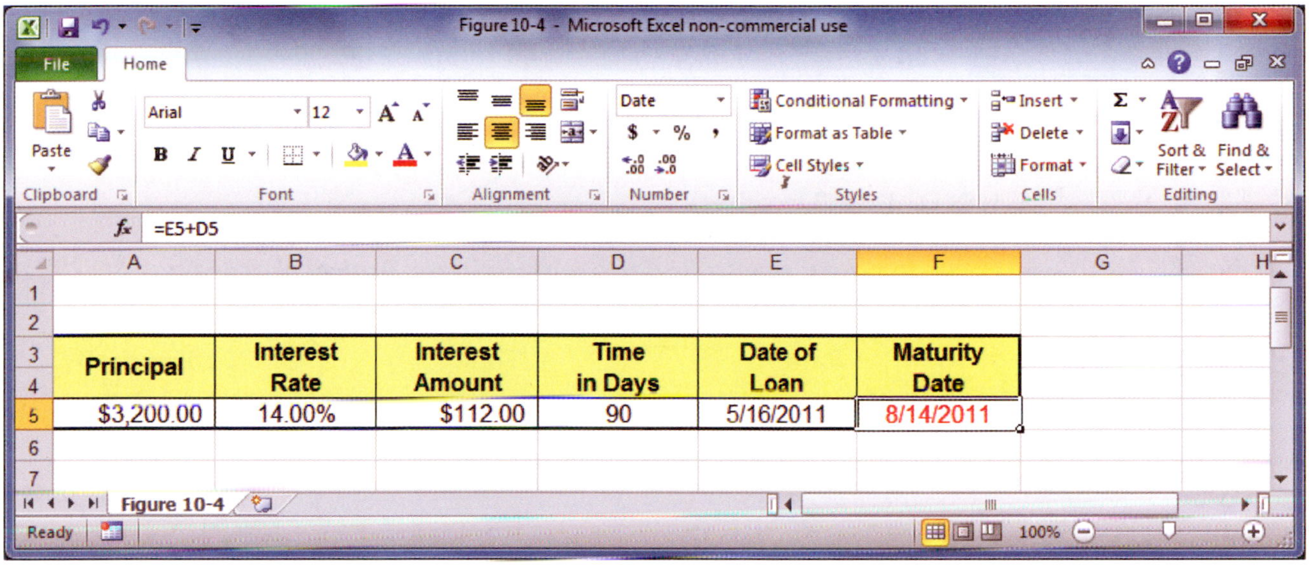

EXAMPLE

Miguel's borrowed $3,200 to purchase additional products. The interest rate was 14% using the ordinary interest method, and the interest was $112. There are 90 interest days. Determine the maturity date.

STEPS

Retrieve the file *ch10pr04.xls*.

1. In Cell F5, enter the formula =E5+D5 to compute the Maturity Date.

2. Format Cell F5 for Date x/xx/xxxx.

3. Save the file as *ch10pr04a.xls*.

Name _____   Date _____

Directions Solve the following problems. Write your answers in the blanks provided. Place commas and dollar signs in answers as needed. Round answers to the nearest hundredth. Use a 360-day year, unless otherwise noted.

A. Calculate simple interest. OBJECTIVE 2

	Principal	Rate	Time	Interest
1.	$1,800	13%	3 years	_____
2.	$5,600	8%	6 months	_____

B. Compute the amount of exact simple interest and the amount of ordinary interest for the following loans. OBJECTIVES 3, 4

Principal	Rate	Time		Exact Interest		Ordinary Interest
$5,000	8%	100 days	3.	_____	4.	_____
$14,450	10%	150 days	5.	_____	6.	_____

C. Calculate ordinary simple interest and the maturity value. OBJECTIVES 3, 6

Principal	Rate	Time		Ordinary Interest		Maturity Value
$7,000	8%	120 days	7.	_____	8.	_____
$1,750	16%	3 m onths	9.	_____	10.	_____

D. Use the ordinary simple interest year to find the missing part. Round percents to the nearest tenth and dollar amounts to the nearest hundredth. OBJECTIVE 7

	Interest	Rate	Time	Principal
11.	$22.50	9%	60 days	_____
12.	$220	_____	120 days	$5,000

E. Calculate the due date. OBJECTIVE 8
(Assume no leap years.)

F. Calculate the number of days. OBJECTIVE 8
(Assume no leap years.)

	Maturity Due Date			Number of Days	
December 15 (90-day)	13.	_____	Jan. 10–Apr. 10	14.	_____
May 16 (120-day)	15.	_____	May 8–Sept. 15	16.	_____

G. Use Excel to calculate interest, maturity value, and due date.

17. Retrieve the file *ch10ex01.xlsx*. Follow the directions. Save the file as *ch10ex01a.xlsx*.

18. Retrieve the file *ch10ex02.xlsx*. Follow the directions. Save the file as *ch10ex02a.xlsx*.

10.2 Promissory Notes and Discounting

OBJECTIVES

1. Identify terms used with promissory notes.
2. Discount notes.
3. Use Excel to discount a note.

OBJECTIVE 1 Identify terms used with promissory notes.

When you borrow money from a financial organization, friend, or family member, you sign a document called a **promissory note** (often called a note), which is a written promise to repay a loan or debt under specific terms. The borrower agrees (1) to pay a specific amount of money at specific times, (2) by a specific date, and (3) to a specific individual or business. The terms of the note may include the deduction of interest from the amount borrowed, which is called a **discount note**.

If a promissory note states an interest rate, the note is called an **interest-bearing note**. In some cases, however, a note may not specify an interest rate, which means it is a **non-interest-bearing note**. In other cases, the interest is collected in advance and is referred to as a **bank discount** to distinguish it from interest paid at maturity. For instance, if a person signs a promissory note for a $2,000 bank loan for 60 days, the bank may discount the note. The person would receive $1,960, which is the face value less the discount. The maturity value would be $2,000 in 60 days, which is what the borrower would repay. The interest ($40) is the same as what would be paid for $2,000 at 12% for 60 days, but the borrower has use of only $1,960 for the 60 days, not $2,000. The amount the borrower receives (maturity value less the bank discount) is called the **proceeds** or loan amount.

A simplified promissory note is illustrated in Figure 10-5. Study the major parts of this promissory note.

Figure 10-5
Promissory Note

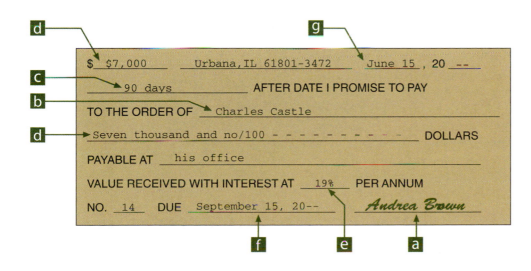

a. The *borrower* or **maker** is the person or business borrowing the money.
b. The *lender* or **payee** is the person or business who lent the money and who will receive the repayment.
c. The *time* or **term** of the note may be expressed as a specific date, in days, or in months.
d. The **face value** or **principal** is the dollar amount, which may be written in word or number form or both.
e. The interest **rate** per year is expressed as a percent of the face value.
f. The **maturity date** or *due date* is the date the loan is to be repaid.
g. The **date** is the date the note is issued.

Due dates on promissory notes are calculated in the same way as due dates on loans. Here are some general procedures to follow.

- When the note is expressed in terms of days, such as a 60-day note, determine the due date by using the exact number of days in the month.
- When the time is expressed in months, such as a 3-month note dated July 15, determine the due date by counting months. The 3-month note dated July 15 is due on October 15. If, however, a 3-month note is dated January 31, the due date is April 30 because April has only 30 days.

OBJECTIVE **2** Discount notes.

A promissory note is a negotiable instrument. Suppose you own a construction business, and, rather than pay for goods received, you sign a note to George Marsch agreeing to pay for the goods at a later time. Mr. Marsch finds that he is running short of cash before you are due to pay him. Rather than request that you pay off the note early, he decides to take the note to his bank to cash the note so he can obtain extra cash for his business. The bank approves Mr. Marsch's request and agrees to give him cash. This procedure is called **discounting commercial paper**. For this privilege, the bank discounts the note, which means that the bank charges a fee based on the maturity value of the note.

kycstudio/iStockphoto.com

To understand bank discounting, you need to learn the following terms. **Maturity date** is when the note is due. **Discount date** is the date the bank discounts the note. **Term** is the period of time from the discount date to the maturity date. **Discount rate** is the percent rate the bank charges against the maturity value. The **discount** is the dollar amount of the bank discount. The actual amount of money received after the discount amount has been subtracted from the maturity value is called the **proceeds**, just as for a non-interest-bearing note.

The concept of calculating simple interest ($I = P \times R \times T$) is applied to calculating maturity value and bank discount interest. The formula for figuring a bank discount is:

$$B = M \times D \times T$$

where

B = Bank discount
M = Maturity value
D = Discount rate
T = Time (in years)

To determine the proceeds, calculate the interest and maturity value. Next, calculate the bank discount. Then figure the proceeds.

EXAMPLE

You have signed a promissory note for $4,000 at 12%. The note is due in 4 months. It is payable to Mr. Marsch. The bank discounts the note for Mr. Marsch at 16%, two months before maturity of the note. Calculate the interest, maturity value, bank discount, and proceeds.

STEPS

1. Calculate the interest.

$$I = P \times R \times T$$
$$I = \$4{,}000 \times 0.12 \times \tfrac{4}{12}$$
$$I = \$160 \qquad \text{interest}$$

2. Calculate the maturity value.

$$M = P + I$$
$$M = \$4{,}000 + \$160$$
$$M = \$4{,}160 \qquad \text{maturity value}$$

3. Calculate the bank discount using the maturity value.

$$B = M \times D \times T$$
$$B = \$4{,}160 \times 0.16 \times \tfrac{2}{12}$$
$$B = \$110.93 \qquad \text{bank discount}$$

4. Calculate the proceeds.

$$P = M - B$$
$$P = \$4{,}160.00 - \$110.93$$
$$P = \$4{,}049.07 \qquad \text{proceeds}$$

Mr. Marsch would receive $4,049.07 cash from the bank if he discounted your note. You would still be obligated to repay the $4,160, but to the bank, not to Mr. Marsch.

Sometimes a note is discounted to the bank when it has a number of days left before maturity. Study the following example.

EXAMPLE

Phillip Williams bought some materials from Wilson Manufacturing Company. Wilson Manufacturing holds a 90-day note dated August 9 with a face value of $2,620 and interest of 14%. The manufacturer is in need of extra cash and decides to sell the note to the bank on September 19 to obtain cash. The bank's discount rate is 12%. Determine the maturity value, term of discount period, bank discount, and proceeds.

STEPS

1. Calculate the interest.

$$I = P \times R \times T$$
$$I = \$2,620.00 \times 14\% \times \frac{90}{360}$$
$$I = \$91.70 \qquad \text{interest}$$

2. Calculate the maturity value.

$$M = P + I$$
$$M = \$2,620.00 + \$91.70$$
$$M = \$2,711.70 \qquad \text{maturity value}$$

3. Find the term of discount period.

a. Determine the original due date.

$$\text{August 9 to November 7} = \text{90-day note}$$

b. Calculate the term of the discount period.

$$\text{September 19 (discount date) to November 7} =$$
$$11 + 31 + 7 = 49 \text{ days}$$

4. Calculate the bank discount.

$$B = M \times D \times T$$
$$B = \$2,711.70 \times 0.12 \times \frac{49}{360}$$
$$B = \$44.29 \qquad \text{bank discount}$$

5. Calculate the proceeds.

$$P = M - B$$
$$P = \$2,711.70 - \$44.29$$
$$P = \$2,667.41 \qquad \text{proceeds}$$

As a result of the bank discounting the note, Wilson Manufacturing will receive $2,667.41. The bank will receive $2,711.70 from the payee, Phillip Williams.

OBJECTIVE 3 Use Excel to discount a note.

Figure 10-6 shows the bank discount and proceeds based on the maturity value and the days remaining on a note. The formula in the Formula Bar, calculates the maturity value, which is the first step taken to discount a note.

CHAPTER 10 INTEREST

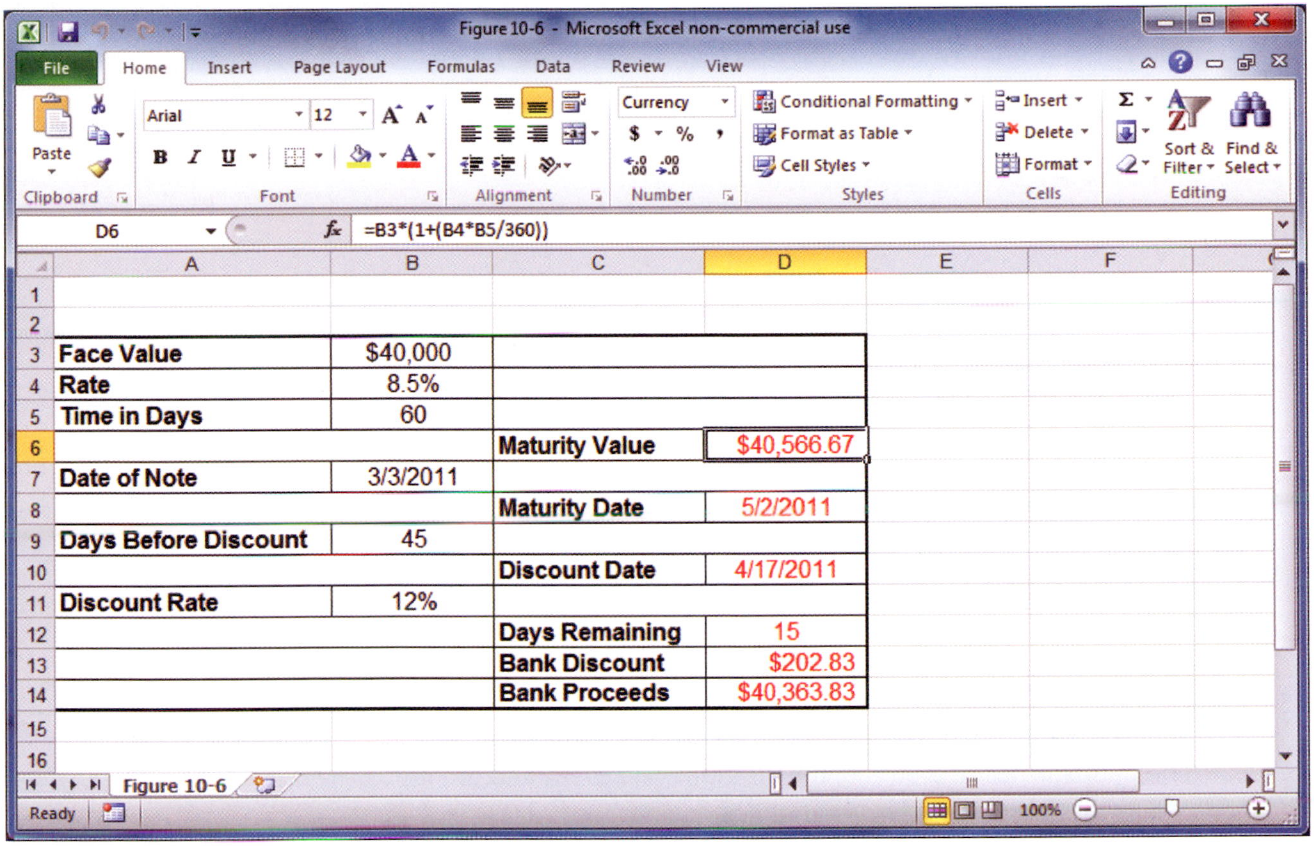

	A	B	C	D
1				
2				
3	Face Value	$40,000		
4	Rate	8.5%		
5	Time in Days	60		
6			Maturity Value	$40,566.67
7	Date of Note	3/3/2011		
8			Maturity Date	5/2/2011
9	Days Before Discount	45		
10			Discount Date	4/17/2011
11	Discount Rate	12%		
12			Days Remaining	15
13			Bank Discount	$202.83
14			Bank Proceeds	$40,363.83

Figure 10-6
Bank Discount and Proceeds

EXAMPLE

Ngoc Truong signed a promissory note on March 3 for $40,000 at 8.5% ordinary interest due in 60 days that was payable to William Hambergen. Forty-five days later, Mr. Hambergen asked his bank to discount the note at a rate of 12%.

STEPS

Retrieve the file ***ch10pr05.xlsx***.

1. In Cell D6, enter the formula to calculate the Maturity Value. The formula is =B3*(1+(B4*B5/360)).
2. In Cell D8, enter the formula to compute the Maturity Date. The formula is =B7+B5.
3. In Cell D10, enter the formula to compute the Discount Date. The formula is =B7+B9.
4. In Cell D12, enter the formula to calculate the Days Remaining. The formula is =B5-B9.
5. In Cell D13, enter the formula to compute the Bank Discount. The formula is =D6*(B11*D12/360).
6. In Cell D14, enter the formula to compute the Bank Proceeds. The formula is =D6-D13.
7. Format dollar amounts for Currency, 2 Decimal places, and $. Format the date entries for Date x/xx/xxxx.
8. Save the file as ***ch10pr05a.xlsx***.

Name _____   Date _____

Directions Solve the following problems. Write your answers in the blanks provided. Round answers to the nearest hundredth.

A. Complete the following statements. OBJECTIVE 1

1. Interest collected in advance on a promissory note is referred to as a(n) _____.

2. The _____ is called the dollar amount on a promissory note.

3. Discount rate is the percent rate the bank charges against the _____ value.

4. To calculate a bank _____, multiply maturity value by the discount percent rate by time.

5. To calculate _____, subtract bank discount from maturity value.

B. Find the bank discount for the following. OBJECTIVE 2

6. The maturity value is $7,195, the discount rate is 11.8%, and the time is 46 days. _____

7. The maturity value is $25,150, the discount rate is 12%, and the time is 65 days. _____

8. The maturity value is $6,770, the discount rate is 9%, and the time is 30 days. _____

C. Find the bank discount and proceeds for these notes. The bank discounted OBJECTIVE 2
these notes at 13% three months before the maturity of the note.

Face Value	Interest Rate	Due	Bank Discount		Proceeds
$2,500	12%	4 months	9. _____	10. _____	
$12,300	13%	3 months	11. _____	12. _____	
$15,700	12%	6 months	13. _____	14. _____	
$15,700	10%	7 months	15. _____	16. _____	

D. Find the due date, interest amount, and maturity value for each of these OBJECTIVE 2
interest-bearing notes. Use the 360-day method.

Face Value	Rate	Date	Time	Due Date	Interest Amount	Maturity Value
$1,550	14%	July 7	90 days	17. _____	18. _____	19. _____
$2,275	12%	Sept. 8	6 months	20. _____	21. _____	22. _____

E. Find the bank discount and proceeds for these notes. Assume that the notes were discounted on June 10 at a 15% discount rate. Use the 360-day method.

OBJECTIVE 2

Face Value	Time	Date	Rate	Bank Discount		Proceeds	
$5,200	90 days	May 10	15%	23. _____		24. _____	
$12,450	120 days	May 20	14%	25. _____		26. _____	
$2,300	60 days	May 12	14%	27. _____		28. _____	
$2,500	90 days	May 10	15%	29. _____		30. _____	

F. Calculate the exact number of days from initial date of note to date interest is due.

OBJECTIVE 2

	Date of Note	Interest Due	Number of Days
31.	May 12	August 27	_____
32.	May 2	August 3	_____
33.	October 12	January 30	_____

G. Find the bank discount and proceeds for these notes. Assume that these notes were discounted on September 11 at a 15% discount rate. Use the 360-day method.

OBJECTIVE 2

Face Value	Time	Date	Rate	Bank Discount		Proceeds	
$3,400	60 days	August 2	15%	34. _____		35. _____	
$25,000	90 days	August 11	14%	36. _____		37. _____	
$8,650	120 days	August 6	15%	38. _____		39. _____	

H. Solve the following word problems. Round to the nearest percent.

OBJECTIVE 2

40. The face value of a note is $12,200, the interest rate is 12%, and the time is based on 120 days (360-day year). The note has been discounted at 15% two months before the maturity of the note. How much were the discount and the proceeds?

   a. Discount _____   b. Proceeds _____

41. Find the time on a principal of $3,600 at 9% and interest earned of $58.50. _____

42. Find the rate on a principal of $2,000 for 90 days with $59.75 interest earned. _____

I. Use Excel to discount notes.

OBJECTIVE 3

43. Retrieve the file *ch10ex03.xlsx*. Follow the directions. Save the file as *ch10ex03a.xlsx*.

44. Retrieve the file *ch10ex04.xlsx*. Follow the directions. Save the file as *ch10ex04a.xlsx*.

10.3 Compound Interest

OBJECTIVE 1 Identify terms used for compounding interest.

For short-term loans, interest may be computed by using simple interest. When interest on a loan or investment is calculated and the interest is added to the principal to make a new principal on which you calculate interest for the next period, you are *compounding interest*. Compound interest results in a higher amount than simple interest because interest is paid on the interest you have earned. Compound interest most often applies to savings accounts, loans, and credit cards.

Compound interest is interest calculated on reinvested interest as well as on the original principal. The **compound amount** (or new principal) is the sum of the original principal and its compound interest. The *interest period* is the time (daily, monthly, quar-

sosb/iStockphoto.com

terly, semiannually, or annually) for which interest has been computed. The **present value** of a future compound amount is the principal invested at a given rate today that will grow to the compound amount at a later date.

OBJECTIVE 2 Calculate compound interest.

Financial institutions consider primarily four variables when calculating interest to be paid on deposits. The four variables are:

1. the amount of money on deposit (the balance)
2. the interest rate applied (sometimes called *stated* rate of interest
3. the method of determining the balance
4. the frequency of compounding (annually semiannually, quarterly, weekly, or daily)

For example, assume the original principal is $1,000, the annual interest rate is 5.25%, and the compounding is annual. Determine the compound amount (principal) at the end of two years.

$1,000 × 0.0525 = $52.50	interest, 1st year
$1,000 + $52.50 = $1,052.50	principal, end of 1st year
$1,052.50 × 0.0525 = $55.26	interest, 2nd year
$1,052.50 + $55.26 = $1,107.76	principal, end of 2nd year

When compounding is quarterly (every three months), you receive a higher return on your money. The table on the next page shows a comparison of quarterly and annual compounding for a $1,000 deposit with a 6% annual interest rate. Determine the quarterly interest rate by dividing the annual interest rate by 4.

$$0.06 \div 4 = 0.015 \qquad \text{quarterly interest rate}$$

Table 10-2

Comparison of Quarterly and Annually Compounded Interest

INTEREST: COMPOUNDED QUARTERLY and ANNUALLY			
Deposit = $1,000.00	Interest rate = 6% per year, 1.5% per quarter		
Quarterly: (1st year)		**Annually: (1st year)**	
$1,000.00	$1,000 × 0.015 = $15.00	$1,000.00	$1,000 × 0.06 = $60.00
+ 15.00	1st quarter interest	+ 60.00	1st year interest
$1,015.00	$1,015.00 × 0.015 = $15.23	$1,060.00	
+ 15.23	2nd quarter interest		
$1,030.23			
+ 15.45	3rd quarter interest		
$1,045.68			
+ 15.69	4th quarter interest	$1,000 earns $60.00 at the end of the 1st year.	
$1,061.37	$1,000 earns $61.37 at the end of the 1st year.		
Quarterly: (2nd year)		**Annually: (2nd year)**	
$1,061.37		$1,060.00	
+ 15.92	5th quarter interest	+ 63.60	2nd year interest
$1,077.29		$1,123.60	
+ 16.16	6th quarter interest		
$1,093.45			
+ 16.40	7th quarter interest		
$1,109.85			
+ 16.65	8th quarter interest	$1,060 earns $63.60 at the end of the 2nd year.	
$1,126.50	$1,061.37 earns $65.13 at the end of the 2nd year.		

If the amount is left on deposit for a second year, then the interest would be worth $65.13 as shown in the table above. In comparing the two methods of compounding, note the following:

- More interest is earned on deposited funds when compounding is used.
- The more frequent the compounding, the greater the return.
- The greatest benefit or value of compounding is realized over longer time periods since greater differences will occur.

Because computers manipulate numbers quickly and reliably, they have had a tremendous impact on the financial field. Most financial analysis and calculations are performed by computers.

The following example summarizes the steps to determine compound interest.

EXAMPLE

The original principal is $2,200 at 12% compounded annually for 2 years. Determine the compound amount and interest at the end of 2 years.

STEPS

1. Calculate interest at the end of the first period (year).

$$I = \$2{,}200 \times 0.12$$
$$I = \$264 \qquad \text{interest, 1st year}$$

2. Add the principal and interest to obtain the new amount on which to base the next period's (year's) interest.

$$\$2{,}200 + \$264 = \$2{,}464 \qquad \text{compound amount, 1st year}$$

3. Calculate the interest at the end of the second period (year).

$$I = \$2{,}464 \times 0.12$$
$$I = \$295.68 \qquad \text{interest, 2nd year}$$

4. Add the interest to the compound amount to obtain the amount at the end of the second period (year).

$$\$2{,}464 + \$295.68 = \$2{,}759.68 \qquad \text{compound amount, 2nd year}$$

5. Subtract the original principal from the last compound amount to find the total compound interest.

$$\text{Compound Interest} = \text{Compound Amount} - \text{Original Principal}$$
$$= \$2{,}759.68 - \$2{,}200$$
$$= \$559.68 \qquad \text{total compound interest}$$

The following summarizes the calculations made in the preceding steps.

$2,200.00	original principal
+ 264.00	1st year's interest, $2,200 × 0.12
$2,464.00	1st year's compound amount
+ 295.68	2nd year's interest, $2,464 × 0.12
$2,759.68	2nd year's compound amount
− 2,200.00	original principal
$ 559.68	total compound interest

If interest is compounded more frequently than once a year, then the interest rate must be changed proportionately to the number of compound periods in the year. For example, if the annual interest rate is 12% and interest is compounded semiannually, interest will be calculated twice a year at a rate of 6%, one-half the annual interest rate.

stevecoleccs/iStockphoto.com

Interest may be compounded more often than once a year. For instance, financial institutions compound interest daily, monthly, quarterly, or semiannually. You must convert the annual interest rate to the interest per compound period. To do so, divide the interest rate by the number of compounding periods per year.

Annual Rate	Time	Interest Compounded	Interest Rate	Number of Periods
10%	2 years	semiannually	10% ÷ 2 = 5%	2 years × twice a year = 4
12%	4 years	quarterly	12% ÷ 4 = 3%	4 years × 4 quarters = 16

EXAMPLE

Calculate the compound amount and interest at the end of 2 years when interest is compounded semiannually.

Principal	$5,000
Interest Rate	10% per year
Time	2 years

STEPS

1. Divide the annual interest rate by 2 compound periods to obtain the semiannual interest rate.

$$10\% \div 2 = 5\%$$

2. Calculate the compound amount and interest.

$5,000.00	original principal
+ 250.00	interest 1st period, $5,000 × 0.05
$5,250.00	
+ 262.50	interest 2nd period, $5,250 × 0.05
$5,512.50	
+ 275.63	interest 3rd period, $5,512.50 × 0.05
$5,788.13	
+ 289.41	interest 4th period, $5,788.13 × 0.05
$6,077.54	compound amount at end of 2 years
− 5,000.00	original principal
$1,077.54	total compound interest

TIPS

When interest is compounded semiannually, use one-half the yearly interest rate and twice the number of compound periods.

To compound interest quarterly, you must know the number of compound periods for each year and the interest rate for each period. There are four compound periods for each year, and the interest rate for each period is one-fourth of the yearly rate.

EXAMPLE

Calculate the compound amount and interest at the end of 2 years when interest is compounded quarterly.

Principal	$5,000
Interest Rate	10% per year
Time	2 years

STEPS

1. Divide the annual interest rate by 4 compound periods to obtain the quarterly interest rate.

$$10\% \div 4 = 2.5\% \text{ or } 0.025$$

2. Calculate the compound amount and interest.

$5,000.00	original principal
+ 125.00	interest 1st period
$5,125.00	
+ 128.13	interest 2nd period
$5,253.13	
+ 131.33	interest 3rd period
$5,384.46	
+ 134.61	interest 4th period
$5,519.07	
+ 137.98	interest 5th period
$5,657.05	
+ 141.43	interest 6th period
$5,798.48	
+ 144.96	interest 7th period
$5,943.44	
+ 148.59	interest 8th period
$6,092.03	
− 5,000.00	principal
$1,092.03	total compound interest

By comparing the last two examples, you can see that the more frequently interest is compounded, the greater the amount of interest earned.

OBJECTIVE 5 Use Excel to calculate compound amount and compound interest.

You can use Excel to compute compound interest as shown in Figure 10-7.

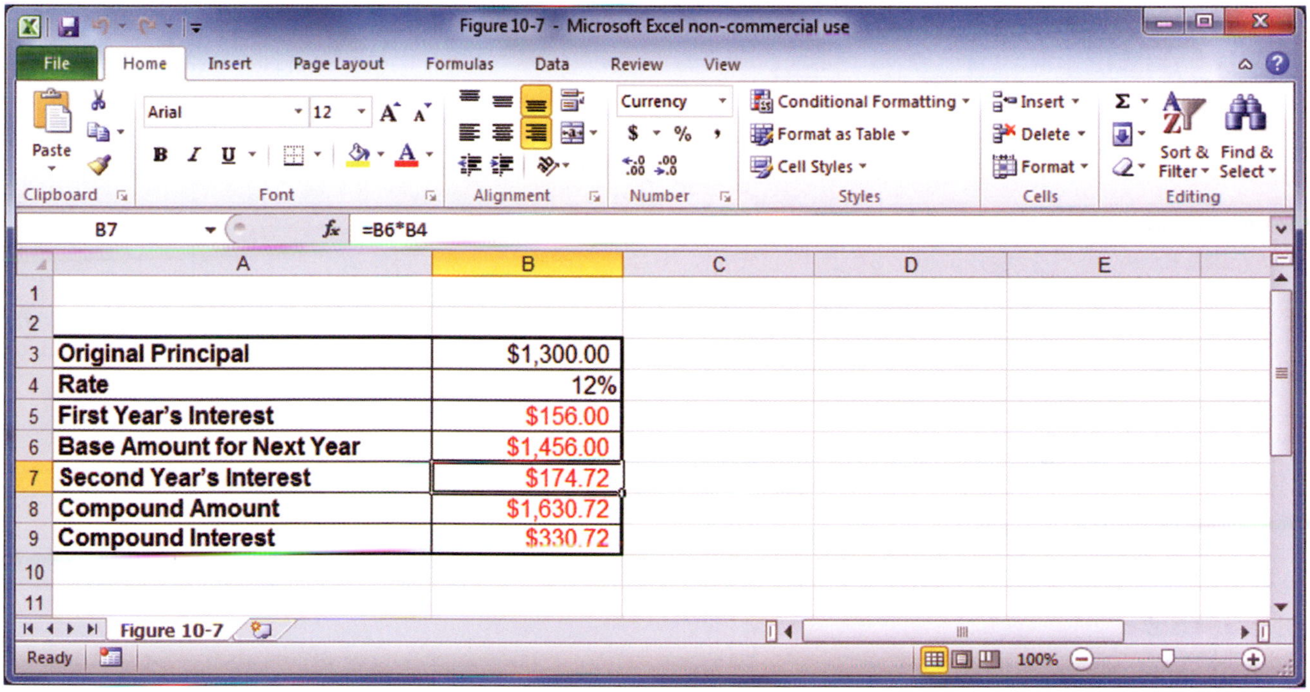

Figure 10-7
Interest for First Year and Second Year

EXAMPLE

The original principal was $1,300 at 12% compounded annually for 2 years. Calculate the first year's interest.

STEPS

Retrieve the file *ch10pr06.xlsx*.

1. In Cell B5, enter the formula =B3*B4 to calculate the interest for the first year.
2. In Cell B6, enter the formula =SUM(B3,B5) to calculate the amount that will be used as the base for the next year's interest. [Click AutoSum and click on Cell B3. Key , (comma) and click on Cell B5. Press Enter.]
3. In Cell B7, enter the formula =B6*B4 to calculate the interest for the second year.
4. In Cell B8, enter the formula =SUM(B6,B7) to compute the Compound Amount.
5. In Cell B9, enter the formula =B8-B3 to compute the Compound Interest.
6. Format dollar amounts for Currency, 2 Decimal places, and $.
7. Save the file as *ch10pr06a.xlsx*.

Figure 10-8 shows the compound amount and the compound interest in Cells E11 and E12, respectively.

		First Quarter	Second Quarter	Third Quarter	Fourth Quarter
5	Base Amount	$4,500.00	$4,646.25	$4,797.25	$4,953.16
6	Yearly Rate	13%	13%	13%	13%
7	Compound Periods	4	4	4	4
8	Quarterly Interest Rate	0.0325	0.0325	0.0325	0.0325
9	Quarterly Interest Amount	$146.25	$151.00	$155.91	$160.98
10	Quarterly Compound Amount	$4,646.25	$4,797.25	$4,953.16	$5,114.14
11				Compound Amount =	$5,114.14
12				Compound Interest =	$614.14

Figure 10-8

Compound Amount and Compound Interest

EXAMPLE

The original principal of $4,500 is to be compounded quarterly for 1 year at 13%. Determine the compound interest.

STEPS

Retrieve the file *ch10pr07.xlsx*.

1. In Cell B8, enter the formula =B6/B7 to compute the Quarterly Interest Rate. Copy the formula into Cells C8 through E8.

2. In Cell B9, enter the formula =B5*B8 to calculate the Quarterly Interest Amount.

3. In Cell B10, enter the formula =SUM(B5,B9) to calculate the Quarterly Compound Amount.

4. In Cell C5, key the Quarterly Compound Amount shown in cell B10.

5. Copy the formula in Cell B9 into Cell C9.

6. Copy the formula in Cell B10 into Cell C10.

7. In Cell D5, key the Quarterly Compound Amount shown in Cell C10.

8. Continue to complete the Third and Fourth Quarter amounts.

9. In Cell E11, key the amount shown in Cell E10.

10. In Cell E12, enter =E11-B5 to calculate the Compound Interest.

11. Format dollar amounts for Currency, 2 Decimal places, and $.

12. Save the file as *ch10pr07a.xlsx*.

Table 10-3 Compound Interest

n	0.5%	1%	1.5%	2%	3%	4%	5%	6%	7%	8%	9%	10%	11%	12%
1	1.00500000	1.01000000	1.01500000	1.02000000	1.03000000	1.04000000	1.05000000	1.06000000	1.07000000	1.08000000	1.09000000	1.10000000	1.11000000	1.12000000
2	1.01002500	1.02010000	1.03022500	1.04040000	1.06090000	1.08160000	1.10250000	1.12360000	1.14490000	1.16640000	1.18810000	1.21000000	1.23210000	1.25440000
3	1.01507513	1.03030100	1.04567837	1.06120800	1.09272700	1.12486400	1.15762500	1.19101600	1.22504300	1.25971200	1.29502900	1.33100000	1.36763100	1.40492800
4	1.02015050	1.04060401	1.06136355	1.08243216	1.12550881	1.16985856	1.21550625	1.26247696	1.31079601	1.36048896	1.41158161	1.46410000	1.51807041	1.57351936
5	1.02525125	1.05101005	1.07728400	1.10408080	1.15927407	1.21665290	1.27628156	1.33822558	1.40255173	1.46932808	1.53862395	1.61051000	1.68505816	1.76234168
6	1.03037751	1.06152015	1.09344326	1.12616242	1.19405230	1.26531902	1.34009564	1.41851911	1.50073035	1.58687432	1.67710011	1.77156100	1.87041455	1.97382269
7	1.03552940	1.07213535	1.10984491	1.14868567	1.22987387	1.31593178	1.40710042	1.50363026	1.60578148	1.71382427	1.82803912	1.94871710	2.07616015	2.21068141
8	1.04070704	1.08285671	1.12649259	1.17165938	1.26677008	1.36856905	1.47745544	1.59384807	1.71818618	1.85093021	1.99256264	2.14358881	2.30453777	2.47596318
9	1.04591058	1.09368527	1.14338998	1.19509257	1.30477318	1.42331181	1.55132822	1.68847896	1.83845921	1.99900463	2.17189328	2.35794769	2.55803692	2.77307876
10	1.05114013	1.10462213	1.16054083	1.21899442	1.34391638	1.48024428	1.62889463	1.79084770	1.96715136	2.15892500	2.36736367	2.59374246	2.83942099	3.10584821
11	1.05639583	1.11566835	1.17794894	1.24337431	1.38423387	1.53945406	1.71033936	1.89829856	2.10485195	2.33163900	2.58042641	2.85311671	3.15175729	3.47854999
12	1.06167781	1.12682503	1.19561817	1.26824179	1.42576089	1.60103222	1.79585633	2.01219647	2.25219159	2.51817012	2.81266478	3.13842838	3.49845060	3.89597599
13	1.06698620	1.13809328	1.21355244	1.29360663	1.46853371	1.66507351	1.88564914	2.13292826	2.40984500	2.71962373	3.06580461	3.45227121	3.88328016	4.36349311
14	1.07232113	1.14947421	1.23175573	1.31947876	1.51258972	1.73167645	1.97993160	2.26090396	2.57853415	2.93719362	3.34172703	3.79749834	4.31044098	4.88711229
15	1.07768274	1.16096896	1.25023207	1.34586834	1.55796742	1.80094351	2.07892818	2.39655819	2.75903154	3.17216911	3.64248246	4.17724817	4.78458949	5.47356576
16	1.08307115	1.17257864	1.26898555	1.37278571	1.60470644	1.87298125	2.18287459	2.54035168	2.95216375	3.42594264	3.97030588	4.59497299	5.31089433	6.13039365
17	1.08848651	1.18430443	1.28802033	1.40024142	1.65284763	1.94790050	2.29201832	2.69277279	3.15881521	3.70001805	4.32763341	5.05447028	5.89509271	6.86604089
18	1.09392894	1.19614748	1.30734064	1.42824625	1.70243306	2.02581652	2.40661923	2.85433915	3.37993227	3.99601950	4.71712042	5.55991731	6.54355291	7.68996580
19	1.09939858	1.20810895	1.32695075	1.45681117	1.75350605	2.10684918	2.52695020	3.02559950	3.61652754	4.31570106	5.14166125	6.11590904	7.26334373	8.61276169
20	1.10489558	1.22019004	1.34685501	1.48594740	1.80611123	2.19112314	2.65329771	3.20713547	3.86968446	4.66095714	5.60441077	6.72749995	8.06231154	9.64629309
21	1.11042006	1.23239194	1.36705783	1.51566634	1.86029457	2.27876807	2.78596259	3.39956360	4.14056237	5.03383372	6.10880774	7.40024994	8.94916581	10.80384826
22	1.11597216	1.24471586	1.38756370	1.54597967	1.91610341	2.36991879	2.92526072	3.60353742	4.43040174	5.43654041	6.65860043	8.14027494	9.93357404	12.10031006
23	1.12155202	1.25716302	1.40837715	1.57689926	1.97358651	2.46471554	3.07152376	3.81974966	4.74052986	5.87146365	7.25787447	8.95430243	11.02626719	13.55234726
24	1.12715978	1.26973465	1.42950281	1.60843725	2.03279411	2.56330416	3.22509994	4.04893464	5.07236695	6.34118074	7.91108317	9.84973268	12.23915658	15.17862893
25	1.13279558	1.28243200	1.45094535	1.64060599	2.09377793	2.66583633	3.38635494	4.29187072	5.42743264	6.84847520	8.62308066	10.83470594	13.58546380	17.00006441
26	1.13845955	1.29525631	1.47270953	1.67341811	2.15659127	2.77246978	3.55567269	4.54938296	5.80735292	7.39635321	9.39915792	11.91817654	15.07986482	19.04007214
27	1.14415185	1.30820888	1.49480018	1.70688648	2.22128901	2.88336858	3.73345632	4.82234594	6.21386763	7.98806147	10.24508213	13.10999419	16.73864995	21.32488079
28	1.14987261	1.32129097	1.51722218	1.74102421	2.28792768	2.99870332	3.92012914	5.11168670	6.64883836	8.62710639	11.16713952	14.42099361	18.57990145	23.88386649
29	1.15562197	1.33450388	1.53998051	1.77584469	2.35656551	3.11865145	4.11613560	5.41838790	7.11425705	9.31727490	12.17218208	15.86309297	20.62369061	26.74993047
30	1.16140008	1.34784892	1.56308022	1.81136158	2.42726247	3.24339751	4.32194238	5.74349117	7.61225504	10.06265689	13.26767847	17.44940227	22.89229657	29.95992212
31	1.16720708	1.36132740	1.58652642	1.84758882	2.50008035	3.37313341	4.53803949	6.08810064	8.14511290	10.86766944	14.46176953	19.19434250	25.41044919	33.55511278
32	1.17304312	1.37494068	1.61032432	1.88454059	2.57508276	3.50805875	4.76494147	6.45338668	8.71527080	11.73708300	15.76332879	21.11377675	28.20559861	37.58172631
33	1.17890833	1.38869009	1.63447918	1.92223140	2.65233524	3.64838110	5.00318854	6.84058988	9.32533975	12.67604964	17.18202838	23.22515442	31.30821445	42.09153347
34	1.18480288	1.40257699	1.65899657	1.96067603	2.73190530	3.79431634	5.25334797	7.25102528	9.97811354	13.69013481	18.72841093	25.54766986	34.75211804	47.14251748
35	1.19072689	1.41660276	1.68388132	1.99988955	2.81386245	3.94608899	5.51601537	7.68608679	10.67658148	14.78534429	20.41396792	28.10243685	38.57485103	52.79961958
36	1.19668052	1.43076878	1.70913954	2.03988734	2.89827832	4.10393255	5.79181614	8.14725280	11.42394218	15.96817184	22.25122503	30.91268053	42.81808464	59.13557393
37	1.20266393	1.44507647	1.73477663	2.08068509	2.98522667	4.26808986	6.08140694	8.63608712	12.22361814	17.24562558	24.25383528	34.00394859	47.52807395	66.23184280
38	1.20867725	1.45952724	1.76079828	2.12229879	3.07478347	4.43881345	6.38547729	9.15425235	13.07927141	18.62527563	26.43668046	37.40434344	52.75616209	74.17966394
39	1.21472063	1.47412251	1.78721025	2.16474477	3.16702697	4.61636599	6.70475115	9.70350749	13.99482041	20.11529768	28.81598170	41.14477779	58.55933991	83.08122361
40	1.22079424	1.48886373	1.81401841	2.20803966	3.26203778	4.80102063	7.03998871	10.28571794	14.97445784	21.72452150	31.40942005	45.25925557	65.00086731	93.05097044
41	1.22689821	1.50375237	1.84122868	2.25220046	3.35989891	4.99306145	7.39198815	10.90286101	16.02266989	23.46248322	34.23626786	49.78518113	72.15096271	104.21708689
42	1.23303270	1.51878989	1.86884712	2.29724447	3.46069588	5.19278391	7.76158756	11.55703267	17.14425678	25.33948187	37.31753197	54.76369924	80.08756861	116.72313732
43	1.23919786	1.53397779	1.89687982	2.34318936	3.56451676	5.40049527	8.14966693	12.25045463	18.34435475	27.36664042	40.67610984	60.24006917	88.89720115	130.72991380
44	1.24539385	1.54931757	1.92533302	2.39005314	3.67145226	5.61651508	8.55715028	12.98548191	19.62845958	29.55597166	44.33695973	66.26407608	98.67589328	146.41750346
45	1.25162082	1.56481075	1.95421301	2.43785421	3.78159583	5.84117568	8.98500779	13.76461083	21.00245175	31.92044939	48.32728610	72.89048369	109.53024154	163.98760387
46	1.25787892	1.58045885	1.98352621	2.48661129	3.89504370	6.07482271	9.43425818	14.59048748	22.47262338	34.47408534	52.67674185	80.17953206	121.57856811	183.66611634
47	1.26416832	1.59626344	2.01327910	2.53634352	4.01189501	6.31781562	9.90597109	15.46591573	24.04570702	37.23201217	57.41764862	88.19748527	134.95221060	205.70605030
48	1.27048916	1.61222608	2.04347829	2.58707039	4.13225186	6.57052824	10.40126965	16.39387173	25.72890651	40.21057314	62.58523700	97.01723379	149.79695377	230.39077633
49	1.27684161	1.62834834	2.07413046	2.63881179	4.25621942	6.83334937	10.92133313	17.37750403	27.52992997	43.42741899	68.21790833	106.71895717	166.27461868	258.03766949
50	1.28322581	1.64463182	2.10524242	2.69158803	4.38390600	7.10668335	11.46739979	18.42015427	29.45702506	46.90161251	74.35752008	117.39085289	184.56482674	289.00218983

Even with a calculator, computing compound interest is very time consuming, particularly when many compound periods are involved. Tables have been developed to help calculate compound interest, and today compound interest is figured using computers. Table 10-3 on the previous page shows $1 compounded at the rates of 0.5% through 12% for interest periods 1 to 50. Use Table 10-3 to complete the following example.

EXAMPLE

Determine the compound amount and interest.

Original Principal	$2,500
Interest Rate	6% compounded annually
Time	2 years

STEPS

1. Find the number of compound periods in the left column, labeled n (meaning number). Move down (vertically) to 2.

2. Read across the table horizontally to the proper interest rate column. Note the column headed 6%.

3. Where the two columns meet, the amount shown, 1.1236, is the compound value of $1 at 6% for 2 years. This means that $1.00 in 2 years compounded annually at 6% equals $1.1236.

4. Multiply the compound value of $1 by the original principal to determine the compound amount of the principal.

   $$1.1236 \times \$2{,}500 = \$2{,}809 \qquad \text{compound amount}$$

5. Subtract the original principal from the compound amount to determine the amount of compound interest.

   $$\begin{array}{r} \$2{,}809 \\ -2{,}500 \\ \hline \$\ \ \ 309 \end{array} \qquad \text{compound interest}$$

Using Compound Interest Tables for Periods Other Than Once a Year

You can also use the table to calculate interest compounded for periods other than once a year.

- To compound *daily*, interest is figured on a balance each day.
- To compound *quarterly*, interest is figured on a balance every 3 months, or every $\frac{1}{4}$ year.
- To compound *semiannually*, interest is figured on a balance every 6 months, or every $\frac{1}{2}$ year.
- To compound *annually*, interest is figured on a balance once a year.

The *rate* is the annual rate divided by the number of times the interest is compounded per year. For example, 8% compounded quarterly is 2%. The *pay period* is figured by multiplying the number of years by the number of times compounded per year.

EXAMPLE

Suppose you had a fund that was to be compounded quarterly for three years. The number of compounding periods is 3 years × 4 quarters, or 12. Determine the compound amount and interest.

Original Principal	$5,000
Interest	8% compounded quarterly
Time	3 years

STEPS

1. Multiply 3 years by 4 quarters. Then find 12 periods in the left column (*n*) of Table 10-3.

2. Take one-fourth of the interest rate (8% ÷ 4 = 2%) and move across the table to the 2% column. The amount, 1.26824179, is the value of $1 compounded quarterly for 3 years at 8%.

3. Multiply the original principal by the compound value found in the table to compute the compound amount.

   $5,000 × 1.26824179 = $6,341.21   compound amount

4. Subtract the original principal from the compound amount to determine the compound interest.

$$
\begin{array}{r}
\$6{,}341.21 \\
-\ 5{,}000.00 \\
\hline
\$1{,}341.21
\end{array}
$$
    compound interest

OBJECTIVE **7** **Calculate present value.**

The present value of a future compound amount is the principal invested at a given rate today that will grow to the compound amount at a later date. For instance, if you want to have a certain amount of money in the future to purchase a large piece of equipment for your business, you need to know how much money to deposit now so the additional interest earned will create the amount of money that you need to meet your goal.

A table showing the present value of $1 at different interest rates is commonly used. Table 10-4 on the next page shows the present value of $1 with compound interest rates from 0.5% to 12%. The amount shown in a present value table is used for multiplying the desired amount by the present value of $1.

Table 10-4 Present Value

n	0.5%	1%	1.5%	2%	3%	4%	5%	6%	7%	8%	9%	10%	11%	12%
1	0.99502488	0.99009901	0.98522167	0.98039216	0.97087379	0.96153846	0.95238095	0.94339623	0.93457944	0.92592593	0.91743119	0.90909091	0.90090090	0.89285714
2	0.99007450	0.98029605	0.97066175	0.96116878	0.94259591	0.92455621	0.90702948	0.88999644	0.87343873	0.85733882	0.84167999	0.82644628	0.81162243	0.79719388
3	0.98514876	0.97059015	0.95631699	0.94232233	0.91514166	0.88899636	0.86383760	0.83961928	0.81629788	0.79383224	0.77218348	0.75131480	0.73119138	0.71178025
4	0.98024752	0.96098034	0.94218423	0.92384543	0.88848705	0.85480419	0.82270247	0.79209366	0.76289521	0.73502985	0.70842521	0.68301346	0.65873097	0.63551808
5	0.97537067	0.95146569	0.92826033	0.90573081	0.86260878	0.82192711	0.78352617	0.74725817	0.71298618	0.68058320	0.64993139	0.62092132	0.59345133	0.56742686
6	0.97051808	0.94204524	0.91454219	0.88797138	0.83748426	0.79031453	0.74621540	0.70496054	0.66634222	0.63016963	0.59626733	0.56447393	0.53464084	0.50663112
7	0.96568963	0.93271805	0.90102679	0.87056018	0.81309151	0.75991781	0.71068133	0.66505711	0.62274974	0.58349040	0.54703424	0.51315812	0.48165841	0.45234922
8	0.96088520	0.92348322	0.88771112	0.85349037	0.78940923	0.73069021	0.67683936	0.62741237	0.58200910	0.54026888	0.50186628	0.46650738	0.43392650	0.40388323
9	0.95610468	0.91433982	0.87459224	0.83675527	0.76641673	0.70258674	0.64460892	0.59189846	0.54393374	0.50024897	0.46047778	0.42409762	0.39092427	0.36061002
10	0.95134794	0.90528695	0.86166723	0.82034830	0.74409391	0.67556417	0.61391325	0.55839478	0.50834929	0.46319349	0.42241081	0.38554329	0.35218448	0.32197324
11	0.94661487	0.89632372	0.84893323	0.80426304	0.72242128	0.64958093	0.58467929	0.52678753	0.47509280	0.42888286	0.38753286	0.35049390	0.31728331	0.28747610
12	0.94190534	0.88744923	0.83638742	0.78849318	0.70137988	0.62459705	0.55683742	0.49696906	0.44401196	0.39711376	0.35553473	0.31863082	0.28584082	0.25667509
13	0.93721924	0.87866260	0.82402702	0.77303253	0.68095134	0.60057409	0.53032135	0.46883902	0.41496445	0.36769792	0.32617865	0.28966438	0.25751426	0.22917419
14	0.93255646	0.86996297	0.81184928	0.75787502	0.66111781	0.57747508	0.50506795	0.44230096	0.38781724	0.34046104	0.29924647	0.26333125	0.23199482	0.20461981
15	0.92791688	0.86134947	0.79985150	0.74301473	0.64186195	0.55526450	0.48101710	0.41726506	0.36244602	0.31524170	0.27453804	0.23939205	0.20900435	0.18269626
16	0.92330037	0.85282126	0.78803104	0.72844581	0.62316694	0.53390818	0.45811152	0.39364628	0.33873460	0.29189047	0.25186976	0.21762914	0.18829220	0.16312166
17	0.91870684	0.84437749	0.77638526	0.71416256	0.60501645	0.51337325	0.43629669	0.37136442	0.31657439	0.27026895	0.23107318	0.19784467	0.16963262	0.14564434
18	0.91413616	0.83601731	0.76491159	0.70015937	0.58739461	0.49362812	0.41552065	0.35034379	0.29586392	0.25024903	0.21199374	0.17985879	0.15282218	0.13003959
19	0.90958822	0.82773992	0.75360747	0.68643076	0.57028603	0.47464242	0.39573396	0.33051301	0.27650833	0.23171206	0.19448967	0.16350799	0.13767764	0.11610678
20	0.90506290	0.81954447	0.74247042	0.67297133	0.55367575	0.45638695	0.37688948	0.31180473	0.25841900	0.21454821	0.17843089	0.14864363	0.12403391	0.10366677
21	0.90056010	0.81143017	0.73149795	0.65977582	0.53754928	0.43883360	0.35894236	0.29415540	0.24151309	0.19865575	0.16369806	0.13513057	0.11174226	0.09255961
22	0.89607971	0.80339621	0.72068763	0.64683904	0.52189250	0.42195539	0.34184987	0.27750510	0.22571317	0.18394051	0.15018171	0.12284597	0.10066870	0.08264251
23	0.89162160	0.79544179	0.71003708	0.63415592	0.50669175	0.40572633	0.32557131	0.26179726	0.21094688	0.17031528	0.13778139	0.11167816	0.09069252	0.07378796
24	0.88718567	0.78756613	0.69954392	0.62172149	0.49193374	0.39012147	0.31006270	0.24697855	0.19714662	0.15769934	0.12640494	0.10152560	0.08170498	0.06588210
25	0.88277181	0.77976844	0.68920583	0.60953087	0.47760557	0.37511680	0.29530277	0.23299863	0.18424918	0.14601790	0.11596784	0.09229600	0.07360809	0.05882331
26	0.87837991	0.77204796	0.67902052	0.59757928	0.46369473	0.36068923	0.28124073	0.21981003	0.17219549	0.13520176	0.10639251	0.08390545	0.06631359	0.05252081
27	0.87400986	0.76440392	0.66898574	0.58586204	0.45018906	0.34681657	0.26784832	0.20736795	0.16093037	0.12518682	0.09760781	0.07627768	0.05974197	0.04689358
28	0.86966155	0.75683557	0.65909925	0.57437455	0.43707675	0.33347747	0.25509364	0.19563014	0.15040221	0.11591372	0.08954845	0.06934335	0.05382160	0.04186927
29	0.86533488	0.74934215	0.64935887	0.56311231	0.42434636	0.32065141	0.24294632	0.18455674	0.14056282	0.10732252	0.08215454	0.06303941	0.04848793	0.03738327
30	0.86102973	0.74192292	0.63976243	0.55207089	0.41198676	0.30831867	0.23137745	0.17411013	0.13136712	0.09937733	0.07537114	0.05730855	0.04368282	0.03337792
31	0.85674600	0.73457715	0.63030781	0.54124597	0.39998715	0.29646026	0.22035947	0.16425484	0.12277301	0.09201605	0.06914783	0.05209868	0.03935389	0.02980172
32	0.85248358	0.72730411	0.62099292	0.53063330	0.38833703	0.28505794	0.20986617	0.15495740	0.11474113	0.08520005	0.06343838	0.04736244	0.03545395	0.02660868
33	0.84824237	0.72010307	0.61181568	0.52022873	0.37702625	0.27409417	0.19987254	0.14618622	0.10723470	0.07888893	0.05820035	0.04305676	0.03194050	0.02375775
34	0.84402226	0.71297334	0.60277407	0.51002817	0.36604490	0.26355209	0.19035480	0.13791153	0.10021934	0.07305481	0.05339481	0.03914251	0.02877522	0.02121227
35	0.83982314	0.70591420	0.59386608	0.50002761	0.35538340	0.25341047	0.18129029	0.13010522	0.09366294	0.06763454	0.04898607	0.03558410	0.02592363	0.01893953
36	0.83564492	0.69892495	0.58508974	0.49022315	0.34503243	0.24366872	0.17265741	0.12274077	0.08753546	0.06262458	0.04494135	0.03234918	0.02335462	0.01691029
37	0.83148748	0.69200490	0.57644309	0.48061093	0.33498294	0.23429685	0.16443563	0.11579318	0.08180884	0.05798572	0.04123059	0.02940835	0.02104020	0.01509848
38	0.82735073	0.68515337	0.56792423	0.47118719	0.32522615	0.22528543	0.15660536	0.10923885	0.07645686	0.05369048	0.03782623	0.02673486	0.01895513	0.01348078
39	0.82323455	0.67836967	0.55953126	0.46194822	0.31575355	0.21662061	0.14914797	0.10305552	0.07145501	0.04971341	0.03470296	0.02430442	0.01707670	0.01203641
40	0.81913886	0.67165314	0.55126232	0.45289042	0.30655684	0.20828904	0.14204568	0.09722219	0.06678038	0.04603093	0.03183758	0.02209493	0.01538441	0.01074680
41	0.81506354	0.66500311	0.54311559	0.44401021	0.29762800	0.20027793	0.13528160	0.09177905	0.06241157	0.04262123	0.02920879	0.02008630	0.01385983	0.00959536
42	0.81100850	0.65841892	0.53508925	0.43530413	0.28895692	0.19257493	0.12883962	0.08652740	0.05832857	0.03946411	0.02679706	0.01826027	0.01248633	0.00856728
43	0.80697363	0.65189992	0.52718153	0.42676875	0.28054294	0.18516820	0.12270440	0.08162962	0.05451268	0.03654084	0.02458446	0.01660025	0.01124895	0.00764936
44	0.80295884	0.64544546	0.51939067	0.41840074	0.27237178	0.17804635	0.11686133	0.07700908	0.05094643	0.03383411	0.02255455	0.01509113	0.01013419	0.00682978
45	0.79896402	0.63905492	0.51171494	0.41019680	0.26443862	0.17119841	0.11129651	0.07265007	0.04761349	0.03132788	0.02069224	0.01371921	0.00912990	0.00609802
46	0.79498907	0.63272764	0.50415265	0.40215265	0.25673653	0.16461386	0.10599668	0.06853781	0.04449859	0.02900730	0.01898371	0.01247201	0.00822513	0.00544466
47	0.79103390	0.62646301	0.49670212	0.39426836	0.24925876	0.15828256	0.10094921	0.06465831	0.04158247	0.02685861	0.01741625	0.01133819	0.00741003	0.00486131
48	0.78709847	0.62026041	0.48936170	0.38653761	0.24199880	0.15219476	0.09614211	0.06099840	0.03886679	0.02486906	0.01597821	0.01030745	0.00667570	0.00434045
49	0.78318250	0.61411921	0.48212975	0.37895844	0.23495029	0.14634112	0.09156391	0.05754566	0.03632410	0.02302693	0.01465891	0.00937041	0.00601415	0.00387540
50	0.77928607	0.60803882	0.47500468	0.37152788	0.22810708	0.14071262	0.08720373	0.05428836	0.03394776	0.02132123	0.01344854	0.00851855	0.00541815	0.00346018

EXAMPLE

How much money should you invest now in the first year (present value) to yield $10,000 (future value) in three years at 8% compounded quarterly?

Future Amount	$10,000
Interest Rate	8% compounded quarterly
Time	3 years

STEPS

1. Find the number of periods.

   3 years × 4 quarters = 12 compound periods

2. Determine the rate.

   8% ÷ 4 = 2%

3. Determine the table amount.
   Read down the left column, n, to 12 periods then across to 2%.

   0.78849318

4. Multiply the desired amount (future value) by the table amount.

   0.78849318 × $10,000 = $7,884.93   present value

Thus, if you invest $7,884.93 today at 8% compounded quarterly for three years, you will have $10,000 at the end of three years.

> **TIPS**
>
> *To prove, use the compound interest table:*
> *12 compound periods,*
> *2% = 1.26824179 ×*
> *$7,884.93 = $10,000.*

To figure the compound interest, subtract the present value from the future value. In the example above, the compound interest is $2,115.07, $10,000 − $7,884.93.

Calculate the present value in the following example.

EXAMPLE

Carol is planning to refurnish and redecorate 2 rooms in her home in 2 years. She expects refurnishing and redecorating to cost $7,000. Calculate how much money she needs to invest today at 12% interest compounded quarterly to have $7,000 in 2 years.

STEPS

1. Multiply the number of years by 4.

   2 years × 4 = 8   compound periods

2. Divide the interest rate by 4 (quarterly).

   12% ÷ 4 = 3%   rate

3. Locate 8 in the left column, n, of the table and move across the table to 3%. Then multiply the table value by the desired amount to obtain the present value.

   0.78940923 × $7,000 = $5,525.86   present value

Thus, if Carol invests $5,525.86 today at 12% compounded quarterly for two years, she will have $7,000 at the end of 2 years. She will have earned $1,474.14 in interest.

Name _____   Date _____

Directions   Solve the following problems. Write your answers in the blanks provided.

A. **Calculate the compound amount and compound interest at the end of a 2-year**   `OBJECTIVE 2`
period. The original principal is $3,000 at $7\frac{1}{4}$% compounded annually.

Interest for first year	1. _____
Interest for second year	2. _____
Compound amount	3. _____
Compound interest	4. _____

B. **Calculate the number of periods, compound amount, and compound interest.**   `OBJECTIVE 3`
Interest is compounded semiannually. Round to nearest cent after each
calculation to avoid rounding errors.

Principal	Annual Rate	Time	No. of Periods	Compound Amount	Compound Interest
$6,200	6%	2 years	5. ____	6. _____	7. _____
$1,500	8%	2 years	8. ____	9. _____	10. _____

C. **Calculate the compound amount and compound interest. Interest is**   `OBJECTIVE 4`
compounded quarterly for one year. Do not use the compound
interest table.

Principal	Annual Rate	Compound Amount	Compound Interest
$1,800	8%	11. _____	12. _____
$965	10%	13. _____	14. _____
$6,470	6%	15. _____	16. _____

D. **Use Table 10-3 to calculate the compound amount and compound interest.**   `OBJECTIVE 5`
Interest is compounded annually.

Principal	Rate	Time	Compound Amount	Compound Interest
$850	9%	2 years	17. _____	18. _____
$912	7%	2 years	19. _____	20. _____
$600	5%	1 year	21. _____	22. _____
$1,370	6%	2 years	23. _____	24. _____

E. Use Table 10-3 to calculate the compound amount and compound interest. OBJECTIVE 5
Interest is compounded quarterly.

Principal	Annual Rate	Time	Compound Amount		Compound Interest	
$4,000	8%	2 years	25.		26.	
$8,900	8%	5 years	27.		28.	
$2,550	6%	3 years	29.		30.	
$6,000	8%	5 years	31.		32.	
$5,000	4%	3 years	33.		34.	
$2,000	6%	4 years	35.		36.	

F. Use Table 10-4 to calculate the present value. OBJECTIVE 6

Future Amount	Period of Time	Annual Interest	Compound Period	Present Value	
$16,000	4 years	9%	annually	37.	
$1,700	1 year	8%	quarterly	38.	
$10,000	4 years	12%	quarterly	39.	
$15,000	6 years	6%	semiannually	40.	
$7,000	3 years	5%	annually	41.	
$25,000	10 years	6%	quarterly	42.	

G. Use Table 10-4 to calculate the present value. Interest is compounded OBJECTIVE 6
quarterly.

Future Amount	Period of Time	Annual Interest	Present Value	
$18,000	3 years	20%	43.	
$6,000	2 years	16%	44.	
$2,200	1 year	12%	45.	
$1,850	2 years	8%	46.	
$10,000	5 years	12%	47.	
$10,000	7 years	16%	48.	

H. Use Excel to discount notes. OBJECTIVE 5

49. Retrieve the file *ch10ex05.xlsx*. Follow the directions. Save the file as *ch10ex05a.xlsx*.

50. Retrieve the file *ch10ex06.xlsx*. Follow the directions. Save the file as *ch10ex06a.xlsx*.

Chapter Review and Assessment

KEY TERMS

bank discount
compound amount
compound interest
date
discount
discount date
discount rate
discounting commercial
   paper
exact simple interest

face value
interest
interest-bearing note
interest period
maker
maturity
maturity date
maturity value
non-interest-bearing note
ordinary simple interest

payee
present value
prime interest
principal
proceeds
promissory note
rate
simple interest
term
time

CONCEPTS	EXAMPLES
10.1 Calculate simple interest. 1. Interest = Principal × Rate × Time $I\ \ =\ \ P\ \ \times R\ \times T$ 2. To calculate interest for months, multiply the principal by the rate by the number of months divided by 12.	Calculate the interest paid on a loan of $5,680 for one year at a 10.2% simple interest rate. $I = \$5,680 \times 0.102 \times 1$ $I = \$579.36$ Find the interest paid on a loan of $3,790 for 8 months at a 9.8% simple interest rate. $I = \$3,790 \times 0.098 \times \frac{8}{12}$ $I = \$247.61$
10.1 Calculate ordinary simple interest and exact simple interest. 1. For ordinary simple interest, divide the number of days by 360 days. 2. For exact simple interest, divide the number of days by 365 days.	Calculate the interest paid on a loan of $4,300 for 90 days at a simple interest rate of 12.4%. $I = \$4,300 \times 0.124 \times \frac{90}{360}$ $I = \$133.30$ ordinary interest $I = \$4,300 \times 0.124 \times \frac{90}{365}$ $I = \$131.47$ exact interest
10.1 Determine the maturity value of a loan. If the principal and interest are known, then Maturity Value = Principal + Interest $M\ \ \ =\ \ P\ +\ \ I$	Compute the maturity value of a loan of $4,300 with $131.47 interest. $M = \$4,300 + \$131.47$ $M = \$4,431.47$

CONCEPTS	EXAMPLES
10.2 Discount notes.	A note for $2,000 at 9% due in 6 months, has been discounted 14% two months before maturity date.
1. Calculate Interest: $I = P \times R \times T$	$P \times R \times T = I$ $2,000 \times 0.09 \times \frac{6}{12} = \$90.00$
2. Calculate Maturity Value: $M = P + I$	$P + I = M$ $2,000 + \$90 = \$2,090$
3. Calculate Bank Discount: $B = M \times D \times T$	$M \times D \times T = B$ $2,090 \times 0.14 \times \frac{2}{12} = \$48.77$
4. Calculate Proceeds: $P = M - B$	$M - B = P$ $2,090 - \$48.77 = \$2,041.23$ If a bank discounts a note when the note has a number of days left before maturity, find the term of the discount period after calculating the maturity value and then calculate the bank discount and proceeds.
10.3 Calculate compound interest.	If $3,000 is invested for 2 years at 12% compounded quarterly, compute the compound amount and compound interest.
1. Find percent per compounded period; divide percent by compounded periods.	12% ÷ 4 = 3% per quarter 4 periods per year; 2 years × 4 = 8 periods
2. Use compound table to find equivalent value.	From Table 10-3, the value = 1.26677008.
3. Multiply the amount in the table by the value.	Compound amount = $3,000 × 1.26677008 = $3,800.31
4. Find compound interest by subtracting the investment from the compound value.	Compound interest = $3,800.31 − $3,000 = $800.31
10.3 Calculate present value.	How much money must be invested today to have $8,000 in 3 years compounded semiannually at 10% interest?
1. Find the compound period.	10% ÷ 2 = 5% per half-year 2 periods per year; 3 years × 2 = 6 periods
2. From a table of compounding values, locate the value.	From Table 10-4, the value = 0.74621540.
3. Multiply the desired amount by the value from the table to find the amount needed.	Amount needed today = $8,000 × 0.74621540 = $5,969.72

Chapter 10 Review Exercises

Directions Complete the following problems. Round dollars to nearest hundredth and percents to the nearest whole percent.

A. Find the simple interest. **10.1** OBJECTIVE **2**

	Principal	Rate	Time	Interest
1.	$5,700	11%	8 months	_____
2.	$9,460	15%	6 months	_____

B. Find the simple interest and maturity value. **10.1** OBJECTIVES **2, 6**

Principal	Rate	Time	Interest	Maturity Value
$820	13%	3 months	3. _____	4. _____
$860	14%	4 months	5. _____	6. _____

C. Calculate the ordinary simple interest and the exact simple interest on these loans. **10.1** OBJECTIVES **3, 4**

Principal	Rate	Time	360-Day Year	365-Day Year
$2,400	13%	60 days	7. _____	8. _____
$1,750	12%	90 days	9. _____	10. _____

D. Find the principal, rate, or time for the following loans. Use the 360-day method. **10.1** OBJECTIVE **7**

	Interest	Principal	Rate	Time
11.	$81.90	_____	13%	120 days
12.	$15.76	$675.50	14%	_____
13.	$296.10	$9,870.00	_____	60 days

E. Find the maturity date. Assume no leap year. **10.1** OBJECTIVE **8**

		Date
14.	March 10 (90-day)	_____
15.	January 20 (120-day)	_____
16.	September 13 (90-day)	_____

F. Find the number of days between the dates. Assume no leap year. 10.1 OBJECTIVE 8

Days

February 15 to April 4   17. _____

June 13 to September 7   18. _____

G. Find the bank discount and proceeds. The bank discounted these notes 12% two months before the maturity of the loan. 10.2 OBJECTIVE 2

Face Value	Interest Rate	Due	Bank Discount	Proceeds
$5,410	9%	3 months	19. _____	20. _____
$975	12%	4 months	21. _____	22. _____

H. Calculate the following problems using the compound interest table. 10.3 OBJECTIVE 5

Principal	Interest Rate	Time	Compound Period	Compound Amount	Compound Interest
$5,000	8%	2 years	quarterly	23. _____	24. _____
$9,200	10%	3 years	annually	25. _____	26. _____

I. Using the present value table, find the present value in each of the following problems. 10.3 OBJECTIVE 6

	Future Amount	Period of Time	Interest Rate	Compound Period	Present Value
27.	$8,000	3 years	6%	quarterly	_____
28.	$7,150	4 years	8%	annually	_____

J. Complete the following word problems.

29. Maria Sanchez borrowed $3,650 at 15% interest for 120 days. How much interest did she pay based on a 360-day year?   _____

30. Tien Chu borrowed $2,000 for 60 days (based on a 360-day year). Her interest amounted to $43.33. What was the interest rate?   _____

31. Lydia's loan date is March 20, and her loan is due in 120 days. What is the due date?   _____

32. Calculate the compound interest on Jerome's principal of $7,500 at 12% interest compounded quarterly for 2 years.   _____

K. Use Excel to calculate compound interest. 10.1 OBJECTIVE 9, 10.2 OBJECTIVE 3, 10.3 OBJECTIVE 5

33. Retrieve the file *ch10ex07xlsx*. Follow the directions. Save the file as *ch10ex07a.xlsx*.

34. Retrieve the file *ch10ex08.xlsx*. Follow the directions. Save the file as *ch10ex08a.xlsx*.

Small business owners often invest a portion of their profit each year to invest for future needs, such as expansion to their current businesses or replacement of equipment. To illustrate the effect of earning interest, look at the example for Bill, who owns a small repair shop.

TRY IT...

Bill received 5% simple interest on his principal of $5,000 over 2 years. In a table similar to Table 10-2, show how his investment grew each year and then compare it to an investment Bill located that could earn 5% compound semiannual interest.

Annually (1st Year)		Semiannually (1st Year)	
$5,000.00 + _____ $	$5,000 × 0.05 = $ ___ 1st year interest	$5,000.00 + _____ $	$5,000 × 0.025 = $ _____ 1st semiannual interest
		$ _____ + _____ $	$ ____ × 0.025 = $ _____ 2nd semiannual interest
	$5,000 earns $ _____ at the end of the first year.		$5,000 earns $ _____ at the end of the first year.
Annually (2nd Year)		Semiannually (2nd Year)	
$ _____ + _____ $	$ ____ × 0.05 = $ _____ 2nd year interest	$ _____ + _____ $	$ _____ × 0.025 = $ _____ 3rd semiannual interest
		$ _____ + _____ $	$ _____ × 0.025 = $ _____ 4th semiannual interest
	$ ____ earns $ _____ at the end of the second year.		$ _____ earns $ _____ at the end of the second year.

Write about Math

1. Maria is interested in borrowing $2,500 from her bank. Would calculating ordinary simple interest or exact simple interest be more beneficial to her? Explain.

2. You are interested in selling a note to your bank at a discount. What does it mean to "sell a note at a discount"?

3. For the bank depositor, is simple interest or compound interest more beneficial? Why?

Personal Finance

What interest are you earning?

It is always beneficial for a person depositing money into a bank account to earn the maximum interest possible. However, various types of bank accounts have different restrictions on what it takes to earn varying amounts of interest. These may include a minimum deposit amount or a minimum amount of time that the money in the account must stay in the account. The purpose of this activity is to help you consider different aspects related to interest.

Suppose you received a bonus of $1,500 for designing a web page for a small business owner of a T-shirt shop. You are interested in investing the bonus and earning the best interest possible.

Henrik5000/iStockphoto.com

Contact three different financial institutions for the following situations.

1. Compare interest rates earned for compound-interest savings accounts. Note the different compounding times, such as daily or monthly.

2. Compare interest rates earned for a certificate of deposit (CD). Consider a one-year time period to hold the CD. Gather the information about the CDs from the same financial institutions used to collect the interest rates in Step 1.

3. Create a table showing the three financial institutions, the interest rates earned for compound-interest savings accounts, and the interest rates earned for certificates of deposit from Steps 1 and 2.

4. Write an explanation of the factors you must consider before making your decision to invest your money. For instance, a CD pays a higher rate of interest than a savings account. However, you must leave your money with the bank for a specified length of time. You pay a penalty for early withdrawal.

5. Using the information you have gathered, answer the following questions:

   a. Suppose you place the bonus in a savings account for one year. How much interest can you earn in a savings account?

   b. What is the difference in the interest earned if you purchased a one-year CD for $1,500 instead of placing the money in the savings account?

   c. Suppose you purchase a $1,500 CD for 6 months. How much interest can you earn on the CD?

   d. How much more interest can you earn by buying a $1,500, 6-month CD?

Name _____ Date _____ Score _____

Directions   Complete the following problems. Round dollars to nearest hundredth and percents to the nearest whole percent.

A. Find the simple interest. 10.1 OBJECTIVE 2

	Principal	Rate	Time	Interest
1.	$1,700	15%	7 months	_____
2.	$8,670	10.5%	6 months	_____

B. Find the simple interest and maturity value. 10.2 OBJECTIVES 2, 6

Principal	Rate	Time	Interest	Maturity Value
$1,680	11.5%	3 months	3. _____	4. _____
$975	12.2%	4 months	5. _____	6. _____

C. Calculate the ordinary simple interest and the exact simple interest on these loans. 10.1 OBJECTIVES 3, 4

Principal	Rate	Time	360-Day Year	365-Day Year
$3,200	10.5%	30 days	7. _____	8. _____
$1,550	9.8%	60 days	9. _____	10. _____

D. Find the principal, rate, or time for the following loans. Use the 360-day method. 10.1 OBJECTIVE 7

	Interest	Principal	Rate	Time
11.	$33.33	$2,500.00	_____	60 days
12.	$18.50	_____	6%	120 days
13.	$48.75	$1,300.00	15%	_____

E. Find the maturity date. Assume no leap year. 10.1 OBJECTIVE 8

		Date
14.	January 15 (60-day)	_____
15.	March 15 (90-day)	_____
16.	May 9 (120-day)	_____

F. Find the number of days between the dates. Assume no leap year. 10.1 OBJECTIVE 8

Days

17. September 15 to November 1 _____

18. October 10 to December 21 _____

G. Find the bank discount and proceeds. The bank discounts rates at 12% two months before the maturity of the loan. 10.2 OBJECTIVE 2

Face Value	Interest Rate	Due	Bank Discount	Proceeds
$6,750	8.9%	3 months	19. _____	20. _____
$840	10.2%	4 months	21. _____	22. _____

H. Calculate the following problems using the compound interest table. 10.3 OBJECTIVE 5

Interest Rate	Period of Time	Principal	Compound Period	Compound Amount	Compound Interest
10%	4 years	$1,600	annually	23. _____	24. _____
12%	3 years	$16,000	quarterly	25. _____	26. _____

I. Using the present value table, find the present value in each of the following problems. 10.3 OBJECTIVE 6

	Future Amount	Period of Time	Interest Rate	Compound Period	Present Value
27.	$10,000	3 years	6%	quarterly	_____
28.	$25,000	4 years	7%	annually	_____

J. Complete the following word problems.

29. Tom Synder has deposited a total of $1,950 in his savings account. The annual interest rate is 5.2%. How much interest did he earn at the end of six months? _____

30. Carolina Maddox borrowed $4,750 at 13.4% interest for 120 days. How much interest did she pay based on a 360-day year? _____

31. Claude borrowed $3,000 for 60 days (based on a 360-day year). His interest amounted to $55.00. What was the interest rate? _____

32. Your loan date is May 27, and your loan is due in 60 days. What is the due date? _____

K. Use Excel to calculate the following problems. 10.1 OBJECTIVE 9, 10.2 OBJECTIVE 3 10.3 OBJECTIVE 5

33. Retrieve the file *ch10qz01.xlsx*. Follow the directions. Save the file as *ch10qz01a.xlsx*.

34. Retrieve the file *ch10qz02.xlsx*. Follow the directions. Save the file as *ch10qz02a.xlsx*.

CHAPTER 11

Consumer Credit and Mortgages

This is a fast-paced era. Many consumer products and services are designed to help people keep up the pace as well as enjoy their leisure time. To afford these products and services, consumers have taken advantage of various credit sources. For instance, they have purchased large TVs on installment plans, bought clothes at department stores on credit, and paid for gasoline with a credit card or debit card. Credit cards are popular because they allow people an extra 30, 60, or more days between the time of purchase and the time of payment. Consumer credit is in two broad categories: open-end and closed-end.

MORTGAGE LOAN OFFICER

Courtesy of Zach Reffitt

Zach Reffitt works in the home mortgage department of a national bank. He meets with prospective clients who are buying a home to determine their qualifications for a mortgage loan in the amount they request. Once the client finds a home in their price range and makes an offer on it, Zach meets with the client again and obtains all necessary documents required for completing the mortgage application process, including paycheck stubs, W2s and other tax forms, homeowner's insurance policy, asset statements, and a draft of the sales contract for the home. Zach sends the application to internal processing for validation of the information that was submitted. Once processing is completed he sends the application to the underwriting team which is responsible for final review and approval. When final approval is granted, the file is then sent to the closing department. In this step the final amount due at closing is given to the buyer and a closing date is set.

Zach says that due to the housing crisis of 2008 caused by loans that were improperly approved, many people have a negative concept of his job. He says, "When working in a bank setting, there are many federal rules and regulations you have to follow. My goal is not to sell you an inappropriate loan program to pad my pocket, nor to set the customer up for financial failure. I hold my customers' best interests first and strive to make the process as painless and enjoyable as possible."

How Math Is Used in the Mortgage Loan Business

Zach says, "Math is an essential tool in mortgage lending when determining payments, taxes, homeowner's insurance, annual percentage rates, and running amortization schedules." Math is also used when calculating debt to income ratios. This is an individual's total outstanding debt divided by the amount of monthly income that is received.

What Do You Think?

What skills do you need to improve in order to work in the mortgage business?

Math Skills Used

Decimals

Percents

Fractions

Time value of money

Other Skills Needed

Communication

Interpersonal Skills

Patience

Organization

11.1 Open-End Credit

OBJECTIVE **1** Identify terms used with open-end credit.

Open-end credit is an agreement to lend up to a certain amount and to allow the amount to be borrowed again once it has been repaid. With open-end credit, loans are made on a continuous basis, and you are expected to make at least a partial payment periodically. A credit card issued by a store, a bank card such as VISA or MasterCard, and overdraft protection are examples of open-end credit. This chapter discusses different methods of calculating card balances and shows you how to use two common methods.

The **Truth in Lending Act** requires creditors to provide certain basic information about the cost of buying on credit or taking out a loan. *Consumer Leasing* disclosures can help you compare the cost and terms of one lease with another and the cost and terms of buying with cash or on credit. The **Credit Card Act of 2009** amends the Truth in Lending Act. It provides better transparency for the consumer so that consumers can better understand their credit card bills. It makes it more difficult to raise your annual percentage rate (APR) without you knowing about it well in advance. It requires lenders to disclose how long it would take to pay off your credit card balance if only minimum payments are made and how much interest you would pay. This chapter discusses only the topics related to Truth in Lending's disclosures, which can help you shop for the best deal.

In the disclosures, the creditors must tell you in writing *before* you sign any agreement what the following terms will be:

- The minimum finance charge
- The annual percentage rate (APR)
- The method of computing the balance at the end of each month
- Any transaction fee for purchases or cash advances

The **finance charge** is the total dollar amount you pay for the use of credit. It includes interest and other costs, such as service charges and some credit-related insurance premiums. The **annual percentage rate (APR)** is the actual rate of interest charged for the privilege of having a loan or using a credit card from month to month. The method is described on a monthly statement, called a billing statement, which is discussed later in this chapter. By remembering the two basic credit terms—finance charge and annual percentage rate (APR)—you can compare prices from different sources.

Credit cards can be used repeatedly, generally until you reach a certain prearranged borrowing limit. The maximum amount of credit you can use is your **credit limit** or **credit line**.

Types of Open-End Credit

A **30-day account** is an agreement allowing a consumer to make purchases or use a service during a 30-day period and pay the full amount within 30 days. With a 30-day account, the maximum amount a consumer can charge may or may not be set. But if the consumer does not pay the specified amount due within the time limit, the lender can assess a late fee on the amount past due or cancel the account. An example of a 30-day service credit account is your telephone company.

The most common forms of open-end credit are *charge cards* and *credit cards*. A **charge card** generally has an annual fee and requires the balance to be paid in full each month. Examples include American Express and Diners Club. This type of charge account is normally used by business people for travel and entertainment expenditures.

Credit cards, also called **bank cards**, are issued on revolving charge accounts. As monthly payments reduce the credit balance on **revolving charge accounts**, new charges are added, resulting in a revolving balance. These accounts are likely to have specified **credit limits**, amounts that cannot be exceeded without penalty. As long as the balance is kept below the credit limit, credit card accounts require only a minimum payment each month. Credit cards permit consumers to make purchases or to obtain a cash advance. Credit cards, such as VISA, MasterCard, Optima, and Discover, can be used worldwide. The consumer has the option of paying the bill in full when it arrives or paying a portion of the amount due over several months. Cash loans, known as cash advances or "instant cash," can be obtained from banks issuing the credit cards and from 24-hour automated teller machines (ATMs). Most credit card companies charge extra fees or interest for this service. Some companies separate cash advance totals from purchase balances and often calculate finance charges at different rates.

Before you open any type of open-end credit account, the creditor must disclose to you the terms to the extent they apply to your particular credit account. Read carefully the terms of the agreement. Your credit rights are protected by the Federal Fair Credit Billing Act.

Balance Calculation Methods

Creditors must tell you when finance charges begin on your account so you know how much time you have to pay your bill before a finance charge is added. Creditors may give you a **grace period**. For example, a grace period of 21 days allows you 21 days to pay your balance in full before you must pay a late fee. If your creditor offers a grace period, you generally can avoid a late fee if you pay your bill in full by the due date each month.

Creditors must tell you the method they use to calculate the balance on which you pay a finance charge. The interest rate they charge is applied to this balance to compute the finance charge. Creditors use different methods to arrive at the balance. Study the following methods carefully, as they can significantly affect your finance charge.

- **Previous balance** Creditors simply use the amount owed at the start of the billing cycle to compute the finance charge. Payments or charges made during the month will not affect your finance charge this billing cycle. A **billing cycle** is the number of days between the last statement date and the current statement date.

- **Average daily balance (ADB)** This balance is figured by adding the outstanding balance, including new purchases, and deducting payments and credits for each day in the billing cycle and then dividing by the number of days in the billing cycle. In many cases, new purchases are included only if you do not pay the previous balance in full by the payment due date. Purchases made during the billing cycle raise your balance and can increase your finance charge. There are variations to this method, but most creditors in the United States favor using the average daily balance method to figure finance charges.
- **Adjusted balance** This balance is figured by deducting payments and credits made during the billing cycle from the outstanding balance at the beginning of the billing cycle. If your beginning balance was $699 and you paid $400 of that, you would be charged interest only on the remaining $299. New purchases are not counted.

OBJECTIVE 2 Calculate finance charge using previous balance.

The previous balance is the balance on the final billing date of the previous month. Monthly rates can range from less than 1% to more than 2%. The following example shows how the finance charge was computed as a percent of the previous balance, ignoring purchases, credit or returns, and payments.

TIPS

Remember to apply the familiar percentage formula P = B × R. In the example, the base is $532.60 and the rate is 1.5%. To determine the unknown part, multiply $532.60 (base) by 0.015 (rate), which is $7.99.

EXAMPLE

Corene Tunnell has an account at Lady Castor Fashions. She has a previous balance on her account of $532.60. Lady Castor Fashions computes 1.5% a month on the previous balance. What is the finance charge?

STEPS

Compute the finance charge by multiplying the previous balance by the monthly rate.

$$\$532.60 \times 0.015 = \$7.99$$ finance charge for the month

Customers receive a monthly statement at the end of each billing period. The **billing statement** describes and summarizes account activity for the month. The statement itemizes purchases along with previous balance, finance charges, payments, credits, new balance, and minimum payment information. Although this information is given on all monthly statements, the forms may vary. In Figure 11-1, the finance charge, $1.50, is computed on the previous

Figure 11-1
Billing Statement

BILLING STATEMENT

Previous Balance	Finance Charge	Payments	Credits	Purchases	Cycle Closing Date	New Balance	Minimum Payment
100.00	1.50	25.00	10.00	80.75	7/24/--	147.25	30.00

If we receive payment of the full amount of the new balances before the next cycle closing date, shown above, you will avoid a finance charge next month. The finance charge, if any, is calculated on the previous balance before deducting any payments or credits shown above. The periodic rates are $1\frac{1}{2}$% of the balance on amounts under $1,000 and 1% of amounts in excess of $1,000, which are annual percentage rates of 18% and 12% respectively.

balance, and added to the balance before payments and credits are deducted. Review your billing statement each month to ensure it is correct. If you find an error, you have the right to question your statement.

Commonly used annual percentage rates (APR) are 21%, 18%, and 15%. For an APR of 18%, the monthly interest rate is 1.5%.

$$18\% \div 12 \text{ months} = 1.5\% \text{ per month}$$

Generally, interest charges are calculated using the monthly rate. The monthly rate can be converted using the percentage formula $R = P \div B$. If the APR is not shown, you can apply the percentage formula again, $P = R \times B$.

If the monthly interest rate is known, you can determine the APR by multiplying the monthly rate (R) by 12 months (B). If the monthly interest rate is 1.5%, the APR is 18%.

$$1.5\% \times 12 = 18\%$$

A retail store may state its credit terms as follows:

- The finance charge, if any, is computed on the previous balance before payments or credits are deducted.
- The monthly rate is 2% on the first $1,000 (24% APR) and 1.75% on amounts over $1,000 (21% APR).
- There is no finance charge if the full amount of the new balance is paid on or before the closing date of the next month's bill.

EXAMPLE

Saleb's account shows a previous balance of $1,325.17. A payment of $290.00 was received during the month. Charges amounted to $375.30. A credit was given in the amount of $37.90. Saleb did not pay the full amount on time. The monthly rate is 2% on the first $1,000 and 1.75% on amounts over $1,000. Compute the finance charge and the new balance.

STEPS

1. Multiply the first $1,000 of the previous amount by the monthly rate of 2%.

$$\$1,000.00 \times 0.02 = \$20.00$$

2. Multiply the difference between the first $1,000 and the amount over $1,000 by the monthly rate of 1.75%.

$$\$325.17 \times 0.0175 = \$5.69$$

3. Add the individual finance charges to obtain the total finance charge.

$$\$20.00 + \$5.69 = \$25.69$$

4. Determine the new balance as shown.

	$1,325.17	previous balance
+	25.69	finance charge
−	290.00	payment
+	375.30	purchases
−	37.90	credit payment
	$1,398.26	new balance

OBJECTIVE 3 Calculate new balance using average daily balance.

This commonly used method computes the finance charge by applying the monthly rate to the average daily balance. The average daily balance (ADB), an average of all the daily balances, is calculated by adding the daily balances and dividing by the number of days in the billing cycle. To find the finance charge for the month, multiply the average daily balance by the monthly interest rate.

EXAMPLE

Jackie's department store card statement shows an unpaid balance on March 1 of $875.90, a payment on March 10 of $125, and a charge on March 15 of $175. The billing cycle is 31 days. The monthly rate is 1.5%. Calculate the new balance and the finance charge.

STEPS

1. The beginning balance was in effect for 9 days—
   March 1 through March 10 (10 − 1 = 9). $875.90

2. Subtract the payment made on March 10 from the
   beginning balance. This new balance is in effect for   − 125.00
   5 days (15 − 10 = 5). $750.90

3. Add the purchase made on March 15 to the balance in
   effect. This new balance is in effect through the billing   + 175.00
   day, April 1, which is 17 days (31 − 15 + 1 = 17). $925.90

4. Find the daily balances by multiplying balances by days in effect, as
   shown. Then add the daily balances.

$$\$875.90 \times \ 9 \text{ days} = \ \$7{,}883.10$$
$$\$750.90 \times \ 5 \text{ days} = \ \$3{,}754.50$$
$$\$925.90 \times 17 \text{ days} = \$15{,}740.30$$
$$31 \text{ days} = \$27{,}377.90$$

5. Divide the total daily balances by the number of days to obtain the
   average daily balance.

$$\$27{,}377.90 \div 31 \text{ days} = \$883.16 \qquad \text{average daily balance}$$

6. Compute the finance charge.

$$\$883.16 \times 0.015 = \$13.25 \qquad \text{finance charge}$$

7. Add the finance charge to the balance from step 2 to find the
   statement balance.

$$\$925.90 + \$13.25 = \$939.15 \qquad \text{statement balance}$$

OBJECTIVE 4 Use Excel to calculate finance charge and new balance.

It is difficult and time-consuming to calculate finance charges and new balances on accounts. To save time and to help eliminate error, businesses make the calculations using special computer software. When you receive a billing statement, you should carefully review it for errors.

EXAMPLE

Mary Scichili owns a small gift shop and allows customers to use inhouse cards to charge items on credit. Without paying for expensive software, she wants to use Excel to save time in calculating finance charges and new balances. Mary can easily convert rates from annual to monthly as well as from monthly to annual, as shown in Figure 11-2. Figure 11-3 on the next page shows that Mary can also compare the results of the previous balance method to calculate finance charges and new balances.

Figure 11-2
Converting Rates

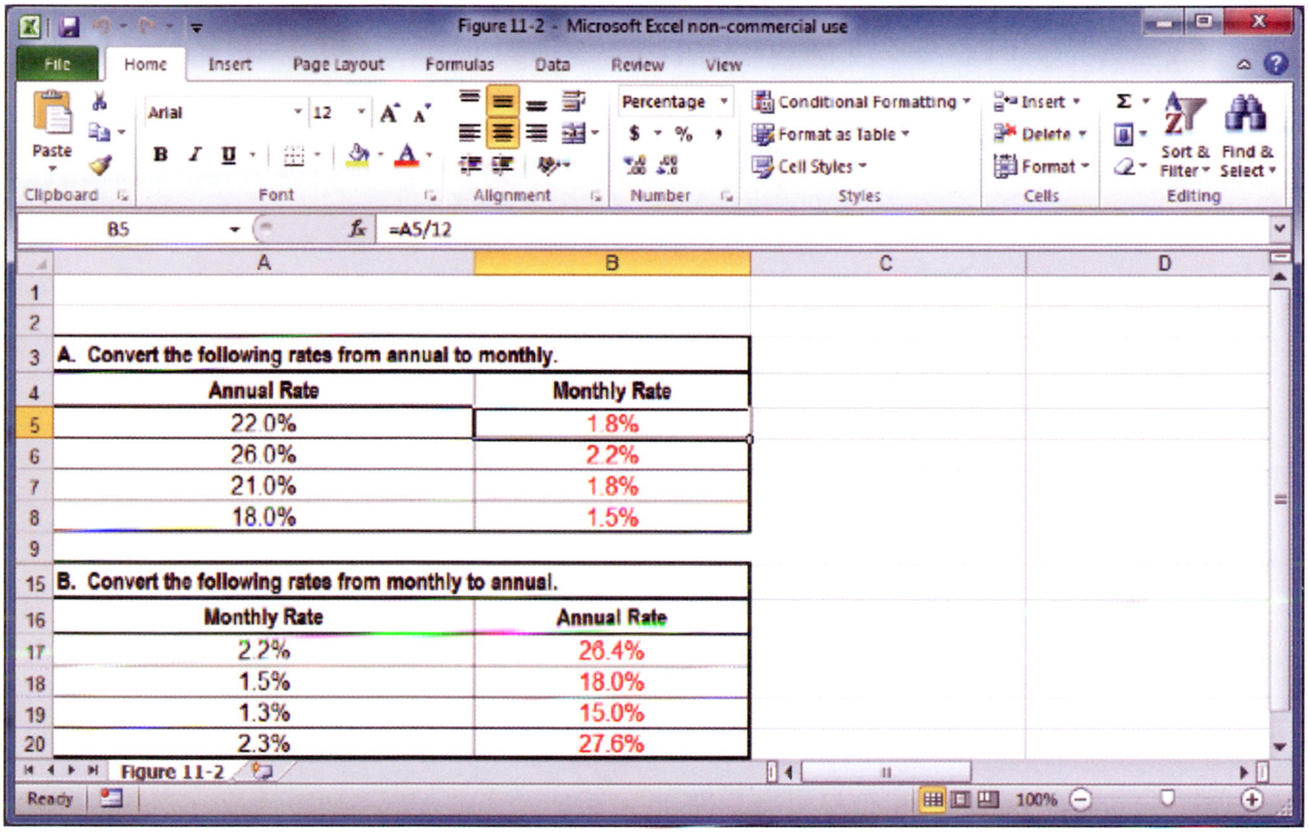

STEPS

Retrieve the file *ch11pr01.xlsx*.

A. Convert the following rates from Annual to Monthly.

1. Enter formulas in Column B to convert the rates from Annual to Monthly. (Use $R = P/B$ formula.)
2. Format Column B for Percentage. Set Decimal places to 1.

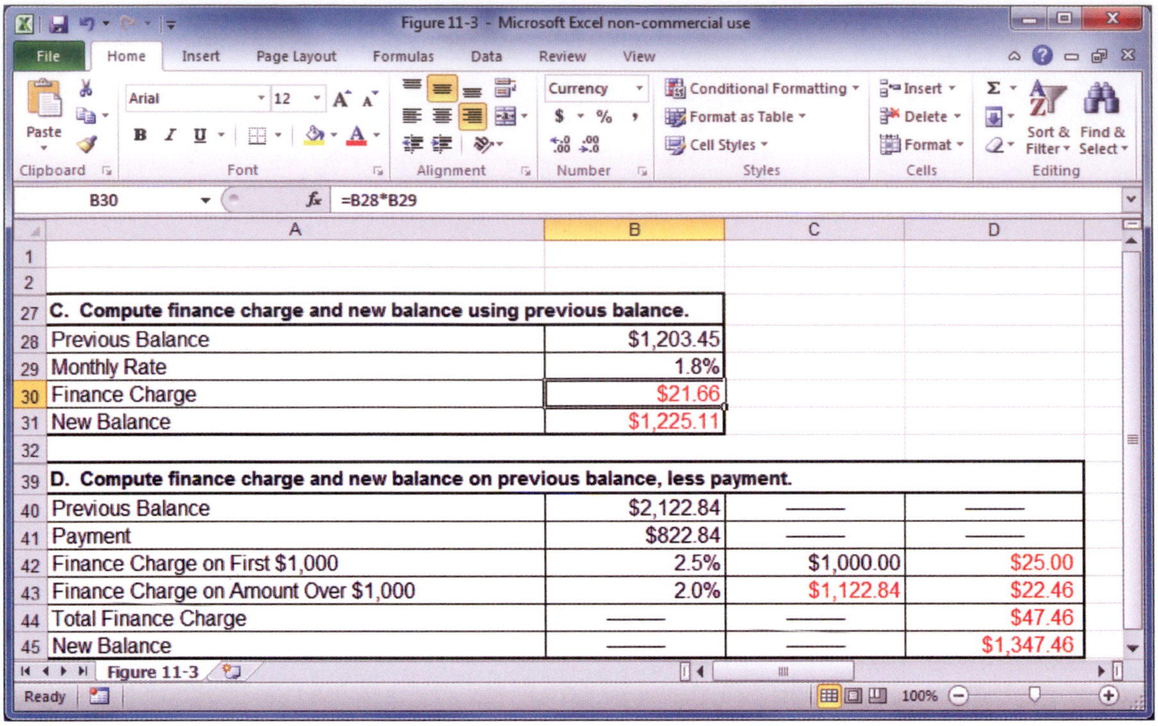

Figure 11-3 - Microsoft Excel non-commercial use

A spreadsheet showing:

	A	B	C	D
27	**C. Compute finance charge and new balance using previous balance.**			
28	Previous Balance	$1,203.45		
29	Monthly Rate	1.8%		
30	Finance Charge	$21.66		
31	New Balance	$1,225.11		
32				
39	**D. Compute finance charge and new balance on previous balance, less payment.**			
40	Previous Balance	$2,122.84	———	———
41	Payment	$822.84	———	———
42	Finance Charge on First $1,000	2.5%	$1,000.00	$25.00
43	Finance Charge on Amount Over $1,000	2.0%	$1,122.84	$22.46
44	Total Finance Charge	———	———	$47.46
45	New Balance	———	———	$1,347.46

Cell B30: =B28*B29

Figure 11-3

Previous Balance Method

B. Convert the following rates from Monthly to Annual.

1. Enter formulas in Column B to convert the rates from Monthly to Annual. (Use $P = B \times R$ formula.)

2. Format Column B for Percentage. Set Decimal places to 1.

C. Compute finance charge and new balance using previous balance.

1. In Cell B30, enter a formula to calculate Finance Charge. (Multiply the Previous Balance by the Monthly Rate.)

2. In Cell B31, enter a formula to calculate New Balance. (Add the Previous Balance and the Finance Charge.)

3. Format Cells B30 and B31 for Currency, 2 Decimal places, and $.

D. Compute finance charge and new balance on previous balance, less payment.

1. In Cell D42, enter a formula to calculate Finance Charge on First $1,000. (Multiply $1,000 by the interest rate on the first $1,000.)

2. In Cell C43, enter a formula to calculate the Amount Over $1,000. (Subtract $1,000 from the Previous Balance.)

3. In Cell D43, enter a formula to calculate Finance Charge on Amount Over $1,000. (Multiply Amount Over $1,000 by Rate.)

4. In Cell D44, enter a formula to calculate Total Finance Charge. (Add the Finance Charge on First $1,000 and the Finance Charge on Amount Over $1,000.)

5. In Cell D45, enter a formula to calculate New Balance. (Subtract the Payment from Previous Balance and add Total Finance Charge.)

6. Format dollar amounts for Currency, 2 Decimal places, and $.

7. Save the file as *ch11pr01a.xlsx*.

You will use the Average Daily Balance Method to calculate finance charges with Excel.

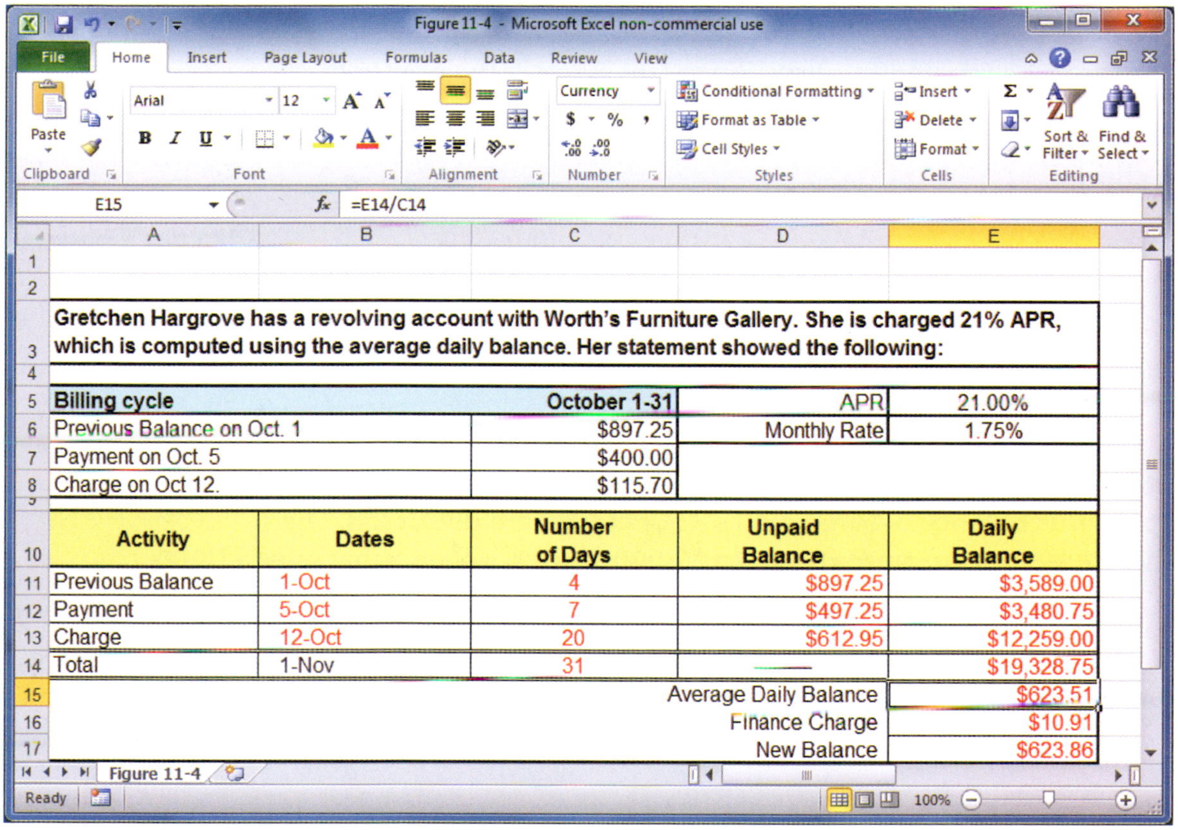

Gretchen Hargrove has a revolving account with Worth's Furniture Gallery. She is charged 21% APR, which is computed using the average daily balance. Her statement showed the following:

Billing cycle		October 1-31	APR	21.00%
Previous Balance on Oct. 1		$897.25	Monthly Rate	1.75%
Payment on Oct. 5		$400.00		
Charge on Oct 12.		$115.70		

Activity	Dates	Number of Days	Unpaid Balance	Daily Balance
Previous Balance	1-Oct	4	$897.25	$3,589.00
Payment	5-Oct	7	$497.25	$3,480.75
Charge	12-Oct	20	$612.95	$12,259.00
Total	1-Nov	31		$19,328.75
			Average Daily Balance	$623.51
			Finance Charge	$10.91
			New Balance	$623.86

Figure 11-4
Average Daily Balance Method

STEPS

Retrieve the file ***ch11pr02.xlsx***.

1. Fill in the Dates in Cells B11 through B13.
2. In Cells C11 through C13, enter a formula to calculate the Number of Days for each Activity.
3. In Cell C14, enter a formula to calculate the Total Number of Days in the billing cycle.
4. In Cell D11 enter a formula to place the Previous Balance in the cell.
5. In Cell D12, enter a formula to calculate the Unpaid Balance after the payment.
6. In Cell D13, enter a formula to calculate the Unpaid Balance after the charge.
7. In Cells E11 through E13, enter formulas to calculate the Daily Balance for each Activity.
8. In Cell E14, enter a formula to calculate the Total Daily Balance.
9. In Cell E15, enter a formula to calculate the Average Daily Balance.
10. In Cell E16, enter a formula to calculate the Finance Charge.
11. In Cell E17, enter a formula to compute the New Balance.
12. Format dollar amounts for Currency, 2 Decimal places, and $.
13. Save the file as ***ch11pr02a.xlsx***.

Name _____   Date _____

Directions   Solve the following problems. Write your answers in the blanks provided. Place commas, dollar signs, and percent symbols in answers as needed. Round dollars to the nearest cent and percents to the nearest tenth.

A. Using the previous balance method, compute the monthly rate and finance charge.   `OBJECTIVE 1`

Previous Balance	APR	Monthly Rate	Finance Charge
$430.50	18%	1. _____	2. _____
$370.40	21%	3. _____	4. _____
$235.60	19.2%	5. _____	6. _____

B. Compute the finance charge and new balance. The finance charge is based on the previous balance before payments or credits are deducted. The monthly rate is 1.5% on amounts up to $1,000 and 1% on amounts over $1,000.   `OBJECTIVE 2`

Previous Balance	Finance Charge	Payment	Credits	Purchases	New Balance
$968.50	7. _____	$230.50	–0–	$89.50	8. _____
$1,645.19	9. _____	$425.00	$122.70	$290.74	10. _____
$1,656.20	11. _____	$589.40	–0–	$187.60	12. _____
$860.30	13. _____	$150.50	–0–	$92.75	14. _____

C. Complete the following word problems.

15. Flair Fashions charges 1.83% per month on the previous balances of its accounts. Account #181-909 shows a beginning balance of $574.65. What is the amount of the finance charge?   _____

16. A charge account statement shows a beginning balance of $278.00 and a billing date of September 5. On September 10, a payment of $60.00 was made. Later two purchases were made: $23.50 on September 20 and $17.38 on September 25. Find the average daily balance on the next billing date of October 5.   _____

17. Compute the average daily balance and finance charge. As of April 1, the credit card balance shows a previous balance of $905.05. A payment of $100 was made on April 10. A purchase of $75 was made on April 15. Finance charges are computed at 3% per month. This balance was in effect through the billing date, May 1.

    Average daily balance   _____   18.   Finance charge   _____

D. Use Excel to calculate finance charge and new balances.   `OBJECTIVE 4`

18. Retrieve the file *ch11ex01.xlsx*. Follow the directions. Save the file as *ch11ex01a.xlsx*.

19. Retrieve the file *ch11ex02.xlsx*. Follow the directions. Save the file as *ch11ex02a.xlsx*.

11.2 Closed-End Credit

OBJECTIVES

1. Identify terms used with closed-end credit.
2. Calculate the installment price and the finance charge.
3. Calculate the monthly installment payment.
4. Calculate the interest refund.
5. Calculate the loan payoff.
6. Use Excel to calculate the cost of an installment loan.

OBJECTIVE 1 Identify terms used with closed-end credit.

Closed-end credit (or *installment* credit) is a type of credit generally used to finance a specific amount of money for a specific purpose for a specific period of time. Businesses use it to finance capital improvements, such as buildings or equipment. Consumers use installment credit to purchase expensive items such as large appliances, furniture, home entertainment equipment, boats, and cars. Credit cards are not always practical for these types of purchases due to low credit limits and high interest rates. Installment credit is often less expensive than revolving credit, especially if the item being purchased is used as collateral to secure the loan, as would be the case with a car loan or a mortgage. Payments may be over a longer period of time making the loan more affordable.

An **installment loan** is one in which you agree to pay back a fixed amount of money, including interest, in a series of equal payments (usually monthly) called **installments**, over a fixed period of time. A **down payment** is a partial payment that may be required in advance and is usually a percent (such as 10% or 20%) of the purchase price of the item you are buying.

When applying for an installment loan, you are likely to be quoted a rate of interest, which is called a *nominal* or **stated interest rate**. But due to the effects of compounding interest, upfront fees, and other charges, the effective interest rate will be higher. These rates are difficult to compute. However, the credit agreement you are asked to sign will disclose the annual percentage rate (the effective rate) along with the amount financed, the total finance charges, the total amount of payments, the monthly payment, and the number of payments.

The **amount financed** is the principal (or purchase price) plus any other costs such as loan origination fees, insurance charges, or extended warranty costs, minus any down payment. The **total amount of payments** is the amount financed plus interest. The **monthly payment** is the total amount of payments divided by the number of payments. If you are financing a purchase with an installment loan, the total amount paid, including the down payment and all the installments, represents the **installment price** of the item as compared to the price you would pay if you paid cash.

When you want to purchase an item on credit, you can obtain an installment loan or a personal loan from a lending institution. In seeking the best finance costs, you should consider these basic elements.

1. The dollar amount of the finance charge
2. The stated rate of interest
3. The annual percentage rate
4. The monthly payment

OBJECTIVE 2 Calculate the installment price and the finance charge.

The installment price is the total of the installments plus the down payment. Determine the installment price and finance charge in the next example.

EXAMPLE

Carmen is buying stereo equipment on installment for her small office. Her down payment is $127. There are 24 monthly payments of $61.91. The retail price is $1,270. How much is the cost of installment buying?

STEPS

1. Determine the total amount of installment payments by multiplying the installment payment by the number of monthly payments.

$$\$61.91 \times 24 = \$1,485.84$$

2. Add any down payment.

$$\$1,485.84 + \$127.00 = \$1,612.84 \qquad \text{installment price}$$

3. Determine the finance charge by subtracting the retail price from the total installment price.

$$\$1,612.84 - \$1,270.00 = \$342.84 \qquad \text{finance charge}$$

OBJECTIVE 3 Calculate the monthly installment payment.

You can calculate the installment payment if you know the installment price, the down payment, and the number of payments. Study the next example.

EXAMPLE

Chambers and Sons sells appliances and offers installment loans. Sara wants to purchase a microwave oven for the employee lounge and pay for it in installments. The installment price is $437.80, the down payment is $100, and the number of payments is 6. What is the total amount of installment payments and the monthly payment?

STEPS

1. To calculate the total amount of installment payments, subtract the down payment from the installment price.

$$\$437.80 - \$100 = \$337.80 \qquad \text{total amount of installment payments}$$

2. To find the installment payment, divide the total of installment payments by the number of payments.

$$\$337.80 \div 6 = \$56.30 \qquad \text{monthly installment payment}$$

TIPS

If a down payment is applicable, it must be subtracted from the cost of the item before the interest is calculated on an installment loan.

If you pay off an installment loan early, you may be entitled to a finance charge refund. **Refund** means to return the unearned portion of the finance charge. According to federal law, the lender must compute the amount of an interest refund by using the **Rule of 78**, also called the **sum-of-digits method**. The number 78 is the sum of the digits for the 12 months of a loan.

$$1 + 2 + 3 + 4 + 5 + 6 + 7 + 8 + 9 + 10 + 11 + 12 = 78$$

This is used to create a refund fraction.

$$\text{Refund Fraction} = \frac{\text{Sum of the digits of the number of payments remaining}}{\text{Sum of the digits of the number of total payments}}$$

EXAMPLE

Suppose you have a one-year loan with a finance charge of $138, which you pay off four months early. The lender could determine your interest refund using the following steps.

STEPS

1. Find the sum of the digits of the number of payments remaining (numerator).

$$1 + 2 + 3 + 4 = 10$$

2. Find the sum of the digits of the number of total payments (denominator).

$$1 + 2 + 3 + 4 + 5 + 6 + 7 + 8 + 9 + 10 + 11 + 12 = 78$$

3. Multiply the finance charge by the refund fraction.

$$\frac{10}{78}\left(\text{or } \frac{5}{39}\right) \times \$138 = \$17.69 \qquad \text{interest refund}$$

You can use the following formula to calculate the refund fraction more easily.

$$\text{Sum} = \frac{N(N+1)}{2}, \text{ where } N = \text{the number of payments}$$

Apply this formula to find the refund fraction for the example.

STEPS

1. Find the sum of the digits of the payments remaining (numerator).

$$N = 4 \qquad \text{payments remaining}$$
$$\frac{4(4+1)}{2} = \frac{20}{2} = 10$$

2. Find the sum of the digits of the total payments (denominator).

$$N = 12 \qquad \text{total payments}$$
$$\frac{12(12+1)}{2} = \frac{156}{2} = 78$$

3. Multiply the refund fraction by the finance charge.

$$\frac{10}{78} \times \$138 = \$17.69 \qquad \text{interest refund}$$

OBJECTIVE **5** Calculate the loan payoff.

Suppose you want to pay off a loan early and want to know the interest refund and amount of the final payment. Study the following example.

EXAMPLE

Shawn had a 12-month installment loan. At the end of 8 months, he wants to pay off the loan. His payments are $86.50, and he has an interest charge of $72.30. What is the interest refund and final payment?

STEPS

1. Find the refund fraction using the formula.

$$\frac{4(4 + 1)}{2} = \frac{20}{2} = 10 \qquad\qquad \frac{12(12 + 1)}{2} = \frac{156}{2} = 78$$

2. Find the interest refund by multiplying the refund fraction by the interest charged.

$$\frac{10}{78} \left(\text{or } \frac{5}{39} \right) \times \$72.30 = \$9.27 \qquad \text{interest refund}$$

3. Determine the amount still owed on the loan by multiplying the amount of the payment by the number of payments still owed.

$$\$86.50 \times 4 = \$346.00$$

4. Find the final payment by subtracting the interest refund from the amount still owed.

$$\$346.00 - \$9.27 = \$336.73 \qquad \text{final payment}$$

Buying on an installment plan allows the customer the privilege of using an item now and paying for it later. As a buyer, you must decide whether to buy an item on an installment plan or wait and purchase the item with cash.

EXAMPLE

One store sells a laptop computer for $1,439, while another store has the same computer for $125 a month for 12 months. What is the difference between the installment price and the cash price?

STEPS

1. Multiply the amount of the monthly payment by the number of monthly payments to find the installment price.

$$\$125 \times 12 = \$1,500 \qquad \text{installment price}$$

2. Subtract the retail price from the installment price.

$$\$1,500 - \$1,439 = \$61 \qquad \text{savings by paying cash}$$

Create a worksheet in Excel to calculate the cost of an installment loan.

EXAMPLE

For her home office, Carlotta wants to purchase a color laser printer that is advertised for a total cash price of $3,059.95. She is interested in obtaining an installment loan. The terms are 10% as a down payment, an interest rate of 18%, and a term of 2 years. What is the amount financed, the finance charge, the amount to be repaid, and the monthly payment?

Figure 11-5

Cost of Installment Loan

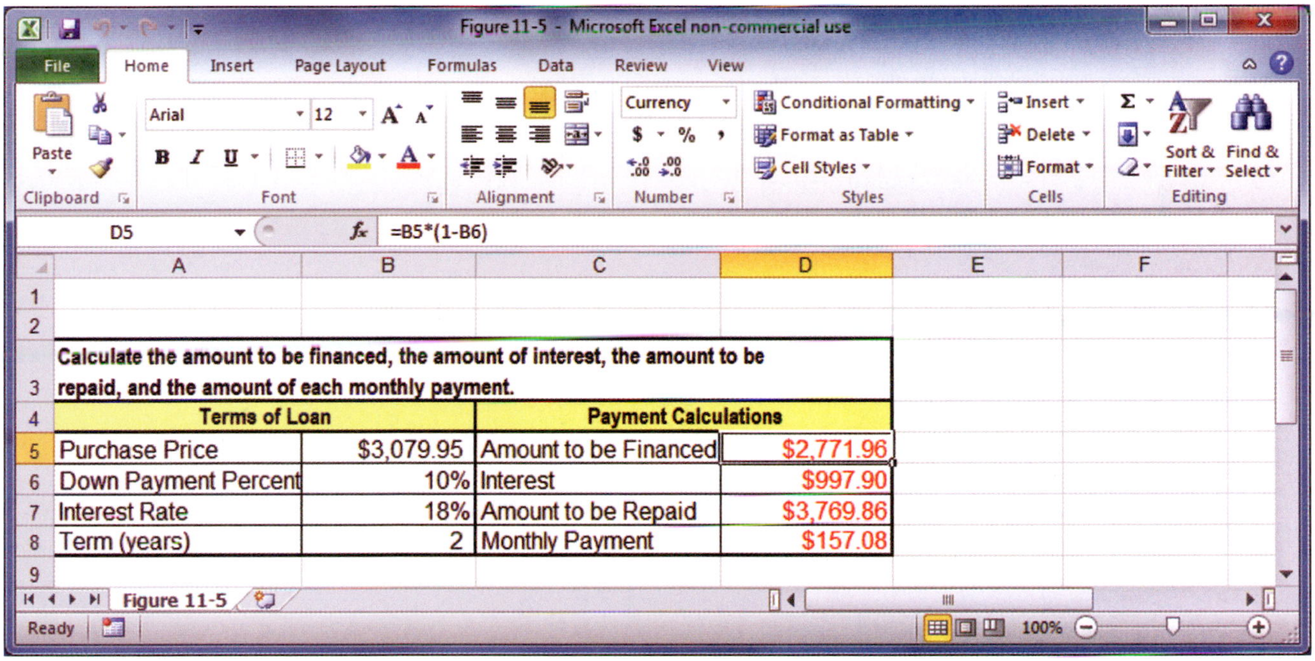

	Terms of Loan		Payment Calculations	
5	Purchase Price	$3,079.95	Amount to be Financed	$2,771.96
6	Down Payment Percent	10%	Interest	$997.90
7	Interest Rate	18%	Amount to be Repaid	$3,769.86
8	Term (years)	2	Monthly Payment	$157.08

Calculate the amount to be financed, the amount of interest, the amount to be repaid, and the amount of each monthly payment.

Formula bar: D5 =B5*(1-B6)

Study the steps below to calculate the amount to be financed, amount of interest, amount to be repaid, and amount of each monthly payment. See Figure 11-5.

STEPS

Retrieve the file *ch11pr03.xlsx*.

1. Enter a formula in Cell D5 to calculate the Amount to be Financed. Multiply the Purchase Price by the complement of the Down Payment Percent. The Excel formula is =B5*(1-B6).

2. Enter a formula in Cell D6 to calculate the Interest. Use the formula $I = P \times R \times T$. The Excel formula is =D5*B7*B8.

3. Enter a formula in Cell D7 to calculate the Amount to be Repaid. Add the Interest to the Amount to be Financed. The Excel formula is =D5+D6.

4. Enter a formula in Cell D8 to calculate the Monthly Payment. Divide the Amount to be Repaid by the number of monthly payments. The Excel formula is =D7/24.

5. Format Column D for Currency. Set Decimal places to 2. Set Currency symbol to $.
6. Save the file as *ch11pr03a.xlsx*.

Study the following example and steps to see how you can use Excel to calculate the finance charge and monthly payment. See Figure 11-6.

EXAMPLE

First State Bank financed Penny's 3-year loan for $15,000 so she could buy new computers for her real estate office. The bank charged 6.5% interest and required 10% down. What is the amount financed, the finance charge, and the monthly payment?

Figure 11-6

Finance Charge and Monthly Payment

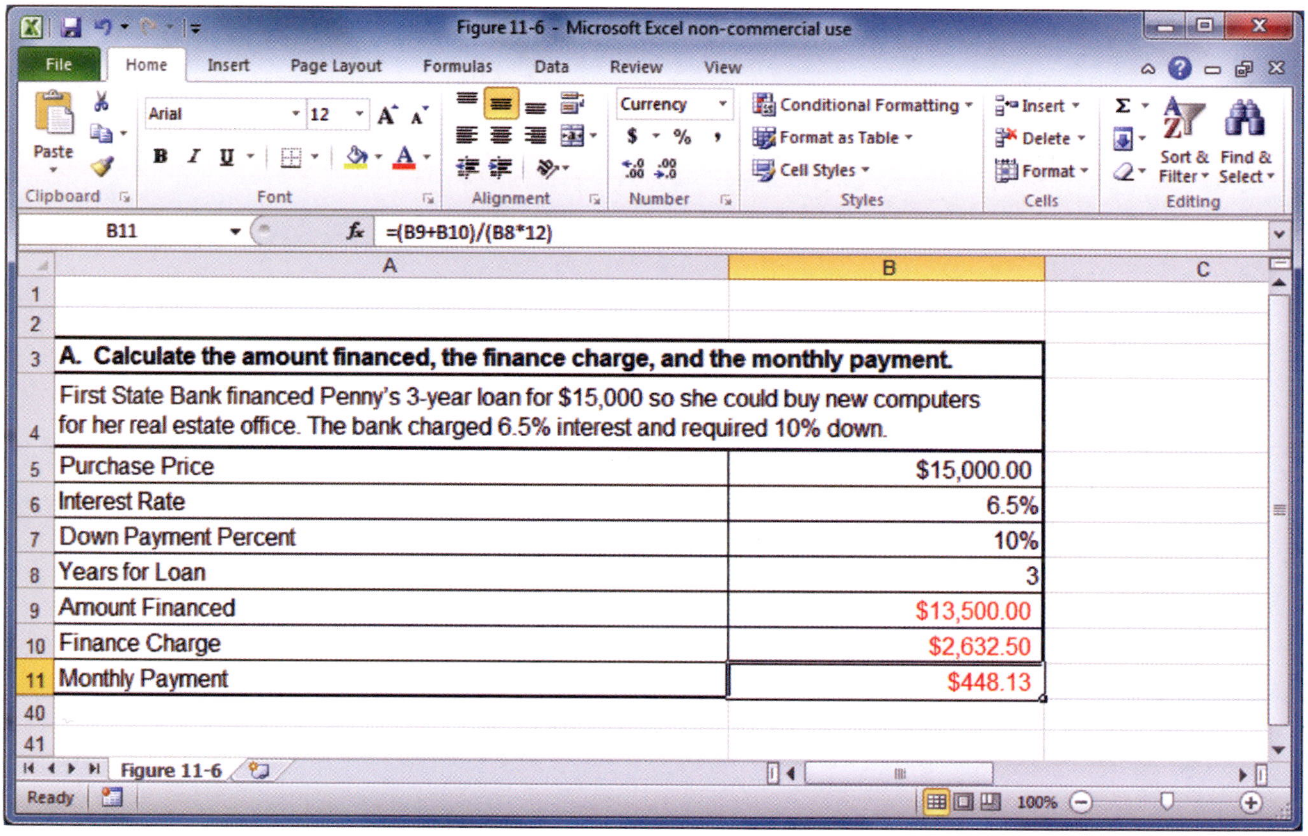

	A	B
3	**A. Calculate the amount financed, the finance charge, and the monthly payment.**	
4	First State Bank financed Penny's 3-year loan for $15,000 so she could buy new computers for her real estate office. The bank charged 6.5% interest and required 10% down.	
5	Purchase Price	$15,000.00
6	Interest Rate	6.5%
7	Down Payment Percent	10%
8	Years for Loan	3
9	Amount Financed	$13,500.00
10	Finance Charge	$2,632.50
11	Monthly Payment	$448.13

STEPS

Retrieve the file *ch11pr04.xlsx*.

1. In Cell B9, enter a formula to calculate the Amount Financed. Multiply the Purchase Price by the complement of the Down Payment Percent. The Excel formula is =B5*(1-B7).
2. In Cell B10, enter a formula to calculate the Finance Charge. Use the formula $I = P \times R \times T$. The Excel formula is =B9*B6*B8.
3. In Cell B11, enter a formula to calculate the Monthly Payment. Divide the amount to be repaid by the number of monthly payments. The Excel formula is =(B9+B10)/(B8*12).
4. Format dollar amounts for Currency, 2 Decimal places, and $.

Penny decided to pay off the loan after 30 months. By paying off the loan early, she is entitled to a refund on the finance charge. She wants to know the amount of the refund and the final payment.

Figure 11-7 shows the multimath formula =B10*(B24/B25) used to calculate the interest refund. In the steps below, you will calculate the remaining balance and loan payoff.

Figure 11-7

Interest Refund and Loan Payoff

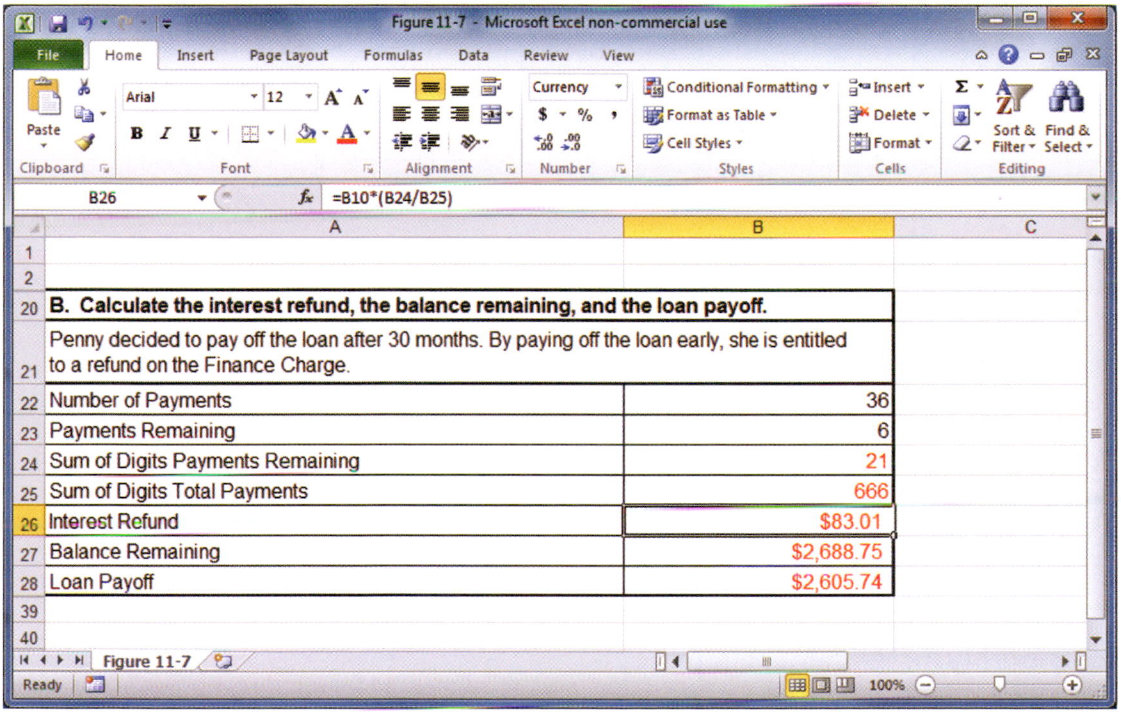

	A	B	C
20	**B. Calculate the interest refund, the balance remaining, and the loan payoff.**		
21	Penny decided to pay off the loan after 30 months. By paying off the loan early, she is entitled to a refund on the Finance Charge.		
22	Number of Payments	36	
23	Payments Remaining	6	
24	Sum of Digits Payments Remaining	21	
25	Sum of Digits Total Payments	666	
26	Interest Refund	$83.01	
27	Balance Remaining	$2,688.75	
28	Loan Payoff	$2,605.74	
39			
40			

STEPS

1. In Cell B24, enter a formula to calculate the Sum of Digits Payments Remaining. Use the formula $N(N+1)$ divided by 2, where N = the Number of Payments Remaining. The Excel formula is =B23*(B23+1)/2.

2. In Cell B25, enter a formula to calculate the Sum of Digits Total Payments. Use the formula $N(N+1)$ divided by 2, where N = the Number of Payments. The Excel formula is =B22*(B22+1)/2.

3. In Cell B26, enter a formula to calculate the Interest Refund. Multiply the Finance Charge by the refund fraction. The Excel formula is =B10*(B24/B25).

4. In Cell B27, enter a formula to compute the Balance Remaining. Multiply the Monthly Payment by the Payments Remaining. The Excel formula is =B11*B23.

5. In Cell B28, enter a formula to find the Loan Payoff. Subtract the Interest R from the Balance Remaining. The Excel formula is =B27-B26.

6. Format dollar amounts for Currency, 2 Decimal places, and $.

7. Save the file as *ch11pr04a.xlsx*.

Name _____ Date _____

Directions   Solve the following problems. Write your answers in the blanks provided. Round dollars to the nearest cent.

A. Compute the total amount of installment payments and installment price.   `OBJECTIVE 2`

Down Payment	Number of Payments	Installment Payment	Total Amount of Installment Payments		Installment Price	
$150	12	$63.75	1. _____		2. _____	
$350	10	$52.00	3. _____		4. _____	
$260	12	$39.75	5. _____		6. _____	

B. Find the total installment price and the finance charge.   `OBJECTIVE 2`

Retail Price	Down Payment	Monthly Installment	Term	Installment Price		Finance Charge	
$ 750	$ 75.00	$90.00	9 months	7. _____		8. _____	
$ 800	$ 80.00	$148.80	6 months	9. _____		10. _____	
$1,400	$350.00	$68.00	24 months	11. _____		12. _____	

C. Calculate the monthly installment payment.   `OBJECTIVE 3`

Down Payment	Installment Price	Number of Payments	Monthly Installment	
$500	$4,978	8	13. _____	
$280	$5,190	12	14. _____	

D. Calculate the interest refund.   `OBJECTIVE 4`

Finance Charge	Length of Loan	Time Left on Loan	Interest Refund	
$190	12 months	6 months	15. _____	
$525	2 years	10 months	16. _____	
$240	12 months	8 months	17. _____	

E. Determine the final payment. OBJECTIVE 5

Length of Loan	Amount of Payments	Interest Charged	Time Left on Loan		Final Payment
12 months	$ 67.30	$110.70	6 months	18.	_____
12 months	$112.20	$220.00	9 months	19.	_____
18 months	$167.40	$450.00	12 months	20.	_____

F. Solve the following word problems.

21. Eliana purchased a piano on installment with a down payment of $600 and 12 payments of $88.40. Find the installment price.   _____

22. Find the total amount of installment payments for Jeffrey. He purchased a wraparound sofa for his den. He agreed to pay 12 installments of $68.60.   _____

23. The installment price for a leather recliner chair was $1,350 for a 12-month loan. Kristen made a $150 down payment. Find the monthly payment.   _____

24. Calculate the rebate fraction on a 12-month loan paid off with 8 months remaining. Calculate the interest rebate with a $78.00 finance charge.

    _____ rebate fraction   _____ interest rebate

25. Gretchen Schmidt purchased an entertainment center on an installment plan. She made a down payment of $210.00 and financed the balance with loan payments for 24 months at $116.92. Determine the total amount of installment payments.   _____

26. Shawn is interested in purchasing a new computer system for $1,650.00 and would like to apply a down payment of 20%. Calculate the down payment amount.   _____

27. Calculate the amount financed by Shawn if he decides to purchase the new computer system.   _____

28. Determine the total amount of installment payments that Shawn will be responsible for if he decides to purchase the computer system on 24 installment payments of $165.00 per month.   _____

29. Tim purchased a new camera that had a cash price of $299.99. He made a down payment of 10% of the cash price. There was a finance charge of $76.50 on the unpaid balance. The unpaid balance, plus the carrying charges were to be paid in 12 equal monthly installments. What was the amount of each monthly payment?   _____

G. Use Excel to calculate amount to be financed, total interest, amount to be repaid, and monthly installment. OBJECTIVE 6

30. Retrieve the file *ch11ex03.xlsx*. Follow the directions. Save the file as *ch11ex03a.xlsx*.

31. Retrieve the file *ch11ex04.xlsx*. Follow the directions. Save the file as *ch11ex04a.xlsx*.

11.3 Mortgage Loans

OBJECTIVE 1 Identify terms used with mortgage loans.

Buying a home is probably the most expensive purchase you will ever make. Because buying a home involves an investment of tens of thousands of dollars, most people buy a home by making a down payment and borrowing the remainder of the purchase price to be paid in monthly installments. A **mortgage loan** is money lent to a borrower by a lender to purchase real estate, with the real estate itself serving as collateral for the loan. **Collateral** is property that is offered to secure a loan and that becomes subject to seizure upon **default**. Default is the failure to meet the terms of a credit agreement. **Foreclosure** is the process of the lender suing the borrower to prove that the borrower cannot repay the loan and asking the court to order the sale of the property in order to pay the debt.

A **first mortgage** is the primary mortgage on a home. Loans for mortgages are available from mortgage companies, savings and loan institutions, and banks. A **second mortgage** is available for homeowners who want to borrow money to make major home improvements, such as adding a room or remodeling a kitchen. Another reason homeowners borrow against their home is to help fund their children's college education. As with any loan, homeowners should give serious consideration to the indebtedness issue and the rights retained by the lenders in case they are no longer able to make their monthly payments.

Amortization is the process of paying off indebtedness by installments of principal and earned interest over a period of time. An **amortization schedule** gives a breakdown of the monthly payments in principal and interest. When potential buyers are considering the purchase of a home, one of the first questions they usually ask is "How much is the monthly payment?"

OBJECTIVE 2 Determine monthly mortgage payments.

Because of the lengthy calculations, it is not practical to calculate monthly payments manually for a home loan that has a term of 15, 20, 25, or 30 years. Specific computer software and financial calculators can provide this information to a potential buyer in a matter of minutes.

You can calculate the monthly mortgage payments by using an amortization table (also referred to as loan payment table). Table 11-1 gives the payment factor required for each $1,000 of a mortgage loan at different interest rates for a variety of terms.

Table 11-1

Loan Payment Table
Based on $1,000

Interest Rate	PAYMENT PERIOD (years)			
	15	20	25	30
8	$ 9.5565	$ 8.3644	$ 7.7182	$ 7.3376
8.5	9.8474	8.6782	8.0528	7.6891
9	10.1427	8.9973	8.3920	8.0462
9.5	10.4422	9.3213	8.7370	8.4085
10	10.7461	9.6505	9.0870	8.7757
10.5	11.0539	9.9838	9.4418	9.1474
11	11.3660	10.3219	9.8011	9.5232
11.5	11.6819	10.6643	10.1647	9.9030
12	12.0017	11.0109	10.5322	10.2861
12.5	12.3252	11.3614	10.9035	10.6726
13	12.6524	11.7158	11.2784	11.0620
13.5	12.9832	12.0737	11.6564	11.4541
14	13.3174	12.4352	12.0376	11.8487
14.5	13.6550	12.8000	12.4216	12.2456
15	13.9959	13.1679	12.8083	12.6444
15.5	14.3399	13.5388	13.1975	13.0452
16	14.6870	13.9126	13.5889	13.4476

EXAMPLE

Ibarhim was approved for his first home mortgage for $84,000. He made a down payment of $16,800, which was 20% of the total purchase price. The loan was financed for $67,200 at 8% for 30 years. Find the monthly payment, which does not include taxes or insurance.

© Monkey Business Images, 2010/Used under license from Shutterstock.com

STEPS

1. Find the amount financed. Remember to apply the percentage formula $(P = B \times R)$. Multiply the purchase price by the interest rate. Then subtract the down payment from the purchase price.

   $84,000 \times 0.20 = $16,800 down payment
   $84,000 - $16,800 = $67,200 amount financed

2. Compute the $1,000 units of amount to be financed. Divide the amount to be financed by $1,000.

   $67,200 \div $1,000 = 67.2 $1,000 units

3. Using the table, locate the term of the loan and interest rate. Where the two columns meet, find the factor or value. Multiply the factor by the $1,000 units computed in step 2 to determine the monthly payment, which includes the principal and the interest.

   $7.3376 \times 67.2 = $493.09 monthly payment

TIPS

If you know the down payment, you can calculate the amount financed using the complement.

In step 1 in the example, $84,000 \times 0.80 = $67,200.

After the monthly payment is determined, the lending institution prepares a loan amortization schedule. The payment schedule shows the monthly payments in principal and interest. The payment schedule below shows the loan amortization calculated for two months on $70,000, the amount financed at 12% interest for a 30-year term.

PAYMENT SCHEDULE				
Payment Number	Monthly Payment	Interest Payment	Principal Payment	Balance of Principal
1	$720.03	$700.00	$20.03	$69,979.97
2	$720.03	$699.80	$20.23	$69,959.74

The monthly payment of $720.03 was computed using the amount in the table: $10.2861 \times 70 = \$720.03$. However, the monthly payment shown here may be different from the payment shown on other schedules because of rounding. With an online amortization schedule or a mortgage calculator, the monthly payment may be rounded to $720.04.

Study these steps to learn how the interest and principal payments and balance of the principal in the payment schedule are computed.

STEPS

1. For the loan payment, compute the interest for 1 month by multiplying the amount of the loan by the interest rate and then dividing by 12 (months).

$$\$70,000 \times 0.12 \div 12 = \$700.00$$

2. Compute the monthly payment on the principal by subtracting the interest payment from the monthly payment.

$$\$720.03 - \$700 = \$20.03$$

3. Compute the balance of the principal after the first payment by subtracting the principal payment from the amount of the loan.

$$\$70,000.00 - \$20.03 = \$69,979.97 \quad \text{balance after first payment}$$

4. For all payments after the first one, compute the interest on the new principal balance. For the second payment

$$\$69,979.97 \times 0.12 \div 12 = \$699.80$$

5. Continue with steps 2, 3, and 4. (In step 3, subtract the principal payment from the new principal balance.)

These calculations show that the payments in the early years of a mortgage loan consist mostly of interest. At this point, only a small portion of each payment is applied to paying off the principal. As each payment is made, the amount of interest decreases so that a larger amount of payment applies to the principal. Only during the last few years of a loan does most of the monthly payment apply toward the principal.

You can use Excel to calculate the monthly payment. See Figure 11-8.

EXAMPLE

Pamela Lopez wants to purchase a home for $95,000. Her 30-year loan will be financed at 8% annual interest with a 20% down payment. She wants to know what her monthly payment will be, and she wants an amortization schedule.

Figure 11-8

Monthly Mortgage Payment

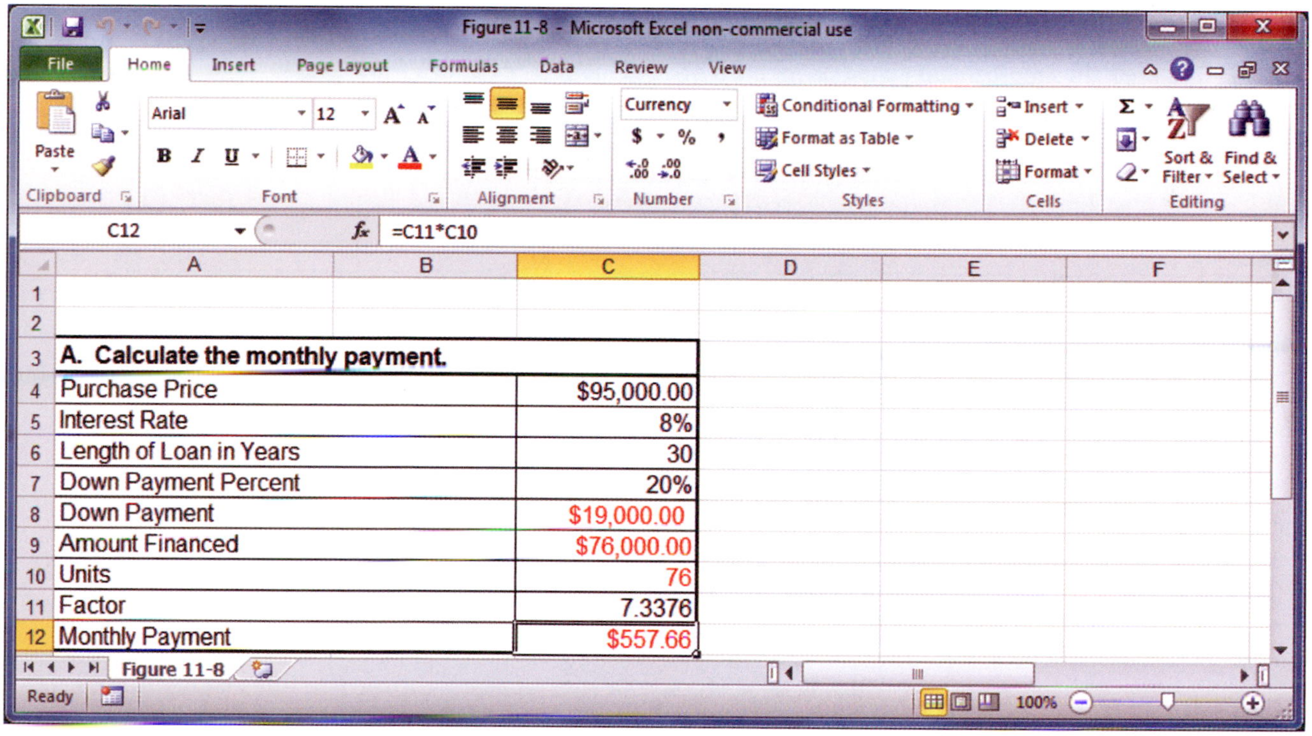

	A	B	C	D	E	F
1						
2						
3	A. Calculate the monthly payment.					
4	Purchase Price		$95,000.00			
5	Interest Rate		8%			
6	Length of Loan in Years		30			
7	Down Payment Percent		20%			
8	Down Payment		$19,000.00			
9	Amount Financed		$76,000.00			
10	Units		76			
11	Factor		7.3376			
12	Monthly Payment		$557.66			

C12 = =C11*C10

STEPS

Retrieve the file *ch11pr05.xlsx*.

A. Calculate the monthly payment.

1. In Cell C8, enter a formula to compute the Down Payment. (Multiply the Purchase Price by the Down Payment Percent.)

2. In Cell C9, enter a formula to compute the Amount Financed. (Subtract the Down payment from the Purchase Price.)

3. In Cell C10, enter a formula to compute the $1,000 Units of Amount Financed. (Divide the Amount Financed by 1,000.)

4. In Cell C12, enter a formula to compute the Monthly Payment. (Multiply the Factor given by the number of $1,000 Units in Cell C10.)

5. Format Cells C8, C9, and C12 for Currency, 2 Decimal places, and $. Format Cell C10 for Number. Set Decimal places to 0.

Figure 11-9 illustrates the first three months of Pamela's amortization schedule. The loan balance is entered in Cell E24 to begin the process of computing the payment schedule. In the steps below, you will compute the interest, principal, and loan balance.

Figure 11-9

Amortization Schedule

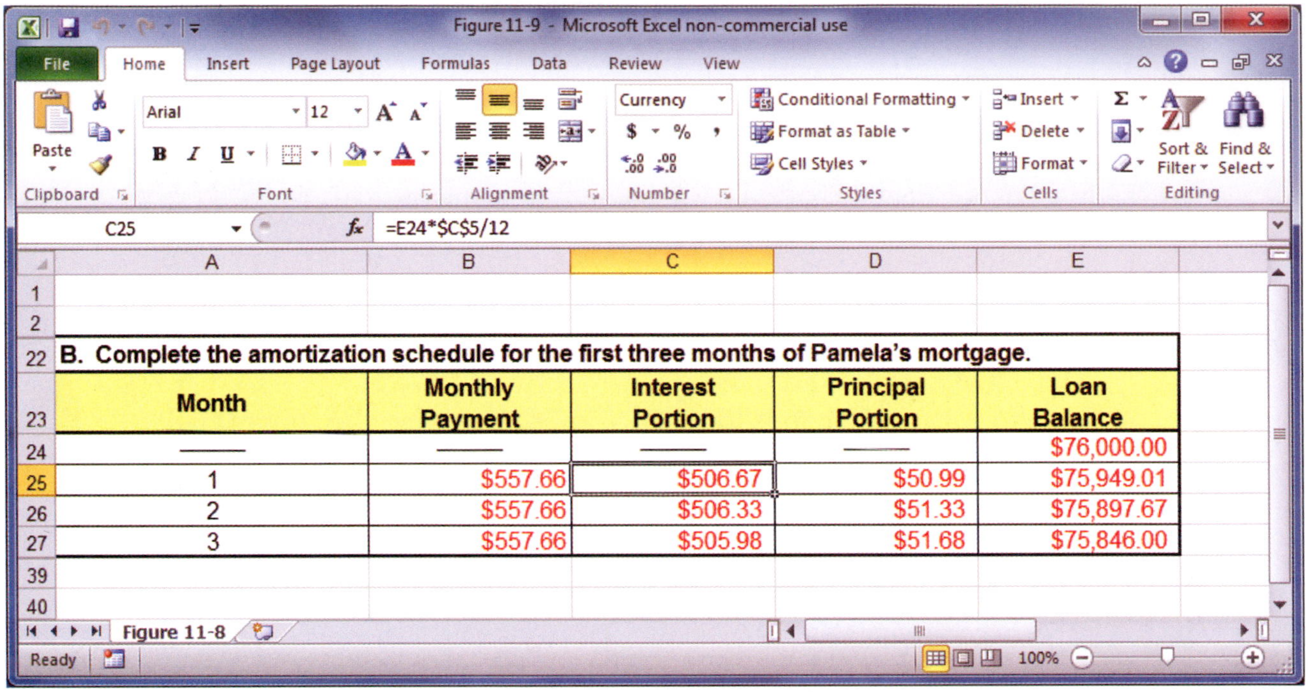

Month	Monthly Payment	Interest Portion	Principal Portion	Loan Balance
B. Complete the amortization schedule for the first three months of Pamela's mortgage.				
——	——	——	——	$76,000.00
1	$557.66	$506.67	$50.99	$75,949.01
2	$557.66	$506.33	$51.33	$75,897.67
3	$557.66	$505.98	$51.68	$75,846.00

B. Complete the amortization schedule for the first three months of Pamela's mortgage.

1. In Cell E24, enter the Amount Financed from Cell C9.
2. In Cell B25, enter the amount of the Monthly Payment. Copy it to Cells B26 and B27.
3. In Cell C25, enter a formula to compute the Interest Portion of the first Monthly Payment. Multiply the Loan Balance by the Interest Rate, divided by 12 months. Use an absolute cell reference for the Interest Rate. The Excel formula is =E24*$C$5/12.
4. In Cell D25, enter a formula to compute the Principal Portion. Subtract the Interest Portion from the Monthly Payment.
5. In Cell E25, enter a formula to calculate the Loan Balance after the first month's payment. Subtract the Principal Portion from the Loan Balance.
6. Copy the formulas in Cells C25, D25, and E25 to Rows 26 and 27 to complete the spreadsheet.
7. Format Columns B, C, D, and E for Currency, 2 Decimal places, and $.
8. Save the file as ***ch11pr05a.xlsx***.

Name _____ Date _____

Directions   Solve the following problems. Write your answers in the blanks provided. Round dollars to the nearest cent.

A. Use Table 11-1 to find the payment factor to 4 decimal places.   OBJECTIVE 2

Interest Rate	Term	Payment Factor
9.5%	15 years	1. _____
10.5%	25 years	2. _____
8%	30 years	3. _____
10%	25 years	4. _____

B. Using Table 11-1, calculate the monthly payment.   OBJECTIVE 2

Loan Amount	Interest Rate	Monthly Term	Payment
$80,000	9.5%	20 years	5. _____
$65,000	9.5%	25 years	6. _____
$169,450	8.5%	30 years	7. _____
$220,500	9%	25 years	8. _____
$175,000	8%	20 years	9. _____
$125,750	8.5%	25 years	10. _____

C. Prepare a payment schedule for the first, second, third, and fourth months   OBJECTIVE 3
of a loan of $80,000 at 12% interest for 30 years. The monthly payment
on this loan is $822.89.

Monthly Payment	Interest Payment	Principal Payment	Balance of Principal
$822.89	11. _____	12. _____	13. _____
$822.89	14. _____	15. _____	16. _____
$822.89	17. _____	18. _____	19. _____
$822.89	20. _____	21. _____	22. _____

D. Use Excel to calculate monthly payment and to prepare   OBJECTIVE 4
an amortization schedule.

23.   Retrieve the file *ch11ex05.xlsx*. Follow the directions. Save the file as *ch11ex05a.xlsx*.

24.   Retrieve the file *ch11ex06.xlsx*. Follow the directions. Save the file as *ch11ex06a.xlsx*.

Chapter Review and Assessment

KEY TERMS

adjusted balance

amortization

amortization schedule

amount financed

annual percentage rate (APR)

average daily balance (ADB)

bank card

billing cycle

billing statement

charge card

closed-end credit

collateral

credit agreement

credit cards

credit limit

credit line

debit card

default

down payment

finance charge

first mortgage

foreclosure

grace period

installment

installment loan

installment price

monthly payment

mortgage loan

open-end credit

previous balance

purchase cash price

refund

revolving charge account

Rule of 78

second mortgage

stated interest rate

sum-of-digits method

30-day account

total amount of installment payments

Truth in Lending

CONCEPTS	EXAMPLES
11.1 Calculate the finance charge using the previous balance. Compute the finance charge by multiplying the previous balance by the monthly rate.	Beginning balance is $302.78 and 1.5% is charged to calculate finance charge. $$\$302.78 \times 0.015 = \$4.54$$ $302.78 = $4.54 − payments + purchases − credits for returns = new balance
11.1 Calculate the new balance using the average daily balance. Find the number of days that have the same balance; total the balance of activities for each group of days and divide by number of days in cycle.	Number of days = 31 and sum of daily unpaid balances = $7,321.98. $7,321.98 ÷ 31 = $236.19 average daily balance $236.19 × 0.015 = $3.54 finance charge

CONCEPTS	EXAMPLES

11.2 Calculate the installment price and the finance charge.

1. Installment price is total of installment payments plus the down payment.

2. Multiply the number of payments by the payment amount. Add any down payment.

3. Finance charge is the difference between the retail price and installment price.

Down payment is $200; 6 installments of $196.25.

$6 \times \$196.25 = \$1,177.50$
$\$1,177.50 + \$200 = \$1,377.50$ total installment price

Retail price is $999.99
$\$1,377.50 - \$999.99 = \$377.51$

11.2 Calculate the monthly installment payment.

Calculate the installment payment by dividing the amount of installments by the number of payments.

Total amount of installment payments is $1,399.58 and number of payments is 6.

$\$1,399.58 \div 6 = \$233.26$ installment payment

11.2 Calculate the interest refund.

If paying off a loan early, a refund may be given. A refund is the unearned portion of finance charge on a loan.

1. Determine the sum of the digits of the payments remaining (numerator).

2. Find the sum of the digits of the total payments (denominator).

3. Multiply the refund fraction by the finance charge.

For a one-year loan with a finance charge of $172, paid off 3 months early:

$$\text{Sum} = \frac{N(N+1)}{2}, \text{ where } N = \text{the number of payments}$$

$N = 3$ payments remaining
$$\frac{3(3+1)}{2} = \frac{12}{2} = 6$$

$N = 12$ total payments
$$\frac{12(12+1)}{2} = \frac{156}{2} = 78$$

$$\frac{6}{78} \times \$172 = \$13.23 \qquad \text{interest refund}$$

11.2 Calculate the loan payoff.

1. Find the refund fraction using the formula.

2. Find the interest rebate by multiplying the refund fraction by the interest charged.

3. Determine the amount still owed on the loan by multiplying the amount of the payment by the number of payments still owed.

4. Find the final payment by subtracting the interest refund from the amount still owed.

For a one-year loan with a payment of $75.10, an interest charge of $62.45, paid off after 10 months:

$$\frac{2(2+1)}{2} = \frac{6}{2} = 3 \qquad \frac{12(12+1)}{2} = \frac{156}{2} = 78$$

$$\frac{3}{78} \text{ or } \frac{1}{26} \times \$62.45 = \$2.40 \qquad \text{interest refund}$$

$\$75.10 \times 2 = \$150.20$

$\$150.20 - \$2.40 = \$147.80 \qquad \text{final payment}$

CONCEPTS	EXAMPLES

11.3 Determine the monthly mortgage payments.

An amortization table provides values that represent a payment factor required for each $1,000 of a mortgage loan at different interest rates for a variety of terms of loans.

1. Find the amount financed. Subtract the down payment from the purchase price.

2. Compute the number of $1,000 units. Divide the amount financed by $1,000.

3. Locate the factor and multiply it by the $1,000 equivalent.

For a loan approved for $79,500 at 9% over a period of 25 years with 10% down payment:

$79,500 × 0.10 = $7,950
$79,500 − $7,950 = $71,550

$71,550 ÷ $1,000 = $71.55

8.3920 × $71.55 = $600.45   monthly payment

11.3 Prepare an amortization schedule.

A loan amortization schedule shows monthly payments in principal and interest.

1. For the loan payment, compute the interest for 1 month by multiplying the amount of the loan by the interest rate and then dividing by 12 (months).

2. Determine the monthly mortgage payment.

3. Compute the monthly payment on the principal by subtracting the interest payment from the monthly payment.

4. Compute the balance of the principal after the first payment by subtracting the principal payment from the amount of the loan.

5. For all payments after the first one, compute the interest on the new principal balance. For the second payment in the example:

6. Continue with steps 2, 3, and 4. (In step 3, subtract the principal payment from the new principal balance.)

For $85,000 financed at 10.5% interest financed for 15 years:

$85,000 × 0.105 ÷ 12 = $743.75

11.0539 × 85 = $939.57

$939.57 − $743.75 = $195.82

$85,000.00 − $195.82 = $84,804.18

balance after first payment

$84,804.18 × 0.105 ÷ 12 = $742.04

Chapter 11 Review Exercises

Name _____   Date _____

Directions   Solve the following problems. Write your answers in the blanks provided. Round dollars to the nearest cent. Round percents to the nearest tenth.

A.   Calculate the finance charge using the previous balance method.   1.1 OBJECTIVE 2

	Previous Balance	Monthly Rate	Finance Charge
1.	$365.30	1.8%	_____
2.	$190.40	1.5%	_____

B.   Determine the finance charge and the new balance. The finance charge is   1.1 OBJECTIVE 2
based on the previous balance before payments or credits are subtracted. The monthly rates are 2% on amounts up to $1,000 and 1.5% on amounts over $1,000. Assume the balance was not paid within the specified period.

Previous Balance		Finance Charge	Payments	Credits	Purchases		New Balance
$1,215.60	3.	_____	$378.50	–0–	$161.30	4.	_____
$1,015.40	5.	_____	$487.65	$39.70	$ 62.00	6.	_____
$1,265.30	7.	_____	$315.00	–0–	$146.00	8.	_____

C.   Determine the annual percentage rate or monthly rate. Round to   1.1 OBJECTIVE 2
2 decimal places.

	Monthly Rate	Annual Percentage Rate		Monthly Rate	Annual Percentage Rate
9.	_____	18%	10.	1.8%	_____
11.	_____	26%	12.	2.35%	_____

D.   Using the previous balance method, calculate the finance charge and   1.1 OBJECTIVE 2
account balance.

Previous Balance	APR		Finance Charge		Account Balance
$542.18	18.5%	13.	_____	14.	_____
$198.08	21.5%	15.	_____	16.	_____

E. Determine the finance charge using the average daily balance method. **1.1 OBJECTIVE 3**
John Richard's charge account shows an opening balance of $500 on
July 1. A payment of $180 was made on July 10. Purchases of $175 were
made on July 15. This amount is in effect until the last day of the billing
cycle. An annual rate of 18% is applied to this account.

17. Average daily balance:

18. Finance charge:

19. New balance:

F. Use the following information to compute the new balance.

Previous balance:	$313.40
Finance charge:	$4.70
Payments:	$113.40
Credits:	$12.50
Purchases:	$37.58

20. New balance: _____

G. Calculate the following information on these installment purchases. **1.2 OBJECTIVES 2, 3**
A 10% cash down payment has already been calculated. The terms
are the balance must be paid in 12 monthly installments and the interest is 18%.

Amount to Be Financed	Finance Charge	Amount to Be Repaid	Monthly Installment
$2,660	21. _____	22. _____	23. _____
$ 999	24. _____	25. _____	26. _____
$1,350	27. _____	28. _____	29. _____

H. Find the interest refund. **1.2 OBJECTIVE 4**

Finance Charge	Length of Loan	Paid in Full	Interest Refund
$150.00	12 months	10 months	30. _____
$224.00	24 months	12 months	31. _____
$337.00	14 months	10 months	32. _____

I. Solve the following word problems.

Find the installment price and expense of using the installment plan for this purchase. The cash price is $4,509. The down payment is $451. The number of payments is 36. The monthly payment is $129.63.

33. Installment price   _____

34. Expense of installment buying   _____

Using the average daily balance method, determine the average daily balance and finance charge. A customer's charge account shows a balance of $255.50 on June 1. A payment of $155.50 was made on June 10. Purchases of $340 were made on June 15. An annual rate of 18.5% is applied to the account. The month of June has 30 days. The next billing date is July 1.

35. Average daily balance   _____

36. Finance charge   _____

37. A credit card account shows a previous balance of $1,740.35. The finance charge is 1.7% on the previous balance of $1,000. A rate of 1.5% is applied to balances that exceed $1,000. Calculate the total finance charge to be applied to this account.   _____

38. An account with a billing date of June 8 shows a beginning balance of $486.32. A charge of $39.64 was made on June 10. A credit of $14.23 was recorded on June 12. A payment of $150.00 was made on June 23. Calculate the average daily balance as of the next billing date of July 8.   _____

39. A finance charge of 1.75% is applied to monthly account balances of $500.00 or less. The rate drops to 1.5% on previous balances that exceed $500.00. Mr. Caster's account has a balance of $368.23. Calculate the finance charge.   _____

40. Find the finance charge of Wanda Lowe's credit card if the unpaid balance is $567 and the rate is 1.5%.   _____

41. Find the monthly rate of interest on John Clevinger's credit card account if the unpaid balance is $159 and the finance charge is $2.86. There were no charges or payments this month.   _____

42. On April 1, the unpaid balance on a credit card is $236. During the month, purchases of $24, $55, and $12.75 are made. Using the previous balance method, find the unpaid balance on May 1 if the finance charge is 1.6% of the unpaid balance and a payment of $45 is made on April 15.   _____

43. Horatio Jeves had a previous balance of $129.88 on his department store credit card. He made purchases of $26.77 and a payment of $55. The interest charge was 1.5%. Find the new unpaid balance of Horatio's credit card using the previous balance method.   _____

J. Use Excel to calculate amounts on open- and closed-end credit and mortgages.

> **11.1** OBJECTIVE **4**, **11.2** OBJECTIVE **6**
> **11.3** OBJECTIVE **4**

44. Retrieve the file *ch11ex07.xlsx*. Follow the directions. Save the file as *ch11ex07a.xlsx*.

45. Retrieve the file *ch11ex08.xlsx*. Follow the directions. Save the file as *ch11ex08a.xlsx*.

46. Retrieve the file *ch11ex09.xlsx*. Follow the directions. Save the file as *ch11ex09a.xlsx*.

A mortgage loan officer uses math on a continual basis during the mortgage lending process. When a prospective borrower applies for a loan, many calculations are made: debt-to-income-ratio, percentage of down payment, real estate commission, amount of prepaid interest, and amount of prepaid taxes. The loan officer also uses an amortization schedule to show buyers how the principal decreases over time.

TRY IT...

Two clients, Maria and Scott Hamilton, applied for a mortgage to buy their first home. Their annual income is $83,288 and they want a monthly house payment of $729. The annual property taxes on the home would be $4,201 and the annual homeowner's insurance premium would be $1,189. The couple pays $575 a month in car payments and $250 a month toward student loans. If the Hamiltons have a debt-to-income ratio that is less than 36%, they will be approved for their loan.

1. Find the monthly amounts to the nearest cent for the Hamiltons' property taxes and homeowner's insurance by dividing the annual figures by 12. Then find the sum of all the monthly payments.

2. Find the Hamiltons' monthly income by dividing their annual income by 12.

3. Calculate the debt-to-income ratio by dividing the monthly debt by the monthly income. What is the ratio? Will the Hamiltons be approved for their loan? Explain.

Write about Math

1. Describe the difference between open-end and closed-end credit.

2. List at least two examples of open-end and closed-end credit.

3. What does it mean to amortize a loan? What information does an amortization table provide?

Personal Finance

Do you use credit cards wisely?

Many adults use credit cards on a regular basis. To make sure you use these efficiently, you should learn how credit cards work. Suppose you have a credit card balance. You realize that overusing your credit cards has been the biggest deterrent to reaching your financial goals.

You are thinking about buying a house, so you want to know what your creditors have said about you. Your credit report includes personal information, such as date of birth, social security number, name, address (current and previous), telephone number, and current and previous employers. Your credit history includes information about each credit account and payment history. In addition, your report contains information obtained from public records, such as job history, whether you own your home and whether you have been sued, arrested, or have filed for bankruptcy.

The Fair Credit Reporting Act allows you to obtain one free credit report from each credit-reporting

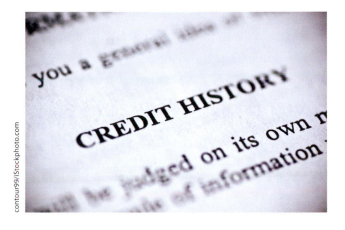

contour99/iStockphoto.com

company every year. Instead of collecting three reports from three different credit bureaus (Equifax, Experian, and TransUnion), you may obtain a combined copy of your credit report from a reputable website.

1. Obtain your credit report and review it. If you find an error in your credit report, call or write to the credit bureau explaining the error in detail. Provide any necessary documents to help prove your statements. Send all your paperwork by certified mail, return receipt requested.

2. A method of reducing debt is transferring credit card balances to a card with a lower interest rate so more of your payment is applied to principal and less to interest each month. Do an online search using keywords, such as *best credit cards* or *top ten credit card offers* to find some credit card offers. Choose three credit cards to consider.

3. In a table format, list your current credit card and the three credit cards you found. List each interest rate. If it is an introductory rate, list the conditions for the rate, and the regular rate.

4. Summarize the information you obtained from your comparison. Reference the website you visited to gather this information. Write a conclusion describing whether you think you should transfer a balance and why or why not.

5. To avoid future mistakes in using your credit card, learn more about common mistakes credit card users make. Do a general online search using keywords such as *top ten credit card mistakes*.

6. Identify one or two of the tips that would be more difficult for you to avoid and provide the reason.

7. Summarize the information.

Name _____   Date _____   Score _____

Directions   Solve the following problems. Write your answers in the blanks provided. Round dollars to the nearest cent. Round percents to the nearest tenth.

A. Using the previous balance method, find the monthly finance charge and account balance.   `11.1 OBJECTIVE 2`

Previous Balance	APR		Finance Charge		Account Balance
$287.44	12%	1. _____		2. _____
$3,200.00	18%	3. _____		4. _____
$1,843.50	16%	5. _____		6. _____

B. Calculate the average daily balance and finance charge.   `11.1 OBJECTIVE 3`

The unpaid balance showed $1,235.45 on June 15; a payment of $300 was made on June 25, and a charge of $57.42 was made on June 28. The billing cycle is 31 days. The monthly rate is 1.6%.

7. _____ average daily balance   8. _____ finance charge

C. Find the installment price and the finance charge. The down payment is 10% of the cash price.   `11.2 OBJECTIVE 2`

Cash Price	Monthly Payment	Length of Loan	Installment Price		Finance Charge
$485	$50.12	12 months	9. _____	10. _____
$780	$90.60	9 months	11. _____	12. _____
$299	$62.30	6 months	13. _____	14. _____

D. Calculate the monthly installment payment.   `11.2 OBJECTIVE 3`

Installment Price	Down Payment	Number of Payments	Monthly Payment
$2,210.48	$ 331.57	10	15. _____
$7,250.40	$1,500.00	24	16. _____
$4,075.28	$ 815.06	12	17. _____

E. Find the interest refund for these problems. Remember to first determine the time left in the loan.   `11.2 OBJECTIVE 4`

	Finance Charge	Length of Loan	Paid in Full	Interest Refund
18.	$192.07	24 months	14 months	_____
19.	$209.04	12 months	8 months	_____
20.	$224.01	12 months	6 months	_____

F. Find the final payment for these loans. 11.2 OBJECTIVE 5

	Length of Loan	Amount of Payments	Interest Charge	Paid in Full	Final Payment
21.	16 month	$110.00	$232.40	12 months	_____
22.	12 month	$ 97.80	$197.30	8 months	_____
23.	14 month	$119.00	$187.20	10 months	_____

G. Solve the following word problems.

24. Using the average daily balance method, compute the finance charge. A customer's charge account shows a balance of $600 on May 1. A payment of $320 was made on May 10. Purchases of $290 were made on May 15. An annual rate of 18% is applied to the account.

   a. Average daily balance _____

   b. Finance charge _____

25. John and Rachel purchased new furniture for their sunroom on an installment plan of 18 monthly payments of $176.67 each, with a down payment of $300. The actual cash price was $2,995. How much more did they pay for buying on the installment plan? _____

26. A loan is being paid in 14 equal monthly payments. At the end of the ninth month, the loan is paid off. What is the rebate fraction? _____

27. The installment price of a breakfast table is $1,450, the down payment is $290, and the number of payments is 8. What is the monthly installment payment? _____

28. If the cash price of an item is $499, the down payment is $50, and there are 18 monthly payments of $29.43, how much is the additional cost of using the installment plan? _____

29. Using Table 11-1, provided on page 421, determine the monthly payment, excluding taxes and insurance, of a $68,000 mortgage loan over a period of 25 years at 10% interest. _____

30. Find the monthly payment for a mortgage loan for a house valued at $102,000 financed at 8% for 30 years. A 20% down payment is required. _____

31. A digital camera with a cash price of $999 can be purchased on the installment plan in 18 monthly payments of $75. Find the amount of finance charge. _____

32. Shirley Lindale borrowed money from her brother-in-law and is repaying it at $55 a month for 12 months. What is the finance charge refund after making 8 payments if the finance charge is $435? _____

H. Use Excel to calculate amounts on open- and closed-end credit and mortgages. 11.1 OBJECTIVE 4, 11.2 OBJECTIVE 6 11.3 OBJECTIVE 4

33. Retrieve the file *ch11qz01.xlsx*. Follow the directions. Save the file as *ch11qz01a.xlsx*.

34. Retrieve the file *ch11qz02.xlsx*. Follow the directions. Save the file as *ch11qz02a.xlsx*.

35. Retrieve the file *ch11qz03.xlsx*. Follow the directions. Save the file as *ch11qz03a.xlsx*.

The most important decisions you make in your lifetime that will have the greatest impact on your quality of life after you retire are those decisions you make early in life about retirement planning. You must be knowledgeable about your choices and decide wisely so you can be assured of comfort in your retirement years. You can achieve this knowledge by studying annuities, stocks, and bonds. This chapter by no means covers all you need to know, but it does introduce some of the basics.

FINANCIAL ADVISOR

Photo courtesy o R. Bryant Moore

Bryant Moore is a financial advisor at a large financial services firm. He specializes in financial planning for medical and dental professionals and entrepreneurs. Bryant helps business owners plan for the future by having a better understanding of their wealth and investments. He says, "Many clients know just enough about their finances and the stock market to be dangerous. It is my job to educate them on the math side, including risk and consequences." Bryant also helps train new advisors on good techniques when working with clients as well as the philosophy of financial planning.

Financial advising is more intricate than number-crunching and investments. Communicating complex data in an easy-to-understand manner is essential. When first meeting with a client, Bryant spends hours interpreting the facts, but he also helps explain the behavioral side of the data. "In order to build a longstanding relationship with a client, conversation needs to be intimate," he says, "Once the trust is built, I can work with them to find their own definition of financial success."

How Math is Used in Financial Advising

In order to plan for a client's current and future finances, financial advisors must perform quick math in their heads. Bryant says, "When going over financial scenarios with someone using lifetime income, it is essential to know percentages on the fly." It is also important to do quick math when reviewing a business budget with a client. Bryant needs to be able to calculate and explain items on an income sheet such as taxes and revenue.

Financial advisors rely heavily on planning software and calculators, but need to understand the math and formulas in order to interpret the information. When analyzing an annuity, Bryant calculates future and present values, compound interest, and rate of return. "Most people aren't looking for a big pot of money at the end of the day," Bryant says, "They are looking for financial stability and for that, efficiency is the key."

What Do You Think?

What skills do you need to improve in order to be a financial advisor?

Math Skills Used

Addition

Subtraction

Multiplication

Statistics

Ratios

Other Skills Needed

Communication

Interpersonal skills

Leadership

Patience

12.1 Annuities

OBJECTIVE **1** Identify terms used with annuities.

To understand annuities better, you must first become familiar with the terminology. Learn the following annuity terms.

Annuity   A regular sequence of equal payments made into an account at regular time intervals; in other words, a stream of payments.

Annuity Certain   A classification of annuities with a certain set number of payments.

Annuity Due   Regular deposits (payments) of an annuity made at the beginning of the period.

Contingent Annuities   An annuity having no fixed number of payments but depending on an uncertain event, such as life insurance payments ceasing at the death of the insured.

Fixed Tax-Deferred Annuity   A contract between an individual and an insurance company for a guaranteed interest-bearing policy with guaranteed income options.

Future Value of an Annuity   The future dollar amount of a series of annuity payments plus interest.

Individual Retirement Account (IRA)   Also referred to as a regular IRA; amounts paid into an account that are usually excluded from federal income taxes in the current year.

Mutual Funds   A professionally managed portfolio of stocks and bonds or other investments divided into shares.

Ordinary Annuity   Regular deposits (payments) of an annuity made at the end of the period.

Payment Period   The time between payments.

Present Value of an Annuity   The amount needed to invest today to receive a stream of payments for a given number of years in the future.

Roth IRA   Amounts paid into an account that are not excluded from federal income taxes, but the interest grows tax free.

Sinking Fund   A fund set up to receive periodic payments to be assured of a certain amount of money.

Tax-Deferred   Postponing taxes on money until a future point in time.

Term of an Annuity   The time from the first annuity payment period to the end of the last annuity payment period.

Variable Annuity   A fund that provides the advantage of a fixed annuity with potential returns available by the investment of money in the stock market.

An *annuity* is a regular sequence of equal payments made into an account at regular time intervals. Companies set up annuities for many purposes. For example, if money is needed in three years to purchase a large piece of equipment, an annuity can be set up to make sure the money is available when the equipment is purchased. An employee can set up an annuity to assure a sum of money on which to live at retirement. Other examples include saving for a vacation, preparing for college expenses, and accumulating money to purchase a building.

Types of Annuities

What is a fixed tax-deferred annuity? A fixed tax-deferred annuity, also referred to as a tax-deferred annuity, is an agreement with an insurance or investment company for a policy that will result in income options at some point in the future. To create money for retirement, money is withheld from an employee's gross earnings or paid by the employer to an insurance or investment company that agrees to pay interest on the money. The employee does not pay taxes on the money paid or on the interest earned as the account grows until he or she makes a withdrawal or begins receiving an annuity income.

An IRS penalty tax, currently 10%, may be imposed on any withdrawal made prior to a person reaching the age of $59\frac{1}{2}$ years old.

What is a variable annuity? A variable annuity provides the advantages of a traditional fixed annuity with the potential return that is available by investing money in the stock market. The investment options you may choose from in a variable annuity are referred to as "sub accounts." These sub accounts are structured as mutual funds or as segregated investment portfolios that are managed by professional investment managers. Of course, an investment of this type can be more risky than an investment in a fixed tax-deferred annuity.

What is an IRA? In many cases, you can create your own retirement plan by paying into an IRA account. Since 2008, the limit you can contribute to a traditional IRA has been $5,000. However, those 50 or older can contribute an extra $1,000 for a $6,000 total contribution limit. IRAs are tax-deferred. The money is subject to income tax when withdrawn. The 10% penalty applies to withdrawals from IRAs until age $59\frac{1}{2}$.

What is a Roth IRA? A Roth individual retirement account is a personal saving plan that offers tax advantages to setting aside money for retirement. Contributions to the Roth IRA are not tax deductible. Therefore, taxes are paid on the money in the current year. One tax break is that interest earned on the money and capital gains are tax free when the money is withdrawn provided guidelines are met. For the most current information regarding Roth IRA contributions, refer to the IRS web site.

To summarize, an IRA can be a sound way to invest for retirement, especially if you are able to deduct a portion of your contributions from your income. This will help you save on taxes. Annuities can be particularly attractive if you are looking for tax-advantage opportunities well into your retirement years, are not planning to make withdrawals for several years, and seek some of the benefits of a life insurance policy. Before you make any decision, determine your goals.

Classification of Annuities

Annuities are classified into two groups—*contingent annuities* and *annuities certain.* A contingent annuity has no fixed number of payments but depends on an uncertain event, such as a person's death. An example of a contingent annuity is life insurance payments that cease when the insured dies. An annuity certain has a set number of payments, such as the mortgage payments on a home. These two groups can be divided into ordinary and annuity due.

OBJECTIVE **3** Calculate the future value of an ordinary annuity.

You will calculate an ordinary annuity using the manual method. Then, you will use a table that simplifies calculating ordinary annuities.

Calculate the future value of an ordinary annuity manually. With an ordinary annuity, you pay your money at the end of the period (monthly, quarterly, annually). The purpose of your calculation is to find the value of the annuity after the stream of payments has been made.

EXAMPLE

Find the value of an investment after 3 years for a $4,000 ordinary annuity at 6%.

STEPS

1. Initial investment at end of year 1	$ 4,000	Year 1
2. Calculate interest at the end of year 2 and add to the balance. $4,000 × 0.06 = $240	$ 240 $ 4,240	Interest
3. Add the additional money invested at the end of year 2	$ 4,000 $ 8,240	Year 2
4. Calculate interest at the end of year 3 and add to the balance. $8,240 × 0.06 = $494 rounded	$ 494 $ 8,734	Interest
5. Add the additional investment at the end of year 3.	$ 4,000 $ 12,734	Year 3

When you deposit $4,000 at the end of each year at an annual interest rate of 6%, the value of the annuity will grow to $12,734. What was called *maturity value* in compounding money is called *future value of the annuity.* This same calculation can be completed more easily using Table 12-1.

Calculate the future value of an ordinary annuity using an annuity table. Use the following steps to calculate the future value of an ordinary annuity by using the ordinary annuity table shown in Table 12-1.

EXAMPLE

Find the value of an investment after 3 years for a $4,000 ordinary annuity at 6%.

Table 12-1 Future Value of an Annuity

Future Value of an Annuity of $1
n = number of periods in annuity; i = interest per period

n	1%	1.5%	2%	2.5%	3%	4%	5%	6%	8%	10%	12%	n
1	1.00000	1.00000	1.00000	1.00000	1.00000	1.00000	1.00000	1.00000	1.00000	1.00000	1.00000	1
2	2.01000	2.01500	2.02000	2.02500	2.03000	2.04000	2.05000	2.06000	2.08000	2.10000	2.12000	2
3	3.03010	3.04522	3.06040	3.07562	3.09090	3.12160	3.15250	3.18360	3.24640	3.31000	3.37440	3
4	4.06040	4.09090	4.12161	4.15252	4.18363	4.24646	4.31013	4.37462	4.50611	4.64100	4.77933	4
5	5.10101	5.15227	5.20404	5.25633	5.30914	5.41632	5.52563	5.63709	5.86660	6.10510	6.35285	5
6	6.15202	6.22955	6.30812	6.38774	6.46841	6.63298	6.80191	6.97532	7.33593	7.71561	8.11519	6
7	7.21354	7.32299	7.43428	7.54743	7.66246	7.89829	8.14201	8.39384	8.92280	9.48717	10.08901	7
8	8.28567	8.43284	8.58297	8.73612	8.89234	9.21423	9.54911	9.89747	10.63663	11.43589	12.29969	8
9	9.36853	9.55933	9.75463	9.95452	10.15911	10.58280	11.02656	11.49132	12.48756	13.57948	14.77566	9
10	10.46221	10.70272	10.94972	11.20338	11.46388	12.00611	12.57789	13.18079	14.48656	15.93742	17.54874	10
11	11.56683	11.86326	12.16872	12.48347	12.80780	13.48635	14.20679	14.97164	16.64549	18.53117	20.65458	11
12	12.68250	13.04121	13.41209	13.79555	14.19203	15.02581	15.91713	16.86994	18.97713	21.38428	24.13313	12
13	13.80933	14.23683	14.68033	15.14044	15.61779	16.62684	17.71298	18.88214	21.49530	24.52271	28.02911	13
14	14.94742	15.45038	15.97394	16.51895	17.08632	18.29191	19.59863	21.01507	24.21492	27.97498	32.39260	14
15	16.09690	16.68214	17.29342	17.93193	18.59891	20.02359	21.57856	23.27597	27.15211	31.77248	37.27971	15
16	17.25786	17.93237	18.63929	19.38022	20.15688	21.82453	23.65749	25.67253	30.32428	35.94973	42.75328	16
17	18.43044	19.20136	20.01207	20.86473	21.76159	23.69751	25.84037	28.21288	33.75023	40.54470	48.88367	17
18	19.61475	20.48938	21.41231	22.38635	23.41444	25.64541	28.13238	30.90565	37.45024	45.59917	55.74971	18
19	20.81090	21.79672	22.84056	23.94601	25.11687	27.67123	30.53900	33.75999	41.44626	51.15909	63.43968	19
20	22.01900	23.12367	24.29737	25.54466	26.87037	29.77808	33.06595	36.78559	45.76196	57.27500	72.05244	20
21	23.23919	24.47052	25.78332	27.18327	28.67649	31.96920	35.71925	39.99273	50.42292	64.00250	81.69874	21
22	24.47159	25.83758	27.29898	28.86286	30.53678	34.24797	38.50521	43.39229	55.45676	71.40275	92.50258	22
23	25.71630	27.22514	28.84496	30.58443	32.45288	36.61789	41.43048	46.99583	60.89330	79.54302	104.60289	23
24	26.97346	28.63352	30.42186	32.34904	34.42647	39.08260	44.50200	50.81558	66.76476	88.49733	118.15524	24
25	28.24320	30.06302	32.03030	34.15776	36.45926	41.64591	47.72710	54.86451	73.10594	98.34706	133.33387	25
26	29.52563	31.51397	33.67091	36.01171	38.55304	44.31174	51.11345	59.15638	79.95442	109.18177	150.33393	26
27	30.82089	32.98668	35.34432	37.91200	40.70963	47.08421	54.66913	63.70577	87.35077	121.09994	169.37401	27
28	32.12910	34.48148	37.05121	39.85980	42.93092	49.96758	58.40258	68.52811	95.33883	134.20994	190.69889	28
29	33.45039	35.99870	38.79223	41.85630	45.21885	52.96629	62.32271	73.63980	103.96594	148.63093	214.58275	29
30	34.78489	37.53868	40.56808	43.90270	47.57542	56.08494	66.43885	79.05819	113.28321	164.49402	241.33268	30
31	36.13274	39.10176	42.37944	46.00027	50.00268	59.32834	70.76079	84.80168	123.34587	181.94342	271.29261	31
32	37.49407	40.68829	44.22703	48.15028	52.50276	62.70147	75.29883	90.88978	134.21354	201.13777	304.84772	32
33	38.86901	42.29861	46.11157	50.35403	55.07784	66.20953	80.06377	97.34316	145.95062	222.25154	342.42945	33
34	40.25770	43.93309	48.03380	52.61289	57.73018	69.85791	85.06696	104.18375	158.62667	245.47670	384.52098	34
35	41.66028	45.59209	49.99448	54.92821	60.46208	73.65222	90.32031	111.43478	172.31680	271.02437	431.66350	35
36	43.07688	47.27597	51.99437	57.30141	63.27594	77.59831	95.83632	119.12087	187.10215	299.12681	484.46312	36
37	44.50765	48.98511	54.03425	59.73395	66.17422	81.70225	101.62814	127.26812	203.07032	330.03949	543.59869	37
38	45.95272	50.71989	56.11494	62.22730	69.15945	85.97034	107.70955	135.90421	220.31595	364.04343	609.83053	38
39	47.41225	52.48068	58.23724	64.78298	72.23423	90.40915	114.09502	145.05846	238.94122	401.44778	684.01020	39
40	48.88637	54.26789	60.40198	67.40255	75.40126	95.02552	120.79977	154.76197	259.05652	442.59256	767.09142	40
41	50.37524	56.08191	62.61002	70.08762	78.66330	99.82654	127.83976	165.04768	280.78104	487.85181	860.14239	41
42	51.87899	57.92314	64.86222	72.83981	82.02320	104.81960	135.23175	175.95054	304.24352	537.63699	964.35948	42
43	53.39778	59.79199	67.15947	75.66080	85.48389	110.01238	142.99334	187.50758	329.58301	592.40069	1081.08262	43
44	54.93176	61.68887	69.50266	78.55232	89.04841	115.41288	151.14301	199.75803	356.94965	652.64076	1211.81253	44
45	56.48107	63.61420	71.89271	81.51613	92.71986	121.02939	159.70016	212.74351	386.50562	718.90484	1358.23003	45
46	58.04589	65.56841	74.33056	84.55403	96.50146	126.87057	168.68516	226.50812	418.42607	791.79532	1522.21764	46
47	59.62634	67.55194	76.81718	87.66789	100.39650	132.94539	178.11942	241.09861	452.90015	871.97485	1705.88375	47
48	61.22261	69.56522	79.35352	90.85958	104.40840	139.26321	188.02539	256.56453	490.13216	960.17234	1911.58980	48
49	62.83483	71.60870	81.94059	94.13107	108.54065	145.83373	198.42666	272.95840	530.34274	1057.18957	2141.98058	49
50	64.46318	73.68283	84.57940	97.48435	112.79687	152.66708	209.34800	290.33590	573.77016	1163.90853	2400.01825	50

1. Determine the number of periods.

Number of periods = 3

2. Determine the interest rate.

Interest rate = 6%

3. Determine the factor from Table 12-1. Read down the left column, n, to 3 period then across to 6%.

3.18360

4. Multiply the payment each period by the number from the table.

Value of annuity = $4,000 × 3.1836 = $12,734   rounded

This answer is the same as the previous example.

OBJECTIVE 4 Calculate the future value of an annuity due.

In the previous example, the annuity payment was made at the end of each period—end of the month, quarter, year, etc. An *annuity due* is paid at the *beginning* of each period, rather than the end; thus, it earns interest throughout the period in which it is paid.

EXAMPLE

Mr. and Mrs. Diaz set up an investment program using an annuity due with payments of $400 *at the beginning of each quarter*. Find the amount of the annuity if they make payments for 8 years in an account paying 10% compounded quarterly.

Four Step Problem Solving Plan

Clues	Action Plan	Solve
$400 payment at the beginning of each quarter Make payments for 8 years. Interest rate is 10% compounded quarterly.	1. Determine number of periods. 2. Add 1 period to number of periods. 3. Determine interest rate. 4. Determine factor from table. 5. Multiply payment each period by number from table. 6. Subtract one payment because it is an annuity due.	8 years × 4 quarters each year = 32 periods 32 + 1 = 33 periods 10% ÷ 4 quarters each year = 2.5% 50.35403 $400 × 50.35403 = $20,142 $20,142 − $400 = $19,742

Conclusion

Based on payments of $400 at the beginning of each quarter for 8 years in an account paying 10% compounded quarterly, the future value of annuity due is $19,742.

OBJECTIVE 5 Calculate the present value of an ordinary annuity.

You just learned how to calculate the *value of ordinary annuity* after you made a series of payments. Calculating the *present value* of an ordinary annuity is determining the amount needed to invest *today* to receive a stream of payments for a given number of years in the future. Another way to look at it is to determine the amount that must be deposited today to be assured of a certain amount at some date in the future. Either way, you need to know what sum must be deposited today as opposed to the future value of an ordinary annuity or an annuity due, where you are making payments and seeking the future value. To calculate the present value of an annuity, use Table 12-2.

EXAMPLE

Jeffrey O'Brien wants to invest in a friend's business that will guarantee him 8% compounded annually for 10 years. He has a choice of giving his friend a lump sum, or he can make payments of $1,000 annually for 10 years. He doesn't want to deplete all his cash. He needs to know what lump sum deposited today at 8% compounded annually will result in the same future value as making the payments.

STEPS

1. Calculate the number of periods and interest rate per period.

   10 years × 1 payment per year = 10 periods

   interest rate = 8%

2. Determine the factor from Table 12-2.

   6.71008

3. Multiply the amount invested by the table factor to determine the present value of an ordinary annuity.

   $1,000 × 6.71008 = $6,710   rounded

A lump sum of $6,710 deposited today at 8% compounded annually will result in the same total after 10 years as annual deposits of $1,000 for 10 years compounded at 8% annually.

> **TIPS**
>
> *Present value calculations can be checked by using the compound interest table.*
>
> *Using the example:*
> *10 periods, 8%, $6,710 or $1,000 payments*
>
> *Using Table 10-3 future value of lump sum investment:*
> *2.15892 × $6,710 = $14,486 (rounded)*
>
> *Using Table 12-1 future value of periodic payments:*
> *$1,000 × 14.48656 = $14,487 (rounded)*
> *The amount is off by $1 due to rounding.*

OBJECTIVE 6 Calculate present value using a sinking fund table.

Often a business or an individual will need a certain amount of money *at some fixed time* in the future. For instance, you might expect that a new sport utility vehicle (SUV) will cost $40,000 in five years, and you want to have the money set aside to pay cash. You could guess at the amount you would need to save but if you use Table 12-3, you can determine the exact payment to have the necessary amount.

A *sinking fund* is a fund set up to receive periodic payments to be assured of a certain amount of money in the future. It is different from an annuity

Table 12-2 Present Value of Annuity

				Present Value of an Annuity								
				n = number of periods in annuity; i = interest per period								

n	1%	1.5%	2%	2.5%	3%	4%	5%	6%	8%	10%	12%	n
1	0.99010	0.98522	0.98039	0.97561	0.97087	0.96154	0.95238	0.94340	0.92593	0.90909	0.89286	1
2	1.97040	1.95588	1.94156	1.92742	1.91347	1.88609	1.85941	1.83339	1.78326	1.73554	1.69005	2
3	2.94099	2.91220	2.88388	2.85602	2.82861	2.77509	2.72325	2.67301	2.57710	2.48685	2.40183	3
4	3.90197	3.85438	3.80773	3.76197	3.71710	3.62990	3.54595	3.46511	3.31213	3.16987	3.03735	4
5	4.85343	4.78264	4.71346	4.64583	4.57971	4.45182	4.32948	4.21236	3.99271	3.79079	3.60478	5
6	5.79548	5.69719	5.60143	5.50813	5.41719	5.24214	5.07569	4.91732	4.62288	4.35526	4.11141	6
7	6.72819	6.59821	6.47199	6.34939	6.23028	6.00205	5.78637	5.58238	5.20637	4.86842	4.56376	7
8	7.65168	7.48593	7.32548	7.17014	7.01969	6.73274	6.46321	6.20979	5.74664	5.33493	4.96764	8
9	8.56602	8.36052	8.16224	7.97087	7.78611	7.43533	7.10782	6.80169	6.24689	5.75902	5.32825	9
10	9.47130	9.22218	8.98259	8.75206	8.53020	8.11090	7.72173	7.36009	6.71008	6.14457	5.65022	10
11	10.36763	10.07112	9.78685	9.51421	9.25262	8.76048	8.30641	7.88687	7.13896	6.49506	5.93770	11
12	11.25508	10.90751	10.57534	10.25776	9.95400	9.38507	8.86325	8.38384	7.53608	6.81369	6.19437	12
13	12.13374	11.73153	11.34837	10.98318	10.63496	9.98565	9.39357	8.85268	7.90378	7.10336	6.42355	13
14	13.00370	12.54338	12.10625	11.69091	11.29607	10.56312	9.89864	9.29498	8.24424	7.36669	6.62817	14
15	13.86505	13.34323	12.84926	12.38138	11.93794	11.11839	10.37966	9.71225	8.55948	7.60608	6.81086	15
16	14.71787	14.13126	13.57771	13.05500	12.56110	11.65230	10.83777	10.10590	8.85137	7.82371	6.97399	16
17	15.56225	14.90765	14.29187	13.71220	13.16612	12.16567	11.27407	10.47726	9.12164	8.02155	7.11963	17
18	16.39827	15.67256	14.99203	14.35336	13.75351	12.65930	11.68959	10.82760	9.37189	8.20141	7.24967	18
19	17.22601	16.42617	15.67846	14.97889	14.32380	13.13394	12.08532	11.15812	9.60360	8.36492	7.36578	19
20	18.04555	17.16864	16.35143	15.58916	14.87747	13.59033	12.46221	11.46992	9.81815	8.51356	7.46944	20
21	18.85698	17.90014	17.01121	16.18455	15.41502	14.02916	12.82115	11.76408	10.01680	8.64869	7.56200	21
22	19.66038	18.62082	17.65805	16.76541	15.93692	14.45112	13.16300	12.04158	10.20074	8.77154	7.64465	22
23	20.45582	19.33086	18.29220	17.33211	16.44361	14.85684	13.48857	12.30338	10.37106	8.88322	7.71843	23
24	21.24339	20.03041	18.91393	17.88499	16.93554	15.24696	13.79864	12.55036	10.52876	8.98474	7.78432	24
25	22.02316	20.71961	19.52346	18.42438	17.41315	15.62208	14.09394	12.78336	10.67478	9.07704	7.84314	25
26	22.79520	21.39863	20.12104	18.95061	17.87684	15.98277	14.37519	13.00317	10.80998	9.16095	7.89566	26
27	23.55961	22.06762	20.70690	19.46401	18.32703	16.32959	14.64303	13.21053	10.93516	9.23722	7.94255	27
28	24.31644	22.72672	21.28127	19.96489	18.76411	16.66306	14.89813	13.40616	11.05108	9.30657	7.98442	28
29	25.06579	23.37608	21.84438	20.45355	19.18845	16.98371	15.14107	13.59072	11.15841	9.36961	8.02181	29
30	25.80771	24.01584	22.39646	20.93029	19.60044	17.29203	15.37245	13.76483	11.25778	9.42691	8.05518	30
31	26.54229	24.64615	22.93770	21.39541	20.00043	17.58849	15.59281	13.92909	11.34980	9.47901	8.08499	31
32	27.26959	25.26714	23.46833	21.84918	20.38877	17.87355	15.80268	14.08404	11.43500	9.52638	8.11159	32
33	27.98969	25.87895	23.98856	22.29188	20.76579	18.14765	16.00255	14.23023	11.51389	9.56943	8.13535	33
34	28.70267	26.48173	24.49859	22.72379	21.13184	18.41120	16.19290	14.36814	11.58693	9.60857	8.15656	34
35	29.40858	27.07559	24.99862	23.14516	21.48722	18.66461	16.37419	14.49825	11.65457	9.64416	8.17550	35
36	30.10751	27.66068	25.48884	23.55625	21.83225	18.90828	16.54685	14.62099	11.71719	9.67651	8.19241	36
37	30.79951	28.23713	25.96945	23.95732	22.16724	19.14258	16.71129	14.73678	11.77518	9.70592	8.20751	37
38	31.48466	28.80505	26.44064	24.34860	22.49246	19.36786	16.86789	14.84602	11.82887	9.73265	8.22099	38
39	32.16303	29.36458	26.90259	24.73034	22.80822	19.58448	17.01704	14.94907	11.87858	9.75696	8.23303	39
40	32.83469	29.91585	27.35548	25.10278	23.11477	19.79277	17.15909	15.04630	11.92461	9.77905	8.24378	40
41	33.49969	30.45896	27.79949	25.46612	23.41240	19.99305	17.29437	15.13802	11.96723	9.79914	8.25337	41
42	34.15811	30.99405	28.23479	25.82061	23.70136	20.18563	17.42321	15.22454	12.00670	9.81740	8.26194	42
43	34.81001	31.52123	28.66156	26.16645	23.98190	20.37079	17.54591	15.30617	12.04324	9.83400	8.26959	43
44	35.45545	32.04062	29.07996	26.50385	24.25427	20.54884	17.66277	15.38318	12.07707	9.84909	8.27642	44
45	36.09451	32.55234	29.49016	26.83302	24.51871	20.72004	17.77407	15.45583	12.10840	9.86281	8.28252	45
46	36.72724	33.05649	29.89231	27.15417	24.77545	20.88465	17.88007	15.52437	12.13741	9.87528	8.28796	46
47	37.35370	33.55319	30.28658	27.46748	25.02471	21.04294	17.98102	15.58903	12.16427	9.88662	8.29282	47
48	37.97396	34.04255	30.67312	27.77315	25.26671	21.19513	18.07716	15.65003	12.18914	9.89693	8.29716	48
49	38.58808	34.52468	31.05208	28.07137	25.50166	21.34147	18.16872	15.70757	12.21216	9.90630	8.30104	49
50	39.19612	34.99969	31.42361	28.36231	25.72976	21.48218	18.25593	15.76186	12.23348	9.91481	8.30450	50

because with an annuity, you know the amount of each payment and must determine its future value. With a sinking fund, you must determine the amount of periodic payments you need to make to be assured of having a certain amount of money. Sinking funds are used by companies, school districts, colleges, cities, and so on, to discharge bonded indebtedness, purchase new equipment, build new facilities, and expand old ones.

EXAMPLE

Mariah Morgan leased a new SUV. She will make payments for three years. Then she must either trade it in for a new one and continue making payments or pay off the balance, thereby owning it. She plans to pay it off and will need $18,000 in three years. What payment must Mariah make at an interest rate of 8% compounded quarterly to have $18,000 in three years?

STEPS

1. Calculate the number of periods and interest rate per period.

    3 years × 4 quarterly payments per year = 12 periods
    8% per year ÷ 4 periods per year = 2% interest per period

2. Determine the factor from Table 12-3.

    0.07456

3. Multiply the amount invested by the table factor to determine the present value of an ordinary annuity.

    $18,000 × 0.07456 = $1,342   rounded

If Mariah makes payments of $1,342 each quarter compounded at 8% for three years, she will have the $18,000 to pay off her SUV.

> **TIPS**
>
> *Sinking fund calculations can be checked by using the Future Value of an Annuity Table. Using Table 12-1, 13.41209 × $1,342 = $17,999 rounded. The amount is off by $1 due to rounding.*

OBJECTIVE **7** **Use Excel to calculate annuities.**

With the sophistication of today's computers and software, when lengthy calculations are required for annuities, present value, or sinking funds, these calculations are accomplished using specialized software. Excel is used when fewer calculations are needed and specialized software is not available.

Annuities

For instance, assume you work for a financial investment agent. This agent represents several companies and handles investments such as *mutual funds* (a professionally managed portfolio of stocks and bonds or other investments divided up into shares). The agent provides assistance to investors, answering questions and handling paperwork related to their investments, selecting funds in which to invest, and providing an annual investment portfolio report. This agent meets with each investor once a year to discuss the investment portfolio report that details the progress of his or her investments. This report might be created using Excel, as shown in the following example.

Table 12-3 Sinking Fund Table

| | | | | | Sinking Fund Table | | | | | | | |
| | | | | n = number of periods in annuity; i = interest per period | | | | | | | | |

n \ i	1%	1.5%	2%	2.5%	3%	4%	5%	6%	8%	10%	12%	i \ n
1	1.00000	1.00000	1.00000	1.00000	1.00000	1.00000	1.00000	1.00000	1.00000	1.00000	1.00000	1
2	0.49751	0.49628	0.49505	0.49383	0.49261	0.49020	0.48780	0.48544	0.48077	0.47619	0.47170	2
3	0.33002	0.32838	0.32675	0.32514	0.32353	0.32035	0.31721	0.31411	0.30803	0.30211	0.29635	3
4	0.24628	0.24444	0.24262	0.24082	0.23903	0.23549	0.23201	0.22859	0.22192	0.21547	0.20923	4
5	0.19604	0.19409	0.19216	0.19025	0.18835	0.18463	0.18097	0.17740	0.17046	0.16380	0.15741	5
6	0.16255	0.16053	0.15853	0.15655	0.15460	0.15076	0.14702	0.14336	0.13632	0.12961	0.12323	6
7	0.13863	0.13656	0.13451	0.13250	0.13051	0.12661	0.12282	0.11914	0.11207	0.10541	0.09912	7
8	0.12069	0.11858	0.11651	0.11447	0.11246	0.10853	0.10472	0.10104	0.09401	0.08744	0.08130	8
9	0.10674	0.10461	0.10252	0.10046	0.09843	0.09449	0.09069	0.08702	0.08008	0.07364	0.06768	9
10	0.09558	0.09343	0.09133	0.08926	0.08723	0.08329	0.07950	0.07587	0.06903	0.06275	0.05698	10
11	0.08645	0.08429	0.08218	0.08011	0.07808	0.07415	0.07039	0.06679	0.06608	0.05396	0.04842	11
12	0.07885	0.07668	0.07456	0.07249	0.07046	0.06655	0.06283	0.05928	0.05270	0.04676	0.04144	12
13	0.07241	0.07024	0.06812	0.06605	0.06403	0.06014	0.05646	0.05296	0.04652	0.04078	0.03568	13
14	0.06690	0.06472	0.06260	0.06054	0.05853	0.05467	0.05102	0.04758	0.04130	0.03575	0.03087	14
15	0.06212	0.05994	0.05783	0.05577	0.05377	0.04994	0.04634	0.04296	0.03683	0.03147	0.02682	15
16	0.05794	0.05577	0.05365	0.05160	0.04961	0.04582	0.04227	0.03895	0.03298	0.02782	0.02339	16
17	0.05426	0.05208	0.04997	0.04793	0.04595	0.04220	0.03870	0.03544	0.02963	0.02466	0.02046	17
18	0.05098	0.04881	0.04670	0.04467	0.04271	0.03899	0.03555	0.03236	0.02670	0.02193	0.01794	18
19	0.04805	0.04588	0.04378	0.04176	0.03981	0.03614	0.03275	0.02962	0.02413	0.01955	0.01576	19
20	0.04542	0.04325	0.04116	0.03915	0.03722	0.03358	0.03024	0.02718	0.02185	0.01746	0.01388	20
21	0.04303	0.04087	0.03878	0.03679	0.03487	0.03128	0.02800	0.02500	0.01983	0.01562	0.01224	21
22	0.04086	0.03870	0.03663	0.03465	0.03275	0.02920	0.02597	0.02305	0.01803	0.01401	0.01081	22
23	0.03889	0.03673	0.03467	0.03270	0.03081	0.02731	0.02414	0.02128	0.01642	0.01257	0.00956	23
24	0.03707	0.03492	0.03287	0.03091	0.02905	0.02559	0.02247	0.01968	0.01498	0.01130	0.00846	24
25	0.03541	0.03326	0.03122	0.02928	0.02743	0.02401	0.02095	0.01823	0.01368	0.01017	0.00750	25
26	0.03387	0.03173	0.02970	0.02777	0.02594	0.02257	0.01956	0.01690	0.01251	0.00916	0.00665	26
27	0.03245	0.03032	0.02829	0.02638	0.02456	0.02124	0.01829	0.01570	0.01145	0.00826	0.00590	27
28	0.03112	0.02900	0.02699	0.02509	0.02329	0.02001	0.01712	0.01459	0.01049	0.00745	0.00524	28
29	0.02990	0.02778	0.02578	0.02389	0.02211	0.01888	0.01605	0.01358	0.00962	0.00673	0.00466	29
30	0.02875	0.02664	0.02465	0.02278	0.02102	0.01783	0.01505	0.01265	0.00883	0.00608	0.00414	30
31	0.02768	0.02557	0.02360	0.02174	0.02000	0.01686	0.01413	0.01179	0.00811	0.00550	0.00369	31
32	0.02667	0.02458	0.02261	0.02077	0.01905	0.01595	0.01328	0.01100	0.00745	0.00497	0.00328	32
33	0.02573	0.02364	0.02169	0.01986	0.01816	0.01510	0.01249	0.01027	0.00685	0.00450	0.00292	33
34	0.02484	0.02276	0.02082	0.01901	0.01732	0.01431	0.01176	0.00960	0.00630	0.00407	0.00260	34
35	0.02400	0.02193	0.02000	0.01821	0.01654	0.01358	0.01107	0.00897	0.00580	0.00369	0.00232	35
36	0.02321	0.02115	0.01923	0.01745	0.01580	0.01289	0.01043	0.00839	0.00534	0.00334	0.00206	36
37	0.02247	0.02041	0.01851	0.01674	0.01511	0.01224	0.00984	0.00786	0.00492	0.00303	0.00184	37
38	0.02176	0.01972	0.01782	0.01607	0.01446	0.01163	0.00928	0.00736	0.00454	0.00275	0.00164	38
39	0.02109	0.01905	0.01717	0.01544	0.01384	0.01106	0.00876	0.00689	0.00419	0.00249	0.00146	39
40	0.02046	0.01843	0.01656	0.01484	0.01326	0.01052	0.00828	0.00646	0.00386	0.00226	0.00130	40
41	0.01985	0.01783	0.01597	0.01427	0.01271	0.01002	0.00782	0.00606	0.00356	0.00205	0.00116	41
42	0.01928	0.01726	0.01542	0.01373	0.01219	0.00954	0.00739	0.00568	0.00329	0.00186	0.00104	42
43	0.01873	0.01672	0.01489	0.01322	0.01170	0.00909	0.00699	0.00533	0.00303	0.00169	0.00092	43
44	0.01820	0.01621	0.01439	0.01273	0.01123	0.00866	0.00662	0.00501	0.00280	0.00153	0.00083	44
45	0.01771	0.01572	0.01391	0.01227	0.01079	0.00826	0.00626	0.00470	0.00259	0.00139	0.00074	45
46	0.01723	0.01525	0.01345	0.01183	0.01036	0.00788	0.00593	0.00441	0.00239	0.00126	0.00066	46
47	0.01677	0.01480	0.01302	0.01141	0.00996	0.00752	0.00561	0.00415	0.00221	0.00115	0.00059	47
48	0.01633	0.01437	0.01260	0.01101	0.00958	0.00718	0.00532	0.00390	0.00204	0.00104	0.00052	48
49	0.01591	0.01396	0.01220	0.01062	0.00921	0.00686	0.00504	0.00366	0.00189	0.00095	0.00047	49
50	0.01551	0.01357	0.01182	0.01026	0.00887	0.00655	0.00478	0.00344	0.00174	0.00086	0.00042	50

Corey Lupinacci has an appointment with Jules Martin to go over Corey's annual investment portfolio. Jules prepares the report in an Excel spreadsheet, as shown in Figure 12-1.

Figure 12-1

Lupinacci's Investment Portfolio Report

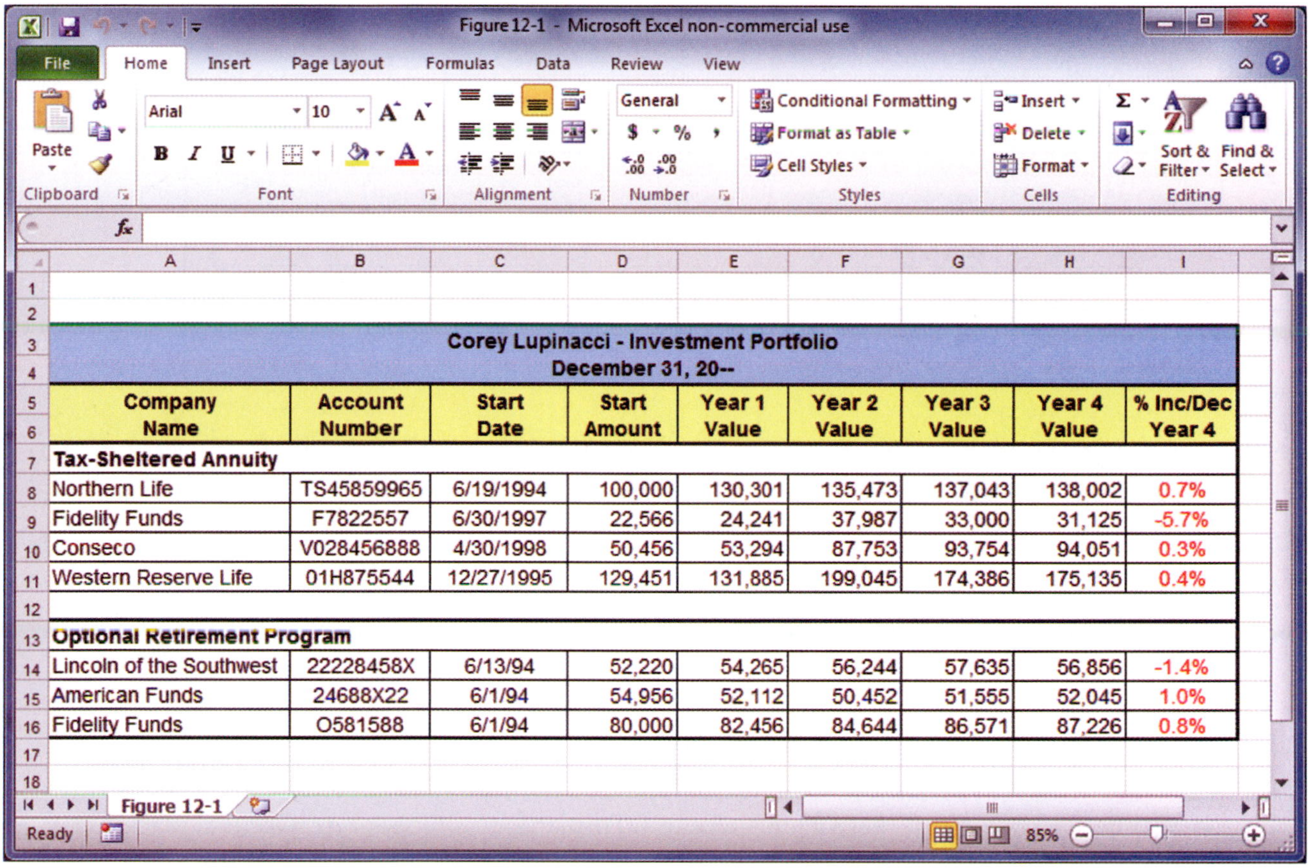

Corey Lupinacci - Investment Portfolio
December 31, 20--

Company Name	Account Number	Start Date	Start Amount	Year 1 Value	Year 2 Value	Year 3 Value	Year 4 Value	% Inc/Dec Year 4
Tax-Sheltered Annuity								
Northern Life	TS45859965	6/19/1994	100,000	130,301	135,473	137,043	138,002	0.7%
Fidelity Funds	F7822557	6/30/1997	22,566	24,241	37,987	33,000	31,125	-5.7%
Conseco	V028456888	4/30/1998	50,456	53,294	87,753	93,754	94,051	0.3%
Western Reserve Life	01H875544	12/27/1995	129,451	131,885	199,045	174,386	175,135	0.4%
Optional Retirement Program								
Lincoln of the Southwest	22228458X	6/13/94	52,220	54,265	56,244	57,635	56,856	-1.4%
American Funds	24688X22	6/1/94	54,956	52,112	50,452	51,555	52,045	1.0%
Fidelity Funds	O581588	6/1/94	80,000	82,456	84,644	86,571	87,226	0.8%

STEPS

Retrieve the file *ch12pr01.xlsx*.

1. Enter formulas in Column I to calculate the Percent of Increase or Decrease from Year 3 to Year 4. Subtract Year 3 from Year 4 and divide by Year 3. Refer to Chapter 3 to review percent of increase and decrease, if needed.

2. Format Column I for Percentage and 1 Decimal place.

3. Save the file as *ch12pr01a.xlsx*.

Present Value

In business today, it is common for a company to sell a note it is holding when it has cash-flow problems. It is necessary to determine today's value of the note to know the amount for which to sell it. For instance, what if a company were receiving payments of $5,000 annually at 8% interest for the next five years, but needed all the money now because of cash-flow problems? The value of the note today can be calculated using the present value table. In Figure 12-2 on the next page, Row 6 shows that the money the company would receive at the end of five years ($25,000) is worth $19,963.55 today. The company should sell the note no lower than $19,963.55. Knowing the present value of the note helps to determine the asking price.

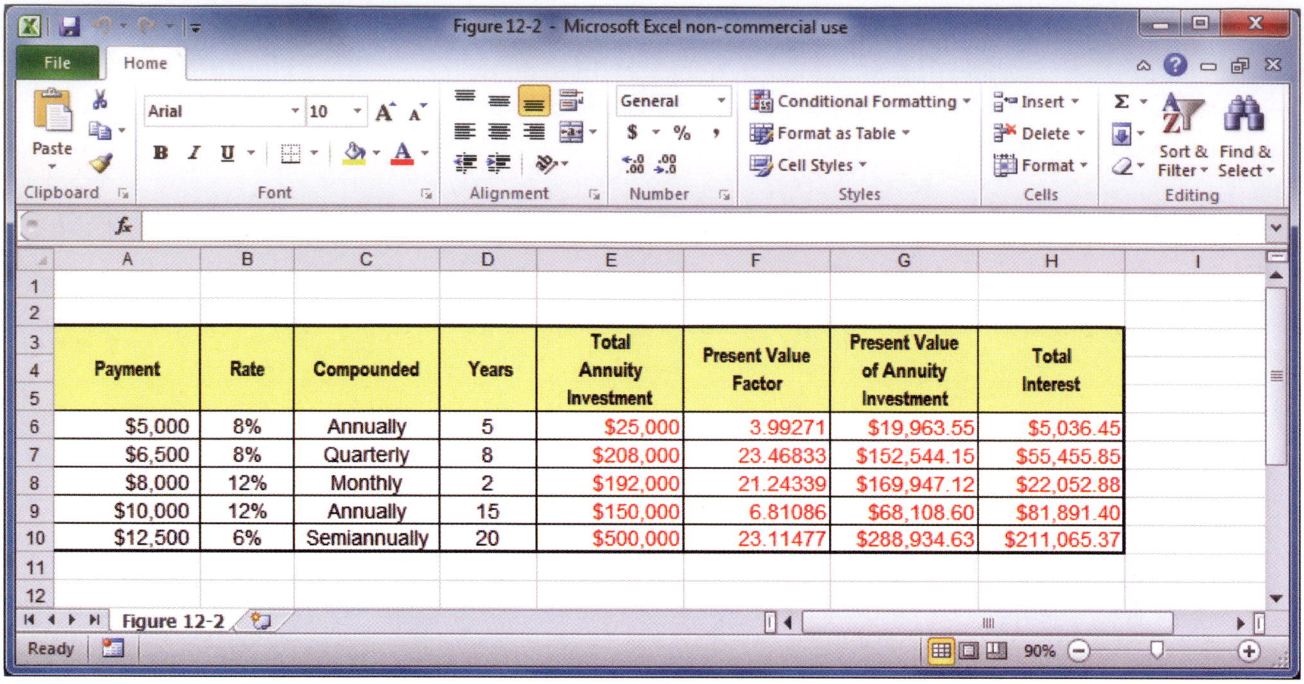

	A	B	C	D	E	F	G	H
1								
2								
3						Total	Present Value	Present Value	Total
4	Payment	Rate	Compounded	Years	Annuity	Factor	of Annuity	Interest
5					Investment		Investment	
6	$5,000	8%	Annually	5	$25,000	3.99271	$19,963.55	$5,036.45
7	$6,500	8%	Quarterly	8	$208,000	23.46833	$152,544.15	$55,455.85
8	$8,000	12%	Monthly	2	$192,000	21.24339	$169,947.12	$22,052.88
9	$10,000	12%	Annually	15	$150,000	6.81086	$68,108.60	$81,891.40
10	$12,500	6%	Semiannually	20	$500,000	23.11477	$288,934.63	$211,065.37
11								
12								

Figure 12-2 /

Figure 12-2

Present Value of a Note

Retrieve the file *ch12pr02.xlsx*.

1. Enter formulas in Column E to calculate the Total Annuity Investment (Payment times periods). Format for Currency, 0 Decimal places, and $.

2. Use the Present Value of Annuity Table and enter the Present Value Factors in Column F. Format for Number and 5 Decimal places.

3. Enter a formula in Cell G6 to calculate the Present Value of Annuity Investment (Present Value Factor times Payment). Round to the nearest cent. The formula is =ROUND((A6*F6),2). Copy the formula down Column G.

4. Enter formulas in Column H to calculate the Total Interest (Total Annuity Investment – Present Value of Annuity Investment).

5. Format Columns G and H for Currency, 2 Decimal places, and $.

6. Save the file as *ch12pr02a.xlsx*.

Sinking Funds

Excel can be used to create a table that shows the interest earned and the accumulated amount of a *sinking fund* at the end of each period.

EXAMPLE

Air-Transport, Inc., has set up a sinking fund to purchase a new corporate jet, costing $135,000, for its charter business. Calculate the payment necessary to purchase this plane earning 8% annually for 5 years. Study the sinking fund for the Cessna in Figure 12-3 on the next page.

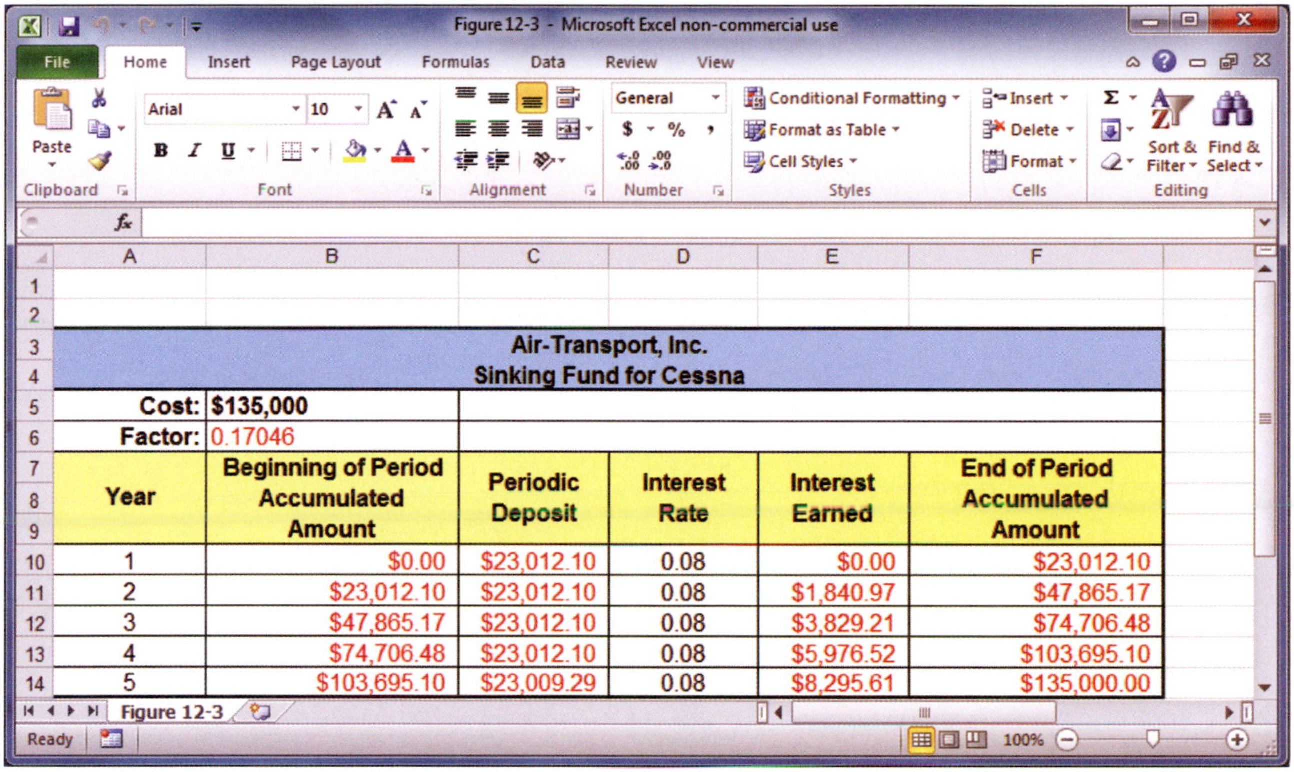

Air-Transport, Inc.					
Sinking Fund for Cessna					
Cost:	**$135,000**				
Factor:	0.17046				
Year	**Beginning of Period Accumulated Amount**	**Periodic Deposit**	**Interest Rate**	**Interest Earned**	**End of Period Accumulated Amount**
1	$0.00	$23,012.10	0.08	$0.00	$23,012.10
2	$23,012.10	$23,012.10	0.08	$1,840.97	$47,865.17
3	$47,865.17	$23,012.10	0.08	$3,829.21	$74,706.48
4	$74,706.48	$23,012.10	0.08	$5,976.52	$103,695.10
5	$103,695.10	$23,009.29	0.08	$8,295.61	$135,000.00

Figure 12-3

Sinking Fund for Cessna

STEPS

Retrieve the file *ch12pr03.xlsx*.

1. Use the Sinking Fund Table to locate the factor for 5 periods at 8% annually (0.17046). Enter the factor in Cell B6.
2. Enter a formula in Cell C10 to multiply the factor by the cost of the airplane. Be sure to use an absolute address. Air-Transport, Inc., must deposit $23,012.10 at the end of each year for 5 years to have the $135,000. Copy the formula down Column C.
3. Enter a formula in Cell E10 to calculate the first year's interest. Notice that Cell E10 is 0 because no interest was earned. Copy the formula down Column E.
4. Enter a formula in Cell F10 to calculate the End of Period Accumulated Amount. (Add Beginning of Period Accumulated Amount + Periodic Deposit + Interest Earned.)
5. Copy the End of Period Accumulated Amount formula from Cell F10 down Column F.
6. Key End of Period Accumulated Amount into Beginning of Period Accumulated Amount cell for the next year. Repeat for each year.
7. The last year's end of period accumulated amount must equal the total amount needed. Adjust the periodic deposit up or down, when necessary, to make it equal the correct amount after interest is calculated for the last year. (Adding a full periodic payment will be $2.81 over the $135,000. Reduce the last periodic payment by $2.81.)
8. Format dollar entries for Currency, 2 Decimal places, and $.
9. Save the file as *ch12pr03a.xlsx*.

Name _____   Date _____

Directions   Solve the following problems. Write your answers in the blanks provided. Round all answers to the nearest cent.

A. Find the amount of the following ordinary annuities and interest earned.   OBJECTIVE 3

	Amount of Each Deposit	Period	Rate	Time (Years)	Amount of Annuity
1.	$1,500	annually	10%	10	_____
2.	$3,000	semiannually	8%	5	_____
3.	$6,500	quarterly	6%	8	_____

B. Find the amount of the following annuities due and interest earned.   OBJECTIVE 4

	Amount of Each Deposit	Period	Rate	Time (Years)	Amount of Annuity
4.	$2,500	annually	12%	10	_____
5.	$4,000	semiannually	6%	5	_____
6.	$7,500	quarterly	8%	8	_____

C. Find the present value of the following ordinary annuities.   OBJECTIVE 5

	Amount per Payment	Payment at End of Each	Time (Years)	Rate of Investment	Present Value
7.	$1,800	year	14	10%	_____
8.	$3,300	6 months	8	12%	_____
9.	$1,500	quarter	5	8%	_____

D. Find the amount of each payment needed to accumulate the indicated amount in a sinking fund.   OBJECTIVE 6

	Amount	Money Earns	Compounded	Years	Payment
10.	$9,300	8%	annually	6	_____
11.	$15,000	6%	semiannually	10	_____
12.	$8,220	5%	annually	9	_____
13.	$14,600	12%	monthly	3	_____

E. Use Excel to complete the following problems.   OBJECTIVE 7

14.   Retrieve the file *ch12ex01.xlsx*. Follow the directions. Save the file as *ch12ex01a.xlsx*.

15.   Retrieve the file *ch12ex02.xlsx*. Follow the directions. Save the file as *ch12ex02a.xlsx*.

12.2 Stocks

OBJECTIVES

1. Identify terms used with stocks.
2. Calculate dividends.
3. Calculate earnings per share.
4. Read a stock table.
5. Calculate the cost of shares, the amount of commission, and the total cost of a stock transaction.
6. Calculate current stock yield.
7. Calculate price-earnings (PE) ratio.
8. Use Excel to calculate and track stock investments.

OBJECTIVE 1 Identify terms used with stocks.

Privately owned companies may need to raise capital (money) to expand, to finance operations, to invest, or to do other things. To raise this capital, they may decide to "go public." Going public means selling part of their ownership to individuals outside the company. Individuals who invest in these companies are known as *stockholders* (also called *shareholders* or *investors*). *Stock*, then, represents ownership in the company. The original owner can maintain control of the company by retaining 51 percent or more of the shares of stock in the company.

To be eligible to sell stock, a corporation must be approved and granted a charter by the state where it incorporated. Any new issues of stock must be registered with the Securities and Exchange Commission (SEC). A booklet known as a *prospectus* must be compiled to give investors details about the issuing corporation.

Stock may be traded (bought or sold) to other investors. Stock exchanges and the over-the-counter (OTC) market permit investors to trade stocks. As of December 31, 2009, the New York Stock Exchange (NYSE) is the largest stock exchange in the world, followed by the Tokyo Exchange. NASDAQ (National Association of Securities Automated Quotes) is an over-the-counter market. Usually, smaller and newer companies are traded on NASDAQ.

The two basic types of stock are *common* and *preferred*. Both types are easily bought and sold through the stock exchanges and the over-the-counter market. Generally, stocks are bought and sold through stockbrokers, who represent buyers and sellers of stocks. The price of the stock depends on factors such as a change in political climate or economic status, national or international conditions, or the corporation's financial condition or earning power. In addition, rumors may affect the sale and purchase of stocks.

To help you learn how to make the calculations involved in dealing with stocks, study the following terms.

Charter A written grant creating a corporation. The charter or certificate of incorporation is granted by a state or by the federal government. The charter must list the number of shares of stock the corporation plans to issue.

Common Stock Stock that carries the right to vote. These voting rights generally are voting for the board of directors and for other important issues. When the board of directors declare a common stock dividend, holders of common stock receive earnings after preferred stockholders have received their earnings.

Dividends A portion of a corporation's profits paid to its stockholders.

Earnings Per Share Net income (earnings) distributed divided by shares outstanding.

Outstanding Shares   Shares of stock issued by a corporation.

Par Value   A value arbitrarily assigned to stock when it is issued; the dollar amount printed on the stock certificate, not the actual value of the stock.

Preferred Stock   Stock characterized by two major features: Its owners do not have voting rights, and its owners must be paid dividends by the corporation before owners of common stock can be paid dividends. Therefore, should the company go bankrupt, preferred stockholders have claim to assets over common stockholders.

Prospectus   Booklet that gives investors financial information about a corporation.

Shares   The parts into which the ownership of a corporation is divided.

Stock   Shares of ownership authorized for sale by a corporation's charter that enable a person to become part owner of a corporation.

Stockholders (or *shareholders*)   Individuals who own stock in a corporation and have certain rights of ownership as a result of their investment.

Stock Certificate   Written evidence of ownership of a share of stock. See the picture below for an example of a stock certificate.

Stock Table   Tables commonly found in newspapers that provide information on stock activity.

OBJECTIVE **2** Calculate dividends.

A group of people known as a **board of directors** represent the stockholders. The board of directors may authorize payment of a dividend. The dividend may be a certain dollar amount per share of stock, or it may be a certain percent of the par value of the shares. However, there is no guarantee that dividends will be paid. The board of directors may wish to reinvest the profits in the corporation in order to further its growth.

If a dividend is authorized, it may be paid to stockholders as a cash dividend or a stock dividend. A stock dividend occurs when stockholders receive a certain number of additional shares of stock for their dividend rather than a cash payment. The specific number of shares paid as a stock dividend is based on a percent of the number of shares held by a stockholder. For example, suppose you own 160 shares of ABC Corp. and a 5% stock dividend is authorized. To find the amount of the stock dividend, multiply the stock dividend rate by the number of shares owned.

$$0.05 \times 160 = 8 \text{ shares}$$

By the 5% stock dividend declaration, you would receive eight additional shares of ABC common stock.

The dividend paid on preferred stock is a fixed rate, whereas the common stock dividend varies with business and economic conditions. If economic or business conditions are good, the common stockholder may receive a larger dividend payment while the preferred stock dividend remains at the fixed rate. However, the dividend paid on preferred stock has priority over any paid on common stock. If certain conditions become critical, the common stockholder may receive a smaller payment or no dividend at all while the preferred stockholder may continue to receive dividends.

Finding a Cash Dividend on Common Stock   Study the following example to determine the dividend per share and the total dividend to be paid to a common stockholder.

EXAMPLE

Rita Garcia has 500 shares of Avery Corp. common stock. The Board of Directors has declared dividends of $175,000 to be distributed among its common stockholders. There are 51,000 shares of common stock outstanding. How much will Rita receive?

STEPS

1. To find the dividend per share, divide the amount of the declared dividends by the number of outstanding shares.

$175,000 ÷ 51,000 = $3.43   dividend per share

2. To find how much Rita will receive, multiply the number of shares of stock owned by the dividend per share.

500 × $3.43 = $1,715   received by Rita

Preferred Stock Dividends   The dividend payment of a preferred stock is usually a fixed percent of the par value. Preferred stock dividends are dependent on particular features, and the effects of these features may vary the dividend payment. For example, if preferred stock is **cumulative stock**, stockholders will receive all dividends not declared in previous years plus the current year's dividends when dividends are authorized. If dividends are not paid, the amount not paid is recorded. These dividends are known as **dividends in arrears**. After preferred stockholders have received their percent share of par value and common stockholders have received their dividend shares, any additional profits may be distributed to both common and preferred stockholders.

Distributing Profits Between Preferred and Common Stockholders   The following example illustrates how profits might be distributed between preferred and common stockholders.

EXAMPLE

The Board of Directors of Macon Corp. has decided to distribute $500,000 to its stockholders. There are 18,000 shares of 8% preferred stock, $100 par value, and 100,000 shares of common stock.

STEPS

1. To determine the dividend amount per share of preferred stock, multiply the dividend rate by the par value (8% × $100).

0.08 × $100 = $8   dividend per share of preferred stock

2. To determine the total dividend amount paid to preferred stockholders, multiply the dividend amount per share by the number of shares of preferred stock.

$8 × 18,000 = $144,000   dividend paid to preferred stockholders

3. To find the remaining dollar amount available to common stockholders, subtract the total amount paid to preferred stockholders from the total profits to be distributed.

$500,000	profits distributed
−$144,000	paid to preferred stockholders
$356,000	to be distributed among common stockholders

4. To find the dividend per share to be paid to common stockholders, divide the total amount available to common stockholders by the total shares of common stock.

$356,000 ÷ 100,000 = $3.56   dividend per share of common stock

OBJECTIVE 3 Calculate earnings per share.

Earnings per share is defined as net income (earnings) distributed divided by shares outstanding. For common stockholders, the corporation's earnings figure may be expressed as earnings per share of stock. Earnings per share are considerably more than the dividends paid to common stockholders. The difference between earnings per share and the dividends paid is accounted for by several things: preferred dividends paid, money reinvested in business operations, and taxes the corporation has to pay.

EXAMPLE

Suppose a corporation has 150,000 shares of common stock. The corporation had total earnings of $940,000, of which $820,000 was distributed to its stockholders and $120,000 was reinvested in its business operations. To find earnings per share, use this formula.

$$\text{Earnings per Share} = \frac{\text{Earnings Distributed}}{\text{Number of Shares of Common Stock}}$$

$$\text{Earnings per Share} = \frac{\$820,000}{150,000}$$

$$\text{Earnings per Share} = \$5.47 \quad \text{rounded}$$

If you are a common stockholder and want to follow a particular stock, it is important to watch a corporation's earnings over a period of time to see whether a dividend is maintained, increased, or decreased.

OBJECTIVE 4 Read a stock table.

You can follow the activity of stocks by reading *stock tables*. Stock tables are found in the financial sections of most daily newspapers, although the most extensive listings appear in *The Wall Street Journal*. You can also find this information on the Internet. In these tables, basic information, such as the highest, lowest, and closing prices for the stocks traded that day, are given. An example of a typical stock exchange table follows. However, the amount of information can vary from newspaper to newspaper. The columns in the table have been numbered to help you locate the information.

Table 12-4

Stock Table

(1)	(2)	(3)	(4)	(5)	(6)	(7)	(8)	(9)	(10)	(11)	(12)
Hi	Lo	Stock	Divi- dend	Yield (YD)	PE Ratio	PPE	Vol. (00s)	Hi	Lo	Close	Chng
33.25	28	SoBun pf	$0.93	2.8	6.9	9	242	36.50	31.13	33.75	+0.50

Read the table by following the information given here.

1. The highest price per share during the past 52 weeks was $33.25.
2. The lowest price per share during the past 52 weeks was $28.
3. SoBun is the abbreviated name of the corporation—South Bundett Corporation. (When pf appears, it represents preferred stock.)
4. The current dividend paid by the corporation is $0.93 per share of stock. Dividends are usually annual payments based on the last quarterly or semiannual report.
5. The yield is reported as a percent. The yield and dividend are related in that the dividend of $0.93 per share represents 2.8% of the current market price of a share of the stock.
6. The price-earnings (PE) ratio is the ratio of the price per share to the earnings per share. The PE is calculated by dividing the closing price of the stock by the earnings per share for the last four quarters.
7. The projected price-earnings ratio (PPE) is based on analysts' estimates for the next 12 months.
8. The number of shares traded that day is reported in hundreds. Therefore, a total of 24,200 (242 × 100) shares of SoBun stock were sold.
9. The highest price paid per share during the day was $36.50.
10. The lowest price paid per share during the day was $31.13.
11. The last sale price at the close of the day was $33.75 per share.
12. The last sale price represents a change of $0.50 increase over the previous day's closing price.

OBJECTIVE 5 Calculate the cost of shares, the amount of commission, and the total cost of a stock transaction.

Calculating the Cost of Stocks   The purchase price of a share of stock includes the market price of the stock and any charges made by the stock-broker. The public usually does not buy and sell stock directly from the stock exchange. Instead, a stockbroker has representatives at the stock exchange who buy and sell stocks. The broker charges a **brokerage fee** or **commission** (a fee charged for handling the purchase or sale of stock) for the transaction. The rates charged depend on factors such as the size of the transaction, the volume of business done by the customer, the services the broker may perform for the customer, or a combination of these factors and other factors. The rates also vary among brokers. The broker's commissions depend on whether the shares of stock are traded according to **round lots** (multiples of 100) or **odd lots** (not multiples of 100). For instance, if you want to purchase an odd lot, the broker may have to buy a round lot, sell you the number of shares you want, and then sell the remaining shares to other buyers. The investor pays the broker the price of the shares plus the commission charges. To find current brokers' commissions, contact several stockbrokers listed in your area on the Internet or in the yellow pages of your local telephone book.

EXAMPLE

You purchase 500 shares of stock at $17.50 per share. The commission is 1.5% of the total transaction.

STEPS

1. To find the cost of the shares, multiply the number of shares to be purchased by the per-share price of the stock.

$$500 \times \$17.50 = \$8,750 \quad \text{cost of shares}$$

2. To find the commission charge, multiply the commission rate by the cost of the shares.

$$0.015 \times \$8,750 = \$131.25 \quad \text{commission charge}$$

3. To find the total cost of the transaction, add the commission to the cost of shares.

$$\$8,750 + \$131.25 = \$8,881.25 \quad \text{total cost of transaction}$$

To calculate the total cost of a transaction that included odd lots, complete these steps.

EXAMPLE

You purchase 250 shares of stock at $10.75 per share. The commission is 3% for round lots and an additional 4% for odd lots. What is the total cost of the transaction?

STEPS

1. Multiply the number of shares to be purchased by the cost per share.

$$250 \text{ shares} \times \$10.75 = \$2,687.50$$

2. Calculate the commission for the round lots by multiplying the maximum round lot number by the cost per share by the percent commission on round lots.

$$200 \times \$10.75 \times 0.03 = \$64.50$$

3. Calculate the commission for the odd lots by multiplying the maximum odd lot number by the cost per share by the percent commission on odd lots.

$$50 \times \$10.75 \times 0.04 = \$21.50$$

4. Add the three amounts to find the total cost of the transaction.

$$\$2,687.50 + \$64.50 + \$21.50 = \$2,773.50$$

TIPS

Remember, round lots are multiples of 100 shares purchased and odd lots are not multiples of 100 shares purchased.

The current percent **yield** on a stock helps you compare two stock investments. A yield is a comparative measure of the annual percentage return to the investor at the current stock price. To find the current yield, use the following formula.

$$\text{Current Yield} = \frac{\text{Annual Dividend per Share}}{\text{Closing Price per Share}}$$

EXAMPLE

Exxon/Mobil pays an annual dividend of $3.70 and lists a closing price of $101.

STEPS

1. Find the current percent yield.

$$\text{Current Yield} = \frac{\$3.70}{\$101}$$

2. Express the answer as a percent rounded to the nearest tenth.

$$\text{Current Yield} = 0.037 = 3.7\%$$

The 3.7% represents a return on your investment of $3.70 for each $100 invested. Suppose you were comparing the 3.7% yield return to a second stock that yielded 7.3%. Of course, the second stock yielding 7.3% has the greater return on investments. However, you must consider other factors, such as price-earnings (PE) ratio, before choosing an investment.

Another factor to consider when purchasing a stock is the **price-earnings ratio** (PE). The PE is the ratio of the price per share to the earnings per share. In other words, it measures how much the stock is selling for compared to its net income earnings per share. Assume a corporation's stock is selling at $52 and its annual earnings per share is $2.90. If the stock is selling at $52, it is selling at 18 times its earnings per share ($52 ÷ $2.90 is about 18). The PE ratio is rounded to a whole number. The PE will vary, usually between 3 and 50, depending on a number of factors, such as whether the stock is undervalued or overpriced or if earnings have been low. The PE ratio is reported in major newspapers and on the Internet. The annual net income earnings per share is found in the financial statements provided by the corporation. If the PE is not listed, it means the company has no earnings. To find the price-earnings ratio, use the following formula.

$$\text{Price-Earnings Ratio} = \frac{\text{Current Price per Share}}{\text{Annual Net Income Earnings per Share}}$$

PepsiCola reports net earnings of $2.70 on stock selling at $44.85.

To find the PE ratio, divide the current price of the stock per share by the annual net income earnings per share.

$$\text{Price - Earnings Ratio} = \frac{\$44.85}{\$2.70} = 17 \quad \text{rounded}$$

PepsiCola's stock is selling at 17 times its earnings per share.

OBJECTIVE 8 Use Excel to calculate and track stock investments.

An investor can use an Excel spreadsheet to track investments and calculate each stock's percent of increase or decrease. Figure 12-4 shows how the treasurer of the Oakcliff Investment Club might use a spreadsheet to track the club's investments for eight stocks.

Figure 12-4

Investment Club Stock

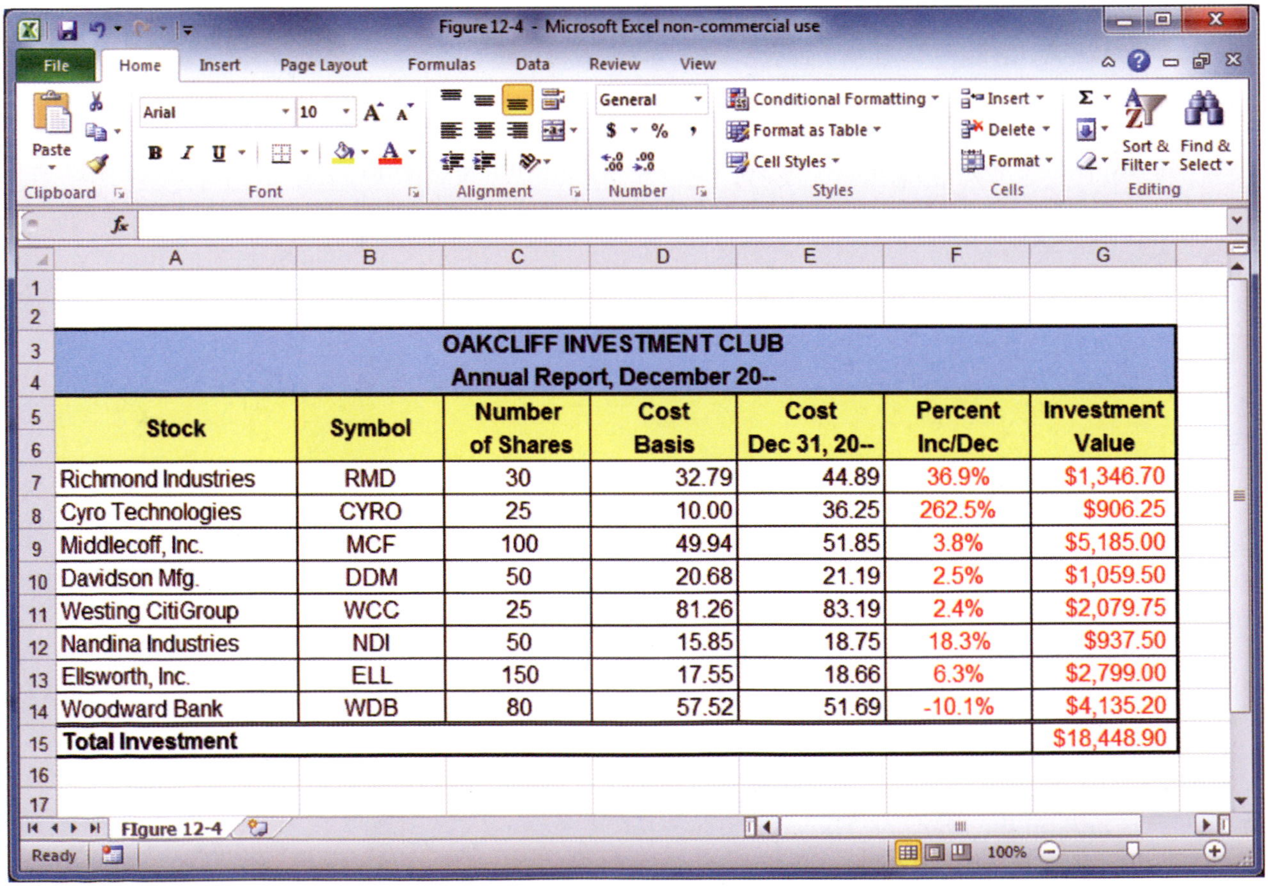

OAKCLIFF INVESTMENT CLUB
Annual Report, December 20--

Stock	Symbol	Number of Shares	Cost Basis	Cost Dec 31, 20--	Percent Inc/Dec	Investment Value
Richmond Industries	RMD	30	32.79	44.89	36.9%	$1,346.70
Cyro Technologies	CYRO	25	10.00	36.25	262.5%	$906.25
Middlecoff, Inc.	MCF	100	49.94	51.85	3.8%	$5,185.00
Davidson Mfg.	DDM	50	20.68	21.19	2.5%	$1,059.50
Westing CitiGroup	WCC	25	81.26	83.19	2.4%	$2,079.75
Nandina Industries	NDI	50	15.85	18.75	18.3%	$937.50
Ellsworth, Inc.	ELL	150	17.55	18.66	6.3%	$2,799.00
Woodward Bank	WDB	80	57.52	51.69	-10.1%	$4,135.20
Total Investment						$18,448.90

Retrieve the file *ch12pr04.xlsx*.

1. Enter formulas in Column F to calculate the Percent of Increase or Decrease.

2. Enter formulas in Column G to calculate the Investment Value (Investment Value = Number of Shares × Cost Dec 31).

3. Total the Investment Value in Column G.

4. Format Column F for Percentage and 1 Decimal place. Format Column G for Currency, 2 Decimal places, and $.

5. Save the file as *ch12pr04a.xlsx*.

Now look at how to use Excel to find the dividend amount paid to preferred and common stockholders. See Figure 12-5.

Figure 12-5

Dividends Paid to Preferred and Common Stockholders

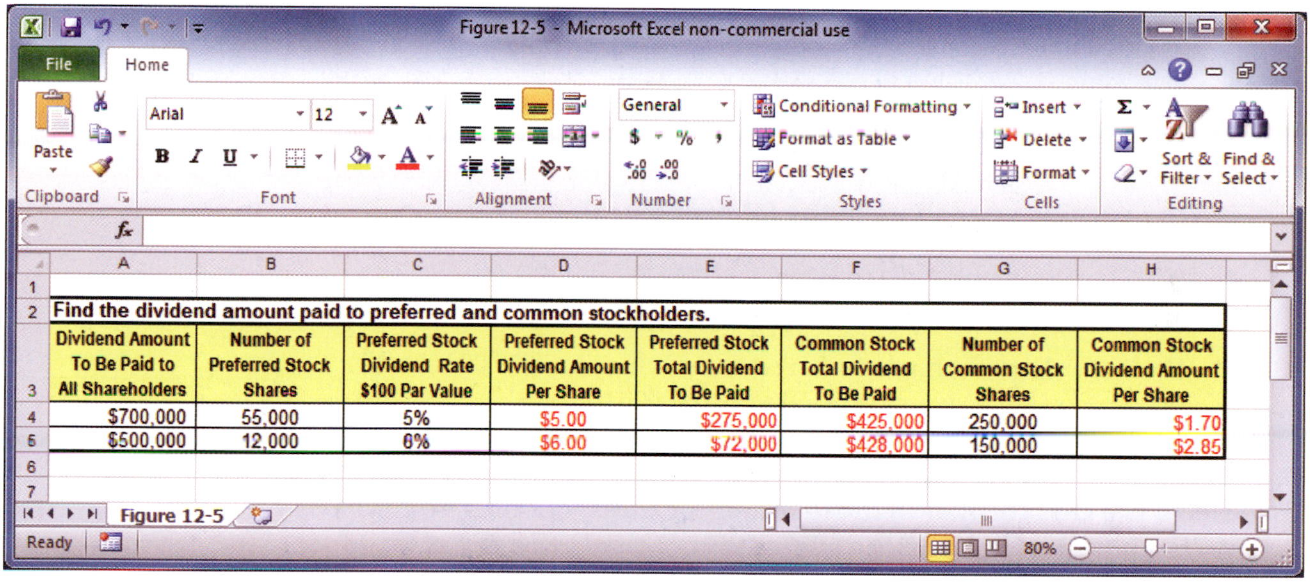

Dividend Amount To Be Paid to All Shareholders	Number of Preferred Stock Shares	Preferred Stock Dividend Rate $100 Par Value	Preferred Stock Dividend Amount Per Share	Preferred Stock Total Dividend To Be Paid	Common Stock Total Dividend To Be Paid	Number of Common Stock Shares	Common Stock Dividend Amount Per Share
$700,000	55,000	5%	$5.00	$275,000	$425,000	250,000	$1.70
$500,000	12,000	6%	$6.00	$72,000	$428,000	150,000	$2.85

STEPS

Retrieve the file *ch12pr05.xlsx*.

1. Enter formulas in Column D to calculate the Preferred Stock Dividend Amount Per Share. Multiply Preferred Stock Dividend Rate by the par value.

2. Enter formulas in Column E to calculate the Preferred Stock Total Dividend To Be Paid. Multiply Preferred Stock Dividend Amount Per Share by Number of Preferred Stock Shares.

3. Enter formulas in Column F to calculate Common Stock Total Dividend To Be Paid. Subtract Preferred Stock Total Dividend To Be Paid from Dividend Amount To Be Paid to All Shareholders.

4. Enter formulas in Column H to calculate Common Stock Dividend Amount Per Share. Divide Common Stock Total Dividend to Be Paid by Number of Common Stock Shares.

5. Format Columns D and H for Currency, 2 Decimal places, and $. Format Columns E and F for Currency and 0 Decimal places, and $.

6. Save the file as *ch12pr05a.xlsx*.

Name _____ Date _____

Directions   Solve the following problems. Round dollar amounts to the nearest hundredth where needed.

A. Compute the dividend per share and the total dividend the common stockholders will receive.   OBJECTIVE 2

	Dividends Declared	Shares Outstanding	Dividend Per Share	Stock Owned	Dividend Received
1.	$500,000	120,000	_____	158	_____
2.	$290,000	140,000	_____	120	_____
3.	$425,000	65,000	_____	600	_____

B. Find the earnings per share in the following problems.   OBJECTIVE 3

4.   ALL Textiles reports total profits of $8,000,000 and has 1,200,000 common shares.   _____

5.   Profits for Kern Technology Corporation, which has 930,000 shares of common stock, were reported at $9,000,000.   _____

C. Compute the cost of shares, amount of commission, and total amount paid to the stockbroker in these round-lot transactions. The commission rate is 1.9% of the cost of the shares.   OBJECTIVE 5

	Purchased	Price per Share	Cost of Shares	Commission	Total Amount Paid
6.	1,000	$32.40	_____	_____	_____
7.	500	$24.20	_____	_____	_____

D. Find the current yield. Round to the nearest tenth of a percent.   OBJECTIVE 6

	Stock	Annual Dividend	Current Price	Current Yield
8.	A	$0.46	$25.73	_____
9.	B	$0.40	$36.42	_____

E. Calculate the PE ratio. Round to the nearest whole number.   OBJECTIVE 7

	Stock	Current Price	Net Earnings	PE Ratio
10.	C	$78.38	$1.56	_____
11.	D	$63.30	$3.41	_____

F. Use Excel to calculate and track stock investments.   OBJECTIVE 8

12.   Retrieve the file *ch12ex03.xlsx*. Follow the directions. Save the file as *ch12ex03a.xlsx*.

13.   Retrieve the file *ch12ex04.xlsx*. Follow the directions. Save the file as *ch12ex04a.xlsx*.

12.3 Bonds

OBJECTIVES

1. Identify terms used with bonds.
2. Read bond quotes.
3. Calculate the market value and the annual interest earned on a bond.
4. Calculate the annual yield on a bond.
5. Use Excel with bond investments.

OBJECTIVE 1 Identify terms used with bonds.

City, state, and federal governments, as well as many corporations, depend on the sale of bonds as a major source of financing. Because of your employment or perhaps because of your own investment interests, you should understand bonds. Municipal, government, and corporate are the three main types of bonds.

Corporate bonds contain the name of the corporation, the face value, the rate of interest, and the maturity date of the bond. Because the price of the bond is set by market conditions, the actual value of the bond may fluctuate as the market fluctuates. When a bond is sold or traded and the market value is less than the face value, the bond is said to sell at a *discount*. Likewise, if the market value is more than the face value of the bond, it is said to sell at a *premium*.

Here are some common terms related to bonds.

Bond A certificate issued by a corporation, the federal government, or a municipality whereby the issuer promises to repay the borrowed money at some specific time plus any interest earned.

Corporate Bonds Bonds are issued by corporations to raise money. For example, a corporation may borrow money from a lending institution for short-term money. A corporation may also issue or sell long-term notes, known as bonds, to provide additional money on which to operate. An individual buying or investing in corporate bonds is lending money to the corporation. Most corporate bonds are issued in denominations of $1,000. Occasionally, however, smaller or larger amounts are issued.

Face Value (Par Value) The amount of money paid to the bondholder when the bond matures, not including interest.

Government Bonds Bonds are issued by the federal government. Some of the more common types are U.S. savings bonds, U.S. treasury bonds, U.S. treasury bills, and U.S. treasury notes. Savings bonds are purchased as an investment to help support the federal government. Treasury bonds, treasury bills, and treasury notes are purchased for investment purposes or are pledged as collateral by individuals, corporations, hospitals, school districts, and banks.

Market Value The amount of money the bond will bring in a competitive and open market.

Maturity The date a bond is due and payable.

Municipal Bonds Bonds are issued by cities, towns, or other municipalities to provide funds for improvement of streets, utilities, and public areas. These bonds are often desirable to the investor because interest earned is usually exempt from federal income tax. The authority to issue municipal bonds must be approved by the voters of the city, town, or other municipality before the bonds may be sold. Common terms used related to voter approval of the sale of bonds are *bond election* and *bond issue*.

Corporations, rather than selling bonds directly to the public, usually sell bonds to an investment company, which in turn sells the bonds at higher prices to the public through stock exchanges or over-the-counter markets. Bond prices are quoted as a percent of face value. For example, a bond quotation of 84.5 means that the bond sold for 0.8450 times $1,000, or $845.00 per bond.

Reading a bond quote is similar to reading a stock market table. A line from a typical daily bond market report is shown in Table 12-5.

Table 12-5

Bond Market Report

①	②	③	④	⑤
Bonds	Cur Yield	Vol	Last	Net Chg
SoBun 13.75s10	6.6	52	84.50	+0.5

1. SoBun is the abbreviated name of the corporation—South Bundett Corporation. The number following the name, 13.75, indicates 13.75 interest rate paid on face value. The *s* indicates that interest is paid by the corporation semiannually. The last two digits, 10, are the abbreviation for the maturing year—2010.
2. Current yield represents the annual percentage return to the purchaser at the current price.
3. Volume is the actual number of bonds that were sold that day—52. Each bond has a face value of $1,000.
4. Last is the closing price the bond sold for that day as a percent of $1,000. To calculate the price of a bond, change the percent to a decimal. Then multiply the percent by $1,000.
5. Net change is the difference between the week's closing price and the previous week's closing price. To calculate the difference in the price from today's listing, find the closing price. In the example, the closing (last) price was $84.50 of its face value, which was up 0.5% from the previous day.

$$84.50 + 0.50 = 85.00$$
$$0.8500 \times \$1,000 = \$850.00, \text{ previous day's bond price}$$

Local newspapers occasionally carry a bond report showing the most actively traded bonds. National financial newspapers carry daily bond market listings.

Each brokerage firm charges a *commission*, sometimes called a *brokerage fee*, for buying or selling bonds. These amounts vary from firm to firm and may be based on a percent of the transaction or a flat dollar amount. Some brokerage firms charge a minimum fee plus a set dollar amount per $1,000 bond. For the examples and exercises in this textbook, the charge will be $10 per $1,000 bond with no minimum per transaction.

When an order is placed for a bond, generally five business days elapse before the bond purchase is completed. The date on which the purchase is completed is called the **settlement date**. Each bond has a specified fixed rate of interest, and the dates the interest will be paid are known. When the settlement date occurs on the interest date, the buyer is due no accrued interest. The buyer will want to know the amount of annual interest that will be paid on the interest dates.

EXAMPLE

You are considering the purchase of six South Bundett bonds. Calculate the market value, the commission, the total expenditure, and the annual interest for the bonds when the settlement date is on the interest date.

Number of bonds purchased	6
Face value of each bond	$1,000
Price per bond	84.5%
Interest rate	10.375%
Commission per $1,000 bond	$10

STEPS

1. To obtain the market value, multiply the number of bonds purchased by the face value of each bond by the price per bond.

$$6 \times \$1,000 \times 84.5\% = \$5,070 \quad \text{market value}$$

2. To obtain the total commission charged, multiply the commission per bond by the number of bonds in the purchase.

$$\$10 \times 6 = \$60 \quad \text{commission}$$

3. To obtain the total expenditure for the bond purchase, add the total market value and the total commission.

$$\$5,070 + \$60 = \$5,130 \quad \text{total expenditure}$$

4. To obtain the annual interest earned, multiply the number of bonds purchased by the face value of each bond by the interest rate.

$$6 \times \$1,000 \times 0.10375 = \$622.50 \quad \text{annual interest}$$

OBJECTIVE **4** Calculate the annual yield on a bond.

The amount of money earned (interest income) by the investor on a bond each year is sometimes referred to as the annual yield. The **rate of annual yield** is the percent the interest income is of the total investment. The formula for computing the rate of annual yield is as follows:

$$\text{Rate of Annual Yield} = \frac{\text{Annual Bond Interest Income}}{\text{Bond Investment}}$$

If a $1,000 bond at a 12.75% interest rate is purchased at 90% of face value, what is the rate of annual yield to the investor? Assume the bond is purchased on the interest date.

STEPS

1. Calculate the market value.

   $1,000 × 0.90 = $900   market value

2. Compute the commission and add it to the market value to obtain the total investment.

   1 × $10 = $10   commission

   $10 + $900 = $910   total investment

3. Calculate the annual bond interest income.

   $1,000 × 0.1275 = $127.50   annual bond interest income

4. To calculate the rate of annual yield, divide the annual bond interest income by the bond investment.

   $127.50 ÷ $910 = 14%   rate of annual yield

OBJECTIVE 5 Use Excel with bond investments.

Bonds are usually issued by governmental bodies or large corporations. When a city, for instance, issues bonds to repair its city streets, a sinking fund might be created to help with the plans to have the money available when the bonds mature. Excel could be used to create a record of this sinking fund. Excel could also be used to track the value of any bonds purchased.

EXAMPLE

Marian Gonzalez creates a spreadsheet as a record of her bond purchases, as shown in Figure 12-6 on the next page.

STEPS

📀 Retrieve the file *ch12pr06.xlsx*.

1. Enter formulas in Column D to calculate the Market Value. Multiply Number of Bonds Purchased times Face Value of Each Bond times Percent Price.

2. Enter formulas in Column F to calculate the Commission. Multiply Number of Bonds Purchased times $10. (Hint: Point to F3.)

3. Enter formulas in Column G to calculate the Total Bond Investment. Add Market Value plus Commission.

4. Enter formulas in Column H to calculate Annual Interest All Bonds. Multiply Number of Bonds Purchased times Face Value times Interest Rate of each Bond.

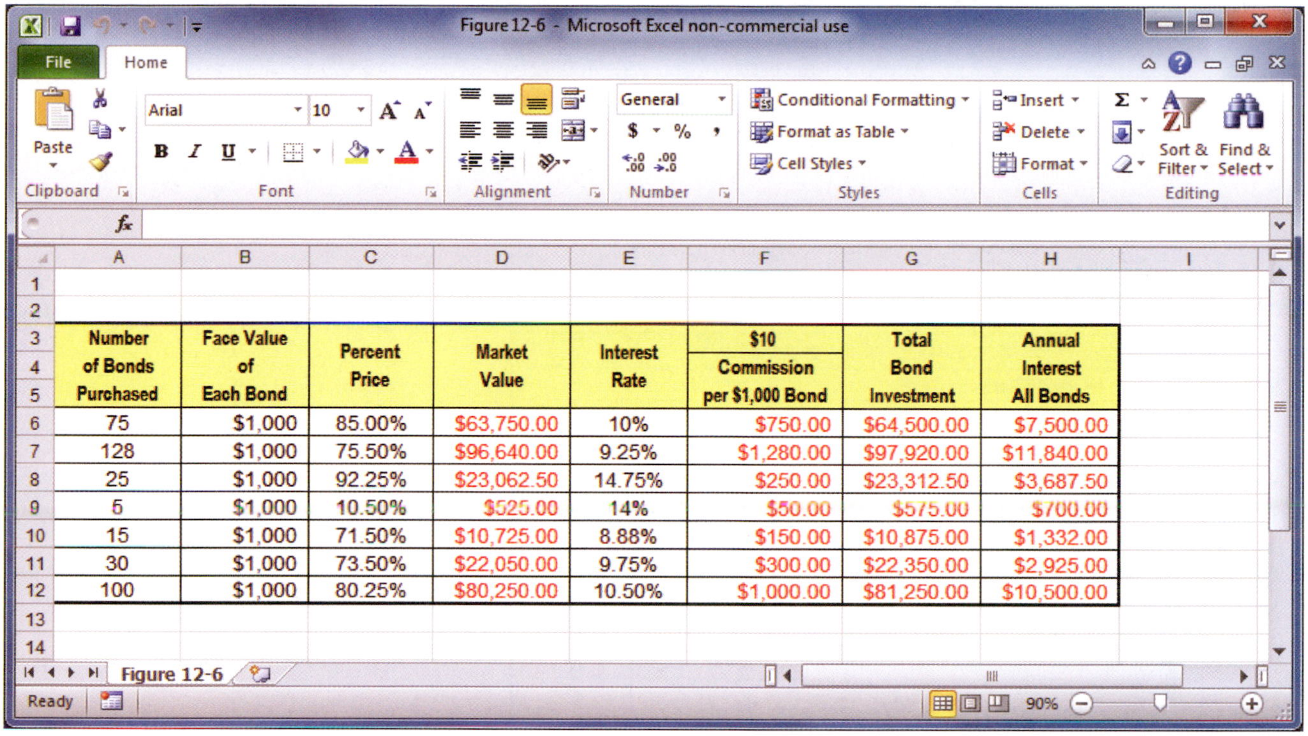

Figure 12-6

Spreadsheet Record of Bond Purchases

Number of Bonds Purchased	Face Value of Each Bond	Percent Price	Market Value	Interest Rate	$10 Commission per $1,000 Bond	Total Bond Investment	Annual Interest All Bonds
75	$1,000	85.00%	$63,750.00	10%	$750.00	$64,500.00	$7,500.00
128	$1,000	75.50%	$96,640.00	9.25%	$1,280.00	$97,920.00	$11,840.00
25	$1,000	92.25%	$23,062.50	14.75%	$250.00	$23,312.50	$3,687.50
5	$1,000	10.50%	$525.00	14%	$50.00	$575.00	$700.00
15	$1,000	71.50%	$10,725.00	8.88%	$150.00	$10,875.00	$1,332.00
30	$1,000	73.50%	$22,050.00	9.75%	$300.00	$22,350.00	$2,925.00
100	$1,000	80.25%	$80,250.00	10.50%	$1,000.00	$81,250.00	$10,500.00

5. Format answers for Currency, 2 Decimal places, and $.

6. Save the file as *ch12pr06a.xlsx*.

Excel can also be used to create a sinking fund table for bonds issued. See Figure 12-7 on the next page.

EXAMPLE

The City of Atlanta needs a new garbage truck in eight years. The truck costs $50,000. They have sold bonds to raise the $50,000 at 8% annually for 8 years and have set up a sinking fund table in Excel.

STEPS

Retrieve the file *ch12pr07.xlsx*.

1. Enter zero in Cell B12 to indicate there is no Periodic Interest in Year 1.

2. Use the Sinking Fund table and locate the factor needed (8 periods, 8%). Enter the factor in Cell B8.

3. Enter a formula in Cell C12 to calculate the Periodic Payment. Multiply factor by Amount Needed. Use absolute cell references. Copy the formula down Column C.

4. Enter a formula in Cell B13 to calculate Periodic Interest. Multiply previous year's Balance at End of Period times Interest Rate. Use =ROUND and absolute cell reference as follows: =ROUND((D12*$B$6),2). Copy the formula down Column B.

5. Key $4,700.50 in Cell D12 for the first year balance since no calculations were necessary.

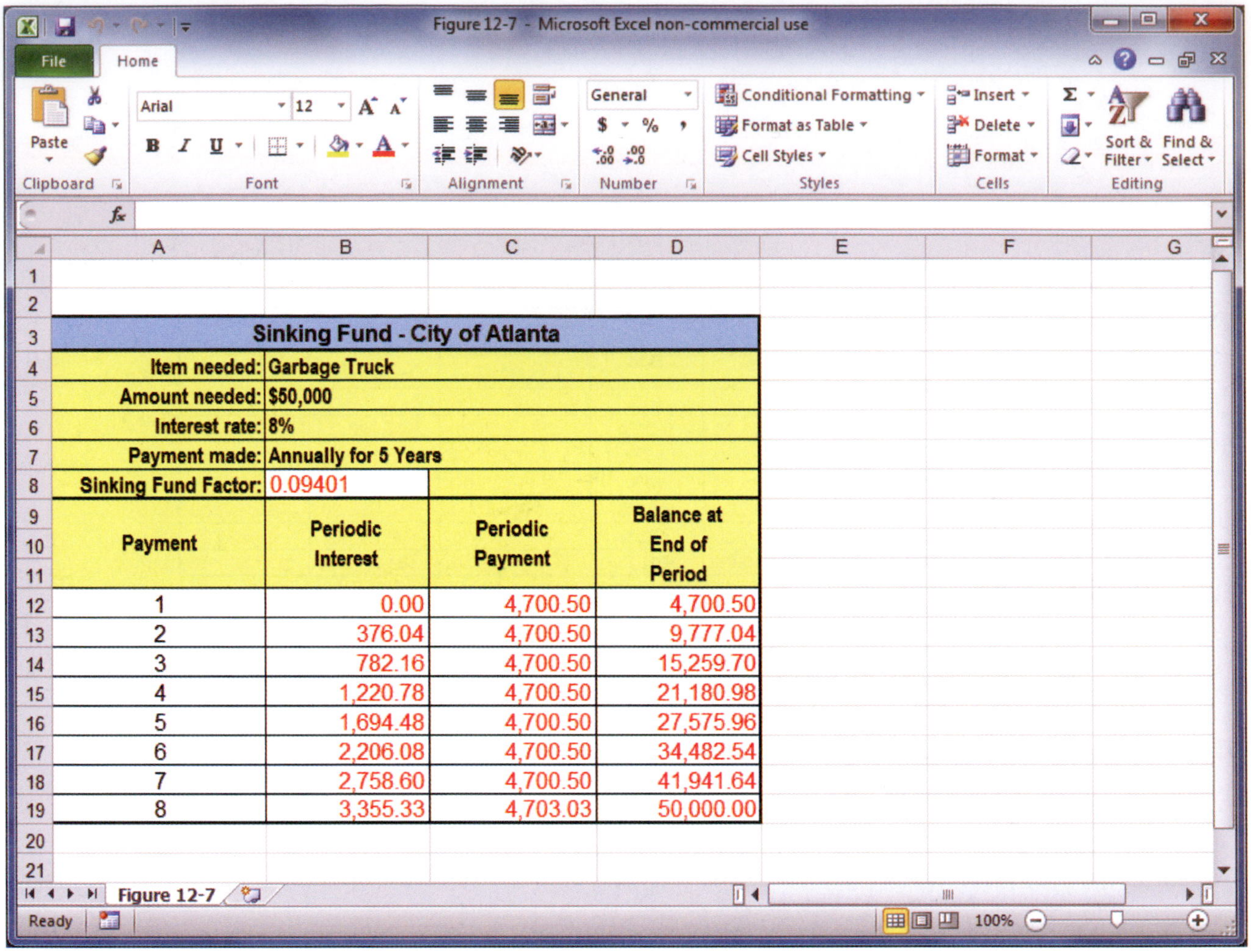

Sinking Fund - City of Atlanta			
Item needed:	Garbage Truck		
Amount needed:	$50,000		
Interest rate:	8%		
Payment made:	Annually for 5 Years		
Sinking Fund Factor:	0.09401		
Payment	Periodic Interest	Periodic Payment	Balance at End of Period
1	0.00	4,700.50	4,700.50
2	376.04	4,700.50	9,777.04
3	782.16	4,700.50	15,259.70
4	1,220.78	4,700.50	21,180.98
5	1,694.48	4,700.50	27,575.96
6	2,206.08	4,700.50	34,482.54
7	2,758.60	4,700.50	41,941.64
8	3,355.33	4,703.03	50,000.00

Figure 12-7
Sinking Fund Table

6. Enter formulas in Column D to calculate the new Balance at End of Period. Add previous year's Balance at End of Period + Periodic Interest + Periodic Payment.
7. After Year 8's Periodic Interest is calculated, subtract Balance at End of Period from Amount Needed and increase the Year 8 Periodic Payment by that amount ($2.53).
8. Format dollar entries for Currency, 2 Decimal places, and no $.
9. Save the file as ***ch12pr07a.xlsx***.

Name _____ Date _____

Directions Solve the following problems. Write your answers in the blanks provided. Give dollar amounts to the nearest cent and percents to the nearest tenth.

A. **Read the following bond market report from left to right for South Bundett Corporation. Provide the information requested.** OBJECTIVE **2**

Bonds	Current Yield	Volume Traded	Last	Net Change
SoBun 10s 05	9.3	62	86	−1

1. SoBun means _____
2. 10 means _____
3. *s* means _____
4. 05 means _____

5. 9.3 means _____
6. 62 means _____
7. 86 means _____
8. −1 means _____

B. **Compute the annual interest per bond, total investment per bond, and rate of annual yield to the nearest tenth. Each bond has a face value of $1,000.** OBJECTIVES **3, 4**

Number of Bonds Purchased	Price per Bond	Commission per Bond	Interest Rate	Annual Interest per Bond	Total Investment per Bond	Rate of Annual Yield
1	80.25%	$10	10.5%	9. _____	10. _____	11. _____
1	87%	$25	9.25%	12. _____	13. _____	14. _____
1	90.50%	$20	11.75%	15. _____	16. _____	17. _____

C. **Solve the following problems using Excel.** OBJECTIVE **5**

18. Retrieve the file *ch12ex05.xlsx*. Follow the directions. Save the file as *ch12ex05a.xlsx*.

19. Retrieve the file *ch12ex06.xlsx*. Follow the directions. Save the file as *ch12ex06a.xls*.

Chapter Review and Assessment

KEY TERMS

annuity
annuity certain
annuity due
Board of Directors
bond
brokerage fee
charter
commission
common stock
contingent annuities
corporate bonds
cumulative stock
dividends
dividends in arrears
earnings per share
face value (par value)

fixed tax-deferred annuity
future value of an annuity
government bonds
Individual Retirement Account (IRA)
market value
maturity value
municipal bonds
mutual funds
odd lots
ordinary annuity
outstanding shares
par value
payment period
preferred stock
present value of an annuity

price-earnings ratio (PE)
prospectus
rate of annual yield
round lots
Roth IRA
settlement date
shares
sinking fund
stock
stock certificate
stock table
stockholders
tax-deferred
term of an annuity
variable annuity
yield

CONCEPTS	EXAMPLES
12.1 Calculate the future value of an ordinary annuity.	2 years, $2,000 ordinary annuity at 6% annually
1. Determine the number of periods.	There are 2 compounding periods.
2. Determine the interest rate.	The interest rate is 6%.
3. Determine the factor from Table 12-1. Read down the left column for the number of periods and across to the interest rate.	The factor from the table is 2.06000.
4. Multiply the payment each period by the number from the table.	$2,000 × 2.06000 = $4,120
12.1 Calculate the future value of an annuity due.	2 years, $2,000 annuity due at 6% annually
1. Determine the number of periods.	There are 2 periods.
2. Add 1 period to the number of periods.	2 + 1 = 3 periods
3. Determine the interest rate.	The interest rate is 6%.
4. Determine the factor from Table 12-1.	The factor from the table is 3.18360.
5. Multiply the payment each period by the number from the table.	$2,000 × 3.18360 = $6,367.20
6. Subtract one payment.	$6,367.20 − $2,000 = $4,367.20

CONCEPTS	EXAMPLES
12.1 Calculate the present value of an ordinary annuity. 1. Calculate the number of periods and interest rate per period. 2. Determine the factor from Table 12-2. 3. Multiply the amount invested by the table factor.	Receive $15,000 for 6 years. Interest is 8% compounded annually. There are 6 periods. The interest rate is 8%. The factor from the table is 4.62288. $15,000 × 4.62288 = $69,343.20 This is the amount you would pay today to have payments of $15,000 for 6 years.
12.1 Calculate present value using a sinking fund table. 1. Calculate the number of periods and interest rate per period. 2. Determine the factor from table 12-3. 3. Multiply the amount invested by the table factor.	$100,000 bond to retire (pay off) 15 years from now. Interest 10% compounded annually. There are 15 periods. The interest rate is 10%. The factor from the table is 0.03147. $100,000 × 0.03147 = $3,147 This is the payment each period to have $100,000 in 15 years.
12.2 Calculate dividends. 1. Multiply the dividend rate by the par value. 2. Multiply the dividend amount per share by the number of shares of preferred stock. 3. Subtract the total amount paid to preferred stockholders from total profits to be distributed. 4. Divide the total amount available to common stock stockholders by the total shares of common stock.	$500,000 to distribute; 20,000 shares of 9% preferred stock, $100 per value; 85,000 shares of common stock 0.09 × $100 = $9 dividend per share of preferred stock $9 × 20,000 = $180,000 dividend paid to preferred shareholders $500,000 − $180,000 = $320,000 $320,000 ÷ 85,000 = $3.76 dividend per share of common stock
12.2 Calculate earnings per share. 1. Divide earnings distributed by number of shares of common stock. $$\text{Earnings per Share} = \frac{\text{Earnings Distributed}}{\text{Number of Shares of Common Stock}}$$	125,000 shares of common stock; $600,000 distributed to stockholders $600,000 ÷ 125,000 = $4.80 earnings per share

CONCEPTS	EXAMPLES
12.2 Calculate the cost of shares, the amount of commission, and the total cost of a stock transaction.	100 shares purchased at $32.45 per share. Commission rate is 1.5% of total transaction.
1. Multiply the number of shares to be purchased by the per-share price of the stock.	$100 \times \$32.45 = \$3,245$ cost of shares
2. Multiply the commission rate by the cost of the shares.	$0.015 \times \$3,245 = \$48.68$ commission charge
3. Add the commission to the cost of shares.	$\$3,245 + \$48.68 = \$3,293.68$ total cost of transaction

12.2 Calculate current stock yield.

$$\text{Current Yield} = \frac{\text{Annual Dividend per Share}}{\text{Closing Price per Share}}$$

$1.80 dividend and a closing price of $72

$\$1.80 \div \$72 = 2.5\%$ current yield

12.2 Calcuate price-earnings (PE) ratio.

$$\text{PE ratio} = \frac{\text{Current Price per Share}}{\text{Annual Net Income Earnings per Share}}$$

Net earnings of $3.42 on stock selling at $30.40

$\$30.40 \div \$3.42 = 9$ PE ratio

12.3 Calcuate the market value and the annual interest earned on a bond.	5 bonds purchased; face value per bond, $1,000; price per bond 89%; interest rate, 8.25%; commission per $1,000 bond, $10
1. Multiply the number of bonds purchased by the face value of each bond times the price per bond.	$5 \times \$1,000 \times 89\% = \$4,450$ market value
2. Multiply the commission per bond by the number of bonds purchased.	$\$10 \times 5 = \$50$ commission
3. Add the total market value and the commission.	$\$4,450 + \$50 = \$4,500$ total cost
4. Multiply the number of bonds by the face value of each bond by the interest rate.	$5 \times \$1,000 \times 8.25\% = \$412.50$ annual interest

12.3 Calculate the annual yield on a bond.	$1,000 bond at a 12% annual interest rate, a $10 commission per $1,000 bond, and a closing price of $90.50
1. Multiply the cost of the bond by the face value.	$\$1,000 \times 0.905 = \$905$ market value
2. Find the commission and add it to the market value.	$\$905 + \$10 = \$915$ cost per bond
3. Multiply the cost of the bond by the annual interest rate.	$\$915 \times 5 \text{ bonds} = \$4,575$ cost all bonds
	$\$1,000 \times 0.12 = \$120$ interest income
4. Divide the annual bond interest income by the bond investment.	$\$120 \div \$4,575 = 2.6\%$ yield

Chapter 12 Review Exercises

Name _____ Date _____

Directions Write your answers in the blanks provided. Round dollar amounts to the nearest hundredth.

A. Find the future value of the following ordinary annuities. `12.1 OBJECTIVE 3`

	Amount of Each Deposit	Period	Rate	Time (Years)	Amount of Annuity
1.	$1,400	annually	10%	10	_____
2.	$2,000	semiannually	8%	5	_____
3.	$3,500	quarterly	6%	8	_____

B. Find the future value of the following annuities. `12.1 OBJECTIVE 4`

	Amount of Each Deposit	Period	Rate	Time (Years)	Amount of Annuity
4.	$3,500	annually	12%	10	_____
5.	$1,000	semiannually	6%	5	_____
6.	$5,500	quarterly	8%	8	_____

C. Find the present value of the following annuities. `12.1 OBJECTIVE 5`

	Amount per Payment	Payment at End of Each	Time (Years)	Rate of Investment	Present Value
7.	$1,200	year	14	10%	_____
8.	$3,100	6 months	8	12%	_____
9.	$2,500	quarter	5	8%	_____

D. Find the payment needed to accumulate the indicated amount in a sinking fund. `12.1 OBJECTIVE 6`

	Amount	Money Earns	Compounded	Years	Payment
10.	$7,300	8%	annually	6	_____
11.	$15,100	10%	quarterly	8	_____
12.	$22,000	6%	semiannually	10	_____
13.	$10,600	12%	monthly	3	_____

E. Find the dividend per share and the total dividends to be received by the holders of common stock. Round Dividend per Share to the nearest cent.

12.2 OBJECTIVE **2**

	Dividends Declared	Shares Outstanding	Dividend Per Share	Stock Owned	Total Dividend Received by Stockholders
14.	$100,000	65,000	_____	100	_____
15.	$500,000	142,000	_____	350	_____
16.	$85,000	36,000	_____	1,000	_____
17.	$150,000	25,000	_____	500	_____

F. Find the earnings per share. **12.2** OBJECTIVE **3**

	Earnings Distributed	Number of Shares of Common Stock	Earnings per Share
18.	$7,000,000	1,500,000	_____
19.	$1,300,000	150,000	_____
20.	$850,000	30,000	_____
21.	$2,400,000	1,000,000	_____

G. Calculate the cost of the shares, the commission, and the total cost of the transaction. The commission rate is 1% of the cost of the round lot shares and 2% on odd lots.

12.2 OBJECTIVE **5**

	Shares Purchased	Per-Share Price	Cost of Shares	Commission	Total Cost
22.	360	$15.25	_____	_____	_____
23.	210	$23.80	_____	_____	_____
24.	600	$16.00	_____	_____	_____

H. Calculate the market value, commission, total expenditure, and annual interest earned on the following bonds. 12.3 OBJECTIVE 3

Bonds Purchased = 7
Face Value of each bond = $1,000
Price per bond = 69.5%
Interest Rate = 9%
Commission per $1,000 bond = $10

Bonds Purchased = 10
Face Value of each bond = $1,000
Price per bond = 87.4%
Interest Rate = 10.2%
Commission per $1,000 bond = $10

25. Market Value = _____

26. Commission = _____

27. Total Expenditure = _____

28. Annual Interest = _____

29. Market Value = _____

30. Commission = _____

31. Total Expenditure = _____

32. Annual Interest = _____

I. Calculate annual yield on the following bonds. Assume a commission of $10 per bond. 12.3 OBJECTIVE 4

	Bond	Purchased/Face Value	Interest Rate	Annual Yield
33.	$1,000	95.1%	8.5%	_____
34.	$1,000	90%	9.7%	_____
35.	$1,000	92.5%	8.3%	_____

J. Solve the following application problems.

Andres Melendez decides to put half the payment from a rental property he owns into an annuity for the education of his two children. At the end of each year for 10 years, he puts $4,200 into an account that pays 6% compounded annually.

36. Find the amount of the annuity. _____

37. Find the interest earned. _____

In five years, Chao-chen Hu plans to purchase his brother's share of their Chinese restaurant when his brother retires. He will need $150,000.

38. What payment into a sinking fund does Chao-chen need to make at an interest rate of 8% compounded quarterly for 5 years? _____

K. Use Excel with annuities, stocks, and bonds. 12.1 OBJECTIVE 7, 12.2 OBJECTIVE 8 12.3 OBJECTIVE 5

39. Retrieve the file *ch12ex07.xlsx*. Follow the directions. Save the file as *ch12ex07a.xlsx*.

40. Retrieve the file *ch12ex08.xlsx*. Follow the directions. Save the file as *ch12ex08a.xlsx*.

41. Retrieve the file *ch12ex09.xlsx*. Follow the directions. Save the file as *ch12ex09a.xlsx*.

Shelly Pearce's financial consultant advised her to invest a portion of her business's profit. After attending a small business investment seminar, Shelly began following several stocks and bonds. She is interested in a stock that is currently trading at $45.25, providing an annual dividend of $2.98. During this period of time, she has also followed a bond that is currently trading at $97.50, with an annual interest rate of 10.5%. Calculate the yield for the stock and bond and compare the two investments.

    1. What is the stock yield?

    2. What is the bond yield?

Shelley shared the advice from her financial consultant with her business partner. He is interested in a stock that is currently trading at $38.95, providing an annual dividend of $2.15. He is also interested in a bond that is currently trading for $99.25 with an annual interest rate of 10.25%. Calculate the yield of Shelley's partner's stock and bond and compare the two investments.

    3. What is the stock yield?

    4. What is the bond yield?

    5. Which of the four options is a better investment for the business? Explain.

Write about Math

1. How are stocks different from bonds?

2. Explain the difference between an annuity and annuity due.

3. Distinguish between *current yield* and *PE ratio*.

Personal Finance

Which would be a better investment?

Suppose you inherited $25,000 from your grandparents with one stipulation—you cannot spend the money. You must invest your inheritance. For now, you have decided to spend $5,000 in the stock market. To prepare for your potential investment, choose stocks in which to invest and follow them for four to eight weeks. Keep a record on the performance of each stock. Check the stocks on the same day each week.

Francesco Carta fotografo/Shutterstock.com

Complete the following activities.

1. Use the newspaper or the Internet to locate a minimum of three stocks and make your initial "play" purchase using those prices. Create an Excel worksheet and keep a weekly record of each stock's performance. Include the date the shares were purchased, stock name, symbol, and number of shares purchased, price per share at the time of purchase, and total value of purchase. Include the date shares were sold, number of shares sold, price per share, total value at time of sale, the amount of profit or loss. Check your stocks once per week and keep your record for at least four weeks.

2. Create a report. Insert the Excel worksheets. Create an Excel line chart showing how the stocks performed. You may create individual graphs per stock. Write a paragraph about each company for which you purchased stock. Include the company name, the stock symbol, the products or services the company sells, a brief history of the company. Refer to Standard & Poor's or Value Line in the library, or research the information online. Include the name of the CEO and/or other key employees, the location of the company's main headquarters, whether the company is international, national, regional, or local.

3. Which stock performed the best during this period of time?

4. What was the percent of increase or decrease from what you paid for the stock at the beginning and the price of it at the end of the four weeks when you sold it?

5. Call a bank, savings and loan, or credit union and obtain the highest rate of interest you could have earned if you had invested the $5,000 for the same number of days in a savings account or money market account at a fixed rate of interest. Create an Excel worksheet and use formulas to calculate the interest for the period you held the stocks compounded daily (see Chapter 10 on Compound Interest) to compare it with the amount earned from your stock market investments. If you had invested the $5,000 in an account that paid a fixed amount during this same period of time, how much would you have earned (or lost) from your investment?

6. Which would have been a better investment? Stock market or a fixed account?

Name _____   Date _____   Score _____

Directions   Write your answers in the blanks provided. Round dollar amounts to the nearest hundredth.

A. Find the future value of the following ordinary annuities.   12.1 OBJECTIVE 3

	Amount of Each Deposit	Period	Rate	Time (Years)	Amount of Annuity
1.	$1,000	annually	10%	10	_____
2.	$3,900	semiannually	6%	5	_____
3.	$4,000	quarterly	8%	8	_____

B. Find the future value of the following annuities due.   12.1 OBJECTIVE 4

	Amount of Each Deposit	Period	Rate	Time (Years)	Amount of Annuity
4.	$4,500	annually	12%	5	_____
5.	$8,000	semiannually	6%	5	_____
6.	$7,500	quarterly	8%	8	_____

C. Find the present value of the following annuities.   12.1 OBJECTIVE 5

	Amount per Payment	Payment at End of Each	Time (Years)	Rate of Investment	Present Value
7.	$600	year	14	10%	_____
8.	$1,100	6 months	8	12%	_____
9.	$1,500	quarter	5	8%	_____

D. Find the amount of each payment needed to accumulate the indicated amount in a sinking fund.   12.1 OBJECTIVE 6

	Amount	Money Earns	Compounded	Years	Payment
10.	$2,400	8%	annually	6	_____
11.	$3,600	10%	quarterly	8	_____
12.	$4,200	6%	semiannually	10	_____
13.	$5,000	12%	monthly	3	_____

E. Find the dividend per share and the total dividends to be received by the stockholders. Round to the nearest cent. **12.2** OBJECTIVE **2**

	Dividend Declared	Shares Outstanding	Dividend per Share	Stock Owned	Total Dividend Received by Stockholder
14.	$200,000	18,000	_____	1,500	_____
15.	$820,000	56,000	_____	502	_____
16.	$708,000	65,000	_____	120	_____

F. Find the earnings per share. **12.2** OBJECTIVE **3**

	Earnings Distributed	Number of Shares of Common Stock	Earnings per Share
17.	$2,400,000	1,000,000	_____
18.	$690,000	145,000	_____
19.	$902,500	852,300	_____

G. Calculate the cost of the shares, the commission, and the total cost of the transaction. The commission is 1.5% of the cost of the shares. **12.2** OBJECTIVE **5**

	Shares Purchased	Per-Share Price	Cost of Shares	Commission	Total Cost
20.	600	$16.00	_____	_____	_____
21.	2,000	$25.50	_____	_____	_____

H. To calculate the market value, the commission, the total expenditure, and the annual interest for bonds, use the following information. **12.3** OBJECTIVE **3**

Number of bonds: 8
Face value of each bond: $1,000
Price per bond: 84.50%
Interest rate: 10.5%
Commission per $1,000 bond: $10

22. _____ market value   23. _____ commission

24. _____ total expenditure   25. _____ interest

I. Use Excel with annuities, stocks, and bonds. **12.1** OBJECTIVE **7**, **12.2** OBJECTIVE **8** **12.3** OBJECTIVE **5**

26. Retrieve the file *ch12qz01.xlsx*. Follow the directions. Save the file as *ch12qz01a.xlsx*.

27. Retrieve the file *ch12qz02.xlsx*. Follow the directions. Save the file as *ch12qz02a.xlsx*.

CHAPTER 13

Depreciation

Business assets such as buildings, automobiles, equipment, and machinery are tangible assets. The Internal Revenue Service (IRS) allows a business to annually deduct as an expense for income tax purposes the declining value due to aging of most of these assets. The aging of these assets is called depreciation. A business must keep accurate records of its expenses so a clear profit picture can be calculated. Because the annual income tax deduction is such a large expense, the IRS carefully monitors the methods by which it is computed.

PURCHASING MANAGER

Kristie Warzala is a senior purchasing manager for a large global consumer goods corporation. For interactive media purchasing she is responsible for seeking and signing professional talent to represent the company's multitude of products in print, on the web and television, and in event appearances. Kristie is part of a large corporation with globally recognized products. She is accountable for managing a big budget and recruiting top name talent.

Many factors come into play when deciding on the total price for a new contract. "The way we think of dollars is number of days and the cost of using someone's name and personality," Kristie says, "The more popular the talent, the more money we will have to spend." Another important factor that impacts the price is usage rights: whether the ads can be run in print, web, or on television, and if the ads will be run regionally or around the globe. A regional print ad will be significantly cheaper than a global, mass media campaign.

Kristie closely monitors how receptive consumers are to ad campaigns and how the popularity of an ad affects product sales. A typical contract is for 12 months, but if she finds that a particular campaign really boosts sales then a contract could be extended. On the other hand, if Kristie finds that consumers have a negative reaction to an ad and that causes sales to decrease, then the ad would be run less frequently or be pulled completely.

How Math is Used in Purchasing

Math can pose a challenge for interactive media purchasing. "I am not buying widgets that can be measured by cost per part," Kristie says, "I'm negotiating intangible goods that could depreciate at the drop of a hat." For example, if the talent is involved in a controversy and an ad must be pulled before the end of a contract, Kristie must find another way to recover the money lost. For every contract Kristie is given a budget, and her primary objective is to save money. Kristie uses Excel to organize her contracts and calculate possible savings. She says, "If I have a budget of $2 million and the final contract is only $1 million, then I am able to show the value of a contract in the amount of money saved."

What Do You Think?

What skills do you need to improve in order to be in purchasing?

photo courtesy of Kristie Warzala

Math Skills Used

Addition

Subtraction

Division

Percents

Other Skills Needed

Collaboration

Communication

Intuition

Listening skills

13.1 Straight-Line Depreciation

OBJECTIVE 1 Identify terms used with straight-line depreciation.

You need to learn the following terms related to depreciation. Many of these terms apply to each of the depreciation methods.

Accumulated Depreciation The total amount of depreciation used from the date the asset was purchased to the present date.

Book Value The original cost of the asset minus total depreciation to date.

Cost The actual cost of the asset.

Depreciable Amount The amount used to calculate the current year's depreciation.

Depreciable Base The cost minus the salvage value.

Depreciation The annual allowance or "paper loss" for the wear and tear, deterioration, or obsolescence of a property.

Depreciation Schedule A table or spreadsheet that shows the cost, salvage value, length of service in years, depreciation amount, annual depreciation, and accumulated depreciation of an asset.

Length of Service or Life of Asset The number of years the asset is expected to be useful, its amount of useful hours, the number of items it may be expected to produce, or the number of miles of travel expected. To be depreciable, property must have a useful life that extends substantially beyond the year it was placed in service.

Residual, Scrap, Salvage, or Trade-In Value The estimated value of the asset at the end of its estimated life, whether it is disposed of, traded in, or continued to be used.

Straight-Line Method Assumes that assets lose an equal amount of value during each year of the assets' useful life.

Tangible Assets Assets such as buildings, vehicles, equipment, furniture, and machinery.

OBJECTIVE 2 Depreciate an asset using straight-line depreciation.

A commonly used method of computing depreciation is the *straight-line method.* The straight-line method calculates depreciation expense less an asset's salvage value evenly over the life of the asset. To compute depreciation using the straight-line method, use this formula.

$$\text{Annual Depreciation} = \frac{\text{Cost} - \text{Salvage Value}}{\text{Length of Service}}$$

EXAMPLE

At the beginning of the year, a delivery truck was bought at a cost of $24,000. The truck has an estimated life of 5 years and a salvage value of $3,000 at the end of the 5-year period. Compute depreciation using the straight-line method. Then create a depreciation schedule.

STEPS

1. Subtract the salvage value from the cost of the asset to get the amount that can be depreciated (depreciable base).

$$\$24,000 - \$3,000 = \$21,000 \quad \text{depreciable base}$$

2. Divide the total depreciation by the length of service to get the annual amount of depreciation.

$$\$21,000 \div 5 = \$4,200 \quad \text{annual depreciation}$$

The truck may be depreciated $4,200 each year for 5 years.

3. Create a depreciation schedule.

Year	Annual Depreciation	Accumulated Depreciation	End-of-Year Book Value
Cost			24,000
1	4,200	4,200	19,800
2	4,200	8,400	15,600
3	4,200	12,600	11,400
4	4,200	16,800	7,200
5	4,200	21,000	3,000

TIPS

If the asset is bought during the year, depreciation is taken on the number of months remaining in that year. If the asset is purchased before the 15th of a month, the full month is taken. If it is purchased after the 15th, no depreciation for that month is taken.

OBJECTIVE 3 Find the book value of an asset using the straight-line method.

The *book value* of an asset is the cost of the asset minus the total depreciation to date. Use the following formula.

$$\text{Book Value} = \text{Cost} - \text{Depreciation}$$

EXAMPLE

Using the previous example, the cost of the asset was $24,000 and the depreciation calculated was $4,200.

$$\$24,000 - \$4,200 = \$19,800 \quad \text{first-year book value}$$

OBJECTIVE 4 Prepare a depreciation schedule in Excel using the straight-line method.

When an asset is purchased, the amount to be depreciated for each year's life of the asset should be calculated. A depreciation schedule is, therefore, created. This schedule is followed each year when the accountant makes the adjusting entries in the general journal to deduct that year's depreciation expense. It is important to make these calculations at this time, when all the information is available and the details of the purchase are known. Fewer errors are likely to occur if all calculations related to the life of the asset are done at the time of purchase rather than yearly.

Using Excel to create a depreciation schedule is quick and easy. Study Figure 13.1. Then follow the steps on the next page.

Figure 13-1
Straight-Line Depreciation Schedule

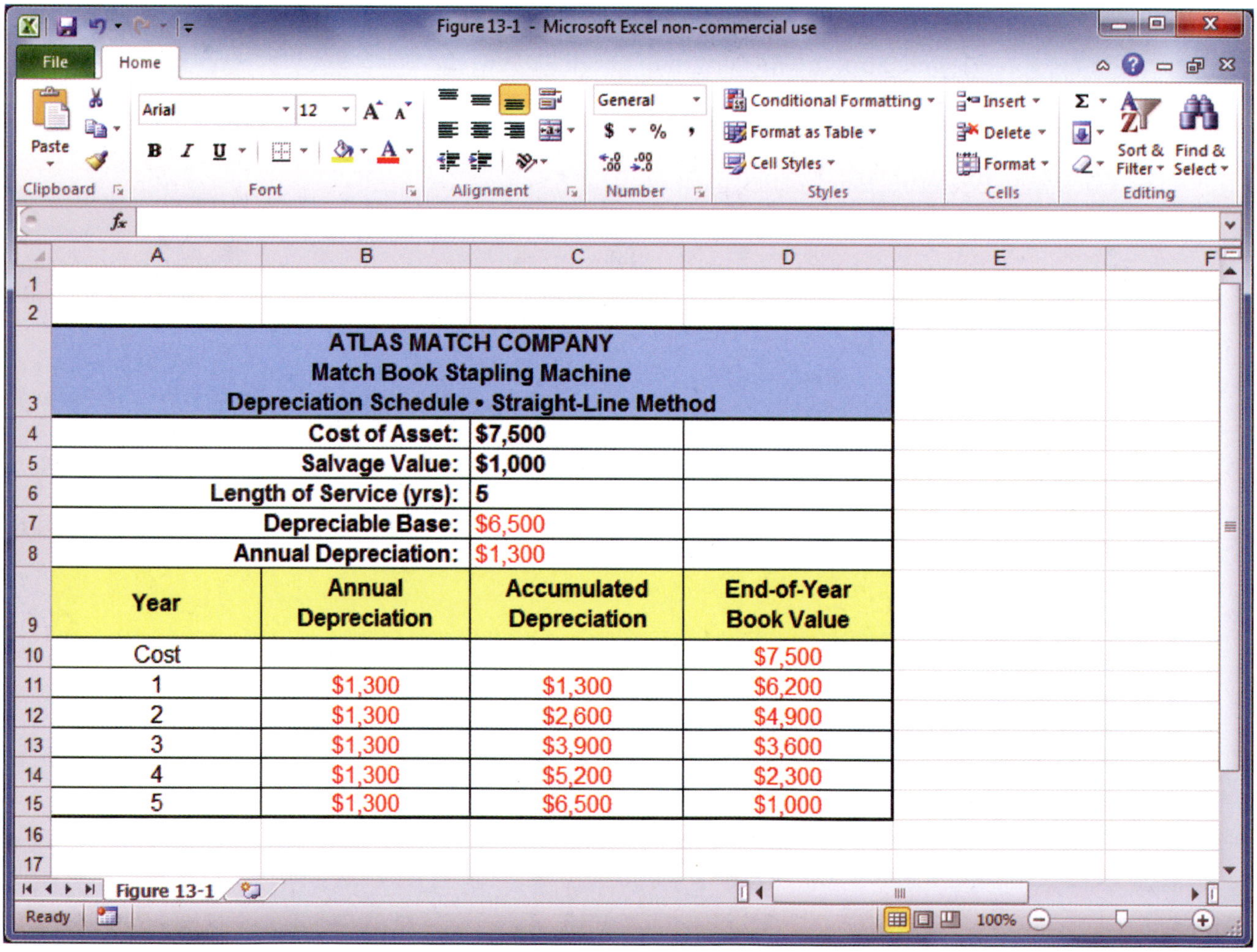

ATLAS MATCH COMPANY Match Book Stapling Machine Depreciation Schedule • Straight-Line Method			
Cost of Asset:		$7,500	
Salvage Value:		$1,000	
Length of Service (yrs):		5	
Depreciable Base:		$6,500	
Annual Depreciation:		$1,300	
Year	Annual Depreciation	Accumulated Depreciation	End-of-Year Book Value
Cost			$7,500
1	$1,300	$1,300	$6,200
2	$1,300	$2,600	$4,900
3	$1,300	$3,900	$3,600
4	$1,300	$5,200	$2,300
5	$1,300	$6,500	$1,000

A machine that manufactures book matches is purchased for $7,500. It is expected to last 5 years and have a salvage value of $1,000. Prepare a depreciation schedule in Excel using the straight-line method of depreciation.

STEPS

Retrieve the file *ch13pr01.xlsx*.

1. Enter a formula in Cell C7 to calculate the Depreciable Base (Cost of Asset minus Salvage Value).

2. Enter a formula in Cell C8 to calculate the Annual Depreciation (Depreciable Base divided by Length of Service). Use absolute cell references.

3. Copy the Annual Depreciation amount down Column B.

4. Enter formulas in Column C to calculate the Accumulated Depreciation (Year multiplied by Annual Depreciation).

5. Enter formulas in Column D to calculate the End-of-Year Book Value (Cost of Asset minus Accumulated Depreciation). Begin with the cost of the asset in Cell D10. Use an absolute cell reference for Cost of Asset. Notice in Year 5 the Book Value is equal to the Salvage Value and the Accumulated Depreciation is equal to the Depreciable Base.

6. Format answers for Currency, 0 Decimal places, and $.

7. Save the file as *ch13pr01a.xlsx*.

> **TIPS**
>
> *Each year's depreciation is added to the previous year's accumulated amount.*

Name _____   Date _____

Directions   Solve the following problems. Write your answers in the blanks provided. Carry all percents to four decimal places and round to the nearest whole number.

A. Use the straight-line method. Assume this is the first year of depreciation.   OBJECTIVES **2, 3**

	Original Cost	Estimated Life	Salvage Value	1st-Year Annual Depreciation
1.	$12,000	3	$3,000	_____
2.	$15,000	5	$5,000	_____
3.	$9,000	2	$2,000	_____
4.	$60,000	19	$10,000	_____

B. Complete the depreciation table using the straight-line method.   OBJECTIVE **2**

Total Cost:	$110,000
Salvage Value:	$15,000
Depreciable Base:	5. _____
Annual Depreciation:	6. _____
Life of asset:	10 years

Year	Annual Depreciation	Accumulated Depreciation	End-of-Year Book Value
1	7. _____	8. _____	9. _____
2	10. _____	11. _____	12. _____
3	13. _____	14. _____	15. _____
4	16. _____	17. _____	18. _____
5	19. _____	20. _____	21. _____
6	22. _____	23. _____	24. _____
7	25. _____	26. _____	27. _____
8	28. _____	29. _____	30. _____
9	31. _____	32. _____	33. _____
10	34. _____	35. _____	36. _____

C. Find the depreciable base and the annual depreciation. OBJECTIVE 2

Using the straight-line method, find the amount of depreciation of an asset that costs $7,600 and has a salvage value of $600. Assume the life of the asset is 6 years.

37. Depreciable base: _____

38. Annual depreciation: _____

39. First year book value: _____

A trailer costs $43,000, has an expected life of 12 years, and has a salvage value of $3,500. Use the straight-line depreciation method.

40. Depreciable base: _____

41. Annual depreciation: _____

42. First year book value: _____

Using the straight-line method, find the amount of depreciation of an asset that costs $11,300 and has a salvage value of $2,000. Assume the life of the asset is 8 years.

43. Depreciable base: _____

44. Annual depreciation: _____

45. First year book value: _____

A set of office furniture costs $9,500. It has an expected life of 10 years and a salvage value of $800. Use the straight-line depreciation method.

46. Depreciable base: _____

47. Annual depreciation: _____

48. First year book value: _____

D. Create a straight-line method depreciation table using Excel. OBJECTIVE 4

49. Retrieve the file *ch13ex01.xlsx*. Follow the directions. Save the file as *ch13ex01a.xlsx*.

50. Retrieve the file *ch13ex02.xlsx*. Follow the directions. Save the file as *ch13ex02a.xlsx*.

13.2 Double-Declining-Balance Method

OBJECTIVE 1 Identify terms used with the double-declining-balance method.

Learn the following terminology related to the double-declining-balance method of depreciation.

Accelerated Depreciation   Larger amounts of depreciation are allowed in the earlier years of the life of an asset and smaller amounts in the later years.

Double-Declining-Balance Method   Assumes that the greatest part of aging, or decline in value, occurs during the first years of use. Uses a constant rate of twice the straight-line rate.

Rate of Depreciation   Obtained by dividing the estimated life in years into 100% and multiplying by 2.

OBJECTIVE 2 Calculate the double-declining-balance rate, annual depreciation, and accumulated depreciation using the double-declining-balance method.

The *double-declining-balance method* assumes that the greatest part of aging, or decline in value, occurs during the first years of use. Since the greatest part of the aging in value is depreciated in the first years, this produces *accelerated depreciation*. A constant rate twice the straight-line rate is determined and applied to the declining balance each year. Depreciation is calculated each year on the end-of-year book value of the asset for the previous year. *Salvage value is not subtracted* when depreciation is computed. However, *you may not depreciate an item below its salvage value.* The double-declining rate is also referred to as the 200%-declining balance method. Other declining-balance rates are possible such as the 150%-declining rate. Each rate is some factor times the straight-line rate. Here are the steps using the double-declining rate.

STEPS

1. Calculate the straight-line rate (100% ÷ years) and multiply by 2 to calculate declining rate. Round your answers to 4 decimal places.

   Example: $1.00 \div 5 \text{ years} = 0.20$
   $0.20 \times 2 = 0.40$, or 40%

   Example: $1.00 \div 7 \text{ years} = 0.1429$
   $0.1429 \times 2 = 0.2858$, or 28.58%

2. Use the end-of-year book value for the previous year (depreciable amount) times the declining rate to calculate the annual depreciation.

3. Do not depreciate below salvage value.

EXAMPLE

Compute the depreciation on the delivery truck used in the straight-line method using the double-declining-balance method.

Original cost of truck	$24,000
Estimated life	5 years
Salvage value	$3,000

STEPS

1. Obtain the rate of depreciation by dividing the estimated life in years into 100%. This is the straight-line rate.

    100% ÷ 5 years = 20%   straight-line rate

2. Double the rate. (This is why the method of using twice the straight-line rate is referred to as the double-declining-balance method.)

    20% × 2 = 40%   annual double-declining-balance rate

3. For the first year, multiply the annual double-declining-balance rate by the cost of the asset.

    $24,000 × 40% = $9,600   first-year depreciation

4. In the first year, the annual depreciation of $9,600 is the accumulated depreciation.

5. Subtract the accumulated depreciation from the cost of the asset to determine the end-of-year book value.

    $24,000 − $9,600 = $14,400   end-of-year book value

Notice that the amount of the first-year depreciation is much larger than when using the straight-line method.

6. The end-of-year book value for the first year is the depreciable amount for the second year. Use the answer in step 5 for the next year's depreciable amount. Multiply the depreciable amount by the annual double-declining-balance rate to determine the amount of depreciation for the second year.

    $14,400 × 40% = $5,760   second-year depreciation

7. For the second year, add the annual depreciation to the accumulated depreciation in the previous year to determine the accumulated depreciation to date.

    $5,760 + $9,600 = $15,360   second-year accumulated depreciation

8. For the second year, subtract the accumulated depreciation from the cost of the asset to determine the end-of-year book value.

    $24,000 − $15,360 = $8,640

TIPS

In step 1, you can divide into 200% instead of 100% and skip step 2. Dividing into 200% doubles the rate.

TIPS

The double-declining-balance (also called the 200%-declining) method of depreciation requires that you double the straight-line rate.

The 150%-declining rate requires that you multiply the straight-line rate by 1.5.

9. Repeat steps 6-9 for the remaining years. Notice that the end-of-year book value in year 5 is $1,866. This is less than the salvage value. So the annual depreciation for year 5 is $3,110 –$3,000 = $110.

   The results are shown in the following table.

Year	Depreciable Amount	Annual Depreciation	Accumulated Depreciation	End-of-Year Book Value
1	$24,000	$9,600	$9,600	$14,400
2	$14,400	$5,760	$15,360	$8,640
3	$8,640	$3,456	$18,816	$5,184
4	$5,184	$2,074	$20,890	$3,110
5	$3,110	$110	$21,000	$3,000

OBJECTIVE 3 Prepare a depreciation schedule in Excel using the double-declining-balance method.

A *depreciation schedule* showing the year, the depreciable amount, the annual double-declining-balance rate, the annual depreciation, the accumulated depreciation, and the end-of-year book value can be created using Excel. See Figure 13-2.

Figure 13-2
Double-Declining-Balance Depreciation Schedule

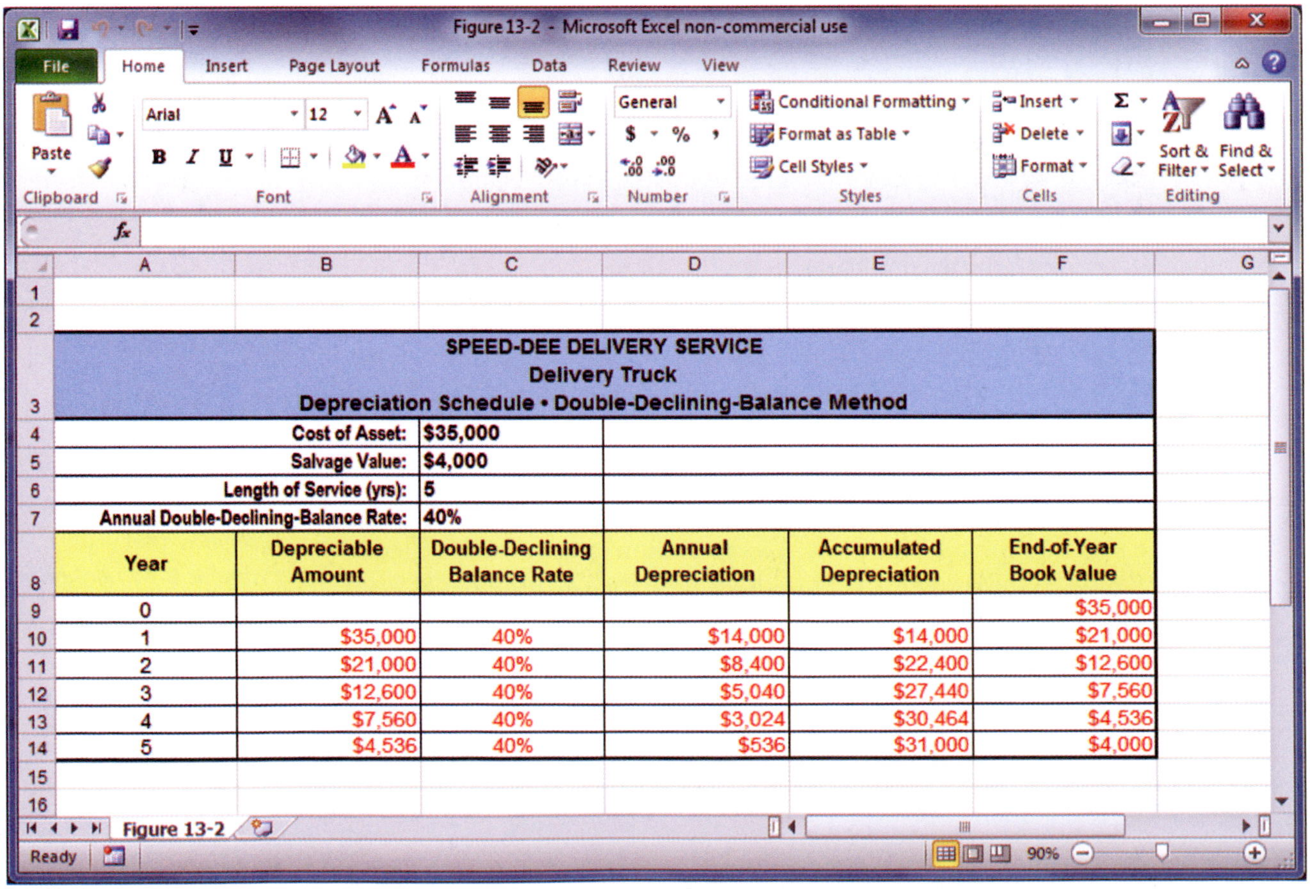

SPEED-DEE DELIVERY SERVICE
Delivery Truck
Depreciation Schedule • Double-Declining-Balance Method

Cost of Asset:	$35,000
Salvage Value:	$4,000
Length of Service (yrs):	5
Annual Double-Declining-Balance Rate:	40%

Year	Depreciable Amount	Double-Declining Balance Rate	Annual Depreciation	Accumulated Depreciation	End-of-Year Book Value
0					$35,000
1	$35,000	40%	$14,000	$14,000	$21,000
2	$21,000	40%	$8,400	$22,400	$12,600
3	$12,600	40%	$5,040	$27,440	$7,560
4	$7,560	40%	$3,024	$30,464	$4,536
5	$4,536	40%	$536	$31,000	$4,000

⚙ Retrieve the file *ch13pr02.xlsx*.

1. In Cells F9 and B10, enter the Depreciable Amount for Year 1 (Cost of Asset).

2. In Cell C10, enter the Annual Double-Declining-Balance Rate. Use an absolute cell reference. Copy the percent down the column. Format for Percentage and 0 Decimal places.

3. In Cell D10, enter the formula to calculate the Annual Depreciation for Year 1 (Depreciable Amount times Double-Declining-Balance Rate). Copy this formula down the column.

4. In Cell E10, enter the Accumulated Depreciation. In the first year, the Accumulated Depreciation is equal to the Annual Depreciation for Year 1.

5. In Cell F10, enter a formula to calculate the End-of-Year Book Value for Year 1 (Cost of Asset minus Accumulated Depreciation). Use an absolute cell reference for Cost of Asset. Copy this formula down the column.

6. In Cell B11, enter the End-of-Year Book Value for Year 1 as the Depreciable Amount for Year 2. Copy this formula down the column.

7. In Cell E11, enter a formula to calculate the Accumulated Depreciation for Year 2 (Accumulated Depreciation for Year 1 plus Annual Depreciation from Year 2). Copy this formula down the column. Notice that all the calculations are done.

8. Notice that the Book Value In Cell F14 is $2,722. This is less than the Salvage Value of $4,000. To correct this, determine the remaining Annual Depreciation and enter this amount in Cell D14. The depreciation in Year 5 is $4,536 − $4,000 = $536.

9. Format dollar entries for Currency, 0 Decimal places, and $.

10. Save the file as *ch13pr02a.xlsx*.

Name _____   Date _____

Directions   Solve the following problems. Write your answers in the blanks provided. Give dollar amounts to the nearest dollar.

A. Determine the double-declining-balance rate. Give answers to the nearest hundredth of a percent.   OBJECTIVE **2**

1.
Cost of bulldozer:	$120,000
Estimated life:	10 years
Salvage value:	$10,000
Double-Declining-balance rate:	_____

2.
Cost of company car:	$60,000
Estimated life:	6 years
Salvage value:	$5,000
Double-Declining-balance rate:	_____

3.
Cost of equipment:	$86,000
Estimated life:	12 years
Salvage value:	$8,000
Double-Declining-balance rate:	_____

4.
Cost of truck:	$40,000
Estimated life:	8 years
Salvage value:	$10,000
Double-Declining-balance rate:	_____

5.
Cost of furniture:	$110,000
Estimated life:	5 years
Salvage value:	$3,000
Double-Declining-balance rate:	_____

B. Use the double-declining-balance method of computing depreciation. Carry the rate to the nearest hundredth, and then round to the nearest dollar. Do not round the percent before doubling the rate.   OBJECTIVE **2**

	Original Cost	Estimated Life	1st-Year Annual Depreciation
6.	$12,000	4	_____
7.	$15,000	6	_____
8.	$18,000	9	_____
9.	$25,000	12	_____
10.	$30,000	7	_____

C. **Complete the following table using the double-declining-balance method** OBJECTIVE **2** **of depreciation. Adjust Year 5 to avoid depreciating below salvage value.**

Total Cost: $13,896
Item: 96 20" Color Monitors
Salvage Value: $1,200
Annual Declining Rate: _____

Year	Depreciable Amount	Annual Depreciation	Accumulated Depreciation	End-of-Year Book Value
1	11. _____	12. _____	13. _____	14. _____
2	15. _____	16. _____	17. _____	18. _____
3	19. _____	20. _____	21. _____	22. _____
4	23. _____	24. _____	25. _____	26. _____
5	27. _____	28. _____	29. _____	30. _____

D. **Solve the following problems.** OBJECTIVE **2**

Use the double-declining-balance method to calculate the first-year depreciation for equipment that costs $4,800 and has a salvage value of $300. The equipment is expected to last five years.

31. First-year depreciation: _____

A sailboat costs $210,000 and has an estimated life of 10 years and a salvage value of $50,000. Find the second-year depreciation using the double-declining-balance method.

32. Second-year depreciation: _____

Dan Martin purchased a Ford Expedition for company use at a cost of $28,000 with a salvage value of $2,000 and an estimated life of 5 years. As Dan's accountant, find the second-year depreciation using the double-declining-balance method of depreciation.

33. Second-year depreciation: _____

E. **Use Excel to prepare a depreciation schedule using the double-declining-** OBJECTIVE **3** **balance method.**

34. Retrieve the file *ch13ex03.xlsx*. Follow the directions. Save the file as *ch13ex03a.xlsx*.

35. Retrieve the file *ch13ex04.xlsx*. Follow the directions. Save the file as *ch13ex04a.xlsx*.

13.3 Sum-of-the-Year's-Digits Method

OBJECTIVE 1 Find the amount of depreciation using the sum-of-the-year's-digits method.

The **sum-of-the-year's-digits method (SYD)** is like the double-declining-balance method in that it also provides larger amounts of depreciation in the early years of the life of an asset and smaller amounts in later years. The book value decreases more slowly than when using the double-declining-balance method. However, it is considered an accelerated depreciation method. A series of fractions are developed to make the computations. To calculate depreciation expense for the method, use the following formula:

$$\text{Annual Depreciation} = (\text{Cost} - \text{Salvage Value}) \times \frac{\text{Years Remaining}}{\text{Sum of the Year's Digits}}$$

EXAMPLE

The life of a delivery truck is 5 years. A fraction is used in each year's calculation in the formula for sum-of-the-year's-digits method of depreciation. To determine the denominator of the fraction, add the digits of the asset's life in years in reverse order. For the numerator of the fraction, write the years in reverse order. This is done because for each year you drop the digit in the numerator previously used and use the next digit in declining order to calculate depreciation. Determine the fractions for the five years of depreciation.

Problem Solving Plan		
Clues	**Action Plan**	**Solve**
Life of truck is 5 years.	Add the digits of the asset's years to determine the denominator.	$5 + 4 + 3 + 2 + 1 = 15$
	Write the years in reverse order to determine each numerator.	5, 4, 3, 2, 1
	Write the fractions for each year.	$\frac{5}{15}, \frac{4}{15}, \frac{3}{15}, \frac{2}{15}, \frac{1}{15}$

Conclusion
The fractions to use in the formula Annual Depreciation = (Cost − Salvage Value) $\times \frac{\text{Years Remaining}}{\text{Sum of Years' Digits}}$ for the first year is $\frac{5}{15}$, the second year is $\frac{4}{15}$, the third year is $\frac{3}{15}$, the fourth year is $\frac{2}{15}$, and the fifth year is $\frac{1}{15}$.

TIPS

You can also divide the numerator by the denominator times cost to determine depreciation.

Determine each year's depreciation for the delivery truck using the SYD method.

Original cost of truck	$24,000
Life in years	5 years
Salvage value	$3,000

1. Subtract the salvage value from the original cost of the asset to find the depreciable amount.

$$\$24,000 - \$3,000 = \$21,000 \quad \text{depreciable amount}$$

2. Multiply the fraction for the first year (found in the previous example) by the total amount to be depreciated in step 1 to find the annual depreciation for the first year.

$$\frac{5}{15} \times \frac{\$21,000}{1} = \$7,000 \quad \text{first-year depreciation}$$

3. Continue finding the depreciation amounts for each year. The following depreciation schedule shows the depreciation for the 5 years using the sum-of-the-year's-digits method.

Year	Fraction	Depreciable Amount	Annual Depreciation	Book Value
Cost				$24,000
1	$\frac{5}{15}$	$21,000	$7,000	$17,000
2	$\frac{4}{15}$	$21,000	$5,600	$11,400
3	$\frac{3}{15}$	$21,000	$4,200	$7,200
4	$\frac{2}{15}$	$21,000	$2,800	$4,400
5	$\frac{1}{15}$	$21,000	$1,400	$3,000

OBJECTIVE 2 Prepare a depreciation schedule in Excel using the sum-of-the-year's-digits method.

You can use Excel to calculate depreciation using the sum-of-the-year's-digits method. Study the spreadsheet in Figure 13-3 on the next page.

Prepare a depreciation schedule using the sum-of-the-year's-digits method for a machine costing $14,000, having a 5-year useful life, and a salvage value of $1,000.

◉ Retrieve *ch13pr03.xlsx*.

1. Enter a formula in Cell D7 to calculate the Depreciable Amount (Cost minus Salvage Value). Use absolute cell references.

TIPS

When determining the denominator of the fraction using the sum-of-the-year's-digits method, you can use the following formula:

$$\frac{N(N+1)}{2}$$

For example, for 5 years of life:

$$\frac{N(N+1)}{2} = \frac{5(5+1)}{2} = \frac{30}{2}$$
$$= 15$$

TIPS

When computing depreciation using the sum-of-the-year's-digits method, always use your largest number of years first as the numerator in your fraction. Also, notice that the depreciable amount is always equal to the cost of the asset minus salvage value. The total annual depreciation should equal the cost minus the salvage value.

	A	B	C	D	E	F	G
1							
2							
3		**WRIGHT'S WELDING SHOP** / Arc-Welding Unit / Depreciation Schedule • Sum-of-the-Year's-Digits Method					
4		Cost of Asset:	$14,000				
5		Salvage Value:	$1,000				
6		Length of Service (yrs.):	5				
7		Depreciable Amount:	$13,000				
8		Sum of the Year's Digits:	15				
9	Year	Depreciable Amount	Fraction for the Years Remaining	Annual Depreciation	Accumulated Depreciation	End-of-Year Book Value	
10	Cost					$14,000	
11	1	$13,000	1/3	$4,333	$4,333	$9,667	
12	2	$13,000	4/15	$3,467	$7,800	$6,200	
13	3	$13,000	1/5	$2,600	$10,400	$3,600	
14	4	$13,000	2/15	$1,733	$12,133	$1,867	
15	5	$13,000	1/15	$867	$13,000	$1,000	
16							
17							

Figure 13-3

Sum-of-the-Year's-Digits Depreciation Schedule

2. Calculate the Sum of the Year's Digits In Cell D8.

3. Copy the Depreciable Amount into each of the cells in Column B.

4. Enter the Fractions for the Years Remaining in Column C. The denominator is the Sum of the Year's Digits. The numerator is the Years Remaining. Format Column C for Fraction and Up to two digits. The fractions will change to lowest terms in Excel. Review fractions in Chapter 2, if necessary.

5. Enter a formula in Cell D11 to calculate the Annual Depreciation (Depreciable Amount times Fraction for the Years Remaining). Copy the formula down Column D.

6. Enter a formula in Cell E11 to calculate the Accumulated Depreciation. For the first year it equals the Annual Depreciation. Enter the Cost of Asset in F10. Use absolute cell references.

7. Enter a formula in Cell F11 to calculate End-of-Year Book Value (Cost minus Annual Depreciation). Copy the formula down Column F.

8. Enter a formula in Cell E12 to calculate the Accumulated Depreciation for the second year (Accumulated Depreciation for previous year plus Annual Depreciation). Copy the formula down Column E.

9. Format dollar entries to Currency, 0 Decimal places, and $.

10. Save the file as *ch13pr03a.xlsx*.

Name _____   Date _____

Directions   Complete the following problems. Write your answers in the blanks provided. Round dollar amounts to the nearest dollar.

A. Determine the fraction to use in the sum-of-the-year's-digits method of depreciation. Reduce fractions to lowest terms.   `OBJECTIVE 1`

	Estimated Life	Depreciation Year	Fraction to Use
1.	5 years	3rd	_____
2.	8 years	5th	_____
3.	5 years	1st	_____
4.	9 years	3rd	_____
5.	6 years	5th	_____

B. Use the sum-of-the-year's-digits method of computing depreciation. Round all answers to the unit position.   `OBJECTIVE 1`

	Original Cost	Estimated Life	Salvage Value	1st-Year Annual Depreciation
6.	$6,000	3	$1,500	_____
7.	$8,000	6	$1,000	_____
8.	$4,000	3	$500	_____
9.	$10,300	4	$2,000	_____
10.	$56,225	10	$8,000	_____

C. Prepare a depreciation schedule using the sum-of-the-year's-digits method.   `OBJECTIVE 1`

Dodge pickup $21,000
Salvage value $1,000
Length of service   4 years

End of Year	Depreciable Amount	Fraction	Annual Depreciation
1	11. _____	12. _____	13. _____
2	14. _____	15. _____	16. _____
3	17. _____	18. _____	19. _____
4	20. _____	21. _____	22. _____

D. Use Excel to create a depreciation schedule using the sum-of-the-year's-digits method.   `OBJECTIVE 2`

23.   Retrieve the file *ch13ex05.xlsx*. Follow the directions. Save the file as *ch13ex05a.xlsx*.

24.   Retrieve the file *ch13ex06.xlsx*. Follow the directions. Save the file as *ch13ex06a.xlsx*.

OBJECTIVES

1. Identify terms used with the Modified Accelerated Cost Recovery System (MACRS) method of depreciation.

2. Find the amount of depreciation using the Modified Accelerated Cost Recovery System (MACRS).

3. Prepare a depreciation schedule in Excel using the Modified Accelerated Cost Recovery System (MACRS).

13.4 Modified Accelerated Cost Recovery System (MACRS)

OBJECTIVE 1 Identify terms used with the Modified Accelerated Cost Recovery System (MACRS) method of depreciation.

The MACRS method of depreciation brings with it several new terms with which you need to become familiar.

Basis   The way of measuring an individual's investment in property for tax purposes; in other words, the cost.

Class Life   A number of years that establishes the property class and recovery period for most types of property.

Convention   A method established under MACRS to determine the portion of the year to depreciate property both in the year the property is placed in service and in the year of disposition.

Nonresidential Real Property   Most real property other than residential rental property.

Placed in Service   Ready and available for a specific use whether in a trade or business, the production of income, a tax-exempt activity, or a personal activity.

Property Class   A category for property under MACRS. It generally determines the depreciation method, recovery period, and convention.

Real Property   Land and buildings.

Recovery Period   The number of years over which the basis (cost) of an item of property is recovered.

Useful Life   An estimate of how long an item of property can be expected to be usable in trade or business or to produce income.

OBJECTIVE 2 Find the amount of depreciation using the Modified Accelerated Cost Recovery System (MACRS).

The depreciation methods presented in the previous sections are used mainly for financial accounting. In 1981 under the Economic Recovery Tax Act, federal tax laws were enacted that identified how depreciation expense may be taken for income tax purposes. A new method of computing depreciation, called the **Accelerated Cost Recovery System (ACRS)**, was introduced for all assets purchased from 1981 through 1986. In 1986 under the Tax Reform Act, a modified form of ACRS was introduced, called the **Modified Accelerated Cost Recovery System (MACRS)**. This act applies to depreciation for all assets put into service after December 31, 1986. Both of these federal laws provide cost recovery tables identifying the useful lives of various assets and the depreciation rates. The methods presented earlier in this chapter are still in effect for property purchased before 1981.

Here is how MACRS differs from the other methods of calculating depreciation expense.

- Salvage value is ignored.
- First-year depreciation for personal property is assumed to have been purchased by midyear.
- Classes 3, 5, 7, and 10 use 200% declining-balance method (double-declining-balance method) for a period of years before switching to straight-line depreciation. The cost recovery table identifies when the switch may be made (see Table 13-1). Switching to straight-line depreciation is made through the table.
- Classes 15 and 20 use a 150% declining-balance method before switching to straight-line depreciation (see Table 13-1). Switching to straight-line depreciation is made through the table.
- Classes 27.5 and 31.5 use straight-line depreciation. (See Table 13-2 for more information.)

To compute depreciation using the MACRS method, find the percentage for the recovery year from Table 13-2. Multiply this percentage by the cost of the asset.

EXAMPLE

Find the annual depreciation using the MACRS method.

Original cost of office furniture	$2,400
Estimated life	5 years

Using the 5-year column of Table 13-2, multiply each percent by the original cost of the office furniture. The depreciation schedule follows:

Year	Original Cost		Percent		Annual Depreciation
1	$2,400	×	20.00%	=	$480
2	$2,400	×	32.00%	=	$768
3	$2,400	×	19.20%	=	$461
4	$2,400	×	11.52%	=	$276
5	$2,400	×	11.52%	=	$276
6	$2,400	×	5.76%	=	$139*
				Total	$2,400

*Check the total and make an adjustment in the last year to make the total equal the original cost. One dollar has been added to Year 6.

TIPS

When you add all annual depreciation, the total should equal the original cost of the item.

Table 13-1 Modified Accelerated Cost Recovery System (MACRS) Classes of Service

		MACRS CLASSES OF SERVICE
Recovery Period	**Life**	**Asset Types**
3-year*	4 years or less	Tractor units for over-the-road use; racehorse over 2 years old when placed in service (All race horses placed in service after December 31, 2008, and before January 1, 2014, are deemed to be 3-year property, regardless of age.), any other horse (other than a race horse) over 12 years old when placed in service; qualified rent-to-own property
5-year*	4 to 10 years	Automobiles; taxis; busses; trucks; computers and peripheral equipment; office machinery (typewriters, calculators, and copiers); breeding cattle and dairy cattle; appliances, carpets, furniture, and so on, used in a residential rental real estate activity; certain geothermal, solar, and wind energy property, certain farm machinery or equipment placed in service before January 1, 2010
7-year*	11 to 15 years	Office furniture and fixtures (desks, files, safes); agricultural machinery and equipment; any property that does not have a class life and has not been designated by law as being in any other class; certain motorsports entertainment complex property placed in service before January 1, 2010; any natural gas gathering line placed in service after April 11, 2005
10-year*	16 to 19 years	Vessels, barges, tugs, and similar water transportation equipment; any single purpose agricultural or horticultural structure; any tree or vine bearing fruit or nuts; qualified small electric meter and qualified smart electric grid system placed in service on or after October 3, 2008
15-year†	20 to 24 years	Certain improvements made directly or added to land (shrubbery, fences, roads, and bridges), any retail motor fuel outlet (convenience store), any municipal wastewater treatment plant, any qualified leasehold improvement property placed in service before January 1, 2010, any qualified restaurant property placed in service before January 1, 2010, initial clearing and grading land improvements for gas utility property, electric transmission property used in the transmission at 69 or more kilovolts of electricity placed in service after April 11, 2005, any natural gas distribution line placed in service after April 11, 2005
20-year†	25 or more	Farm buildings (other than single-purpose agricultural or horticultural structures), municipal sewers not classified as 25-year property, initial clearing and grading land improvements for electric utility transmission and distribution plants
25-year‡	Any life	Property that is an integral part of the gathering, treatment, or commercial distribution of water, and that, without regard to this provision, would be 20-year property, municipal sewers other than property placed in service under a binding contract in effect at all times since June 9, 1996
27.5-year‡	Any life	Residential rental property such as any building or structure, such as a rental home (including a mobile home), if 80% or more of its gross rental income for the tax year is from dwelling units. A dwelling unit is a house or apartment used to provide living accommodations in a building or structure. It does not include a unit in a hotel, motel, or other establishment where more than half the units are used on a transient basis. If you occupy any part of the building or structure for personal use, its gross rental income includes the fair rental value of the part you occupy.
31.5-year‡	Any life	Non-residential property, such as an office building, store, or warehouse, that is neither residential rental property nor property with a class life of less than 27.5 years.

* These classes use 200% declining-balance method/straight-line method.
† These classes use 150% declining-balance method/straight-line method.
‡ These classes use straight-line method.

Table 13-2 Modified Accelerated Cost Recovery Table

		MODIFIED ACCELERATED COST RECOVERY TABLE				
			Appropriate Percentage			
Year	3-Year Class (200% D.B.)	5-Year Class (200% D.B.)	7-Year Class (200% D.B.)	10-Year Class (200% D.B.)	15-Year Class (150% D.B.)	20-Year Class (150% D.B.)
1	33.33	20.00	14.29	10.00	5.00	3.750
2	44.45	32.00	24.49	18.00	9.50	7.219
3	14.81	19.20	17.49	14.40	8.55	6.677
4	7.41	11.52	12.49	11.52	7.70	6.177
5		11.52*	8.93	9.22	6.93	5.713
6		5.76	8.92	7.37	6.23	5.285
7			8.93*	6.55*	5.90*	4.88
8			4.46	6.55	5.90	4.522
9				6.56	5.91	4.462*
10				6.55	5.90	4.461
11				3.28	5.91	4.462
12					5.90	4.661
13					5.91	4.462
14					5.90	4.461
15					5.91	4.462
16					2.95	4.461
17						4.462
18						4.461
19						4.462
20						4.461
21						2.231

* Identifies when switch is made to straight-line depreciation.

OBJECTIVE 3 Prepare a depreciation schedule in Excel using the Modified Accelerated Cost Recovery System (MACRS).

Consider office furniture costing $55,000 that falls into the 7-year class from Table 13-2. Create a depreciation schedule in Excel using the MACRS method of depreciation (see Figure 13-4).

Follow these steps to compute the depreciation.

EXAMPLE

Office furniture cost basis	$55,000
Life of asset	7-year class

STEPS

Retrieve the file *ch13pr04.xlsx*.

1. In Column B, enter the percentage rates for the 7-year class from Table 13-2. Format for Percentage and 2 Decimal places.

2. In Cell C8, enter the Cost Basis for the office furniture. Use an absolute cell reference. Copy it down Column C.

Figure 13-4

MACRS Depreciation Schedule

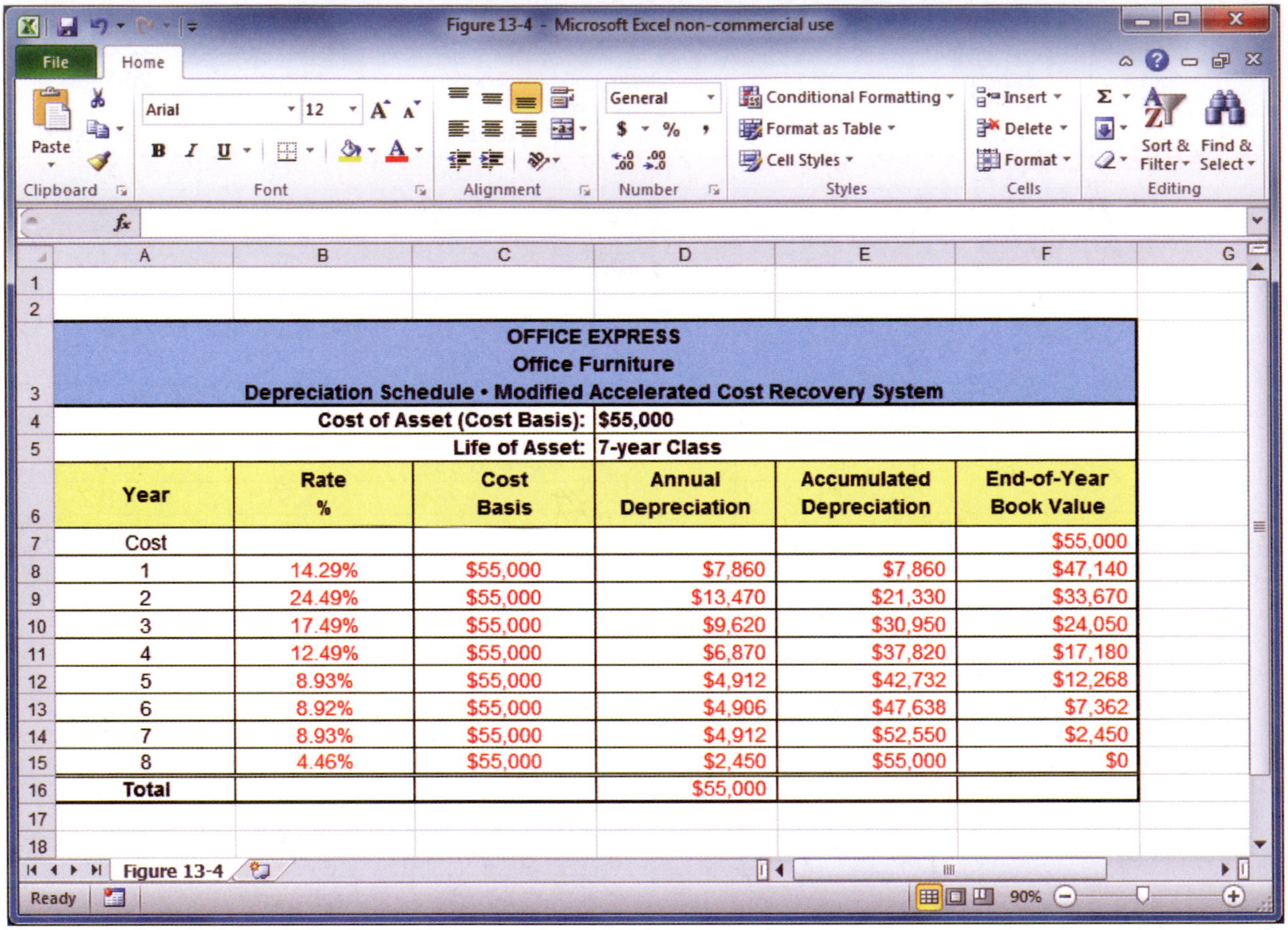

OFFICE EXPRESS Office Furniture Depreciation Schedule • Modified Accelerated Cost Recovery System					
	Cost of Asset (Cost Basis):		$55,000		
	Life of Asset:		7-year Class		
Year	Rate %	Cost Basis	Annual Depreciation	Accumulated Depreciation	End-of-Year Book Value
Cost					$55,000
1	14.29%	$55,000	$7,860	$7,860	$47,140
2	24.49%	$55,000	$13,470	$21,330	$33,670
3	17.49%	$55,000	$9,620	$30,950	$24,050
4	12.49%	$55,000	$6,870	$37,820	$17,180
5	8.93%	$55,000	$4,912	$42,732	$12,268
6	8.92%	$55,000	$4,906	$47,638	$7,362
7	8.93%	$55,000	$4,912	$52,550	$2,450
8	4.46%	$55,000	$2,450	$55,000	$0
Total			$55,000		

3. In Cell D8, enter a formula to calculate Depreciation for Year 1 (Rate times Cost Basis). Round to the nearest whole number. The formula is =ROUND((B8*C8),0). Copy the formula down Column D.
4. Use the AutoSum button to total Column D. If necessary, adjust the Depreciation in Cell D15 to make the Total Depreciation agree with the Cost of Asset.
5. In Column E, enter formulas to calculate Accumulated Depreciation. In Year 1, the Accumulated Depreciation equals the Annual Depreciation. In Years 2-8, the Accumulated Depreciation equals the previous year's Accumulated Depreciation plus the current year's Annual Depreciation.
6. In Column F, enter the Cost Basis in Cell F7, then enter formulas to calculate End-of-Year-Book Value. (Cost Basis minus Accumulated Depreciation)
7. Format all dollar amounts for Currency, 0 Decimal places, and $.
8. Save the file as ***ch13pr04a.xlsx***.

TIPS

When using an asset for business and personal use, the asset can be depreciated only for the amount of business use. Determine what percentage the asset is used for business purposes. Multiply the cost by that percentage to determine the depreciable amount for the asset.

Name _____ Date _____

Directions   Complete the following problems. Round all dollar amounts to the nearest dollar. Round percentages to the nearest hundredth of a percent.

A. Identify the MACRS property class and appropriate percentage for the following assets using Tables 13-1 and 13-2.

OBJECTIVE 1

Asset	Year	Class	Percentage
Farm buildings	3rd	1. _____	2. _____
File cabinet	2nd	3. _____	4. _____
Barge	5th	5. _____	6. _____
Calculator	4th	7. _____	8. _____
Copier	1st	9. _____	10. _____
Appliances	5th	11. _____	12. _____

B. Complete the following problems.   OBJECTIVE 1

13. Randy O'Malley purchased a new F-150 Ford pickup for his O'Malley Delivery Service. The truck cost $26,800 and has a salvage value of $3,500. Randy plans to use the truck 80% for business purposes and 20% for personal use. (a) What depreciation class is used? (b) What amount depreciation expense can he deduct the first year?

    a. _____   b. _____

14. Frank Rodriguez is an independent trucker. He purchased a Peterbilt 18-wheel truck costing $150,000 and having a salvage value of $35,000. IRS allows the 5-year class. Calculate (a) first-year and (b) second-year depreciation.

    a. _____   b. _____

15. Legacy Shuttle Service purchased a new Chevrolet van costing $32,000. It has a salvage value of $4,500. Use the 5-year class and calculate (a) first-year and (b) fifth-year depreciation.

    a. _____   b. _____

16. Anne Hamilton purchased a new heavy-duty riding lawn mower for her Stay-Green Lawn Service. It cost $3,750 and has a salvage value of $300. Use the 7-year class and calculate the depreciation for the (a) first year and (b) second year.

    a. _____   b. _____

C. Use Excel to create a depreciation schedule using the MACRS method of depreciation.

OBJECTIVE 2

17. Retrieve the file *ch13ex07.xlsx*. Follow the directions. Save the file as *ch13ex07a.xlsx*.

18. Retrieve the file *ch13ex08.xlsx*. Follow the directions. Save the file as *ch13ex08a.xlsx*.

Chapter Review and Assessment

KEY TERMS

accelerated depreciation
accumulated depreciation
basis
book value
class life
convention
cost
depreciable amount
depreciable base
depreciation

depreciation schedule
double-declining-balance method
length of service
life of asset
Modified Accelerated Cost Recovery System method (MACRS)
nonresidential real property
placed in service
property class

rate of depreciation
real property
recovery period
residual, scrap, salvage, or trade-in value
straight-line method
sum-of-the-year's-digits method
tangible assets
useful life

CONCEPTS	EXAMPLES
13.1 Depreciate an asset using straight-line depreciation. Annual Depreciation = $\dfrac{\text{Cost} - \text{Salvage Value}}{\text{Length of Service}}$	Truck: $27,000, $5,000 salvage value, 5-year life Annual Depreciation $= \dfrac{\$27{,}000 - \$5{,}000}{5}$ $= \$4{,}400$
13.1 Find the book value of an asset using the straight-line method. Book value = Cost − Depreciation	Truck: $27,000 Depreciation calculated: $4,400 per year Book value = $27,000 − $4,400 = $22,600
13.2 Calculate the double-declining-balance rate, annual depreciation, and accumulated depreciation using the double-declining-balance method. Annual Depreciation = Depreciable Amount × Depreciation Rate Cannot depreciate asset below its salvage value.	Truck: $27,000, $5,000 salvage value, 5-year life 100% ÷ 5 yrs = 20% 20% × 2 = 40% depreciation rate Annual Depreciation = $27,000 × 40% $= \$10{,}800$

CONCEPTS	EXAMPLES
13.3 Find the amount of depreciation using the sum-of-the-year's digits method. Annual Depreciation = $(\text{Cost} - \text{Salvage Value}) \times \dfrac{\text{Years Remaining}}{\text{Sum of the year's digits}}$ Cannot depreciate asset below its salvage value.	Truck: $27,000, $5,000 salvage value, 5-year life Sum of year's digits = 5 + 4 + 3 + 2 + 1 = 15 First yr. fraction $\dfrac{5}{15}$; second yr. fraction = $\dfrac{4}{15}$ Depreciable amt: $27,000 − $5,000 = $22,000 Depreciation = $\dfrac{5}{15} \times \$22,000 = \$7,333$ year 1 Depreciation = $\dfrac{4}{15} \times \$22,000 = \$5,867$ year 2
13.4 Find the amount of depreciation using the Modified Accelerated Cost Recovery System (MACRS). Annual Depreciation = Cost × Rate Each Year (from table) Assets are depreciated 100%.	Truck: $27,000, $5,000 salvage value, 5-year class Depreciation = $27,000 × 20% = $5,400 year 1 Depreciation = $27,000 × 32% = $8,640 year 2

Chapter 13 Review Exercises

Name _____   Date _____

Directions   Complete the following problems. Round dollar amounts to the nearest dollar.

A. Use the straight-line depreciation method.   `13.1 OBJECTIVE 2`

	Original Cost	Estimated Life	Salvage Value	Annual Depreciation
1.	$15,000	5	$2,500	_____
2.	$9,500	3	$1,500	_____
3.	$21,000	4	$1,500	_____
4.	$18,400	6	$2,000	_____
5.	$33,800	10	$5,000	_____
6.	$12,000	4	$2,000	_____

B. Use the double-declining-balance method of depreciation. Carry the rate to the nearest hundredth, and then round to the nearest dollar. Do not round the percent before doubling the rate.

	Original Cost	Estimated Life	1st-Year Annual Depreciation
7.	$17,000	4	_____
8.	$22,000	6	_____
9.	$16,000	9	_____
10.	$28,000	12	_____
11.	$36,000	7	_____
12.	$51,000	8	_____

C. Use the sum-of-the-year's-digits method of depreciation.   `13.3 OBJECTIVE 1`

	Original Cost	Estimated Life	Salvage Value	1st-Year Annual Depreciation
13.	$5,000	2	$400	_____
14.	$9,800	3	$1,200	_____
15.	$12,000	5	$1,500	_____
16.	$18,000	4	$3,000	_____
17.	$25,000	6	$5,000	_____
18.	$8,800	3	$1,100	_____

D. Use the Modified Accelerated Cost Recovery System method of depreciation.   13.4 OBJECTIVE 2

Asset: Office furniture

Cost of asset: $18,000

Life of Asset: 7-year class

Year	Annual Percent	Depreciation	End-of-Year Book Value
1	0.1429	19. _____	20. _____
2	21. _____	22. _____	23. _____
3	24. _____	25. _____	26. _____
4	27. _____	28. _____	29. _____
5	30. _____	31. _____	32. _____
6	33. _____	34. _____	35. _____
7	36. _____	37. _____	38. _____
8	39. _____	40. _____	41. _____

E. Use Excel to calculate depreciation.   13.1 OBJECTIVE 4, 13.2 OBJECTIVE 3
13.3 OBJECTIVE 2, 13.4 OBJECTIVE 3

42. Retrieve the file *ch13ex09.xlsx*. Follow the directions. Save the file as *ch13ex09a.xlsx*.

43. Retrieve the file *ch13ex10.xlsx*. Follow the directions. Save the file as *ch13ex10a.xlsx*.

44. Retrieve the file *ch13ex11.xlsx*. Follow the directions. Save the file as *ch13ex11a.xlsx*.

45. Retrieve the file *ch13ex12.xlsx*. Follow the directions. Save the file as *ch13ex12a.xlsx*.

Emily works as an Accounting Assistant for Morris & Martin, Certified Public Accountants. Morris & Martin provide accounting services for several small businesses in their area. When Technology Depot purchased computer equipment, it was Emily's responsibility to create a depreciation schedule for the life of the computer assets. Examine the invoice below. Compute a depreciation schedule using the MACRS method of depreciation. Round dollar amounts to the nearest dollar.

TECHNOLOGY DEPOT
1700 East I-20 • Arlington, TX 76008-0000
(817) 555-0186

CASHIER: KB1   **INVOICE:** 30930
REGISTER: 001   **DATE:** 11/11/—

12299	MOUSE PAD, COMPUTER PRC CHG TO .00	1	5.00
			−5.00
10277	CCITY PARALLEL CABLE PRC CHG TO .00	1	7.00
			−7.00
10163	HP PAVILION 761N PC 4423000802	1	899.00
12442	22 FLAT PANEL MONITOR S173952L	1	259.99
19900	HP LASER JET 2200D PRINTER VENDOR REBATE 32.00	1	129.00

WARRANTY FOR:

10163	HP PAVILION 761N PC EXPIRES 11/11/20—	1	40.00
12242	22 FLAT PANEL MONITOR EXPIRES 11/11/20—	1	42.00
19900	HP LASER JET 2200D PRINTER EXPIRES 11/11/20—	1	45.00
		SUBTOTAL	1,414.99
	7.5% SALES TAX		106.12
	TOTAL		1,521.11
	CHECK #28899		−1,521.11
	BALANCE		0.00

Thank you for shopping at TECHNOLOGY DEPOT!

Write about Math

1. When you purchase a new vehicle and drive it off the dealer's lot, it automatically depreciates a considerable amount. What is the reason for the depreciation? Discuss the advantages and disadvantages of purchasing a new car as opposed to a used car that has depreciated only slightly. What minimum number of miles would you accept on the car to consider purchasing it? Why?

2. Consider an asset that is fully depreciated yet the asset has several years of life left. What can a business do with the asset?

Personal Finance

Have you thought about owning your own business and becoming an entrepreneur?

Establishing a small business can help you build a secure financial future. Small businesses are started because people are willing to put their ideas into action. Some start from a small one-or-two-person venture. Success is due to a willingness to take risk and to work hard. Some examples of small home businesses are virtual assistants that (from a remote location, usually their home or office) support multiple clients by providing administrative, creative, and technical services; accounting services that provide bookkeeping, payroll, and bill paying services; a house-cleaning service; a lawn and landscaping service for businesses, apartments, or restaurants; or a carpet-cleaning service for residential sites and commercial companies.

Dmitrijs Dmitrijevs/Shutterstock.com

Identify a business you hope to someday own. Provide the following information about your business.

1. Decide on the name of your company. Research the procedure for establishing a company name in your state. Explain this procedure.

2. Decide if your business would be online, home-based, or rented space; include the approximate annual cost, if any.

3. Assume you will use your personal vehicle at least 50% of the time. Determine its present value from www.kbb.com (Kelly Blue Book). Assume the salvage value would be $1,500 (adjust this figure as needed). Create a depreciation schedule using the MACRS method of depreciation.

4. Determine each piece of equipment you would need; research each piece of equipment's cost online; total all the equipment costs; create a depreciation schedule for equipment using the MACRS method.

5. Determine each piece of furniture you would need; research its cost online; total the cost of all the furniture; create a depreciation schedule for the furniture using the MACRS method.

6. Explain your expected cash flow—how much money you estimate will come in (revenue) and go out (expenses). What is your expected net profit before taxes?

7. Identify the assets you have that you could sell if your business failed. This information is needed by your lenders.

8. How much money do you have to put down or how much will you need?

9. What is your target market? How many customers will you have? Create statistics for the lender to see—how many customers in an approximate 5-mile radius of where your business is located.

10. Define your leadership skills; how much experience do you have?

11. How will you advertise—by a website, on facebook, twitter, flyers, press releases (research how to write a press release), newspaper?

12. Do you have a passion for the work you will be doing? Will you enjoy working and providing good service or products?

Name _____ Date _____ Score _____

Directions Solve the following problems. Write your answers in the blanks provided. Round dollar amounts to the nearest dollar.

A. **Use the straight-line method of computing depreciation.** `13.1 OBJECTIVE 2`

	Original Cost	Estimated Life	Salvage Value	1st-Year Annual Depreciation
1.	$18,000	3	$3,000	_____
2.	$25,000	5	$5,000	_____
3.	$17,000	2	$2,000	_____
4.	$30,000	8	$10,000	_____
5.	$25,000	6	$8,000	_____

B. **Use the double-declining-balance method of computing depreciation. Carry the rate to the nearest hundredth, and then round to the nearest dollar. Do not round the percent before doubling the rate.** `13.2 OBJECTIVE 2`

	Original Cost	Estimated Life	1st-Year Annual Depreciation
6.	$12,000	3	_____
7.	$15,000	7	_____
8.	$18,000	5	_____
9.	$25,000	8	_____
10.	$30,000	6	_____

C. **Determine the fraction to use in the sum-of-the-year's-digits method of depreciation. Reduce fractions to lowest terms.** `13.3 OBJECTIVE 1`

	Estimated Life	Depreciation Year	Fraction to Use
11.	5 years	2nd	_____
12.	8 years	3rd	_____
13.	6 years	4th	_____
14.	4 years	3rd	_____
15.	10 years	1st	_____

D. Use the sum-of-the-year's-digits method of computing depreciation. 13.3 OBJECTIVE 1

	Original Cost	Estimated Life	Salvage Value	1st-Year Annual Depreciation
16.	$6,000	4	$1,500	_____
17.	$8,000	5	$1,000	_____
18.	$4,000	2	$500	_____
19.	$9,000	6	$800	_____

E. Identify the MACRS property class and appropriate percentage for the following assets using Tables 13-1 and 13-2. Round percentages to the nearest hundredth. 13.4 OBJECTIVE 2

Asset	Year	Class	Percentage
Automobiles	3rd	20. _____	21. _____
Desk	4th	22. _____	23. _____
Barge	1st	24. _____	25. _____

F. Use Excel to create depreciation schedules. 13.1 OBJECTIVE 4, 13.2 OBJECTIVE 3 13.3 OBJECTIVE 2, 13.4 OBJECTIVE 3

26. Retrieve the file *ch13qz01.xlsx*. Follow the directions. Save the file as *ch13qz01a.xlsx*.

27. Retrieve the file *ch13qz02.xlsx*. Follow the directions. Save the file as *ch13qz02a.xlsx*.

28. Retrieve the file *ch13qz03.xlsx*. Follow the directions. Save the file as *ch13qz03a.xlsx*.

29. Retrieve the file *ch13qz04.xlsx*. Follow the directions. Save the file as *ch13qz04a.xlsx*.

14.1 INCOME STATEMENT

14.2 BALANCE SHEET

14.3 FINANCIAL RATIOS

The income statement and the balance sheet are two of the most important financial statements used in the successful operation of a business. Management depends on these statements to help make sound business decisions. The income statement determines how a company is performing based on its profitability (net profit or net income) for a given period of time (month, year, and so on). The balance sheet determines the worth of a company on a given day.

Financial ratios provide a way for a company to compare its financial condition with other companies' financial conditions. Calculating financial ratios helps management identify areas that need further investigation.

Math@Work

FINANCIAL ACCOUNTANT

Jeff Lewis is a financial accountant for a global aerospace and defense corporation. He is responsible for booking journal entries, which is the logging of business and accounting transactions. Because journal entries are an essential piece of the financial statement puzzle, it is imperative for Jeff to be accurate when making an entry. Jeff says, "We use support such as invoices, check copies, and amortization tables to ensure the income statement amounts we book are accurate." He ensures accuracy by keeping up to date on any new accounting and regulation literature released by the SEC, Financial Accounting Standards Board (FASB), and American Institute of Certified Public Accountants (AICPA). Jeff also researches regulations when the company has new transactions that he has not accounted for yet.

When researching potential financial accounting positions, Jeff recommends seeking companies that fit your personal definition of a work and life balance. His previous position required longer hours. Despite the more complex accounting issues Jeff deals with in his current position, he is much happier. "I like my position because I'm challenged to meet deadlines and resolve issues in a timely manner. I'm also given opportunities to work on special projects throughout the year," Jeff says.

How Math is Used in Financial Accounting

When preparing for the company's quarterly filing with the SEC, Jeff must complete earnings per share (EPS) calculations. Jeff says, "To calculate basic EPS we take our net income and divide it by the shares of company stock issued and outstanding at period end." Jeff also uses arithmetic when calculating the interest added to the cost of the construction of a new building or machinery. He says, "We multiply our weighted average cost of financing by our construction in progress balance each month to come up with the amount of interest to be capitalized."

What Do You Think?

What skills do you need to become a financial accountant?

Math Skills Used

Addition

Subtraction

Multiplication

Division

Ratios

Other Skills Needed

Collaboration

Detail-oriented

Time management

Organization

OBJECTIVES

1. Identify terms used with income statements.

2. Create an income statement for a service business.

3. Create an income statement for a merchandise business.

4. Create a vertical analysis of an income statement.

5. Use Excel to create an income statement.

14.1 Income Statement

OBJECTIVE 1 Identify terms used with income statements.

To understand the computations necessary to complete an income statement, you must be familiar with the terminology used. Some of the basic terms follow.

Cost of Merchandise (Goods) Sold   The cost incurred for merchandise, such as material used in the manufacture of clothing.

Gross Profit (Gross Margin)   The difference between net sales and cost of goods sold.

Income Statement   A financial statement showing total revenue, total expenses, and net income (net profit or net loss) of a business; also called a *profit and loss statement,* statement of financial performance, earnings statement, operating statement, or statement of operations.

Merchandise Available for Sale   Beginning inventory plus net purchases.

Merchandise Business   A business engaged in the sale of goods.

Merchandise Inventory (Beginning)   The cost of inventory available for sale at the beginning of the period.

Merchandise Inventory (Ending)   The cost of inventory that remains to be sold at the end of the period.

Net Income (Net Profit)   Gross profit less total operating expenses.

Net Purchases   The total of all purchases minus any purchases returned (purchases returns and allowances) or discounts earned by paying early.

Net Sales   Gross sales after sales returns and allowances and sales discounts.

Operating Expenses   All costs incurred in the normal operation of a business, such as rent, supplies, and wages.

Purchase Discounts   A deduction from a purchase invoice, usually expressed as a percent, for paying early.

Purchases   The cost of additional merchandise purchased for resale during the period.

Purchases Returns and Allowances   The cost of merchandise returned to the seller due to damage, defects, or any other reason.

Revenue   Income earned for the period from the sale of goods or services.

Sales   Total sales made before all returned merchandise and discounts are allowed.

Sales Discounts   An amount, usually expressed as a percent, deducted from a sales invoice for a customer paying within a specified number of days.

Sales Returns and Allowances   The value of returned goods resulting from a refund or credit to a customer.

Service Business   A business engaged in selling a service; doctors, lawyers, barbers, and accountants all sell a service.

Vertical Analysis of an Income Statement   An expression of each item on an income statement as a percent of net sales displayed in a vertical format.

A service business is one in which the principal product is a service. To determine the net profit for a service business, use the following basic formula:

$$\boxed{\text{Net Profit}} = \boxed{\text{Revenue Received}} - \boxed{\text{Operating Expenses}}$$

EXAMPLE

Assume that Celeste Casey, M.D., received revenue (professional fees) totaling $400,000 for the year ending December 31, 20--. Her operating expenses were as follows: $132,800 for salaries for two nurses and one receptionist; $2,230 for payroll taxes; $18,000 for rent for her office; $4,500 for depreciation of equipment; $30,000 for supplies; $5,540 for utilities; $2,900 for miscellaneous expenses; $2,400 for automobile expense; and $1,500 for equipment repair expense. Complete an income statement for Dr. Casey.

STEPS

1. Total all operating expenses.

   $132,800 + $2,230 + $18,000 + $4,500 + $30,000 + $5,540 + $2,400 + $1,500 + $2,900 = $199,870

2. Subtract operating expenses from revenue (professional fees).

   $400,00 − $199,870 = $200,130   net profit before taxes

3. List the revenue and operating expenses as shown below.

Celeste Casey, M.D.
INCOME STATEMENT
For the year ending December 31, 20--

Revenue		
Professional fees		$400,000
Operating expenses		
Salary expense	$132,800	
Payroll taxes expense	2,230	
Rent expense	18,000	
Depreciation expense—equipment	4,500	
Supplies expense	30,000	
Utilities expense	5,540	
Automobile expense	2,400	
Equipment repair expense	1,500	
Miscellaneous expense	2,900	
Total operating expenses		$199,870
Net profit before federal income tax		$200,130

The computation of net income for a merchandise business is more involved than for a service business. Study the following formula.

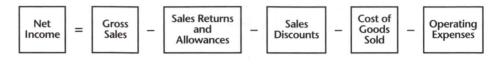

Net Sales

A merchandise business makes its money from sales. But gross sales is not pure profit. Net sales shows profit. Notice how gross sales are affected by returned goods and any discounts given to customers.

EXAMPLE

Mr. Ortiz's store is a small family-owned corner grocery store. The gross sales for the first quarter of the year amounted to $80,000. There was $1,611 in returned merchandise and $1,050 in sales discounts for customers paying early. Find the net sales.

STEPS

To obtain the net sales, subtract merchandise or goods that have been returned and sales discounts from gross sales.

Sales		$80,000
Less: Sales returns and allowances	$1,611	
Less: Sales discounts	+1,050	– 2,661
Net sales 1st quarter		$77,339

Cost of Goods Sold

The next part of the income statement that must be computed is cost of goods sold. To obtain cost of goods sold, use this formula.

TIPS

When there are shipping charges (freight), the formula for Net Purchases is:

Net Purchases = Purchases + Freight Charges

EXAMPLE

Mr. Ortiz's beginning merchandise inventory was $98,000, and his ending inventory was $60,000. He purchased $21,000 of additional merchandise for sale during the quarter, returned $5,300 worth of merchandise damaged in shipment, and received $4,800 in purchase discounts for paying early. Find the cost of goods sold.

Merchandise inventory, January 1, 20--		$ 98,000
Purchases	$21,000	
Less: Purchases returns and allowances $5,300		
Less: Purchase discounts + 4,800	− 10,100	
Net Purchases		+ 10,900
Total cost of merchandise available for sale		$108,900
Less merchandise inventory, March 31, 20--		− 60,000
Cost of goods sold		$ 48,900

Gross Profit

Now that you have computed net sales and cost of goods sold, you can determine the gross profit for Ortiz's Grocery Store. To determine gross profit, you subtract cost of goods sold from net sales.

Net sales	$77,339
Cost of goods sold	− 48,900
Gross profit	$28,439

Operating Expenses

Operating expenses are computed the same as they were for Dr. Casey. Here are the expenses for Ortiz's Grocery Store.

Delivery expense	$ 211
Depreciation expense—equipment	1,800
Payroll taxes expense	154
Salary expense	2,200
Supplies expense	50
Telephone expense	60
Utilities expense	+ 900
Total operating expenses	$5,375

Net Profit (Net Income)

To compute the net profit (net income) for Ortiz's Grocery Store, subtract total operating expenses from gross profit.

Gross profit	$28,439
Total operating expenses	− 5,375
Net profit before federal income tax	$23,064

Federal income tax is due quarterly. Therefore, it must be subtracted from net profit.

Net profit before federal income tax	$23,064
Federal income tax	− 3,459
Net profit after federal income tax	$19,605

A completed income statement for Ortiz's Grocery Store follows.

Ortiz's Grocery Store
INCOME STATEMENT
For the quarter ending March 31, 20--

Revenue

Sales			$80,000
Less: Sales returns and allowances		$ 1,611	
Less: Sales discounts		1,050	2,661
Net sales			$77,339

Cost of goods sold

Merchandise inventory, January 1, 20--		$ 98,000	
Purchases	$21,000		
Less: Purchases returns and allowances	$5,300		
Less: Purchase discounts	4,800	10,100	
Net purchases		10,900	
Total cost of merchandise available for sale		108,900	
Less: Merchandise inventory, March 31, 20--		60,000	
Cost of goods sold			48,900
Gross profit			$28,439

Operating expenses

Delivery expense	$ 211		
Depreciation expense—equipment	1,800		
Payroll taxes expense	154		
Salary expense	2,200		
Supplies expense	50		
Telephone expense	60		
Utilities expense	900		
Total operating expenses			5,375
Net income before federal income tax			$23,064
Federal income tax			3,459
Net income after federal income tax			$19,605

OBJECTIVE 4 Create a vertical analysis of an income statement.

Not only can a business determine its income by completing an income statement, it can also make comparisons of items on the income statement to net sales. Such a comparison is called a *vertical analysis*. Net sales are considered to be the base of 100%. All other parts of the income statement are reported as a percent of net sales. This information can then be compared with previous quarters, other businesses, or budget figures to help make decisions.

EXAMPLE

Determine what percent each item is of net sales on the income statement for Nichols Furniture Mart.

STEPS

1. Divide each item in the Amount column by the net sales figure ($99,160). Remember to use $R = P \div B$.

2. Round percents to 1 decimal place.

Nichols Furniture Mart
INCOME STATEMENT
1st Quarter Ending March 31, 20--

	Amount	Percent
Revenue		
Sales	$100,000	100.8
Less: Sales returns and allowances	840	0.8
Net sales	$ 99,160	100.0
Cost of goods sold		
Merchandise inventory, January 1, 20--	$ 66,000	66.6
Purchases less returns and allowances	39,200	39.5
Total cost of merchandise available for sale	$105,200	106.1
Less: Merchandise inventory, March 31, 20--	60,225	60.7
Cost of goods sold	$ 44,975	45.4
Gross profit	$ 54,185	54.6
Operating expenses		
Delivery expense	$ 467	0.5
Depreciation expense—equipment	3,600	3.6
Payroll taxes expense	388	0.4
Salary expense	10,739	10.8
Supplies expense	204	0.2
Telephone expense	175	0.2
Utilities expense	1,907	1.9
Total operating expenses	$ 17,480	17.6
Net income before federal income tax	$ 36,705	37.0
Federal income tax	12,113	12.2
Net income after federal income tax	$ 24,592	24.8

A vertical analysis of an income statement can be particularly useful when comparing data from different companies. In the previous example, Nichols Furniture Mart's net profit before taxes was $36,705, whereas their larger main competitor, So-Low Furniture's net profit before taxes was $45,500. Simply comparing the two net profit figures before taxes can be somewhat misleading. To better understand the difference between the two company's net profits, the net profit figures can be expressed as a percentage of net sales for each company. Since Nichol's net sales were $99,160 and SoLow's net sales were $129,000, Nichol's net profit as a percentage of net sales was about 37.1% and So-Low's was about 35.3%.

Nichols = $36,705 ÷ $99,160 = 0.3701 or 37.1%

Quick Carpet Clean = $45,500 ÷ $129,000 = 0.3527 or 35.3%

The comparison shows that even though SoLow had larger sales than Nichols, Nichols managed costs much better than SoLow.

OBJECTIVE 5 Use Excel to create an income statement.

Excel provides a way to display financial reports. It enables any professional to create complex spreadsheets that provide information necessary for companies to make critical decisions quickly and economically.

Income Statement

The **income statement** provides management information about whether the business is making a profit or a loss. This report is used as a basis for most fundamental business decisions. Study Figure 14-1.

STEPS

Retrieve the file *ch14pr01.xlsx*.

1. Enter a formula in Cell E7 to add Sales returns and allowances and Sales discounts.

2. Enter a formula in Cell E8 to subtract the total in Cell E7 from Sales.

3. Enter a formula in Cell C13 to add Purchases returns and allowances and Purchases discounts.

4. Enter a formula in Cell D14 to subtract the total in Cell C13 from Purchases.

5. Enter a formula in Cell E17 to calculate Cost of goods sold (Subtract Merchandise Inventory, March 31, from Cost of Merchandise available for sale).

6. Enter a formula in Cell E18 to calculate Gross profit. (Subtract Cost of goods sold from Net sales.)

7. Enter a formula in Cell E27 to total all Operating expenses.

8. Enter a formula in Cell E28 to subtract total Operating expenses from Gross profit.

9. Enter a formula in Cell E30 to subtract Federal income tax from Net income before Federal income tax.

10. Format Cells E8, E18, E28, and E30 to Currency Style, 0 Decimal places, and $. Format all other answers for Number, 0 Decimal places, and Use 1000 Separator (,).

11. Save the file as *ch14pr01a.xlsx*.

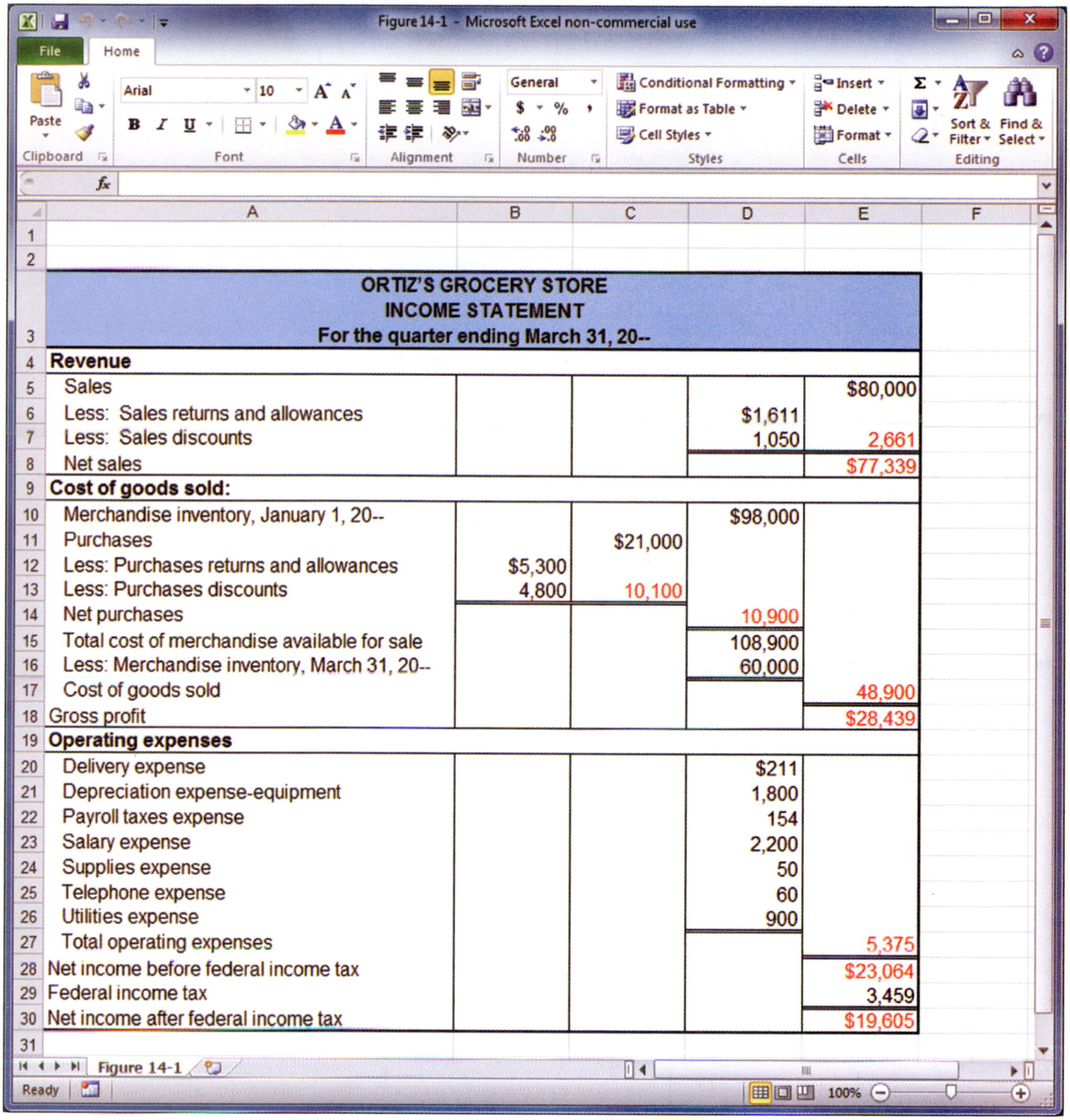

Figure 14-1 - Microsoft Excel non-commercial use

	A	B	C	D	E	F
1						
2						
3	**ORTIZ'S GROCERY STORE** **INCOME STATEMENT** **For the quarter ending March 31, 20--**					
4	**Revenue**					
5	Sales				$80,000	
6	Less: Sales returns and allowances			$1,611		
7	Less: Sales discounts			1,050	2,661	
8	Net sales				$77,339	
9	**Cost of goods sold:**					
10	Merchandise inventory, January 1, 20--			$98,000		
11	Purchases		$21,000			
12	Less: Purchases returns and allowances	$5,300				
13	Less: Purchases discounts	4,800	10,100			
14	Net purchases			10,900		
15	Total cost of merchandise available for sale			108,900		
16	Less: Merchandise inventory, March 31, 20--			60,000		
17	Cost of goods sold				48,900	
18	Gross profit				$28,439	
19	**Operating expenses**					
20	Delivery expense			$211		
21	Depreciation expense-equipment			1,800		
22	Payroll taxes expense			154		
23	Salary expense			2,200		
24	Supplies expense			50		
25	Telephone expense			60		
26	Utilities expense			900		
27	Total operating expenses				5,375	
28	Net income before federal income tax				$23,064	
29	Federal income tax				3,459	
30	Net income after federal income tax				$19,605	
31						

Vertical Analysis of an Income Statement

Figure 14-1
Income Statement

Excel can be used to compare the items on an income statement to net sales to complete a vertical analysis of an income statement. Remember, net sales are considered to be the base of 100%. All other parts of the income statement are reported as a percent of net sales. Study Figure 14-2.

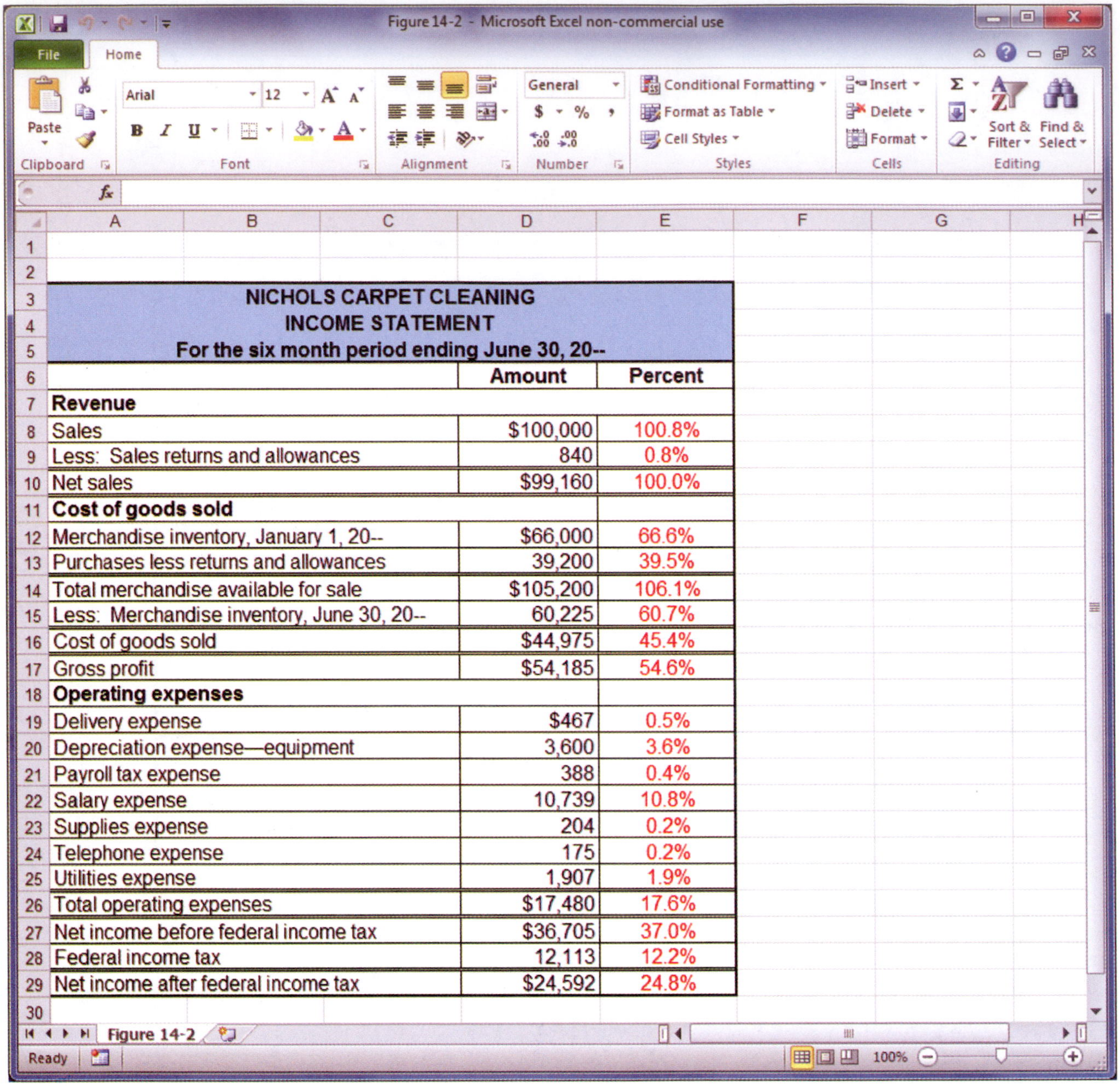

	Amount	Percent
NICHOLS CARPET CLEANING		
INCOME STATEMENT		
For the six month period ending June 30, 20--		
Revenue		
Sales	$100,000	100.8%
Less: Sales returns and allowances	840	0.8%
Net sales	$99,160	100.0%
Cost of goods sold		
Merchandise inventory, January 1, 20--	$66,000	66.6%
Purchases less returns and allowances	39,200	39.5%
Total merchandise available for sale	$105,200	106.1%
Less: Merchandise inventory, June 30, 20--	60,225	60.7%
Cost of goods sold	$44,975	45.4%
Gross profit	$54,185	54.6%
Operating expenses		
Delivery expense	$467	0.5%
Depreciation expense—equipment	3,600	3.6%
Payroll tax expense	388	0.4%
Salary expense	10,739	10.8%
Supplies expense	204	0.2%
Telephone expense	175	0.2%
Utilities expense	1,907	1.9%
Total operating expenses	$17,480	17.6%
Net income before federal income tax	$36,705	37.0%
Federal income tax	12,113	12.2%
Net income after federal income tax	$24,592	24.8%

Figure 14-2

Vertical Analysis of an Income Statement

STEPS

Retrieve the file *ch14pr02.xlsx*. You will use the income statement presented earlier in the chapter for Nichols Carpet Cleaning.

1. Format Column E for Percentage and 1 Decimal place.
2. Enter a formula in Cell E8 to determine what percent Sales is of Net sales. Divide Sales by Net sales. Be sure to use an absolute cell reference (=D8/$D$10).
3. Copy the formula in Cell E8 down Column E to determine what percent each item is of Net Sales.
4. Save the file as *ch14pr02a.xlsx*.

Name _____ Date _____

Directions Solve the following problems. Write your answers in the blanks provided. Give dollar amounts to the nearest dollar and percents to the nearest tenth.

A. Compute the total operating expenses and net profit before taxes for Thomas Harden, D.D.S., for the first quarter of the year. OBJECTIVE 2

Thomas Harden, D.D.S.
INCOME STATEMENT
For the quarter ending March 31, 20--

Revenue		
Professional fees		$128,000
Operating expenses		
Depreciation expense—equipment	$6,500	
Miscellaneous expense	1,900	
Payroll taxes expense	5,113	
Automobile expense	960	
Rent expense	7,000	
Salary expense	42,000	
Supplies expense	3,100	
Utilities expense	2,380	
Total operating expenses		_____ 1.
Net profit before federal income tax		_____ 2.

B. Compute the cost of goods sold. OBJECTIVE 3

Merchandise inventory, January 1, 20-- $56,000

Purchases $18,000

Less: Purchases returns and allowances $800

Less: Purchase discounts .... 350 _____ 3.

Net purchases .... _____ 4.

Total cost of merchandise available for sale ...... _____ 5.

Less: Merchandise inventory, March 31, 20-- $12,000

Cost of goods sold .... _____ 6.

C. Compute gross profit. OBJECTIVE 3

Net sales	$85,555		Net sales	$63,640	
Cost of goods sold	64,225		Cost of goods sold	25,892	
Gross profit		7.	Gross profit		8.

D. Compute operating expenses. OBJECTIVE 3

Delivery expense	$180
Depreciation expense—equipment	2,500
Payroll taxes expense	311
Salary expense	4,800
Supplies expense	150
Telephone expense	280
Utilities expense	590
Miscellaneous expense	175
Total operating expenses	9.

E. Compute net profit before federal income tax. OBJECTIVE 3

Gross profit	$88,500	
Total operating expense	51,990	
Net profit before federal income tax		10.

Gross profit	$91,234	
Total operating expenses	48,222	
Net profit before federal income tax		11.

Gross profit	$63,745	
Total operating expenses	38,295	
Net profit before federal income tax		12.

F. **Create a vertical analysis of an income statement. Find the percent of each item based on net sales for this partial income statement. Make your percents accurate to 1 decimal place. Write your answers in the blanks provided.**

The Fashion Place
INCOME STATEMENT
For the period ending June 30, 20--

	Amount	Percent	
Revenue			
Sales	$386,000	_____	13.
Less: Sales returns and allowances	5,840	_____	14.
Net sales	$380,160	_____	15.
Cost of goods sold			
Merchandise inventory, January 1, 20--	$220,000	_____	16.
Purchases less returns and allowances	39,200	_____	17.
Total cost of merchandise available for sale	$259,200	_____	18.
Less: Merchandise inventory, June 30, 20--	71,225	_____	19.
Cost of goods sold	$187,975	_____	20.
Gross profit	$192,185	_____	21.

G. **Use Excel to complete an income statement and a vertical analysis of an income statement.**

22. Retrieve the file *ch14ex01.xlsx*. Follow the directions. Save the file as *ch14ex01a.xlsx*.

23. Retrieve the file *ch14ex02.xlsx*. Follow the directions. Save the file as *ch14ex02a.xlsx*.

14.2 Balance Sheet

OBJECTIVE 1 Identify terms used with balance sheets.

Here are some of the terms used when a balance sheet is completed.

Accounting Equation   Assets = Liabilities + Owner's equity (capital). This equation shows the relationship among what the owner owns, owes, and is worth at all times.

Assets   What is owned.

Capital   The owner's equity in a business. It is a claim against the assets of the business after the total liabilities are deducted.

Current Assets   Cash and other assets that may reasonably be expected to be converted to cash or sold or consumed, usually within a year or less, through the normal operation of a business.

Current Liabilities   Liabilities that will be due within a short time (usually one year or less).

Horizontal Analysis of a Balance Sheet   Also called a *comparative analysis*, a financial statement that compares each item on a balance sheet to total assets, displayed in a horizontal format.

Liabilities   What is owed to creditors.

Long-Term Assets   Assets such as equipment, buildings, or furniture that gradually wear out or otherwise lose their usefulness with the passage of time (sometimes referred to as *fixed assets*).

Long-Term Liabilities   Liabilities that will not be due for a comparatively long time (usually more than one year).

Owner's Equity   The owner's worth in the enterprise; sometimes called proprietorship, net worth, stockholder's equity, or capital.

Vertical Analysis of a Balance Sheet   A financial statement comparing each item on the balance sheet as a percent of assets or total liabilities and owner's equity, displayed in a vertical format.

OBJECTIVE 2 Create a balance sheet.

Like the income statement, the balance sheet is a very important financial statement. A **balance sheet** summarizes the balances of the assets, liability, and owner's equity accounts for a business on a given date. A balance sheet is usually completed at the end of a month or year and shows the financial condition of the company on that day. The balance sheet shows an exact financial picture of the business and, thereby, aids management in its decision making.

A balance sheet has three parts: assets, liabilities, and owner's equity. The total assets (what one owns) are equal to the sum of the liabilities (what one owes) and owner's equity (what one is worth). To complete a balance sheet, follow these steps.

TIPS

An important thing to remember about the balance sheet is that it represents a single moment in time.

STEPS

1. Total all assets, both current and long-term assets (sometimes called *fixed assets*).

2. Total all liabilities, both current and long-term.

3. Total all owner's equity.

4. Add total liabilities and owner's equity. (The total should be equal to the total of all assets.)

Balance sheets are completed using a particular format. Study the following example of a completed balance sheet that shows one format.

Benson's Bike Shop
BALANCE SHEET
March 31, 20--

Assets

Current assets

Cash	$ 3,200
Supplies	545
Prepaid insurance	600

Long-term assets

Office equipment	4,900
Building	45,000
Land	12,000
Total assets	$66,245

Liabilities

Current liabilities

Notes payable	$ 4,000
Accounts payable	8,000

Long-term liabilities

Mortgage payable	40,000
Total liabilities	$52,000

Owner's Equity

Shaw Benson, capital	$14,245
Total liabilities and owner's equity	$66,245

Vertical analysis of a balance sheet is used to compare data in two or more balance sheets. It is completed like the vertical analysis of the income statement presented earlier in this chapter. The analysis is based on the total assets (or total liabilities and owner's equity). A vertical analysis of a balance sheet is completed by dividing each item on the balance sheet by the base, which is the total asset figure for assets and the total liability and owner's equity figure for liabilities and equity. To facilitate a comparison, the two balance sheets are placed side by side in one financial statement.

In the following example, to determine what percent the first item, cash, is of total assets, divide cash ($3,200) by the total assets ($66,245). To determine what percent the notes payable is of total liabilities and owner's equity, divide notes payable ($4,000) by the total liabilities and owner's equity ($66,245). Study the vertical analysis below.

Benson's Bike Shop
BALANCE SHEET
March 31, 20--

Assets	Amount	Percent
Current assets		
Cash	$ 3,200	4.9*
Supplies	545	0.8
Prepaid insurance	600	0.9
Long-term assets		
Office equipment	4,900	7.4
Building	45,000	67.9
Land	12,000	18.1
Total assets	$66,245	100.0
Liabilities		
Current liabilities		
Notes payable	$ 4,000	6.0
Accounts payable	8,000	12.1
Long-term liabilities		
Mortgage payable	40,000	60.4
Total liabilities	$52,000	78.5
Owner's Equity		
Shaw Benson, capital	$14,245	21.5
Total liabilities and owner's equity	$66,245	100.0

* Number has been rounded up by 0.1% so total equals 100%.

4 Create a horizontal analysis of a balance sheet.

Another method used to compare items on a balance sheet is *horizontal analysis*. This method makes use of the concept of percent of increase and decrease concept presented in Chapter 3. To complete the analysis, you subtract the current year from the previous year for each item and write the difference in the amount of change column. Then you divide the difference by the previous year for each item to determine the percent of change. The following example is the assets portion of a horizontal analysis of a balance sheet.

STEPS

1. Subtract the previous (Year 1) year from the current (Year 2) year for each item to find the amount of change (difference).

2. Divide the amount of change (difference) by the previous year for each item to determine the percent of change.

Grant Washington, Consultant
COMPARATIVE (HORIZONTAL) BALANCE SHEET (Partial)
Year 2 and Year 1

	Year 2	Year 1	Amount of Change	Percent of Change
Current assets				
Cash	$ 69,000	$ 62,000	$ 7,000	11.3
Notes receivable	32,000	25,000	7,000	28.0
Accounts receivable	99,000	100,200	1,200*	1.2*
Supplies	1,300	1,400	100*	7.1*
Total current assets	$201,300	$188,600	$12,700	6.7
Fixed assets				
Professional equipment	$ 38,000	$ 25,000	$13,000	52.0
Building	58,000	54,000	4,000	7.4
Total fixed assets	$ 96,000	$ 79,000	$17,000	21.5
Total assets	$297,300	$267,600	$29,700	11.1

*Decrease

A main advantage of analyzing a balance sheet this way is that you can easily compare the balance sheet of any size business with your own business. Also, the comparison can target annual changes in your business.

OBJECTIVE 5 Use Excel to create a balance sheet.

Since a balance sheet describes the financial condition of a company *at one point in time*, such as a month or a year, accountants are called upon to create balance sheets more often than any other financial statement. A balance sheet may be requested, for instance, when a company is borrowing money. The lending institution might require a balance sheet to determine the financial status of the company at that given time.

Balance Sheet

You can create a balance sheet using Excel. Study Figure 14-3.

Figure 14-3
Balance Sheet

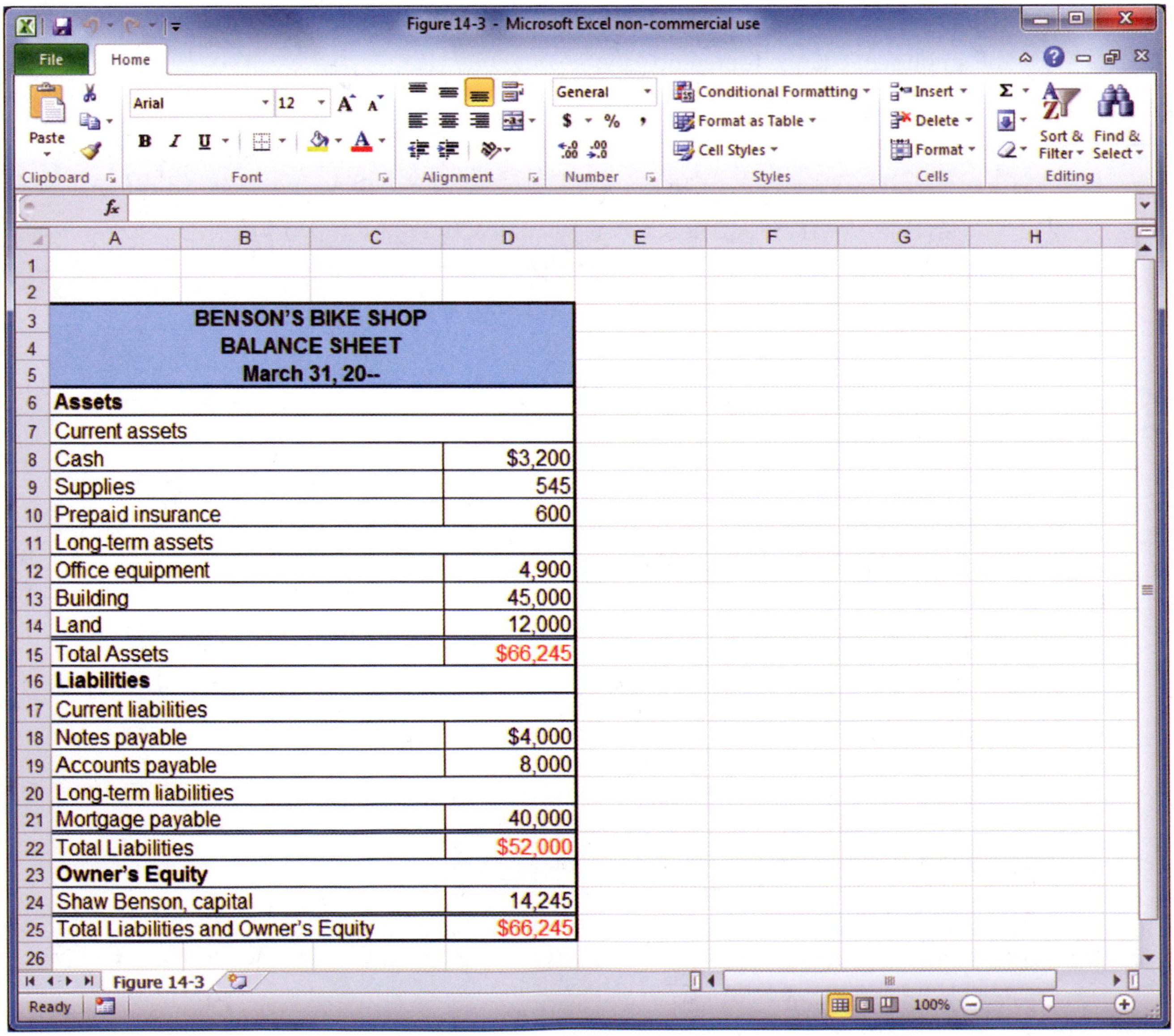

BENSON'S BIKE SHOP BALANCE SHEET March 31, 20--	
Assets	
Current assets	
Cash	$3,200
Supplies	545
Prepaid insurance	600
Long-term assets	
Office equipment	4,900
Building	45,000
Land	12,000
Total Assets	$66,245
Liabilities	
Current liabilities	
Notes payable	$4,000
Accounts payable	8,000
Long-term liabilities	
Mortgage payable	40,000
Total Liabilities	$52,000
Owner's Equity	
Shaw Benson, capital	14,245
Total Liabilities and Owner's Equity	$66,245

STEPS

Retrieve the file *ch14pr03.xlsx*.

1. Enter a formula in Cell D15 to total all Assets, both Current and Long-term.

2. Enter a formula in Cell D22 to total all Liabilities, both Current and Long-term.

3. Enter a formula in Cell D25 to add Total Liabilities and Owner's Equity.

4. Format answers to Currency, 0 Decimal places, and $.

5. Save the file as *ch14pr03a.xlsx*.

Vertical analysis of a balance sheet

Completing a vertical analysis for Benson's Bike shop can also be done using Excel. Study Figure 14-4.

Figure 14-4

Vertical Analysis of a Balance Sheet

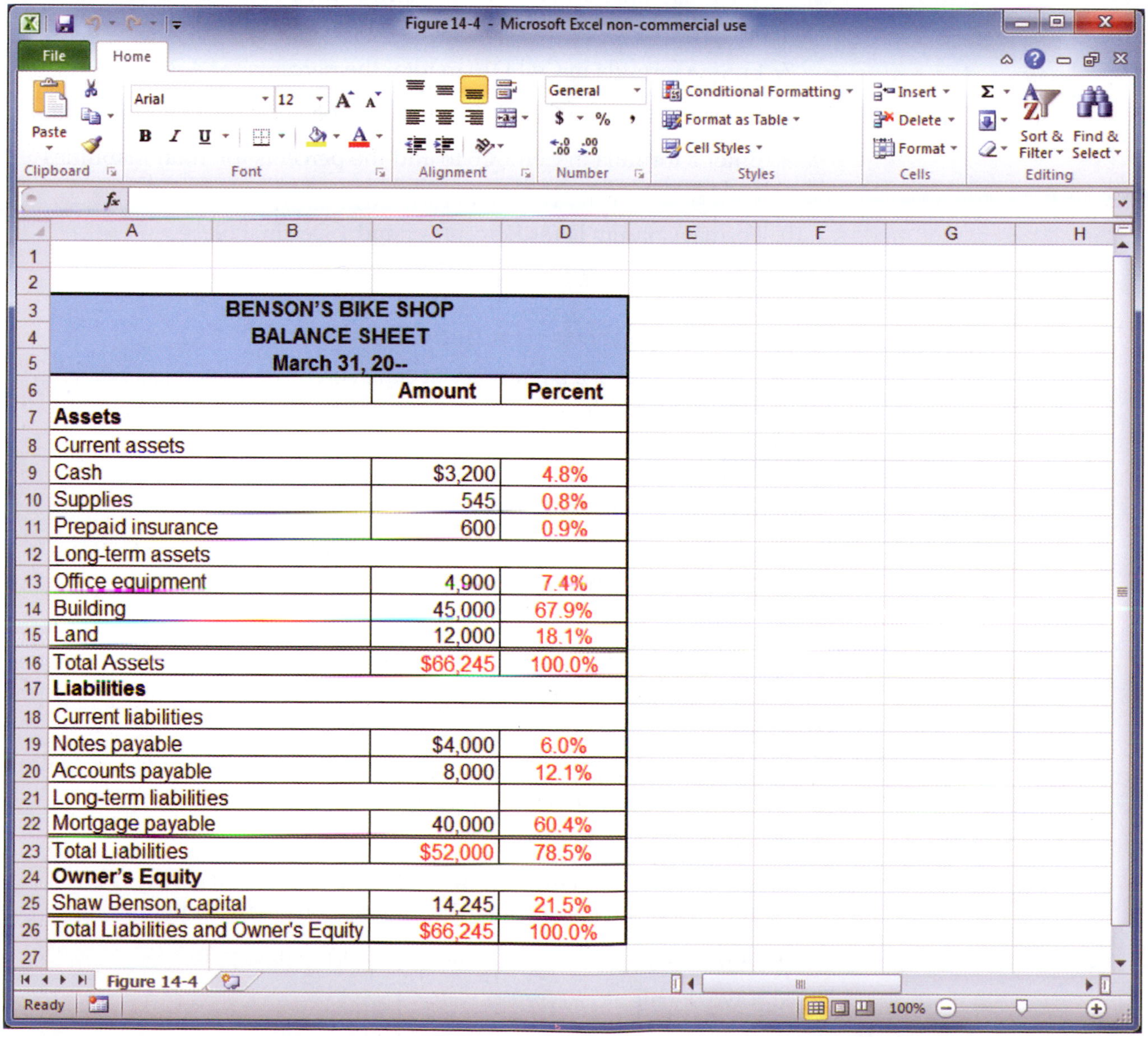

	A	B	C	D
		BENSON'S BIKE SHOP		
		BALANCE SHEET		
		March 31, 20--		
6			**Amount**	**Percent**
7	**Assets**			
8	Current assets			
9	Cash		$3,200	4.8%
10	Supplies		545	0.8%
11	Prepaid insurance		600	0.9%
12	Long-term assets			
13	Office equipment		4,900	7.4%
14	Building		45,000	67.9%
15	Land		12,000	18.1%
16	Total Assets		$66,245	100.0%
17	**Liabilities**			
18	Current liabilities			
19	Notes payable		$4,000	6.0%
20	Accounts payable		8,000	12.1%
21	Long-term liabilities			
22	Mortgage payable		40,000	60.4%
23	Total Liabilities		$52,000	78.5%
24	**Owner's Equity**			
25	Shaw Benson, capital		14,245	21.5%
26	Total Liabilities and Owner's Equity		$66,245	100.0%

Retrieve the file *ch14pr04.xlsx*.

1. Enter a formula in Cell C16 to total all Assets, both Current and Long-term.

2. Enter a formula in Cell C23 to total all Liabilities, both Current and Long-term.

3. Enter a formula in Cell C26 to add Total Liabilities and Owner's Equity.

4. Format the answers in Column C for Currency, 0 Decimal places, and set Currency Symbol to $.

5. Divide each Asset in Column D by Total Assets. Remember to use an absolute cell reference.

6. Divide each Liability and the Owner's Equity in Column D by the Total Liabilities and Owner's Equity. Remember to use an absolute cell reference.

7. Enter a formula in Cell D16 to total the percents for Assets.

8. Enter a formula in Cell D23 to total the percents for Liabilities.

9. Enter a formula in Cell D26 to add the percents for Total Liabilities and Owner's Equity.

10. Format Column D for Percentage and 1 Decimal place.

11. Save the file as *ch14pr04a.xlsx*.

Comparative analysis of a balance sheet

A horizontal analysis of a balance sheet can also be completed easily using Excel. Study Figure 14-5.

STEPS

Retrieve the file *ch14pr05.xlsx*.

1. Enter formulas in Columns C and D to total Current Assets, Fixed Assets, and Total Assets for Year 1 and Year 2.

2. Format answers in Columns C and D for Currency. Set Decimal places to 0. Set Currency symbol to $.

3. Enter formulas in the Amount of Change column to subtract Year 1 from Year 2 for each item.

4. Format Column E for Currency. Set Decimal places to 0. Set Currency symbol to $. Set negative numbers to be shown in parentheses and in red.

5. Enter formulas in the Percent of Change column to divide the Amount of Change by Year 1 (original year) for each item.

6. Format Column F for Percentage and 1 Decimal place.

7. Save the file as *ch14pr05a.xlsx*.

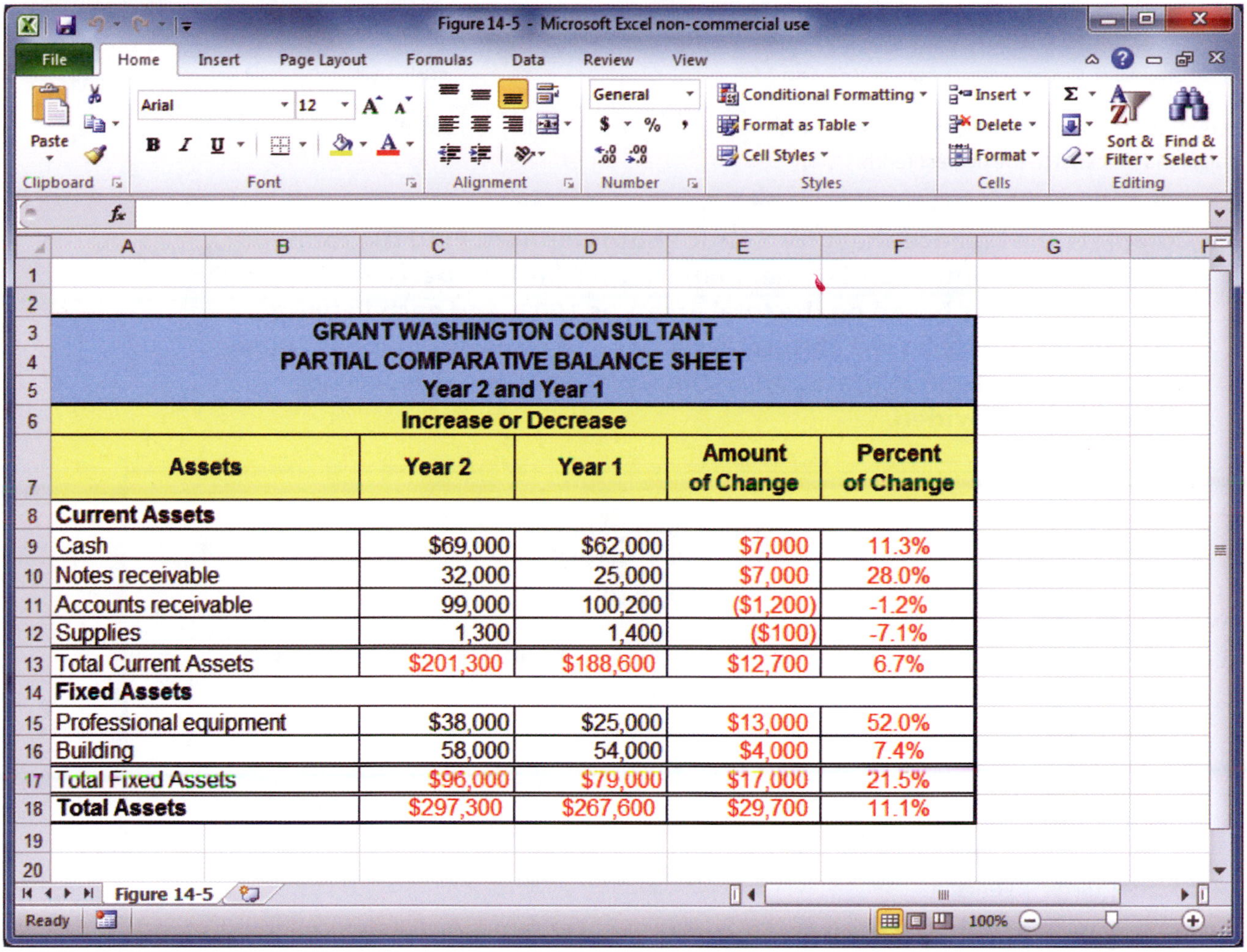

				GRANT WASHINGTON CONSULTANT	
		PARTIAL COMPARATIVE BALANCE SHEET			
		Year 2 and Year 1			
		Increase or Decrease			
Assets	Year 2	Year 1	Amount of Change	Percent of Change	
Current Assets					
Cash	$69,000	$62,000	$7,000	11.3%	
Notes receivable	32,000	25,000	$7,000	28.0%	
Accounts receivable	99,000	100,200	($1,200)	-1.2%	
Supplies	1,300	1,400	($100)	-7.1%	
Total Current Assets	$201,300	$188,600	$12,700	6.7%	
Fixed Assets					
Professional equipment	$38,000	$25,000	$13,000	52.0%	
Building	58,000	54,000	$4,000	7.4%	
Total Fixed Assets	$96,000	$79,000	$17,000	21.5%	
Total Assets	$297,300	$267,600	$29,700	11.1%	

Figure 14-5

Partial Horizontal Analysis of a Balance Sheet

Name _____   Date _____

Directions   Solve the following problems. Write your answers in the blanks provided. Round dollar amounts to the nearest dollar and percents to the nearest tenth.

A. Complete the balance sheet for Scenic Photographers. Find the total   OBJECTIVE **2, 3**
assets, total liabilities, and owner's equity. Also find the percent of
each of the assets based on the total assets as 100% and each liability
and owner's equity based on total liabilities and owner's equity as 100%.
Make your percents accurate to 1 decimal place. Write your answers
in the blanks provided.

Scenic Photographers
BALANCE SHEET
April 30, 20- -

Assets	Amount	Percent	
Current assets			
Cash	$ 5,000	_____	4.
Supplies	1,865	_____	5.
Prepaid insurance	205	_____	6.
Long-term assets			
Photographic equipment	2,390	_____	7.
Building	61,000	_____	8.
Land	11,000	_____	9.
Total assets	_____ 1.	_____	10.
Liabilities			
Current liabilities			
Notes payable	$ 5,900	_____	11.
Accounts payable	7,300	_____	12.
Long-term liabilities			
Mortgage payable	48,000	_____	13.
Total liabilities	_____ 2.	_____	14.
Owner's Equity			
R. T. Page, capital	$20,260	_____	15.
Total liabilities and owner's equity	_____ 3.	_____	16.

B. Complete the following comparative balance sheet using horizontal analysis. Round percents to 1 decimal place. Show decreases with an asterisk (*). OBJECTIVE 4

Corrigan Counselors					BALANCE SHEET Year 1 and Year 2
Assets	Year 2	Year 1	Amt. of Change	% of Change	
Current assets					
Cash	$ 72,000	$ 56,000	_____	_____	17.
Notes receivable	7,000	9,000	_____	_____	18.
Accounts receivable	14,600	21,800	_____	_____	19.
Supplies	1,193	1,700	_____	_____	20.
Total current assets	$ 94,793	$ 88,500	_____	_____	21.
Fixed assets					
Professional equipment	$ 14,000	$ 10,000	_____	_____	22.
Building	58,000	60,000	_____	_____	23.
Total fixed assets	$ 72,000	$ 70,000	_____	_____	24.
Total assets	$ 166,793	$ 158,500	_____	_____	25.
Liabilities					
Current liabilities					
Notes payable	10,000	$ 14,900	_____	_____	26.
Accounts receivable	11,000	12,000	_____	_____	27.
Payroll taxes payable	14,600	13,100	_____	_____	28.
Total current liabilities	$ 35,600	$ 40,000	_____	_____	29.
Long-term liabilities					
Mortgage payable	$ 54,000	$ 55,000	_____	_____	30.
Notes payable (over 1 year)	42,000	39,000	_____	_____	31.
Total long-term liabilities	$ 96,000	$ 94,000	_____	_____	32.
Total liabilities	$ 131,600	$ 134,000	_____	_____	33.
Owner's Equity					
John Corrigan, capital	$ 35,193	$ 24,500	_____	_____	34.
Total liabilities and owner's equity	$ 166,793	$ 158,500	_____	_____	35.

*Decrease

C. Use Excel to create a balance sheet. OBJECTIVE 5

36. Retrieve the file *ch14ex03.xlsx*. Follow the directions. Save the file as *ch14ex03a.xlsx*.

37. Retrieve the file *ch14ex04.xlsx*. Follow the directions. Save the file as *ch14ex04a.xlsx*.

38. Retrieve the file *ch14ex05.xlsx*. Follow the directions. Save the file as *ch14ex05a.xlsx*.

OBJECTIVES

1. Identify terms used with ratios.
2. Find the current ratio.
3. Find the acid test ratio.
4. Find the return on investment.
5. Use Excel to calculate ratios.

14.3 Financial Ratios

OBJECTIVE 1 Identify terms used with ratios.

To better understand how to calculate and use ratios, learn the following terms.

Acid Test Ratio   (Also called *quick ratio*) A ratio comparing liquid assets to current liabilities.

Accounts Payable   An account that tracks what you owe your creditors on account (credit).

Accounts Receivable   An account that tracks what your charge customers owe you for services performed or goods delivered.

Current Ratio   A ratio comparing current assets to current liabilities.

Financial Ratios   A series of comparisons of financial statement components expressed as ratios used to evaluate the financial performance of a company.

Liquid Assets   Assets that are cash or can be converted to cash quickly, such as accounts receivable and notes receivable.

Liquidity Ratios   A comparison of how well a company can pay off its short-term debts and yet maintain cash flow.

Ratio   A comparison of one amount to another.

OBJECTIVE 2 Find the current ratio.

Financial ratios help management identify areas that need investigation. A financial ratio that is not in line with other similar companies or its industry averages might mean a company is heading toward financial difficulty in a certain area. Managers, investors, and creditors often use publications such as *Industry Norms and Key Business Ratios*, by Dun & Bradstreet. This publication provides financial norm and business ratio data developed from actual company income statements and balance sheets. The *Survey of Current Business*, published by the Bureau of Economic Analysis, an agency of the U.S. Department of Commerce provides industry statistics for similar-sized companies for comparison purposes. Figures can also be obtained from a company's banker, accountants, local small business centers, libraries, and newspaper articles.

As a part of producing financial statements for a company, accountants often provide comparisons of financial information in the form of ratios. Managers, creditors, and investors, in turn, study these ratios to help with decision making.

Ratios can be stated several ways.

As a ratio	2:1	
As a fraction	$\frac{2}{1}$	
As a number	2	Use a denominator of 1.
As a percent	200%	
As money	$2	

A lending institution might calculate a current ratio to help determine whether to approve a loan by comparing a company's current assets to current liabilities. Use this formula to calculate the *current ratio*.

Current ratio = Current assets ÷ Current liabilities

EXAMPLE

Thorndike Manufacturing's current assets were $100 million and current liabilities were $50 million. Find the current ratio.

$$\text{Current ratio} = \text{Current assets} \div \text{Current liabilities}$$
$$= \$100 \text{ million} \div \$50 \text{ million}$$
$$= 2:1 \quad \text{current ratio}$$

The company has two assets for each liability or assets are 200% of liabilities or for each $2 of assets, the company has $1 of liabilities.

OBJECTIVE **3** Find the acid test ratio.

Even though the current ratio is a valid way to determine a company's financial standing, some accountants prefer to use the acid test ratio to determine a company's financial strength. The *acid test ratio* considers only liquid assets (assets that can be converted to cash quickly). Other than cash, these accounts are usually *accounts receivable* (what your customers owe you for services performed or goods delivered) and *accounts payable* (what you owe creditors on account). This ratio measures how quickly a company can liquidate assets to pay off current debt.

Acid test ratio = (Cash + Accounts receivable) ÷ Current liabilities

EXAMPLE

Compute the acid test ratio for Sun 'n Fun Sporting Goods.

Cash	$ 85,000
Accounts receivable	145,000
Total cash and receivables	$230,000
Accounts payable	$110,000

Acid test ratio = (Cash + Accounts receivable) ÷ Current liabilities
$$= \$230,000 \div \$110,000 = 2.1$$

Note the ratio 2.1:1 is stated as a number.

TIPS

As a rule of thumb, the current ratio should be at least 2:1 (stated as 2 to 1). This, of course, is a general measure and does not apply to all companies.

TIPS

The acid-test ratio does not include inventory and prepaid amounts, such as prepaid insurance, as assets that can be liquidated.

OBJECTIVE 4 Find the return on investment.

The company's profitability picture is one area in which not only management but also investors are especially interested. A company can compare its return on investment with competitors to determine whether the company is showing enough profit on sales. Investors, on the other hand, expect a return on their investment in the form of dividends, which are determined by the company's profitability. The return on investment compares the net income to owner's equity (amount invested by owners). The result is expressed as a percent of owner's equity. Study the following formula.

$$\text{Return on investment} = \text{Net income} \div \text{Owner's equity}$$

EXAMPLE

Crafters Corner wants to know what its return on investment was for the year.

$$\text{Return on investment} = \text{Net income} \div \text{Owner's equity}$$
$$= \$98,500 \div \$153,300 = 0.643$$

The return on investment is 64.3% or $0.64 in net profit for each $1.00 invested, an excellent return on the investor's money.

OBJECTIVE 5 Use Excel to calculate ratios.

Excel provides a way to calculate helpful information such as ratios.

STEPS

Retrieve the file *ch14pr06.xlsx.*

A. Calculate the Current Ratio for Max's Lawn & Garden Equipment for the years shown.

1. Enter formulas in Column D to calculate the Current Ratio.

2. Format Column D for Number. Set Decimal places to 1.

3. In Column E, key in the Current Ratio Expressed as a Ratio.

4. Format Column E for General.

B. Calculate the acid test Ratio for Max's Lawn & Garden Equipment for the years shown.

1. Enter the formulas in Column E to calculate the Acid Test Ratio.

2. Format Column E for Number. Set Decimal places to 1.

3. In Column F, key in the Acid Test Ratio Expressed as a Ratio.

4. Format Column F for General.

A. Calculate the current ratio for Max's Lawn & Garden Equipment for the years shown.

Year	Current Assets	Current Liabilities	Current Ratio	Expressed as a Ratio
2006	90,800	45,380	2.0	2.0:1
2007	110,000	59,000	1.9	1.9:1
2008	125,000	67,000	1.9	1.9:1
2009	143,000	80,000	1.8	1.8:1
2010	196,500	85,000	2.3	2.3:1

B. Calculate the acid test ratio for Max's Lawn & Garden Equipment for the years shown.

Year	Cash	Accounts Receivable	Accounts Payable	Acid Test Ratio	Expressed as a Ratio
2006	72,000	23,000	41000	2.3	2.3:1
2007	80,000	25,500	62000	1.7	1.7:1
2008	96,000	16,000	88000	1.3	1.3:1
2009	87,000	22,000	53000	2.1	2.1:1
2010	106,000	31,000	77000	1.8	1.8:1

C. Calculate the return on investment for Max's Lawn & Garden Equipment for the years shown.

Year	Net Income	Owner's Equity	Return on Investment
2006	125,000	444,000	28.2%
2007	136,000	469,000	29.0%
2008	110,800	498,000	22.2%
2009	112,300	589,000	19.1%
2010	108,000	637,000	17.0%

Figure 14-6
Calculating Ratios

C. Calculate the return on investment for Max's Lawn & Garden Equipment for the years shown.

1. Enter the formulas in Column D to calculate Return on Investment.

2. Format Column D for Percentage and 1 Decimal place.

3. Save the file as *ch14pr06a.xlsx.*

Name _____ Date _____

Directions   Solve the following problems. Write your answers in the blanks provided. Round ratios to the nearest tenth. Round percents to the nearest percent.

A. Find the current ratio.   OBJECTIVE 2

	Company	Current Assets	Current Liabilities	Current Ratio
1.	Acme Hardware, Inc.	$110,460	$75,855	_____
2.	Just-A-Click Camera Shop	$145,610	$89,900	_____
3.	Hair Masters	$95,325	$32,800	_____
4.	A-Thousand-And-One Books	$192,220	$134,210	_____
5.	Tia's Café	$36,875	$15,440	_____
6.	Taco Express	$6,600	$2,005	_____
7.	Chicken On-the-Go	$13,550	$18,500	_____
8.	Acme Tire Company	$440,500	$400,300	_____
9.	Landscapes Galore	$1,000,900	$880,990	_____
10.	Sammy's Ice Cream Shoppe	$10,200	$1,500	_____

B. Find the acid test ratio. (Hint: Add Cash and Accounts Receivable to determine Current Assets.)   OBJECTIVE 3

	Company	Cash	Accounts Receivable	Accounts Payable	Acid-Test Ratio
11.	Kola Auto Repair	$15,200	$5,890	$32,000	_____
12.	Regents Dry Cleaners	$18,920	$1,400	$25,000	_____
13.	Weekly Times Herald	$94,660	$32,395	$125,300	_____
14.	Garden World	$54,880	$12,500	$59,650	_____
15.	Elite Dance Studio	$6,050	$1,010	$1,545	_____
16.	Continental Photographers	$3,255	$6,890	$10,188	_____
17.	Nails 2000	$21,200	–0–	$56,900	_____
18.	The Pearl Restaurant	$6,560	$7,500	$36,808	_____
19.	Lee's Chinese Food	$12,300	$5,890	$75,400	_____
20.	Delco Distributors	$68,442	$83,875	$235,625	_____

C. Calculate the return on investment. Show ratios as a percent of net income. `OBJECTIVE 4`

	Company	Net Income	Owner's Equity	Return on Investment
21.	Shield Enterprises	$150,675	$135,990	_____
22.	The Busy Bee, Inc.	$68,400	$85,900	_____
23.	Trust Securities, Inc.	$350,000	$1,495,000	_____
24.	One-On-One Training	$46,000	$58,390	_____
25.	Karma Tae Kwon-Do	$42,450	$168,900	_____
26.	Smith & Carlson, P.C.	$90,000	$610,300	_____
27.	Big John's Self Storage	$130,000	$1,500,000	_____
28.	Ruth's Caribbean Tan	$45,210	$312,000	_____
29.	Action Electric, Inc.	$150,875	$2,350,000	_____
30.	Oasis Pool Service	$110,786	$1,675,500	_____

D. Use Excel to calculate ratios. `OBJECTIVE 5`

31. Retrieve the file *ch14ex06.xlsx*. Follow the directions. Save the file as *ch14ex06a.xlsx*.

32. Retrieve the file *ch14ex07.xlsx*. Follow the directions. Save the file as *ch14ex07a.xlsx*.

Chapter Review and Assessment

KEY TERMS

accounting equation

accounts payable

accounts receivable

acid test ratio

assets

balance sheet

capital

cost of merchandise
 (goods) sold

current assets

current liabilities

current ratio

financial ratios

gross profit (gross margin)

horizontal analysis of a balance sheet

income statement

liabilities

liquid assets

liquidity ratios

long-term liabilities

merchandise available for sale

merchandise business

merchandise inventory (beginning)

merchandise inventory (ending)

net income (net profit)

net purchases

net sales

operating expenses

owner's equity

plant and equipment

purchase discounts

purchases

purchases returns and allowances

ratio

revenue

sales

sales discounts

sales returns and allowances

service business

vertical analysis of a balance sheet

vertical analysis of an income
 statement

CONCEPTS	EXAMPLES

14.1 Create an income statement for a service business.
 	
1. Total all operating expenses.
 	
2. Subtract operating expenses from revenues.
	Revenue
	    Professional fees $300,000
	Operating expenses
	    Rent expense $12,000
	    Salary expense 99,000
	    Automobile expense 65,000
	Total operating expenses $176,000
	Net profit before federal income tax $124,000

14.1 Create an income statement for a merchandise business. 1. Net Sales = Sales – Sales Returns and Allowances – Sales Discounts 2. Cost of Goods Sold = Beginning Merchandise Inventory + Purchases – Purchases Returns and Allowances – Purchase Discounts – Ending Merchandise Inventory 3. Gross Profit = Net Sales – Cost of Goods Sold 4. Operating Expenses = Total of all Operating Expenses 5. Net Profit before Federal Income Tax = Gross Profit – Total Operating Expenses 6. Net Profit after Federal Income Tax = Net Profit before Federal Income Tax – Federal Income Tax	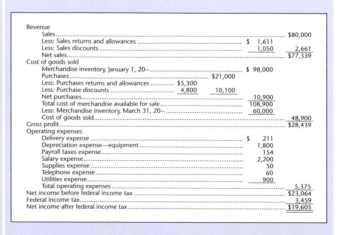

CONCEPTS	EXAMPLES

14.2 Create a balance sheet.

1. Total all assets.

2. Total all liabilities.

3. Total all owner's equity.

4. Add total liabilities and owner's equity. (The total should be equal to total assets.)

Use Excel to create balance sheets using the same format as shown in the example.

Assets	
Current assets	
Cash	$ 3,200
Supplies	545
Prepaid insurance	600
Long-term assets	
Office equipment	4,900
Building	45,000
Land	12,000
Total assets	$66,245
Liabilities	
Current liabilities	
Notes payable	$ 4,000
Accounts payable	8,000
Long-term liabilities	
Mortgage payable	40,000
Total liabilities	$52,000
Owner's Equity	
Shaw Benson, capital	$14,245
Total liabilities and owner's equity	$66,245

14.2 Create a horizontal analysis of a balance sheet.

1. Subtract current year from last year to get the amount of change.

2. Divide each amount of change by last year's amount.

	Year 2	Year 1	Amt of Change	% of Change
Current assets				
Cash	$ 69,000	$ 62,000	$ 7,000	11.3
Notes receivable	32,000	25,000	7,000	28.0
Accounts receivable	99,000	100,200	1,200*	1.2*
Supplies	1,300	1,400	100*	7.1*
Total current assets	$201,300	$188,600	$12,700	6.7
Fixed assets				
Professional equipment	$ 38,000	$ 25,000	$13,000	52.0
Building	58,000	54,000	4,000	7.4
Total fixed assets	$ 96,000	$ 79,000	$17,000	21.5
Total assets	$297,300	$267,600	$29,700	11.1
*Decrease				

14.3 Find the current ratio.

$$\text{Current ratio} = \frac{\text{Current assets}}{\text{Current liabilities}}$$

Current assets = $100 million

Current liabilities = $500 million

$100 ÷ $50 = 2:1   current ratio

14.4 Find the acid test ratio.

$$\text{acid test ratio} = \frac{(\text{Cash} + \text{Accounts receivable})}{\text{Current liabilities}}$$

Cash	$ 85,000
Accounts receivable	$145,000
Total cash and receivables	$230,000
Accounts Payable	$110,000

$230,000 ÷ $110,000 = 2.1:1   acid test ratio

14.4 Find the return on investment.

Return on investment = Net income ÷ Owner's equity

Net income	$98,500
Owner's equity	$153,300

$98,500 ÷ $153,300 = 64.3%   return on investment

Chapter 14 Review Exercises

Name _____ Date _____

Directions Solve the following problems. Write your answers in the blanks provided.

A. Compute the quarterly total operating expenses and net profit before taxes for each of the following companies. `14.1 OBJECTIVE 2`

Cowboy's Western Wear
INCOME STATEMENT
For the quarter ending June 30, 20--

Revenue
    Professional fees... $132,455
Operating expenses
    Depreciation expense—equipment .... $ 6,500
    Payroll taxes expense 10,500
    Rent expense 15,000
    Salary expense 49,000
    Supplies expense 1,500
    Utilities expense.. 4,380
    Automobile expense 1,400
    Equipment repair expense.............................. 500
    Miscellaneous expense................................... 1,900
Total operating expenses .... _____ **1.**
Net profit before federal income tax......................... _____ **2.**

Lavender Financial Services
INCOME STATEMENT
For the quarter ending September 30, 20--

Revenue
    Professional fees... $285,550
Operating expenses
    Depreciation expense—equipment $25,500
    Payroll taxes expense 10,500
    Rent expense 20,000
    Salary expense 150,000
    Supplies expense.. 14,000
    Utilities expense 5,500
    Automobile expense 25,500
    Equipment repair expense.............................. 6,000
    Miscellaneous expense................................... 2,500
Total operating expenses .... _____ **3.**
Net profit before federal income tax......................... _____ **4.**

B. Complete the following income statement for the first quarter of this year. 14.1 OBJECTIVE 3

Ellsworth Jewelry
INCOME STATEMENT
For the quarter ending March 31, 20--

Revenue

    Sales $225,875

    Less: Sales returns and allowances... $23,458

    Less: Sales discounts... 5,050   _____ **5.**

    Net sales... _____ **6.**

Cost of goods sold

    Merchandise inventory, January 1, 20-- $88,000

    Purchases $35,600

    Less: Purchases returns and allowances... $5,300

    Less: Purchase discounts......................... 3,800   _____ **7.**

    Net purchases .... _____ **8.**

    Total cost of product available for sale .... _____ **9.**

    Less: Product inventory, March 31, 20-- 50,000

    Cost of goods sold.. _____ **10.**

Gross profit.. _____ **11.**

Operating expenses

    Delivery expense .... $ 2,700

    Depreciation expense—equipment... 6,800

    Payroll taxes expense 15,303

    Salary expense 92,800

    Supplies expense... 1,456

    Telephone expense 2,355

    Utilities expense 6,890

    Total operating expenses .... _____ **12.**

Net income before federal income tax .... _____ **13.**

Federal income tax.. 684

Net income after federal income tax .... _____ **14.**

C. Complete a vertical analysis of an income statement. Round percents to the tenth place.

RICHARDSON ELECTRONICS
INCOME STATEMENT
1st Quarter, March 31, 20--

Revenue	Amount	Percent	
Sales	$450,000	_____	15.
Less: Sales returns and allowances	42,000	_____	16.
Net sales...	$408,000	_____	17.
Cost of goods sold			
Merchandise inventory, January 1, 20--	$185,000	_____	18.
Purchases...	105,400	_____	19.
Net Purchases	290,400	_____	20.
Purchases returns and allowances	29,200	_____	21.
Total cost of merchandise available for sale	$261,200	_____	22.
Less: Merchandise inventory, March 31, 20-- ..	62,300	_____	23.
Cost of goods sold	$198,900	_____	24.

D. Complete the following balance sheet for Kaminski Clothiers. 14.2 OBJECTIVE 2

Kaminski Clothiers
BALANCE SHEET
March 31, 20--

Assets		
Current assets		
Cash	$ 6,325	
Supplies	445	
Prepaid insurance	1,830	
Long-term		
Office equipment	10,990	
Building	155,000	
Land	32,000	
Total assets		25.
Liabilities		
Current liabilities		
Notes payable	$ 56,850	
Accounts payable	86,000	
Long-term liabilities		
Mortgage payable	51,235	
Total liabilities		26.
Owner's Equity		
Carl Kaminski, capital	$ 12,505	
Total liabilities and owner's equity		27.

E. Complete the following vertical analysis of a balance sheet for Valdez Plumbing Supply.

Valdez Plumbing Supply
BALANCE SHEET
March 31, 20--

	Amount	Percent	
Assets			
Current assets			
Cash	$ 5,200		28.
Supplies	345		29.
Prepaid insurance	900		30.
Long-term			
Office equipment	7,900		31.
Building	72,000		32.
Land	21,000		33.
Total assets		34.	35.
Liabilities			
Current liabilities			
Notes payable	$ 22,395		36.
Accounts payable	15,811		37.
Long-term liabilities			
Mortgage payable	37,500		38.
Total liabilities		39.	40.
Owner's Equity			
Mark Valdez, capital	$31,639		41.
Total liabilities and owner's equity		42.	43.

*Number has been rounded up so total equals 100%.

F. Complete the following comparative balance sheets for Clubfinders Golf Shop and Capella Chiropractic Center.

Clubfinders Golf Shop
COMPARATIVE (HORIZONTAL) BALANCE SHEET
Year 2 and Year 1

Assets	Year 2	Year 1	Amt. of Change	% of Change	
Current assets					
Cash	$ 59,000	$ 72,000	$13,000*	_____	44.
Notes receivable	42,000	35,000	7,000	_____	45.
Accounts receivable	89,000	101,200	12,200*	_____	46.
Supplies	3,300	3,400	100*	_____	47.
Total current assets	_____ 48.	_____ 49.	_____ 50.	_____	51.
Fixed assets					
Equipment	$ 67,510	$ 75,000	$ 7,490*	_____	52.
Building	98,000	98,000	– 0 –	_____	53.
Total fixed assets	_____ 54.	_____ 55.	_____ 56.	_____	57.
Total assets	_____ 58.	_____ 59.	_____ 60.	_____	61.

*Decrease

Capella Chiropractic Center
COMPARATIVE (HORIZONTAL) BALANCE SHEET
Year 2 and Year 1

Assets	Year 2	Year 1	Amt. of Change	%of Change	
Current assets					
Cash	$ 59,000	$ 42,000	$17,000	_____	62.
Notes receivable	32,000	25,000	7,000	_____	63.
Accounts receivable	109,000	101,000	8,000	_____	64.
Supplies	1,400	1,000	400	_____	65.
Total current assets	_____ 66.	_____ 67.	_____ 68.	_____	69.
Fixed assets					
Equipment	$ 99,000	$ 75,000	$24,000	_____	70.
Building	56,000	50,000	6,000	_____	71.
Total fixed assets	_____ 72.	_____ 73.	_____ 74.	_____	75.
Total assets	_____ 76.	_____ 77.	_____ 78.	_____	79.

*Decrease

G. Find the current ratio. Round each ratio to the nearest tenth. 14.3 OBJECTIVE 2

	Company	Current Assets	Current Liabilities	Current Ratio
80.	Ross Avenue Ignition	$25,420	$15,825	_____
81.	Metro Salon Equipment	$45,610	$19,480	_____
82.	Blair Rentals	$75,340	$23,110	_____

H. Find the acid test ratio. Round each ratio to the nearest tenth. 14.3 OBJECTIVE 3

	Company	Cash	Accounts Receivable	Accounts Payable	Acid-Test Ratio
83.	Anderson Air Conditioning	$15,000	$6,890	$2,000	_____
84.	Henley Aircraft Services	$68,920	$73,400	$25,000	_____
85.	Best Little Car Wash in Texas	$12,000	– 0 –	$23,700	_____

I. Calculate the return on investment as a percent of owner's equity. Round to the nearest percent. 14.3 OBJECTIVE 4

	Company	Net Income	Owner's Equity	Return on Investment
86.	Lucky Bail Bonds	$140,575	$35,990	_____
87.	Cactus Bank	$268,400	$185,900	_____
88.	Indulgence Salon	$90,000	$78,000	_____
89.	Key Security Systems	$36,000	$28,390	_____

J. Use Excel to create an income statement, create a balance sheet, and calculate ratios. 14.1 OBJECTIVE 5, 14.2 OBJECTIVE 5 14.3 OBJECTIVE 5

90. Retrieve the file *ch14ex08.xlsx*. Follow the directions. Save the file as *ch14ex08a.xlsx*.

91. Retrieve the file *ch14ex09.xlsx*. Follow the directions. Save the file as *ch14ex09a.xlsx*.

92. Retrieve the file *ch14ex10.xlsx*. Follow the directions. Save the file as *ch14ex10a.xlsx*.

A comparative vertical analysis is done using the same procedure used for vertical analysis, with one exception. The difference is that two or more prior years are given in a comparative vertical analysis. This allows a visual comparison to be made.

TRY IT...

Complete the percent columns for Year 1 and Year 2 for the following partial comparative vertical analysis. Find the percent of each amount based on net sales. Round all answers to the nearest tenth percent.

Uniform Service Company
COMPARATIVE INCOME STATEMENT with VERTICAL ANALYSIS
Year 2 and Year 1

	Year 2		Year 1	
	Amount	Percent	Amount	Percent
Revenue				
Sales	$855,000 **1.** _____		$818,000 **10.** _____	
Less: Sales returns and allowances	24,000 **2.** _____		37,800 **11.** _____	
Net sales	$831,000 **3.** _____		$780,200 **12.** _____	
Cost of product sold				
Product inventory, January 1	$111,000 **4.** _____		$210,000 **13.** _____	
Purchases less returns and allowances	455,000 **5.** _____		401,000 **14.** _____	
Total cost of product available for sale	$566,000 **6.** _____		$611,000 **15.** _____	
Less: Product inventory, December 31	110,000 **7.** _____		122,000 **16.** _____	
Cost of product sold	$456,000 **8.** _____		$489,000 **17.** _____	
Gross profit	$375,000 **9.** _____		$291,200 **18.** _____	

Write about Math

1. Identify three reasons how an owner or manager might use the information in a vertical analysis of an income statement?

2. Explain how to create a comparative analysis of a balance sheet. Why are the percents not summed vertically?

Personal Finance

How important is your credit score?

Each time you purchase an item on credit, such as a car, house, appliance, you are establishing your credit history. Based on how good your credit history is, future requests for credit will be granted. It is important to know your credit score and what it means. You can get your credit score from credit reporting agencies - Experian, TransUnion, and Equifax. Your credit score is often used to determine whether or not you qualify for credit, the terms of the credit, and the interest rate that will be charged. Your credit score is calculated based on the data in your credit reports. For instance, if you are one day late on a payment, that information goes into your credit report. You should constantly monitor your credit and make all payments on time.

Feng Yu/Shutterstock.com

1. Determine your financial status by completing a personal income statement that will show your assets, liabilities, and net worth. Complete all lines that apply to you.

PERSONAL FINANCIAL STATEMENT	
Name: _____	Date: _____
Assets	**Amount in Dollars**
Cash - checking accounts	$
Cash - savings accounts	
Certificates of deposit/stocks/bonds/mutual funds	
Notes & contracts receivable	
Life insurance (*cash surrender value*)	
Personal property (*autos, jewelry, etc.*)	
Retirement Funds (*eg. IRAs, 401k*)	
Real estate (*market value*)	
Other assets (*specify*)	
Total Assets	$
Liabilities	**Amount in Dollars**
Current Debt (*Credit cards, Accounts*)	$
Notes payable (*describe*)	
Taxes payable	
Real estate mortgages (*describe*)	
Other liabilities (*specify*)	
Total Liabilities	$
Net Worth	$

2. Calculate your debt ratio using the following formula.
   Total Liabilities ÷ Total Assets = Debt Ratio

   _____ ÷ _____ = _____

Name   Date   Score

Directions   Solve the following problems. Write your answers in the blanks provided. Place commas and dollar signs in answers as needed.

A. Compute the quarterly total operating expenses and net profit before taxes for each of the following companies.   `14.1 OBJECTIVE 2`

Air Wave Flying Service
INCOME STATEMENT
For the quarter ending September 30, 20--

Revenue

Flight service..	$120,000	
Training	96,500	
Maintenance service	180,000	
Total revenue...		1.

Expenses

Depreciation expense—equipment	$42,000	
Rent expense	12,000	
Telephone expense	980	
Supplies expense...	18,000	
Salary expense	80,000	
Payroll tax expense	5,600	
Total expenses		2.
Net profit before federal income tax..............................		3.

Blue Bayou Kennels
INCOME STATEMENT
For the quarter ending September 30, 20--

Revenue

Boarding revenue	$ 85,000	
Obedience training	52,500	
Grooming service	79,000	
Total revenue...		4.

Expenses

Depreciation expense—van	$12,000	
Rent expense	12,000	
Advertising expense	22,980	
Dog/cat food and supplies expense	36,000	
Salary expense	40,000	
Payroll tax expense	5,600	
Total expenses		5.
Net profit before federal income tax..............................		6.

B. Complete the following income statement. 14.1 OBJECTIVES 3, 4

Blackwell Computer Center
INCOME STATEMENT
For the six month period ending June 30, 20--

Revenue	Amount		Percent	
Sales	$220,000		_____	7.
Less: Sales returns and allowances	1,840		_____	8.
Net sales	_____	9.	_____	10.
Cost of goods sold				
Merchandise inventory, January 1, 20--	$ 56,000		_____	11.
Purchases less returns and allowances	29,200		_____	12.
Total cost of merchandise available for sale ...	_____	13.	_____	14.
Less: Merchandise inventory, June 30, 20--....	30,225		_____	15.
Cost of goods sold	_____	16.	_____	17.

C. Complete the following balance sheet for AZ Tech Publishing Services. 14.2 OBJECTIVE 2

AZ Tech Publishing Services
BALANCE SHEET
March 31, 20--

Assets
Current assets
    Cash $ 4,075
    Supplies   1,445
    Prepaid insurance   1,550
Long-term assets
    Office equipment   20,490
    Building   135,000
    Land   31,000
Total assets   _____ 18.
Liabilities
Current liabilities
    Notes payable $ 46,500
    Accounts payable   81,245
Long-term liabilities
    Mortgage payable   50,355
Total liabilities   _____ 19.
Owner's Equity
Alisa Ortega, capital $ 15,460
Total liabilities and owner's equity   _____ 20.

D. Complete the following comparative balance sheet for Ms. Clean House Cleaners.

Ms. Clean House Cleaners
COMPARATIVE BALANCE SHEET with VERTICAL ANALYSIS
Year 2 and Year 1

	Year 2		Year 1	
	Amount	Percent	Amount	Percent
Assets				
Current assets				
Cash	$ 82,550	**21.** _____	$ 75,000	**22.** _____
Office supplies	710	**23.** _____	480	**24.** _____
Prepaid insurance......................	2,100	**25.** _____	1,990	**26.** _____
Accounts receivable	5,500	**27.** _____	4,000	**28.** _____
Total current assets	$ 90,860	**29.** _____	$ 81,470	**30.** _____
Long-term assets				
Building	$ 45,000	**31.** _____	$ 40,000	**32.** _____
Land	27,000	**33.** _____	25,000	**34.** _____
Total plant and equipment	$ 72,000	**35.** _____	$ 65,000	**36.** _____
Total assets	$162,860	**37.** _____	$146,470	**38.** _____
Liabilities				
Current liabilities				
Accounts payable......................	$ 13,500	**39.** _____	$ 12,500	**40.** _____
Salaries payable........................	36,400	**41.** _____	25,000	**42.** _____
Total current liabilities	$ 49,900	**43.** _____	$ 37,500	**44.** _____
Long-term liabilities				
Mortgage payable.....................	$ 34,000	**45.** _____	$ 38,000	**46.** _____
Total liabilities	$ 83,900	**47.** _____	$ 75,500	**48.** _____
Owner's Equity				
D. L. Barton, capital	$ 78,960	**49.** _____	$ 70,970	**50.** _____
Total liabilities and owner's equity ..	$162,860	**51.** _____	$146,470	**52.** _____

E. Find the current ratio. Round each ratio to the tenths position. 14.3 OBJECTIVE 2

Company	Current Assets	Current Liabilities	Current Ratio
53. Entech Sales & Service	$225,420	$105,825	_____
54. Metro Equipment Company	$66,610	$29,480	_____
55. Answer First	$85,340	$27,110	_____

F. Find the acid test ratio. Round the ratio to the tenths position. 14.3 OBJECTIVE 3

Company	Cash	Accounts Receivable	Accounts Payable	Acid-Test Ratio
56. Alco Door Repair	$25,000	$6,890	$12,000	_____
57. Little Beaver Drills	$88,920	$83,400	$55,000	_____
58. Lancaster & Associates	$101,000	$61,450	$22,700	_____

G. Calculate the return on investment. Show ratios as a percent of owner's equity. Round to the nearest whole percent. 14.3 OBJECTIVE 4

Company	Net Income	Owner's Equity	Return on Investment
59. Cowtown Storage	$40,575	$25,990	_____
60. Ambrosia Flowers & Gifts	$88,400	$55,900	_____
61. Pamper Yourself Salon	$109,000	$48,000	_____

H. Use Excel to create a vertical analysis of an income statement; to create a partial comparative balance sheet; and to calculate current ratio, acid test ratio, and return on investment ratio. 14.1 OBJECTIVE 5, 14.2 OBJECTIVE 5 14.3 OBJECTIVE 5

62. Retrieve the file *ch14qz01.xlsx*. Follow the directions. Save the file as *ch14qz01a.xlsx*.

63. Retrieve the file *ch14qz02.xlsx*. Follow the directions. Save the file as *ch14qz02a.xlsx*.

64. Retrieve the file *ch14qz03.xlsx*. Follow the directions. Save the file as *ch14qz03a.xlsx*.

Many businesses today are faced with trying to reduce costs and yet maintain a reasonable profit margin. Business statistics can play an important role in helping a business predict what direction to take to do both.

In this chapter, you will learn only a few of the basic methods used in business statistics. You will make calculations as well as create charts that illustrate your findings graphically.

ACTUARIAL ANALYST

Photo courtesy of Kyle Huss

Kyle Huss is an actuarial analyst for a multiregional human resources consulting firm. He performs calculations and runs studies to help companies plan the structure of their retirement and pension programs. This allows companies to ensure that they will have the proper funds for the retirement accounts of their employees. Kyle works with consultants and actuaries to analyze companies' financial risks during different periods of change. This could include large-scale decisions such as mergers and acquisitions within the company or the growth or the reduction in the number of employees.

Another main goal for an actuary when forecasting retirement structure is to guarantee that a company is compliant with the ever-changing standards of government and accounting regulations. Kyle works with 30 to 40 clients at any given time, so time management is essential when conducting research and running evaluations.

In order to become an accredited actuary, you must go through a rigorous exam process. Each of the five preliminary tests is topic-specific, covering subject areas such as financial mathematics and life contingencies. "Although I work specifically with practices related to retirement," Kyle says, "there are two other main silos of actuary work, life insurance and the property and causality side."

How Math is Used in Actuarial Analysis

Performing benefit calculations and organizing data in spreadsheets is fundamental to Kyle's role as an actuarial analyst. Kyle creates graphs and charts for an easy to understand display of information for presentations to clients. Kyle says, "I use graphs to display how numbers have shifted over the years, not where they currently stand." He says it is an easy way for a company to see how their liability might change as their population or rates change. It is also important for clients to see the extremes in their numbers. Kyle sorts large amounts of data in Excel to find the top and bottom five percent of data to show the outliers.

What Do You Think?

What skills do you need to improve in order to work as an actuarial analyst?

Math Skills Used

Addition

Subtraction

Percents

Time value of money

Other Skills Needed

Collaboration

Communication

Multitasking

Time management

OBJECTIVES

1. Identify terms used with calculating the mean, median, and mode.

2. Calculate the mean of a set of data.

3. Calculate the median of a set of data.

4. Calculate the mode of a set of data.

5. Use Excel to calculate the mean, median, and mode.

15.1 Measures of Central Tendency: Mean, Median, and Mode

OBJECTIVE 1 Identify terms used with calculating the mean, median, and mode.

The mean, median, and mode are different ways of finding the center of a set of data. That is why these three ways are called measures of central tendency. Some terms used with mean, median, and mode are the following.

Grouped Data   Numbers arranged into a group so they are more easily understood.

Mean   An average of a set of data.

Median   A number that is the middle value when numbers are arranged in ascending or descending order.

Mode   The value(s) in a set of data that occur most often.

Numerical Average   A value that represents a group of data.

Ordered Array   A list of numbers shown in order from the smallest number to the largest number.

Raw Data   Information in the form of facts and figures. Data is something that is known. It is a set of data that has not been manipulated or analyzed. Also called *ungrouped data*.

OBJECTIVE 2 Calculate the mean of a set of data.

You worked with averages when you were asked to average grades. A *numerical average* is a value that represents a group of data. In other words, the one average grade that you calculated was representative of all the grades you earned in a course. Businesses use averages to describe or represent a variety of situations. Suppose you were in charge of sales for a car dealership. If you were asked to present to the sales personnel a report on the overall sales of automobiles by salesperson for the first quarter of the year, you could show a listing of each salesperson's individual sales. A more easily understood report might be one that shows the average sales for each salesperson. These averages could be compared to generate discussion on successful sales techniques.

The *mean* (or average) is a common calculation used in business decision making. People usually say average rather than mean, but the two words mean the same thing. Study the following formula.

Mean = Sum of all values ÷ Number of all values

When working with sets of data, you often begin with *ungrouped* or *raw* data—data that has yet to be manipulated or analyzed. Raw data is ideal for calculating the mean because it does not need to be arranged in any particular order for the calculations to be completed.

EXAMPLE

Salaries are one of the greatest expenses a business incurs. Therefore, when making payroll decisions, a business should know the average salary paid for each job. Imagine you are a small business owner who has six employees doing the same job and making the following annual salaries: $14,500, $15,300, $16,800, $19,200, $22,400, and $22,500. Before considering raises, you may want to figure the average salary. Calculate your employee's average salary.

STEPS

1. Add the salaries to obtain a total.

   $14,500 + $15,300 + $16,800 + $19,200 + $22,400 + $22,500 = $110,700

2. Divide the total by the number of employees in this group. The result is the mean (average) salary for the group.

   $$\$110{,}700 \div 6 = \$18{,}450$$

You could think that $18,450 is an excellent salary for the job, and half the employees already make well above the mean. Based on other factors, you decide not to raise salaries for this quarter.

Note: When numbers appear in a data set more than once, a **weighted mean** is more meaningful. It differs from the previous procedures because you weigh each number by how often it occurs. To calculate the weighted mean, count the number of times each amount occurs (frequency), total the frequencies, total the amounts, and divide the amounts by the total of the frequencies.

Weighted mean = Sum of amounts ÷ Sum of frequencies

OBJECTIVE **3** **Calculate the median of a set of data.**

Business statistics can be interpreted to mean different things. The mean is often a poor indicator of the midpoint in a set of numbers. The *median* may be a better indicator of the middle of a set of numbers. It divides the set in half, with one-half of the numbers above the median (middle) and one-half below the median. Calculating the median requires that you work with numbers arranged in an ordered array. An *ordered array* is a list of numbers shown in order from the smallest number to the largest number.

Odd number array

When there is an odd number of values in the array, the middle value is the median. For example, for the numbers 1 to 7, 4 would be the median.

Assume you are purchasing T-shirts for your employees. You gather all the prices and decide that you want a midpriced T-shirt. Calculate the median value for the following prices.

$14.80, $27.50, $18.90, $12.50, $13.25, $15.00, $28.00, $14.50, $16.50, $19.95, $23.00, $17.50, $12.75

STEPS

1. Complete an ordered array by arranging the prices from the smallest to the largest.

$12.50	
$12.75	
$13.25	
$14.50	
$14.80	
$15.00	
$16.50	7th number
$17.50	
$18.90	
$19.95	
$23.00	
$27.50	
$28.00	

2. Count the values in the array. Then divide the total number by 2. Disregard any remainder.

$$13 \div 2 = 6$$

3. Add one to the result.

$$6 + 1 = 7$$

4. Count down the array to the 7th number. The 7th value is $16.50. So, the median is $16.50.

Even number array

When there is an even number of values in the array, the median is the average between the two middle numbers. For example, for the numbers 1 to 8, 4.5 is the median.

EXAMPLE

Use the previous example but delete $16.50 from the list of prices.

$14.80, $27.50, $18.90, $12.50, $13.25, $15.00, $28.00, $14.50, $19.95, $23.00, $17.50, $12.75

1. Complete an ordered array arranging the prices from the smallest to the largest.

$12.50
$12.75
$13.25
$14.50
$14.80
$15.00   6th number
$17.50   7th number
$18.90
$19.95
$23.00
$27.50
$28.00

2. Divide the total number in the array by 2.

$$12 \div 2 = 6$$

3. Count down to and identify the 6th and 7th numbers.

$$\$15.00 \text{ and } \$17.50$$

4. Calculate the average of the numbers in step 3.

$$(\$15.00 + \$17.50) \div 2 = \$32.50 \div 2 = \$16.25$$

The median of this set of numbers is $16.25.

OBJECTIVE 4 Calculate the mode of a set of data.

The *mode* is the number that occurs most often in a set of numbers. If all the values are different, as in the previous example, there is no mode. If the same number appears more than once, that number is the mode. If two sets of numbers appear more than once, each set is considered a mode. You do not need to arrange the numbers in an ordered array.

EXAMPLE

$$4, 5, 9, 3, 4, 6, 4, 10, 4, 7, 8, 12, 4, 2, 1$$

The mode is 4 since it is listed 5 times and no other number appears five times.

A set of data may have more than one mode if two numbers appear the same number of times.

EXAMPLE

$$7, 8, 15, 9, 3, 9, 8$$

Both 8 and 9 occur two times so they are both modes.

OBJECTIVE 5 Use Excel to calculate the mean, median, and mode.

Excel provides functions to calculate the mean (=AVERAGE), median (=MEDIAN), and mode (=MODE). Study Figure 15-1.

🔲 Retrieve the file **ch15pr01.xlsx**.

A. Calculate the mean for the set of numbers in Row 4.

   1. In Cell B5, key =AVERAGE(.

   2. Use the Pointing Method to select each of the 5 cells in Row 4, placing a comma between each cell address.

   3. Key a right parenthesis to close the formula and press Enter.

B. Calculate the median for the set of numbers in Row 14.

   1. In Cell B15, key =MEDIAN(.

   2. Use the Pointing Method to select each of the 5 cells in Row 14, placing a comma between each cell address.

   3. Key a right parenthesis to close the formula and press Enter.

C. Calculate the mode for the set of numbers in Row 24.

   1. In Cell B25, key =MODE(.

   2. Use the Pointing Method to select each of the 5 cells in Row 24, placing a comma between each cell address.

   3. Key a right parenthesis to close the formula and press Enter.

   4. Save the file as **ch15pr01a.xlsx**.

TIPS

Excel provides a searchable list of most of the functions (formulas) normally used in business. To view the functions in Excel, key = in the Formula bar, then click on the drop-down arrow to the left of the Formula bar. A list will appear. Click on More Functions. The Insert Function dialog box will appear. Select the desired function and enter the needed information. Excel will remember the most common functions you use in the drop-down list.

Figure 15-1

=AVERAGE, =MEDIAN, and =MODE Function in Excel

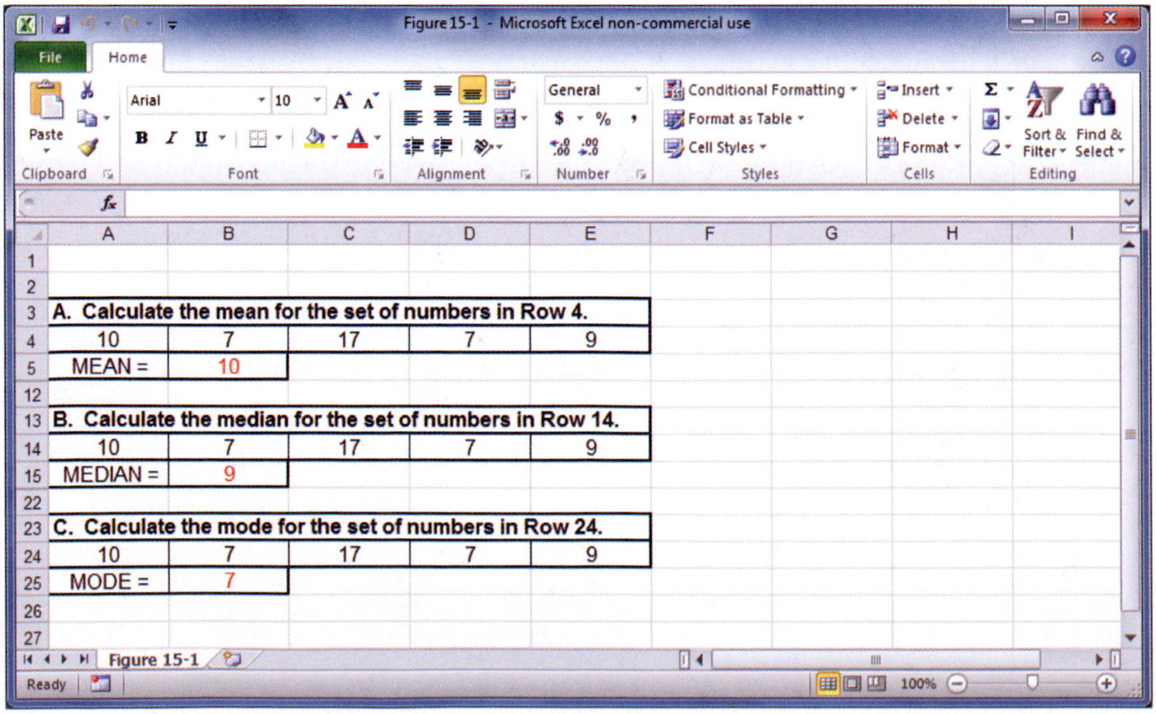

Name _____ Date _____

Directions   Complete the following problems. Write your answers in the blanks provided. Give answers to the nearest tenth.

A. Calculate the mean.   OBJECTIVE 2

1.   2, 7, 5, 8, 9, 2, 1, 6, 8, 4, 5   _____   6.   8, 9, 11, 9, 12, 15, 18, 20, 15   _____

2.   9, 10, 11, 15, 18, 12, 8, 7, 20   _____   7.   45, 22, 94, 36, 77, 28, 89, 11   _____

3.   1, 5, 1, 6, 8, 10, 15, 25, 45   _____   8.   104, 254, 870, 232, 119, 450   _____

4.   26, 32, 43, 12, 84, 36, 14, 10   _____   9.   26, 28, 29, 31, 42, 39, 29, 19   _____

5.   95, 88, 72, 65, 81, 90, 100, 70   _____   10.   5, 9, 12, 24, 56, 10, 34, 25, 6   _____

B. Calculate the median.   OBJECTIVE 3

11.   10, 14, 22, 15, 18, 20, 25   _____   16.   120, 132, 159, 146, 138, 161   _____

12.   45, 67, 55, 32, 98, 75, 41, 30   _____   17.   7, 19, 8, 17, 12, 4, 9, 3, 5, 6, 1   _____

13.   21, 23, 43, 45, 56, 87, 98   _____   18.   21, 23, 24, 28, 30, 32, 33, 22   _____

14.   8, 28, 32, 7, 9, 15, 19, 49   _____   19.   8, 2, 5, 3, 9, 10, 11, 19, 6, 7, 1   _____

15.   92, 101, 78, 59, 88, 110, 43   _____   20.   112, 119, 124, 133, 109, 117   _____

C. Calculate the mode.   OBJECTIVE 4

21.   12, 15, 17, 19, 12, 33, 45, 33, 25   _____   26.   501, 5001, 105, 1001, 1005, 5001   _____

22.   18, 92, 87, 102, 92, 77, 87, 92   _____   27.   9, 3, 7, 8, 2, 4, 8, 1, 6   _____

23.   1, 4, 6, 3, 5, 4, 7, 8, 4, 9, 2, 4, 11   _____   28.   21, 22, 28, 27, 25, 38, 28, 20, 33   _____

24.   1223, 1221, 2224, 1223, 1225   _____   29.   01, 07, 09, 02, 05, 03, 08, 01, 10   _____

25.   18, 19, 17, 15, 17, 21, 30, 16, 14   _____   30.   10, 30, 50, 60, 90, 30, 20, 40, 70   _____

D. Use Excel to calculate the mean, median, and mode.   OBJECTIVE 5

31.   Retrieve the file *ch15ex01.xlsx*. Follow the directions. Save the file as *ch15ex01a.xlsx*.

32.   Retrieve the file *ch15ex02.xlsx*. Follow the directions. Save the file as *ch15ex02a.xlsx*.

OBJECTIVES

1. Identify terms used with frequency distribution tables and graphs.

2. Create a frequency distribution table.

3. Use Excel to create a frequency distribution table.

4. Create a line graph.

5. Use Excel to create a line graph.

6. Create a bar graph.

7. Use Excel to create a bar graph.

8. Create a pie graph.

9. Use Excel to create a pie graph.

15.2 Frequency Distributions and Graphs

OBJECTIVE **1** Identify terms used with frequency distribution tables and graphs.

Here are some common terms used when working with frequency distribution tables and graphs.

Bar Graph   A graph that displays data using bars.

Pie Graph   Also called a pie chart, a 360° circle broken up into several pie-shaped parts to display data. This is sometimes called a circle graph.

Frequency Distribution Table   A table showing the number of times one or more numbers appear.

Graph   A visual presentation of numeric data.

Line Graph   Compares two variables of data along points on a line showing how the data changes.

***x*-axis**   The horizontal axis that measures units of time (such as days, weeks, months, or years).

***y*-axis**   The vertical axis that measures magnitude (such as dollars).

OBJECTIVE **2** Create a frequency distribution table.

In today's business world, a lot of money is spent on obtaining data. The next step is to analyze and present this data in a meaningful way. This section introduces how data is manipulated so it can be understood, and inferences can be drawn from what is shown. Common ways to present this data are frequency distribution tables and various graphs.

Large sets of numbers can be difficult to interpret. A way to analyze the data is to put the numbers in a table so you can identify how frequently a number occurs. This table is called a *frequency distribution table*. Study the raw data in the following example.

EXAMPLE

Jed, owner of Jed Golf Carts, Inc., believes he sells more golf carts to men and women who are over the age of 50 than he does to younger individuals. To determine whether this is true so he will know which group to market to in the coming season, Jed uses his database of past customers to determine at what age each person purchased his or her golf cart. Here are the ages of the individuals in raw data form.

25	36	28	62	44	36
55	48	33	48	32	56
43	54	59	55	25	25
64	21	65	32	60	59
68	39	70	40	41	48
41	67	41	56	27	32
27	50	45	60	32	67

STEPS

1. List the data from lowest to highest. List each number only once.

21	41	59
25	43	60
27	44	62
28	45	64
32	48	65
33	50	67
36	54	68
39	55	70
40	56	

2. Place a tally mark (|) beside a number each time it occurs in the data.

Age	Tally	Age	Tally	Age	Tally
21			41					59			
25					43			60			
27				44			62		
28			45			64		
32						48					65		
33			50			67			
36				54			68		
39			55				70		
40			56					

3. Simplify the table by grouping the data by age ranges of five each.

Age Range	Number of Tallies	Age Range	Number of Tallies
21 – 25	4	46 – 50	4
26 – 30	3	51 – 55	3
31 – 35	5	56 – 60	6
36 – 40	4	61 – 65	3
41 – 45	6	66 – 70	4

You can see from the regrouping that the largest age group is from 21 to 50 (26 occurrences), not over 50 (16 occurences). This information tells Jed he should market to the 50-and-under age group.

Excel provides a way to create tables and graphs. You are already familiar with how it is used to create a table.

Frequency distribution table   The purpose of a frequency distribution table is to help organize large amounts of data into a form that is more understandable. Excel is ideal for this use. Study the following example and steps for creating a frequency distribution table in Excel. Study Figure 15-2, which shows the =FREQUENCY formula which counts the number of test scores that fall within various ranges of scores.

> **EXAMPLE**
>
> Jonathan Biery, a college professor, averaged his students' final grades in his Business Math class. The grading scale he uses is less than 70, 71–80, 81–90, and 91–100. He is interested in knowing how many grades fell in each of these ranges. The following are the grades students received:
>
> | 78 | 89 | 65 | 72 | 95 | 82 | 88 | 70 | 98 | 80 | 56 | 89 |
> | 75 | 83 | 94 | 80 | 92 | 89 | 91 | 90 | 77 | 73 | 66 | 84 |

Figure 15-2

=FREQUENCY Formula Results

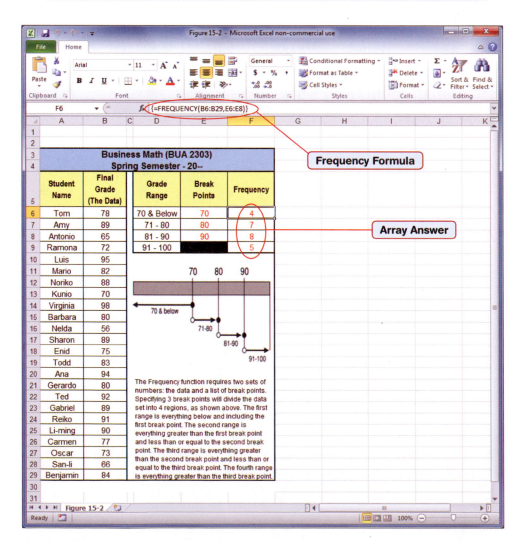

⊗ Retrieve the file *ch15pr02.xlsx*.

1. In Cell E6 enter 70, the first break point.

2. In Cell E7 enter 80, the second break point.

3. In Cell E8 enter 90, the third break point.

4. Select Cells F6 through F9. Key =FREQUENCY(B6:B29, E6:E8. Do NOT key the final parenthesis.

5. Press CTRL + SHIFT + Enter to apply the results of the Frequency formula to the selected cells.

6. Save the file as *ch15pr02a.xlsx*.

OBJECTIVE **4** Create a line graph.

A *line graph* compares two variables of data along points on a line, showing how the data changes. One variable is displayed along the horizontal axis (called the *x-axis*), which usually represents time (days, months, years), and one variable is shown along the vertical axis (called the *y-axis*), which displays sales, production units, money, or any value that changes.

EXAMPLE

Construct a line graph showing the increase in the installed base of Digital Subscriber Lines (DSL) over the past five years. Use the following data:

Year	DSL Lines
2007	5,000
2008	12,000
2009	14,000
2010	20,000
2011	25,000

STEPS

1. Draw an *x*-axis. Label it *Years*. Evenly space the time values along the *x*-axis. The time values are:

    2007   2008   2009   2010   2011

2. Draw a *y*-axis. Label it *Thousands*. Evenly space the amount values along the *y*-axis. The amount values are:

    0   5,000   10,000   15,000   20,000   25,000   30,000

3. Using the data table, place a dot (data point) where each amount and time value intersect. For example, place a dot to the right of 5,000 on the *y*-axis and above 2007 on the *x*-axis.

4. Connect the data points with straight lines, as shown in Figure 15-3.

Figure 15-3
Line Graph

TIPS

Graphs can often be misleading. Ask someone to look at your graph and tell you what it means in order to verify that the graph displays the information correctly.

TIPS

One advantage of line graphs is that two or more sets of data can be shown on the same graph.

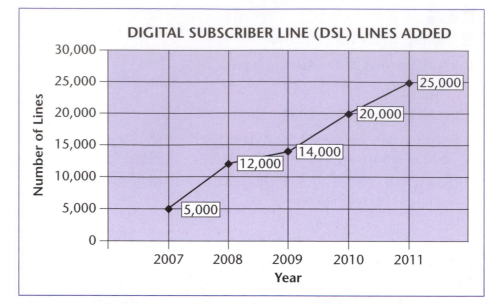

OBJECTIVE 5 Use Excel to create a line graph.

Excel provides a way to create line graphs. Study the following steps which show how to create a line graph using Excel. Use the data from Objective 4. To create a chart, go to the Insert tab. In the charts group, click the chart type you want to use. To see all available chart types, click any chart, and then click All Chart Types to display the Insert Chart dialog box shown in Figure 15-4.

Figure 15-4
Insert Chart Dialog Box

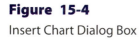

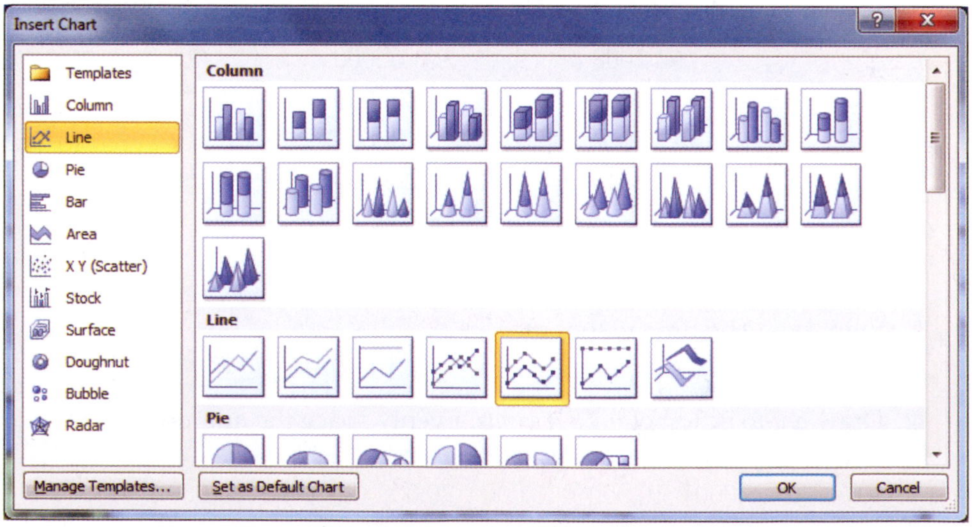

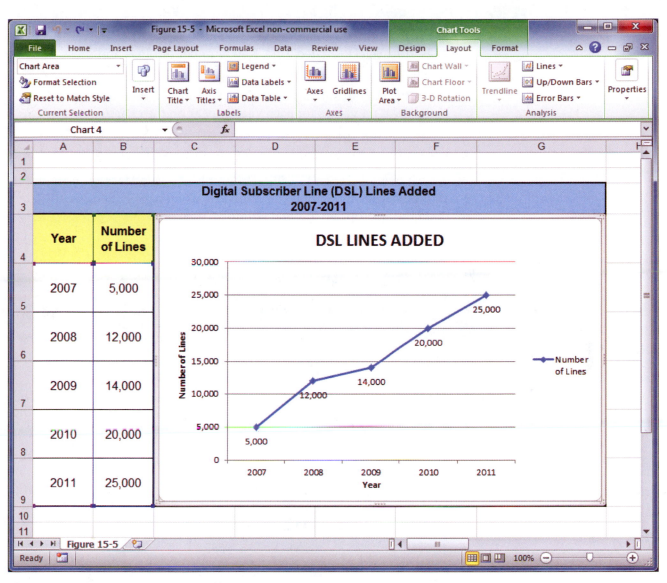

Figure 15-5

Line Graph in Excel

STEPS

Retrieve the file *ch15pr03.xlsx*.

1. Select Cells B4 through B9 by highlighting them.

2. Click the Insert tab. In the Chart Group, click "Line." Then hover over the various types of line graphs to display their titles. Click on the one named "Stacked line with Markers." A chart is displayed in the Excel spreadsheet.

3. Now the chart can be modified to meet your needs. Click anywhere on the chart and a new tab labeled Chart Tools will be displayed on the ribbon. This tab has three subtabs: Design, Layout, and Format. These allow modifications to any chart. Click the Design subtab. Click Select Data. For the Horizontal (Category) Axis Labels, click Edit. Highlight Cells A5 through A9. Then Click OK twice.

4. Select the Layout subtab. Click Axis Titles. Select Primary Horizontal Axis Title. Select Title Below Axis. Key Year and press Enter.

5. Select the Layout subtab. Click Axis Titles. Select Primary Vertical Axis Title. Select Rotated Title. Key Number of Lines and press Enter.

6. Select the Layout subtab. Click Data Labels. Select Below. This will make the data values for each year appear on the chart.

7. Because a title already exists in the chart, click once on the chart title to select it and then again to modify it. Key DSL LINES ADDED.

8. Adjust overall size and position of graph as needed. Make cosmetic changes as desired. Double click on any element of the graph to open the appropriate Format window.

9. Save the file as *ch15pr03a.xlsx*.

OBJECTIVE 6 Create a bar graph.

Bar graphs are an excellent way to present data that occur at one time. Examples include surveys, inventories, and so on. The horizontal *x*-axis is usually the base of the bars and displays the type of data being graphed. The vertical *y*-axis is the scale that is a measure of the frequency or amounts of the data. The bars can be shown horizontally or vertically.

EXAMPLE

Construct a bar graph showing the fluctuations in the price of gold in the United States last year. Use the following data:

Month	Price ($)	Month	Price ($)	Month	Price ($)
JAN	875	MAY	882	SEP	955
FEB	915	JUN	982	OCT	1,005
MAR	938	JUL	936	NOV	1,062
APR	915	AUG	960	DEC	1,198

STEPS

1. Draw an *x*-axis. Label it *January – December, 20--*. Evenly space the time values along the *x*-axis. The time values are:

   JAN, FEB, MAR, APR, MAY, JUN, JUL, AUG, SEP, OCT, NOV, DEC

2. Draw a *y*-axis. Label it *Price Per Troy Ounce ($US)*. Evenly space the price values along the *y*-axis. The price values are:

   870, 900, 930, 960, 990, 1020, 1,050, 1,070, 1,100, 1,130, 1,160, 1,190, 1,220

3. Add the bars with their base on the *x*-axis above each date, making their height correspond with the price on that date.

4. Add the following labels:

   Title: U.S. GOLD PRICES
   Legend: Gold

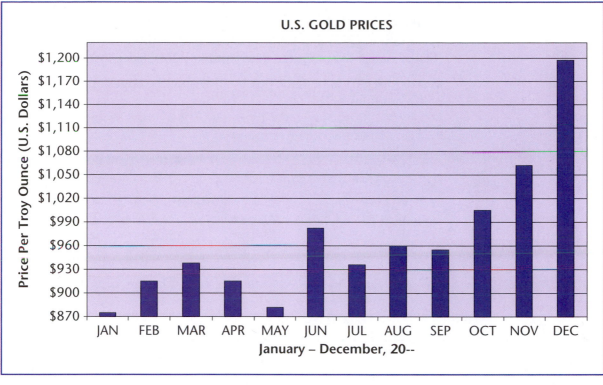

U.S. GOLD PRICES

Figure 15-6

Bar Graph

OBJECTIVE **7** Use Excel to create a bar graph.

Excel provides a way to create bar graphs. Study the following steps which show how to create the bar graph in Figure 15-7 using Excel. Use the data from the example in Objective 6.

STEPS

Retrieve the file *ch15pr04.xlsx*.

1. Select Cells A4 through B16 by highlighting them.

2. Click the Insert tab. In the Charts group, click on Column. Pictures of various column graphs (vertical bar graphs) will drop down. Hover over the pictures with the mouse to see the names of the graphs. Select Stacked Column.

3. A bar graph is created and can be modified. Because a title already exists, click once on the title to select it and then again to modify it. Key U.S. GOLD PRICES.

4. Click the Layout subtab on the Chart Tools tab. Click Axis Titles. Select Primary Horizontal Axis Title. Select Title Below Axis. Key January-December, 20-- and press enter.

5. Click the Layout subtab. Click Axis Titles. Select Primary Vertical Axis Title. Select Rotated Title. Key Price Per Troy Ounce (U.S. dollars). Press enter.

6. To change the *y*-axis scale, double-click the numbers on the *y*-axis to get the Format Axis dialog box. On the Axis Options menu, change Minimum to Fixed and key 870. Change Maximum to Fixed and key 1,230. Change Major unit to Fixed and key 30. Click Close.

7. Resize the chart to fit in the box by dragging the edges of the chart with your mouse.

8. Save the file as *ch15pr04a.xlsx.*

Figure 15-7

Bar Graph in Excel

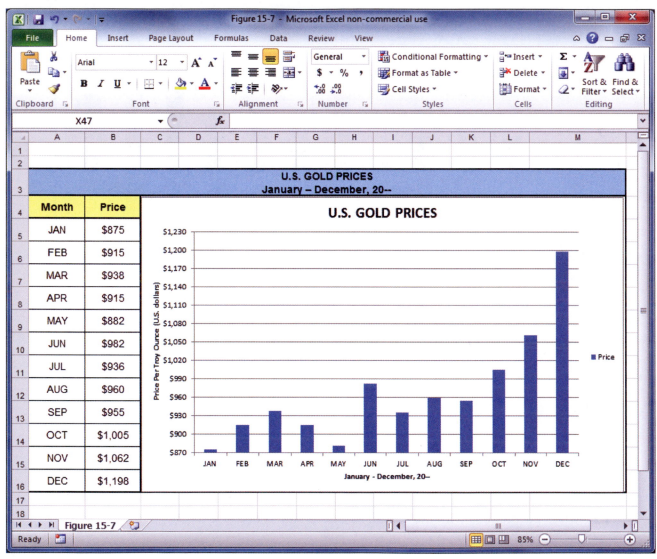

Pie graphs are excellent illustrations of the division of 100%. The whole, 100%, is the circle, and the pie-shaped sections are the parts of the whole. The total of all the parts must equal 100%.

EXAMPLE

Most people have had to cope with setting a monthly budget so money is available for all the things they need. Construct a circle graph showing monthly expenditures. Use the following data:

Expenditure	Amount ($)
Rent	550
Utilities	110
Phone	28
Credit Cards	80
Car Payment	375
Groceries	250
Gasoline	100
Entertainment	150
Savings	75
TOTAL	**$1,718**

STEPS

1. Use the percentage formula Rate = Part ÷ Base to calculate each pie-shaped component of the graph. Divide each part (rent, utilities, and so on) by the total amount of all expenditures to obtain the percent. Give answers to the nearest hundredth of a percent.

Rent	=	$550 ÷ $1,718 = 0.3201 or 32.01%
Utilities	=	$110 ÷ $1,718 = 0.0640 or 6.40%
Phone	=	$28 ÷ $1,718 = 0.0163 or 1.63%

Continue with the remainder of the expenditures.

2. A full circle is 360°, which represents 100% in the pie graph. Multiply each component's percent by 360° to determine how many degrees each component's slice of the pie will be. Round to the nearest whole degree.

Rent	=	0.3201 × 360° = 115°
Utilities	=	0.0640 × 360° = 23°
Phone	=	0.0163 × 360° = 6°

Continue with the remainder of the expenditures.

3. Use a compass to draw a circle. Mark the center.

4. Use a protractor to mark the degrees on the circle each component represents, indicating the component's beginning and ending points on the edge of the circle.

5. Create each slice of the pie by drawing straight lines from each point marked on the edge of the circle to the center.

6. Name, color, or shade each component of the pie graph, as shown in Figure 15-8.

Figure 15-8

Pie Graph

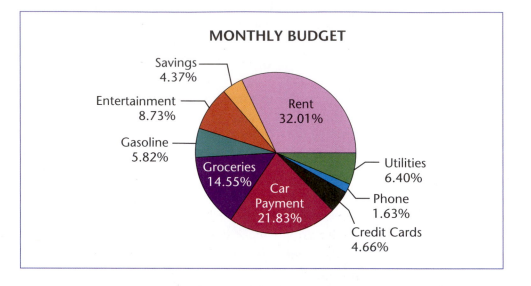

OBJECTIVE 9 **Use Excel to create a pie graph.**

Excel provides a way to create pie graphs. Study the following steps which show how to create the pie graph in Figure 15-9 using Excel. Use the data from the previous Objective.

STEPS

Retrieve the file *ch15pr05.xlsx*.

1. Select Cells A6 through B14 by highlighting them.

2. Click the Insert tab. In the Charts group, then click on Pie. Pictures of various pie graphs will drop down. Hover over each picture with the mouse to see the names of the types of pie graphs. Click on Pie.

3. In the Layout subtab of the Chart Tools, Click on Chart Title, then select Above Chart. Add Chart Title: MONTHLY BUDGET.

4. Click the Layout subtab in Chart Tools. Click Data Labels. Select More Data Label Options to get the Format Data labels dialog box. On the Label Options menu, click Category Name to add a check mark, click Value to remove the check from the box. Click Percentage to add a check mark. Show Leader Lines should already be checked. Click Best Fit under Label Position. Click Close. Click the legend at the right and press the delete key.

5. On the graph, double-click one of the data labels (such as 22%) to open the Format Data Labels dialog box window. Click the Number menu. Select Percentage. Key 2 in Decimal Places and click close. Repeat this procedure for each data label.

6. Adjust the overall size and position of graph as needed. Make cosmetic changes as desired. Double click on any element of the graph to open the appropriate Format window.

7. Save the file as *ch15pr05a.xlsx*.

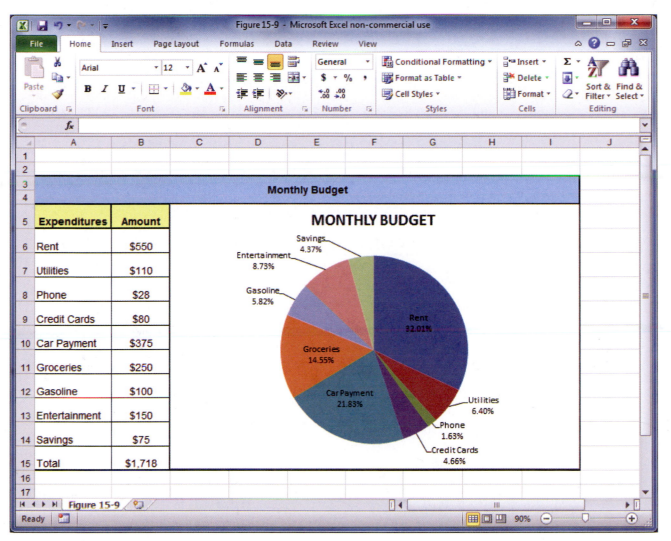

Figure 15-9

Pie Graph in Excel

Name _____ *Date* _____

Directions Complete the following problems. Write your answers in the blanks provided.

A. Manually create frequency distribution tables. OBJECTIVE 2

You are the manager of the Finger Lickin' Good fast-food restaurant. You hire several college students. Last month they worked the following total hours.

65	56	88	32	56	75	48	88	56	32
73	48	56	88	72	36	40	48	73	56
40	36	32	56	75	88	48	40	50	56

Group the hours worked into six equal classes (0–39, 40–49, 50–59, 60–69, 70–79, 80–89).

1. 0–39 _____ 2. 40–49 _____

3. 50–59 _____ 4. 60–69 _____

5. 70–79 _____ 6. 80–89 _____

Calculate the mean of the ungrouped data to the nearest tenth. 7. _____

You are the finance manager for the Mega Construction Company. You have been asked to create a report for management that shows the hourly wages for first-line supervisors. The following are the hourly wages.

$9.90	$12.40	$13.50	$10.10	$11.25
$13.00	$10.50	$9.90	$11.25	$12.40
$12.40	$10.50	$9.90	$11.25	$13.50
$13.00	$13.50	$10.50	$12.40	$11.25
$12.40	$10.10	$9.90	$11.25	$10.50
$10.50	$13.00	$10.50	$12.40	$13.00

Group the wages into five-equal size classes ($9.01–$10.00, $10.01–$11.00, $11.01–$12.00, $12.01–$13.00, $13.01–$14.00).

8. $9.01–$10.00 _____

9. $10.01–$11.00 _____

10. $11.01–$12.00 _____

11. $12.01–$13.00 _____

12. $13.01–$14.00 _____

Calculate the mean salary to the nearest hundredth. 13. _____

The following are the scores made by students on a chemistry exam.

78	88	98	98	77	90	82	99	93	82	80
65	87	45	95	70	69	85	71	67	80	45
98	57	63	73	79	81	92	70	68	77	84

Use the numbers to complete the following table. Enter the number of grades that fall into each range.

Score Ranges	Frequency	
0–50	14.	_____
51–60	15.	_____
61–70	16.	_____
71–80	17.	_____
81–90	18.	_____
91–100	19.	_____

Calculate the mean to the nearest whole number.   20. _____

Identify the mode(s).   21. _____

B. Create a line, a bar, and a pie graph.

22. Create a line graph using the data from the chemistry exam above.   **OBJECTIVE 4**

Title the graph CHEMISTRY 1303 – SECTION 14777

Title the *x*-axis: Student Number

Title the *y*-axis: Grade

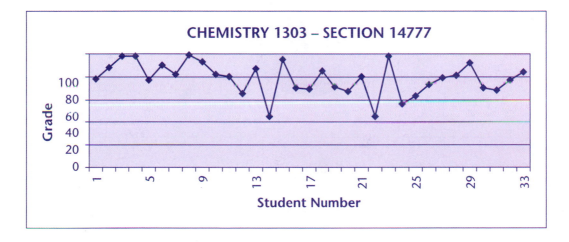

23. Create a bar graph using the Score Ranges and Frequency shown in answers 14-19.

Title the graph: CHEMISTRY 1303 – GRADE FREQUENCY

Title the *x*-axis: Grade Range

Title the *y*-axis: Grade Frequency

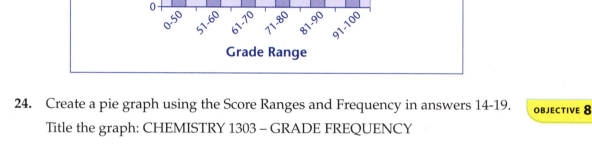

24. Create a pie graph using the Score Ranges and Frequency in answers 14-19.

Title the graph: CHEMISTRY 1303 – GRADE FREQUENCY

Show each pie slice with the grade range and percent.

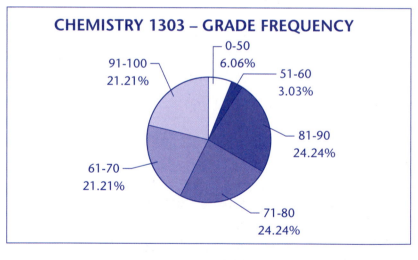

C. **Use Excel to create a frequency distribution table, a line graph, a bar graph, and a pie graph.**

25. Retrieve the file *ch15ex03.xlsx*. Follow the directions. Save the file as *ch15ex03a.xlsx*.

26. Retrieve the file *ch15ex04.xlsx*. Follow the directions. Save the file as *ch15ex04a.xlsx*.

27. Retrieve the file *ch15ex05.xlsx*. Follow the directions. Save the file as *ch15ex05a.xlsx*.

28. Retrieve the file *ch15ex06.xlsx*. Follow the directions. Save the file as *ch15ex06a.xlsx*.

15.3 Measures of Dispersion

OBJECTIVES
1. Identify terms used with measures of dispersion.
2. Calculate the range.
3. Calculate the standard deviation.
4. Use Excel to calculate the range.
5. Use Excel to calculate the standard deviation.

OBJECTIVE 1 Identify terms used with measures of dispersion.

You should become familiar with the following terms used with dispersion.

Measure of dispersion A number that describes how the numbers of a set of data are spread out or dispersed within the set.

Range The difference between the highest and lowest values in a group of values or set of data.

Standard deviation The measure of the spread of data around the mean (average) in a data set.

OBJECTIVE 2 Calculate the range.

Two measures of dispersion are the *range* and the *standard deviation*. The range is the difference between the greatest and least numbers—the two extremes—in a set of data. It is the simplest measure of dispersion. The second measure of dispersion you will learn about in this section is standard deviation. Standard deviation measures the spread of data around the mean (average).

You often need to know how data is scattered, or spread, within a set of data. For instance, a common practice in hiring procedures is to ask each member of an interviewing committee to rank each applicant's ability on a scale of 1 to 5. Another example is using a similar ranking for job performance to determine raises and promotions. Study the following formula for the range.

Range = Greatest value – Least value

If you were talking about the weather and said the highest temperature in June was 95°F and the lowest °F temperature was 68°F, the range would be the difference between the two numbers—27.

High temperature	=	95
Low temperature	=	$-$ 68
Range	=	27

If during the period, temperatures dropped drastically or warmed considerably, these changes would have an effect on the range. Because of the effect variables can have on a range, the range can provide only a general idea of the spread of values in a data set.

Standard deviation measures the spread of data around the mean. To calculate standard deviation, begin by calculating the mean. Once you know how far a number deviates from the mean, you can make comparisons. An example might be that a student believes a test was too difficult for a class. The teacher could calculate how well each class member did compared to the average grade (mean). This might be a basis for discussion and understanding.

EXAMPLE

Find the standard deviation for the following set of data.

$$25, 44, 51, 59, 63$$

STEPS

1. Calculate the mean (average) of the set of data.

$$25 + 44 + 51 + 59 + 63 = 242$$
$$242 \div 5 = 48.4 = 48 \quad \text{rounded}$$

2. Calculate the deviation for each number by subtracting each number from the mean.

$$25 - 48 \quad = \quad -23$$
$$44 - 48 \quad = \quad -4$$
$$51 - 48 \quad = \quad 3$$
$$59 - 48 \quad = \quad 11$$
$$63 - 48 \quad = \quad 15$$

3. Square each answer (deviation) found in step 2. To square a number, multiply it by itself.

$$(-23) \times (-23) \quad = \quad 529$$
$$(-4) \times (-4) \quad = \quad 16$$
$$3 \times 3 \quad = \quad 9$$
$$11 \times 11 \quad = \quad 121$$
$$15 \times 15 \quad = \quad 225$$

4. Add all of the squared deviations.

$$529 + 16 + 9 + 121 + 225 = 900$$

5. Divide the sum of the squared deviations by the total number of deviations minus 1.

$$900 \div 4 = 225$$

6. Find the square root of the answer in step 5 using Table 15-1. (The square root is a number that, when multiplied by itself, equals the amount shown inside the square root symbol.)

$$\sqrt{225} = 15 \quad \text{standard deviation}$$

TIPS

Remember in Algebra a negative number times a negative number equals a positive number.

TIPS

When using a calculator to figure standard deviation, your decimal places can vary from the manual method due to the number of decimal places used in your calculations.

CHAPTER 15 BUSINESS STATISTICS

Number	Sq. Root	Number	Sq. Root	Number	Sq. Root	Number	Sq. Root
150 – 151	12.2	180 – 182	13.4	214 – 216	14.6	250 – 252	15.8
152 – 153	12.3	183 – 184	13.5	217 – 219	14.7	253 – 255	15.9
154 – 156	12.4	185 – 187	13.6	220 – 222	14.8	256 – 259	16.0
157 – 158	12.5	188 – 190	13.7	223 – 224	14.9	260 – 262	16.1
159 – 161	12.6	191 – 193	13.8	225 – 228	15.0	263 – 265	16.2
162 – 163	12.7	194 – 195	13.9	229 – 231	15.1	266 – 268	16.3
164 – 166	12.8	196 – 198	14.0	232 – 234	15.2	269 – 272	16.4
167 – 168	12.9	199 – 201	14.1	235 – 237	15.3	273 – 275	16.5
169 – 171	13.0	202 – 204	14.2	238 – 240	15.4	276 – 278	16.6
172 – 174	13.1	205 – 207	14.3	241 – 243	15.5	279 – 282	16.7
175 – 176	13.2	208 – 210	14.4	244 – 246	15.6	283 – 285	16.8
177 – 179	13.3	211 – 213	14.5	247 – 249	15.7	286 – 288	16.9

Table 15-1

Partial Square Root Table (rounded to the nearest tenth)

OBJECTIVE **4** **Use Excel to calculate the range.**

Calculating the range in Excel is done with a basic operation since it involves simply finding the greatest and least values and completing a subtraction problem. Study Figure 15-10 showing the range of the average high and low temperatures in Phoenix, Arizona. The range is calculated by using the functions =MAXA (to find the highest value) and =MINA (to find the lowest value) and then subtracting the highest figure from the lowest figure in each column.

> **TIPS**
>
> *The maximum (MAXA) and minimum (MINA) functions are available in Excel's list of functions found in the drop-down menu after keying = in the Formula bar.*

STEPS

Retrieve the file *ch15pr06.xlsx*.

1. Enter a formula in Cell B17 to find the greatest high temperature. Key =MAXA(B5:B16). Press Enter.

2. Enter a formula in Cell B18 to find the least high temperature. Key =MINA(B5:B16). Press Enter.

3. Enter a formula in Cell B19 to find the range of average high temperatures. (Range = Greatest value – Least value)

4. Enter a formula in Cell D17 to find the greatest low temperature. Key =MAXA(D5:D16). Press Enter.

5. Enter a formula in Cell D18 to find the least low temperature. Key =MINA(D5:D16). Press Enter.

6. Enter a formula in Cell D19 to find the range of average low temperatures. (Range = Greatest value – Least value)

7. Save the file as *ch15pr06a.xls*.

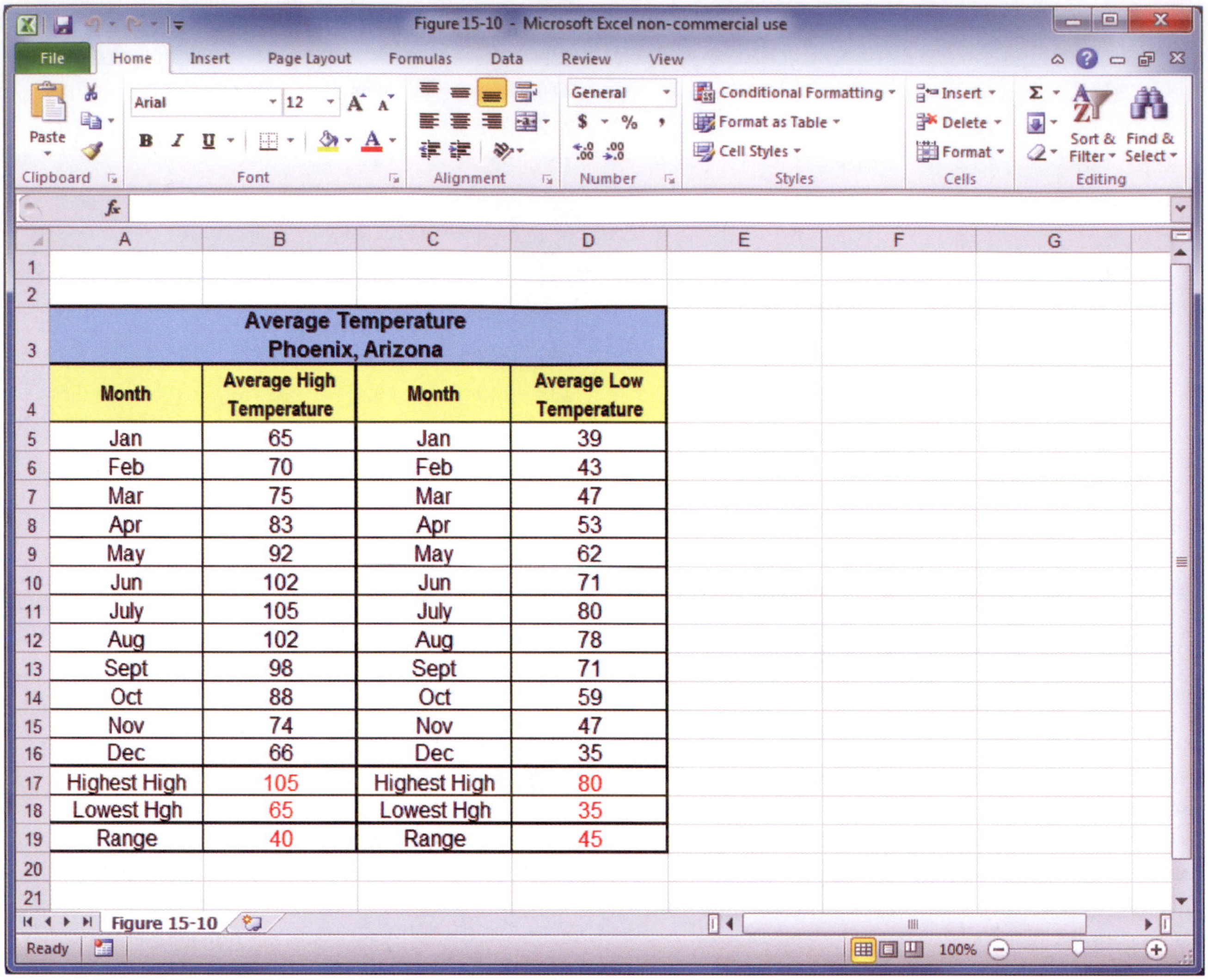

	A	B	C	D
3	Average Temperature Phoenix, Arizona			
4	Month	Average High Temperature	Month	Average Low Temperature
5	Jan	65	Jan	39
6	Feb	70	Feb	43
7	Mar	75	Mar	47
8	Apr	83	Apr	53
9	May	92	May	62
10	Jun	102	Jun	71
11	July	105	July	80
12	Aug	102	Aug	78
13	Sept	98	Sept	71
14	Oct	88	Oct	59
15	Nov	74	Nov	47
16	Dec	66	Dec	35
17	Highest High	105	Highest High	80
18	Lowest Hgh	65	Lowest Hgh	35
19	Range	40	Range	45

Figure 15-10
Calculating the Range

OBJECTIVE 5 Use Excel to calculate the standard deviation.

Excel provides the function =STDEV to calculate the standard deviation. Study Figure 15-11.

STEPS

Retrieve the file *ch15pr07.xlsx*.

1. Enter a formula in Cell B25 to compute the standard deviation. Key =STDEV(B5:B24). Press Enter.
2. Format Cell B25 for Number. Set Decimal places to 1.
3. Save the file as *ch15pr07a.xlsx*.

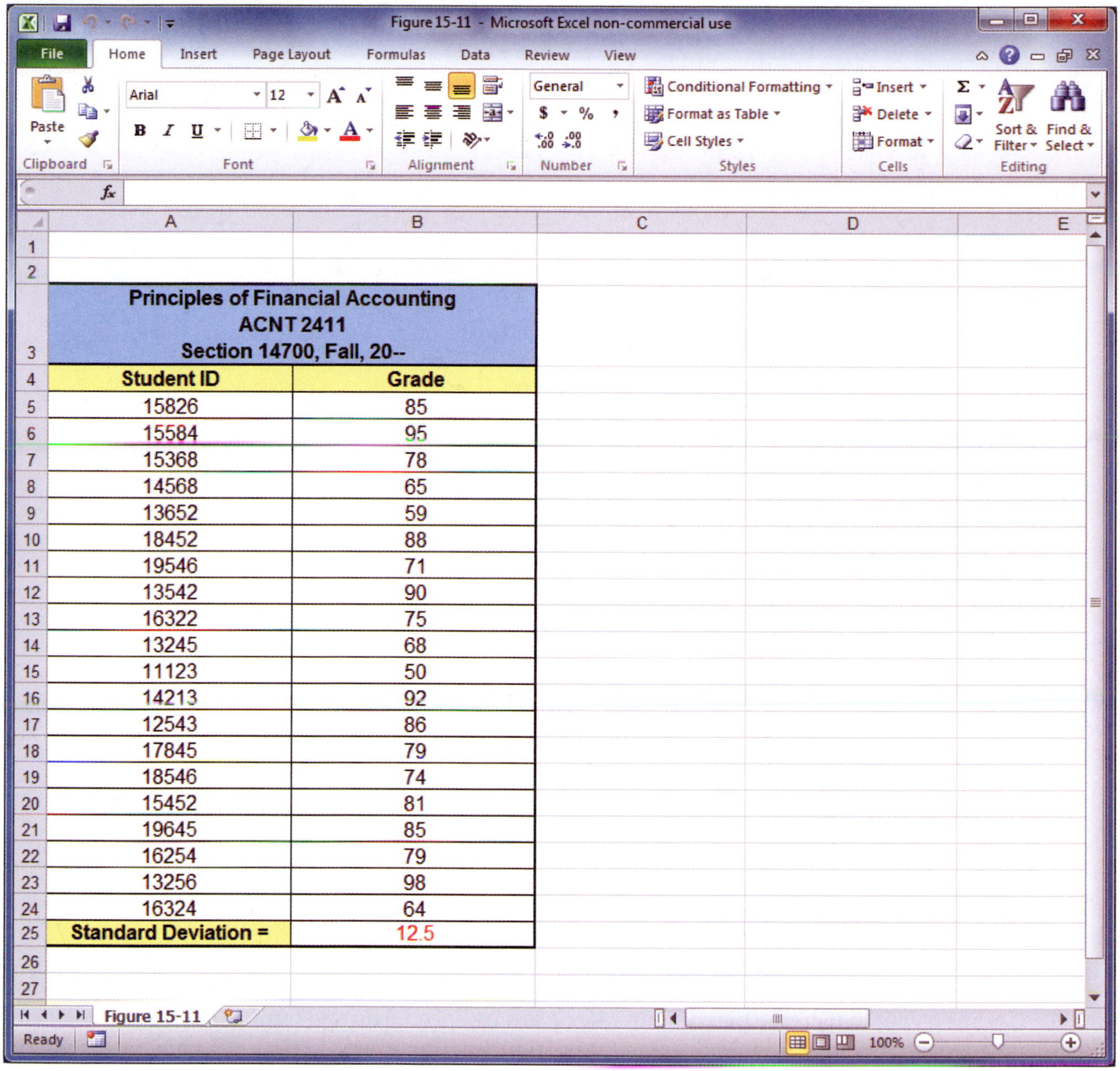

Principles of Financial Accounting ACNT 2411 Section 14700, Fall, 20--	
Student ID	**Grade**
15826	85
15584	95
15368	78
14568	65
13652	59
18452	88
19546	71
13542	90
16322	75
13245	68
11123	50
14213	92
12543	86
17845	79
18546	74
15452	81
19645	85
16254	79
13256	98
16324	64
Standard Deviation =	12.5

Figure 15-11

Calculating the Standard Deviation

Name _____   Date _____

Directions   Complete the following problems. Write your answers in the blanks provided.

A. Calculate the range.   OBJECTIVE 2

1. The girls' basketball team scored the following points in the first ten games of the season. What is the range of the points?

| 67 | 75 | 88 | 89 | 77 | 82 | 94 | 101 | 90 | 78 |

   Range: _____

2. Han Nugyen made ten trips from Dallas to Houston. His driving times were as follows. What is the range of his driving times?

5.6 hours	5 hours	4.9 hours	5.1 hours	4.8 hours
5.3 hours	5.2 hours	4.7 hours	4.3 hours	6.0 hours

   Range: _____

3. Sharon walked two miles each morning for a week. The minutes it took her to walk are as follows. What is the range of minutes?

30 minutes	25 minutes	20 minutes	35 minutes	45 minutes
28 minutes	32 minutes			

   Range: _____

4. Randy races dirt bikes. His times on his favorite track are as follows. What is the range of his times?

12.5 minutes	10.2 minutes	14.4 minutes	11.9 minutes
13.8 minutes	9.9 minutes	13.6 minutes	10.1 minutes

   Range: _____

5. Josh is trying to increase his computer keyboarding speed. His one-minute practice timings are as follows. What is his words-per-minute (wpm) range?

57.2 wpm	45.9 wpm	50.1 wpm	68.9 wpm	75 wpm	49 wpm
66.9 wpm	59.8 wpm	72.0 wpm	63.4 wpm	76 wpm	50 wpm

   Range: _____

6. The following are toy sales for a department store for one week. What is the range of sales?

$18,200.30	$15,900.25	$17,821.22	$18,203.25
$16,890.45	$17,909.50	$18,750.45	

   Range: _____

B. Calculate standard deviation for the following sets of data. OBJECTIVE **3**

7. 20, 25, 32, 44, 50

   Standard Deviation: _____

8. 31, 43, 44, 61, 65

   Standard Deviation: _____

9. 52, 33, 28, 35, 69

   Standard Deviation: _____

10. 27, 38, 49, 55, 65

    Standard Deviation: _____

11. 20, 30, 36, 50, 55

    Standard Deviation: _____

12. 25, 28, 34, 41, 63

    Standard Deviation: _____

13. 61, 35, 39, 42, 64

    Standard Deviation: _____

14. 28, 66, 43, 47, 59

    Standard Deviation: _____

15. 20, 30, 40, 50, 60

    Standard Deviation: _____

16. 22, 28, 30, 56, 45

    Standard Deviation: _____

C. Use Excel to calculate the range and standard deviation. OBJECTIVES **3, 4**

17. Retrieve the file *ch15ex07.xlsx*. Follow the directions. Save the file as *ch15ex07a.xlsx*.

18. Retrieve the file *ch15ex08.xlsx*. Follow the directions. Save the file as *ch15ex08a.xlsx*.

Chapter Review and Assessment

KEY TERMS

bar graph	mean	range
circle graph	measure of dispersion	raw data
frequency distribution table	median	standard deviation
graph	mode	weighted mean
grouped data	numerical average	*x*-axis
line graph	ordered array	*y*-axis

CONCEPTS	EXAMPLES
15.1 Calculate the mean of a set of data. The mean is the sum of all values divided by the number of all values. Use =AVERAGE formula in Excel. To calculate mean: 1. Add the data values. 2. Divide by the number of data values.	Bowling scores: $$\frac{200 + 175 + 189 + 166 + 180}{5}$$ = 182 team average
15.1 Calculate the median of a set of data. The median is the middle value when numbers are arranged in ascending or descending order. Use =MEDIAN formula in Excel. **Odd Number Array** 1. Complete an ordered array by arranging the values from the least to the greatest. 2. Divide the total number in the array by 2. Ignore the remainder. 3. Add one. 4. Count down the array that number of times. **Even Number Array** 1. Complete an ordered array by arranging the values from the least to the greatest. 2. Divide the total number in the array by 2. 3. Identify the two middle values. 4. Calculate the average of the numbers in step 3.	**Odd Number Array** 19, 16, 21, 12, 18, 21, 35 1. The order is: 12, 16, 18, 19, 21, 21, 35. 2. $7 \div 2 = 3.5$. Ignore the remainder. 3. $3 + 1 = 4$ 4. The median is the 4th value, 19. **Even Number Array** 6, 15, 10, 4, 4, 13 1. The order is: 4, 4, 6, 10, 13, 15. 2. $6 \div 2 = 3$ 3. The middle numbers are 6 and 10. 4. $6 + 10 = 16$; $16 \div 2 = 8$; the median is 8.

CONCEPTS	EXAMPLES
15.1 Calculate the mode of a set of data. The mode is the number that occurs most often in a set of data. Use =MODE formula in Excel.	7, 3, 5, 1, 3, 2, 3 Because 3 is the number that occurs most often, it is the mode.

15.2 Create a frequency distribution table.

Use =FREQUENCY formula in Excel.

1. List the data from least to greatest.
2. Place a tally mark (|) beside a number each time it occurs in the data.
3. Simplify the grouping of the data if necessary.

Number of doughnuts consumed after the meeting.

1, 5, 3, 5, 7, 4, 5, 3

No.	Tally	Frequency
1	|	1
3	||	2
4	|	1
5	|||	3
7	|	1

15.2 Create a line graph.

A line graph compares two variables on a line and shows trends.

Use the Insert tab and Charts group to select a line graph type in Excel.

Wages from 2003 through 2005.

2003 – $12.50

2004 – $12.75

2005 – $13.00

15.2 Create a bar graph.

In a bar graph, the height of the bar represents frequency. A bar graph can be vertical or horizontal.

Use the Insert tab and Charts group to select a bar or column graph type in Excel.

Record of ice cream sales by flavor.

CONCEPTS	EXAMPLES
15.2 Create a pie graph.	Survey of what refreshments the staff prefers
In a pie graph, the circle equals 360°. Each slice equals a percent of 360°. All slices must total 360°.	
Use the Insert tab and Charts group to select a pie graph type in Excel.	

RESULTS OF STAFF SURVEY

- ■ Doughnuts
- ■ Cookies
- ▫ Cake

25% 15% 60%

15.3 Calculate the range.

Range = Greatest value – Least value

Use =MAXA function in Excel to find the greatest value.
Use =MINA function in Excel to find the least value.

Use a subtraction formula in Excel to find the range.

25, 35, 43, 53

MAXA(25, 35, 43, 53) = 53
MINA(25, 35, 43, 53) = 25

Greatest value – Least value = Range
          53   –   25   =   28   range

15.3 Calculate the standard deviation.

Standard deviation measures the spread of data around the mean.

Use =STDEV formula in Excel.

1. Calculate the mean (average) of the set of data.

2. Calculate the deviation for each number by subtracting each number from the mean.

3. Square each answer (deviation) found in step 2.

4. Add all of the squared deviations.

5. Divide the sum of the squared deviations by the total number of deviations minus 1.

6. Find the square root of the answer in step 5.

53, 32, 72, 65, 35

1. 53 + 32 + 72 + 65 + 38 = 260; 260 ÷ 5 = 52

2. 53 − 52 = 1; 32 −52 = −20; 72 −52 = 20;
   65 −52 = 13; 38 −52 = −14

3. 1 x 1 = 1; (−20) x (−20) = 400; 20 x 20 = 400;
   13 x 13 = 169; (−14) x (−14) = 196

4. 1 + 400 + 400 + 169 + 196 = 1,166

5. 1,166 ÷ 4 = 291.5

6. $\sqrt{291.5} \approx 17.07$

Chapter 15 Review Exercises

Name _____   Date _____

Directions   Complete the following problems. Write your answers in the blanks provided. Give answers to the nearest tenth.

A. Calculate the mean.   `15.1 OBJECTIVE 2`

1.   3, 7, 5, 10, 9, 2, 1, 6, 8, 4, 5   _____

2.   17, 10, 11, 15, 18, 12, 8, 7, 20   _____

3.   20, 32, 53, 12, 84, 36, 14, 10   _____

4.   85, 88, 72, 65, 81, 60, 100, 70   _____

5.   55, 22, 94, 56, 77, 58, 89, 11   _____

6.   124, 234, 570, 232, 119, 450   _____

B. Calculate the median.   `15.1 OBJECTIVE 3`

7.   30, 14, 22, 15, 18, 20, 25   _____

8.   45, 67, 55, 32, 28, 75, 41, 30   _____

9.   8, 28, 32, 7, 9, 15, 19, 29   _____

10.   92, 82, 78, 59, 88, 90, 43   _____

11.   7, 10, 8, 13, 12, 4, 9, 3, 5, 6, 1   _____

12.   112, 119, 124, 143, 109, 117   _____

C. Calculate the mode.   `15.1 OBJECTIVE 4`

13.   12, 15, 17, 25, 12, 33, 25, 30, 25   _____

14.   18, 92, 87, 65, 35, 77, 87, 92   _____

15.   16, 19, 16, 15, 17, 21, 30, 16, 14   _____

16.   304, 308, 304, 305, 307, 304   _____

17.   9, 3, 1, 8, 2, 4, 1, 1, 6   _____

18.   60, 20, 50, 60, 90, 30, 20, 40, 60, 20   _____

D. Create frequency distribution tables manually. 15.2 OBJECTIVE 2

You are the manager of Haley's Dry Cleaners. You hire several college students to work for you part-time. Last month they worked the following total hours.

45	65	29	32	21	43	39	49	55	32
37	44	25	20	44	36	28	50	37	51
30	42	32	15	57	51	19	23	40	56

Group the hours worked into six classes (1–20, 21–30, 31–40, 41–50, 51–60, 61–70).

		Tally	Frequency
19.	1–20	_____	_____
20.	21–30	_____	_____
21.	31–40	_____	_____
22.	41–50	_____	_____
23.	51–60	_____	_____
24.	61–70	_____	_____

Calculate the mean of the ungrouped data to the nearest tenth.

25. _____

You are the sales manager for Prestige Ford in Cheyenne, Wyoming. You have been asked to create a report for management that shows September sales by sales persons for the store's three locations. Here are the sales figures.

$5,800	$12,300	$7,100	$1,500	$4,900	$8,200
$10,500	$3,250	$9,300	$11,990	$4,100	$5,600
$1,800	$2,900	$7,500	$2,100	$6,900	$14,700
$10,800	$6,200	$5,900	$7,300	$9,150	$16,800

Group the sales into four equal-size classes ($1–$5,000; $5,001–$10,000; $10,001–$15,000; $15,001–$20,000)

		Tally	Frequency
26.	$1–$5,000	_____	_____
27.	$5,001–$10,000	_____	_____
28.	$10,001–$15,000	_____	_____
29.	$15,001–$20,000	_____	_____

Calculate the mean salary to the nearest hundredth.

30. _____

E. Calculate the range. 15.3 OBJECTIVE 2

31. Your softball team scored the following points in the first ten games of the season. What is the range of the points?

    3   5   12   9   0   2   4   6   1   5

    Range: _____

32. Your bowling team had these averages. What is the range of the bowler's averages?

    222   185   169   175   201

    Range: _____

33. Maria Ramirez made ten trips from Dallas to El Paso. Her driving times were as follows. What is her range of time?

9.6 hours	10 hours	8.9 hours	10.1 hours	9.8 hours
8.3 hours	9.2 hours	9.7 hours	12.3 hours	9.0 hours

    Range: _____

34. Mary and Sharon walked two miles each morning for a week. The minutes it took them to walk were as follows. What is their range of time?

35 minutes	40 minutes	27 minutes	46 minutes
32 minutes	38 minutes	30 minutes	

    Range: _____

F. Calculate the standard deviation for the following sets of data. Give your answers to the nearest tenth. 15.3 OBJECTIVE 3

35. 60, 35, 22, 44, 49

    Standard Deviation: _____

36. 26, 43, 44, 51, 59

    Standard Deviation: _____

37. 37, 27, 29, 50, 60

    Standard Deviation: _____

38. 29, 38, 59, 55, 60

    Standard Deviation: _____

G. Use Excel with business statistics.

15.1 OBJECTIVE 5
15.2 OBJECTIVES 3, 5, 7, 9
15.3 OBJECTIVES 4, 5

39. Retrieve the file *ch15ex09.xlsx*. Follow the directions. Save the file as *ch15ex09a.xlsx*.

40. Retrieve the file *ch15ex10.xlsx*. Follow the directions. Save the file as *ch15ex10a.xlsx*.

41. Retrieve the file *ch15ex11.xlsx*. Follow the directions. Save the file as *ch15ex11a.xlsx*.

42. Retrieve the file *ch15ex12.xlsx*. Follow the directions. Save the file as *ch15ex12a.xlsx*.

43. Retrieve the file *ch15ex13.xlsx*. Follow the directions. Save the file as *ch15ex13a.xlsx*.

44. Retrieve the file *ch15ex14.xlsx*. Follow the directions. Save the file as *ch15ex14a.xlsx*.

The world of statistics consists of figuring out ways to gather data, organize the data, and then draw meaningful conclusions *about the data*. The conclusions drawn *often* show the average and the spread around the average. As you have learned in this chapter, you *can* use computations with formulas or charts and graphs to present information.

In the teaching profession, instructors are called upon to present statistics as clearly and neutrally as possible. For example, the dean of the Math Department has asked John William to chair a committee to assess students' learning outcomes. The committee has agreed to give a project to students in three introductory statistics classes to determine if they are meeting the program's goals. Based on the students' scores, the committee will review several areas, including their teaching strategies and students' learning styles, and identify areas for improvement. To present a meaningful report to John's committee, he must be able to organize the data, do computations, draw conclusions, and make predictions. Assume the role of John William to complete the following:

The first group of students made the following scores:

54	76	60	78	80	67	82	88	67	77
79	83	73	89	81	71	65	62	70	84

Using either paper or Excel, complete the following:

1. Calculate the mean of the scores.
2. Calculate the median of the scores.
   a. What do the mean and median suggest regarding the students' scores?

3. Calculate the standard deviation of the scores.

Write about Math

1. Define mean, median, and mode.

2. Identify three kinds of graphs and explain how each graph best presents data.

3. Explain standard deviation and give an example of when it might be used.

Personal Finance

How much money do you spend on average per week for groceries?

Inflation is an increase in the general level of prices for goods and services. In a period of inflation, everything gets more valuable—except money. When prices are rising faster than a person's income, buyers lose purchasing power. It means you can buy fewer things with the amount of money you have. There are many causes of inflation, but the effects are all the same. One tip on how to beat inflation is to make wise decisions at the grocery store. With the increased prices of many food items, you need to perfect your "consumerism." The list below shows the differences in average U.S. prices of some food staples in September 2009 and September 2010.

Mona Makela/Shutterstock.com

1. Estimate how much of each item you purchase in a month. For example, suppose you purchase 10 gallons of whole milk in a month. How much more are you spending?

2. If you increased your spending for whole milk by $1.15 on a monthly basis, how much more are you spending for the year for this one item?

3. Choose 2 other food items, such as ground chuck or spaghetti. Repeat Questions 1 and 2 for the price increases for these food items.

4. If your grocery costs have increased as a whole, what adjustments, can you make in your monthly budget?

5. Identify five grocery items that you buy regularly. Over a period of four weeks, keep track of the five items. Complete the following:

   a. Calculate the price change if any. What percentage increase or decrease occurred during each week?
   b. What effect has the price change had on your purchasing this item? What choices have you made because of this change?
   c. What decisions will you make if the price continues to rise?

Food Staple	9/1/2010	9/1/2009
Vegetable Oil/24 oz	2.79	2.46
Ground Chuck/1 lb.)	3.10	2.95
Peanut Butter/18 oz	2.28	2.27
Whole Milk/1 gal	3.82	2.86
White Bread/1 lb	1.09	.79
Eggs/1 dz	1.60	1.01
Spaghetti/1 lb box	1.08	1.00

   d. Calculate the average price of each item. For example, what is the average price for sliced ham for all four weeks?

6. Keep your grocery receipts for a month, total them, and calculate the average for the month. If you eat out, keep the receipts for the same period of time. Add the total of the grocery receipts and the total from the eating out. Calculate the average for your food for the month. What conclusions can you draw from these calculations? What changes, if any, could you make to save additional money?

7. Savvy grocery shoppers can save hundreds of dollars a month for their families. Conduct several Internet searches for ways to save on your grocery bill. Identify at least five tips to save money on your grocery shopping.

Directions   Complete the following problems. Write your answers in the blanks provided. Give answers to the nearest tenth.

A. Calculate the mean.   `15.1 OBJECTIVE 2`

1. 9, 5, 10, 9, 12, 11, 6, 18, 4, 5 _____

2. 20, 10, 11, 16, 18, 32, 8, 17, 20 _____

3. 17, 25, 12, 6, 38, 10, 15, 25, 45 _____

B. Calculate the median.   `15.1 OBJECTIVE 3`

4. 21, 14, 22, 15, 18, 30, 45 _____

5. 55, 77, 56, 32, 15, 75, 41, 30 _____

6. 11, 23, 43, 45, 66, 37, 38 _____

C. Calculate the mode(s).   `15.1 OBJECTIVE 4`

7. 33, 25, 17, 33, 12, 33, 25, 30, 25 _____

8. 1, 2, 6, 3, 5, 1, 7, 8, 11, 9, 1, 4, 14 _____

9. 42, 24, 45, 42, 44, 224, 444, 42 _____

D. Manually create a frequency distribution table.   `15.1 OBJECTIVE 2; 15.2 OBJECTIVE 2`

You are the owner of Cherries Sports Bar & Grill. You have 20 employees. Last month they worked the following total hours.

45	35	29	32	21	43	39	49	25	32
37	44	25	20	44	36	28	50	37	41

Group the hours worked into four equal classes (1–20, 21–30, 31–40, 41–50).

		Tally	Frequency
10.	1–20	_____	_____
11.	21–30	_____	_____
12.	31–40	_____	_____
13.	41–50	_____	_____

Calculate the mean of the ungrouped data to the nearest tenth.

14. _____

E. **Calculate the range and standard deviation for the following sets of numbers.**   **15.3** OBJECTIVES **2, 3**

62; 51; 48; 33; 25

15. Range _____   **16.** Standard deviation _____

147; 135; 169; 175; 149

17. Range _____   **18.** Standard deviation _____

18; 50; 55; 42; 23

19. Range _____   **20.** Standard deviation _____

419; 636; 698; 354; 498

21. Range _____   **22.** Standard deviation _____

4,005; 3,462; 4,633; 5,000; 3,898

23. Range _____   **24.** Standard deviation _____

15.1 OBJECTIVE **5**
15.2 OBJECTIVES **3, 5, 7, 9**
15.3 OBJECTIVES **4, 5**

F. **Use Excel to complete the following business statistics problems.**

25. Retrieve the file *ch15qz01.xlsx*. Follow the directions. Save the file as *ch15qz01a.xlsx*.

26. Retrieve the file *ch15qz02.xlsx*. Follow the directions. Save the file as *ch15qz02a.xlsx*.

27. Retrieve the file *ch15qz03.xlsx*. Follow the directions. Save the file as *ch15qz03a.xlsx*.

28. Retrieve the file *ch15qz04.xlsx*. Follow the directions. Save the file as *ch15qz04a.xlsx*.

29. Retrieve the file *ch15qz05.xlsx*. Follow the directions. Save the file as *ch15qz05a.xlsx*.

30. Retrieve the file *ch15qz06.xlsx*. Follow the directions. Save the file as *ch15qz06a.xlsx*.

Answers to Selected Exercises

1.1 Exercises 11

1. 4 tens   **3.** 2 hundredths   **5.** 2 millions   **7.** 4 units

9. 7 units   **11.** 3 hundred thousands   **13.** 9 hundred thousandths   **15.** 130

17. 73.65   **19.** 5,600.034   **21.** 0.26   **23.** 51.006

25. 7,462.03   **27.** five hundred ninety-five

29. five hundred million four hundred sixty-five thousand six hundred two

31. two and four hundred sixty-nine thousandths   **33.** three million four hundred fifty-two thousand and forty-two thousandths

35. nine thousand ninety and ninety-nine hundredths   **37.** $585.00   **39.** $802.00

41. $1.00   **43.** $111.00   **45.** $50.00   **47.** $5,270

49. 422   **51.** 4.2   **53.** 249.957   **55.** 4.0

57. 3,610

1.2 Exercises 20

1.
$$\begin{array}{r} 14 \\ 890 \\ 1,092 \\ + 1,463 \\ \hline 3,459 \end{array}$$

3.
$$\begin{array}{r} 387 \\ 6,780 \\ 1,000.1 \\ + 9,046 \\ \hline 17,213.1 \end{array}$$

5.
$$\begin{array}{r} 829.2 \\ 270.2968 \\ 8.00 \\ + 110.43 \\ \hline 1,217.9268 \end{array}$$

7a. 11
7b. 14
7c. 22
7d. 27
7e. 33

7f. 38   **7g.** 40   **9a.** 12   **9b.** 15

9c. 17   **9d.** 24   **9e.** 29   **9f.** 35

9g. 38   **11a.** –   **11b.** 10   **11c.** 20

13a. –   **13b.** 10   **13c.** 20   **15a.** 10

15b. –   **15c.** 20   **17a.** –   **17b.** –

17c. 10   **17d.** 20   **17e.** 30   **19a.** –

19b. 10   **19c.** 10   **19d.** –   **19e.** 20

21. 4,764   **23.** 88,579   **25.** 60,161   **27.** 2.686

29. 202.62   **31.** 8.987   **33.** $128.55   **35.** $223.26

37. $850.24   **39.** $129,625.54   **41.** 13,241   **43.** 1,444

45. 3,322   **47.** 8,741,818   **49.** 429   **51.** 40

53. $843   **55.** $957.90   **57.** 280

1.3 Exercises 30

1. 466   **3.** $63.52   **5.** 1,818   **7.** 181.93

9. $389.96   **11.** $558,680   **13.** 1,721.019   **15.** 6,541.38

17. 4.6756   **19.** 98.987   **21.** 316   **23.** 813

25. $11.67   **27.** 0.008   **29.** $49.75   **31.** 9,938

33. 31,570   **35.** $7.89   **37.** 1.368   **39.** 16.045

41. −520   **43.** −40,001   **45.** −21.545   **47.** −$17.54

49. −$1,016   **51.** −3,110   **53.** −39   **55.** −13.17

57. −215   **59.** −28.57   **61.** $27.98   **63.** $70.87

65. $277.30   **67.** $489.00   **69.** $10.12   **71.** $9,920

73. $1,679.88

1.4 Exercises 39

1. 184,769   **3.** 4,770   **5.** 7,544   **7.** $20,958

9. 5,355,253   **11.** 496,755   **13.** 966,889   **15.** 279,790

17. 6,624   **19.** 21,508   **21.** 90,068   **23.** 6,956

25. 457,555   **27.** 3,706.58   **29.** $4.3460   **31.** $6.64

33. $29.70   **35.** $320.04   **37.** $5.36   **39.** $4,014.00

41. $17.55   **43.** 150,450   **45.** 370,800   **47.** $80,800

49. $179,340   **51.** 20,800   **53.** 15,422   **55.** 1,674; 3,149; 2,520; 7,343

57. $10.62; $19.72; $71.28; $101.62   **59.** $3,230.00   **61.** $54,000.00

63. $24.85   **65.** $265.00   **67.** $16,100.40   **69.** $412.20

71. $67.50   **73.** $127.25

1.5 Exercises 47

1. 166   **3.** 293   **5.** 3,098   **7.** 106

9. 192   **11.** 88   **13.** 101   **15.**
$$\begin{array}{r} 4.576 = 4.58 \\ 1\times9.\overline{)8\times6{,}950} \\ \underline{7\,6} \\ 1\,0\,9 \\ \underline{9\,5} \\ 1\,45 \\ \underline{1\,33} \\ 120 \\ \underline{114} \\ 6 \end{array}$$

17.
$$\begin{array}{r} 15.145 = 15.15 \\ 6\times37.\overline{)96\times48{,}000} \\ \underline{63\,7} \\ 32\,78 \\ \underline{31\,85} \\ 93\,0 \\ \underline{63\,7} \\ 29\,30 \\ \underline{25\,48} \\ 3\,820 \\ \underline{3\,185} \\ 635 \end{array}$$
   19. 270.721   **21.** 0.132

23. 6.521   **25.** 4,281.429   **27.** 270.60   **29.** 14.12

31. 86.93   **33.** 74.27   **35.** $300 \div 60 = 5.00$; 5.20   **37.** $900 \div 200 = 4.50$; 4.77

39. 42   **41.** 3,592   **43.** $500.00

Chapter 1 Review Exercises 55

1. 8 millions   **3.** 3 ten thousands   **5.** 7 tenths   **7.** 89.65

9. 4,600.026   **11.** 6,000,000,000,000   **13.** one million eight hundred thousand one

15. six billion four hundred twenty-nine million one thousand nineteen   **17.** 40

19. $400   **21.** 10,000   **23.** 1.0   **25.** 9.46

27. 7.649   **29.** 12.99   **31.** 21.73   **33.** 2,176

35. 45.93   **37.** 1,000   **39.** 1,000   **41.** 1,600

43. 111   **45.** 237   **47.** $758,680   **49.** 33,9198

51. $54.43   **53.** 3,880   **55.** −67   **57.** −7.01

59. −18.67   **61.** 62,038,139   **63.** $14.46016   **65.** 260.70; 3.70; 47.76; 312.16

67. $3,047.80   **69.** 12.10   **71.** 5.00; 4.64   **73.** 4.00; 4.18

75. $24.41

Chapter 1 Quiz 60

1. 9 tens   **3.** 3 thousandths   **5.** 93.11   **7.** six hundred seventy-two

9. three and one hundred eleven thousandths   **11.** $90.00   **13.** 0.7

15. $446.77   **17.** 31,156   **19.** 4,721.96   **21.** 911.86

23. −20.594   **25.** −$30.19   **27.** 4,527   **29.** 67

31. 35   **33.** 53.33   **35.** $5.9052   **37.** 3.9910893

39. 71.64; 95.88; 60.25; 227.77   **41.** 39.430   **43.** $5,778.000   **45.** 2.777

47. 70   **49.** $7,313.60

Chapter 2   62

2.1 Exercises 77

1. I   **3.** M   **5.** I   **7.** P

9. 4   **11.** 5   **13.** 6   **15.** 21

17. $9\frac{3}{8}$ **19.** $1\frac{2}{5}$ **21.** 33   **23.** 8

25. $\frac{25}{4}$ **27.** $\frac{16}{3}$ **29.** $\frac{603}{8}$ **31.** $\frac{19}{4}$

33. $\frac{1}{2}$ **35.** $\frac{1}{6}$ **37.** $\frac{3}{7}$ **39.** $\frac{1}{2}$

41. $\frac{3}{4}$ **43.** $\frac{50}{125}$ **45.** $\frac{20}{96}$ **47.** $\frac{12}{57}$

49. $\frac{35}{50}$ **51.** $\frac{30}{48}$ **53.** 0.16   **55.** 9.42

57. 0.44   **59.** 7.14   **61.** 0.60   **63.** $\frac{3}{4}$

65. $\frac{3}{100}$ **67.** $\frac{17}{25}$ **69.** $\frac{43}{50}$ **71.** $\frac{6}{25}$

2.2 Exercises 91

1. $1\frac{3}{4}$ **3.** $\frac{19}{25}$ **5.** $1\frac{2}{5}$ **7.** $1\frac{1}{3}$

9. $\frac{1}{2}$ **11.** $\frac{1}{5}$ **13.** $\frac{1}{2}$ **15.** $\frac{1}{4}$

17. 75   **19.** 20   **21.** 12   **23.** 45

25. $\frac{7}{8}$ **27.** $1\frac{1}{84}$ **29.** $1\frac{1}{6}$ **31.** $2\frac{1}{16}$

33. $\frac{5}{12}$ **35.** $\frac{3}{8}$ **37.** $\frac{1}{10}$ **39.** $\frac{2}{15}$

41. $79\frac{1}{4}$ **43.** $21\frac{1}{2}$ **45.** $12\frac{2}{5}$ **47.** $12\frac{1}{13}$

49. $48\frac{1}{24}$ **51.** $24\frac{59}{72}$ **53.** $23\frac{11}{56}$ **55.** $122\frac{3}{10}$

57. $6\frac{1}{8}$ **59.** $4\frac{11}{21}$ **61.** $9\frac{1}{2}$ **63.** $102\frac{1}{4}$

65. $12\frac{11}{35}$ **67.** $5\frac{8}{21}$ **69.** $1\frac{1}{12}$ **71.** $6\frac{5}{18}$

73. $4\frac{3}{4}$ **75.** $14\frac{5}{6}$ **77.** $96\frac{2}{3}$ **79.** $1\frac{1}{2}$

81. $15\frac{7}{8}$ miles   **83.** $12\frac{1}{12}$ gallons   **85.** 0.33   **87.** $29\frac{1}{4}$ hours

2.3 Exercises 101

1. $\frac{5}{36}$ **3.** $\frac{1}{3}$ **5.** $\frac{5}{12}$ **7.** $\frac{5}{3}$

9. $1\frac{13}{27}$ **11.** $2\frac{7}{9}$ **13.** $12\frac{11}{24}$ **15.** $7\frac{3}{16}$

17. $2\frac{2}{3}$ **19.** $\frac{7}{8}$ **21.** $1\frac{7}{9}$ **23.** $1\frac{11}{19}$

25. $2\frac{2}{5}$ **27.** $2\frac{22}{39}$ **29.** $\frac{56}{75}$ **31.** $\frac{7}{9}$

33. $\frac{8}{15}$ or 0.533 yard   **35.** 120 people

Chapter 2 Review Exercises 105

1. $4\frac{11}{12}$
3. 11
5. $6\frac{1}{4}$
7. $4\frac{1}{3}$
9. $\frac{135}{30}$
11. $\frac{73}{16}$
13. $\frac{53}{16}$
15. $\frac{30}{5}$
17. 0.80
19. 2.29
21. 4.38
23. 15.67
25. $3\frac{3}{5}$
27. $8\frac{39}{1000}$
29. $9\frac{469}{1000}$
31. $3\frac{33}{50}$
33. $1\frac{29}{48}$
35. $1\frac{3}{8}$
37. $1\frac{11}{20}$
39. $5\frac{1}{6}$
41. $7\frac{1}{4}$
43. $10\frac{1}{2}$
45. $\frac{1}{2}$
47. $\frac{3}{32}$
49. $3\frac{1}{12}$
51. $\frac{1}{3}$
53. $1\frac{1}{4}$
55. $3\frac{2}{3}$
57. $4\frac{2}{3}$
59. $2\frac{5}{6}$
61. $1\frac{1}{8}$
63. $\frac{9}{10}$
65. $2\frac{6}{17}$
67. $1\frac{11}{21}$
69. $1\frac{5}{9}$
71. $2\frac{3}{8}$ yards
73. $10\frac{1}{4}$ hours
75. $102\frac{9}{10}$ lots
77. $151\frac{1}{2}$ loads
79. $25,000
81. $1,125.83

Chapter 2 Quiz 110

1. $6\frac{1}{5}$
3. $20\frac{1}{9}$
5. $\frac{87}{4}$
7. $\frac{21}{8}$
9. $\frac{1}{4}$
11. $\frac{12}{13}$
13. $\frac{60}{180}$
15. $\frac{64}{72}$
17. 0.300
19. 6.500
21. $\frac{61}{100}$
23. $\frac{3}{10}$
25. $1\frac{7}{12}$
27. $6\frac{5}{8}$
29. $\frac{1}{2}$
31. $\frac{1}{15}$
33. 120
35. 36
37. $10\frac{2}{3}$
39. $\frac{2}{25}$
41. 1
43. 2
45. $28\frac{5}{24}$ yards
47. $38\frac{1}{4}$ sq. ft.

Chapter 3 112

3.1 Exercises 119

1. 0.03
3. 0.152
5. 0.312
7. 0.0254
9. 630%
11. 7%
13. 43%
15. 89.7%
17. $\frac{2}{25}$
19. $\frac{1}{1,000}$
21. $\frac{1}{15}$
23. $\frac{3}{2,000}$
25. 275%
27. 60%
29. 91.7%
31. 855.6%

3.2 Exercises 128

1. ?; 34%; 65
3. 108.3; 100%; ?
5. 85.7; 56%; ?
7. 0.75
9. 20.82
11. 2.88
13. 270.00
15. 21.92
17. 47.50%
19. 17.33%
21. 9.99%
23. 125.0%
25. 22.58
27. 162.96
29. 20.00
31. 1,614.04
33. 800.00
35. $P = B \times R$; $416.85
37. $B = \frac{P}{R}$; $182.25
39. $B = \frac{P}{R}$; $1,200.00
41. $P = B \times R$; $9,548.00
43. $B = \frac{P}{R}$; $1,008.40
45. $P = B \times R$; $27.06
47. $B = \frac{P}{R}$; $140,000.00
49. $R = \frac{P}{B}$; 6%

3.3 Exercises 138

1. $1,570; 6.1%
3. $1,778.70; $37,352.70
5. $0.03; 2.7%
7. $99.00; $396.00
9. +16.2%
11. −4.8%
13. +7.7%
15. 4.6%
17. 19.2%
19. 130; 100%
21. $37,895
23. $197.65
25. $561; 2.6%
27. −34.0%

Chapter 3 Review Exercises 143

1.	0.155	**3.**	0.30	**5.**	0.72	**7.**	0.00625
9.	0.007	**11.**	66.7%	**13.**	47%	**15.**	145%
17.	41.7%	**19.**	0.3%	**21.**	$\frac{9}{100}$	**23.**	$\frac{13}{20}$
25.	$\frac{14}{25}$	**27.**	$1\frac{1}{4}$	**29.**	250%	**31.**	25%
33.	175%	**35.**	$1,396.08	**37.**	15.1%	**39.**	$200.00
41.	$175.80	**43.**	$82.05	**45.**	$582.56	**47.**	18.1%
49.	$449,108.47	**51.**	$43.27	**53.**	71.4%	**55.**	7.4%
57.	4,669	**59.**	33.3%	**61.**	10.9%	**63.**	$30,687.83

Chapter 3 Quiz 148

1.	0.000235	**3.**	0.085	**5.**	41%	**7.**	11.15%
9.	$\frac{13}{20}$	**11.**	$1\frac{11}{100}$	**13.**	20%	**15.**	50%
17.	240	**19.**	7.5	**21.**	20.0%	**23.**	$90.00
25.	$386.67	**27.**	87.59%	**29.**	42.76%	**31.**	9.98%
33.	29.35%	**35.**	9.5%	**37.**	525	**39.**	400

Chapter 4 150

4.1 Exercises 162

1.	e	**3.**	a	**5.**	c	**7.**	Overdraft protection
9.	Debit card	**11.**	direct deposit	**13.**	$250,000	**15.**	payee
17.	drawee	**19.**	ABA number	**21.**	restrictive	**23.**	350 00; 600 00
25.	36 90; 490 70	**27.**	127 75; 588 15	**29.**	12 70; 533 25	**31.**	$686.80

33.

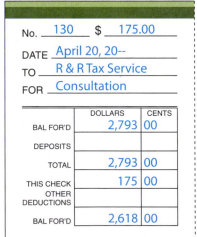

No. <u>130</u> $ <u>175.00</u>

DATE <u>April 20, 20--</u>

TO <u>R & R Tax Service</u>

FOR <u>Consultation</u>

	DOLLARS	CENTS
BAL FOR'D	2,793	00
DEPOSITS		
TOTAL	2,793	00
THIS CHECK	175	00
OTHER DEDUCTIONS		
BAL FOR'D	2,618	00

35.

CHECK NUMBER	DATE	DESCRIPTION OF TRANSACTION	AMOUNT OF CHECK		✓	AMOUNT OF DEPOSIT	BALANCE BROUGHT FORWARD	
							$ 1,968	80
321	6/10/--	June's Deli	9	95			9	95
		Lunch					1,958	85

37.		6/10/--	Deposit				814	00	814	00
									2,752	45

4.2 Exercises 172

1.	Outstanding checks	**3.**	Service charges	**5.**	12/17/–	**7.**	$1,167.90
9.	$1,167.90	**11.**	$957.87	**13.**	$1,257.87	**15.**	$7.00
17.	$785.37	**19.**	$472.50	**21.**	$1,693.50	**23.**	$21.72

Chapter 4 Review Exercises 175

1.	164 20; 359 45	**3.**	303 14; 633 13	**5.**	75 00; 520 73	**7.**	303 14; 741 47
9.	800 90	**11.**	767 80	**13.**	767 80	**15.**	761 25
17.	761 25	**19.**	729 75	**21.**	729 75	**23.**	716 30
25.	716 30	**27.**	693 60	**29.**	1,443 60	**31.**	1,346 40
33.	d	**35.**	b	**37.**	c	**39.**	$1,753.00
41.	$235.91	**43.**	$2,878.88	**45.**	$2,362.15	**47.**	$65,574.07; $65,574.07
49.	$2,333.47						

Chapter 4 Quiz 180

1.	51 47; 763 18	**3.**	73 21; 1,551 63	**5.**	42 00; 1,497 88	**7.**	820 50
9.	755 11	**11.**	755 11	**13.**	730 11	**15.**	730 11
17.	690 66	**19.**	690 66	**21.**	684 45	**23.**	no; $5.93
25.	$350.97	**27.**	$1,112.48				

Chapter 5 182

5.1 Exercises 188

1.	$823.08	**3.**	$2,284.62	**5.**	$2,475.00	**7.**	$375.00
9.	$500.00	**11.**	$293.80	**13.**	$471.75	**15.**	$193.50
17.	$118.80	**19.**	$212.00	**21.**	$964.00	**23.**	$1,397.80
25.	$204.75	**27.**	$700.00	**29.**	$910.00	**31.**	$357.00
33.	$484.00	**35.**	$665.50				

5.2 Exercises 193

1.	$4,025.00	**3.**	$701.00	**5.**	$594.00	**7.**	$615.00
9.	90	**11.**	$420.50	**13.**	$48.00	**15.**	$1,456.00
17.	108	**19.**	$141				

5.3 Exercises 204

1.	$25.30	**3.**	$32.00	**5.**	$20.64	**7.**	$43.91
9.	$5.62	**11.**	$15.91	**13.**	$7.55	**15.**	$54.62
17.	$37.93	**19.**	$24.63	**21.**	$15	**23.**	–0–

25. $30   **27.** $68   **29.** $24   **31.** $73.83

33. $99.34   **35.** $65.26   **37.** $45.47   **39.** $39.41

41. $2,412.46

5.4 Exercises 210

1. 36.00; 47.10; 11.01; 40.50; 15.00; 149.61; 609.99; 5,055.71

3. 32.00; 49.59; 11.60; 40.50; 15.00; 148.69; 651.21; 6,642.56

5. 32.00; 49.08; 11.48; 40.50; 15.00; 148.06; 643.54; 8,193.76

7. 66.00; 42.66; 9.98; 28.25; 20.00; 166.89; 521.21; 2,897.95

9. 66.00; 37.84; 8.85; 28.25; 20.00; 160.94; 449.46; 4,208.60

11. 516.00; 174.15; 690.15; 39.00; 42.79; 10.01; 124.80; 565.35

13. 696.00; 208.80; 904.80; 51.00; 56.10; 13.12; 141.22; 763.58

15. 428.00; 160.50; 588.50; 54.00; 36.49; 8.53; 125.02; 463.48

17. 888.00; 0.00; 888.00; 50.00; 55.06; 12.88; 131.94; 756.06

19. 800.00; 0.00; 800.00; 16.00; 49.60; 11.60; 98.20; 701.80

21. 452.00; 33.90; 485.90; 17.00; 30.13; 7.05; 87.18; 398.72

23. 776.00; 116.40; 892.40; 39.00; 55.33; 12.94; 140.27; 752.13

25. 50.64; 48.10; 11.25; 164.99; 610.81

27. 63.15; 45.90; 10.74; 174.79; 565.59

29. 56.48; 43.15; 10.09; 164.72; 531.18

Chapter 5 Review Exercises 215

1. $625.00   **3.** $1,237.50   **5.** $178.20   **7.** $970.20

9. $186.00   **11.** $961.00   **13.** $899.00   **15.** $40.66

17. $88.82   **19.** $56.03   **21.** $63.00   **23.** $0.00

25. $45.24   **27.** $28.99   **29.** $22.65   **31.** $10,129.89

33. $190.46; $44.54; $49.15; $38.25; $2,327.24

Chapter 5 Quiz 220

1. $1,519   **3.** $1,158   **5.** $4,583   **7.** $127.50

9. $568   **11.** $227.20   **13.** $274.82   **15.** $1,298.18

17. $881.50   **19.** $231.25   **21.** $12.69   **23.** $9.00

25. $5.29   **27.** $4.09   **29.** $5.99   **31.** $20.16

33. $14.11   **35.** 380; 14.25; 394.25; 6.01; 24.44; 5.72; 13.75; 3.00; 52.92; 341.33; 5,095.92

Chapter 6   222

6.1 Exercises 229

1. $61.20   **3.** $29.63   **5.** $3,600.00   **7.** $1,728.00

9. $156.00   **11.** 8%   **13.** 6%   **15.** 4%

17. 1%   **19.** 7%

21. 8 − 4.5 = 3.5 mills; 3.5 mills ÷ 1,000 = $0.0035; $0.0035 × $1,200,000,000 = $4,200,000

23. $190,800 × 40% = $76,320; 49.708 mills + 3.5 mills = 53.208 mills; 53.208 ÷ 1,000 = $0.053208; $0.053208 × $76,320 = $4,060.83

25. $842.40   **27.** $802.09

6.2 Exercises 234

1. $270.00   **3.** $269.70   **5.** $270.00   **7.** $235.50

9. $264.00   **11.** $56.00   **13.** $56.00   **15.** $33.80

17. $16.47

6.3 Exercises 249

1. $678	**3.** $1,208	**5.** $923	**7.** $1,133
9. $853	**11.** $788	**13.** $1,038	**15.** $7,050
17. $1,287 refund	**19.** $1,244	**21.** $10,900	**23.** $81 owed
25. $528	**27.** $7,660	**29.** $1,178 refund	**31.** $578

33. $45,500; $12,600; $58,100; − $6,500; $51,600; $4,450; − $3,870; $580; $13,200; $540; $10,800; $24,540; − $25,120; − $21,000; $5,480; $548; − $1,515; Refund due; $967

Chapter 6 Review Exercises 254

1. $177.00	**3.** $2,400.00	**5.** 5%	**7.** $270.00
9. $267.00	**11.** $471.54	**13.** $772.00	**15.** $11,110
17. $ 246	**19.** $43 tax due		

Chapter 6 Quiz 258

1. $221.49	**3.** $3,285.00	**5.** 3%	**7.** $196.65
9. $150.02	**11.** $12,400	**13.** /Refund due; $263	**15.** $562 refund

Chapter 7   260

7.1 Exercises 269

1. $25.00	**3.** $4.17	**5.** −0−	**7.** $58.33
9. $100.00	**11.** $56.25	**13.** $0.83	**15.** −0−
17. $893.75	**19.** $5,500.00	**21.** $1,437.05	**23.** $189.75
25. −0−; $1,245; $756; $2,268; $4,536;		**27.** $123.75	**29.** $19,500; $325.00; $475.00;

7.2 Exercises 278

1. $50,000	**3.** $60,000	**5.** $47,000	**7.** $57,000
9. $660.00	**11.** $49.50	**13.** $80,000	**15.** $1,600,000
17. $396,000	**19.** $200,000	**21.** $184,000	**23.** $100,000
25. $12,000	**27.** $8,300	**29.** $11,500	**31.** −0−

Chapter 7 Review Exercises 281

1. $117.50	**3.** $36.67	**5.** $137.50	**7.** $2,340
9. $6,300	**11.** $40,000	**13.** $11,950	**15.** $10,000
17. $192.50	**19.** $392.00	**21.** $50,922.16	**23.** $2,800,000
25. $410.97	**27.** $42,400		

Chapter 7 Quiz 286

1. $59.00	**3.** $172.50	**5.** $85.42	**7.** $36,000
9. $46,000	**11.** $82.65	**13.** $89,000	**15.** $75,680
17. $49,309			

Chapter 8 288

8.1 Exercises 295

1. a   **3.** c   **5.** l   **7.** k

9. q   **11.** o   **13.** n

8.2 Exercises 303

1. $12.47   **3.** $139.07   **5.** $62.51   **7.** $10.70

9. $6.05   **11.** 0   **13.** $295.92   **15.** $5.92

17. $543.70   **19.** $675.51   **21.** $676.17

8.3 Exercises 308

1. $61.96   **3.** $154.02   **5.** $505.05   **7.** $60.05

9. 7.56; 113.40   **11.** 7.70; 154.00   **13.** 33.95; 101.85   **15.** $630.59

17. $13.98, $20.96

8.4 Exercises 313

1. 0.72675   **3.** 0.684   **5.** $341.11   **7.** $141.43

9. $3,721.12   **11.** 0.72   **13.** $670.35   **15.** $1,835.04, April 4

8.5 Exercises 318

1. False   **3.** $224.83   **5.** $120.02   **7.** $20.95

9. $17.59   **11.** $52.07   **13.** $97.22   **15.** $90.02

17. $72.16   **19.** $38.51   **21.** $62.02   **23.** $24.23

25. $630.00   **27.** $519.94   **29a.** no, it is not correct

29b. sales tax was charged on shipping; $715.58   **29c.** $41.29   **31.** $305.87

33. $1.44   **35.** $18.79; $1.17   **37.** $568.54

Chapter 8 Review Exercises 323

1. $7.50   **3.** $6.22   **5.** $24.60   **7.** $31.25

9. $3.07   **11.** $6.89   **13.** 0   **15.** $60.92

17. $877.55   **19.** $17.55   **21.** $430.68   **23.** $1,903.06

25. $38.06   **27.** $772.24   **29.** $2,130.30   **31.** $1,608.90

33. $4,102.05   **35.** $626.66   **37.** $926.05   **39.** $500.66

41. $380.01   **43.** $305.32   **45.** $1,216.55   **47.** $459.22

49. $514.10   **51.** $7.88   **53.** $4,213.40   **55.** $1,298.33; August 14

57. $1,848.80   **59.** $119.80   **61.** $389.85   **63.** $1,940.00

65. $447.00   **67.** $14,775.00   **69.** $1,195.03   **71.** $21,201.18

73. $20,603.67

Chapter 8 Quiz 328

1. $51.32   **3.** $49.56   **5.** $12.00   **7.** $1.87

9. $3.38   **11.** $367.35   **13.** $7.35   **15.** $445.75

17. $248.60   **19.** $476.45   **21.** $299.23   **23.** $640.11

25. $1,871.00   **27.** $645.57   **29.** $232.69   **31.** $753.88

33. $39.25   **35.** $2,328.00   **37.** $229.47   **39.** $65.00

41. $86.05   **43.** April 15

Chapter 9   330

9.1 Exercises 334

1. f   **3.** c   **5.** b   **7.** f: selling price; a: cost

9. $17.67   **11.** $52.30   **13.** $38.90   **15.** $442.25

17. $108.85   **19.** $56.23

9.2 Exercises 339

1. $9.73   **3.** $13.28   **5.** $1,078.96   **7.** $72.40

9. $6.85   **11.** $330.00 markup; $1,650.00 selling price   **13.** $17.86

9.3 Exercises 345

1. 17%   **3.** $25.25   **5a.** $24.19   **5b.** 40%

7. $10.50   **9.** 76%   **11.** $49.82   **13.** $116.54

9.4 Exercises 349

1. $393.79   **3.** $21.44   **5.** 42%   **7.** $25.85

9. $115.46   **11.** $45.60   **13.** $90.00   **15.** $29.75; 20%

Chapter 9 Review Exercises 352

1. 37.98   **3.** 7.00   **5.** 26.60; 102.60   **7.** 125.81; 69.20

9. 59%; 19.25   **11.** 12.00; 4.00   **13.** 12.87; 26.13   **15.** 18.75; 56.25

17a. $350.00   **17b.** 67%   **19.** 14%   **21.** $32.40

23. $81.25   **25.** $110.00   **27.** 60%

Chapter 9 Quiz 356

1. 184.95   **3.** 80.90   **5.** 39.00; 91.00   **7.** 768.97; 346.04

9. 78%; 33.25   **11.** 113.75; 211.25   **13.** 53.40; 35.60   **15.** 52.50; 122.50

17. $44.50; 50%   **19.** $34.00; 18%   **21.** $470.91   **23.** $128.70

25. $156.00   **27.** $57.60   **29.** $52.00

Chapter 10   358

10.1 Exercises 370

1. $702.00   **3.** $109.59   **5.** $593.84   **7.** $186.67

9. $70.00   **11.** $1,500.00   **13.** March 15   **15.** September 13

10.2 Exercises 376

1. bank discount   **3.** maturity (or face)   **5.** proceeds   **7.** $544.92

9. $84.50   **11.** $412.74   **13.** $540.87   **15.** $540.01

17. Oct. 5   **19.** $1,604.25   **21.** $136.50   **23.** $132.63

25. $537.53   **27.** $30.40   **29.** $63.76   **31.** 107

33. 110 **35.** $3,455.96 **37.** $25,238.91 **39.** $8,764.61

41. 65 days

10.3 Exercises 390

1. $217.50	**3.** $3,450.77	**5.** 4	**7.** $778.16
9. $1,754.79	**11.** $1,948.37	**13.** $1,065.19	**15.** $6,867.02
17. $1,009.89	**19.** $1,044.15	**21.** $630.00	**23.** $1,539.33
25. $4,686.64	**27.** $13,224.93	**29.** $3,048.83	**31.** $8,915.68
33. $5,634.13	**35.** $2,537.97	**37.** $11,334.80	**39.** $6,231.67
41. $6,046.87	**43.** $10,023.07	**45.** $1,954.67	**47.** $5,536.76

Chapter 10 Review Exercises 394

1. $418.00	**3.** $26.65	**5.** $40.13	**7.** $52.00
9. $52.50	**11.** $1,890.00	**13.** 18%	**15.** May 20
17. 48	**19.** $110.63	**21.** $20.28	**23.** $5,858.30
25. $12,245.20	**27.** $6,691.10	**29.** $182.50	**31.** July 18

Chapter 10 Quiz 398

1. $148.75	**3.** $48.30	**5.** $39.65	**7.** $28.00
9. $25.32	**11.** 8%	**13.** 90 days	**15.** June 13
17. 47	**19.** $138.00	**21.** $17.37	**23.** $2,342.56
25. $22,812.17	**27.** $8,363.87	**29.** $50.70	**31.** 11%

Chapter 11   400

11.1 Exercises 410

1. 1.5%	**3.** 1.75%	**5.** 1.6%	**7.** $14.53
9. $21.45	**11.** $21.56	**13.** $12.90	**15.** $10.52
17. $875.05			

11.2 Exercises 418

1. $765.00	**3.** $520.00	**5.** $477.00	**7.** $885.00
9. $972.80	**11.** $1,982.00	**13.** $559.75	**15.** $51.15
17. $110.77	**19.** $882.88	**21.** $1,660.80	**23.** $100.00
25. $2,806.08	**27.** $1,320.00	**29.** $28.87	

11.3 Exercises 425

1. $10.4422	**3.** $7.3376	**5.** $745.70	**7.** $1,302.92
9. $1,463.77	**11.** $800.00	**13.** $79,977.11	**15.** $23.12
17. $799.54	**19.** $79,930.64	**21.** $23.58	

Chapter 11 Review Exercises 429

1. $6.58	**3.** $23.23	**5.** $20.23	**7.** $23.98
9. 1.50%	**11.** 2.17%	**13.** $8.36	**15.** $3.55

17. $468.23; (9 days × $500) + (5 days × $320) + (17 days × $495) = $14,515; $14,515 ÷ 31 = ADB

19. $502.02; $495 (ending balance) + $7.02 (finance charge) = New Balance **21.** $478.80

23. $261.57	**25.** $1,178.82	**27.** $243.00	**29.** $132.75
31. $58.24	**33.** $5,117.68	**35.** $327.98	**37.** $28.11
39. $6.44	**41.** 1.8%	**43.** $103.60	

Chapter 11 Quiz 434

1. $2.87	**3.** $48.00	**5.** $24.58	**7.** $1,065.56
9. $649.94	**11.** $893.40	**13.** $403.70	**15.** $187.89
17. $271.69	**19.** $26.80	**21.** $422.91	**23.** $458.17
25. $485.06	**27.** $145.00	**29.** $617.92	**31.** $351

Chapter 12   436

12.1 Exercises 450

1. $23,906.13	**3.** $264,473.89	**5.** $47,231.20	**7.** $13,260.04
9. $24,527.15	**11.** $558.30	**13.** $338.87	

12.2 Exercises 460

1. $4.17	**3.** $6.54	**5.** $9.68	**7.** $12,100, $229.90, $12,329.90
9. 1.1%	**11.** 19		

12.3 Exercises 467

1. Abbreviated name of corporation, South Bundett Corporation   **3.**   Interest paid semiannually

5. Current yield represents the annual percentage return to the purchase at the current price.

7. The closing price the bond sold for that day as a percent of $1,000   **9.** $105.00

11. 12.9%	**13.** $895.00	**15.** $117.50	**17.** 12.7%

Chapter 12 Review Exercises 471

1. $22,312.39	**3.** $142,409.02	**5.** $11,807.80	**7.** $8,840.03
9. $40,878.58	**11.** $313.63	**13.** $246.03	**15.** $3.52, $1,232
17. $6.00, $3,000	**19.** $8.67	**21.** $2.40	**23.** $4,998, $52.36, $5,050.36
25. $4,865	**27.** $4,935	**29.** $8,740	**31.** $8,840
33. 8.8%	**35.** 8.9%	**37.** $13,359.32	

Chapter 12 Quiz 476

1. $15,937.42	**3.** $176,908.12	**5.** $94,462.40	**7.** $4,420.01
9. $24,527.15	**11.** $74.77	**13.** $116.05	**15.** $14.64, $7,349.28
17. $2.40	**19.** $1.06	**21.** $51,000, $765, $51,765	**23.** $80.00
25. $840.00			

Chapter 13   478

13.1 Exercises 484

1. $3,000	**3.** $3,500	**5.** $95,000	**7.** $9,500
9. $100,500	**11.** $19,000	**13.** $9,500	**15.** $81,500
17. $38,000	**19.** $9,500	**21.** $62,500	**23.** $57,000

25. $9,500   **27.** $43,500   **29.** $76,000   **31.** $9,500

33. $24,500   **35.** $95,000   **37.** $7,000   **39.** $6,433

41. $3,292   **43.** $9,300   **45.** $10,137   **47.** $870

13.2 Exercises 490

1. 20%   **3.** 16.67%   **5.** 40%   **7.** $4,950

9. $4,250   **11.** $13,896   **13.** $5,558   **15.** $8,338

17. $8,893   **19.** $5,003   **21.** $10,894   **23.** $3,002

25. $12,095   **27.** $1,801   **29.** $12,696   **31.** $1,920

33. $6,720

13.3 Exercises 495

1. 1/5   **3.** 1/3   **5.** 2/21   **7.** $2,000

9. $3,320   **11.** $20,000   **13.** $8,000   **15.** 3/10

17. $20,000   **19.** $4,000   **21.** 1/10

13.4 Exercises 501

1. 20-year   **3.** 7-year   **5.** 10-year   **7.** 5-year

9. 5-year   **11.** 5-year   **13a.** 5-year class   **13b.** $4,288

15a. $6,400   **15b.** $3,686

Chapter 13 Review Exercises 504

1. $2,500   **3.** $4,875   **5.** $2,880   **7.** $8,500

9. $3,520   **11.** $10,440   **13.** $3,067   **15.** $3,500

17. $5,714   **19.** $2,572   **21.** 0.2449   **23.** $11,020

25. $3,148   **27.** 0.1249   **29.** $5,624   **31.** $1,607

33. 0.0892   **35.** $2,411   **37.** $1,607   **39.** 0.0446

41 $0

Chapter 13 Quiz 508

1. $5,000   **3.** $7,500   **5.** $2,833   **7.** $4,350

9. $6,250   **11.** 4/15   **13.** 1/7   **15.** 2/11

17. $2,333   **19.** $2,343   **21.** 19.20   **23.** 12.49

25. 10.00

Chapter 14 510

14.1 Exercises 521

1. $68,953   **3.** $1,150   **5.** $72,850   **7.** $21,330

9. $8,986   **11.** $43,012   **13.** 101.5%   **15.** 100.0%

17. 10.3%   **19.** 18.7%   **21.** 50.6%

14.2 Exercises 532

1. $81,460   **3.** $81,460   **5.** 2.3%   **7.** 2.9%

9. 13.5%   **11.** 7.2%   **13.** 58.9%   **15.** 24.9%

17. $ 16,000, 28.6   **19.** 7,200*, 33.0*   **21.** $6,293; 7.1   **23.** 2,000*; 3.3*

25. $8,293; 5.2   **27.** 1,000*, 8.3*   **29.** $4,400*, 11.0*   **31.** 3,000; 7.7

33. $2,400*; 1.8*   **35.** $8,293; 5.2

14.3 Exercises 538

1. 1.5:1   **3.** 2.9:1   **5.** 2.4:1   **7.** 0.7:1

9. 1.1:1   **11.** 0.7:1   **13.** 1.0:1   **15.** 4.6:1

17. 0.4:1   **19.** 0.2:1   **21.** 111%   **23.** 23%

25. 25%   **27.** 9%   **29.** 6%

Chapter 14 Review Exercises 542

1. $90,680   **3.** $259,500   **5.** 28,508   **7.** 9,100

9. 114,500   **11.** $132,867   **13.** $4,563   **15.** 110.3

17. 100.0   **19.** 25.8   **21.** 7.2   **23.** 15.3

25. $206,590   **27.** $206,590   **29.** 0.3   **31.** 7.4

33. 19.6   **35.** 100.0   **37.** 14.7   **39.** $75,706

41. 29.5   **43.** 100.0   **45.** 0.2   **47.** 2.9*

49. $211,600   **51.** 8.6*   **53.** –0–   **55.** $173,000

57. 4.3*   **59.** $384,600   **61.** 6.7*   **63.** 28.0

65. 40.0   **67.** $169,200   **69.** 19.2   **71.** 12.0

73. $125,000   **75.** 24.0   **77.** $294,000   **79.** 21.2

81. 2.3:1   **83.** 10.9:1   **85.** 0.5:1   **87.** 144%

89. 127%

Chapter 14 Quiz 550

1. $396,500   **3.** $237,920   **5.** $128,580   **7.** 100.8%

9. $218,160   **11.** 25.7%   **13.** $ 85,200   **15.** 13.9%

17. 25.2%   **19.** $178,100   **21.** 50.7   **23.** 0.4

25. 1.3   **27.** 3.4   **29.** 55.8   **31.** 27.6

33. 16.6   **35.** 44.2   **37.** 100.0   **39.** 8.2*

41. 22.4   **43.** 30.6   **45.** 20.9   **47.** 51.5

49. 48.5   **51.** 100.0   **53.** 2.1:1   **55.** 3.1:1

57. 3.1:1   **59.** 156%   **61.** 227%

Chapter 15   554

15.1 Exercises 561

1. 5.2   **3.** 12.9   **5.** 82.6   **7.** 50.3

9. 30.4   **11.** 18   **13.** 45   **15.** 88

17. 7   **19.** 7   **21.** 12, 33   **23.** 4

25. 17   **27.** 8   **29.** 01

15.2 Exercises 574

1. 5   **3.** 8   **5.** 5   **7.** 56.9

9. 8   **11.** 10   **13.** $11.53   **15.** 1

17. 8   **19.** 7   **21.** 98

23.

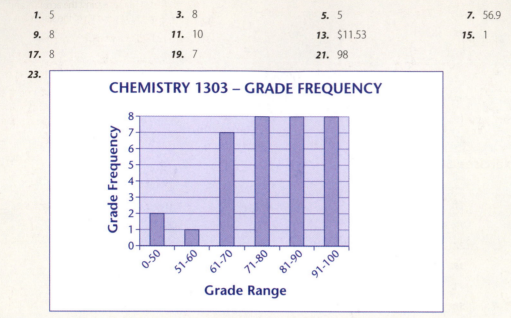

CHEMISTRY 1303 – GRADE FREQUENCY

15.3 Exercises 582

1. 34   **3.** 25 minutes   **5.** 30.1 wpm   **7.** 12.6

9. 16.9   **11.** 14.4   **13.** 13.3   **15.** 15.8

Chapter 15 Review Exercises 587

1. 5.5   **3.** 32.6   **5.** 57.8   **7.** 20

9. 17   **11.** 7   **13.** 12, 25   **15.** 16

17. 1   **19.** |||, 3   **21.** ⦀⦀|||, 8   **23.** ⦀⦀, 5

25. 38.2   **27.** ⦀⦀ ⦀⦀|, 11   **29.** |, 1   **31.** 12

33. 4 hours   **35.** 14.4   **37.** 14.1

Chapter 15 Quiz 592

1. 8.9   **3.** 21.4   **5.** 48.0   **7.** 25, 33

9. 42   **11.** ⦀⦀, 5   **13.** ⦀⦀||, 7   **15.** 37

17. 40   **19.** 37   **21.** 344   **23.** 1,538

Glossary

3/10 EOM a payment term that may appear on an invoice that states that a 3% discount is calculated if the amount is paid during the first 10 days of the month after the invoice date.

30-day account an agreement allowing a consumer to make purchases or use a service during a 30-day period and pay the full amount within 30 days.

A

absolute cell reference a reference used by Excel to indicate Excel must return to a specific cell for part of a formula. A $ precedes the cell letter and number in an absolute cell reference.

accumulated earnings the accumulation or collection of earnings each pay period for an employee.

actuary a person who works with the collection and interpretation of numerical data, for instance, someone who uses statistics to calculate insurance rates.

addend each number being added.

addition the process of combining two or more numbers into a sum.

adjusted balance balance that is calculated by deducting payments and credits made during the billing cycle from the outstanding balance at the beginning of the billing cycle.

adjusted gross income the amount of income remaining after adjustments.

adjustments to income allowable deductions from income including certain business expenses, contributions to a health savings account, moving expenses, alimony, IRA contributions, student loan interest, and tuition and fees.

American Bankers Association (ABA) an association that issues check transit numbers.

amortization the process of paying off indebtedness by installments of principal and earned interest over a period of time.

amortization schedule a timeline that gives a breakdown of the monthly payments in principal and interest.

amount see sum.

amount financed the principal (or purchase price) plus any other costs such as loan origination fees, insurance charges, or extended warranty costs, minus any down payment.

annexing see appending.

annual percentage rate (APR) the actual rate of interest charged for the privilege of having a loan or using a credit card from month to month.

appending when multiplying numbers ending in zero, ignore the zeros. Then, count the number of zeros ignored and add them to the right of the product.

approximate to come near to an amount rather than give an exact amount.

are the base unit for measuring area in the metric system.

assessed rate an arbitrary rate set by the taxing body, usually regarding property value.

assessed value the amount of money for which property is listed in the public tax records for tax purposes.

assessor the elected or appointed public official responsible for the collection of property tax.

automated clearing house (ACH) an electronic network that enables banks (and other financial institutions) to transfer funds among themselves.

automated teller machine (ATM) machines are located outside of banks and in supermarkets, convenience stores, and shopping malls that allow 24-hour access to bank accounts.

automatic payments bill payments made directly from an individual's checking account on a regularly scheduled basis.

automobile liability insurance insurance that covers damages for bodily injury and property damage for which an insured person becomes legally responsible because of an auto accident.

AutoSum command a shortcut command in Excel used to add a row or column of numbers.

average daily balance (ADB) balance that is calculated by adding the outstanding balance, including new purchases, and deducting payments and credits for each day in the billing cycle and then dividing by the number of days in the billing cycle.

averaging the result of adding two or more values together and then dividing this total by the number of values.

B

bank card see credit cards.

bank discount a loan where the interest is collected in advance to distinguish it from interest paid at maturity.

bank statement a report showing the activity in a checking account including paid checks, deposits, charges against the account, and the balance on the date of the statement.

base 100% or the whole of something.

beneficiary person or persons designated to receive the proceeds of a life insurance policy in the event of the insured's death.

bill of lading a contract between the seller and the carrier that is prepared and sent with the shipment.

billing cycle the number of days between the last statement date and the current statement date.

billing statement statement that describes and summarizes account activity for the month.

blank endorsement the signature signed on the back of a check.

borrowing see regrouping.

C

cancellation the process of determining a common number that will evenly divide any one of the numerators and any one of the denominators in the fractions being multiplied. Then crossing out the numbers that were divided and writing in the new number that is remaining after the division.

cancelled checks checks that have cleared the bank.

cash discount reduction of cost extended to a business that pays its bill within a designated time period, usually 10 days.

Celsius the base unit of temperature in the metric system.

centigram unit of weight measurement in the metric system; equivalent to 1/100 of a gram.

centiliter unit of volume measurement in the metric system; equivalent to 1/100 of a meter.

centimeter unit of length measurement in the metric system; equivalent to 1/100 of a meter.

charge card card that has an annual fee and requires the balance to be paid in full each month.

check a written order (also called a draft) used to tell a bank to pay money (transfer funds) from an account to the check holder.

check register a record of each check number and date, the amount of each check, the deposits made, debit card transactions, and the balance in the checking account.

check stub see check register.

checkbook a book containing blank checks and deposit slips, along with a check register or check stubs for recording checks written on the account and deposits made into the account.

checking account an account opened at a bank for the purpose of making payments from funds on deposit in that account, a demand deposit account.

claim a form filed to request payment for losses covered on an insurance policy.

closed-end credit a type of credit generally used to finance a specific amount of money for a specific purpose for a specific period of time.

coinsurance a clause allowing the insured to bear part of the loss when there is damage due to fire.

collateral property that is offered to secure a loan and that becomes subject to seizure upon default.

collect on delivery (COD) the buyer must pay for the goods plus shipping charges upon delivery.

collision coverage pays for damage to the insured's vehicle as a result of an accident.

commission compensation in the form of a percentage of total sales.

common denominator a number that can be divided evenly by all the unlike denominators.

compensation salary, wages, pay, or benefits received for the performance of a service.

complement the difference between 100% and the discount rate.

compound amount the sum of the original principal and its compound interest.

compound interest money that builds on itself; that is, it earns money on the interest that is reinvested as well as on the original principal.

comprehensive coverage pays to fix an individuals vehicle less any deductible for damage not caused by an accident, such as vandalism, theft, storm, or fire.

converted check a check that initiates an electronic funds transfer.

co-payment a fixed payment made to a care provider by a medical patient at the time of service.

copy command a button on the Quick Access toolbar in Excel used to select items for copying.

cost what the retailer pays to the manufacturer.

coverage a term used to describe the type or amount of loss protected against by an insurance policy.

credit agreement agreement signed for a loan that will disclose the annual percentage rate (the effective rate) along with the amount financed, the total finance charges, the total amount of payments, the monthly payment, and the number of payments.

credit card card issued on revolving charge accounts.

Credit Card Act of 2009 an act amending the Truth in Lending Act so that consumers can better understand their credit card bills.

credit limit the maximum amount of credit available.

credit line see credit limit.

credit memorandum memo which notifies a company that they have received a credit on their account for the amount of the returned merchandise.

cubic decimeter unit of volume measurement in the metric system; equivalent to 1 liter.

cubic meters unit of volume measurement in the metric system; equivalent to 1 kiloliter.

currency the money in circulation within a country.

Currency Style command a method used in Excel for rounding a number to two decimal places when working with values of money.

D

date the day the note is issued.

debit card an electronic checkbook; a plastic card (like a credit card) that is linked to a checking account with a personal identification number or PIN.

decaliter unit of volume measurement in the metric system; equivalent to 10 liters.

decameter unit of length measurement in the metric system; equivalent to 10 meters.

decigram unit of weight measurement in the metric system; equivalent to 1/10 of a gram.

deciliter unit of volume measurement in the metric system; equivalent to 1/10 of a meter.

decimal equivalent what is shown in the formula bar in Excel when a fraction is entered into a cell.

decimal number system (also called the Hindu-Arabic system) a number system using base 10.

decimal part digits to the right of the decimal point.

decimal point a dot (.) which separates the whole number part from the decimal part.

decimeter unit of length measurement in the metric system; equivalent to 1/10 of a meter.

Decrease Decimal command a command used in Excel to remove a decimal place from the value in the selected cell.

deductible an amount deducted from an insurance settlement; the amount of loss the insured agrees to accept.

default the failure to meet the terms of a credit agreement.

dekagram unit of weight measurement in the metric system; equivalent to 10 grams.

denominator bottom number in a fraction, expresses the number of equal parts the whole number is divided into.

deposit a transaction that adds funds to a bank account.

deposit insurance the Federal Deposit Insurance Corporation (FDIC) insures depositors' accounts up to $250,000 per person per institution, except for some retirement accounts.

deposit slip a written record of credit to an account.

depositor person who is depositing money into an account.

difference solution obtained by subtracting the subtrahend from the minuend.

digit the ten single numbers: 1, 2, 3, 4, 5, 6, 7, 8, 9, and 0.

digital check images an electronic image of both the front and back of a cleared check.

direct deposit a payment made by a deposit directly to the receiver's bank account rather than by mailing a check; the other end of an automatic payment.

discount date the date the bank discounts the note.

discount note the terms of the note may include the deduction of interest from the amount borrowed.

discount period the time period when a discount will be offered; the second number of the terms of payment.

discount rate the percentage rate offered as a discount; the first number on the terms of payment.

discounting commercial paper the procedure of giving a promissory note to a bank in exchange for cash.

dividend the number that is to be divided by another number.

division the process of determining how many times one number is contained in another.

divisor the number by which to divide.

double time wages paid at twice an employee's hourly rate.

down payment a partial payment that may be required in advance and is usually a percent (such as 10% or 20%) of the purchase price of the item bought.

drawee the drawer's bank.

drawer the person or business who writes the check; the person who pays.

due date the date payment is due.

E

earned income tax credit a federal program for low- to moderate-income workers who meet certain requirements that offers a refund of federal income taxes withheld. In some cases, the earned income credit can exceed the amount of taxes withheld. The maximum benefit in 2009 was $5,028 for those with incomes not exceeding $43,415.

electronic bill paying the process of paying a bill over the Internet which is initiated from a computer.

electronic funds transfer (EFT) the process of moving funds electronically from an account in one bank to an account in another bank.

employee's earnings record a record showing an employee's personal payroll information, yearly earnings, and deductions.

employee's withholding allowance certificate this is Form W-4, which specifies the number of withholding allowances claimed by an employee for tax purposes.

equivalent fraction another fraction equal to the original fraction.

escrow account an account created by the lender to hold money, collected monthly along with the property owner's mortgage payment, to insure that property taxes get paid. The owner receives a statement when the lender pays the tax.

estimated tax payments quarterly tax payments to the IRS that are required if an individual expects to owe at least $1,000 in tax (2009) after subtracting withholding and credits. Other qualifications apply based on the amount of withholding and credits and prior year taxes or estimated payments.

estimation an approximate calculation. Estimation can be used to check the reasonableness of a calculation.

exact simple interest a loan that is stated in a certain number of days; computing interest is based on a 365-day year.

exchange rate the cost of one currency in terms of another currency.

exemptions a deduction from taxable income for each dependent.

F

face value the amount of insurance purchased.

face value the initial amount borrowed or invested for a certain period of time.

factors the multiplicand and multiplier.

Fahrenheit unit of temperature measurement in the English system.

Fair Labor Standards Act (FLSA) an act of law (sometimes called the Wage and Hour Law) establishing minimum wages and requiring employers whose firms are involved in interstate commerce (sale of goods from state to state) to pay their employees time and one-half for all hours worked in excess of 40 hours per week. There is no requirement that time and one-half be paid for weekends or holidays. The act also provides that certain employees (management and supervisory) are exempt from its regulations.

federal income tax (FIT) the amount of money a U.S. citizen must pay the federal government based on his or her wages.

Federal Insurance Contributions Act (FICA) a law, originally passed in 1935, providing for retirement income after an employee reaches a minimum age of 62, disability benefits for any employee who becomes disabled (and for his or her dependents), and a health insurance program after an employee reaches the age of 65.

Federal Unemployment Tax Act (FUTA) tax authorizing the IRS to collect a tax on each employer's payroll to fund state workforce agencies. FUTA covers the costs of administering the Unemployment Insurance (UI) and Job Service programs in all states.

fill handle the bottom right corner of a cell in Excel. When the fill handle is clicked and dragged across a row or down a column, the formulas in the original cell will be copied to the others.

finance charge the interest paid for the use of credit.

first mortgage the primary mortgage on a home.

FOB destination the seller maintains ownership of the goods until they are delivered to the buyer and bears the cost of shipping.

FOB shipping point the buyer takes title to the goods at the seller's point of shipment and pays the freight to the buyer's business location.

footing a method of checking that amounts balance.

foreclosure the process of the lender suing the borrower to prove that the borrower cannot repay the loan and asking the court to order the sale of the property in order to pay the debt.

Format Cells command a command used in Excel to round numbers to a specific decimal place.

format cells dialog box a tabbed menu in Excel used to select various formatting characteristics for the information entered into cells.

formula (also called a **function**) a method for entering calculations in a cell in Excel. The formula must begin with the equals (=) sign.

fraction part of a whole; the part is written above the whole and the numbers are separated by a bar.

free on board (FOB) used to identify the point at which the buyer takes ownership and responsibility for the goods, the point at which the shipper is free of responsibility for the shipment; also called freight on board.

freight collect the buyer must pay freight charges to the carrier before taking delivery.

full endorsement used when the payee wants to transfer a check to a third party. The endorsement would be written as, "pay to the order of' and the name of the third party.

function (also called a **formula**) a method for entering calculations in a cell in Excel. The function must begin with the equals (=) sign.

G

grace period period to pay off balance before finance charges begin.

gram the base unit of weight in the metric system.

greatest common divisor the largest number that will divide evenly into both the numerator and denominator.

gross earnings the total amount of an employee's pay before deductions.

H

health insurance covers a predetermined portion of the cost of health care.

Health Maintenance Organization (HMO) a managed health care organization which attempts to lower costs by negotiating discounted rates for their policyholders; focuses on preventive care, and limiting choices; providing access to their own network of health care professionals, hospitals, clinics, etc.; differs from other organizations in the amount of control plan members have in their choice of health care providers and the cost of premiums, co-payments, and deductibles.

health savings account (HSA) a qualifying employer-sponsored plan allowing employees to have pre-tax deductions from their paychecks deposited into a savings account that can be used only for medical expenses.

hectare unit of measure used for selling land in the metric system; equivalent to approximately 2.471 acres (A).

hectogram unit of weight measurement in the metric system; equivalent to 100 grams.

hectoliter unit of volume measurement in the metric system; equivalent to 100 liters.

hectometer unit of length measurement in the metric system; equivalent to 100 meters.

homeowner's insurance insurance that provides coverage of property against damage or loss.

hourly wage (hourly rate) wages paid according to the number of hours worked.

I

Increase Decimal command a command used in Excel to add a decimal place to the value in the selected cell.

improper fraction fraction in which the numerator is equal to or greater than the denominator and expresses one or more whole numbers.

individual retirement account (IRA) with some restrictions set by the IRS, employed individuals can set aside pre-tax funds for their retirement years in a traditional IRA or a Roth IRA. Contributions to a traditional IRA are deducted from earnings as a tax savings. The money is taxed when it is withdrawn. There are penalties for early withdrawal.

installment loan a loan in which an individual agrees to pay back a fixed amount of money, including interest, in a series of equal payments over a fixed period of time.

installment price the price of the item as compared to the price you would pay if you paid cash.

installments a series of equal payments (usually monthly).

insurance protection against the cost of loss.

insurance agent a person who sells insurance and provides claims service to the policyholders.

insurance claims adjuster a person representing an insurance company who investigates claims and determines the amount of damage for which the insurance company is responsible.

insured the individual or company receiving the insurance protection.

interest period the term of the loan.

interest-bearing checking account a checking account that pays interest.

interest-bearing note a promissory note that states an interest rate.

invoice a record of the sales transaction showing the quantity of each item sold with its individual price, any added charges or discounts, the total price, and the payment terms.

invoice date the date an invoice was issued.

itemized deductions amounts subtracted from adjusted gross income before tax is computed.

K

kilogram unit of weight measurement in the metric system; equivalent to 1,000 grams.

kiloliter unit of volume measurement in the metric system; equivalent to 1,000 liters.

kilometer unit of length measurement in the metric system; equivalent to 1,000 meters.

L

least common denominator (LCD) the smallest number that can be divided evenly by all the unlike denominators.

levied assessed or collected, as with a tax.

liability an obligation for which someone is responsible.

life insurance an agreement providing for the payment of a stipulated sum to one or more beneficiaries upon the death of the insured person.

like fractions two or more fractions that have the same denominator.

list price suggested retail price, the price that the manufacturer suggests be charged to retail customers.

liter the base unit of volume in the metric system.

lowest terms the smallest numerator and denominator possible to represent the original value of the fraction.

M

maker borrower; the person or business borrowing the money.

manufacturers businesses that purchase raw materials and/or parts to make finished products and sell their products to other manufacturers, wholesalers, or other sales intermediaries.

markdown a percentage of the original selling price by which the selling price is reduced.

markdown amount the difference between the original selling price of the merchandise and the reduced selling price.

markdown rate the markdown expressed as a percent or a fraction.

market value the amount of money property would sell for in a competitive open market.

markup the difference between the cost and the selling price; gross profit.

markup amount markup expressed in dollars.

markup rate markup expressed as a percentage.

maturity the length of time until the principal amount of the loan must be repaid.

maturity date the date on which a loan must be paid in full.

maturity value the full amount of money that must be repaid when the loan is due, the principal plus the interest, abbreviated as M.

medical payment coverage protects the insured and other occupants of the insured's vehicle against the cost of bodily injury in an accident.

Medicare a U.S. federal health program that subsidizes individuals over 65 or the disabled.

meter the base unit of length in the metric system.

Metric Conversion Act of 1975 act signed by Gerald Ford to initiate the adoption of the metric system of measurement. The act does not identify a specific date for complete U.S. conversion, nor is it mandatory for companies.

metric ton unit of weight measurement in the metric system; there are 0.907 t in 1 short ton.

mill a unit in which tax rate is expressed; 1/10 of a cent (0.1¢) or 1/1,000 of a dollar ($0.001).

milligram unit of weight measurement in the metric system; equivalent to 1/1,000 of a gram.

milliliter unit of volume measurement in the metric system; equivalent to 1/1000 of a liter.

millimeter unit of length measurement in the metric system; equivalent to 1/1000 of a meter.

minuend the number from which another number is subtracted.

mixed number a whole number and a fraction.

monthly payment the total amount of payments divided by the number of payments.

mortgage loan money lent to a borrower by a lender to purchase real estate, with the real estate itself serving as collateral for the loan.

multimath formula a formula created in Excel that uses more than one of the basic math operations.

multiplicand the number to be multiplied.

multiplication the mathematical procedure for finding the product of two numbers.

multiplier the number by which another number is multiplied; indicates how many groups of the multiplicand will be in the final product.

N

n/30 ROG a payment term that may appear on an invoice that states that the net is due 30 days after the receipt of goods (ROG) rather than the invoice date.

n/EOM a payment term that may appear on an invoice that states that the net is due at the end of the month (EOM) in which the invoice is dated.

negative number the result when a larger number is subtracted from a smaller number.

net pay the total amount of an employee's pay after deductions; that is, gross pay minus deductions.

net price the price the seller charges the customer.

net price equivalent the result of multiplying the complements of the discounts in a series discount; a faster way to calculate the net price and the discount amount than the chain method.

net profit the amount of profit left over (if any) after expenses have been paid.

net sales total sales less returned merchandise over a set quota.

no-fault automobile insurance form of coverage where the insured's own insurance company pays for property damage and bodily injury no matter who is at fault.

non-interest-bearing note a note that does not specify an interest rate.

nonsufficient funds (NSF) checks that are drawn against an account that does not contain sufficient funds to cover the amount of the checks and will be returned to the holder—usually the payee.

numeral any grouping of 1 or more digits.

numerator top number in a fraction, expresses the number of equal parts of the whole number.

O

online banking a banking transaction conducted over the Internet.

open-end credit an agreement to lend up to a certain amount and to allow the amount to be borrowed again once it has been repaid.

operating expenses the expenses incurred by a business, such as rent, utilities, salaries, insurance, supplies, advertising, and so on.

ordinary simple interest a loan that is stated in a certain number of days; computing interest is based on a 360-day year.

other bank services services offered by a bank that are not directly linked to a checking account such as the purchase of certified or cashier's checks, money orders, traveler's checks, notary service, and foreign currency exchange.

outstanding checks checks that have been written and deducted from the check register or check stubs but do not appear on the monthly bank statement.

outstanding deposits deposits that have been made by the depositor but do not appear on the monthly bank statement.

overdraft protection a security measure where banks link a checking account with a savings account, credit line or credit card so that if more money is withdrawn than is in the checking account it can be taken from the linked account to prevent overdraft fees.

overtime all time worked in excess of straight time.

P

part a selected piece of the base.

paste command a button on the Quick Access tool bar in Excel used to paste items that have been selected for copying.

payee an individual or a business paid a certain sum from a checking account as authorized by a check.

payee lender; the person or business who lends the money and who will receive the repayment.

payroll register a summary of payroll information for a particular pay period.

percent represents a part of a whole; means parts per 100; the symbol for percent is %.

percentage when the rate is expressed as a percent.

percentage distribution the percent each part is of the total.

percentage method a method to calculate federal income tax withholding using tables in publication *Circular E, Employer's Tax Guide (Publication 15)*.

personal property possessions such as jewelry, autos, boats, and furniture.

piece rate the amount paid for each piece produced.

piecework compensation based on the number of pieces completed.

places the digits to the left and right of the decimal point. Each position has a name representing its value.

Pointing Method a method that eliminates keyboarding in Excel by using the mouse to point to the cells that are to be selected for a formula.

Point of Service (POS) plan a managed health care organization which attempts to lower costs by negotiating discounted rates for their policyholders; focuses on preventive care, and limiting choices; providing access to their own network of health care professionals, hospitals, clinics, etc.; differs from other organizations in the amount of control plan members have in their choice of health care providers and the cost of premiums, co-payments, and deductibles.

policy a written contract between the insurance company and the insured that explains the benefits and limitations of the protection purchased.

policyholder the person or business that purchases an insurance policy.

positions the digits to the left and right of the decimal point. Each position has a name representing its value.

Preferred Provider Organization (PPO) a managed health care organization which attempts to lower costs by negotiating discounted rates for their policyholders; focuses on preventive care, and limiting choices; providing access to their own network of health care professionals, hospitals, clinics, etc.; differs from other organizations in the amount of control plan members have in their choice of health care providers and the cost of premiums, co-payments, and deductibles.

premium payment to the insurance company for the insurance policy.

prepaid freight (prepaid shipping) the buyer will require the seller to prepay the shipping charges to the carrier.

present value the principal invested at a given rate today that will grow to the compound amount at a later date.

pre-tax deductions some deductions are made from gross earnings before calculating taxable earnings; these include (but are not limited to) medical, dental, and vision insurance premiums; flexible spending account (FSA) contributions; 401(k) and 403(b) retirement plan contributions; and some prepaid parking fees.

previous balance the amount owed at the start of the billing cycle.

primary care physician a doctor who monitors an individual's health, provides primary care, and makes referrals to specialists inside the network as needed.

prime factorization a number written as a product of primes.

prime interest the interest rate that banks charge their best or most creditworthy customers.

prime number a whole number larger than 1 that can be divided evenly only by itself and 1; the six smallest prime numbers are 2, 3, 5, 7, 11, and 13.

prime number method a method of determining the least common denominator of a group of fractions in which the denominators are repeatedly divided by prime numbers common to at least 2 of the denominators. When no more division can be done, the prime numbers from division are multiplied to calculate the least common denominator.

principal see face value, abbreviated as *P*.

proceeds loan amount, the amount the borrower receives (maturity value less the bank discount).

product the result or the answer.

promissory note (note) a written promise to repay a loan or debt under specific terms.

proper fraction fraction in which the numerator is less than the denominator.

property tax a tax imposed on a property owner to help fund public services such as fire and police protection, schools, and parks.

purchase order a document issued by a buyer to a vendor listing products or services wanted.

purchase requisition an internal order form sent to the purchasing department from another department so purchasing knows what supplies to buy.

R

radical the symbol √ to indicate division, drawn over the dividend.

rate the percentage or fraction the part is of the base.

rate the percent charged to lend or borrow money, abbreviated as *R*.

rate of decrease the percent obtained when the amount of decrease is divided by the base or previous amount.

rate of increase the percent obtained when the amount of increase is divided by the base or previous amount.

ratio when the rate is expressed as a fraction.

real property property such as land and buildings.

receiving report document listing each item received and is prepared by the person or department that receives the order when the merchandise arrives. It may be a copy of the purchase order.

reconciliation the process of comparing the check register or check stubs with the bank statement so that the balance agrees. If there are discrepancies, an adjustment or correction is made.

reconciliation form form used to complete the reconciliation process.

reduced price the selling price once marked down; discounted sale price.

refund to return to the borrower who is paying off a loan early the unearned portion of the finance charge on the loan.

regrouping When a number cannot be subtracted from a smaller number, you must borrow 10 from the position to it's left. This process is called regrouping.

regular time hours paid at an employee's regular wage, usually the first 40 hours worked per week. This number may vary from company to company.

relative cell reference a reference to a cell in Excel based on the position of the formula.

remainder the number left over if a dividend cannot be divided evenly, often placed over the divisor making a fraction.

repeating decimal in division, when one or more numbers repeat in a pattern, represented by a line above the last digit(s) to indicate that these digit(s) will always repeat.

restrictive endorsement the words "for deposit only" written on the back of a check, making it only valid for deposit and not for receiving funds.

retailers businesses that sell directly to the consumer.

returned (dishonored) check a check not honored and returned to the owner because of insufficient funds.

returned merchandise goods returned due to defects, errors, or other reasons.

revolving charge accounts card where monthly payments reduce credit balance and new charges are added, resulting in a revolving balance.

Round function a function used in Excel to round a number or calculation to a specific number of digits.

rounding the process of replacing a number by another number of approximately the same value but having fewer digits.

Rule of 78 rule based on the number 78, which is used to calculate a loan refund.

running balance the current balance in an account after all deposits and withdrawals.

S

salaried an employee who is paid a set annual amount; salaried employees usually do not receive overtime pay.

sales tax a specified percent charged when certain merchandise is sold to a customer.

second mortgage another mortgage available for homeowners who want to borrow money to make major home improvements, such as adding a room or remodeling a kitchen.

selling price also called retail price; what the customer pays.

series discount a chain discount such as 5%, 10%, and 5% which represents a 5% reduction from the list price, a 10% reduction on the remainder after the first discount has been subtracted, and another 5% reduction on the remainder after the second discount has been subtracted.

service charges bank charges; monthly fees charged to the depositor for providing a checking account.

settlement the amount an insurance company agrees to pay on a claim.

simple interest interest computed on the principal for the time of the transaction.

single discount equivalent one discount rate that is equal to applying the separate rates one at a time.

Social Security a program which includes retirement benefits, unemployment, health, disability, and survivors insurance maintained by the federal government through required payments from employers.

standard deductions a dollar amount that reduces the amount of income on which an individual is taxed. An individual cannot take the standard deduction if you claim itemized deductions.

state and local income tax withholding the amount withheld from earnings for taxes imposed by some states and local governments on gross earnings.

State Unemployment Tax Act (SUTA) tax collected by state governments to fund state workforce agencies, is used solely for the payment of benefits to eligible unemployed workers. The rates vary by state based upon their individual needs.

stated interest rate nominal, quoted rate of interest when applying for an installment loan.

statement of account document sent monthly by a business to each customer with an open account balance indicating the month's transactions, including the balance at the beginning of the month, payments made during the month, any credit from credit memorandums, and the balance owed at the end of the month.

stop payment a service provided by banks to cease payment on a check.

straight time see regular time.

subtotal the total of two or more numbers within the column being added.

subtraction the process of determining the difference between two numbers.

subtrahend the number being subtracted.

sum the solution to an addition problem.

sum-of-digits method see the Rule of 78.

T

tax the amount of money paid by a property owner.

tax credits items that reduce calculated income tax; for example, credit for child and dependent care expenses.

tax rate the percent set by the taxing body that is used to calculate tax owed.

taxable amount the total of the taxable items on an invoice.

taxable earnings the tax base on which the income tax withholding is calculated.

taxable income the amount of income subject to tax after adjustments, deductions, and exemptions.

template file a file that has the design, layout, and formulas that can be used over and over.

term the time for which an insurance policy is in effect.

term the time of the note expressed as a specific date in days or in months.

terms of payment the way a business communicates the way it will accept payment on its invoice, shown in an abbreviated form: 2/10, n/30, for example.

time the period of time to repay a loan or to earn interest on invested money, expressed in days, months, or years, abbreviated as *T*.

time and one-half wages paid at one and one-half times an employee's hourly rate.

total see sum.

total amount of payments amount financed plus interest.

total income all the income you receive, such as wages, salaries, tips, dependent care benefits, employer-provided adoption benefits, interest income, ordinary dividend income, taxable refunds, credits or offsets of state and local income tax, alimony, business income, capital gain distributions, pensions, IRA distributions, annuities, rents, royalties, partnerships, certain scholarships and fellowship grants, prizes and awards, gambling winnings, jury fees, rental income, unemployment compensation, and Social Security benefits.

trade discount a deduction from a list price.

Truth in Lending Act an act requiring creditors to provide certain basic information about the cost of buying on credit or taking out a loan.

U

uninsured motorist coverage protects the insured and the insured's passengers against bodily/personal injuries as well as against property damage caused by another at-fault driver without liability insurance.

unlike fractions two or more fractions that have different denominators.

V

voucher checks the detachable portion of a check showing the invoice number (or numbers) being paid by the check.

W

wage bracket method a method to look up federal income tax withholding using tables provided in publication Circular E, Employer's Tax Guide.

whole number part digits to the left of the decimal point.

wholesalers middlemen who buy merchandise from manufacturers or other wholesalers and sell to retailers.

word form numbers or amounts that are spelled out.

Index